A Sanskrit Reader

Seneca — de Beneficiis
ii. 33

Perfecit opus suum Phidias,
etiamsi non vendidit

A SANSKRIT READER

Text and Vocabulary and Notes

BY

CHARLES ROCKWELL LANMAN

Professor at Harvard University; Honorary Fellow of the Asiatic Society of Bengal, of France, of England, and of Germany; Corresponding Member of the Society of Sciences at Göttingen, the Russian Academy of Sciences, and the Académie des Inscriptions et Belles-Lettres of the Institute of France

CAMBRIDGE, MASSACHUSETTS

Harvard University Press

1920

Typography of the Text by Gebrueder Unger, Berlin, Germany
Typography of the Vocabulary and Notes by J. S. Cushing & Co., Boston
Printed from electrotype plates by the
Harvard University Press, Cambridge, Massachusetts, U. S. A.

PREFACE.

THE results of comparative philology are now so generally incorporated into our modern classical grammars, lexicons, and text-books, that even a slight knowledge of Sanskrit, if it be accurate so far as it goes, is of great service to the classical teacher in making his instruction interesting and effective. As independent disciplines, moreover, Sanskrit and comparative philology, and the literatures and religions of India, are constantly gaining in importance, so that, for example, Sanskrit is now taught at all but one of the twenty universities of the German Empire.

The design of this work, then, is twofold. In the first place, it is to serve as an introduction to these subjects for the students of our colleges and universities. The excellent Chrestomathy of BOEHTLINGK has no vocabulary; and few persons can be expected to buy the costly dictionary of WILLIAMS or that of BOEHTLINGK AND ROTH, at the outset, when they are uncertain whether Sanskrit will be of sufficient interest or use to them to warrant their continuing its study. What the beginner needs is an elementary work comprehending both text and vocabulary in a single volume. And accordingly, this Reader is meant to furnish ample material for about fifty weeks' reading, in a course of three hours a week, and, with the text, the appropriate lexical apparatus. The Reader is made as a companion-volume to WHITNEY's *Sanskrit Grammar*, and these two books supply all that is needed for the first year's study.

This Reader is designed, in the second place, to render a knowledge of Sanskrit accessible to the classical teachers of high-schools, academies, and colleges. These teachers, if they pursue this study at all, usually do so without the aid of an instructor. And it is especially *the requirements of unaided private study* that I have taken constant pains to meet. I state this fact thus explicitly, because, both here at Cambridge, and during my connection with the Johns Hopkins University (where the plan for this work was formed), numerous inquiries for such a book have been addressed to me by persons very remote from any of the higher institutions of learning.

If, incidentally, this work should help to correct some of the false notions which are prevalent respecting the relations of Sanskrit to other languages of the Indo-European family, and to save the literature from undue depreciation and from exaggerated praise, it will have served a worthy object.

So cumbrous or so meagre have been hitherto the appliances for acquiring even a moderate knowledge of Sanskrit, that classical students, when seeking such knowledge as an auxiliary to their special work, have found the labor discouragingly great. These students unquestionably have a legitimate and sufficient reason for undertaking Sanskrit, and I venture to hope that the difficulties of the beginning (see p. xv) have been so materially lessened that they will now find even a modicum of Sanskrit well worth the trouble of attainment.

In making my selections[1] from the various Sanskrit writings, I have had two practical aims in view: first, to provide abundant material for thorough drill in the language of the classical period; and, secondly, to furnish a brief introduction to the works of the Vedic period, Mantra, Brāhmana, and Sūtra. Accordingly I have not sought to give any thing new, but rather that which is best suited for beginners. The easy Nala is the Xenophon's Anabasis of Sanskrit students, and quotations from it appear very often in the grammars. And the first five chapters here given form a complete story. For an elementary reader, the Hitopadeça is unrivalled, and to leave it out would have been an inexcusable omission, unless, indeed, its place were taken by the Panchatantra. From this latter work I attempted to prepare some selections; but the text is in so unsatisfactory a condition, that I relinquished the plan. And so, although the Hitopadeça has been printed very often, I have given a considerable part[2] of it here, choosing the fables on the ground of their intrinsic excellence and their interest as originals of well-known occidental stories.[3] For similar reasons the six tales from the Kathā-sarit-sāgara were selected. On account of their easy style and simple narrative, they furnish admirable matter for exercise in rapid reading. The selections from "Manu" are so made as to illustrate some of the most important and interesting matters of Hindu custom and belief.[4]

Among the Vedic hymns (or Mantra-material) are, first, some of the easiest[5]; then some taken on account of their poetic[6] or dramatic[7] merit, or

[1] These include 68 pages of classical Sanskrit and 37 pages of Vedic Sanskrit.

[2] Nineteen fables: there are forty-three in all.

[3] See the introductions to the fables in the Notes.

[4] Compare the table of contents. The text-selections are intended to be mutually illustrative as far as may be. Thus the passage 64⁶ ff. is given for its interesting bearing on Rigveda x.18.7 (86¹⁷), the verse which was appealed to as scriptural authority for the practice of widow-burning. Compare also the notes on 28²⁰, 57⁵, and 65⁹ ff., with those on 65⁶, 91¹⁶, and 97² respectively.

[5] Such are selections xxxi. (Rigveda i.1), xxxiii., xxxviii., xxxix., xli., xlv., xlvi., and lix.

[6] Selection xxxii. is the best.

[7] Selections xxxv., xxxvii., and lvi. are in dramatic form (see WHITNEY, page xviii), and are among the most difficult.

their ethical interest[1]; and finally some taken because of their historical importance.[2] For the most part, a repetition of the hymns given by DELBRUECK and by BOEHTLINGK in their Chrestomathies has been avoided. The Brāhmana pieces are chosen in such a way as to show the relation of this kind of literature to the hymns or Mantras.[3] The selections from the Grihya-sûtras are the two most interesting chapters of Indian private antiquities, the wedding and the burial service. These texts are, to a certain extent, rubrics, and prescribe that numerous specified stanzas of the Rigveda be repeated at these ceremonials. Care has therefore been taken that all the stanzas here cited by their first words should be given in full among the selections from the hymns.[4]

Concerning the text, little need be said. It would have been either folly or idle pretense to make elaborate text-studies for the short extracts of which the Reader is composed.[5] I have accordingly contented myself, in the main, with reprinting the text of the best editions. Misprints have of course been corrected, and I have endeavored to make the orthography conformable to the best standard[6] and consistent throughout.[7] Of some slight emendations, due mention will be made in the Notes. For the Nala, I followed the edition of BUEHLER in his *Third Book of Sanskrit*[8]; for the Hitopadeça, the text of BOEHTLINGK in the second edition of his Chrestomathy,[8] and MUELLER; for the Kathā-sarit-sāgara, BROCKHAUS; and for "Manu," LOISELEUR DESLONGCHAMPS. I regret that the results of the studies of BUEHLER, BURNELL, HOPKINS, and JOLLY on the text of "Manu" are not yet available.

---

[1] Such are the Varuna-hymns, selections xliii.–xlv.

[2] Such are the hymns for the dead and the wedding-hymn; likewise selection xxxvii., and selection xxxvi. (which contains the Sāvitrī). Selection lxii. is the Maitrāyanī version of the Hiranya-garbha hymn, Rigveda x. 121, and is given partly in order that those who possess copies of the Rigveda may study the two versions comparatively.

[3] Thus the Brāhmana selections lxvi., lxvii., lxviii., and lxxii. stand in connection with the Mantra selections lvi., xlvii., lxii., and xlvi. respectively.

[4] The stanzas required for the wedding ceremonial are given in selections lviii., lvii., and lv. From this the student will see why there are some selections consisting of only one or two stanzas. The burial-stanzas are from Rigveda x. 9, 14, 16, 17, 18, 53, 154, and 155 (selections xlix. ff.), and i. 97 (selection xxxiv.). This last hymn is mere trash, and would not have been included among the texts, had not Açwalāyana (at iv.6.18) prescribed that it be used as a burial-hymn; but I could not allow room for the "Sun-hymns" (sauryāṇi) and the "Blessings" (svasty-ayanāni), which are also mentioned at iv.6.18.

[5] See A. WEBER, *Indische Studien*, ii. 151.

[6] Especially in the use of *anusvāra* and of the nasal mutes, of b and of ç. I have written cch where WHITNEY (see § 227) writes ch.

[7] But some of the interesting orthographical peculiarities of the Maitrāyanī Sanhitā I have allowed to stand.

[8] See the "Brief List," page xvii.

It is a pleasant duty to acknowledge my thanks to BOEHTLINGK, who, in a way no less generous than unexpected, volunteered to look over all the proofs of the classical part of the text. For the well-established and well-edited Vedic texts, such help was of course not needed.

For the Rigveda, AUFRECHT's second edition was made the standard. For the selections from the Maitrāyaṇī Sanhitā, I am indebted to the kindness of its editor,[1] Dr. LEOPOLD VON SCHROEDER, of Dorpat. The extracts from the Brāhmaṇas naturally follow the editions of WEBER and AUFRECHT. The chapters from Açwalāyana are a reprint from STENZLER's edition, with some unimportant typographical licenses.

The vocabulary, it is almost needless to say, is based on the great Lexicon of BOEHTLINGK AND ROTH. I should of course deviate from it only with the utmost circumspection; but I trust that I have not followed it slavishly.

As for the extent of the vocabulary, it is designed to be complete for the text given in the Reader, and also, it may be added, for the text in the Appendix to the Grammar.

It is proper to mention here several matters touching the general plan of the vocabulary. It is not a mere list of the actually occurring Sanskrit words with their English equivalents. So far as possible, it aims to do with thoroughness two things:

First, as regards the *forms*, To enable the student to trace every word back to its root, by giving references to WHITNEY's chapters (xvi. and xvii.) on word-formation, and by giving the root itself, and, in the case of secondary and tertiary derivatives, the intermediate forms, even when these do not occur in the text at all. Thus, for the complete explanation of mithyopacāra (p. 217), are given, first, mithyá, then the older form thereof, mithuyá,[2] then the adjective mithu from which the adverb is derived, and finally the root mith, although neither the adverbs nor the adjective nor any verbal form of the root occurs in the text. In like manner, car + upa is given solely on account of upacāra.

Secondly, as regards the *meanings*, To enable the student to trace every signification back to the radical idea, by giving not only the meaning required for translating a particular passage, but also, if this is a secondary or tertiary or later meaning, the intermediate meanings, and in their logical order of development. Thus the only meanings of the word pāda, as it

---

[1] He gave them to me in manuscript, before he himself began printing.

[2] By looking out the reference to 1112e (under mithu), the student will have his attention drawn to the peculiar form and accent of the adverb and will find the explanation thereof.

occurs in the text of this Reader, are 'foot' or 'leg,' in ten passages, and 'verse of a three-versed stanza,' in one passage (60¹³). The history and uses of the word may be clearly understood from BOEHTLINGK AND ROTH. The original meaning 'foot' was extended to that of 'leg'; then specialized to the meaning 'limb of a quadruped'; then generalized to the meaning 'quarter' (as, conversely. the English word *quarter* is specialized to the meaning 'fourth part of a quadruped, including a leg,' e.g., in *quarter of beef*); once more it is specialized to the meaning 'quarter of a four-versed stanza,' i.e. 'verse'; and then, at last, the use of the word is illogically extended, and it is made to denote a verse of even a three-versed stanza. To have given the meanings 'foot, leg, verse,' in three words, and perhaps in the order 'verse, leg, foot,' would have sufficed, it is true, for the purpose of making a translation; but such translation demands of the student only the most thoughtless and mechanical labor. On the other hand, by indicating briefly the development and connection of meanings, the attention of the student is directed to the processes which are constantly going on in the life and growth of language; and thus, although Sanskrit is a dead language, the *study* of Sanskrit may be made a study of life and growth.

The illustration of the transitions of meaning by analogies from the English and other familiar tongues would, it seemed to me, greatly increase the interest and usefulness of the vocabulary. And so, considerable space has been devoted to this matter. Thus under vyāma (p. 254, top), 'a stretch-out,' i.e. 'a fathom,' are adduced the closely parallel English *fathom*, from Anglo-Saxon *fæðm*, 'the extended arms,' and also ὀργυιά and French *toise*, both meaning 'fathom,' and of common origin respectively with ὀρέγω and Latin *tendere*, 'stretch.'[1]

In a book intended partly for persons whose chief interest in Sanskrit is from the side of its relations to the classical languages and to our mother-tongue, etymological comparisons are plainly called for. Accordingly, the kindred words from the Greek, Latin, Anglo-Saxon, and English have been given,[2] and always along with their meanings. It is hoped that these comparisons, presenting, as they do, many familiar words with which the learner can associate what is new and strange, will prove a useful aid to the memory. Etymology is a subject in which there is large room for reasonable

---

[1] For other parallels, compare, for example, ābharaṇa, barhis, bhavana, vañça, varṇa. Sometimes the understanding of the parallelism depends on a knowledge of the etymology of an English word; thus under root nud + vi, are adduced the English *di-vert*, *dis-port*, and *s-port*, and a reference to SKEAT's dictionary or to WEBSTER's may be necessary for the student, in order to find how these words are parallel in specialization and metaphor. On this subject in general, compare CURTIUS, *Grundzüge*⁵, pp. 111–116, and BRINKMANN, *Die Metaphern*, Bonn, 1878.

[2] To give them without their meanings and without showing the connection of ideas is, for an elementary book, a useless task.

difference of opinion on matters of detail, and on such matters well-recognized authorities often disagree. I have tried to use the standard works of reference in the light of the best and latest etymological criticism at my command. and to distinguish with care between what is certain and what is mere conjecture. In the revision of the greater part of my manuscript for the press, I had the benefit of KLUGE's valuable dictionary.[1] His acceptance of the current comparisons has often given me assurance, and his sober judgment has often confirmed me in scepticism or silence on doubtful points. In the numerous cases where the undoubtedly allied words are too many to be given in full, I have usually selected those forms which were the simplest or the most interesting, or those whose kinship was clearest.[2]

These comparisons include only genuinely cognate words, as distinguished from borrowed words; the latter have as a rule been excluded, or, if given, have been characterized as borrowings.[3] Thus ἷνος, Latin sen-ex, and English sen-green are given on page 266, all as genuine cognates of sana; the words senate, senator, senatorial, senescent, senile, senility, senior, sire, sir, seigniorage, etc., are not mentioned, because they are not genuine English cognates, but only more or less ancient borrowings or more or less direct derivatives from the Latin.[4] So under the root sṛp (p. 276) are given Latin serpens and reptilis, and it would be superfluous to add the borrowed English serpent and reptile.

The accents of all words have been regularly marked in the headings of the articles, so far as the accents are known from the occurrence of the words in any accentuated texts of the literature.[5] But in addition to these words, the verb-forms immediately following the root have been uniformly accented, according to the rules, except in a few doubtful cases; and a number of compounds occurring on the pages of Nala have been accented.

---

[1] Entitled *Etymologisches Wörterbuch der deutschen Sprache.* Strassburg, Karl J. Trübner. 1883. Royal 8°. Price 10 Mark 50 Pfennige.

[2] Thus under sana (p. 266) might have been given, in addition to Latin senex, the words senior, senectus, senilis, senesco, senator, senatus, etc.; but these are readily suggested by senex.

[3] Thus the interesting compound sene-schal is added under sana, not as a genuine English cognate, but as a borrowing through the French from Continental Germanic, where its first member is indeed a genuine cognate.

[4] Compare note [3], above.

[5] For these accents I have relied on BOEHTLINGK's *Sanskrit-Wörterbuch in Kürzerer Fassung* as far as it has appeared, i.e. to the end of bh, and for the rest of the alphabet, on the great thesaurus of BOEHTLINGK AND ROTH. There are many words accented in more than one way (e.g., rājyá, rājyà, rājya, ásana, ásaná, dáridra, daridrá, dáiva, dáivá, bhūtí, bhūti, vṛṣṭí, vṛṣṭi, venú, vénu); such have generally been left unmarked; but of a few common words like mánu, dvipád, paçú, pāpá, and matí, the prevailing accent is given, especially, if (as in the case of bhṛtí or pātṛí) the other accent is rare, or (as in the case of çúṣka) not authenticated.

according to the rules, in order to make more tangible the difference between homonymous determinatives and possessives.[1]

What form should be given to the headings of articles is often a question. For denominative verbs, I have chosen the stem-form (e.g., mantraya rather than mantray) ; to this is prefixed the root-sign (√), merely in order to catch the eye ; the sign must not be understood as meaning that such stems are in any wise co-ordinate with roots. The stems of the perfect active participle and of the primary comparatives are given as ending in vāńs and yāńs, but without any implication that these are theoretically better than the weaker forms. Roots with medial or final ar or ṛ are given in the latter form, and so are the stems in ar or ṛ.[2]

The synopses of conjugational forms which follow each verbal root are based on the collections, still in manuscript, made by Professor WHITNEY.[3] These were placed at my disposal by him with the greatest kindness. They include all the verb-forms cited by the St. Petersburg Lexicon and BOEHT-LINGK's Abridgment, as occurring in the actual literature, besides very extensive gleanings made independently by Professor WHITNEY from texts represented in the Lexicon,[4] and from others published since its completion,[5] or even not yet published.[6] In the description and classification of the forms, I have followed WHITNEY. It often happens that there are several forms in actual use for the same tense ; in such cases, the commonest one has been given, or else the one prescribed by the Hindu Root-book (dhātu-pāṭha), or sometimes more than one form. Although in the case of many roots the aorist is confined almost exclusively to the Vedic language, I have neverthe-less given the aorist in such cases in order to fill out the conjugational scheme, since this seemed desirable from a pedagogical point of view. For pedagogical reasons, also, the secondary conjugations have been for the most part omitted. Many roots which are conjugated regularly in only one voice show forms of the other voice in the Epos, especially where the metre demands them. It is very difficult to say just how far such forms should be included, and my course in accepting or rejecting them has been, I fear, not wholly consistent.

The Notes, which form the third part of this work, will be issued as soon as is practicable. It is designed that they shall be as brief as possible, but shall render ample assistance in the interpretation of difficult passages and

[1] Compare bhímaparākramá and bhímá-parākrama, p. 206.

[2] See WHITNEY, §§ 107 and 108, and com-pare § 370.

[3] See *Proceedings of the American Oriental Society* for May, 1882, p. xiii.

[4] For example, the Çatapatha and Aita-reya Brāhmanas.

[5] Especially GARBE's edition of Apastam-ba's Çrauta Sūtra, and VON SCHROEDER's Maitrāyanī.

[6] The Jaiminīya Brāhmana.

the explanation of allusions to the antiquities of India. The plan includes also concise literary introductions to the various selections.

An open acknowledgment of my thanks is due to the printers of the vocabulary, Messrs. J. S. CUSHING & Co. They have performed their part with such intelligence, accuracy, and skill as to merit most cordial recognition.

In conclusion, I desire to make public expression of my gratitude to my honored teacher, Professor WILLIAM DWIGHT WHITNEY, for his constant interest in this undertaking and for his generous aid. I can only hope that the book may do something to further the cause in which he has labored long and devotedly, and that it may help to enlarge the scope of classical teaching, to quicken the interest in the history of our mother-tongue, and to make Sanskrit study among us increasingly fruitful.

C. R. L.

HOLLIS HALL, HARVARD COLLEGE,
CAMBRIDGE, MASSACHUSETTS,
December, 1883.

NOTE TO THE FOURTH ISSUE (1908).

THE references to Whitney's Sanskrit Grammar which are given in Parts II. and III. of this book are, I believe, absolutely correct throughout for the first edition of the Grammar. The second edition of the Grammar did not appear until after the plates for Parts II. and III. of the Reader were made. The section-numbers of the second edition of the Grammar (see Whitney's Preface thereto) are substantially unchanged from those of the first; but there are some slight alterations, notably in the sequence from § 98 to § 108, and again in the sequence from § 708 to § 713 (whereby the references to the section on the important verb çru are thrown out of gear). Occasionally, too, a statement has been taken from one section and put into another and more appropriate section: thus the euphonic treatment of bhos has been shifted from § 176a to § 174b. Moreover, the subsections are much more thoroughly marked (with a, b, c, etc.) in the second edition. Users of the second or third edition of the Grammar will often have to make a slight allowance for these changes, seeking, for example, 844^2 under 844a, 371^{12} under 371k, and the like. It seemed hardly worth while to alter the plates to suit these changes; a little practical common sense will usually offset the apparent inaccuracy. Mention of these matters has already been made by me below, in the Postscript, p. 405; but as it seems usually to be overlooked there, I have thought it well to repeat the mention in this more conspicuous place.

C. R. L.

JUNE, 1908.

CONTENTS.

———◦◦◦———

PART I.

A. From the Mahā-bhārata.

B. From the Hitopadeça.

C. From the Kathā-sarit-sāgara.

* For detailed synopsis, see Notes.

INTRODUCTORY SUGGESTIONS.

It is chiefly at the beginning that the difficulties of Sanskrit present themselves. The variety of forms, the strange alphabet, the peculiarities of word and sentence combination,—all these simultaneously confront the student at the very outset. Accordingly, the plan followed with my classes, and for which provision is here made, is to distribute these difficulties over the first few weeks of the course. The common paradigms of nouns and verbs should first be learned. These are given by the Grammar in transliteration. The reading of the first four pages of the Nala in Roman letters should then be taken up. The Reader gives these in transliteration on an inset conveniently facing the same text in *nāgarī* letters. The student may thus become familiar with the *form* and *sound* of the vocables, without being embarrassed by the alphabet and the running together of the words. Next, the same familiar text should be read aloud over and over again in *nāgarī* letters. I am convinced that the easiest way to master the alphabet is to read frequently in it words which one already knows. The next step will be the reading of pages five to nine without the help of a transliteration, but with the aid given by the typographical separation of the words, which has been carried out so far as is practicable, though in violation of Indian usage. Finally, from this point on, the reading may be continued without other help for the difficulties of euphonic and graphic combination than is offered by the notes.

After finishing the Nala, the student should take up the Hitopadeça. Selections xvii., xx., and xi. are very easy and are good to begin with. The remaining short ones from vi. to xxi. may then follow in order; and finally the long selections ii. to v.

It is recommended that the student use the stories from the Kathā-sarit-sāgara for exercise in rapid reading, as soon as he has acquired a fair vocabulary from what precedes. The passages from "Manu" may be read as they stand.

Of the Vedic selections, the easiest are numbers xxxi. (Rigveda i. 1), xxxiii., xxxviii., xxxix., xli., xlv., xlvi., and lix.; and it is advisable to read these first and in the order here mentioned. Selection xxxii., as being one of poetic merit and not over-hard, may next be taken up, and after it, the Varuna-hymns, selections xliii.-xliv.; then the hymns in dramatic form, selections xxxv., xxxvii., and lvi.

After these, selections **xxxvi., xl., xlii., xlvii., xlviii., liv.,** and **lxii.** may be rapidly read. There will then remain the selections for the burial-service, **xlix.–liii., lvii., lx., lxi.,** and **xxxiv.,** and those for the wedding, **lviii., lvii.,** and **lv.** These may properly be read last, in order that they may be fresh in the mind when reading the Sūtras, where constant reference is made to them.

The Brāhmaṇa pieces may be read in the order in which they are printed; but selections **lxvi., lxvii., lxviii.,** and **lxxii.** ought not to be taken up, unless selections **lvi., xlvii., lxii.,** and **xlvi.** have previously been studied.

It is very undesirable to attempt to read the Sūtra chapters until one is familiar with the burial and wedding stanzas just mentioned. It is advisable to write out a translation of these chapters, and to insert therein each *mantra* in its proper place, writing out the original of the *mantra* in full, and its translation, the latter also in metre, if possible.

Since the synopses following each verbal root in the vocabulary represent the great mass of all the forms in actual use (rather than those simply prescribed by the grammarians), and so correspond to the "principal parts" of the Latin and Greek verbs, the student should make it his duty to learn the synopsis for each root when he first meets verbal forms of that root in the text.

Attention is called to the explanations and abbreviations (pages 289-294): these should be looked over carefully before using the vocabulary.

A BRIEF LIST OF BOOKS FOR STUDENTS OF SANSKRIT.

———❖❖❖———

THIS list has a purely practical aim,[1] and is restricted to a few of the more important and useful books and[2] to such as are neither rare nor out of print. It includes (a) a grammar, (b) readers, (c) dictionaries, (d) classical works, books for the study (e) of the Rigveda and its literature, and (f) of the Atharvaveda, and last (g) some books on antiquities and the history of the literature and the religions of India.

1. **Whitney**, William Dwight. A Sanskrit Grammar, including both the classical language, and the older dialects, of Veda and Brahmana. Leipzig, Breitkopf and Härtel. London, Trübner & Co. 1879. 8°. Price (bound in cloth) 12 shillings.

This may be had in Boston of Ginn and Company. The work exists also in a German translation, which may be had of the Leipzig publishers.

2. **Bühler**, Georg. Third Book of Sanskrit. With a glossary by Vishnu P. Shastri Pandit. Second edition. Bombay. 1877. 12°. 128 pages of text and 97 of glossary. Price 9 annas.

This book can be procured from Trübner & Co. in London (price 3 shillings). It contains the entire Story of Nala (26 chapters), Daçaratha's Death (Rāmāyana, ii. 63-64), and four stories from the Panchatantra. For beginners, the typography proves troublesome and the glossary too meagre; but the little volume is inexpensive and contains excellent material for easy and rapid reading, and so is highly to be recommended to those who have finished the classical part of this Reader and wish to continue their Sanskrit. For such students the glossary would be quite sufficient.

3. **Böhtlingk**, Otto. Sanskrit-Chrestomathie. Zweite, gänzlich umgearbeitete Auflage. St. Petersburg. 1877. Large 8°. 372 pages. Price 4 Mark 80 Pfennige.

This work and the two following are publications of the Russian Imperial Academy, and should be ordered through the Academy's agent, Leopold Voss, of Leipzig. The volume contains selections from the Veda (Mantra, Brāhmana, and Sūtra), from the Mahā-bhārata, Rāmāyana, Vishnu-purāna, Kathā-sarit-sāgara, Hitopadeça, "Manu's Laws," and Pānini's Grammar, and from various other books ; a rich collection of proverbs ; the Vedānta-sāra, a philosophical treatise, in text and translation ; and the entire drama, Ratnāvali. The Vedic hymns are all translated in the volume mentioned below, no. 15 ; and the notes show where many of the other selections may be found translated. Like all publications of the Academy, this is sold at an extremely low price. Since the book has no vocabulary, the student will at this point need to get a dictionary.

[1] Hence the prices are included. Both the Mark and the shilling may be reckoned as a quarter of a dollar. The prices given with the titles are publishers' prices. To these prices, except when given in dollars, should be added the duty, which is 25 per cent. The books will cost the American purchaser somewhat more or less according to his facilities for obtaining foreign books.

[2] With perhaps one exception, no. 18, which can, however, be had of second-hand dealers.

4. Böhtlingk, Otto. Sanskrit-Wörterbuch in kürzerer Fassung. St. Petersburg. 1879–. 4°.

To be ordered through Voss (see above). Parts I. to IV. have appeared, and reach to the end of bh; they cover 1167 pages, i.e. nigh two-thirds of the whole, and cost 34 Mark 80 Pfennige. The rest may be expected in the course of 1885. The manuscript is ready as far as varṇa. The work is an abridgment of the following.

5. Böhtlingk, Otto, and Rudolph **Roth**. Sanskrit-Wörterbuch. St. Petersburg. 1855–1875. Seven volumes. 4°. Price 177 Mark 90 Pfennige.

To be ordered through Voss (see above). This work, which is often called the "St. Petersburg Lexicon," is by far the most important production of Sanskrit scholarship. To such as wish to make any special study of the language and literature, it is absolutely indispensable.

6. Williams, Monier. A Sanskrit-English Dictionary, etymologically and philologically arranged, with special reference to Greek, Latin, Gothic, German, Anglo-Saxon, and other cognate Indo-European languages. London and New York, Macmillan and Co. 1872. 4°. 1186 pages. Price 94 shillings 6 d. in England, or $24 in the United States.

This is the only dictionary of Sanskrit into English which approaches completeness. It is in one compact and handy volume and is very convenient for reading works of the classical period. Unfortunately, the common meanings of a word are not distinguished from those which are seldom or never found. All Sanskrit words are given in transliteration, and the roots and more important words in *nāgarī* letters also.

7. Williams, Monier. S'akuntalā, a Sanskrit drama in seven acts, by Kālidāsa. Second edition. London and New York, Macmillan and Co. 1876. 8°. 339 pages. Price 21 shillings in England, or $5.25 in the U.S.

This gives literal English translations of all the metrical passages, explanatory notes, and the Sanskritization of the Prakrit passages, and all on the same page with the text of this, the most famous of the plays.

8. Kielhorn, Franz, and Georg **Bühler**. Panchatantra. Edited with notes. Bombay. 1868. 8°.

The work constitutes numbers IV., III., and I. of the "Bombay Sanskrit Series." Number IV. (comprehending book I.) appeared in a second edition in 1873. The book may be had of Trübner & Co., London. The price of the entire work is 8 shillings; but the first book may be had separately for 3 shillings. The Panchatantra is easy and entertaining reading. It has been admirably translated into German by Benfey: Pantschatantra. Leipzig, F. A. Brockhaus. 1859. 2 vols. 8°. Price 24 Mark. The translation is accompanied by a very valuable history of fable-literature.

9. Delbrück, Berthold. Vedische Chrestomathie. Mit Anmerkungen und Glossar. Halle, Buchhandlung des Waisenhauses. 1874. 8°. Price 3 Mark.

This contains 47 hymns from the Rigveda. Of these, only five are repeated in this Reader. Both text and glossary are in transliteration. On account of the small price of the book, its mention may prove useful to such as do not wish to buy the two complete editions following (numbers 11 and 12).

10. Windisch, Ernst. Zwölf Hymnen des Rigveda. Mit Sāyaṇa's Commentar. Text. Wörterbuch zu Sāyaṇa. Appendices. Leipzig, S. Hirzel. 1883. 8°. Price 5 Mark.

This gives the text, and the comment of the great scholiast, both in *nāgarī* letters. The text is printed with the genuine accentuation (as in this Reader). The book serves a useful purpose as introduction to the native Hindu or traditional exegesis of the Veda. The vocabulary does not cover the hymns themselves; but seven of the twelve hymns are translated in the little book mentioned below, no. 15.

11. **Aufrecht**, Theodor. Die Hymnen des Ṛigveda. Herausgegeben. Zweite Auflage. Bonn, Adolph Marcus. 1877. 2 volumes. 8°. Price 20 Mark.

The entire *sanhita* text is given in transliteration, and extracts from the *pada* text at the foot of each page. The exceedingly valuable appendix contains lists of the poets, divinities, and metres, and a complete table of first lines of every stanza, with references to the concordant texts of other Vedas.

12. **Müller**, F. Max. The Hymns of the Rigveda, in the Samhita and Pada texts, reprinted from the editio princeps. Second edition. London, Trübner & Co. 1877. 2 volumes. 8°. Price 32 shillings.

This edition gives the two texts complete on parallel pages and in *nāgari* letters. The names of the poets, divinities, and metres are given at the beginning of each hymn.

13. **Grassmann**, Hermann. Wörterbuch zum Rig-veda. Leipzig, F. A. Brockhaus. 1873[-1875]. 8°. Price 30 Mark.

This is not only a dictionary, but also a complete concordance to the Rigveda. It is a work of wonderful industry, method, clearness, and accuracy. Aside from the St. Petersburg Lexicon, this dictionary stands next in importance, for Vedic students, after the Vedic text itself.

14. **Grassmann**, Hermann. Rig-veda. Uebersetzt und mit kritischen und erläuternden Anmerkungen versehen. Leipzig, F. A. Brockhaus. 1876. 1877. 2 volumes. 8°. Price 24 Mark.

This translation is entirely in metre, except for a few corrupt or difficult hymns. The student can almost invariably see just what word Grassmann intended as the rendering of any given word of the text. This work is especially useful as giving a convenient general view of the contents of the Rigveda, and as enabling the student to grasp easily many matters touching the metres, the arrangement, and the textual condition of the original.

15. **Geldner**, Karl, und Adolf **Kägi**. Siebenzig Lieder des Rigveda. Uebersetzt. Mit Beiträgen von R. Roth. Tübingen. H. Laupp'sche Buchhandlung. 1875. 12°. Price 3 Mark.

Thirty-six of the seventy hymns of which this book gives metrical translations were later incorporated by Böhtlingk into his Chrestomathy (no. 3, above).

16. **Aufrecht**, Theodor. Das Aitareya Brāhmaṇa. Mit Auszügen aus dem Commentare von Sāyaṇācārya und anderen Beilagen herausgegeben. Bonn, Adolph Marcus. 1879. 8°. Price 11 Mark.

This Brāhmaṇa belongs to the Rigveda. The text is in transliteration. The translation of Haug (London, Trübner & Co. 1863) would be of help; but it is inaccurate and hard to get. A good many passages are translated in volumes I., II., and V. of Muir (below, no. 26). Using these as an introduction, and the St. Petersburg Lexicon for help in hard places, an advanced student can make good progress with this text.

17. **Stenzler**, Adolf Friedrich. Indische Hausregeln. Sanskrit und deutsch herausgegeben. I. Açvalāyana. Erstes Heft. Text. Leipzig. 1864. 8°. Price 2 Mark. — Zweites Heft. Uebersetzung. 1865. Price 3 Mark.

Published by the German Oriental Society, in volumes III. and IV. of the Abhandlungen für die Kunde des Morgenlandes. To be ordered through the Society's agent, F. A. Brockhaus, in Leipzig. These are the Grihya-sūtras belonging to the Rigveda.

18. **Roth**, R., und **Whitney**, W. D. Atharva Veda Sanhita. Herausgegeben. Erster Band. Text. Berlin, Ferd. Dümmler. 1856. Royal 8°. Price 28 Mark 50 Pfennige.

This is the most important and interesting of the Vedas, after the Rik. It is full of magic incantations and other products of curious superstitions.

19. **Garbe**, Richard. Vaitāna Sûtra. The Ritual of the Atharvaveda. Edited with critical notes and indices. London, Trübner & Co. 1878. 8°. Price 5 shillings.

20. **Garbe**, Richard. Vaitāna Sûtra. Das Ritual des Atharvaveda. Aus dem Sanskrit übersetzt und mit Anmerkungen versehen. London, Trübner & Co. 1878. 8°. Price 5 shillings.

Since this is the only Çranta-sûtra published with translation, and since it is to be had easily and cheaply, it is recommended as an introduction to the works of this class.

21. **Weber**, Albrecht. The history of Indian Literature. Translated from the second German edition by John Mann and Theodor Zachariae. Second edition. London, Trübner & Co. 1878. 8°. Price 10 shillings 6 pence.

This is a systematic treatise covering both the Vedic and the classical Sanskrit literature. It gives abundant and practical bibliographical information. As a guide and as a work of reference it is of the utmost value.

22. **Zimmer**, Heinrich. Altindisches Leben. Die Cultur der vedischen Arier. Nach den Samhitā dargestellt. Berlin, Weidmannsche Buchhandlung. 1879. 8°. Price 10 Mark.

Under the different categories — geography, climate, minerals, plants, animals, agriculture, commerce, dress, food, amusements, family relations, art, etc. — the Vedic texts touching these subjects are discussed, and the results deducible from them are put together in a very readable and pleasant way.

23. **Kägi**, Adolf. Der Rigveda. Die älteste Literatur der Inder. Zweite, umgearbeitete und erweiterte, mit vollständigem Sach- und Wortregister versehene Auflage. Leipzig, Otto Schulze. 1881. 12°. Price 4 Mark.

This contains an account of the Vedic writings in general, descriptions of the gods in language agreeing closely with the actual words of the original as cited in the notes, and sketches of some of the more important phases of Vedic life and thought. The numerous notes are highly useful as a guide to the already extensive literature of these subjects, and point out many interesting parallels of custom, belief, and expression to be found in biblical and classical antiquity.

24. **Barth**, Auguste. The religions of India. Authorized translation by Rev. J. Wood. London, Trübner & Co. 1882. 8°. Price 16 shillings.

The subject is treated in five chapters corresponding to the five grand phases of religious development in India : the Vedic religion ; Brahmanism (ritual, philosophic speculation, decline); Buddhism ; Jainism ; and Hinduism (the sects and their great deities, Vishnuism and Çivaism, reforming sects, cultus). The copious references to the literature of the subjects in hand add greatly to the value of the work.

25. **Oldenberg**, Hermann. Buddha; his life, his doctrine, his order. Translated from the German by William Hoey. London, Williams and Norgate. 1882. 8°. Price 18 shillings.

Oldenberg has recently finished editing (in five volumes) the Vinaya Piṭakam, one of the most important among the Buddhist sacred books. He has a wide and deep knowledge of the original Pāli sources, and in his use of them he is guided by rare critical acumen and good common-sense. His account of Buddha's life, doctrine, and order contains the best results of his studies and they are presented in an extremely attractive form.

26. **Muir**, John. Original Sanskrit texts on the origin and history of the people of India, their religions and institutions. Collected, translated, and illustrated. London, Trübner & Co. 1872–1874. 5 volumes. 8°.

The first four volumes have appeared in a second edition, and the second volume in a third edition. The third volume costs 16 shillings. The price of each of the others is 21 shillings. The first volume discusses the origin of caste. The fifth is devoted to the cosmogony, mythology, religious ideas, life, and manners of the Indians in the Vedic age.

PART I.
THE SANSKRIT TEXT.

[Page 1.]

atha nalopākhyānam.

bṛhadaçva uvāca.

āsīd rājā, nalo nāma, vīrasenasuto balī,
upapanno guṇāir iṣṭāi, rūpavān, açvakovidaḥ.

5 atiṣṭhan manujendrāṇām mūrdhni devapatir yathā,
upary upari sarveṣām āditya iva tejasā ;
brahmaṇyo, vedavic, chūro, niṣadheṣu mahīpatiḥ,
akṣapriyaḥ, satyavādī, mahān akṣāuhiṇīpatiḥ ;
īpsito naranārīṇām, udāraḥ, saṁyatendriyaḥ,

10 rakṣitā, dhanvinām çreṣthaḥ, sākṣād iva manuḥ svayam.
tathāivāsīd vidarbheṣu bhīmo, bhīmaparākramaḥ,
çūraḥ, sarvaguṇāir yuktaḥ, prajākāmaḥ, sa cāprajaḥ.
sa prajārthe param yatnam akarot, susamāhitaḥ.
tam abhyagacchad brahmarṣir, damano nāma, bhārata.

15 taṁ sa bhīmaḥ, prajākāmas, toṣayām āsa, dharmavit,
mahiṣyā saha, rājendra, satkāreṇa, suvarcasam.
tasmāi prasanno damanaḥ sabhāryāya varaṁ dadāu,

[Page 3.]

70 tato 'ntarikṣago vācaṁ vyājahāra nalaṁ tadā :
hantavyo 'smi na te, rājan ; kariṣyāmi tava priyam ;

21 damayantīsakāçe tvāṁ kathayiṣyāmi, nāiṣadha,
yathā tvad anyam puruṣaṁ na sā maṁsyati karhi cit.

22 5 evam uktas tato haṁsam utsasarja mahīpatiḥ.
te tu haṁsāḥ samutpatya vidarbhān agamaṁs tataḥ.

23 vidarbhanagarīṁ gatvā, damayantyās tadāntike
nipetus te garutmantaḥ, sā dadarça ca tān gaṇān.

24 sā, tān adbhutarūpān vāi dṛṣṭvā, sakhigaṇāvṛtā,
10 hṛṣṭā grahītuṁ khagamāṁs tvaramāṇepacakrame.

25 atha haṁsā visasṛpuḥ sarvataḥ pramadāvane.
ekāikaças tadā kanyās tān haṁsān samupādravan.

26 damayantī tu yaṁ haṁsaṁ samupādhāvad antike,
sa, mānuṣīṁ giraṁ kṛtvā, damayantīm athābravīt :

27 15 damayanti, nalo nāma, niṣadheṣu mahīpatiḥ,
açvinoḥ sadṛço rūpe ; na samās tasya mānuṣāḥ.

28 tasya vāi yadi bhāryā tvam bhavethā, varavarṇini,
saphalaṁ te bhavej janma, rūpaṁ cedaṁ, sumadhyame.
vayaṁ hi devagandharvamānuṣoragarākṣasān

20 dṛṣṭavanto ; na cāsmābhir dṛṣṭapūrvas tathāvidhaḥ.
tvaṁ cāpi ratnaṁ nārīṇām, nareṣu ca nalo varaḥ ;
viçiṣṭāyā viçiṣṭena saṁgamo guṇavān bhavet.
evam uktā tu haṁsena damayantī, vicāṁ pate,

kanyāratnaṁ, kumārāṅç ca trīn udārān, mahāyaçāḥ,
damayantīṁ, damaṁ, dāntaṁ, damanaṁ ca suvarcasam,
upapannān guṇāiḥ sarvāir, bhīmān, bhīmaparākramān.
damayantī tu rūpeṇa, tejasā, yaçasā, çriyā,
5 sāubhāgyena ca, lokeṣu yaçaḥ prāpa, sumadhyamā.
atha tāṁ, vayasi prāpte, dāsīnāṁ samalaṁkṛtam
çataṁ, çataṁ sakhīnāṁ ca, paryupāsac, chacīm iva.
tatra sma rājate bhāimī, sarvābharaṇabhūṣitā,
sakhīmadhye, 'navadyāṅgī, vidyut sāudāmanī yathā,
10 atīva rūpasampannā, çrīr ivāyatalocanā.
na deveṣu, na yakṣeṣu, tādṛg rūpavatī kva cit,
mānuṣeṣv api cānyeṣu, dṛṣṭapūrvātha vā çrutā,
cittapramāthinī bālā devānām api sundarī.
nalaç ca naraçārdūlo, lokeṣv apratimo bhuvi,
15 kandarpa iva rūpeṇa mūrtimān abhavat svayam.
tasyāḥ samīpe tu nalam praçaçaṁsuḥ kutūhalāt,
nāiṣadhasya samīpe tu damayantīm punaḥ punaḥ.
17 tayor adṛṣṭakāmo 'bhūc chṛṇvatoḥ satataṁ guṇān ;
anyonyam prati, kāunteya, sa vyavardhata hṛcchayaḥ.
18 20 açaknuvan nalaḥ kāmam tadā dhārayituṁ hṛdā,
antaḥpurasamīpasthe vana āste raho gataḥ.
19 sa dadarça tato haṁsāñ jātarūpapariṣkṛtān ;
vane vicaratāṁ teṣām ekaṁ jagrāha pakṣiṇam.

abravīt tatra taṁ haṁsaṁ : tvam apy evaṁ nale vada.
tathety uktvāṇḍajaḥ kanyāṁ vidarbhasya, viçāṁ pate,
punar āgamya niṣadhān, nale sarvaṁ nyavedayat.
iti nalopākhyāne prathamaḥ sargaḥ.

5   bṛhadaçva uvāca.
damayantī tu, tac chrutvā vaco haṁsasya, bhārata,
tataḥ prabhṛti na svasthā nalam prati babhūva sā.
tataç cintāparā, dīnā, vivarṇavadanā, kṛçā,
babhūva damayantī tu, niḥçvāsaparamā tadā.
10 ūrdhvadṛṣṭir, dhyānaparā, babhūvonmattadarçanā,
pāṇḍuvarṇā kṣaṇenātha, hṛcchayāviṣṭacetanā.
na çayyāsanabhogeṣu ratiṁ vindati karhi cit.
na naktaṁ, na divā çete, hā heti rudatī punaḥ.
tato vidarbhapataye damayantyāḥ sakhījanaḥ
15 nyavedayat tām asvasthāṁ damayantīṁ nareçvare.
tac chrutvā nṛpatir bhīmo damayantīsakhīgaṇāt,
cintayām āsa tat kāryam sumahat svāṁ sutām prati.
sa samīkṣya mahīpālaḥ svāṁ sutām prāptayāuvanām,
apaçyad ātmanā kāryaṁ damayantyāḥ svayaṁvaram.
20 sa saṁnimantrayām āsa mahīpālān viçām patiḥ :
anubhūyatām ! ayaṁ, vīrāḥ, svayaṁvara iti, prabho.

॥ अथ नलोपाख्यानम् ॥

बृहदश्व उवाच ।

आसीद् राजा नलो नाम वीरसेनसुतो बली ।
उपपन्नो गुणैर् इष्टै रूपवान् अश्वकोविदः ॥१॥

5 अतिष्ठन् मनुजेन्द्राणां मूर्ध्नि देवपतिर् यथा ।
उपर्य् उपरि सर्वेषाम् आदित्य इव तेजसा ॥२॥

ब्रह्मण्यो वेदविच् छूरो निषधेषु महीपतिः ।
अक्षप्रियः सत्यवादी महान् अक्षौहिणीपतिः ॥३॥

ईप्सितो नरनारीणाम् उदारः संयतेन्द्रियः ।
10 रक्षिता धन्विनां श्रेष्ठः साक्षाद् इव मनुः स्वयम् ॥४॥

तथैवासीद् विदर्भेषु भीमो भीमपराक्रमः ।
शूरः सर्वगुणैर् युक्तः प्रजाकामः स चाप्रजः ॥५॥

स प्रजार्थे परं यत्नम् अकरोत् सुसमाहितः ।
तम् अभ्यगच्छद् ब्रह्मर्षिर् दमनो नाम भारत ॥६॥

15 तं स भीमः प्रजाकामस् तोषयामास धर्मवित् ।
महिष्या सह राजेन्द्र सत्कारेण सुवर्चसम् ॥७॥

तस्मै प्रसन्नो दमनः सभार्याय वरं ददौ ।

1

कन्यारत्नं कुमारांश् च त्रीन् उदारान् महायशाः ॥८॥

दमयन्तीं दमं दान्तं दमनं च सुवर्चसम् ।

उपपन्नान् गुणैः सर्वैर् भीमान् भीमपराक्रमान् ॥९॥

दमयन्ती तु रूपेण तेजसा यशसा श्रिया ।

सौभाग्येन च लोकेषु यशः प्राप सुमध्यमा ॥१०॥

अथ तां वयसि प्राप्ते दासीनां समलंकृतम् ।

शतं शतं सखीनां च पर्युपासच् छचीम् इव ॥११॥

तत्र स्म राजते भैमी सर्वाभरणभूषिता ।

सखीमध्ये ऽनवद्याङ्गी विद्युत् सौदामनी यथा ॥१२॥

अतीव रूपसंपन्ना श्रीर् इवायतलोचना ।

न देवेषु न यक्षेषु ताहृग् रूपवती क्व चित् ॥१३॥

मानुषेष्व् अपि चान्येषु हृष्टपूर्वाथ वा श्रुता ।

चित्तप्रमाथिनी बाला देवानाम् अपि सुन्दरी ॥१४॥

नलश् च नरशार्दूलो लोकेष्व् अप्रतिमो भुवि ।

कन्दर्प इव रूपेण मूर्तिमान् अभवत् स्वयम् ॥१५॥

तस्याः समीपे तु नलं प्रशशंसुः कुतूहलात् ।

नैषधस्य समीपे तु दमयन्तीं पुनः पुनः ॥१६॥

तयोर् अदृष्टकामो ऽभूच् छृण्वतोः सततं गुणान् ।

अन्योन्यं प्रति कौन्तेय स व्यवर्धत हृच्छयः ॥१७॥

अशक्नुवन् नलः कामं तदा धारयितुं हृदा ।

अन्तःपुरसमीपस्थे वन आस्ते रहो गतः ॥१८॥

स ददर्श ततो हंसाञ् जातरूपपरिष्कृतान् ।

वने विचरतां तेषाम् एकं जग्राह पक्षिणम् ॥१९॥

ततो ऽन्तरिक्षगो वाचं व्याजहार नलं तदा ।
हन्तव्यो ऽस्मि न ते राजन् करिष्यामि तव प्रियम् ॥२०॥
दमयन्तीसकाशे त्वां कथयिष्यामि नैषध ।
यथा त्वद् अन्यं पुरुषं न सा मंस्यति कर्हि चित् ॥२१॥
5 एवम् उक्तस् ततो हंसम् उत्ससर्जे महीपतिः ।
ते तु हंसाः समुत्पत्य विदर्भान् अगमंस् ततः ॥२२॥
विदर्भनगरीं गत्वा दमयन्त्यास् तदन्तिके ।
निपेतुस् ते गरुत्मन्तः सा ददर्शे च तान् गणान् ॥२३॥
सा तान् अद्भुतरूपान् वै दृष्ट्वा सखिगणावृता ।
10 हृष्टा ग्रहीतुं खगमांस् त्वरमाणोपचक्रमे ॥२४॥
अथ हंसा विससृपुः सर्वतः प्रमदावने ।
एकैकशस् तदा कन्यास् तान् हंसान् समुपाद्रवन् ॥२५॥
दमयन्ती तु यं हंसं समुपाधावद् अन्तिके ।
स मानुषीं गिरं कृत्वा दमयन्तीम् अथाब्रवीत् ॥२६॥
15 दमयन्ति नलो नाम निषधेषु महीपतिः ।
अश्विनोः सदृशो रूपे न समास् तस्य मानुषाः ॥२७॥
तस्य वै यदि भार्या त्वं भवेथा वरवर्णिनि ।
सफलं ते भवेज् जन्म रूपं चेदं सुमध्यमे ॥२८॥
वयं हि देवगन्धर्वमानुषोरगराक्षसान् ।
20 दृष्टवन्तो न चास्माभिर् दृष्टपूर्वस् तथाविधः ॥२९॥
त्वं चापि रत्नं नारीणां नरेषु च नलो वरः ।
विशिष्टाया विशिष्टेन संगमो गुणवान् भवेत् ॥३०॥
एवम् उक्ता तु हंसेन दमयन्ती विशां पते ।

अब्रवीत् तच्च तं हंसं त्वम् अप् य॑वं नले वद ॥३१॥

तथेत्य् उक्त्वाण्डजः कन्यां विदर्भस्य विशां पते ।

पुनर् आगम्य निषधान् नले सर्वं न्यवेदयत् ॥३२॥

॥ इति नलोपाख्याने प्रथमः सर्गः ॥१॥

———

5   बृहदश्व उवाच ।

दमयन्ती तु तच् छ्रुत्वा वचो हंसस्य भारत ।

ततः प्रभृति न स्वस्था नलं प्रति बभूव सा ॥१॥

ततश् चिन्तापरा दीना विवर्णवदना कृशा ।

बभूव दमयन्ती तु निःश्वासपरमा तदा ॥२॥

10 ऊर्ध्वेहष्टिर् ध्यानपरा बभूवोन्मत्तदर्शना ।

पाण्डुवर्णा क्षणेनाथ हृच्छयाविष्टचेतना ॥३॥

न शय्यासनभोगेषु रतिं विन्दति कार्हि चित् ।

न नक्तं न दिवा शेते हा हेति रुदती पुनः ॥४॥

ततो विदर्भपतये दमयन्त्याः सखीजनः ।

15 न्यवेदयत् ताम् अस्वस्थां दमयन्तीं नरेश्वरे ॥५॥

तच् छ्रुत्वा नृपतिर् भीमो दमयन्तीसखीगणात् ।

चिन्तयामास तत् कार्यं सुमहत् स्वां सुतां प्रति ॥६॥

स समीक्ष्य महीपालः स्वां सुतां प्राप्तयौवनाम् ।

अपश्यद् आत्मना कार्यं दमयन्त्याः स्वयंवरम् ॥७॥

20 स संनिमन्त्रयामास महीपालान् विशां पतिः ।

अनुभूयताम् अयं वीराः स्वयंवर इति प्रभो ॥८॥

श्रुत्वा तु पार्थिवाः सर्वे दमयन्त्याः स्वयंवरम् ।
अभिजग्मुस् ततो भीमं राजानो भीमशासनात् ॥९॥
हस्त्यश्वरथघोषेण पूरयन्तो वसुंधराम् ।
विचित्रमाल्याभरणैर् बलैर् हृद्यैः स्वलंकृतैः ॥१०॥
तेषां भीमो महाबाहुः पार्थिवानां महात्मनाम् ।
यथार्हम् अकरोत् पूजां ते ऽवसंस् तत्र पूजिताः ॥११॥
एतस्मिन् एव काले तु सुराणाम् ऋषिसत्तमौ ।
अटमानौ महात्मानाव् इन्द्रलोकम् इतो गतौ ॥१२॥
नारदः पर्वतश् चैव महाप्राज्ञौ महाव्रतौ ।
देवराजस्य भवनं विविशाते सुपूजितौ ॥१३॥
ताव् अर्चयित्वा मघवा ततः कुशलम् अव्ययम् ।
पप्रच्छानामयं चापि तयोः सर्वगतं विभुः ॥१४॥

नारद उवाच ।

आवयोः कुशलं देव सर्वत्र गतम् ईश्वर ।
लोके च मघवन् कृत्स्ने नृपाः कुशलिनो विभो ॥१५॥

बृहदश्व उवाच ।

नारदस्य वचः श्रुत्वा पप्रच्छ बलवृत्रहा ।
धर्मज्ञाः पृथिवीपालास् त्यक्तजीवितयोधिनः ॥१६॥
शस्त्रेण निधनं काले ये गच्छन्त्य् अपराङ्मुखाः ।
अयं लोको ऽक्षयस् तेषां यथैव मम कामधुक् ॥१७॥
क्व नु ते क्षत्रियाः शूरा न हि पश्यामि तान् अहम् ।
आगच्छतो महीपालान् दयितान् अतिथीन् मम ॥१८॥

एवम् उक्तस् तु शक्रेण नारदः प्रत्यभाषत ।

मृगयु मे मघवन् येन न दृश्यन्ते महीक्षितः ॥१९॥

विदर्भराज्ञो दुहिता दमयन्तीति विश्रुता ।

रूपेण समतिक्रान्ता पृथिव्यां सर्वयोषितः ॥२०॥

तस्याः स्वयंवरः शक्र भविता नचिराद् इव ।

तत्र गच्छन्ति राजानो राजपुत्राश् च सर्वशः ॥२१॥

तां रत्नभूतां लोकस्य प्रार्थयन्तो महीक्षितः ।

काङ्क्षन्ति स विशेषेण बलवृत्रनिषूदन ॥२२॥

एतस्मिन् कथ्यमाने तु लोकपालाश् च सामिकाः ।

आजग्मुर् देवराजस्य समीपम् अमरोत्तमाः ॥२३॥

ततस् ते शुश्रुवुः सर्वे नारदस्य वचो महत् ।

श्रुत्वैव चाब्रुवन् हृष्टा गच्छामो वयम् अप् उत ॥२४॥

ततः सर्वे महाराज सगणाः सहवाहनाः ।

विदर्भान् अभिजग्मुस् ते यतः सर्वे महीक्षितः ॥२५॥

नलो ऽपि राजा कौन्तेय श्रुत्वा राज्ञां समागमम् ।

अभ्यगच्छद् अदीनात्मा दमयन्तीम् अनुव्रतः ॥२६॥

अथ देवाः पथि नलं ददृशुर् भूतले स्थितम् ।

साक्षाद् इव स्थितं मूर्त्या मन्मथं रूपसंपदा ॥२७॥

तं दृष्ट्वा लोकपालास् ते भ्राजमानं यथा रविम् ।

तस्थुर् विगतसंकल्पा विस्मिता रूपसंपदा ॥२८॥

ततो ऽन्तरिक्षे विष्टभ्य विमानानि दिवौकसः ।

अब्रुवन् नैषधं राजन् अवतीर्य नभस्तलात् ॥२९॥

भो भो नैषध राजेन्द्र नल सत्यव्रतो भवान् ।

अस्माकं कुरु साहाय्यं दूतो भव नरोत्तम ॥ ३० ॥

॥ इति नलोपाख्याने द्वितीयः सर्गः ॥ २ ॥

———

बृहदश्च उवाच ।

तेभ्यः प्रतिज्ञाय नलः करिष्ये इति भारत ।

अथैतान् परिपप्रच्छ कृताञ्जलिर् उपस्थितः ॥ १ ॥

के वै भवन्तः कम् चासौ यस्याहं दूत ईप्सितः ।

किं च तद् वो मया कार्यं कथयध्वं यथातथम् ॥ २ ॥

एवम् उक्ते नैषधेन मघवान् अभ्यभाषत ।

अमरान् वै निबोधास्मान् दमयन्त्यर्थम् आगतान् ॥ ३ ॥

अहम् इन्द्रो ऽयम् अग्निश् च तथैवायम् अपां पतिः ।

शरीरान्तकरो नॄणां यमो ऽयम् अपि पार्थिव ॥ ४ ॥

त्वं वै समागतान् अस्मान् दमयन्त्यै निवेदय ।

लोकपाला महेन्द्राद्याः समायान्ति दिदृक्षवः ॥ ५ ॥

प्राप्तुम् इच्छन्ति देवास् त्वां शक्रो ऽग्निर् वरुणो यमः ।

तेषाम् अन्यतमं देवं पतित्वे वरयस्व ह ॥ ६ ॥

एवम् उक्तः स शक्रेण नलः प्राञ्जलिर् अब्रवीत् ।

एकार्थं समुपेतं मां न प्रेषयितुम् अर्हथ ॥ ७ ॥

कथं नु जातसंकल्पः स्त्रियम् उत्सहते पुमान् ।

परार्थम् ईहशं वक्तुं तत् क्षमन्तु महेश्वराः ॥ ८ ॥

देवा ऊचुः ।

करिष्ये इति संश्रुत्य पूर्वम् अस्मासु नैषध ।

न करिष्यसि कस्मात् त्वं व्रज नैषध माचिरम् ॥ ९ ॥

बृहदश्व उवाच ।

एवम् उक्तः स देवैस् तैर् नैषधः पुनर् अब्रवीत् ।

सुरक्षितानि वेश्मानि प्रवेष्टुं कथम् उत्सहे ॥ १० ॥

प्रवेक्ष्यसीति तं शक्रः पुनर् एवाभ्यभाषत ।

जगाम स तथेत्य् उक्ता दमयन्त्या निवेशनम् ॥ ११ ॥

ददर्श तत्र वैदर्भीं सखीगणसमावृताम् ।

देदीप्यमानां वपुषा श्रिया च वरवर्णिनीम् ॥ १२ ॥

अतीव सुकुमाराङ्गीं तनुमध्यां सुलोचनाम् ।

आक्षिपन्तीम् इव प्रभां शशिनः स्वेन तेजसा ॥ १३ ॥

तस्य दृष्ट्वैव ववृधे कामस् तां चारुहासिनीम् ।

सत्यं चिकीर्षमाणस् तु धारयामास हृच्छयम् ॥ १४ ॥

ततस् ता नैषधं दृष्ट्वा संभ्रान्ताः परमाङ्गनाः ।

आसनेभ्यः समुत्पेतुस् तेजसा तस्य धर्षिताः ॥ १५ ॥

प्रशशंसुश् च सुप्रीता नलं ता विस्मयान्विताः ।

न चैनम् अभ्यभाषन्त मनोभिस् त्व् अभ्यपूजयन् ॥ १६ ॥

अहो रूपम् अहो कान्तिर् अहो धैर्यं महात्मनः ।

को ऽयं देवो ऽथ वा यक्षो गन्धर्वो वा भविष्यति ॥ १७ ॥

न तास् तं शक्नुवन्ति स्म व्याहर्तुम् अपि किं चन ।

तेजसा धर्षितास् तस्य लज्जावत्यो वराङ्गनाः ॥ १८ ॥

अथैनं स्मयमानं तु सितपूर्वाभिभाषिणी ।

दमयन्ती नलं वीरम् अभ्यभाषत विस्मिता ॥ १९ ॥

कस् त्वं सर्वानवद्याङ्ग मम हृच्छयवर्धन ।

प्राप्तो ऽस्य् अमरवद् वीर ज्ञातुम् इच्छामि ते ऽनघ ॥२०॥

कथम् आगमनं चेह कथं चासि न लक्षितः ।

सुरक्षितं हि मे वेश्म राजा चैवोग्रशासनः ॥२१॥

एवम् उक्तस् तु वैदर्भ्या नलस् तां प्रत्युवाच ह ।

नलं मां विद्धि कल्याणि देवदूतम् इहागतम् ॥२२॥

देवास् त्वां प्राप्तुम् इच्छन्ति शक्रो ऽग्निर् वरुणो यमः ।

तेषाम् अन्यतमं देवं पतिं वरय शोभने ॥२३॥

तेषाम् एव प्रभावेन प्रविष्टो ऽहम् अलक्षितः ।

प्रविशन्तं न मां कश् चिद् अपश्यन् नाप्य् अवारयत् ॥२४॥

एतदर्थम् अहं भद्रे प्रेषितः सुरसत्तमैः ।

एतच् छ्रुत्वा शुभे बुद्धिं प्रकुरुष्व यथेच्छसि ॥२५॥

॥ इति नलोपाख्याने तृतीयः सर्गः ॥३॥

बृहदश्व उवाच ।

सा नमस्कृत्य देवेभ्यः प्रहस्य नलमब्रवीत् ।

प्रणयस्व यथाश्रद्धं राजन्किं करवाणि ते ॥१॥

अहं चैव हि यच्चान्यन्ममास्ति वसु किं चन ।

तत्सर्वं तव विश्रब्धं कुरु प्रणयमीश्वर ॥२॥

हंसानां वचनं यत्तु तन्मां दहति पार्थिव ।

त्वत्कृते हि मया वीर राजानः संनिपातिताः ॥३॥

यदि त्वं भजमानां मां प्रत्याख्यास्यसि मानद ।

विषमयिं जलं रज्जुमास्यास्ये तव कारणात् ॥४॥×

एवमुक्तस्तु वैदर्भ्या नलस्तां प्रत्युवाच ह ।

तिष्ठत्सु लोकपालेषु कथं मानुषमिच्छसि ॥५॥

येषामहं लोककृतामीश्वराणां महात्मनाम् ।

न पादरजसा तुल्यो मनस्ते तेषु वर्तताम् ॥६॥

विप्रियं ह्याचरन्मर्त्यो देवानां मृत्युमृच्छति ।

त्राहि मामनवद्याङ्गि वरयस्व सुरोत्तमान् ॥७॥

विरजांसि च वासांसि दिव्याभ्यर्चिताः सजस्तथा ।

भूषणानि च मुख्यानि देवानाप्य तु भुङ्क्ष्व वै ॥८॥

य इमां पृथिवीं कृत्स्नां संक्षिप्य ग्रसते पुनः ।

हुताशमीशं देवानां का तं न वरयेत्पतिम् ॥९॥

यस्य दण्डभयात्सर्वे भूतग्रामाः समागताः ।

धर्ममेवानुरुध्यन्ति का तं न वरयेत्पतिम् ॥१०॥

धर्मात्मानं महात्मानं दैत्यदानवमर्दनम् ।

महेन्द्रं सर्वदेवानां का तं न वरयेत्पतिम् ॥११॥×

क्रियतामविशङ्केन मनसा यदि मन्यसे ।

वरणं लोकपालानां सुहृद्वाक्यमिदं शृणु ॥१२॥×

निषधेनैवमुक्ता सा दमयन्ती वचो ऽब्रवीत् ।

समाश्रुताभ्यां नेत्राभ्यां शोकजेनाथ वारिणा| ॥१३॥

देवेभ्यो ऽहं नमस्कृत्य सर्वेभ्यः पृथिवीपते ।

वृणे त्वामेव भर्तारं सत्यमेतद्ब्रवीमि ते ॥१४॥

तामुवाच ततो राजा वेपमानां कृताञ्जलिम् ।

दौत्येनागत्य कस्याणि कथं स्वार्थमिहोत्सहे ॥१५॥

कथं ह्यहं प्रतिश्रुत्य देवतानां विशेषतः ।
परार्थं यत्नमारभ्य कथं स्वार्थमिहोत्सहे ॥१६॥

एष धर्मो यदि स्वार्थो ममापि भविता ततः ।
एवं स्वार्थं करिष्यामि तथा भद्रे विधीयताम् ॥१७॥

5 ततो बाष्पाकुलां वाचं दमयन्ती शुचिस्मिता ।
प्रत्याहरन्ती शनकैर्नलं राजानमब्रवीत् ॥१८॥

उपायोऽयं मया दृष्टो निरपायो नरेश्वर ।
येन दोषो न भविता तव राजन्कथं चन ॥१९॥

त्वं चैव हि नरश्रेष्ठ देवाश्चेन्द्रपुरोगमाः ।
10 आयान्तु सहिताः सर्वे मम यत्र स्वयंवरः ॥२०॥

ततोऽहं लोकपालानां संनिधौ त्वां नरेश्वर ।
वरयिष्ये नरव्याघ्र नैवं दोषो भविष्यति ॥२१॥

एवमुक्तस्तु वैदर्भ्या नलो राजा विशां पते ।
आजगाम पुनस्तत्र यत्र देवाः समागताः ॥२२॥

15 तमपश्यंस्तथायान्तं लोकपाला महेश्वराः ।
दृष्ट्वा चैनं ततोऽपृच्छन्वृत्तान्तं सर्वमेव तम् ॥२३॥

कच्चिद्दृष्टा त्वया राजन्दमयन्ती शुचिस्मिता ।
किमब्रवीच्च नः सर्वान्वद भूमिपते ऽनघ ॥२४॥

नल उवाच ।

20 भवद्भिरहमादिष्टो दमयन्त्या निवेशनम् ।
प्रविष्टः सुमहाकक्षं दण्डिभिः स्थविरैर्वृतम् ॥२५॥

प्रविशन्तं च मां तत्र न कश्चिददृष्टवान्नरः ।
ऋते तां पार्थिवसुतां भवतामेव तेजसा ॥२६॥

सख्यश्चास्या मया हृष्टाभिषाणुपलक्षितः ।
विस्मिताश्चाभवन्सर्वी हृष्ट्वा मां विबुधेश्वराः ॥ २७ ॥
वर्यमानेषु च मया भवत्सु रुचिरानना ।
मामेव गतसंकल्पा वृणीते सा सुरोत्तमाः ॥ २८ ॥
अब्रवीच्चैव मां बाला आयान्तु सहिताः सुराः ।
त्वया सह नरव्याघ्र मम यत्र स्वयंवरः ॥ २९ ॥
तेषामहं सन्निधौ त्वां वरयिष्यामि नैषध ।
एवं तव महाबाहो दोषो न भवितेति ह ॥ ३० ॥
एतावदेव विबुधा यथावृत्तमुदाहृतम् ।
मया शेषे प्रमाणं तु भवन्तस्त्रिदशेश्वराः ॥ ३१ ॥

॥ इति नलोपाख्याने चतुर्थः सर्गः ॥४॥

_____

बृहदश्व उवाच ।
अथ काले शुभे प्राप्ते तिथौ पुण्ये क्षणे तथा ।
आजुहाव महीपालानभीमो राजा स्वयंवरे ॥ १ ॥
तच्छ्रुत्वा पृथिवीपालाः सर्वे हृच्छयपीडिताः ।
त्वरिताः समुपाजग्मुर्दमयन्तीमभीप्सवः ॥ २ ॥
कनकस्तम्भरुचिरं तोरणेन विराजितम् ।
विविशुस्ते नृपा रङ्गं महासिंहा इवाचलम् ॥ ३ ॥
तत्रासनेषु विविधेष्वासीनाः पृथिवीक्षितः ।
सुरभिस्रग्धराः सर्वे प्रमृष्टमणिकुण्डलाः ॥ ४ ॥
तत्र स्म पीना हृश्यन्ते बाहवः परिघोपमाः ।

आकारवन्तः सुखक्ष्णाः पञ्चशीर्षा इवोरगाः ॥ ५ ॥
मुकेशान्तानि चारूणि सुनासाक्षिभुवाणि च ।
मुखानि राज्ञां शोभन्ते नक्षत्राणि यथा दिवि ॥ ६ ॥
दमयन्ती ततो रङ्गं प्रविवेश शुभानना ।
5 मुष्णन्ती प्रभया राज्ञां चक्षूंषि च मनांसि च ॥ ७ ॥
तस्या गात्रेषु पतिता तेषां दृष्टिर्महात्मनाम् ।
तत्र तत्रैव सक्ताभून्न चचाल च पश्यताम् ॥ ८ ॥
ततः संकीर्त्यमानेषु राज्ञां नामसु भारत ।
ददर्शे भैमी पुरुषान्पञ्च तुल्याकृतीनथ ॥ ९ ॥
10 तान्समीक्ष्य ततः सर्वानिर्विशेषाकृतीन्स्थितान् ।
संदेहादथ वैदर्भी नाभ्यजानान्नलं नृपम् ॥ १० ॥
यं यं हि ददर्शे तेषां तं तं मेने नलं नृपम् ।
सा चिन्तयन्ती बुद्ध्याथ तर्कयामास भाविनी ॥ ११ ॥
कथं हि देवाञ्ज्ञानीयां कथं विद्यां नलं नृपम् ॥ १२ ॥
15 एवं संचिन्तयन्ती सा वैदर्भी भृशदुःखिता ।
श्रुतानि देवलिङ्गानि तर्कयामास भारत ॥ १३ ॥
देवानां यानि लिङ्गानि स्थविरेभ्यः श्रुतानि मे ।
तानीह तिष्ठतां भूमावेकस्यापि न लक्ष्ये ॥ १४ ॥
सा विनिश्चित्य बहुधा विचार्य च पुनः पुनः ।
20 शरणं प्रति देवानां प्राप्तकालममन्यत ॥ १५ ॥
वाचा च मनसा चैव नमस्कारं प्रयुज्य सा ।
देवेभ्यः प्राञ्जलिर्भूत्वा वेपमानेदमब्रवीत् ॥ १६ ॥
हंसानां वचनं श्रुत्वा यथा मे नैषधो वृतः ।

पतित्वे तेन सत्येन देवास्तं प्रदिशन्तु मे ॥१७॥

बचसा मनसा चैव यथा नाभिचराम्यहम् ।

तेन सत्येन विबुधास्तमेव प्रदिशन्तु मे ॥१८॥

यथा देवैः स मे भर्ता विहितो निषधाधिपः ।

तेन सत्येन मे देवास्तमेव प्रदिशन्तु मे ॥१९॥

यथेदं व्रतमारब्धं नलस्याराधने मया ।

तेन सत्येन मे देवास्तमेव प्रदिशन्तु मे ॥२०॥

स्वं चैव रूपं कुर्वन्तु लोकपाला महेश्वराः ।

यथाहमभिजानीयां पुण्यश्लोकं नराधिपम् ॥२१॥

निशम्य दमयन्त्यास्तत्करुणं परिदेवितम् ।

यथोक्तं चक्रिरे देवाः सामर्थ्यं लिङ्गधारणे ॥२२॥

सापश्यद्विबुधान्सर्वानस्वेदान्स्तब्धलोचनान् ।

हृषितस्रग्जोहीनान्स्थितानस्पृशतः क्षितिम् ॥२३॥

छायाद्वितीयो म्लानस्रग्रजःस्वेदसमन्वितः ।

भूमिष्ठो नैषधश्चैव निमेषेण च सूचितः ॥२४॥

सा समीक्ष्य तु तान्देवान्पुण्यश्लोकं च भारत ।

नैषधं वरयामास भैमी धर्मेण पाण्डव ॥२५॥

विलज्जमाना वस्त्रान्ते जग्राहायतलोचना ।

स्कन्धदेशेऽसृजत्तस्य स्रजं परमशोभनाम् ॥२६॥

वरयामास चैवैनं पतित्वे वरवर्णिनी ।

ततो हा हेति सहसा मुक्तः शब्दो नराधिपैः ॥२७॥

देवैर्महर्षिभिस्तत्र साधु साध्विति भारत ।

विस्मितैरीरितः शब्दः प्रशंसद्भिर्नलं नृपम् ॥२८॥

दमयन्तीं तु कौरव्य वीरसेनसुतो नृपः ।
आश्वासयद्वरारोहां प्रहृष्टेनान्तरात्मना ॥२९॥
यत्त्वं भजसि कल्याणि पुमांसं देवसन्निधौ ।
तस्मान्मां विद्धि भर्तारमेवं ते वचने रतम् ॥३०॥
यावच्च मे धरिष्यन्ति प्राणा देहे शुचिस्मिते ।
तावत्त्वयि भविष्यामि सत्यमेतब्रवीमि ते ॥३१॥
दमयन्तीं तथा वाग्भिरभिनन्द्य कृताञ्जलिः ।
. . . . ॥३२॥

तौ परस्परतः प्रीतौ दृष्ट्वा त्रिदिवपुरोगमान् ।
तानेव शरणं देवानगमत्तुर्मनसा तदा ॥३३॥
वृते तु नैषधे भैम्या लोकपाला महौजसः ।
प्रहृष्टमनसः सर्वे नलायाष्टौ वरान्ददुः ॥३४॥
प्रत्यक्षदर्शनं यज्ञे गतिं चानुत्तमां शुभाम् ।
नैषधाय ददौ शक्रः प्रीयमाणः शचीपतिः ॥३५॥
अग्निरात्मभवं प्रादाद्यत्र वाञ्छति नैषधः ।
लोकानात्मप्रभांश्चैव ददौ तस्मै हुताशनः ॥३६॥
यमस्त्वन्नरसं प्रादाद्धर्मे च परमां स्थितिम् ।
अपां पतिरपां भावं यत्र वाञ्छति नैषधः ॥३७॥
स्रजश्चोत्तमगन्धाढ्याः सर्वे च मिथुनं ददुः ।
वरानेवं प्रदायास्य देवास्ते त्रिदिवं गताः ॥३८॥
पार्थिवाश्चानुभूयास्य विवाहं विस्मयान्विताः ।
दमयन्त्याश्च मुदिताः प्रतिजग्मुर्यथागतम् ॥३९॥
गतेषु पार्थिवेन्द्रेषु भीमः प्रीतो महामनाः ।

विवाहं कारयामास दमयन्त्या नलस्य च ॥४०॥

उष्य तत्र यथाकामं नैषधो द्विपदां वरः ।

भीमेन समनुज्ञातो जगाम नगरं स्वकम् ॥४१॥

अतीव मुदितो राजा भाजमानोंऽशुमानिव ।

5 अरञ्जयत्प्रजा वीरो धर्मेण परिपालयन् ॥४२॥

ईजे चाप्यश्वमेधेन ययातिरिव नाहुषः ।

अन्यैश्च बहुभिर्धीमान्क्रतुभिश्चाप्तदक्षिणैः ॥४३॥

पुनश्च रमणीयेषु वनेषूपवनेषु च ।

दमयन्त्या सह नलो विजहारामरोपमः ॥४४॥

10 जनयामास च नलो दमयन्त्यां महामनाः ।

इन्द्रसेनं सुतं चापि इन्द्रसेनां च कन्यकाम् ॥४५॥

एवं स यजमानश्च विहरंश्च नराधिपः ।

रक्ष वसुसंपूर्णां वसुधां वसुधाधिपः ॥४६॥

॥ इति नलोपाख्याने पञ्चमः सर्गः ॥५॥

---

15   ॥ अथ हितोपदेशः ॥

II.

श्रुतो हितोपदेशोऽयं पाटवं संस्कृतोक्तिषु ।
वाचां सर्वत्र वैचित्र्यं नीतिविद्यां ददाति च ॥

अजरामरवत्प्राज्ञो विद्यामर्थं च चिन्तयेत् ।
गृहीत इव केशेषु मृत्युना धर्ममाचरेत् ॥

सर्वद्रव्येषु विद्यैव द्रव्यमाहुरनुत्तमम् ।
अहार्यत्वादनर्घ्यत्वादक्षयत्वाच्च सर्वदा ॥

3 विद्या शस्त्रं च शास्त्रं च द्वे विद्ये प्रतिपत्तये ।
4 आद्या हास्याय वृद्धत्वे द्वितीयाद्रियते सदा ॥

5 यन्नवे भाजने लग्नः संस्कारो नान्यथा भवेत् ।
कथाच्छलेन बालानां नीतिस्तदिह कथ्यते ॥

7 मित्रलाभः सुहृद्भेदो विग्रहः संधिरेव च ।
8 पञ्चतन्त्रात्तथान्यस्माद्ग्रन्थादाकृष्य लिख्यते ॥

अस्ति भागीरथीतीरे पाटलिपुत्रनामधेयं नगरम् । तत्र स-
10 र्वस्वामिगुणोपेतः सुदर्शनो नाम नरपतिरासीत् । स भूपतिरे-
कदा केनापि पठ्यमानं श्लोकद्वयं शुश्राव ।

अनेकसंशयोच्छेदि परोक्षार्थस्य दर्शकम् ।
सर्वस्य लोचनं शास्त्रं यस्य नास्त्यन्ध एव सः ॥

यौवनं धनसंपत्तिः प्रभुत्वमविवेकता ।
15 एकैकमप्यनर्थाय किं पुनस्तु चतुष्टयम् ॥

इत्याकर्ण्यात्मनः पुत्राणामनधिगतशास्त्राणां नित्यमुन्मार्गगा-
मिनां शास्त्राननुष्ठानेनोद्विग्नमनाः स राजा चिन्तयामास ।

को ऽर्थः पुत्रेण जातेन यो न विद्वान्न धार्मिकः ।
काणेन चक्षुषा किं वा चक्षुःपीडैव केवलम् ॥

20 अजातमृतमूर्खाणां वरमाद्यौ न चान्तिमः ।
सकृद्दुःखकरावाद्यावन्तिमस्तु पदे पदे ॥

किं च । स जातो येन जातेन याति वंशः समुन्नतिम् ।

2

परिवर्त्तिनि संसारे मृतः को वा न जायते ॥

अपरं च । वरमेको गुणी पुत्रो न च मूर्खशतैरपि ।

एकश्चन्द्रस्तमो हन्ति न च तारागणैरपि ॥

यस्य तस्य प्रसूतो ऽपि गुणवान्पूज्यते नरः ।

5 धनुर्वेदविज्ञुद्रो ऽपि निर्गुणाः किं करिष्यति ॥

हा हा पुत्रक नाधीत सुगतैतासु राभिषु ।

तेन त्वं विदुषां मध्ये पङ्के गौरिव सीदसि ॥

तत्कथमिदानीमेते मम पुत्रा गुणवन्तः क्रियन्ताम् ।   यच्चो-

च्यते । यद्भावि न तद्भावि भावि चेन्न तदन्यथा ।

10 इति चिन्ताविषघ्नो ऽयमगदः किं न पीयते ॥

एतत्कार्याक्षमाणां केषां चिदालस्यवचनम् ।

न दैवमिति संचिन्त्य त्यजेदुद्योगमात्मनः ।

अनुद्योगेन कस्तैलं तिलेभ्यः प्राप्तुमर्हति ॥

अन्यच्च । उद्योगिनं पुरुषसिंहमुपैति लक्ष्मीर्

15 दैवेन देयमिति कापुरुषा वदन्ति ।

दैवं निहत्य कुरु पौरुषमात्मशक्त्या

यत्ने कृते यदि न सिध्यति को ऽत्र दोषः ॥

यथा ह्येकेन चक्रेण रथस्य न गतिर्भवेत् ।

एवं पुरुषकारेण विना दैवं न सिध्यति ॥

20 तथा च । पूर्वेजन्मकृतं कर्म तद्दैवमिति कथ्यते ।

तस्मात्पुरुषकारेण यत्नं कुर्यादतन्द्रितः ॥

उद्यमेन हि सिध्यन्ति कार्याणि न मनोरथैः ।

न हि सुप्तस्य सिंहस्य प्रविशन्ति मुखे मृगाः ॥

मूर्खो ऽपि शोभते तावत्सभायां वस्त्रवेष्टितः ।
तावच्च शोभते मूर्खो यावत्किं चिन्न भाषते ॥
एतच्चिन्तयित्वा स राजा पण्डितसभां कारितवान् । राजोवाच ।
भो भोः पण्डिताः । श्रूयताम् । अस्ति कश्चिद्देवंभूतो विद्वान्यो
6 मम पुत्राणां नित्यमुन्मार्गगामिनामनधिगतशास्त्राणामि-
दानीं नीतिशास्त्रोपदेशेन पुनर्जन्म कारयितुं समर्थः ।
यतः । काचः काञ्चनसंसर्गाद्धत्ते मारकतीं द्युतिम् ।
तथा सत्सन्निधानेन मूर्खो याति प्रवीणताम् ॥
उक्तं च । हीयते हि मतिस्तात हीनैः सह समागमात् ।
10 समैश्च समतामेति विशिष्टैश्च विशिष्टताम् ॥
अथान्तरे विष्णुशर्मनामा महापण्डितः सकलनीतिशास्त्रतत्त्व-
ज्ञो बृहस्पतिरिवाब्रवीत् । देव । महाकुलसंभूता एते राजपुत्राः ।
तन्मया नीतिं ग्राहयितुं शक्यन्ते ।
यतः । नाद्रव्ये निहिता काचित्क्रिया फलवती भवेत् ।
15 न व्यापारशतेनापि शुकवत्पाठ्यते बकः ॥
अन्यच्च । असिंस्तु निर्गुणे गोत्रे नापत्यमुपजायते ।
आकरे पद्मरागाणां जन्म काचमणेः कुतः ॥
अतो ऽहं षण्मासाभ्यन्तरे तव पुत्राम्बीतिशास्त्राभिज्ञान्करि-
ष्यामि । राजा सविनयं पुनरुवाच ।
20 कीटो ऽपि सुमनःसङ्गादारोहति सतां शिरः ।
अश्मापि याति देवत्वं महद्भिः सुप्रतिष्ठितः ॥
तदेतेषामसत्पुत्राणां नीतिशास्त्रोपदेशाय भवन्तः प्रमाणम् ।
इत्युक्त्वा तस्य विष्णुशर्मणो बहुमानपुरःसरं पुत्रान्समर्पित-

वान् । अथ प्रासादपृष्ठे सुखोपविष्टानां राजपुत्राणां पुरस्ता-
त्रस्तावक्रमेण स पण्डितो ऽब्रवीत् ।

काव्यशास्त्रविनोदेन कालो गच्छति धीमताम् ।
व्यसनेन तु मूर्खाणां निद्रया कलहेन वा ॥

तन्नवतां विनोदाय काककूर्मादीनां विचित्रां कथां कथयामि ।
राजपुत्रैरुक्तम् । आर्य । कथ्यताम् । विष्णुशर्मोवाच । शृणुत
यूयम् । संप्रति मित्रलाभः प्रस्तूयते ।

III.

अहमेकदा दक्षिणारण्ये चरन्नपश्यम् । एको वृद्धव्याघ्रः स्ना-
तः कुशहस्तः सरस्तीरे ब्रूते । भो भोः पान्थाः । इदं सुवर्णकङ्क-
णं गृह्यताम् । तद्वचनमाकर्ण्य भयात्को ऽपि तत्पार्श्वं न भज-
ते । ततो लोभाकृष्टेन केन चित्पान्येनालोचितम् । भाग्येनै-
तत्संभवति । किं तस्मिन्नात्मसंदेहे प्रवृत्तिर्न विधेया । यतः ।

अनिष्टादिष्टलाभे ऽपि न गतिर्जायते शुभा ।
यत्रास्ति विषसंसर्गो ऽमृतं तदपि मृत्यवे ॥

किं तु सर्वत्रार्थार्जने प्रवृत्तिः संदेह एव । तथा चोक्तम् ।

न संशयमनारुह्य नरो भद्राणि पश्यति ।
संशयं पुनरारुह्य यदि जीवति पश्यति ॥

तन्निरूपयामि तावत् । प्रकाशं ब्रूते । कुत्र तव कङ्कणम् ।
व्याघ्रो हस्तं प्रसार्य दर्शयति । पान्थो ऽवदत् । कथं मारात्मके
त्वयि विश्वासः । व्याघ्र उवाच । शृणु रे पान्थ । प्रागेव यौ-

वनदशायामतिदुर्वृत्त आसम् । अनेकगोब्राह्मणमनुघ्नवधान्मे
पुत्रा अनेकशो मृता दाराश्च । सांप्रतं निर्वंशो ऽस्मि । ततः के-
नापि धार्मिकेणाहमुपदिष्टः । दानधर्ममाचरतु भवानिति । त-
दुपदेशदिदानीमहं स्नानशीलो दाता वृद्धो गलितनखदन्तो
5 दयावांश्च कथं न विश्वासभूमिः । उक्तं च ।

इज्याध्ययनदानानि तपः सत्यं क्षमा दमः ।
अलोभ इति मार्गो ऽयं धर्मस्याष्टविधः स्मृतः ॥
तत्र पूर्वश्चतुर्वर्गो दम्भार्थमपि सेव्यते ।
उत्तरश्च चतुर्वर्गो नामहात्मसु विद्यते ॥

10 मम चैतावालैं लोभविह्नो येन स्वहस्तगतमपि सुवर्णकङ्कणं
यस्मै कस्मै चिह्नातुमिच्छामि । तथापि व्याघ्रो मानुषं खादतीति
लोकप्रवादो दुर्निवारः । यतः ।

गतानुगतिको लोकः कुट्टनीमुपदेशिनीम् ।
प्रमाणयति नो धर्मे यथा गोघ्नमपि द्विजम् ॥

15 मया च धर्मशास्त्राण्यधीतानि । शृणु ।

महस्थल्यां यथा वृष्टिः क्षुधार्ते भोजनं तथा ।
दरिद्रे दीयते दानं सफलं पाण्डुनन्दन ॥
प्राणा यथात्मनो ऽभीष्टा भूतानामपि ते तथा ।
आत्मौपम्येन सर्वत्र दयां कुर्वन्ति साधवः ॥

20 अपरं च । प्रत्याख्याने च दाने च सुखदुःखे प्रियाप्रिये ।
आत्मौपम्येन पुरुषः प्रमाणमधिगच्छति ॥

अन्यच्च । मातृवत्परदारांश्च परद्रव्याणि लोष्टवत् ।
आत्मवत्सर्वभूतानि यः पश्यति स पश्यति ॥

र्यं च दुर्गतः। तेन तत्तुभ्यं दातुं सयत्नो ऽहम्। तथा चोक्तम्।

दरिद्रान्भर कौन्तेय मा प्रयच्छेश्वरे धनम्।

व्याधितस्यौषधं पथ्यं नीरुजस्तु किमौषधैः ॥

अन्यच्च। दातव्यमिति यद्दानं दीयते ऽनुपकारिणे।

देशे काले च पात्रे च तद्दानं सात्त्विकं स्मृतम् ॥

तदत्र सरसि स्नात्वा सुवर्णकङ्कणमिदं प्रतिगृह्याण। ततो जात-
विश्वासो यावदसौ सरः स्नातुं प्रविष्टस्तावदेव महापङ्के निम-
ग्नः पलायितुमक्षमः। पङ्के पतितं दृष्ट्वा व्याघ्रो ऽवदत्। अ-
हह। महापङ्के पतितो ऽसि। अतस्त्वामुन्थापयामि। इत्युक्ता
शनैः शनैरुपगम्य तेन व्याघ्रेण धृतः स पान्थो ऽचिन्तयत्।

न धर्मशास्त्रं पठतीति कारणं

न चापि वेदाध्ययनं दुरात्मनः।

स्वभाव एवात्र तथातिरिच्यते

यथा प्रकृत्या मधुरं गवां पयः ॥

किं च। अवशेन्द्रियचित्तानां हस्तिस्नानमिव क्रिया।

दुर्भगाभरणप्रायो ज्ञानं भारः क्रियां विना ॥

तन्न मया भद्रं कृतं यदत्र मारात्मके विश्वासः कृतः। तथा चु-
क्तम्। नखिनां च नदीनां च शृङ्गिणां शस्त्रपाणिनाम्।

विश्वासो नैव कर्तव्यः स्त्रीषु राजकुलेषु च ॥

अपरं च। सर्वस्य हि परीक्ष्यन्ते स्वभावा नेतरे गुणाः।

अतीत्य हि गुणान्सर्वान्स्वभावो मूर्ध्नि वर्तते ॥

अन्यच्च। स हि गगणविहारी कल्मषध्वंसकारी

दशशतकरधारी ज्योतिषां मध्यचारी।

विधुरपि विधियोगाङ्कृस्यते राहुणासौ
लिखितमपि ललाटे प्रोज्झितुं कः समर्थः ॥
इति चिन्तयन्नेव तेनासौ व्याघ्रेण व्यापादितः खादितश्च ।

IV.

अस्ति मगधदेशे चम्पकवती नामारण्यानी । तस्यां चिरा-
न्महता स्नेहेन मृगकाकौ निवसतः । स च मृगः स्वेच्छया भा-
म्यन्पुष्टाङ्गः केन चित्सृगालेनावलोकितः । तं हृष्ट्वा सृगालो
ऽचिन्तयत् । आः । कथमेतन्मांसं सुललितं भक्षयामि । भ-
वतु । विश्वासं तावदुत्पादयामि । इत्यालोच्योपसृत्याब्रवीत् ।
मित्र । कुशलं ते । मृगेणोक्तम् । कस्त्वम् । जम्बुको ब्रूते । क्षु-
द्रबुद्धिनामा जम्बुको ऽहम् । अचारण्ये मित्रबन्धुहीनो मृतव-
देकाकी निवसामि । इदानीं भवन्तं मित्रमासाद्य पुनः स-
न्त्रुजीविलोकं प्रविष्टो ऽस्मि । अधुना मया तवानुचरेण सर्वे-
था भवितव्यम् । मृगेणोक्तम् । एवमस्तु । ततो ऽस्तं गते स-
वितरि भगवति मरीचिमालिनि मृगस्य वासभूमिं प्रति मृ-
गजम्बुकौ गतौ । तत्र चम्पकवृक्षशाखायां सुबुद्धिनामा काको
मृगस्य चिरमित्रं निवसति । तौ हृष्ट्वा काको ऽवदत् । सखे
चित्राङ्ग । को ऽयं द्वितीयः । मृगो ब्रूते । जम्बुको ऽयमस-
त्सख्यमिच्छन्नागतः । काको ब्रूते । मित्र । अकस्मादागन्तुना
सह विश्वासो नैव युक्तः । तत्र भद्रमाचरितम् । तथा चोक्तम् ।
अज्ञातकुलशीलस्य वासो देयो न कस्य चित् ।
मार्जारस्य हि दोषेण हतो गृघ्रो जरद्ध्वजः ॥

इत्याकर्ण्य स जम्बुकः सकोपमाह । मृगस्य प्रथमदर्शनदिने भ-
वानप्यज्ञातकुलशील एवासीत् । तन्नवता सह कथमद्य या-
वदेतस्य स्नेहानुवृत्तिरुत्तरोत्तरं वर्धते ।

यत्र विद्वज्जनो नास्ति श्लाघ्यस्तत्राल्पधीरपि ।
5 निरस्तपादपे देशे एरण्डो ऽपि द्रुमायते ॥

अयं निजः परो वेति गणना लघुचेतसाम् ।
उदारचरितानां तु वसुधैव कुटुम्बकम् ॥

यथा चायं मृगो मम बन्धुस्तथा भवानपि । मृगो ऽब्रवीत् ।
किमनेनोत्तरोत्तरेण । सर्वैरेकत्र विश्रम्भालापैः सुखमनुभवद्भिः
10 स्थीयताम् । यतः ।

न कस्यचित्कस्य चिन्मित्रं न कस्यचित्कश्चिद्रिपुः ।
व्यवहारेण मित्राणि जायन्ते रिपवस्तथा ॥

काकेनोक्तम् । एवमस्तु । अथ प्रातः सर्वे यथाभिमतदेशं ग-
ताः । एकदा निभृतं सृगालो ब्रूते । सखे मृग । एतस्मिन्नेव व-
15 नैकदेशे सस्यपूर्णं क्षेत्रमस्ति । तदहं त्वां तत्र नीत्वा दर्शयामि ।
तथा कृते सति मृगः प्रत्यहं तत्र गत्वा सस्यं खादति । अथ
क्षेत्रपतिना तद्दृष्ट्वा पाशास्तत्र नियोजिताः । अनन्तरं पुनरा-
गतो मृगस्तत्र चरन्पाशैर्बद्धो ऽचिन्तयत् । को मामितः का-
लपाशादिव व्याधपाशान्त्रातुं मित्रादन्यः समर्थः । अथान्तरे
20 जम्बुकस्तत्रागत्योपस्थितो ऽचिन्तयत् । फलितं तावदस्माकं
कपटप्रबन्धेन । मनोरथसिद्धिरपि बाहुल्यान्मे भविष्यति । ए-
तस्योत्कृत्यमानस्य मांसासृग्नुलिप्तान्यस्थीनि मयावश्यं प्रा-
प्स्यानि । स च मृगस्तं दृष्ट्वोल्लसितो ब्रूते । सखे । छिन्धि ता-

बन्धनम् बन्धनम्। सत्वरं घातयस्व माम्। यतः।

आपत्सु मित्रं जानीयाद्युद्धे शूरमृणे शुचिम्।
भार्यां क्षीणेषु वित्तेषु व्यसनेषु च बान्धवान्॥

अपरं च। उत्सवे व्यसने चैव दुर्भिक्षे शत्रुसंकटे।

5 राजद्वारे श्मशाने च यस्तिष्ठति स बान्धवः॥

जम्बुकः पाशं मुहुर्मुहुर्विलोक्याचिन्तयत्। हठबन्धनबद्धो ऽस्ति
तावद्यं मृगः। ब्रूते च। आयुनिर्मिताः पाशाः। तद्य भट्टा-
रकद्वारे कथमेतान्दन्तैः स्पृशामि। मित्र। यदि नान्यथा मन्य-
से तदा प्रभाते यत्त्वयोच्यते तन्मया कर्तव्यम्। इत्युक्ता तात्स-
10 मीप आत्मानमाच्छाद्य स्थितः सः। अनन्तरं स काकः प्रदोष-
काले मृगमनागतमवलोक्येतस्ततो ऽन्विष्य तथाविध दृष्ट्वो-
वाच। सखे। किमेतत्। मृगेणोक्तम्। अवधीरितसुहृद्वाक्यस्य
फलमेतत्। तथा चोक्तम्।

सुहृदां हितकामानां यः शृणोति न भाषितम्।
15 विपत्संनिहिता तस्य स नरः शत्रुनन्दनः॥

काको ब्रूते। स सृगालः क्व। मृगेणोक्तम्। मन्मांसार्थी तिष्ठत्य-
त्रैव। काको ब्रूते। मित्र। उक्तमेव मया पूर्वम्।

अपराधो न मे ऽस्तीति नैतद्विश्वासकारणम्।
विद्यते हि नृशंसेभ्यो भयं गुणवतामपि॥

20 परोक्षे कार्यहन्तारं प्रत्यक्षे प्रियवादिनम्।
वर्जयेत्तादृशं मित्रं विषकुम्भं पयोमुखम्॥

दीर्घं निःश्वस्य। अरे वञ्चक। किं त्वया पापकर्मणा कृतम्।
यतः।

संलापितानां मधुरैर्वचोभिर्मिथ्योपचारैश्च वशीकृतानाम् ।

आशावतां अदधतां च लोके किमर्षिनां वञ्चयितव्यमस्ति ॥

अन्यच्च । उपकारिणि विश्रब्धे मुग्धमतौ यः समाचरति पापम् ।

तं जनमसत्यसंधं भगवति वसुधे कथं वहसि ॥

5 दुर्जनेन समं सख्यं प्रीतिं चापि न कारयेत् ।

उष्णो दहति चाङ्गारः शीतः कृष्णायते करम् ॥

अथ वा स्थितिरियं दुर्जनानाम् ।

प्राक्पादयोः पतति खादति पृष्ठमांसं

कर्णे कलं किमपि रौति शनैर्विचिषम् ।

10 छिद्रं निरूप्य सहसा प्रविशत्यशङ्कः

सर्वं खलस्य चरितं मशकः करोति ॥

तथा च । दुर्जनः प्रियवादी च नैतद्विश्वासकारणम् ।

मधु तिष्ठति जिह्वाये हृदये तु हलाहलम् ॥

अथ प्रभाते स क्षेत्रपतिर्लगुडहस्तस्तं प्रदेशमागच्छन्काकेनाव-

15 लोकितः । तमालोक्य काकेनोक्तम् । सखे मृग । त्वमात्मानं

मृतवत्संदर्श्य वातेनोदरं पूरयित्वा पादान्स्तब्धीकृत्य तिष्ठ । य-

दाहं शब्दं करोमि तदा त्वं सत्वरमुत्थाय पलायिष्यसि । मृग-

स्तथैव काकवचनेन स्थितः । ततः क्षेत्रपतिना हर्षोन्मुल्ललो-

चनेनावलोकितः । तथाविधं मृगमवलोक्यासौ आः स्वयंमृ-

20 तो ऽयमित्युक्त्वा मृगं बन्धनान्मोचयित्वा पाशान्संवरितुं सय-

त्नो बभूव । ततः कियद्दूरे उन्तरिते क्षेत्रपतौ स मृगः काकस्य

शब्दं श्रुत्वा ससंभ्रमः समुत्थाय पलायितः । तमुद्दिश्य तेन क्षे-

त्रपतिना प्रकोपात्क्षिप्तलगुडेन सृगालो व्यापादितः । तथा

चोक्तम् । पिबिर्वेषैस्तिभिर्मासैस्तिभिः पक्षैस्तिभिर्दिनैः ।
अत्युग्रपुण्यपापानामिहैव फलमश्नुते ॥
अतो ऽहं ब्रवीमि ।

भक्ष्यभक्षकयोः प्रीतिर्विपत्तेरेव कारणम् ।
सृगालात्याश्रबद्धो ऽसौ मृगः काकेन रक्षितः ॥

V.

अस्ति भागीरथीतीरे गृभ्रकूटनाम्नि पर्वते महान्पर्केाटीवृक्षः ।
तस्य कोटरे दैवदुर्विपाकात्गलितनयनो जरद्गवो नाम गृध्रः प्र-
तिवसति । अथ कृपया तज्जीवनाय तद्वृक्षवासिनः पक्षिणः
स्वाहारात्किं चिल्किं चिद्ददति । तेनासौ जीवति । अथ कदा-
चिद्दीर्घकर्णेनामा मार्जारः पक्षिशावकान्भक्षयितुं तत्रागतः ।
ततस्तमायान्तं दृष्ट्वा पक्षिशावकैर्भयातैः कोलाहलः कृतः ।
तच्छ्रुत्वा जरद्गवेनोक्तम् । को ऽयमायाति । दीर्घकर्णो गृध्रम-
वलोक्य सभयमाह । हा हतो ऽस्मि । अधुनातिसंनिधानेन
पलायनमप्यशक्यम् । तद्यथा भवितव्यं तथा भवतु । एतत्समी-
पमुपगच्छामि । इत्यालोच्योपसृत्याब्रवीत् । आर्य । त्वामभि-
वन्दे । गृध्रो ऽवदत् । कस्त्वम् । सो ऽब्रवीत् । मार्जारो ऽहम् ।
गृध्रो ब्रूते । तदूरमपसर । नो चेद्धन्तव्यो ऽसि मया । मार्जा-
रो ऽवदत् । श्रूयतां तावदस्मद्वचनम् । ततो यद्यहं वध्यस्तदा
हन्तव्यः । यतः ।

जातिमात्रेण किंचित्किं वध्यते पूज्यते क्व चित् ।
व्यवहारं परिज्ञाय वध्यः पूज्यो ऽथ वा भवेत् ॥

गृध्रो ब्रूते । ब्रूहि । कीहग्व्यापारवान् । सो ऽवदत् । अहमत्र
गङ्गातीरे नित्यस्त्रायी निरामिषाशी ब्रह्मचर्येण चान्द्रायणव्र-
तमाचरन्तिष्ठामि । युष्मांश्च धर्मज्ञानरतान्विश्वासभूमयः प-
क्षिणः सर्वे सर्वदा ममाग्रे स्तुवन्ति । अतो भवद्भ्यो विद्याव-
5 योवृद्धेभ्यो धर्मं श्रोतुमिहागतः । भवन्तश्चेताहशा धर्मज्ञा य-
न्मामतिथिं हन्तुमुद्यताः । गृहस्थस्य धर्मश्चैष समुदीरितः ।

अरावप्युचितं कार्यमातिथ्यं गृहमागते ।
छेत्तुमप्यागते छायां नोपसंहरते द्रुमः ॥

किं च । यद्द्रव्यं नास्ति तदा प्रीतिवचसाप्यतिथिः पूज्यः । यतः ।

10 तृणानि भूमिरुदकं वाक्चतुर्थी च सूनृता ।
एतान्यपि सतां गेहे नोच्छिद्यन्ते कदा चन ॥

अन्यच्च । बालो वा यदि वा वृद्धो युवा वा गृहमागतः ।
तस्य पूजा विधातव्या सर्वैश्चाभ्यागतो गुरुः ॥

अन्यच्च । निर्गुणेष्वपि सत्त्वेषु दयां कुर्वन्ति साधवः ।
15 न हि संहरते ज्योत्स्नां चन्द्रश्चाण्डालवेश्मनि ॥

अन्यच्च । अतिथिर्यस्य भग्नाशो गृहात्प्रतिनिवर्तते ।
स दत्त्वा दुष्कृतं तस्मै पुण्यमादाय गच्छति ॥

अन्यच्च । उत्तमस्यापि वर्णस्य नीचो ऽपि गृहमागतः ।
पूजनीयो यथायोग्यं सर्वदेवमयो ऽतिथिः ॥

20 गृध्रो ऽवदत् । मार्जारा हि मांसरुचयो भवन्ति पक्षिशावका-
श्च निवसन्ति । तेनैवं ब्रवीमि । मार्जारो ऽथैवं श्रुत्वा भू-
मिं स्पृष्ट्वा कर्णौ स्पृशति ब्रूते च । मया धर्मशास्त्रं श्रुत्वा वी-
तरागेणेदं दुष्करं व्रतं चान्द्रायणमध्यवसायितम् । यतः पर-

स्वरं विवदमानानामपि धर्मशास्त्राणामहिंसा परमो धर्म इ-
त्यचैकमत्यम् । यतः ।

सर्वे हिंसानिवृत्ताश्च नराः सर्वसहाश्च ये ।
सर्वस्याश्रयभूताश्च ते नराः स्वर्गगामिनः ॥

5 अन्यच्च । एक एव सुहृद्धर्मो निधने ऽप्यनुयाति यः ।
शरीरेण समं नाशं सर्वमन्यद्धि गच्छति ॥

किं च । यो ऽत्ति यस्य यदा मांसमुभयोः पश्यतान्तरम् ।
एकस्य क्षणिकी प्रीतिरन्यः प्राणैर्विमुच्यते ॥

अपि च । मर्तव्यमिति यद्दुःखं पुरुषस्योपजायते ।

10 शक्यस्तेनानुमानेन परो ऽपि परिरक्षितुम् ॥ शृणु
पुनः । स्वच्छन्दवनजातेन शाकेनापि प्रपूर्यते ।
अस्य दग्धोदरस्यार्थे कः कुर्यात्पातकं महत् ॥

एवं विश्वास्य स मार्जारस्तरुकोटरे स्थितः । ततो दिनेषु ग-
च्छत्सु पक्षिशावकानाक्रम्य कोटरमानीय प्रत्यहं खादति । अथ
15 येषामपत्यानि खादितानि तैः शोकार्तैर्विलपद्भिरितस्ततो जि-
ज्ञासा समारब्धा । तत्परिज्ञाय मार्जारः कोटराद्बिःसृत्य पला-
यितः । पश्चात्यतद्भिरितस्ततो निरूपयद्भिस्तत्र तरुकोटरे शा-
वकास्थीनि प्राप्तानि । अनन्तरं चानेनैव शावकाः खादिता
इति निश्चित्य मिलित्वा तैः पक्षिभिः स गृध्रो व्यापादितः ।
20 अतो ऽहं ब्रवीमि ।

अज्ञातकुलशीलस्य वासो देयो न कस्य चित् ।
मार्जारस्य हि दोषेण हतो गृध्रो जरद्ववः ॥

VI.

अस्ति वाराणस्यां कर्पूरपटो नाम रजकः । स चैकदा नि-
र्भरं प्रसुप्रः । तदनन्तरं द्रव्याणि हर्तुं तद्गृहं चौरः प्रविष्टः । त-
स्य प्राङ्गणे गर्दभो बद्धस्तिष्ठति कुक्कुरश्चोपविष्टः । तं चौरम-
वलोक्य गर्दभः श्वानमाह । तव तावदयं व्यापारः । तत्किमि-
ति त्वमुच्चैः शब्दं कृत्वा स्वामिनं न जागरयसि । कुक्कुरो ब्रूते ।
माम । नियोगस्यास्य चर्चा किं त्वया कर्तव्या ।त्वमेव जानासि
यथाहमेतस्याहर्निशं गृहरक्षां करोमि । यतो ऽयं चिरान्निवृ-
त्तो ममोपयोगं न जानाति तेनाधुना ममाहारदाने ऽपि
मन्दादरः । विना विधुरदर्शनं स्वामिनो ऽनुजीविषु मन्दा-
दरा भवन्ति । गर्दभो ब्रूते । शृणु रे बर्बर ।

याचते कार्यकाले यः स किंभृत्यः स किंसुहृत् । कुक्कु-
रो ब्रूते । भृत्यान्संभावयेद्यस्तु कार्यकाले स किंप्रभुः ॥

किं च ।　आश्रितानां भृतौ स्वामिसेवायां धर्मसेवने ।

पुत्रस्योत्पादने चैव न सन्ति प्रतिहस्तकाः ॥

ततो गर्दभः सकोपमाह । आः । पापीयांस्त्वं यः स्वामिकार्यो-
पेक्षां करोषि ।भवतु । यथा स्वामी जागर्ति तथा मया कर्तव्यम् ।
यतः ।　पृष्टतः सेवयेद्वह्निं जठरेण हुताशनम् ।

स्वामिनं सर्वभावेन परलोकममायया ॥

इत्युक्ता स अतीव चीत्कारं कृतवान् । ततः स रजकस्तेन ची-
त्कारेण प्रबुद्धो निद्राविमर्दकोपादुत्थाय गर्दभं लगुडेन ताड-
यामास । अतो ऽहं ब्रवीमि ।

पराधिकारचर्चां यः कुर्यात्स्वामिहितेच्छया ।

स विषीदति चीत्काराज्जाडितो गर्देभो यथा ॥

VII.

अस्त्युत्तरापथे ऽर्बुदशिखरनाम्नि पर्वते महाविक्रमो नाम
सिंहः । तस्य पर्वतकन्दरमधिशयानस्य केसराग्रं मूषिकः कश्चि-
च्छिनत्ति । स सिंहः केसराग्रं लूनं बुद्ध्वा कुपितो विवरान्तर्गतं
मूषिकमलभमानो ऽचिन्तयात् । किं विधेयमत्र । भवतु । एवं
श्रूयते । क्षुद्रशत्रुर्भवेद्यस्तु विक्रमान्न स नम्यते ।
तं निहन्तुं पुरस्कार्यः सहशस्त्रस्य सैनिकः ॥

इत्यालोच्य तेन ग्रामं गत्वा दधिकर्णनामा बिडालो मांसा-
ह्याहारेण संतोष्य प्रयत्नादानीय स्वकन्दरे धृतः । ततस्तद्भया-
न्मूषिको बहिर्ने निःसरति । तेनासौ सिंहो ऽक्षतकेसरः सुखं
स्वपिति । मूषिकशब्दं यदा यदा शृणोति तदा तदा सविशेषं
तं बिडालं मांसाहारदानेन संवर्धयति । अथैकदा स मूषिकः
क्षुधा पीडितो बहिः संचरंस्तेन मार्जारेण प्राप्तो व्यापादितः
खादितश्च । अनन्तरं स सिंहो यदा कदा चिदपि मूषिकशब्दं
न शुश्राव तदोपयोगाभावात्तस्य बिडालस्याहारदाने मन्दा-
दरो बभूव । अतो ऽहं ब्रवीमि ।
निरपेक्षो न कर्तव्यो भृत्यैः स्वामी कदा चन ।
निरपेक्षं प्रभुं कृत्वा भृत्यः स्याद्धिकर्णवत् ॥

VIII. IX.

कस्मिंश्चित्तरौ वायसदंपती निवसतः । तयोश्चापत्यानि त-

रुकोटरावस्थितकृष्णसर्पेण खादितानि । ततः पुनर्गर्भवती वा-
यसी ब्रूते । स्वामिन् । त्यज्यतामयं तरुः । अथ यावत्कृष्णस-
र्पेणावदावयोः संततिः कदा चिदपि न भविष्यति । यतः ।

दुष्टा भार्या शठं मित्रं भृत्यश्चोत्तरदायकः ।
⁵ सर्सर्पे च गृहे वासो मृत्युरेव न संशयः ॥

वायसो ब्रूते । प्रिये । न भेतव्यम् । वारं वारं मयैतस्य महा-
पराधः सोढः । इदानीं पुनर्न क्षन्तव्यः । वायस्याह । कथमनेन
बलवता कृष्णसर्पेण साधं भवान्विग्रहीतुं समर्थः । वायसो ब्रू-
ते । अलमनया चिन्तया । यतः ।

¹⁰ यस्य बुद्धिर्बलं तस्य निर्बुद्धेस्तु कुतो बलम् ।
वने सिंहो बलोन्मत्तः शशकेन निपातितः ॥

वायस्याह । कथमेतत् । वायसः कथयति । अस्ति मन्दरना-
म्नि पर्वते दुर्दान्तो नाम सिंहः । स च सर्वदा पशूनां वधं
विद्धान एवास्ते । ततः सर्वैः पशुभिर्मेलकं कृत्वा स सिं-
¹⁵ हो विज्ञप्तः । देव । किमर्थं सर्वेषांपशुवधः क्रियते । वयमेव
भवदाहारार्थं प्रत्यहमेकैकं पशुमुपढौकयामः । सिंहेनोक्तम् ।
यद्येतदभिमतं भवतां तर्हि भवतु । ततः प्रभृति प्रत्यहमेकैकं
पशुमुपकल्पितं भक्षयन्नास्ते । अथ कदा चित्कस्यापि वृ-
द्धशशकस्य वासरः प्राप्तः । ततः सो ऽचिन्तयत् ।

²⁰ त्रासहेतोर्विनीतिस्तु क्रियते जीविताशया ।
पञ्चत्वं चेद्गमिष्यामि किं सिंहानुनयेन मे ॥

तन्मन्दं मन्दमुपगच्छामि । ततः सिंहो ऽपि क्षुधा पीडितः
कोपादुवाच । कुतस्त्वं विलम्ब्यागतो ऽसि । शशको ऽब्र-

वीत । नाहमपराधः । पथि सिंहान्तरेण बलात्कृतत्तस्याये
पुनरागमनाय शपथं कृत्वा स्वामिनं निवेदयितुमभागतो
ऽस्मि । सिंहः सकोपमाह । सत्वरं गत्वा मां दर्शय । क्कासौ
दुरात्मा तिष्ठति । ततः शशकर्त्त गृहीत्वा गम्भीरकूपसमीपं
5 गतः । अवागत्य पश्यतु स्वामीत्युक्का तस्मिन्कूपजले त-
स्यैव प्रतिबिम्बं दर्शितवान् । ततो ऽसौ दर्पाध्मातत्तस्यो-
पर्यात्मानं निक्षिप्य पञ्चत्वं गतः । अतो ऽहं ब्रवीमि । यस्य
बुद्धिर्बलं तस्येत्यादि ।

वायसी ब्रूते । श्रुतं मया । कर्त्तव्यतां ब्रूहि । वायसो ऽवदत् ।
10 प्रिये । आसन्ने सरसि राजपुत्रः सततमागत्य क्ष्णाति । तस्मिन्स्-
तरे तदङ्गादवतारितं कनकसूत्रं चञ्च्वा धृत्वानीयास्मिन्कोटरे
धरिष्यसि । अथ कनकसूत्रानुसरणप्रवृत्तै राजपुरुषैः कोटरे नि-
रूप्यमाणे कृष्णसर्पो द्रष्टव्यो व्यापादयितव्यश्च । अथ कदा चि-
त्क्ष्णातुं प्रविष्टे राजपुत्रे वायस्या तदनुष्ठितम् । तथानुष्ठिते तद्वृ-
15 त्तम् । अतो ऽहं ब्रवीमि ।

उपायेन हि तत्कुर्याद्वन्न शक्यं पराक्रमैः ।
काक्या कनकसूत्रेण कृष्णसर्पो निपातितः ॥

X.

अस्ति नर्मदातीरे पर्वतोपत्यकायां विशालः शाल्मलीतरुः ।
तत्र निर्मितनीडक्रोडे पक्षिणः सुखेन वर्षास्वपि निवसन्ति ।
20 अथ नीलपटैरिव जलधरपटलैरावृते नभस्तले धारासारैर्महती

3

वृष्टिर्बभूव । ततो वानरांस्तलतले ऽवस्थिताञ्छीतार्तांत्कम्प-
मानानवलोक्य पक्षिभिरुक्तम् । भो भो वानराः । श्रूयताम् ।

अस्माभिर्निर्मिता नीडाश्चञ्चुमात्राहृतैस्तृणैः ।
हस्तपादादिसंयुक्ता यूयं किमवसीदथ ॥

5 तच्छ्रुत्वा वानरैर्जातामर्षैरालोचितम् । अहो । निर्वातनीडग-
भावस्थिताः सुखिनः पक्षिणो ऽस्मान्निन्दन्ति । तन्नवतु ताव-
द्वृष्टेरुपशमः । अनन्तरं शान्ते पानीयवर्षे तैर्वानरैर्वृक्षमारुह्य
सर्वे नीडा भग्नाः । तेषां पक्षिणामण्डानि चाधः पतितानि ।
अतो ऽहं ब्रवीमि ।

10 विज्ञानेनोपदेष्टव्यो नाविज्ञांस्तु कदा चन ।
वानरानुपदिश्याज्ञान्स्थानभ्रंशं ययुः खगाः ॥

<hr/>

XI.

अस्ति हस्तिनापुरे कर्पूरविलासो नाम रजकः । तस्य गर्द-
भो ऽतिभारवाहनादुर्बलो मुमूर्षुरिवाभवत् । ततस्तेन रज-
केनासौ व्याघ्रचर्मणा प्रच्छाद्यारण्यसमीपे सस्यक्षेत्रे मोचितः ।
15 ततो दूरादवलोक्य व्याघ्रबुद्ध्या क्षेत्रपतयः सत्वरं पलायन्ते । स
च सुखेन सस्यं चरति । अथैकदा केनापि सस्यरक्षकेण धूसर-
कम्बलकृततनुत्राणेन धनुष्कारं सज्जीकृत्यावनतकायेनैकान्ते
स्थितम् । तं च दूरे हृष्ट्वा गर्दभः पुष्टाङ्गो गर्दभीयमिति मत्वा
शब्दं कुर्वाणस्तदभिमुखं धावितः । ततस्तेन सस्यरक्षकेण गर्द-
20 भो ऽयमिति ज्ञात्वा लीलयैव व्यापादितः । अतो ऽहं ब्रवीमि ।

सुचिरं हि चरन्मीनं श्रेयः पश्यत्यबुद्धिमान् ।
द्वीपिचर्मपरिच्छन्नो वाग्दोषाद्गर्दभो हतः ॥

XII.

यदा चिन्तयेास्वपि वृद्धेर्भावाच्चृषार्तो गजयूथो यूथपतिमा-
ह । नाथ । को ऽप्युपायो ऽस्माकं जीवनाय नास्ति । अस्त्यत्र
खुद्रजन्तूनां निमज्जनस्थानम् । वयं च निमज्जनाभावादन्धा
इव क यामः किं वा कुर्मः । ततो हस्तिराजो नातिदूरं गत्वा
निर्मलं हृदं दर्शितवान् । ततस्तत्तीरावस्थिताः शशका गजयू-
थपादाहतिभिर्बहवश्चूर्णिताः । अनन्तरं शिलीमुखो नाम श-
शकः सर्वानाहूय चिन्तयामास । अनेन गजयूथेन पिपासा-
10 कुलितेन प्रत्यहमेवाचागन्तव्यम् । अतो विनङ्क्ष्यत्यस्मत्कुलम् ।
अथ विजयो नाम वृद्धशशको ऽवदत् । मा विषीदत । प्रती-
कारो मया कर्तव्यः । इति प्रतिज्ञाय चलितः । गच्छता च
तेनालोचितम् । कथं मया गजयूथपनिकटे गत्वा वक्तव्यम् ।
यतः । स्पृशन्नपि गजो हन्ति जिघ्रन्नपि भुजंगमः ।
15 हसन्नपि नृपो हन्ति मानयन्नपि दुर्जनः ॥

अतो ऽहं पर्वतशिखरमारुह्य यूथनाथमभिवादयामि । तथा-
नुष्ठिते सति यूथनाथ उवाच । कस्त्वम् । कुतः समायातः । स
ब्रूते । दूतो ऽहं भगवता चन्द्रेण प्रेषितः । यूथपतिराह । का-
र्यमुच्यताम् । विजयो वदति । शृणु गजेन्द्र ।

20 उद्यतेष्वपि शस्त्रेषु दूतो वदति नान्यथा ।
सदैवावध्यभावेन यथार्थस्य हि वाचकः ॥

तदहं तदाज्ञया ब्रवीमि । शृणु । यदेते शशकाश्चन्द्रसरोरक्षका-
स्त्वया निःसारितास्तन्न युक्तं कृतम् । यतो रक्षकास्ते शशका
मदीया अत एव लोके मे शशाङ्क इति प्रसिद्धिः । एवमुक्त्व-
ति दूते स यूथपतिर्भयादिदमाह । इदमज्ञानतः कृतम् । पुनर्न
5 गमिष्यामि । दूत उवाच । तदत्र सरसि भगवन्तं चन्द्रमसं प्रको-
पात्कम्पमानं प्रणम्य प्रसाद्य च गच्छ । ततस्तेन रात्रौ नीत्वा तस्मिन्
जले चञ्चलं चन्द्रप्रतिबिम्बं दर्शयित्वा स यूथपतिः प्रणामं का-
रितः । देव । अज्ञानादेवानेनापराधः कृतस्तत्क्षम्यतामित्युक्त्वा
तेन शशकेन स यूथपतिः प्रस्थापितः । अतो ऽहं ब्रवीमि ।

10 व्यपदेशेन महतां सिद्धिः संजायते परा ।
　शशिनो व्यपदेशेन वसन्ति शशकाः सुखम् ॥

XIII.

अस्ति सृगालः कश्चित्स्वेच्छया नगरोपान्ते भ्रमन्बीलसंधा-
नभाण्डे निपतितः । पश्चात्तत उत्थातुमसमर्थः प्रातरात्मानं मृ-
15 तवत्संदर्श्य स्थितः । अथ नीलीभाण्डस्वामिनासावुत्थाप्य दूरे
नीत्वा परित्यक्तः । ततो ऽसौ वनं गत्वात्मानं नीलवर्णमवलो-
क्याचिन्तयत् । अहमिदानीमुत्तमवर्णः । तदात्मनः किमुत्कर्षं
न साधयामि । इत्यालोच्य सृगालानाहूय तेनोक्तम् । अहं भ-
गवत्या वनदेवतया स्वहस्तेनारण्यराज्ये सर्वौषधिरसेनाभिषि-
20 क्तः । पश्यत मम वर्णम् । तद्द्यारभ्यास्मदाज्ञया स्मिन्नरण्ये
व्यवहारः कार्यः । सृगालाश्च तं विशिष्टवर्णमवलोक्य साष्टा-
ङ्गपातं प्रणम्योचुः । यथाज्ञापयति देवः । ततो ऽनेन क्रमेण

सर्वेश्वरराख्यवासिष्ववाधिपत्यं तस्य बभूव । ततस्तेन सिंहव्याघ्रा-
दीनुत्तमपरिजनाश्राप्य सृगालानवलोक्य लज्जमानेनावज्ञया
दूरीकृताः स्वज्ञातयः । ततो विषख्नासृगालानवलोक्य वृद्धसृ-
गालेन केन चित्प्रतिज्ञातम् । मा विषीदत । एवं चेदनेनानी-
तिज्ञेन वयं मर्मज्ञाः परिभूताः तद्यद्यायं नश्यति तन्मया
विधेयम् । यतो ऽमी व्याघ्रादयो वयमाभाविप्रलब्धाः सृगा-
लमज्ञात्वा राजानममुं मन्यन्ते तद्यद्यायं परिचीयते तथा
कुरुत । तच्च चैवमनुष्ठेयं यथा वदामि । यदा सर्वे संध्यासमये
तत्सन्निधाने महारावमेकदा करिष्यथ ततस्त्वं शब्दमाकर्ण्य स्व-
भावासेनापि शब्दः कर्तव्यः । यतः ।

यः स्वभावो हि यस्य स्यात्तस्यासौ दुरतिक्रमः ।
श्वा यदि क्रियते भोगी तत्किं नाश्नात्युपानहम् ॥

ततः शब्दाद्विज्ञाय व्याघ्रेण हन्तव्यः । तथानुष्ठिते सति तद्वृ-
त्तम् । तथा चोक्तम् ।

छिद्रं मर्म च वीर्यं च विजानाति निजो रिपुः ।
दहत्यन्तर्गतश्चैव शुष्कवृक्षमिवानलः ॥

अतो ऽहं ब्रवीमि ।

आत्मपक्षं परित्यज्य परपक्षे च यो रतः ।
स परैर्हन्यते मूढो नीलवर्णसृगालवत् ॥

_____

XIV. XV. XVI.

अस्ति मगधदेशे पुल्लोत्पलाभिधानं सरः । तत्र विरार्तक-
टविकटनामानौ हंसौ निवसतः । तयोर्मित्रं कथ्रुयीबनामा

कूर्मः प्रतिवसति । अचेकदा धीवरैरागत्य तत्रोक्तं यद्व्यासा-
भिरूषिता प्रातः कूर्ममत्स्यादयो व्यापादयितव्याः । तदाक-
र्ण्ये कूर्मो हंसावाह । सुहृदौ । श्रुतो ऽयं धीवरालापः । अधुना
किं मया कर्तव्यम् । हंसावाहतुः । ज्ञायतां तावत् । पश्चाद-
दुचितं तत्कर्तव्यम् । कूर्मो ब्रूते । मैवं यतो हृदृश्यतिकरो ऽह-
मत्र । तथा चोक्तम् ।

अनागतविधाता च प्रत्युत्पन्नमतिश्च यः ।
द्वावेतौ सुखमेधेते यद्भविष्यो विनश्यति ॥

तावाहतुः । कथमेतत् । कूर्मः कथयति । पुरैतस्मिन्नेव सर-
स्येवंविधेष्वेव धीवरेषूपस्थितेषु मत्स्यत्रयेणालोचितम् ।
तत्रानागतविधाता नामैको मत्स्यः । तेनोक्तम् । अहं ताव-
ज्जलाशयान्तरं गच्छामि । इत्युक्त्वा स हृदान्तरं गतः । अ-
परेण प्रत्युत्पन्नमतिनाख्या मत्स्येनाभिहितम् । भाविन्यर्थे प्र-
माणाभावात्कुत्र मया गन्तव्यम् । तदुत्पन्ने कार्ये यथाकार्य-
मनुष्ठेयम् । ततो यद्भविष्येणोक्तम् ।

यद्भावि न तद्भावि भावि चेन्न तदन्यथा ।
इति चिन्ताविषघ्नो ऽयमगदः किं न पीयते ॥

ततः प्रातर्जालेन बद्धः प्रत्युत्पन्नमतिर्मृतवदात्मानं संदर्श्य
स्थितः । ततो जालादपसारितः स्थलादुत्प्लुत्य गम्भीरं नीरं
प्रविष्टः । यद्भविष्यश्च धीवरैः प्राप्तो व्यापादितः । अतो ऽहं
ब्रवीमि । अनागतविधातेत्यादि ।

तद्यथाहमन्यह्रदं प्राप्नोमि तदेष विधीयताम् । हंसावाहतुः ।
जलाशयान्तरे प्राप्ते तव कुशलम् । स्थले गच्छतस्ते को कि-

पिः । कूर्मो ब्रूते । यथाहं भवद्भ्यां सहाकाशवर्त्मेना यामि स
उपायो विधीयताम् । हंसौ ब्रूतः । कथमुपायः संभवति । क-
च्छपो वदति । युवाभ्यां चञ्चुधृतं काष्ठमेकं मया मुखेनावल-
म्बितव्यम् । अतो भवतोः पक्षबलेन मयापि सुखं गन्तव्यम् ।
5 हंसौ ब्रूतः । संभवत्येष उपायः । किं तु ।

उपायं चिन्तयेत्प्राज्ञस्तथापायं च चिन्तयेत् ।
पश्यतो बकमूर्खस्य नकुलैर्भक्षिता बकाः ॥

कूर्मः पृच्छति । कथमेतत् । तौ कथयतः । अस्त्युत्तरापथे
गृध्रकूटो नाम पर्वतः । तत्रैव रेवातीरे न्यग्रोधपादपे बका
10 निवसन्ति । तस्य वटस्याधस्ताद्विवरे सर्पस्तिष्ठति । स च
बकानां बालापत्यानि खादति । ततः शोकातौनां बकानां
प्रलापं श्रुत्वा केन चिद्वृद्धबकेनोक्तम् । भोः । एवं कुरुत
यूयम् । मत्स्यानानीय नकुलविवरादारभ्य सर्पविवरं या-
वत्पङ्क्तिक्रमेणैकैकशो मत्स्यान्धत्त । ततस्तदाहारवर्त्मेना नकु-
15 लैरागत्य सर्पो द्रष्टव्यः स्वभावद्वेषाद्घातयितव्यश्च । तथा-
नुष्ठिते सति तद्वृत्तम् । अथ नकुलैर्वृक्षोपरि पक्षिशावका-
नां रावः श्रुतः । पश्चात्तैर्वृक्षमारुह्य शावकाः सर्वे एव खा-
दिताः । अत आवां ब्रूवः । उपायं चिन्तयेदित्यादि ।

आवाभ्यां नीयमानं त्वां दृष्ट्वा लोकैः किं चिद्वक्तव्यमेव । त-
20 दाकर्ण्य यदि त्वमुत्तरं ददासि तदा तव मरणं भविष्यति । त-
त्सर्वथाचैव स्थीयताम् । कूर्मो वदति । किमहमज्ञः । न कि-
मपि मया वक्तव्यम् । तत एवमनुष्ठिते सत्याकाशे नीयमानं
तं कूर्ममालोक्य सर्वे गोरक्षकाः पश्चाद्धावन्ति वदन्ति च ।

अहो महदाश्चर्यम् । पक्षिभ्यां कूर्मः समुद्यते । तत्र कश्चिदाह । य-
द्ययं कूर्मः पतति तदाचैव पक्का खादितव्यः । को ऽपि निगदति ।
गृहं नेतव्यः । कश्चिद्वदति । सरसः समीपे पक्का भक्षितव्यः ।
तत्परुषवचनमाकर्ण्य स कूर्मः क्रोधाद्विस्मृतसंस्कारो ऽवदत् ।
5 युष्माभिर्भस्म भक्षितव्यम् । इति वद्त्रेव काष्ठात्पतितो गोर-
क्षकैर्व्यापादितः । अतो ऽहं ब्रवीमि ।

मुहृदां हितकामानां न करोतीह यो वचः ।
स कूर्म इव दुर्बुद्धिः काष्ठाद्भ्रष्टो विनश्यति ॥

XVII.

अस्ति गौतमारण्ये महातपा नाम मुनिः । तेनाश्रमसंनि-
10 धाने मूषिकाशावकः काकमुखाद्भ्रष्टो दृष्टः । ततो दयालुना
तेन मुनिना नीवारकणैः स संवर्धितः । तं च मूषिकं खादि-
तुमनुधावन्बिडालो मुनिना दृष्टः । पश्चात्तपःप्रभावात्तेन मुनि-
ना मूषिको बलिष्ठो बिडालः कृतः । स बिडालः कुक्कुराद्विभेति ।
ततो ऽसौ कुक्कुरः कृतः । कुक्कुरस्य व्याघ्रान्महद्भयम् । तदनन्तरं स
15 व्याघ्रः कृतः । अथ व्याघ्रमपि तं मूषिकानिर्विशेषं पश्यति मु-
निः । अतः सर्वे तत्रस्था जनास्तं व्याघ्रं दृष्ट्वा वदन्ति । अनेन
मुनिना मूषिको ऽयं व्याघ्रतां नीतः । एतच्छ्रुत्वा स व्याघ्रः स-
व्यथो ऽचिन्तयत् । यावदनेन मुनिना जीवितव्यं तावदिदं मम
स्वरूपाख्यानमकीर्तिकरं न पलायिष्यते । इति समालोच्य मु-
20 निं हन्तुं समुद्यतः । ततो मुनिना तस्य चिकीर्षितं ज्ञात्वा पु-
नर्मूषिको भवेत्युक्त्वा मूषिक एव कृतः । अतो ऽहं ब्रवीमि ।

नीचः स्वाध्यपदं प्राप्य स्वामिनं लोप्तुमिच्छति ।
मूषिको व्याघ्रतां प्राप्य मुनिं हन्तुं गतो यथा ॥

XVIII.

अस्ति मालवविषये पद्मगर्भाभिधानं सरः । तत्रैको वृद्ध-
बकः सामर्थ्यहीनस्त्वधोव्रियमिवात्मानं दर्शयित्वा स्थितः । स
च केन चित्कुलीरेण दूरादेव पृष्टः । किमिति भवानाहारपरि-
त्यागेन तिष्ठति । बकेनोक्तम् । मत्स्या मम जीवनहेतवः ।
ते चावश्यमेव कैवर्तैर्व्यापादयितव्या इति नगरोपान्ते पर्या-
लोचना मयाकर्णिता । तदितो वर्तनाभावादस्मन्मरणमुपस्थि-
तम् । इति ज्ञात्वाहमाहारे ऽपि मन्दादरः कृतः । तच्छ्रुत्वा स-
र्वैर्मत्स्यैरालोचितम् । इह समये तावदुपकारक एवायमुपल-
भ्यते ऽस्माकम् । तदयमेव यथाकर्तव्यं पृच्छ्यताम् । तथा
चोक्तम् ।

उपकर्त्रारिणा संधिर्न मित्रेणापकारिणा ।
उपकारापकारी हि लक्ष्यं लक्षणमेतयोः ॥

मत्स्या ऊचुः । भो बक । अस्माकं कुत्र रक्षणोपायः । बको ब्रू-
ते । अस्ति रक्षणहेतुर्जलाशयान्तरम् । तत्राहमेकैकशो युष्मान्न-
यामि । मत्स्यैरपि भयादुक्तम् । एवमस्तु । ततो ऽसौ दुष्टबक-
स्तान्मत्स्यानेकैकाबीला कस्मिंश्चिद्देशे खादित्वा पुनरागत्य व-
दति । ते मया जलाशयान्तरे स्थापिताः । अनन्तरं कुलीरस्त-
मुवाच । भो बक । मामपि तत्र नय । ततो बको ऽप्यपूर्वंकु-
लीर्मांसार्थी सादरं तं नीत्वा स्थले धृतवान् । कुलीरो ऽपि

मत्स्यकङ्कालाकीर्णां भूमिं दृष्ट्वाचिन्तयत् । हा हतो ऽस्मि म-
न्दभाग्यः । भवतु । इदानीं समयोचितं व्यवहरामि । यतः ।

तावद्भयातु भेतव्यं यावद्भयमनागतम् ।
आगतं तु भयं दृष्ट्वा प्रहर्तव्यमभीतवत् ॥

5 अपरं च । अयुद्धे हि यदा पश्येन् किं चिज्जितमात्मनः ।
युध्यमानस्तदा प्राज्ञो म्रियते रिपुणा सह ॥

इत्यालोच्य स कुलीरस्तस्य बकस्य ग्रीवां चिच्छेद । स बकः
पञ्चत्वं गतः । अतो ऽहं ब्रवीमि ।

भक्षयित्वा बहून्मत्स्यानुत्तमाधममध्यमान् ।
10 अतिलौल्याद्बकः कश्चिन्मृतः कर्कटकग्रहात् ॥

_____

XIX.

अस्ति देवीकोट्टनगरे देवशर्मा नाम ब्राह्मणः । तेन विषु-
वत्संक्रान्तौ सक्तुपूर्णशरावः प्राप्तः । ततस्तमादायासौ भा-
ण्डपूर्णकुम्भकारमण्डपिकैकदेशे शय्यानिक्षिप्तदेहः सन्नाचाव-
चिन्तयत् । यद्यहमिमं सक्तुशरावं विक्रीय दश कपर्दकान्प्रा-
15 प्नोमि तदा तैरिह समये शरावांस्ततो घटादीनुपक्रीय विक्री-
यानेकधा वृद्धैर्धनैः पुनः पुनः पूगवस्त्रादिकमुपक्रीय लक्षसं-
ख्यानि धनान्युत्पाद्य विवाहचतुष्टयं करोमि । ततस्तासु पत्नीषु
याधिकरूपवती तस्यामधिकानुरागं करोमि । अनन्तरं जाते-
र्ष्यास्तत्पत्न्यो यदा द्वंद्वं कुर्वन्ति तदा कोपाकुलो ऽहं ताः
20 पत्नीर्लगुडेनेत्थं ताडयामि । इत्यभिधायोत्थाय तेन लगुडः
क्षिप्तः । अतः सक्तुशरावश्चूर्णितो भाण्डानि च बहूनि भग्ना-

नि। ततो भाराऽभङ्गश्छेनागतकुम्भकारेण तदृष्ट्वा स ब्राह्म-
णस्तिरस्कृतो मण्डपिकागर्भाऽबहिष्कृतः। अतो ऽहं ब्रवीमि।

अनागतवतीं चिन्तां कृत्वा यस्तु प्रहृष्यति।
स तिरस्कारमाप्नोति भग्नभाण्डो द्विजो यथा॥

<hr>

XX.

5 अस्ति गौतमारण्ये प्रस्तुतयज्ञः कश्चिद्ब्राह्मणः। स च य-
ज्ञार्थे ग्रामान्तराच्छागमुपक्रीय स्कन्धे कृत्वा गच्छन्धूर्तैत्रयेणा-
वलोकितः। ततस्ते धूर्ता यद्येष छागः केनाप्युपायेन प्राप्य
खाद्यते तदा मतिप्रकर्षो भवतीत्यालोच्य ग्रान्तरे वृक्षत्रयतले
ब्राह्मणस्य वर्त्मन्युपविश्य स्थिताः। तत्रैकेन धूर्तेन स ब्राह्मणो
10 गच्छन्नभिहितः। भो ब्राह्मण। किमिति त्वया कुक्कुरः स्क-
न्धेनोह्यते। ब्राह्मणो ब्रूते। नायं श्वा। यज्ञच्छागो ऽयं। अन-
न्तरं पुनर्द्वितीयेन क्रोशमात्रावस्थितेन तदेवोक्तम्। तदाकर्ण्ये
ब्राह्मणस्तं छागं भूमौ निधाय मुहुर्मुहुर्निरीक्ष्य पुनः स्कन्धे कृ-
त्वा दोलायमानमतिः स्खलितः। तदनन्तरं पुनर्गच्छन्स ब्राह्मण-
15 स्तृतीयेन धूर्तेनोक्तः। भो ब्राह्मण। किमिति कुक्कुरं स्कन्धेन
भवान्वहति। तदाकर्ण्ये निश्चितमेवायं कुक्कुर इति मत्वा
छागं त्यक्ता स्नात्वा स्वगृहं ययौ। स च्छागो तैर्धूर्तैर्नीत्वा भ-
क्षितः। अतो ऽहं ब्रवीमि।

आत्मौपम्येन यो वेत्ति दुर्जनं सत्यवादिनम्।
20 स तथा वञ्च्यते धूर्तैर्ब्राह्मणश्छागतो यथा॥

XXI.

अस्त्युज्जयिन्यां माठरो नाम ब्राह्मणः । तस्य ब्राह्मणी बा-
लापत्यस्य रक्षार्थं ब्राह्मणमवस्थाप्य स्नातुं गता । अथ ब्राह्म-
णस्य कृते राज्ञः श्राद्धं दातुमाह्वानमागतम् । तच्छ्रुत्वा ब्राह्मणः
सहजदारिद्र्यादचिन्तयत् । यदि सत्वरं न गच्छामि तदान्यः क-
श्चिच्छ्राद्धं ग्रहीष्यति । उक्तं च ।

आदानस्य प्रदानस्य कर्त्तव्यस्य च कर्मणः ।
क्षिप्रमक्रियमाणस्य कालः पिबति तद्रसम् ॥

किं तु बालकस्याच रक्षको नास्ति । तत्किं करोमि । यातु ।
चिरकालपालितमिमं पुत्रनिर्विशेषं नकुलं बालकरक्षार्थम-
वस्थाप्य गच्छामि । तथा कृत्वा स तत्र गतः । ततस्तेन नकु-
लेन बालकसमीपमागच्छता कृष्णसर्पो दृष्टो व्यापादितश्च ।
अथासौ नकुलो ब्राह्मणमायान्तमवलोक्य रक्तविलिप्तमुख-
पादः सत्वरमुपागम्य तस्य चरणयोर्लुलोठ । ततो ऽसौ ब्राह्म-
णस्तं तथाविधं दृष्ट्वा मम पुत्रो ऽनेन भक्षित इत्यवधार्य व्या-
पादितवान् । अनन्तरं यावदसावुपसृत्य पश्यति ब्राह्मणस्ता-
वद्बालकः सुस्थः सर्पश्च व्यापादितस्तिष्ठति । ततस्तमुपकार-
कमेव नकुलं निरूप्य विभावितकृत्यः संतप्तचेताः स परं वि-
षादमगमत् । अतो ऽहं ब्रवीमि ।

यो ऽर्थतत्त्वमविज्ञाय क्रोधस्यैव वशं गतः ।
स तथा तप्यते मूढो ब्राह्मणो नकुलाद्यथा ॥

॥ अथ कथासरित्सागरः ॥

XXII.

अथान्तरे स राजापि पुष्पकः सत्यसंगरः ।
विवेश विन्ध्यकान्तारं विरक्तः स्वेषु बन्धुषु ॥
भ्रमन्नवाप तत्रासौ बाहुयुद्धैकतत्परौ ।
पुरुषौ द्वौ ततस्तौ स पृष्टवान्कौ युवामिति ॥ ५
मयासुक्षुतावावां तदीयं चास्ति नौ धनम् ।
इदं भाजनमेषा च यष्टिरेते च पादुके ॥
तन्निमित्तेन युद्धं नौ यो बली स हरेदिति ।
एतत्तद्वचनं श्रुत्वा हसन्नोवाच पुष्पकः ॥
कियदेतद्वनं पुंसस्ततस्तौ समवोचताम् । १०
पादुके परिधायैते खेचरत्वमवाप्यते ॥
यच्छया यल्लिख्यते किं चित्तत्सत्यं संपद्यते हि तत् ।
भाजने यो य आहारश्चिन्त्यते स स तिष्ठति ॥
तच्छ्रुत्वा पुष्पको ऽवादीत्किं युद्धेनास्त्वयं पणः ।
धावन्बलाधिको यः स्यात्स एवैतद्धरेदिति ॥ १५
एवमस्त्विति तौ मूढौ धावितौ सो ऽपि पादुके ।
अध्यास्योदपतद्व्योम गृहीत्वा यष्टिभाजने ॥
अथ दूरं क्षणाद्गत्वा ददर्श नगरीं शुभाम् ।
आकर्षिकाख्यां तस्यां च नभसो ऽवततार सः ॥

XXIII.

अर्थैः संचयवानर्थान्नाप्नोति कियदद्भुतम् ।
मया पुनर्विनैवार्थै लक्ष्मीरासादिता पुरा ॥

गर्भस्थस्यैव मे पूर्वे पिता पञ्चत्वमागतः ।
मन्मातुश्च तदा पापैर्गोत्रजैः सकलं हृतम् ॥

5 ततः सा तद्भयाज्ञत्वा रक्षन्ती गर्भमात्मनः ।
तस्थौ कुमारदत्तस्य पितृमित्रस्य वेश्मनि ॥

तत्र तस्याश्च जातो ऽहं साध्व्या वृत्तिनिबन्धनम् ।
ततश्चावर्धयत्सा मां कृच्छ्रकर्माणि कुर्वती ॥

उपाध्यायमथाभ्यर्थे तया किं चन दीनया ।
10 क्रमेण शिक्षितश्चाहं लिपिं गणितमेव च ॥

वणिक्पुत्रो ऽसि तन्मुञ्च वाणिज्यं कुरु साम्प्रतम् ।
विशाखिलाख्यो देशे ऽस्मिन्वणिक्चास्ति महाधनः ॥

दरिद्राणां कुलीनानां भाण्डमूल्यं ददाति सः ।
गच्छ याचस्व तं मूल्यमिति माताब्रवीच्च माम् ॥

15 ततो ऽहमगमं तस्य सकाशं सो ऽपि तत्क्षणम् ।
इत्यवोचत्कुधा कं चिद्वणिक्पुत्रं विशाखिलः ॥

मूषको ह्रियते यो ऽयं गतप्राणो ऽत्र भूतले ।
एतेनापि हि पण्येन कुशलो धनमर्जयेत् ॥

दत्तास्तव पुनः पाप दीनारा बहवो मया ।
20 दूरे तिष्ठतु तद्वृद्धिस्त्वया ते ऽपि न रक्षिताः ॥

तच्छ्रुत्वा सहसैवाहं तमवोचं विशाखिलम् ।
गृहीतो ऽयं मया लब्धो भाण्डमूल्याय मूषकः ॥

इत्युक्ता मूषकं हस्ते गृहीला संपुटे च तम् ।
लिखिलास्य गतो ऽभूवमहं सो ऽप्यहसन्बणिक् ॥
चणकाञ्जलियुग्मेन मूल्येन स च मूषकः ।
मार्जारस्य कृते दत्तः कस्य चिद्वणिजो मया ॥
5 कृला तांक्षणकान्पिष्टान्गृहीला जलकुम्भिकाम् ।
अतिश्रं चन्दरे गला छायायां नगराद्बहिः ॥
तच श्रान्तागतायाम्भः शीतलं चरणांश्च तान् ।
काष्ठभारिकसंघाय समभ्ययमदामहम् ॥
एकैकः काष्ठिकः प्रीला काष्ठे द्वे द्वे ददौ मम ।
10 विक्रोतवानहं तानि नीला काष्ठानि चापणे ॥
ततः स्तोकेन मूल्येन क्रीला तांक्षणकांस्ततः ।
तथैव काष्ठिकेभ्यो ऽहमन्येद्युः काष्ठमाहरम् ॥
एवं प्रतिदिनं कृला प्राप्य मूल्यं क्रमान्मया ।
काष्ठिकेभ्यो ऽखिलं दारु क्रीतं तेभ्यो दिनत्रयम् ॥
15 अकस्माद्च संजाते काष्ठच्छेदे ऽतिवृष्टिभिः ।
मया तद्दारु विक्रोतं पणानां बहुभिः शतैः ॥
तेनैव विपणीं कृला धनेन निजकौशलात् ।
कुर्वन्वाणिज्यं क्रमशः संपन्नो ऽस्मि महाधनः ॥
सौवर्णो मूषकः कृला मया तस्मै समर्पितः ।
20 विशाखिलाय सो ऽपि स्वां कन्यां मह्यमदात्ततः ॥
अत एव च लोके ऽहं प्रसिद्धो मूषकाख्यया ।
एवं लक्ष्मीरियं प्राप्ता निर्धनेन सता मया ॥

XXIV.

तथा च पूर्वे राजाभूत्तपस्वी करुणापरः ।
दाता धीरः शिविर्नाम सर्वसत्त्वाभयप्रदः ॥

तं वञ्चयितुमिन्द्रो ऽथ कृत्वा श्येनवपुः स्वयम् ।
मायाकपोतवपुषं धर्ममन्वपतद्द्रुतम् ॥

5 कपोतः स भयाक्रान्ता शिबेरङ्कमशिश्रियत् ।
मनुष्यवाचा श्येनो ऽथ स तं राजानमब्रवीत् ॥

राजन्भक्ष्यमिदं मुञ्च कपोतं क्षुधितस्य मे ।
अन्यथा मां मृतं विद्धि कस्ते धर्मस्ततो भवेत् ॥

ततः शिबिरुवाचैनमेष मे शरणागतः ।

10 अत्याज्यस्तद्ददाम्यन्यन्मांसमेतत्समं तव ॥

श्येनो जगाद यद्येवमात्ममांसं प्रयच्छ मे ।
तथेति तद्ग्रह्यः सन्स राजा प्रत्यपद्यत ॥

यथा यथा च मांसं स्वमुत्कृत्यारोपयन्नृपः ।
तथा तथा तुलायां स कपोतो ऽभ्यधिको ऽभवत् ॥

15 ततः शरीरं सकलं तुलां राजाध्यरोपयत् ।
साधु साधु समं त्वेतद्दिव्या वागुदभूत्ततः ॥

इन्द्रधर्मौ ततस्त्यक्त्वा रूपं श्येनकपोतयोः ।
तुशावक्षतदेहं तं राजानं चक्रतुः शिबिम् ॥

दत्त्वा चास्मै वरानन्यांस्तावनन्तर्धानमीयतुः ॥

XXV.

20 पुराभूज्जैतमो नाम त्रिकालज्ञो महामुनिः ।

अहल्येति च तस्यासीद्भार्या रूपजिताप्सराः ॥
एकदा रूपलुब्धस्तामिन्द्रः प्रार्थितवानह ।
प्रभूणां हि विभूत्यन्धा धावत्यविषये मतिः ॥
सानुमेने च तं मूढा वृषस्यन्ती शचीपतिम् ।
5 तच्च प्रभावतो बुद्ध्वा तत्रागाद्गौतमो मुनिः ॥
मार्जारूपं चक्रे च भयादिन्द्रो ऽपि तत्क्षणम् ।
कः स्थितो ऽत्रेति सो ऽपृच्छदहल्यामथ गौतमः ॥
एषो ठिछ्ठो खु मज्जाओ इत्यपभ्रष्टवक्रया ।
गिरा सत्यानुरोधिन्या सा तं प्रत्यब्रवीत्पतिम् ॥
10 सत्यं तज्जार इत्युक्ता विहसन्स ततो मुनिः ।
सत्यानुरोधकुप्रान्तं शापं तस्यामपातयत् ॥
पापशीले शिलाभावं भूरिकालमवाप्नुहि ।
आ वनान्तरसंचारिराघवालोकनादिति ॥
दत्तशापो यथाकामं तपसे स मुनिर्ययौ ।
15 अहल्यापि शिलाभावं दारुणं प्रत्यपद्यत ॥

XXVI.

ततः कदा चिद्द्याख्य वसन्तसमयोत्सवे ।
देवीकृतं तदुद्यानं स राजा सातवाहनः ॥
विहरन्स चिरं तत्र महेन्द्र इव नन्दने ।
वापीजले ऽवतीर्णो ऽभूत्क्रीडितुं कामिनीसखः ॥
20 असिञ्चत्तम दयिताः सहेलं करवारिभिः ।
असिच्यत स ताभिश्च वशाभिरिव वारणः ॥

अथैका तस्य महिषी राज्ञः स्तनभरालसा ।
शिरीषमृदुकुमाराङ्घ्री क्रीडन्ती ह्ममभ्यगात् ॥
सा जलैरभिषिञ्चन्तं राजानमसहा सती ।
अब्रवीन्मोदकैर्देव परिताडय मामिति ॥
तच्छ्रुत्वा मोदकानाज्ञा द्रुतमानाययत्तदा । ५
ततो विहस्य सा राज्ञी पुनरेवमभाषत ॥
राजन्नवसरः को ऽच मोदकानां जलान्तरे ।
उदकैः सिञ्च मा त्वं मामित्युक्तं हि मया तव ॥
संधिमात्रं न जानासि माशब्दोदकशब्दयोः ।
न च प्रकरणं वेत्सि मूर्खस्त्वं कथमीदृशः ॥ १०
इत्युक्तः स तया राज्ञ्या शब्दशास्त्रविदा नृपः ।
परिवारे हसत्यन्तर्लज्जाक्रान्तो ऽभूत्स्फुटीभूत ॥
परित्यक्तजलक्रीडो वीतदर्पश्च तत्क्षणम् ।
जातावमानो निर्लक्ष्यः प्राविशन्निजमन्दिरम् ॥
ततश्चिन्तापरो मुह्यन्नाहारादिपराङ्मुखः । १५
चित्रस्थ इव पृष्टो ऽपि नैव किं चिद्भाषत ॥
पाठयितव्यं शरणं वा मे मृत्युर्वेति विचिन्तयन् ।
शयनीयपरित्यक्तगात्रः संतापवानभूत ॥
अकस्मादथ राज्ञस्तां दृष्ट्वावस्थां तथाविधाम् ।
किमेतदिति संभ्रान्तः सर्वः परिजनो ऽभवत् ॥ २०
ततो ऽहं शर्ववर्मा च ज्ञातवन्तौ क्रमेण ताम् ।
अथान्तरे च स प्रायः पर्यहीयत वासरः ॥
प्रातरावामगच्छाव वासवेश्म महीपतेः ॥

तत्र सर्वस्य रुद्धे ऽपि प्रवेशे कथमप्यहम् ।
प्राविशं मम पश्चाच्च शर्ववर्मा लघुक्रमम् ॥
उपविश्याथ निकटे विज्ञप्रः स मया नृपः ।
अकारणं कर्थं देव वर्तसे विमना इति ॥
5 तच्छ्रुत्वापि तथैवासीत्स तूष्णीं सातवाहनः ।
शर्ववर्मा ततश्चेदमद्भुतं वाक्यमब्रवीत् ॥
श्रुतिमन्तं मां कुर्विति प्रागुक्तं देव मे त्वया ।
तेनाहं कृतवानद्य स्वप्नमाणवकं निशि ॥
स्वप्ने ततो मया हृदं नभसश्च्युतमम्बुजम् ।
10 तच्च दिव्येन केनापि कुमारेण विकासितम् ॥
ततश्च निर्गता तस्मादिव्या स्त्री धवलाम्बरा ।
तव देव मुखं सा च प्रविष्टा समनन्तरम् ॥
इत्यदृष्ट्वा प्रबुद्धो ऽस्मि सा च मन्ये सरस्वती ।
देवस्य वदने साक्षात्संप्रविष्टा न संशयः ॥
15 एवं निवेदितस्वप्ने शर्ववर्मणि तत्क्षणम् ।
मामक्तमौनः साकूतमवदात्सातवाहनः ॥
शिक्ष्यमाणः प्रयत्नेन कालेन कियता पुमान् ।
अधिगच्छति पाणिनीत्यमेतन्मे कथ्यतां त्वया ॥
मम तेन विना ह्येषा लक्ष्मीर्न प्रतिभासते ।
20 विभवैः किं नु मूर्खस्य काचस्याभरणैरिव ॥
ततो ऽहमवदं राजन्वर्षैर्द्वादशभिः सदा ।
ज्ञायते सर्वविद्यानां मुखं व्याकरणं नृभिः ॥
अहं तु शिक्षयामि त्वां वर्षेषड्भेन तद्विभो ।

श्रुत्वैतत्सहसा सेर्ष्यं शर्ववर्मा किलावदत् ॥

सुखोचितो जनः क्लेशं कथं कुर्यादियच्चिरम् ।
तदहं मासषड्वेन देव त्वां शिक्षयामि तात् ॥

श्रुत्वैवैतदसंभाव्यं तमवोचमहं रुषा ।

5 षड्भिर्मासैस्त्वया देवः शिक्षितश्चेत्ततो मया ॥

संस्कृतं प्राकृतं तद्देशभाषा च सर्वदा ।
भाषाश्चयमिदं त्यक्ता यन्मनुष्येषु संभवेत् ॥

शर्ववर्मा ततो ऽवादीच्चेदेवं करोम्यहम् ।
द्वादशाब्दान्वहाम्येष शिरसा तव पादुके ॥

10 इत्युक्त्वा निर्गते तस्मिन्नहमप्यगमं गृहम् ।
राजाप्युभयतः सिद्धिं मत्वा शक्तो बभूव सः ॥

शर्ववर्मा च वीहस्तः प्रतिज्ञां तां सुदुस्तराम् ।
पश्यन्सानुशयः सर्वां स्वभार्यायै शशंस तात् ॥

सापि तं दुःखितावोचत्संकटे ऽसि स्त्वव प्रभो ।

15 विना स्वामिकुमारेण गतिरन्या न दृश्यते ॥

तथेति निश्चयं कृत्वा पश्चिमे प्रहरे निशि ।
शर्ववर्मा निराहारस्त्वेव प्रस्थितो ऽभवत् ॥

सो ऽपि वात्तैकभक्षः सन्कृतमौनः सुनिश्चयः ।
प्राप स्वामिकुमारस्य शर्ववर्मान्तिकं क्रमात् ॥

20 शरीरनिरपेक्षेण तपसा तत्र तोषितः ।
प्रसादमकरोत्तस्य कार्त्तिकेयो यथेप्सितम् ॥

आगत्य शर्ववर्मा ऽथ कुमारवरसिद्धिमान् ।
चिन्तितोपस्थिता राज्ञे सर्वा विद्याः प्रदत्तवान् ॥

प्रादुरासंश्च तात्तस्य सातवाहनभूपतेः ।
तत्क्षणं किं न कुर्याद्धि प्रसादः पारमेश्वरः ॥

XXVII.

एवं गुणाढ्यवचसा साथ सप्तकथामयी ।
स्वभाषया कथा दिव्या कथिता काण्यभूतिना ॥
5 तथैव च गुणाढ्येन पैशाच्या भाषया तया ।
निबद्धा सप्तभिर्वर्षैर्येन्थलक्षाणि सप्त सा ॥
मैतां विद्याधरा हार्षुरिति तामात्मशोणितैः ।
अटव्यां मष्यभावाच्च लिलेख स महाकविः ॥
तथा च श्रोतुमायातैः सिद्धविद्याधरादिभिः ।
10 निरन्तरमभूत्तन्न सवितानमिवाम्बरम् ॥
गुणाढ्येन निबद्धां च तां दृष्ट्वैव महाकथाम् ।
जगाम मुक्तशापः सन्काण्यभूतिर्निजां गतिम् ॥
पिशाचा ये ऽपि तत्रासन्नन्ये तत्सहचारिणः ।
ते ऽपि प्रापुर्दिवं सर्वे दिव्यामाकर्ण्ये तां कथाम् ॥
15 प्रतिष्ठां प्रापणीयैषा पृथिव्यां मे बृहत्कथा ।
अयमर्थो ऽपि मे देव्या शापान्तोक्तावुदीरितः ॥
तत्कथं प्रापयाम्येनां कस्मै तावत्समर्पये ।
इत्येवाचिन्तयत्तत्र स गुणाढ्यो महाकविः ॥
अथैको गुणदेवाख्यो नन्दिदेवाभिधः परः ।
20 तमूचतुरुपाध्यायं शिष्यावनुगताबुभौ ॥

तत्काव्यस्यार्पणस्थानमेकः श्रीसातवाहनः ।
रसिको हि वहेत्काव्यं पुष्पामोदमिवानिलः ॥
एवमस्त्विति तौ शिष्यावन्तिकं तस्य भूपतेः ।
प्राहिणोत्पुस्तकं दत्त्वा गुणाढ्यो गुणशालिनौ ॥
5 स्वयं च गत्वा तत्रैव प्रतिष्ठाने पुराद्बहिः ।
कृतसंकेत उद्याने तस्यौ देवीविनिर्मिते ॥
तच्छिष्याभ्यां च गत्वा तत्सातवाहनभूपतेः ।
गुणाढ्यकृतिरेषेति दर्शितं काव्यपुस्तकम् ॥
पिशाचभाषां तां श्रुत्वा तौ च दृष्ट्वा तदाकृती ।
10 विद्यामदेन सासूयं स राजैवमभाषत ॥
प्रमाणं सप्त लक्षाणि पैशाचं नीरसं वचः ।
शोणितेनाक्षराण्यासौ धिक्किपशाचकथामिमाम् ॥
ततः पुस्तकमादाय गत्वा ताभ्यां यथागतम् ।
शिष्याभ्यां तद्गुणाढ्याय यथावृत्तमकथ्यत ॥
15 गुणाढ्यो ऽपि तदाकर्ण्यं सद्यः खेदवशो ऽभवत् ।
तत्स्वज्ञेन कृतावज्ञः को नामान्तर्न तप्यते ॥
सखिष्यश्च ततो गत्वा नातिदूरं शिलोच्चयम् ।
विविक्तरम्यभूभागमम्बिकुण्डं व्यधात्पुरः ॥
तत्रामी पत्रमेकैकं शिष्याभ्यां साधु वीक्षितः ।
20 वाचयित्वा स चिक्षेप श्रावयन्मृगपक्षिणः ॥
नरवाहनदत्तस्य चरितं शिष्ययोः कृते ।
यन्यलक्षं कथामेकां वर्जयित्वा तदीप्सिताम् ॥
तल्लिख च तां कथां दिव्यां पठत्यपि दहत्यपि ।

परित्यक्ततृणाहाराः भृक्तन्तः साश्रुलोचनाः ॥
आसन्नभ्येत्य तच्चैव निश्चला बद्धमण्डलाः ।
निखिलाः खलु सारङ्गवराहमहिषादयः ॥
   अवान्तरे स राजाभूदस्वस्थः सातवाहनः ।
5 दोषं चास्यावदन्वैद्याः शुष्कमांसोपभोगजम् ॥
आश्रित्राप्तन्निमित्तं च सूपकारा बभाषिरे ।
अस्माकमीदृशं मांसं ददते लुब्धका इति ॥
पृष्टाश्च लुब्धका ऊचुर्नातिदूरे गिराविति ।
पठित्वा पन्नमेकैकं कोऽप्ययौ क्षिपति द्विजः ॥
10 तत्समेत्य निराहाराः भृक्तन्ति प्राणिनोऽखिलाः ।
नान्यतो यान्ति तेनैषां शुष्कं मांसमिदं क्षुधा ॥
इति व्याधवचः श्रुत्वा कृत्वा तानेव चायतः ।
स्वयं स कौतुकाद्राजा गुणाढ्यस्यान्तिकं ययौ ॥
ददर्शे तं समाकीर्णं जटाभिर्वेनवासतः ।
15 प्रशान्तशेषशापाग्निधूमिकाभिरिवाभितः ॥
अथैनं प्रत्यभिज्ञाय सबाष्पमृगमध्यगम् ।
नमस्कृत्य च पप्रच्छ तं वृत्तान्तं महीपतिः ॥
सोऽपि स्वं पुष्पदन्तस्य राज्ञे शापादिचेष्टितम् ।
ज्ञानी कथावतारं तमाचख्यौ भूतभाषया ॥
20 ततो गणावतारं तं मत्वा पादानतो नृपः ।
ययाचे तां कथां तस्मादिष्ठां हरमुखोन्नताम् ॥
अथोवाच स तं भूपं गुणाढ्यः सातवाहनम् ।
राजन्नड्यन्धलक्षाणि मया दग्धानि षड्ध्वया ॥

लक्ष्मेकमिदं ब्रूत्ति कथैका सैव गृह्यताम् ।
मन्ज्रिषौ तव चाचैतौ व्याख्यातारौ भविष्यतः ॥
इत्युक्ता नृपमामन्त्र्य त्यक्त्वा योगेन तां तनुम् ।
गुणाढ्यः शापनिर्मुक्तः प्राप दिव्यं निजं पदम् ॥
अथ तां गुणाढ्यदत्तामादाय कथां बृहत्कथां नाम्ना ।
नृपतिरगाद्बिजनगरं नरवाहनदत्तचरितमयीम् ॥
गुणदेवनन्दिदेवी तत्र च तौ तत्कथाकवेः शिष्यौ ।
क्षितिकनकवस्त्रवाहनभवनधनैः संविभेजे सः ॥
ताभ्यां सह च कथां तामाश्वास्य स सातवाहनस्तस्याः ।
तत्राषयावतारं वक्तुं चक्रे कथापीठम् ॥
सा च विचरसनिर्भरा कथा विसृतामरकथा कुतूहलात् ।
तद्बिधाय नगरे निरन्तरां ख्यातिमच भुवनत्रये गता ॥
॥ इति कथासरित्सागरे ऽष्टमस्तरङ्गः ॥

XXVIII.

॥ अथ मानवधर्मशास्त्रम् ॥

आसीदिदं तमोभूतमप्रज्ञातमलक्षणम् ।
अप्रतर्क्यमविज्ञेयं प्रसुप्तमिव सर्वतः ॥५॥ ॥अध्या॰१॥
ततः स्वयंभूर्भगवानव्यक्तो व्यञ्जयन्निदम् ।
महाभूतादि वृत्तौजाः प्रादुरासीत्तमोनुदः ॥६॥
यो ऽसावतीन्द्रियग्राह्यः सूक्ष्मो ऽव्यक्तः सनातनः ।
सर्वभूतमयो ऽचिन्त्यः स एव स्वयमुद्भभौ ॥७॥

सो ऽभिध्याय शरीरात्स्वात्सिसृक्षुर्विविधाः प्रजाः ।
अप एव ससर्जादौ तासु बीजमवासृजत् ॥ ८ ॥

तदण्डमभवद्वैमं सहस्रांशुसमप्रभम् ।
तस्मिञ्जज्ञे स्वयं ब्रह्मा सर्वलोकपितामहः ॥ ९ ॥

आपो नारा इति प्रोक्ता आपो वै नरसूनवः ।
ता यदस्यायनं पूर्वं तेन नारायणः स्मृतः ॥ १० ॥

यत्तत्कारणमव्यक्तं नित्यं सदसदात्मकम् ।
तद्विसृष्टः स पुरुषो लोके ब्रह्मेति कीर्त्यते ॥ ११ ॥

तस्मिन्नण्डे स भगवानुषित्वा परिवत्सरम् ।
स्वयमेवात्मनो ध्यानात्तदण्डमकरोद्द्विधा ॥ १२ ॥

ताभ्यां स शकलाभ्यां च दिवं भूमिं च निर्ममे ।
मध्ये व्योम दिशश्चाष्टावपां स्थानं च शाश्वतम् ॥ १३ ॥

अग्निवायुरविभ्यस्तु त्रयं ब्रह्म सनातनम् ।
दुदोह यज्ञसिद्ध्यर्थमृग्यजुःसामलक्षणम् ॥ २३ ॥

लोकानां तु विवृद्ध्यर्थं मुखबाहूरुपादतः ।
ब्राह्मणं क्षत्रियं वैश्यं शूद्रं च निरवर्तयत् ॥ ३१ ॥

अहोरात्रे विभजते सूर्यो मानुषदैविके ।
रात्रिः स्वप्नाय भूतानां चेष्टायै कर्मणामहः ॥ ६५ ॥

पित्र्ये रात्र्यहनी मासः प्रविभागस्तु पक्षयोः ।
कर्मचेष्टास्वहः कृष्णः शुक्लः स्वप्नाय शर्वरी ॥ ६६ ॥

दैवे रात्र्यहनी वर्षं प्रविभागस्तयोः पुनः ।
अहस्तत्रोदगयनं रात्रिः स्याद्दक्षिणायनम् ॥ ६७ ॥

ब्राह्मस्य तु क्षपाहस्य यत्प्रमाणं समासतः ।

एकैकशो युगानां तु क्रमशस्तन्निबोधत ॥६८॥

चत्वार्याहुः सहस्राणि वर्षाणां तु कृतं युगम् ।

तस्य तावच्छती संध्या संध्यांशश्च तथाविधः ॥६९॥

इतरेषु ससंध्येषु ससंध्यांशेषु च त्रिषु ।

एकापायेन वर्तन्ते सहस्राणि शतानि च ॥७०॥

यदेतत्परिसंख्यातमादावेव चतुर्युगम् ।

एतद्द्वादशसाहस्रं देवानां युगमुच्यते ॥७१॥

दैविकानां युगानां तु सहस्रं परिसंख्यया ।

ब्राह्ममेकमहर्ज्ञेयं तावती रात्रिरेव च ॥७२॥

भूतानां प्राणिनः श्रेष्ठाः प्राणिनां बुद्धिजीविनः ।

बुद्धिमत्सु नराः श्रेष्ठा नरेषु ब्राह्मणाः स्मृताः ॥९६॥

ब्राह्मणेषु च विद्वांसो विद्वत्सु कृतबुद्धयः ।

कृतबुद्धिषु कर्तारः कर्तृषु ब्रह्मवेदिनः ॥९७॥

वेदो ऽखिलो धर्ममूलं स्मृतिशीले च तद्विदाम् ।

आचारश्चैव साधूनामात्मनस्तुष्टिरेव च ॥६॥   ॥अध्या॰ २॥

श्रुतिस्मृत्युदितं धर्ममनुतिष्ठन्हि मानवः ।

इह कीर्तिमवाप्नोति प्रेत्य चानुत्तमं सुखम् ॥९॥

श्रुतिस्तु वेदो विज्ञेयो धर्मशास्त्रं तु वै स्मृतिः ।

ते सर्वार्थेष्वमीमांस्ये ताभ्यां धर्मो हि निर्बभौ ॥१०॥

यो ऽवमन्येत ते मूले हेतुशास्त्राश्रयाद्द्विजः ।

स साधुभिर्बहिष्कार्यो नास्तिको वेदनिन्दकः ॥११॥

वेदः स्मृतिः सदाचारः स्वस्य च प्रियमात्मनः ।

एतच्चतुर्विधं प्राहुः साक्षाद्धर्मस्य लक्षणम् ॥१२॥

वैदिकैः कर्मभिः पुण्यैर्निषेकादिर्द्विजन्मनाम् ।
कार्यः शरीरसंस्कारः पावनः प्रेत्य चेह च ॥२६॥
गार्भैर्होमैर्जातकर्मचौडमौञ्जीनिबन्धनैः ।
बैजिकं गार्भिकं चैनो द्विजानामपमृज्यते ॥२७॥
स्वाध्यायेन व्रतैर्होमैस्त्रैविद्येनेज्यया सुतैः ।
महायज्ञैश्च यज्ञैश्च ब्राह्मीयं क्रियते तनुः ॥२८॥
प्राङ्नाभिवर्धनात्पुंसो जातकर्म विधीयते ।
मन्त्रवत्प्राशनं चास्य हिरण्यमधुसर्पिषाम् ॥२९॥
नामधेयं दशम्यां तु द्वादश्यां वास्य कारयेत् ।
पुण्ये तिथौ मुहूर्ते वा नक्षत्रे वा गुणान्विते ॥३०॥
मङ्गल्यं ब्राह्मणस्य स्यात्क्षत्रियस्य बलान्वितम् ।
वैश्यस्य धनसंयुक्तं शूद्रस्य तु जुगुप्सितम् ॥३१॥
शर्मवद्ब्राह्मणस्य स्याद्राज्ञो रक्षासमन्वितम् ।
वैश्यस्य पुष्टिसंयुक्तं शूद्रस्य प्रेष्यसंयुतम् ॥३२॥
स्त्रीणां सुखोद्यमक्रूरं विस्पष्टार्थं मनोहरम् ।
मङ्गल्यं दीर्घवर्णान्तमाशीर्वादाभिधानवत् ॥३३॥
चतुर्थे मासि कर्तव्यं शिशोर्निष्क्रमणं गृहात् ।
षष्ठे ऽन्नप्राशनं मासि यद्वेष्टं मङ्गलं कुले ॥३४॥
चूडाकर्म द्विजातीनां सर्वेषामेव धर्मतः ।
प्रथमे ऽब्दे तृतीये वा कर्तव्यं श्रुतिचोदनात् ॥३५॥
गर्भाष्टमे ऽब्दे कुर्वीत ब्राह्मणस्योपनायनम् ।
गर्भादेकादशे राज्ञो गर्भात्तु द्वादशे विशः ॥३६॥
प्रतिगृह्येप्सितं दण्डमुपस्थाय च भास्करम् ।

प्रदक्षिणं परीत्यायिं चरेन्नैनं यथाविधि ॥४८॥

भवत्पूर्वं चरेन्नैक्षमुपनीतो द्विजोत्तमः ।

भवन्मध्यं तु राजन्यो वैश्यस्तु भवदुत्तरम् ॥४९॥

व्यत्यस्तपाणिना कार्यमुपसंयहणं गुरोः ।

5 सव्येन सव्यः स्पृष्टव्यो दक्षिणेन च दक्षिणः ॥७२॥

अध्येष्यमाणं तु गुर्निंत्यकालमतन्द्रितः ।

अधीष्व भो इति ब्रूयाद्विरामो ऽस्त्विति चारमेत् ॥७३॥

ब्रह्मणः प्रणवं कुर्यादादावन्ते च सर्वदा ।

स्रवत्यनोंकृतं पूर्वं परस्ताच्च विशीर्यते ॥७४॥

10 अकारं चाप्युकारं च मकारं च प्रजापतिः ।

वेदत्रयान्निरदुहद्भूर्भुवः स्वरितीति च ॥७६॥

त्रिभ्य एव तु वेदेभ्यः पादं पादमदूदुहत् ।

तदित्यृचो ऽस्याः सावित्र्याः परमेष्ठी प्रजापतिः ॥७७॥

एतदक्षरमेतां च जपन्व्याहृतिपूर्विकाम् ।

15 संध्ययोर्वेदविद्विप्रो वेदपुण्येन युज्यते ॥७८॥

ऊर्ध्वं प्राणा ह्युत्क्रामन्ति यूनः स्थविर आयति ।

प्रत्युत्थानाभिवादाभ्यां पुनस्तान्प्रतिपद्यते ॥१२०॥

अभिवादनशीलस्य नित्यं वृद्धोपसेविनः ।

चत्वारि तस्य वर्धन्ते आयुर्विद्या यशो बलम् ॥१२१॥

20 अभिवादात्परं विप्रो ज्यायांसमभिवादयन् ।

असौ नामाहमस्मीति स्वं नाम परिकीर्तयेत् ॥१२२॥

नामधेयस्य ये के चिदभिवादं न जानते ।

तानाह्मो ऽहमिति ब्रूयात्स्त्रियः सर्वास्तथैव च ॥१२३॥

भोःशब्दं कीर्तयेदन्ते स्वस्य नाम्नो ऽभिवादने ।
नाम्नां स्वरूपभावी हि भोभाव ऋषिभिः स्मृतः ॥१२४॥

आयुष्मान्भव सौम्येति वाच्यो विप्रो ऽभिवादने ।
अकारश्चास्य नाम्नो ऽन्ते वाच्यः पूर्वाक्षरः प्लुतः ॥१२५॥

यो न वेत्त्यभिवादस्य विप्रः प्रत्यभिवादनम् ।
नाभिवाद्यः स विदुषा यथा शूद्रस्तथैव सः ॥१२६॥

ब्राह्मणं कुशलं पृच्छेत्क्षत्रबन्धुमनामयम् ।
वैश्यं क्षेमं समागम्य शूद्रमारोग्यमेव च ॥१२७॥

अवाच्यो दीक्षितो नाम्ना यवीयानपि यो भवेत् ।
भोभवत्पूर्वकं त्वेनमभिभाषेत धर्मवित् ॥१२८॥

परपत्नी तु या स्त्री स्यादसंबन्धा च योनितः ।
तां ब्रूयाद्भवतीत्येवं सुभगे भगिनीति च ॥१२९॥

मातुलांश्च पितृव्यांश्च श्वशुरानृत्विजो गुरून् ।
असावहमिति ब्रूयात्प्रत्युत्थाय यवीयसः ॥१३०॥

ब्राह्मस्य जन्मनः कर्ता स्वधर्मस्य च शासिता ।
बालो ऽपि विप्रो वृद्धस्य पिता भवति धर्मतः ॥१५०॥

अध्यापयामास पितॄञ्छिशुराङ्गिरसः कविः ।
पुत्रका इति होवाच ज्ञानेन परिगृह्य तान् ॥१५१॥

ते तमर्थमपृच्छन्त देवानागतमन्यवः ।
देवांश्चैतान्समेत्योचुर्न्याय्यं वः शिशुरुक्तवान् ॥१५२॥

अज्ञो भवति वै बालः पिता भवति मन्त्रदः ।
अज्ञं हि बालमित्याहुः पितेत्येव तु मन्त्रदम् ॥१५३॥

यदि हंशदाष्टिकं चर्यं गुरौ चैवैदिकं व्रतम् ।

तदर्धिकं पादिकं वा यहणान्तिकमेव वा ॥१॥ ॥ अध्या॰ ३॥

वेदानधीत्य वेदौ वा वेदं वापि यथाक्रमम् ।
अविप्लुतब्रह्मचर्यो गृहस्थाश्रममावसेत् ॥२॥

तं प्रतीतं स्वधर्मेण ब्रह्मदायहरं पितुः ।
स्रग्विणं तल्प आसीनमर्हयेत्प्रथमं गवा ॥३॥

गुरुणानुमतः स्नात्वा समावृत्तो यथाविधि ।
उद्वहेत द्विजो भार्यां सवर्णां लक्षणान्विताम् ॥४॥

सर्वान्परित्यजेदर्थान्स्वाध्यायस्य विरोधिनः ।
यथा तथाध्यापयंस्तु सा ह्यस्य कृतकृत्यता ॥१७॥ अध्या॰ ४॥

कॢप्तकेशनखश्मश्रुर्दान्तः शुक्लाम्बरः शुचिः ।
स्वाध्याये चैव युक्तः स्यान्नित्यमात्महितेषु च ॥३५॥

वैणवीं धारयेद्यष्टिं सोदकं च कमण्डलुम् ।
यज्ञोपवीतं वेदं च शुभे रौक्मे च कुण्डले ॥३६॥

नेक्षेतोद्यन्तमादित्यं नास्तं यान्तं कदा चन ।
नोपसृष्टं न वारिस्थं न मध्यं नभसो गतम् ॥३७॥

न लङ्घयेद्वत्सतन्त्रीं न प्रधावेच्च वर्षति ।
न चोदके निरीक्षेत स्वं रूपमिति धारणा ॥३८॥

मृदं गां दैवतं विप्रं घृतं मधु चतुष्पथम् ।
प्रदक्षिणानि कुर्वीत प्रज्ञातांश्च वनस्पतीन् ॥३९॥

वायुमग्निं विप्रमादित्यमपः पश्यंस्तथैव गाः ।
न कदा चन कुर्वीत विण्मूत्रस्य विसर्जनम् ॥४८॥

मूत्रोच्चारसमुत्सर्गं दिवा कुर्यादुदङ्मुखः ।
दक्षिणाभिमुखो रात्रौ संध्ययोश्च यथा दिवा ॥५०॥

न वारयेन्नो धयन्तीं न चाचक्षीत कस्य चित् ।
न दिवीन्द्रायुधं दृष्ट्वा कस्य चिद्दर्शयेद्बुधः ॥५९॥

सामध्वनावृग्यजुषी नाधीयीत कदा चन ।
वेदस्याधीत्य वाप्यन्तमारण्यकमधीत्य च ॥१२३॥

ऋग्वेदो देवदैवत्यो यजुर्वेदस्तु मानुषः ।
सामवेदः स्मृतः पित्र्यस्तस्मात्तस्यानुचिर्ध्वनिः ॥१२४॥

नाधर्मश्चरितो लोके सद्यः फलति गौरिव ।
शनैरावर्तमानस्तु कर्तुर्मूलानि कृन्तति ॥१७२॥

यदि नात्मनि पुत्रेषु न चेत्पुत्रेषु नप्तृषु ।
न त्वेव तु कृतोऽधर्मः कर्तुर्भवति निष्फलः ॥१७३॥

धर्मं शनैः संचिनुयाद्वल्मीकमिव पुत्तिकाः ।
परलोकसहायार्थं सर्वभूतान्यपीडयन् ॥२३८॥

नामुत्र हि सहायार्थं पिता माता च तिष्ठतः ।
न पुत्रदारं न ज्ञातिर्धर्मस्तिष्ठति केवलः ॥२३९॥

एकः प्रजायते जन्तुरेक एव प्रलीयते ।
एकोऽनुभुङ्क्ते सुकृतमेक एव च दुष्कृतम् ॥२४०॥

मृतं शरीरमुत्सृज्य काष्ठलोष्टसमं क्षितौ ।
विमुखा बान्धवा यान्ति धर्मस्तमनुगच्छति ॥२४१॥

तस्माद्धर्मं सहायार्थं नित्यं संचिनुयाच्छनैः ।
धर्मेण हि सहायेन तमस्तरति दुस्तरम् ॥२४२॥

प्राणस्यान्नमिदं सर्वं प्रजापतिरकल्पयत् ।
स्थावरं जङ्गमं चैव सर्वं प्राणस्य भोजनम् ॥२८॥ अध्या० ५॥

चराणामन्नमचरा दंष्ट्रिणामप्यदंष्ट्रिणः ।

अहस्ताश्च सहस्रानां शूराणां चैव भीरवः ॥२९॥

कुर्यादृतपशुं सङ्गे कुर्यात्पिष्टपशुं तथा ।
न त्वेव तु वृथा हन्तुं पशुमिच्छेत्कदा चन ॥३७॥

यावन्ति पशुरोमाणि तावत्कृत्वो ह मारणम् ।
5 वृथापशुघ्नः प्राप्नोति प्रेत्य जन्मनि जन्मनि ॥३८॥

मां स भक्षयितामुत्र यस्य मांसमिहाद्म्यहम् ।
एतन्मांसस्य मांसत्वं प्रवदन्ति मनीषिणः ॥५५॥

नास्ति स्त्रीणां पृथग्यज्ञो न व्रतं नाप्युपोषितम् ।
पतिं शुश्रूषते येन तेन स्वर्गे महीयते ॥१५५॥

10 पाणिग्राहस्य साध्वी स्त्री जीवतो वा मृतस्य वा ।
पतिलोकमभीप्सन्ती नाचरेत्किं चिदप्रियम् ॥१५६॥

कामं तु क्षपयेद्देहं पुष्पमूलफलैः शुभैः ।
न तु नामापि गृह्णीयात्पत्यौ प्रेते परस्य तु ॥१५७॥

आसीता मरणात्क्षान्ता नियता ब्रह्मचारिणी ।
15 यो धर्म एकपत्नीनां काङ्क्षन्ती तमनुत्तमम् ॥१५८॥

एवं गृहाश्रमे स्थित्वा विधिवत्स्नातको द्विजः ।
वने वसेत्तु नियतो यथावद्विजितेन्द्रियः ॥१॥   ॥अध्या॰६॥

वसीत चर्म चीरं वा सायं स्नायात्प्रगे तथा ।
जटाश्च बिभृयान्नित्यं श्मश्रुलोमनखानि च ॥६॥

20 ग्रीष्मे पञ्चतपास्तु स्याद्वर्षास्वभ्रावकाशिकः ।
आर्द्रवासास्तु हेमन्ते क्रमशो वर्धयंस्तपः ॥२३॥

वनेषु तु विहृत्यैवं तृतीयं भागमायुषः ।
चतुर्थमायुषो भागं त्यक्ता सङ्गान्परिव्रजेत् ॥३३॥

आश्रमादाश्रमं गत्वा हुतहोमो जितेन्द्रियः ।
भिक्षाबलिपरिश्रान्तः प्रेत्यजन्मेत्य वर्धते ॥ ३४ ॥

ब्रह्मचारी गृहस्थश्च वानप्रस्थो यतिस्तथा ।
एते गृहस्थप्रभवाश्चत्वारः पृथगाश्रमाः ॥ ८७ ॥

5 एकैकं ह्रासयेत्पिण्डं कृष्णे शुक्ले च वर्धयेत् ।
उपस्पृश्यत्रिषवणमेतच्चान्द्रायणं स्मृतम् ॥ २१६ ॥ अध्या० ११ ॥

एतमेव विधिं कृत्स्नमाचरेद्यवमध्यमे ।
शुक्लपक्षादि नियतश्चरंश्चान्द्रायणं व्रतम् ॥ २१७ ॥

शुभाशुभफलं कर्म मनोवाग्देहसंभवम् ।
10 कर्मजा गतयो नृणामुत्तमाधममध्यमाः ॥ ३ ॥ ॥ अध्या० १२ ॥

तस्येह त्रिविधस्यापि अधिष्ठानस्य देहिनः ।
दशलक्षणयुक्तस्य मनो विद्यात्प्रवर्तकम् ॥ ४ ॥

परद्रव्येष्वभिध्यानं मनसानिष्टचिन्तनम् ।
वितथाभिनिवेशश्च त्रिविधं कर्म मानसम् ॥ ५ ॥

15 पारुष्यमनृतं चैव पैशुन्यं चापि सर्वशः ।
असंबद्धप्रलापश्च वाङ्मयं स्याच्चतुर्विधम् ॥ ६ ॥

अदत्तानामुपादानं हिंसा चैवाविधानतः ।
परदारोपसेवा च शारीरं त्रिविधं स्मृतम् ॥ ७ ॥

मानसं मनसैवायमुपभुङ्क्ते शुभाशुभम् ।
20 वाचा वाचा कृतं कर्म कायेनैव च कायिकम् ॥ ८ ॥

शरीरजैः कर्मदोषैर्याति स्थावरतां नरः ।
वाचिकैः पक्षिमृगतां मानसैरन्त्यजातिताम् ॥ ९ ॥

यद्याचरति धर्मं स प्रायशो ऽधर्ममल्पशः ।

तैरेव चावृतो भूतैः स्वर्गे सुखमुपाश्नुते ॥२०॥

यदि तु प्रायशो ऽधर्मं सेवते धर्ममल्पशः ।

तैर्भूतैः स परित्यक्तो यामीः प्राप्नोति यातनाः ॥२१॥

यामीस्ता यातनाः प्राप्य स जीवो वीतकल्मषः ।

तान्येव पञ्च भूतानि पुनरभ्येति भागशः ॥२२॥

एता दृष्ट्वास्य जीवस्य गतीः स्वेनैव चेतसा ।

धर्मतो ऽधर्मतश्चैव धर्मे दध्यात्सदा मनः ॥२३॥

सत्त्वं रजस्तमश्चैव त्रीन्विद्यादात्मनो गुणान् ।

वैर्याप्येमान्स्थितो भावान्महान्सर्वानशेषतः ॥२४॥

यत्कर्मे कृत्वा कुर्वंश्च करिष्यंश्चैव लज्जते ।

तज्ज्ञेयं विदुषा सर्वं तामसं गुणलक्षणम् ॥३५॥

येनास्मिन्कर्मणा लोके ख्यातिमिच्छति पुष्कलाम् ।

न च शोचत्यसंपत्तौ तद्विज्ञेयं तु राजसम् ॥३६॥

यत्सर्वेणेच्छति ज्ञातं यन्न लज्जति चाचरन् ।

येन तुष्यति चात्मास्य तत्सत्त्वगुणलक्षणम् ॥३७॥

तमसो लक्षणं कामो रजसस्त्वर्थ उच्यते ।

सत्त्वस्य लक्षणं धर्मः श्रैष्ठ्यमेषां यथाक्रमम् ॥३८॥

येन यांस्तु गुणेनैषां संसारान्प्रतिपद्यते ।

तान्समासेन वक्ष्यामि सर्वस्यास्य यथाक्रमम् ॥३९॥

देवत्वं सात्त्विका यान्ति मनुष्यत्वं च राजसाः ।

तिर्यक्त्वं तामसा नित्यमित्येषा त्रिविधा गतिः ॥४०॥

त्रिविधा त्रिविधैषा तु विज्ञेया गौणिकी गतिः ॥

अधमा मध्यमाग्र्या च कर्मविद्याविशेषतः ॥४१॥

स्थावराः कृमिकीटाश्च मत्स्याः सर्पाः सकच्छपाः ।
पशवश्च मृगाश्चैव जघन्या तामसी गतिः ॥४२॥
हस्तिनश्च तुरंगाश्च शूद्रा म्लेच्छाश्च गर्हिताः ।
सिंहा व्याघ्रा वराहाश्च मध्यमा तामसी गतिः ॥४३॥
5 चारणाश्च सुपर्णाश्च पुरुषाश्चैव दाम्भिकाः ।
रक्षांसि च पिशाचाश्च तामसीषूत्तमा गतिः ॥४४॥
झल्ला मल्ला नटाश्चैव पुरुषाः शस्त्रवृत्तयः ।
द्यूतपानप्रसक्ताश्च जघन्या राजसी गतिः ॥४५॥
राजानः क्षत्रियाश्चैव राज्ञां चैव पुरोहिताः ।
10 वादयुद्धप्रधानाश्च मध्यमा राजसी गतिः ॥४६॥
गन्धर्वा गुह्यका यक्षा विबुधानुचराश्च ये ।
तथैवाप्सरसः सर्वा राजसीषूत्तमा गतिः ॥४७॥
तापसा यतयो विप्रा ये च वैमानिका गणाः ।
नक्षत्राणि च दैत्याश्च प्रथमा सात्त्विकी गतिः ॥४८॥
15 यज्वान ऋषयो देवा वेदा ज्योतींषि वत्सराः ।
पितरश्चैव साध्याश्च द्वितीया सात्त्विकी गतिः ॥४९॥
ब्रह्मा विश्वसृजो धर्मो महानव्यक्त एव च ।
उत्तमां सात्त्विकीमेतां गतिमाहुर्मनीषिणः ॥५०॥
असूकरखरोष्ट्राणां गोऽजाविमृगपक्षिणाम् ।
20 चण्डालपुल्कसानां च ब्रह्महा योनिमृच्छति ॥५५॥
हिंसा भवन्ति क्रव्यादाः कृमयोऽभक्ष्यभक्षिणः ।
परस्परादिनः स्तेनाः प्रेता ऽन्यस्त्रीनिषेविणः ॥५९॥
धान्यं हृत्वा भवत्याखुः कांस्यं हंसो जलं प्लवः ।

मधु दंशः पयः काको रसं श्वा नकुलो घृतम् ॥६२॥

छुछुन्दरिः शुभान्गन्धान्पत्तशार्कं तु बर्हिणः ।

ग्रावित्कृताबं विविधमकृताबं तु शल्यकः ॥६५॥

स्त्रियो ऽप्येतेन कल्पेन हत्वा दोषमवाप्नुयुः ।

5 एतेषामेव जन्तूनां भार्यात्वमुपयान्ति ताः ॥६९॥

वेदाभ्यासस्तपो ज्ञानमिन्द्रियाणां च संयमः ।

अहिंसा गुरुसेवा च निःश्रेयसकरं परम् ॥८३॥

प्रवृत्तं कर्म संसेव्य देवानामेति साम्यताम् ।

निवृत्तं सेवमानस्तु भूतान्यत्येति पञ्च वै ॥९०॥

10   या वेदबाह्याः स्मृतयो याश्च काश्च कुहृदयः ।

सर्वास्ता निष्फलाः प्रेत्य तमोनिष्ठा हि ताः स्मृताः ॥९५॥

उत्पद्यन्ते च्यवन्ते च यान्यतो ऽन्यानि कानि चित् ।

तान्यर्वाक्कालिकतया निष्फलान्यनृतानि च ॥९६॥

अज्ञेभ्यो ग्रन्थिनः श्रेष्ठा ग्रन्थिभ्यो धारिणो वराः ।

15 धारिभ्यो ज्ञानिनः श्रेष्ठा ज्ञानिभ्यो व्यवसायिनः ॥१०३॥

XXIX. XXX.

एकोना विंशतिर्नार्यः क्रीडां कर्तुं वने गताः ।

विंशतिगृहमायाताः शेषो व्याघ्रेण भक्षितः ॥

समादिशत्पिता पुत्रं लिख लेखं ममाज्ञया ।

न तेन लिखितो लेखः पितुराज्ञा न खण्डिता ॥

XXXI. RIGVEDA I. 1.

अग्निमीळे पुरोहितं यज्ञस्य देवमृत्विजम् ।
होतारं रत्नधातमम् ॥१॥
अग्निः पूर्वेभिर्ऋषिभिरीड्यो नूतनैरुत ।
स देवाँ एह वक्षति ॥२॥
अग्निना रयिमश्नवत्पोषमेव दिवे दिवे ।
यशसं वीरवत्तमम् ॥३॥
अग्ने यं यज्ञमध्वरं विश्वतः परिभूरसि ।
स इद्देवेषु गच्छति ॥४॥
अग्निर्होता कविक्रतुः सत्यश्चित्रश्रवस्तमः ।
देवो देवेभिरा गमत् ॥५॥
यदङ्ग दाशुषे त्वमग्ने भद्रं करिष्यसि ।
तवेत्तत्सत्यमङ्गिरः ॥६॥
उप त्वाग्ने दिवे दिवे दोषावस्तर्धिया वयम् ।
नमो भरन्त एमसि ॥७॥
राजन्तमध्वराणां गोपामृतस्य दीदिविम् ।
वर्धमानं स्वे दमे ॥८॥
स नः पितेव सूनवे ऽग्ने सूपायनो भव ।
सचस्वा नः स्वस्तये ॥९॥

मधु दंशः पयः काको रसं श्वा नकुलो घृतम् ॥६२॥

छुच्छुन्दरिः शुभाङ्गन्धान्यच्छशकं तु बर्हिणः ।

श्वाविल्कृतार्बं विविधमकृतार्बं तु शल्यकः ॥६५॥

स्त्रियो ऽप्येतेन कल्पेन हत्वा दोषमवाप्नुयुः ।

5 एतेषामेव जन्तूनां भार्यात्वमुपयान्ति ताः ॥६९॥

वेदाभ्यासस्तपो ज्ञानमिन्द्रियाणां च संयमः ।

अहिंसा गुरुसेवा च निःश्रेयसकरं परम् ॥८३॥

प्रवृत्तं कर्म संसेव्य देवानामेति साम्यताम् ।

निवृत्तं सेवमानस्तु भूतान्यत्येति पञ्च वै ॥९०॥

10   या वेदबाह्याः स्मृतयो याश्च काश्च कुदृष्टयः ।

सर्वास्ता निष्फलाः प्रेत्य तमोनिष्ठा हि ताः स्मृताः ॥९५॥

उत्पद्यन्ते च्यवन्ते च यान्यतो ऽन्यानि कानि चित् ।

तान्यर्वाक्कालिकतया निष्फलान्यनृतानि च ॥९६॥

अङ्गेभ्यो यज्ञिनः श्रेष्ठा यज्ञिभ्यो धारिणो वराः ।

15 धारिभ्यो ज्ञानिनः श्रेष्ठा ज्ञानिभ्यो व्यवसायिनः ॥१०३॥

———

XXIX. XXX.

एकोना विंशतिर्नार्यः क्रीडां कर्तुं वने गताः ।

विंशतिगृहमायाताः शेषो व्याघ्रेण भक्षितः ॥

समादिशत्पिता पुत्रं लिख लेखं ममाज्ञया ।

न तेन लिखितो लेखः पितुराज्ञा न खण्डिता ॥

———

XXXI. RIGVEDA I. 1.

अग्निमीळे पुरोहितं यज्ञस्य देवमृत्विजम् ।
होतारं रत्नधातमम् ॥१॥

अग्निः पूर्वेभिर्ऋषिभिरीड्यो नूतनैरुत ।
स देवाँ एह वक्षति ॥२॥

अग्निना रयिमश्नवत्पोषमेव दिवे दिवे ।
यशसं वीरवत्तमम् ॥३॥

अग्ने यं यज्ञमध्वरं विश्वतः परिभूरसि ।
स इद्देवेषु गच्छति ॥४॥

अग्निर्होता कविक्रतुः सत्यश्चित्रश्रवस्तमः ।
देवो देवेभिरा गमत् ॥५॥

यदङ्ग दाशुषे त्वमग्ने भद्रं करिष्यसि ।
तवेत्तत्सत्यमङ्गिरः ॥६॥

उप त्वाग्ने दिवे दिवे दोषावस्तर्धिया वयम् ।
नमो भरन्त एमसि ॥७॥

राजन्तमध्वराणां गोपामृतस्य दीदिविम् ।
वर्धमानं स्वे दमे ॥८॥

स नः पितेव सूनवे ऽग्ने सूपायनो भव ।
सचस्वा नः स्वस्तये ॥९॥

XXXII. RIGVEDA I. 32.

इन्द्रस्य नु वीर्याणि प्र वोचं यानि चकार प्रथमानि वज्री ।

अहन्नहिमन्वपस्ततर्दं प्र वक्षणा अभिनत्पर्वतानाम् ॥१॥

अहन्नहिं पर्वते शिश्रियाणं त्वष्टास्मै वज्रं स्वर्यं ततक्ष ।

वाश्रा इव धेनवः स्यन्दमाना अञ्जः समुद्रमव जग्मुरापः ॥२॥

5 वृषायमाणो ऽवृणीत सोमं त्रिकद्रुकेष्वपिबत्सुतस्य ।

आ सायकं मघवादत्त वज्रमहन्नेनं प्रथमजामहीनाम् ॥३॥

यदिन्द्राहन्प्रथमजामहीनामान्मायिनामर्मिणाः प्रोत मायाः ।

आत्सूर्यं जनयन्द्यामुषासं तादीत्ना शत्रुं न किला विवित्से ॥४॥

अहन्वृत्रं वृत्रतरं व्यंसमिन्द्रो वज्रेण महता वधेन ।

10 स्कन्धांसीव कुलिशेना विवृक्णाहिः शयत उपपृक्पृथिव्याः॥५॥

अयोद्धेव दुर्मद आ हि जुह्वे महावीरं तुविबाधमृजीषम् ।

नातारीदस्य समृतिं वधानां सं रुजानाः पिपिष इन्द्रशत्रुः ॥६॥

अपादहस्तो अपृतन्यदिन्द्रमास्य वज्रमधि सानौ जघान ।

वृष्णो वध्रिः प्रतिमानं बुभूषन्पुरुत्रा वृष्णो अशयद्व्यस्तः ॥७॥

15 नदं न भिन्नममुया शयानं मनो रुहाणा अति यन्त्यापः ।

याश्चिद्वृत्रो महिना पर्यतिष्ठत्तासामहिः पत्सुतःशीर्बभूव ॥८॥

नीचावया अभवद्वृत्रपुत्रेन्द्रो अस्या अव वधर्जभार ।

उत्तरा सूर्यधः पुत्र आसीदानुः शये सहवत्सा न धेनुः ॥९॥

अतिष्ठन्तीनामनिवेशनानां काष्ठानां मध्ये निहितं शरीरम् ।

20 वृत्रस्य निण्यं वि चरन्त्यापो दीर्घं तम आशयदिन्द्रशत्रुः ॥१०॥

दासपत्नीरहिगोपा अतिष्ठन्निरुद्धा आपः पणिनेव गावः ।

अपां बिलमपिहितं यदासीवृत्रं जघन्वाँ अप तद्ववार ॥१९॥

अग्न्यो वारो अभवत्तदिन्द्र सृके यत्त्वा प्रत्यहन्देव एकः ।

अजयो गा अजयः शूर सोममवासृजः सर्तवे सप्त सिन्धून् ॥१२॥

नास्मै विद्युन्न तन्यतुः सिषेध न यां मिहमकिरद्धादुनिं च ।

इन्द्रश्च यद्युयुधाते अहिश्चोतापरीभ्यो मघवा वि जिग्ये ॥१३॥

अहेर्यातारं कमपश्य इन्द्र हृदि यत्ते जघ्नुषो भीरगच्छत् ।

नव च यन्नवतिं च स्रवन्तीः श्येनो न भीतो अतरो रजांसि ॥१४॥

इन्द्रो यातो ऽवसितस्य राजा शमस्य च शृङ्गिणो वज्रबाहुः ।

सेदु राजा क्षयति चर्षणीनामरान्न नेमिः परि ता बभूव ॥१५॥

XXXIII. RIGVEDA I. 50.

उदु त्यं जातवेदसं देवं वहन्ति केतवः ।

दृशे विश्वाय सूर्यम् ॥१॥

अप त्ये तायवो यथा नक्षत्रा यन्त्यक्तुभिः ।

सूराय विश्वचक्षसे ॥२॥

अदृश्रमस्य केतवो वि रश्मयो जनाँ अनु ।

भ्राजन्तो अग्नयो यथा ॥३॥

तरणिर्विश्वदर्शतो ज्योतिष्कृदसि सूर्य ।

विश्वमा भासि रोचनम् ॥४॥

प्रत्यङ्देवानां विशः प्रत्यङ्ङुदेषि मानुषान् ।

प्रत्यङ्विश्वं स्वर्दृशे ॥५॥

येना पावक चक्षसा भुरण्यन्तं जनाँ अनु ।

त्वं वरुण पश्यसि ॥६॥

वि द्यामेषि रजस्पृथ्वहा मिमानो अक्तुभिः ।

पश्यञ्जन्मानि सूर्य ॥७॥

सप्त त्वा हरितो रथे वहन्ति देव सूर्य ।

5 शोचिष्केशं विचक्षण ॥८॥

अयुक्त सप्त शुन्ध्युवः सूरो रथस्य नप्त्यः ।

ताभिर्याति स्वयुक्तिभिः ॥९॥

_____

XXXIV. RIGVEDA I. 97.

अप नः शोशुचदघमग्ने शुशुग्ध्या रयिम् ।

अप नः शोशुचदघम् ॥१॥

10 सुक्षेत्रिया सुगातुया वसूया च यजामहे ।

अप नः शोशुचदघम् ॥२॥

प्र यद्भन्दिष्ठ एषां प्रास्माकासश्च सूर्यः ।

अप नः शोशुचदघम् ॥३॥

प्र यत्ते अग्ने सूर्यो जायेमहि प्र ते वयम् ।

15 अप नः शोशुचदघम् ॥४॥

प्र यदग्ने सहस्वतो विश्वतो यन्ति भानवः ।

अप नः शोशुचदघम् ॥५॥

त्वं हि विश्वतोमुख विश्वतः परिभूरसि ।

अप नः शोशुचदघम् ॥६॥

20 द्विषो नो विश्वतोमुखाति नावेव पारय ।

अप नः शोशुचद्घम् ॥७॥

स नः सिन्धुमिव नावयाति पर्षा स्वस्तये ।

अप नः शोशुचद्घम् ॥८॥

XXXV. RIGVEDA I. 165.

कया शुभा सवयसः सनीळाः समान्या मरुतः सं मिमिक्षुः ।

कया मती कुत एतास एते ऽर्चन्ति शुष्मं वृषणो वसूया ॥१॥

कस्य ब्रह्माणि जुजुषुर्युवानः को अध्वरे मरुत आ ववर्त ।

श्येनाँ इव ध्रजतो अन्तरिक्षे केन महा मनसा रीरमाम ॥२॥

कुतस्त्वमिन्द्र माहिनः सन्नेको यासि सत्पते किं त इत्था ।

सं पृच्छसे समराणः शुभानैर्वोचेस्तन्नो हरिवो यत्ते अस्मे ॥३॥

ब्रह्माणि मे मतयः शं सुतासः शुष्मं इयर्ति प्रभृती मे अद्रिः ।

आ शासते प्रति हर्यन्त्युक्थेमा हरी वहतस्ता नो अच्छ ॥४॥

अतो वयमन्तमेभिर्युजानाः स्वक्षत्रेभिस्तन्वः शुम्भमानाः ।

महोभिरेताँ उप युज्महे न्विन्द्र स्वधामनु हि नो बभूथ ॥५॥

क्व स्या वो मरुतः स्वधासीद्यन्मामेकं समधत्ताहिहत्ये ।

अहं ह्युग्रस्तविषस्तुविष्मान्विश्वस्य शत्रोरनमं वधस्नैः ॥६॥

भूरि चकर्थ युज्येभिरस्मे समानेभिर्वृषभ पौंस्येभिः ।

भूरीणि हि कृणवामा शविष्ठेन्द्र क्रत्वा मरुतो यद्वशाम ॥७॥

वधीं वृत्रं मरुत इन्द्रियेण स्वेन भामेन तविषो बभूवान् ।

अहमेता मनवे विश्वश्चन्द्राः सुगा अपश्चकर वज्रबाहुः ॥८॥

अनुत्तमा ते मघवन्नकिर्नु न त्वावाँ अस्ति देवता विदानः ।

न जायमानो नश्यते न जातो यानि करिष्या कृणुहि प्रवृद्ध ॥९॥

एकस्य चिन्मे विभ्वस्त्वोजो या नु दधृष्वान्कृणवै मनीषा ।

अहं ह्यूर्यो मरुतो विदानो यानि च्यवमिन्द्र इदीश एषाम् ॥१०॥

अमन्दन्मा मरुत स्तोमो अत्र यन्मे नरः श्रुत्यं ब्रह्म चक्र ।

5 इन्द्राय वृष्णे सुमखाय मह्यं सख्ये सखायस्तन्वे तनूभिः ॥११॥

एवेदेते प्रति मा रोचमाना अनेद्यः श्रव एषो दधानाः ।

संचक्ष्या मरुतश्चन्द्रवर्णा अच्छान्त मे छदयाथा च नूनम् ॥१२॥

को न्वत्र मरुतो मामहे वः प्र यातन सखीँ रच्छा सखायः ।

मन्मानि चित्रा अपिवातयन्त एषां भूत नवेदा म ऋतानाम् ॥१३॥

10 आ यद्दुवस्याद्दुवसे न कारुरस्माञ्चक्रे मान्यस्य मेधा ।

ओ षु वर्त्त मरुतो विप्रमच्छेमा ब्रह्माणि जरिता वो अर्चत् ॥१४॥

एष व स्तोमो मरुत इयं गीर्मान्दार्यस्य मान्यस्य कारोः ।

एषा यासीष्ट तन्वे वयां विद्यामेषं वृजनं जीरदानुम् ॥१५॥

XXXVI. RIGVEDA III. 62.

तात्सवितुर्वरेण्यं भर्गो देवस्य धीमहि ।

15 धियो यो नः प्रचोदयात् ॥१०॥

देवस्य सवितुर्वयं वाजयन्तः पुरंध्या ।

भगस्य रातिमीमहे ॥११॥

देवं नरः सवितारं विप्रा यज्ञैः सुवृक्तिभिः ।

नमस्यन्ति धियेषिताः ॥१२॥

XXXVII. RIGVEDA IV. 42.

मम द्विता राष्ट्रं क्षत्रियस्य विश्वायोर्विश्वे अमृता यथा नः ।
क्रतुं सचन्ते वरुणस्य देवा राजामि कृष्टेरुपमस्य वव्रेः ॥१॥

अहं राजा वरुणो मह्यं तान्यसुर्याणि प्रथमा धारयन्त ।
क्रतुं सचन्ते वरुणस्य देवा राजामि कृष्टेरुपमस्य वव्रेः ॥२॥

अहमिन्द्रो वरुणस्ते महित्वोर्वी गभीरे रजसी सुमेके ।
तष्टेव विश्वा भुवनानि विद्वान्समैरयं रोदसी धारयं च ॥३॥

अहमपो अपिन्वमुक्षमाणा धारयं दिवं सदन ऋतस्य ।
ऋतेन पुत्रो अदितेर्ऋतावोत त्रिधातु प्रथयद्भि भूम ॥४॥

मा नः स्वश्वा वाजयन्तो मा वृताः समरणे हवन्ते ।
कृणोम्याजिं मघवाहमिन्द्र इर्यामि रेणुमभिभूत्योजाः ॥५॥

अहं ता विश्वा चकरं नकिर्मा दैव्यं सहो वरते अप्रतीतम् ।
यन्मा सोमासो ममदन्यदुक्थोभे भयेते रजसी अपारे ॥६॥

विदुष्टे विश्वा भुवनानि तस्य ता प्र ब्रवीषि वरुणाय वेधः ।
त्वं वृषाणि भूरिणे जघन्वान्त्वं वृताँ अरिणा इन्द्र सिन्धून् ॥७॥

XXXVIII. RIGVEDA IV. 52.

16 प्रति षा सूनरी जनी व्युच्छन्ती परि स्वसुः ।
दिवो अदर्शि दुहिता ॥१॥

अश्वेव चित्रारुषी माता गवामृतावरी ।
सखाभूदश्विनोरुषाः ॥२॥

उत सखास्यश्विनोरुत माता गवामसि ।

उतोषो वस्व ईशिषे ॥३॥

यावयद्द्वेषसं त्वा चिकित्सित्सूनृतावरि ।

प्रति स्तोमैरभुत्स्महि ॥४॥

प्रति भद्रा अद्वक्षत गवां सर्गा न रश्मयः ।

⁵ ओषा अप्रा उरु ज्रयः ॥५॥

आपप्रुषी विभावरि व्यावर्ज्योतिषा तमः ।

उषो अनु स्वधामव ॥६॥

आ द्यां तनोषि रश्मिभिरान्तरिक्षमुरु प्रियम् ।

उषः शुक्रेण शोचिषा ॥७॥

XXXIX. RIGVEDA V. 24.

¹⁰ अग्ने त्वं नो अन्तम उत त्राता शिवो भवा वरूथ्यः ॥१॥

वसुरग्निर्वसुश्रवा अच्छा नक्षि द्युमत्तमं रयिं दाः ॥२॥

स नो बोधि श्रुधी हवमुरुष्या णो अघायतः समस्मात् ॥३॥

तं त्वा शोचिष्ठ दीदिवः सुम्नाय नूनमीमहे सखिभ्यः ॥४॥

XL. RIGVEDA V. 40.

स्वर्भानोरध यदिन्द्र माया अवो दिवो वर्तमाना अवाहन् ।

¹⁵ गूळ्हं सूर्यं तमसापव्रतेन तुरीयेण ब्रह्मणाविन्दद्दत्रिः ॥६॥

मा मामिमं तव सन्तमत्र इर्स्या दुग्धो भियसा नि गारीत् ।

त्वं मित्रो असि सत्यराधास्त्वौ मेहावर्तं वरुणश्च राजा ॥७॥

याद्ब्राह्मो ब्रह्मा युयुजानः सपर्यन्कीरिणा देवान्नमसोपशिक्षन्॥

अग्निः सूर्य्यस्य दिवि चक्षुराधात्स्वभानोरप माया अघुक्षत ॥८॥

XLI. RIGVEDA VII. 55.

अमीवहा वास्तोष्पते विश्वा रूपाण्याविशन् ।
सखा सुशेव एधि नः ॥१॥

यदर्जुन सारमेय दूतः पिंशङ्ग यच्छसे ।
वीव भाजन्त ऋष्टय उप स्रक्वेषु बप्सतो नि षु स्वप ॥२॥

स्तेनं राय सारमेय तस्करं वा पुनःसर ।
स्तोतॄनिन्द्रस्य रायसि किमस्मान्दुच्छुनायसे नि षु स्वप ॥३॥

त्वं सूकरस्य दर्दृहि तव दर्दर्तु सूकरः ।
स्तोतॄनिन्द्रस्य रायसि किमस्मान्दुच्छुनायसे नि षु स्वप ॥४॥

सस्तु माता सस्तु पिता सस्तु श्वा सस्तु विश्पतिः ।
ससन्तु सर्वे ज्ञातयः सस्त्वयमभितो जनः ॥५॥

य आस्ते यश्च चरति यश्च पश्यति नो जनः ।
तेषां सं हन्मो अक्षाणि यथेदं हर्म्यं तथा ॥६॥

सहस्रशृङ्गो वृषभो यः समुद्रादुदाचरत् ।
तेना सहस्येना वयं नि जनान्स्वापयामसि ॥७॥

प्रोष्ठेश्या वह्येश्या नारीर्यास्तल्पशीवरीः ।
स्त्रियो याः पुण्यगन्धास्ताः सर्वाः स्वापयामसि ॥८॥

XLII. RIGVEDA VII. 56.

क ईं व्यक्ता नरः सनीळा हुद्रस्य मर्या अधा स्वश्वाः ॥१॥

नकिर्येषां जनूंषि वेद् ते अङ्ग विद्रे मिथो जनित्रम् ॥२॥

अभि स्वपूर्भिर्मिथो वपन्त वातस्वनसः श्येना असृप्रन् ॥३॥

एतानि धीरो निःया चिकेत पृश्निर्यदूधो मही जभार ॥४॥

सा विट्सुवीरा मरुद्भिरस्तु सनात्सहन्ती पुर्यन्ती नृम्णम् ॥५॥

यामं येष्ठाः शुभा शोभिष्ठाः श्रिया संमिश्ला ओजोभिरह्याः ॥

उग्रं व ओज स्थिरा शवांस्यधा मरुद्भिर्गणस्तुविष्मान् ॥७॥

शुभ्रो वः शुष्मः क्रुध्मी मनांसि धुनिर्मुनिरिव शर्धस्य धृष्णोः ॥

सनेम्यस्मद्युयोत दिद्युं मा वो दुर्मतिरिह प्रणङ्नः ॥९॥

प्रिया वो नाम हुवे तुराणामा यत्तृपन्मरुतो वावशानाः ॥१०॥

XLIII. RIGVEDA VII. 86.

धीरा त्वस्य महिना जनूंषि वि यस्तस्तम्भ रोदसी चिदुर्वी ।

प्र नाकमृष्वं नुनुदे बृहन्तं द्विता नक्षत्रं पप्रथच्च भूम ॥१॥

उत स्वया तन्वा सं वदे तत्कदा न्वन्तर्वरुणे भुवानि ।

किं मे हव्यमहृणानो जुषेत कदा मृळीकं सुमना अभि ख्यम् ॥

पृच्छे तदेनो वरुण दिदृक्षूपो एमि चिकितुषो विपृच्छम् ।

समानमिन्मे कवयश्चिदाहुरयं ह तुभ्यं वरुणो हृणीते ॥३॥

किमागास आस वरुण ज्येष्ठं यत्स्तोतारं जिघांससि सखायम् ।

प्र तन्मे वोचो दूळभ स्वधावो ऽव त्वानेना नमसा तुर इयाम् ॥

अव द्रुग्धानि पित्र्या सृजा नो ऽव या वयं चकृमा तनूभिः ।

अव राजन्पशुतृपं न तायुं सृजा वत्सं न दाम्नो वसिष्ठम् ॥५॥

न स स्वो दक्षो वरुण ध्रुतिः सा सुरा मन्युर्विभीदको अचित्तिः

अस्ति ज्यायान्कनीयस उपारे स्वप्नश्चनेदनृतस्य प्रयोता ॥६॥

अरे दासो न मीळ्हुषे कराण्यहं देवाय भूर्णये अनागाः ।

अचेतयदचितो देवो अर्यो गृत्से राये कवितरो जुनाति ॥७॥

अयं सु तुभ्यं वरुण स्वधावो हृदि स्तोम उपश्रितश्चिदस्तु ।

५ शं नः क्षेमे शमु योगे नो अस्तु यूयं पात स्वस्तिभिः सदा नः ॥

XLIV. RIGVEDA VII. 88.

प्र शुन्ध्युवं वरुणाय प्रेष्ठां मतिं वसिष्ठ मीळ्हुषे भरस्व ।

य ईमर्वाञ्चं करते यजत्रं सहस्रामघं वृषणं बृहन्तम् ॥१॥

अधा न्वस्य संदृशं जगन्वानमेरनीकं वरुणस्य मंसि ।

स्व१येदश्मन्नधिपा उ अन्धो अभि मा वपुर्दृशये निनीयात् ॥

१० आ यद्रुहाव वरुणश्च नावं प्र यत्समुद्रमीरयाव मध्यम् ।

अधि यदपां स्नुभिश्चराव प्र प्रेङ्ख ईङ्खयावहै शुभे कम् ॥३॥

वसिष्ठं ह वरुणो नाव्याधाद्दषिं चकार स्वपा महोभिः ।

स्तोतारं विप्रः सुदिनत्वे अह्नां यान्नु द्यावस्ततनन्यादुषासः ॥४॥

क्व१ त्यानि नौ सख्या बभूवुः सचावहे यदवृकं पुरा चित् ।

१५ बृहन्तं मानं वरुण स्वधावः सहस्रद्वारं जगमा गृहं ते ॥५॥

य आपिर्नित्यो वरुण प्रियः सन्त्वामागांसि कृणवत्सखा ते ।

मा त एनस्वन्तो यक्षिन्भुजेम यन्धि ष्मा विप्रः स्तुवते वरूथम् ॥

ध्रुवासु त्वासु क्षितिषु क्षियन्तो व्य१स्मत्पाशं वरुणो मुमोचत् ।

अवो वन्वाना अदितेरुपस्थाद्यूयं पात स्वस्तिभिः सदा नः ॥

XLV. RIGVEDA VII. 89.

मो षु वरुण मृन्मयं गृहं राजन्नहं गमम् ।
मृळा सुक्षत्र मृळय ॥१॥

यदेमि प्रस्फुरन्निव हतिनें ध्मातो अद्रिवः ।
मृळा सुक्षत्र मृळय ॥२॥

5 क्रत्वः समह दीनता प्रतीपं जगमा शुचे ।
मृळा सुक्षत्र मृळय ॥३॥

अपां मध्ये तस्थिवांसं तृष्णाविदज्जरितारम् ।
मृळा सुक्षत्र मृळय ॥४॥

यत्किं चेदं वरुण दैव्ये जनें ऽभिद्रोहं मनुष्याश्चरामसि ।
10 अचित्ती यत्तव धर्मा युयोपिम मा नस्तस्मादेनसो देव रीरिषः ॥

XLVI. RIGVEDA VIII. 14.

यदिन्द्राहं यथा त्वमीशीय वस्व एक इत् ।
स्तोता मे गोषखा स्यात् ॥१॥

शिक्षेयमस्मै दित्सेयं शचीपते मनीषिणे ।
यदहं गोपतिः स्याम् ॥२॥

15 धेनुष्ट इन्द्र सूनृता यजमानाय सुन्वते ।
गामश्वं पिप्युषी दुहे ॥३॥

न ते वर्तास्ति राधस इन्द्र देवो न मर्त्यः ।
यद्दित्ससि स्तुतो मघम् ॥४॥

यज्ज इन्द्रमवर्धयद्धूमिं व्यवर्तयत् ।

चक्राण ओपशं दिवि ॥५॥

वावृधानस्य ते वयं विश्वा धनानि जिग्युषः ।

ऊतिमिन्द्रा वृणीमहे ॥६॥

व्यश्नन्तरिक्षमतिरन्मदे सोमस्य रोचना ।

6 इन्द्रो यदभिनद्बलम् ॥७॥

उद्गा आजदङ्गिरोभ्य आविष्कृण्वन्गुहा सतीः ।

अर्वाञ्चं नुनुदे वलम् ॥८॥

इन्द्रेण रोचना दिवो दृऴ्हानि दृंहितानि च ।

स्थिराणि न पराणुदे ॥९॥

10 अपामूर्मिर्मदन्निव स्तोम इन्द्राजिरायते ।

वि ते मदा अराजिषुः ॥१०॥

त्वं हि स्तोमवर्धन इन्द्रास्युक्थवर्धनः ।

स्तोतॄणामुत भद्रकृत् ॥११॥

इन्द्रमित्केशिना हरी सोमपेयाय वक्षतः ।

15 उपं यज्ञं सुराधसम् ॥१२॥

अपां फेनेन नमुचेः शिर इन्द्रोदवर्तयः ।

विश्वा यदजय स्पृधः ॥१३॥

मायाभिरुत्सिसृप्सत इन्द्र द्यामारुरुक्षतः ।

अव दस्यूँरधूनुथाः ॥१४॥

20 असुन्वामिन्द्र संसदं विषूचीं व्यनाशयः ।

सोमपा उत्तरो भवन् ॥१५॥

XLVII. RIGVEDA VIII. 85.

वृषस्य त्वा ध्वसयादीर्षमाणा विश्वे देवा अंजहुर्ये सखायः ।
मरुद्भिरिन्द्र सख्यं ते अस्त्वथेमा विश्वाः पृतना जयासि ॥७॥
भिः षडिस्त्वा मरुतो वावृधाना उद्धा इव राश्यो यज्ञियासः ।
उप त्वेमः कृधि नो भागधेयं शुष्मो त एना हविषा विधेम ॥८॥
तिग्ममायुधं महतामनीकं कत्स्वे इन्द्र प्रति वज्रं दधर्ष ।
अनायुधासो असुरा अदेवाश्चक्रेण तॉ अप वप ऋजीषिन् ॥

XLVIII. RIGVEDA VIII. 91.

अग्ने घृतस्य धीतिभिस्तेपानो देव शोचिषा ।
आ देवान्वक्षि यक्षि च ॥१६॥
तं त्वाजनन्त मातरः कविं देवासो अङ्गिरः ।
10 हव्यवाहममर्त्यम् ॥१७॥
प्रचेतसं त्वा कवे ऽग्ने दूतं वरेण्यम् ।
हव्यवाहं नि षेदिरे ॥१८॥
नहि मे अस्त्यघ्ना न स्वधितिर्वनन्वति ।
अथैताहग्भरामि ते ॥१९॥
15 यद्मे कानि कानि चिदा ते दारूणि दध्मसि ।
ता जुषस्व यविष्ठ्य ॥२०॥
अग्निमिन्धानो मनसा धियं सचेत मर्त्यः ।
अग्निमीधे विवस्वभिः ॥२२॥

XLIX. RIGVEDA X. 9.

आपो हि ष्ठा मयोभुवस्ता न ऊर्जे दधातन ।

महे रणाय चक्षसे ॥१॥

यो वः शिवतमो रसस्तस्य भाजयतेह नः ।

उशतीरिव मातरः ॥२॥

5 तस्मा अरं गमाम वो यस्य क्षयाय जिन्वथ ।

आपो जनयथा च नः ॥३॥

L. RIGVEDA X. 14.

परेयिवांसं प्रवतो महीरनु बहुभ्यः पन्थामनुपस्पशानम् ।

वैवस्वतं संगमनं जनानां यमं राजानं हविषा दुवस्य ॥१॥

यमो नो गातुं प्रथमो विवेद नैषा गव्यूतिरपभर्तवा उ ।

10 यत्रा नः पूर्वे पितरः परेयुरेना जज्ञानाः पथ्या अनु स्वाः ॥२॥

प्रेहि प्रेहि पथिभिः पूर्व्येभिर्यत्रा नः पूर्वे पितरः परेयुः ।

उभा राजाना स्वधया मदन्ता यमं पश्यासि वरुणं च देवम् ॥७॥

सं गच्छस्व पितृभिः सं यमेनेष्टापूर्तेन परमे व्योमन् ।

हित्वायावद्यं पुनरस्तमेहि सं गच्छस्व तन्वा सुवर्चाः ॥८॥

15 अपेत वीत वि च सर्पतातो ऽस्मा एतं पितरो लोकमक्रन् ।

अहोभिरद्भिरक्तुभिर्व्यक्तं यमो ददात्यवसानमस्मै ॥९॥

अति द्रव सारमेयौ श्वानौ चतुरक्षौ शबलौ साधुना पथा ।

अथा पितॄन्सुविदत्रां उपेहि यमेन ये सधमादं मदन्ति ॥१०॥

यौ ते श्वानौ यम रक्षितारौ चतुरक्षौ पथिरक्षी नृचक्षसौ ।

ताभ्यामेनं परि देहि राजन्त्स्वस्ति चास्मा अनमीवं च धेहि ॥

उहूषसार्वसुतृपा उदुखलौ यमस्य दूती चरतो जनाँ अनु ।

ताव॒स्मभ्यं दृश्ये सूर्याय॒ पुनर्दातामसुम॒द्येह भद्रम् ॥१२॥

LI. RIGVEDA X. 16.

मैनमग्ने॒ वि द॒हो माभि शोचो मास्य॒ त्वचं चिक्षिपो मा शरीरम् ।

५ यदा॒ शृतं कृणवो जातवेदो ऽधेमेनं प्र हि॒णुतात्पितृभ्यः ॥१॥

शृतं यदा॒ करसि जातवेदो ऽथेमेनं परि॒ दत्तात्पितृभ्यः ।

यदा॒ गच्छात्यसुनीतिमेतामथा देवानां॑ वशनीर्भवाति ॥२॥

सूर्यं॑ चक्षुर्गच्छतु॒ वातमात्मा द्यां॑ च गच्छ पृथिवीं च धर्मणा ।

अ॒पो वा॑ गच्छ यदि॒ तत्र॑ ते॒ हितमोषधीषु प्रति॒ तिष्ठा शरीरैः ॥३॥

१० अ॒जो भागस्तपसा तं तपस्व॒ तं ते॑ शोचिस्तपतु॒ तं ते॑ अर्चिः ।

यास्ते॑ शिवास्तन्वो जातवेदस्ताभिर्वहैनं सुकृतामु लोकम् ॥४॥

अव॑ सृज॒ पुनरग्ने॑ पितृभ्यो यस्त॑ आहुतश्चरति स्वधाभिः ।

आयुर्वसान॒ उप॑ वेतु॒ शेषः॒ सं गच्छतां त॒न्वा॑ जातवेदः ॥५॥

यत्ते॑ कृष्णः॒ शकुन॑ आतुतोद॑ पिपीलः स॒र्प उत वा॒ श्वापदः ।

१५ अग्निष्टद्विश्वादग॑दं कृणोतु सोमश्च॒ यो ब्राह्मणाँ॑ आविवेश॑ ॥६॥

अग्नेर्वर्म॒ परि॒ गोभिर्व्ययस्व॒ सं प्रोर्णुष्व॒ पीवसा मेदसा च ।

नेत्त्वा॑ धृष्णुर्हर॑सा जर्हृषाणो॑ दधृग्विधक्ष्यन्पर्यङ्ख्याते ॥७॥

इममग्ने॑ चमसं॒ मा वि॑ जिह्वरः प्रियो देवानामुत सोम्यानाम् ।

एष यश्चम॒सो देवपान॒स्तस्मि॑न्देवा अमृता॑ मादयन्ते ॥८॥

२० क्र॒व्यादम॒ग्निं प्र हि॒णोमि दूरं यमराज्ञो गच्छतु रिप्रवाहः ।

इहैवायमितरो जातवेदा देवेभ्यो हव्यं वहतु प्रजानन् ॥९॥

यो अग्निः क्रव्यात्प्रविवेश वो गृहमिमं पश्यन्नितरं जातवेदसम् ।

तं हरामि पितृयज्ञाय देवं स घर्ममिन्वात्परमे सधस्थे ॥१०॥

यो अग्निः क्रव्यवाहनः पितृन्यक्षद्‌ऋतावृधः ।

5 प्रेदु हव्यानि वोचति देवेभ्यश्च पितृभ्य आ ॥११॥

उशन्तस्त्वा नि धीमह्युशन्तः समिधीमहि ।

उशन्नुशत आ वह पितृन्हविषे अत्तवे ॥१२॥

यं त्वमग्ने समदहस्तमु निर्वापया पुनः ।

कियाम्बुर्वं रोहतु पाकदूर्वा व्यल्कशा ॥१३॥

10 शीतिके शीतिकावति ह्लादिके ह्लादिकावति ।

मण्डूक्या३ः सु सं गम इमं स्वग्निं हर्षय ॥१४॥

LII. RIGVEDA X. 17.

त्वष्टा दुहित्रे वहतुं कृणोतीतीदं विश्वं भुवनं समेति ।

यमस्य माता पर्युह्यमाना महो जाया विवस्वतो ननाश ॥१॥

अपागूहन्नमृतां मर्त्येभ्यः कृत्वी सवर्णामददुर्विवस्वते ।

15 उताश्विनावभरद्यत्तदासीदजहादु द्वा मिथुना सरण्यूः ॥२॥

पूषा त्वेतश्च्यावयतु प्र विद्वानन्ष्टपशुर्भुवनस्य गोपाः ।

स त्वैतेभ्यः परि दददत्पितृभ्यो ऽग्निर्देवेभ्यः सुविदत्रियेभ्यः ॥३॥

आयुर्विश्वायुः परि पासति त्वा पूषा त्वा पातु प्रपथे पुरस्तात् ।

यत्रासते सुकृतो यत्र ते ययुस्तत्र त्वा देवः सविता दधातु ॥४॥

20 पूषेमा आशा अनु वेद सर्वाः सो अस्माँ अभयतमेन नेषत् ।

स्वस्तिदा आधृष्णिः सर्ववीरो ऽमयुञ्छन्तुर एंतु प्रजानन् ॥५॥

प्रपंथे पथामंजनिष्ट पूषा प्रपंथे दिवः प्रपंथे पृथिव्याः ।

उभे अभि प्रियतमे सधस्थे आ च परा च चरति प्रजानन् ॥

LIII. RIGVEDA X. 18.

परं मृत्यो अनु परेहि पन्थां यस्ते स्व इतरो देवयानात् ।

⁵ चक्षुष्मते शृक्षते ते ब्रवीमि मा नः प्रजां रीरिषो मोत वीरान् ॥

मृत्योः पदं योपयन्तो यदैत द्राधीय आयुः प्रतरं दधानाः ।

आप्यायमानाः प्रजया धनेन शुद्धाः पूता भवत यज्ञियासः ॥२॥

इमे जीवा वि मृतैराववृत्रन्नभूद्भद्रा देवहूतिर्नो अद्य ।

प्राञ्चो अगाम नृतये हसाय द्राधीय आयुः प्रतरं दधानाः ॥३॥

¹⁰ इमं जीवेभ्यः परिधिं दधामि मैषां नु गादपरो अर्थमेतम् ।

शतं जीवन्तु शरदः पुरूचीरन्तर्मृत्युं दधतां पर्वतेन ॥४॥

यथाहान्यनुपूर्वं भवन्ति यथ ऋतवऋतुभिर्यन्ति साधु ।

यथा न पूर्वमपरो जहात्येवा धातरायूंषि कल्पयैषाम् ॥५॥

आ रोहतायुर्जरसं वृणाना अनुपूर्वं यतमाना यति ष ।

¹⁵ इह त्वष्टा सुजनिमा सजोषा दीर्घमायुः करति जीवसे वः ॥६॥

इमा नारीरविधवाः सुपत्नीराञ्जनेन सर्पिषा सं विशन्तु ।

अनश्रवो अनमीवाः सुरत्ना आ रोहन्तु जनयो योनिमग्रे ॥७॥

उदीर्ष्व नार्यभि जीवलोकं गतासुमेतमुप शेष एहि ।

हस्तग्राभस्य दिधिषोस्तवेदं पत्युर्जनित्वमभि सं बभूथ ॥८॥

²⁰ धनुर्हस्तादाददानो मृतस्यास्मे क्षत्राय वर्चसे बलाय ।

अचैव तमिह वयं सुवीरा विश्वा स्पृधो अभिमातीर्जयेम ॥१०॥

उप सर्प मातरं भूमिमेतामुरुव्यचसं पृथिवीं सुशेवाम् ।

ऊर्णमदा युवतिर्दक्षिणावत एषा त्वा पातु निर्ऋतेरुपस्थात् ॥

उच्छ्वञ्चस्व पृथिवि मा नि बाधथाः सूपायनास्मै भव सूपवञ्चना ।

5 माता पुत्रं यथा सिचाभ्येनं भूम ऊर्णुहि ॥११॥

उच्छ्वञ्चमाना पृथिवी सु तिष्ठतु सहस्रं मित उप हि श्रयन्ताम् ।

ते गृहासो घृतश्चुतो भवन्तु विश्वाहास्मै शरणाः सन्त्वत्र ॥१२॥

उत्ते स्तभ्नामि पृथिवीं त्वत्परीमं लोगं निदधन्मो अहं रिषम् ।

एतां स्थूणां पितरो धारयन्तु ते ऽत्रा यमः सादना ते मिनोतु ॥

10 प्रतीचीने मामहनीष्वाः पर्णमिवा दधुः ।

प्रतीचीं जग्रभा वाचमश्वं रशनया यथा ॥१४॥

LIV. RIGVEDA X. 33.

कुरुश्रवणमावृणि राजानं त्रासदस्यवम् ।

मंहिष्ठं वाघतामृषिः ॥४॥

यस्य मा हरितो रथे तिस्रो वहन्ति साधुया ।

15 स्तवै सहस्रदक्षिणे ॥५॥

यस्य प्रस्वादसो गिर उपमश्रवसः पितुः ।

क्षेत्रं न रण्वमूचुषे ॥६॥

अधि पुत्रोपमश्रवो नपान्मित्रातिथेरिहि ।

पितुष्टे अस्मि वन्दिता ॥७॥

20 यदीशीयामृतानामुत वा मर्त्यानाम् ।

जीवेदिन्मघवा ममं ॥८॥

न देवानामति व्रतं शतात्मा चन जीवति ।

तथा युजा वि वावृते ॥९॥

LV. RIGVEDA X. 40. 10.

जीवं रुदन्ति वि मयन्ते अध्वरे दीर्घामनु प्रसितिं दीधियुर्नरः ।

वामं पितृभ्यो य इदं समेरिरे मयः पतिभ्यो जनयः परिष्वजे ॥

LVI. RIGVEDA X. 52.

विश्वे देवाः शास्तन मा यथेह होता वृतो मनवै यद्विषद्ध ।

प्र मे ब्रूत भागधेयं यथा वो येन पथा हव्यमा वो वहानि ॥१॥

अहं होता न्यसीदं यजीयान्विश्वे देवा मरुतो मा जुनन्ति ।

अहरहरश्विनाध्वर्यवं वां ब्रह्मा समिध्यते साहुतिर्वाम् ॥२॥

अयं यो होता किरु स यमस्य कमप्यूहे यात्समञ्जन्ति देवाः ।

अहरहर्जायते मासि मास्यथा देवा दधिरे हव्यवाहम् ॥३॥

मां देवा दधिरे हव्यवाहमपम्लुक्तं बहु कृच्छ्रा चरन्तम् ।

अग्निर्विद्वान्यज्ञं नः कल्पयाति पञ्चयामं त्रिवृतं सप्ततन्तुम् ॥

आ वो यक्ष्यमृतत्वं सुवीरं यथा वो देव वरिवः कराणि ।

आ बाह्वोर्वज्रमिन्द्रस्य धेयामथेमा विश्वाः पृतना जयाति ॥५॥

त्रीणि शता त्री सहस्राण्यग्निं त्रिंशच्च देवा नव चासपर्यन् ।

औक्षन्घृतैरस्तृणन्बर्हिरस्मा आदिद्धोतारं न्यसादयन्त ॥६॥

LVII. RIGVEDA X. 53.

तन्नु तन्वबजंसो भानुमन्विंहि ज्योतिष्मतः पथो रक्ष धिया कृतान् ।
अनुल्बणं वयत जोगुवामपो मनुर्भव जनया दैव्यं जनम् ॥६॥

अश्मन्वती रीयते सं रभध्वमुत्तिष्ठत प्र तरता सखायः ।
अत्रा जहाम ये असन्नशेवाः शिवान्वयमुत्तरेमाभि वाजान् ॥८॥

LVIII. RIGVEDA X. 85. 36, 24-26, 32-33, 27, 43-47.

5 गृभ्णामि ते सौभगत्वाय हस्तं मया पत्या जरदष्टिर्यथासः ।
भगो अर्यमा सविता पुरंधिर्मह्यं त्वादुर्गार्हपत्याय देवाः ॥३६॥

प्र त्वा मुञ्चामि वरुणस्य पाशाद्येन त्वाबध्नात्सविता सुशेवः ।
ऋतस्य योनौ सुकृतस्य लोके अरिष्टां त्वा सह पत्या दधामि ॥२४॥

प्रेतो मुञ्चामि नामुतः सुबद्धाममुतस्करम् ।
10 यथेयमिन्द्र मीढ्वः सुपुत्रा सुभगासति ॥२५॥

पूषा त्वेतो नयतु हस्तगृह्याश्विना त्वा प्र वहतां रथेन ।
गृहान्गच्छ गृहपत्नी यथासो वशिनी त्वं विदथमा वदासि ॥२६॥

मा विदन्परिपन्थिनो य आसीदन्ति दंपती ।
सुगेभिर्दुर्गमतीतामप द्रान्त्वरातयः ॥३२॥

15 सुमङ्गलीरियं वधूरिमां समेत पश्यत ।
सौभाग्यमस्यै दत्त्वायाथास्तं वि परेतन ॥३३॥

इह प्रियं प्रजया ते समृध्यतामस्मिन्गृहे गार्हपत्याय जागृहि ।
एना पत्या तन्वं सं सृजस्वाधा जिव्री विदथमा वदाथः ॥२७॥

आ नः प्रजां जनयतु प्रजापतिराजरसाय समनक्त्वर्यमा ।

अदुर्मङ्गलीः पतिलोकमा विश शं नों भव द्विपदे शं चतुष्पदे॥

अघोरचक्षुरपतिघ्न्येधि शिवा पशुभ्यः सुमनाः सुवर्चाः ।

वीरसूर्देवकामा स्योना शं नों भव द्विपदे शं चतुष्पदे ॥४४॥

इमां त्वमिन्द्र मीढुः सुपुत्रां सुभगां कृणु ।

दशास्यां पुत्राना धेहि पतिमेकादशं कृधि ॥४५॥

सम्राज्ञी श्वशुरे भव सम्राज्ञी श्वश्र्वां भव ।

ननान्दरि सम्राज्ञी भव सम्राज्ञी अधि देवृषु ॥४६॥

समञ्जन्तु विश्वे देवाः समापो हृदयानि नौ ।

सं मातरिश्वा सं धाता समु देष्ट्री दधातु नौ ॥४७॥

LIX. RIGVEDA X. 137.

उत देवा अवहित देवा उन्नयथा पुनः ।

उतागश्चक्रुषं देवा देवा जीवयथा पुनः ॥१॥

द्वाविमौ वातौ वात आ सिन्धोरा परावतः ।

दक्षं ते अन्य आ वातु परान्यो वातु यद्रपः ॥२॥

आ वात वाहि भेषजं वि वात वाहि यद्रपः ।

त्वं हि विश्वभेषजो देवानां दूत ईयसे ॥३॥

आ त्वागमं शंतातिभिरथो अरिष्टतातिभिः ।

दक्षं ते भद्रमाभार्षं परा यक्ष्मं सुवामि ते ॥४॥

त्रायन्तामिह देवास्त्रायतां मरुतां गणः ।

त्रायन्तां विश्वा भूतानि यथायमरपा असत् ॥५॥

आप इद्वा उ भेषजीरापो अमीवचातनीः ।

आपः सर्वस्य भेषजीस्तास्ते कृणन्तु भेषजम् ॥६॥
हस्ताभ्यां दशशाखाभ्यां जिह्वा वाचः पुरोगवी ।
अनामयित्नुभ्यां त्वा ताभ्यां त्वोप स्पृशामसि ॥७॥

LX. RIGVEDA X. 154.

सोम एकेभ्यः पवते घृतमेक उपासते ।
येभ्यो मधु प्रधावति तांश्चिदेवापि गच्छतात् ॥१॥
तर्पसा ये अनाधृष्यास्तर्पसा ये स्वर्ययुः ।
तपो ये चक्रिरे महस्तांश्चिदेवापि गच्छतात् ॥२॥
ये युध्यन्ते प्रधनेषु शूरासो ये तनूत्यजः ।
ये वा सहस्रदक्षिणास्तांश्चिदेवापि गच्छतात् ॥३॥
ये चित्पूर्व ऋतसाप ऋतावान ऋतावृधः ।
पितॄन्तपस्वतो यम तांश्चिदेवापि गच्छतात् ॥४॥
सहस्रणीथाः कवयो ये गोपायन्ति सूर्यम् ।
ऋषीन्तपस्वतो यम तपोजाँ अपि गच्छतात् ॥५॥

LXI. RIGVEDA X. 155.

परीमे गामनेषत पर्यग्निमहृषत ।
देवेष्वक्रत श्रवः क इमाँ आ दधर्षति ॥५॥

LXII. MAITRAYANI SANHITA II. 13. 23.

हिरण्यगर्भः समवर्तताग्रे भूतस्य जातः पतिरेक आसीत् ।

सं दाधार पृथिवीं द्यामुतेमां कस्मै देवाय हविषा विधेम ॥१॥

यः प्राणतो निमिषतश्च राजा पतिर्विश्वस्य जगतो बभूव ।

ईशे यो अस्य द्विपदश्चतुष्पदः कस्मै देवाय हविषा विधेम॥२॥

य ओजोदा बलदा यस्य विश्व उपासते प्रशिषं यस्य देवाः ।

5 यस्य छायामृतं यस्य मृत्युः कस्मै देवाय हविषा विधेम ॥३॥

यस्येमे विश्वे गिरयो महित्वा समुद्रं यस्य रसया सहाहुः ।

दिशो यस्य प्रदिशः पञ्च देवीः कस्मै देवाय हविषा विधेम ॥

येन द्यौरुग्रा पृथिवी च दृढा येन स्व स्तभितं येन नाकः ।

यो अन्तरिक्षं विममे वरीयः कस्मै देवाय हविषा विधेम॥५॥

10 य इमे द्यावापृथिवी तस्तभाने अधारयद्रोदसी रेजमाने ।

यस्मिन्नधि विततः सूरा एति कस्मै देवाय हविषा विधेम॥६॥

आपो ह यन्महतीर्विश्वमायन्गर्भे दधाना जनयन्तीरग्निम् ।

ततो देवानां निरवर्ततासुः कस्मै देवाय हविषा विधेम ॥७॥

LXIII. MAITRAYANI SANHITA I. 5. 12.

यमो वा अम्रियत । ते देवा यम्या यममपाब्रुवन् । ता

15 यदपृच्छन्त्साब्रवीदद्यामृतेति । ते ऽब्रुवन्त वा इयमिमंमित्थं

मृष्यते रात्रीं सृजावहा इति । अहर्वाव तर्ह्यासीन्न रात्रिः । ते

देवा रात्रिमसृजन्त । ततः श्वस्तनमभवत् । ततः सा तममृ-

ष्यत । तस्मादाहुरहोरात्राणि वावाघं मर्षयन्तीति ।

LXIV. MAITRAYANI SANHITA I. 10. 13.

प्रजापतेर्वा एतज्ज्येष्ठं तोकं यत्सर्ववेताः । ते परिक्षिण आ-

सन् । ते परापीतमासत यंच यचाकामयन्त । अध वा इयं
तर्हि शिथिरासीत् । तेषामिन्द्रः पक्षानछिनत् । तैरिमामद॰-
हत । ये पक्षा आस॰स्ते जीमूता अभवन् । तस्मादेते सद्दि
पर्वतमुप प्लवन्ते । योनिर्हैषामेषः ।

---

5 ऐन्द्राबार्हस्पत्य॰ हविर्निर्वपेद्यो राष्ट्रीयो नैव प्रतिङ्नुयात् ।
अदितिर्वै प्रजाकामौदनमपचत् । सौञ्छिष्टमाश्रात् । त॰ वा
इन्द्रमन्तरेव गर्भ॰ सन्तमयसंयेन दार्बापौम्भात् । सो ऽपोब्यो
ऽजायत । त॰ वा एतेन बृहस्पतिरयाजयदैन्द्राबार्हस्पत्येन ।
तस्य तर्हीमं स्वयमेव व्युपद्यत । स इमा दिशो व्रजेणाभिप-
10 र्यावर्तत । यो राष्ट्रीयो नैव प्रतिङ्नुयात्तमेतेन याजयेदैन्द्रा-
बार्हस्पत्येन । परजितो हि वा एष पाप्मना । अथैष न प्र-
तिङ्नोति । बृहस्पतये निरुप्यता इन्द्राय क्रियते सर्वत एवैनं
मुञ्चति । व्रजेणेमा दिशो ऽभिपर्यावर्तते ।

अग्नेस्त्रयो ज्यायांसो भ्रातर आसन् । ते देवेभ्यो हव्यं वह-
15 न्तः प्रामीयन्त । सो ऽग्निरबिभेत्त्यर्थं वाव स्य आर्तिमारिष्य-
तीति । स निलायत । सो ऽपः प्राविशत् । तं देवताः प्रैषमै-
च्छन् । तं मत्स्यः प्राब्रवीत् । तमशपद्विया धिया त्वा वध्या-
सुर्यो मा प्रावोच इति । तस्मान्मत्स्यं धिया धिया घ्नन्ति । श-
प्तो हि । तमन्वविन्दन् । तमब्रुवन्नुप न आ वर्तस्व हव्यं नो

वहेति । सो ऽब्रवीद्वरं वृणै यदेव गृहीतस्याहुतस्य बहिःपरि-
धि स्कन्दात्तन्मे भ्रातृणां भागधेयमसदिति । तस्माद्गृहीतस्या-
हुतस्य बहिःपरिधि स्कन्दति तेषां तन्द्रागधेयम् ।

LXVII. AITAREYA BRAHMANA III. 20.

इन्द्रो वै वृत्रं हनिष्यन्त्सर्वा देवता अब्रवीदनु मोप तिष्ठ-
ध्वमुप मा ह्वयध्वमिति । तथेति । तं हनिष्यन्त आद्रवन् । सो
ऽवेन्मां वै हनिष्यन्त आ द्रवन्ति हन्तेमान्भीषया इति । ता-
नभि प्राक्षसीत् । तस्य ख्यसखादीषमाणा विश्वे देवा आद्रवन् ।
मरुतो हैनं नाजहुः प्रहर भगवो जहि वीर्यस्वेत्येवैनमेतां
वाचं वदन्त उपातिष्ठन्त । तदेतदृचिः पश्यन्नभ्यनूवाच वृत्रस्य
त्वा ख्वसखादिति । सो ऽवेदिमे वै किल मे सचिवा इमे मा-
कामयन्त हन्तेमानसिन्नुक्थ आ भजा इति । तानेतस्मिन्नुक्थ
आभजत् ।

LXVIII. AITAREYA BRAHMANA III. 21.

इन्द्रो वै वृत्रं हत्वा सर्वा विजितीर्विजित्याब्रवीत्प्रजापति-
र्महमेतदसानि यत्त्वमहं महानसानीति । स प्रजापतिरब्रवी-
दथ को ऽहमिति । यदेवैतदवोच इत्यब्रवीत् । ततो वै को
नाम प्रजापतिरभवत् । को वै नाम प्रजापतिः । यन्महानि-
न्द्रो ऽभवत्तन्महेन्द्रस्य महेन्द्रत्वम् ।

LXIX. ÇATAPATHA BRAHMANA II. 2. 2.

इया वै देवाः । देवा अहैव देवाः । अथ ये ब्राह्मणाः शुश्रुवां-

सो ऽनूचानास्ते मनुष्यदेवाः । तेषां त्रेधा विभक्त एव यज्ञः ।
आहुतय एव देवानां दक्षिणा मनुष्यदेवानां ब्राह्मणानां भु-
ञ्जुवुषामनूचानानाम् । आहुतिभिरेव देवाञ्छ्रीणाति दक्षिणा-
भिर्मनुष्यदेवान्ब्राह्मणाञ्जुञ्जुवुषो ऽनूचानान् । त एनमुभये
देवाः प्रीताः सुधायां दधति ॥६॥

तस्य वा एतस्याग्न्याधेयस्य सत्यमेवोपचारः । स यः सत्यं
वदति यथायिमं समिद्धं तं घृतेनाभिषिञ्चेद्वं हैनं स उद्दीपयति
तस्य भूयो भूय एव तेजो भवति श्वः श्वः श्रेयाम्भवति । अथ यो
ऽनृतं वदति यथायिमं समिद्धं तमुदकेनाभिषिञ्चेद्वं हैनं स जा-
सयति तस्य कनीयः कनीय एव तेजो भवति श्वः श्वः पापी-
याम्भवति । तस्मादु सत्यमेव वदेत् ॥१९॥ तदु हारुणमौ-
पवेशिं ज्ञातय ऊचुः स्थविरो वा अस्यमी आ धत्स्वेति । स
होवाच ते मैतद्रूप वाचंयम एवैधि न वा आहितापिनानृतं
वदितव्यं न वद्ग्रातु नानृतं वदेतावास्त्यमेवोपचार इति ॥२०॥

एष वै मृत्युर्यत्संवत्सरः । एष हि मर्त्यानामहोरात्राभ्यामा-
युः क्षिणोति । अथ म्रियन्ते । तस्मादेष एव मृत्युः । स यो
हैतं मृत्युं संवत्सरं वेद न हास्यैष पुरा जरसो ऽहोरात्राभ्यामा-
युः क्षिणोति । सर्व हैवायुरेति ॥१॥ एष उ एवान्तकः । एष
हि मर्त्यानामहोरात्राभ्यामायुषी ऽन्तं गच्छति । अथ म्रियन्ते ।

तस्मादेष एवान्तकः । स यो हैतमन्तकं मृत्युं संवत्सरं वेद न
हास्यैष पुरा जरसो ऽहोरात्राभ्यामायुषो ऽन्तं गच्छति । सर्व
हैवायुरेति ॥२॥ ते देवा एतस्मादन्तकान्मृत्योः संवत्सरात्प्रजा-
पतेर्बिभयां चक्रुर्यद्वै नो ऽयमहोरात्राभ्यामायुषो ऽन्तं न ग-
5 च्छेदिति ॥३॥ त एतान्यज्ञक्रतूंस्तेनिरे ऽग्निहोत्रं दर्शपूर्णमा-
सौ चातुर्मास्यानि पशुबन्धं सौम्यमध्वरम् । त एतैर्यज्ञक्रतुभि-
र्यजमाना नामृतत्वमानशिरे ॥४॥ ते हाग्निं चिक्रिरे । ते
ऽपरिमिता एव परिश्रित उप दधुरपरिमिता यजुष्मतीरपरि-
मिता लोकंपृणा यथेदमप्येतर्ह्येक उपदधति । इति देवा अ-
10 कुर्वन् । इति ते ह नैवामृतत्वमानशिरे ॥५॥ ते ऽचैन्तः आ-
म्यन्तर्हेररमृतत्वमवरुरुत्समानाः । ताम्ह प्रजापतिरुवाच न
वै मे सर्वाणि रूपाण्युप धत्याति वैव रेचयथ न वाभ्यापयथ
तस्मान्नामृता भवथेति ॥६॥ ते होचुस्त्वेभ्यो वै नस्त्वमेव त-
द्ब्रूहि यथा ते सर्वाणि रूपाण्युपदधामेति ॥७॥ स होवाच
15 षष्टिं च त्रीणि च शतानि परिश्रित उप धत्स षष्टिं च त्रीणि
च शतानि यजुष्मतीरधि षट्त्रिंशतमथ लोकंपृणा दश च स-
हस्राण्यष्टौ च शतान्युप धत्साथ मे सर्वाणि रूपाण्युप धास्य-
थाथामृता भविष्यथेति । ते ह तथा देवा उप दधुः । ततो दे-
वा अमृता आसुः ॥८॥ स मृत्युर्देवानब्रवीदित्थमेव सर्वे मनु-
20 ष्या अमृता भविष्यन्त्यथ को मह्यं भागो भविष्यतीति । ते हो-
चुर्नातो ऽपरः कश्चन सह शरीरेणामृतो ऽसच्छदैव त्वमेतं भागं
हरासा अथ ध्यावृत्य शरीरेणामृतो ऽसच्छो ऽमृतो ऽसच्छिद्यया
वा कर्मणा वेति । यद्वै तद्ब्रुवन्विद्यया वा कर्मणा वेत्येषा

हैव सा विद्या यदग्निरेतदु हैव तत्कर्म यदग्निः ॥८॥ ते य ए-
वमेतद्विदुर्ये वैतत्कर्म कुर्वते मृत्वा पुनः सं भवन्ति । ते संभ-
वन्त एवामृतत्वमभिसं भवन्ति । अथ य एवं न विदुर्ये वैत-
त्कर्म न कुर्वते मृत्वा पुनः सं भवन्ति त एतस्यैवान्नं पुनः पु-
र्नभवन्ति ॥१०॥

LXXII. ÇATAPATHA BRAHMANA XII. 7. 3.

इन्द्रस्येन्द्रियमन्नस्य रसं सोमस्य भक्षं सुरयासुरो नमुचिरह-
रत् । सो ऽश्विनौ च सरस्वतीं चोपाधावच्छेपानो ऽसि न-
मुचये न त्वा दिवा न नक्तं हनानि न दण्डेन न धन्वना न पृ-
थेन न मुष्टिना न मुष्केण नार्द्रेणाथ म इदमहार्षीं दिदं म
आ जिहीर्षेति । ते ऽब्रुवन्नस्तु नो ऽनाप्यथा हरामेति । सह
न एतदथा हरेत्यब्रवीत् । इति तावश्विनौ च सरस्वती च
अपां फेनं वज्रमसिञ्चन्न मुष्को नार्द्रे इति । तेनेन्द्रो नमुचे-
रासुरस्य थुष्टायां उषायां यद्यावनुदित आदित्ये न दिवा न नक्तमि-
ति शिर उद्वासयत् । तस्मादेतदृषिणाभ्यनूक्तमपां फेनेनेति ।

LXXIII. NIRUKTA II. 16.

अतिछन्नीनामनिविश्यमानानामित्यस्थावराणां काष्ठानां
मध्ये निहितं शरीरं मेघः । शरीरं शृणातेः शब्बातेर्वा । वृत्रस्य
निहयं निर्णामं विचरन्ति विजानन्त्याप इति । दीर्घं द्राघतेः ।
तमस्तनोतेः । आशयदाशेतेः । इन्द्रशत्रुरिन्द्रो ऽस्य शमयिता वा
शातयिता वा तस्मादिन्द्रशत्रुः । तत्को वृत्रः । मेघ इति नैरु-

क्काः । त्वाष्ट्रो ऽसुर इत्यैतिहासिकाः । अपां च ज्योतिषश्च
मिश्रीभावकर्मणो वर्षकर्म जायते । तत्रोपमार्थेन युक्तवर्षा
भवन्ति । अहिवत्तु खलु मन्त्रवर्णो ब्राह्मणवादाश्च । विवृद्ध्या
शरीरस्य स्त्रोतांसि निवार्यां चकार । तस्मिन्हते प्रसस्यन्दिर
5 आपः । तदभिवादिन्येषगर्भवति ।

LXXIV. AÇVALAYANA'S GRIHYASUTRA I. 5, 7, 8.

कुलमग्ये परीक्षेत ये मातृतः पितृतश्चेति यथोक्तं पुरस्तात्।१।
बुद्धिमते कन्यां प्रयच्छेत।२।बुद्धिरूपशीललक्षणसंपन्नामरोगा-
मुपयच्छेत ।३। दुर्विज्ञेयानि लक्षणान्यष्टौ पिण्डान्कृत्व आत्तमग्ये
प्रथमं जङ्घ छुते सत्यं प्रतिष्ठितम् । यदियं कुमार्यभिजाता
10 तदियमिह प्रतिपद्यताम् । यत्सत्यं तदृश्यतामिति पिण्डान-
भिमन्त्र्य कुमारीं ब्रूयादेषामेकं गृहाणेति ।४। छेवाचेद्भयतः-
सस्याग्रृह्णीयादन्नवत्यस्याः प्रजा भविष्यतीति विद्यान्मृद्भात्य-
शुमती वेदिपुरीषाद्ब्रह्मवर्चस्विन्यविदासिनो हृदात्सर्वसंपन्ना-
देवनात्कितवी चतुष्पथादिव्रमग्राजिनीरिणाद्धन्या श्मशाना-
15 त्पतिघ्नी ।५। ॥५॥

अथ खलूच्चावचा जनपदधर्मा ग्रामधर्माश्च तान्विवाहे प्र-
तीयात् ।१। यत्तु समानं तद्वक्ष्यामः ।२। पश्चादग्नेर्हेषदमश्मानं
प्रतिष्ठाप्योत्तरपुरस्तादुदकुम्भं समन्वारब्धायां हुत्वा तिष्ठन्नत्य-
क्रमुखः प्राङ्मुख्या आसीनाया गृभ्णामि ते सौभगत्वाय हस्त-
20 मित्यङ्गुष्ठमेव गृह्णीयाद्यदि कामयीत पुमांस एव मे पुत्रा
जायेरन्निति ।३। अङ्गुलीरिव स्त्रीकामः ।४। रोमान्ते हस्तं साङ्गुष्ठ-

मुभयकामः ।५। प्रदक्षिणमयिमुदकुम्भं च चिः परिणयं जपति

अमो ऽहमस्मि सा त्वं सा त्वमस्यमो ऽहम् ।

द्यौरहं पृथिवी त्वं सामाहमृक्त्वम् ॥

तावेहि विवहावहै प्रजां प्रजनयावहै ।

5 संप्रियौ रोचिष्णू सुमनस्यमानौ जीवेव शरदः शतम् ॥

इति ।६। परिणीय परिणीयाश्मानमारोहयति

इममश्मानमारोहाश्मेव त्वं स्थिरा भव ।

सहस्व पृतनायतो ऽभितिष्ठ पृतन्यतः ॥

इति ।७। वध्वञ्जला उपस्तीर्ये आता आतृष्ठानो वा द्विलो-

10 जानावपति ।८। चिर्णोमदन्यानाम् ।९। प्रत्यभिघार्यं हविः ।१०।

अवत्तं च ।११। एषो ऽवदानधर्मः ।१२।

अर्यमणं नु देवं कन्या अग्निमयक्षत ।

स इमां देवो अर्यमा प्रेतो मुञ्चातु नामुतः स्वाहा ॥

वरुणं नु देवं कन्या अग्निमयक्षत ।

15 स इमां देवो वरुणः प्रेतो मुञ्चातु नामुतः स्वाहा ॥

पूषणं नु देवं कन्या अग्निमयक्षत ।

स इमां देवः पूषा प्रेतो मुञ्चातु नामुतः स्वाहा ॥

इत्यविच्छिन्दत्यञ्जलिं स्रुचेव जुहुयात् ।१३। अपरिणीय शूर्प-

पुटेनाभ्यात्मं तूष्णीं चतुर्धम् ।१४। ओप्योप्य हैके लाजाम्परिण-

20 यन्ति तथोत्तमे आहुती न संनिपतत ।१५। अस्यै शिखे वि-

मुञ्चति यदि कृते भवत ऊर्णास्तुके केशपक्षयोर्बद्धे भवतः ।१६।

प्र त्वा मुञ्चामि वरुणस्य पाशादिति ।१७। उत्तरामुत्तरया ।१८।

अथैनामपराजितायां दिशि सप्त पदान्यभ्युत्क्रामयति

7°

इष एकपदी   ऊर्जे द्विपदी

रायस्पोषाय त्रिपदी   मायोभव्याय चतुष्पदी

प्रजाभ्यः पञ्चपदी   ऋतुभ्यः षट्पदी

सखा सप्तपदी भव सा मामनुव्रता भव ।

⁵ पूषान्विन्दावहै बहूंस्ते सन्तु जरदष्टयः ॥

इति ।१९। उभयोः संनिधाय शिरसी उत्कुम्भेनावसिच्य ।२०।

ब्राह्मख्याश्च वृद्धाया जीवपत्या जीवप्रजाया अगार एतां रा-

त्रीं वसेत् ।२१। ध्रुवमरुन्धतीं सप्त ऋषीनिति दृष्ट्वा वाचं वि-

सृजेत जीवपत्नी प्रजां विन्देयेति ।२२। ॥७॥

¹⁰   प्रयाण उपपद्यमाने पूषा त्वेतो नयतु हस्तगृह्णेति यानमा-

रोहयेत् ।१। अश्मन्वती रीयते सं रभध्वमित्यर्धर्चेन नावमारो-

हयेत् ।२। उत्तरेणोत्क्रमयेत् ।३। जीवं रुदन्तीति रुदत्याम् ।४।

विवाहाग्निमयतो ऽजस्रं नयन्ति ।५। कल्याणेषु देशवृक्ष-

चतुष्पथेषु मा विदत्परिपन्थिन इति जपेत् ।६। वासे वासे

¹⁵ सुमङ्गलीरियं वधूरितीक्षकानीक्षेत ।७। इह प्रियं प्रजया ते

समृध्यतामिति गृहं प्रवेशयेत् ।८। विवाहाग्निमुपसमाधाय

पश्चादस्यानडुहं चर्मास्तीर्ये प्राग्ग्रीवमुत्तरलोम तस्मिन्नुपवि-

श्यार्या समन्वारब्धायामा नः प्रजां जनयतु प्रजापतिरिति च-

तसृभिः प्रत्यृचं हुत्वा समञ्जन्तु विश्वे देवा इति दभ्रः प्राश्य

²⁰ प्रतिप्रयच्छेदाज्यशेषेण वानक्ति हृदये ।९। अत ऊर्ध्वमक्षारा-

लवणाशिनौ ब्रह्मचारिणावलंकुर्वाणावधःशायिनौ स्यातां

त्रिरात्रं द्वादशरात्रम् ।१०। संवत्सरं वैक ऋत्विजीयात इति ।११।

चरितवतः सूर्यायां विदे वधूवस्त्रं दद्यात् ।१०। अन्नं ब्राह्मणेभ्यः ।१३। अथ स्वस्त्ययनं वाचयीत ।१४। ॥ ८ ॥

LXXV. AÇVALAYANA'S GRIHYASUTRA IV. 1—6.

आहितामिं चेदुपत्पेत्राच्यामुदीच्यामपराजितायां वा दि-
ष्युदवस्येत् ।१। यामकामा अमय इत्युदाहरन्ति ।२। आशंसन्त
5 एनं यामंमाजिगमिषन्तो ऽगदं कुर्युरिति ह विज्ञायते ।३। अ-
गदः सोमेन पशुनेष्ट्वावस्येत् ।४। अनिष्ट्वा वा ।५। संस्थिते
भूमिभागं खानयेद्द्क्षिणपूर्वस्यां दिशि दक्षिणापरस्यां वा ।६।
दक्षिणाप्रवणं प्राग्दक्षिणाप्रवणं वा ।७। प्रत्यग्दक्षिणाप्रवण-
मित्येके ।८। यावानुबाहुकः पुरुषस्तावदायामम् ।९। व्याममात्रं
10 तिर्यक् ।१०। वितस्त्यवाक् ।११। अभित आकाशं श्मशानम् ।१२।
बहुलौषधिकम् ।१३। कठकिक्षीरिणस्त्विति यथोक्तं पुरस्तात्
।१४। यत्र सर्वत आपः प्रस्यन्देरन्नेतदाहुरेतस्य लक्षणं श्मशा-
नस्य ।१५। केशश्मश्रुलोमनखानि वापयन्तीत्युक्तं पुरस्तात् ।१६।
विगुल्फे बहिराज्यं च ।१७। उधन्यच सर्पिरानयन्ति ।१८। एत-
15 त्पित्र्यं पृषदाज्यम् ।१९। ॥ १ ॥

अथैतां दिशमभीचयन्ति यज्ञपात्राणि च ।१। अन्वञ्चं प्रे-
तमयुजो ऽमिथुनाः प्रवयसः ।२। पीठचक्रेण गोयुक्तेनेत्येके ।३।
अनुत्तरणीम् ।४। गाम् ।५। अजां वैकवर्णाम् ।६। कृष्णामेके
७। स्वये बाहौ बद्ध्वानुसंकालयन्ति ।८। अन्वञ्चो ऽमात्या अ-
20 धोनिवीताः प्रचृत्तशिखा ज्येष्ठप्रथमाः कनिष्ठजघन्याः ।९। प्रा-
ग्वैवं भूमिभागं कर्तोदकेन शमीशाखया चिः प्रसव्यमायतनं

परिव्रजन्मोक्षान्यपेत वीत वि च सर्पेतात इति।१०। दक्षिणपूर्वे
उत्ततान्त आहवनीयं निदधाति।११। उत्तरपश्चिमे गार्हेपत्यम्
।१२। दक्षिणपश्चिमे दक्षिणम्।१३। अथैनमन्तर्वेदीध्मचितिं चि-
नोति यो जानाति।१४। तस्मिन्बर्हिराल्तीयं कृष्णाजिनं चो-
त्तरलोम तस्मिन्त्रेतं संवेशयन्युत्तरेण गार्हेपत्यं हृताहवनीयम-
भिशिरसम्।१५। उत्तरतः पत्नीम्।१६। धनुष्च क्षत्रियाय।१७।
तामुन्थापयेद्देवरः पतिस्थानीयो ऽन्तेवासी जरद्दासो वोदीध्वे
नार्येभि जीवलोकमिति।१८। कातो वृषले जपेत।१९। धनुर्हे-
स्तादाददानो मृतस्येति धनुः।२०। उक्तं वृषले।२१। अधिज्यं
कृत्वा संचितिमचिला संश्रीयानुप्रहरेत।२२। ॥२॥

अथैतानि पात्राणि योजयेत।१। दक्षिणे हस्ते जुहूम।२। स-
व्य उपभृतम्।३। दक्षिणे पार्श्वे स्रुवं सव्ये ऽग्निहोत्रहवणीम्
।४। उरसि ध्रुवां शिरसि कपालानि दाद्सु याव्णः।५। नासि-
कयोः स्रुवौ।६। भित्त्वा चैकम्।७। कर्णयोः प्राश्चित्रहरणे।८।
भित्त्वा चैकम्।९। उदरे पात्रीम्।१०। समवत्तधानं च चम-
सम्।११। उपस्थे शम्याम्।१२। अरणी ऊर्वोः।१३। उलूखल-
मुसले जङ्घयोः।१४। पादयोः भूर्वे।१५। छित्त्वा चैकम्।१६।
आसेचनवन्ति पृषदाज्यस्य पूरयन्ति।१७। अमा पुत्रो हषदु-
पले कुर्वीत।१८। लौहायसं च कौलालम्।१९। अनुत्तरण्या
वपामुत्सिच्च शिरोमुखं प्रच्छादयेदग्रेवेस्मे परि गोभिर्य्यस्खेति
।२०। वृक्षा उद्हृत्य पाख्योरादध्यादति द्रव सारमेयौ श्वानाविति
दक्षिणे दक्षिणं सव्ये सव्यम्।२१। हृदये हृदयम्।२२। पिराश्मौ
चैके।२३। वृक्षापचार इत्येके।२४। सर्वां यथाङ्गं विनिश्चिप्य च-

मैणा प्रक्षाद्येममये चमसं मा वि जिह्वर इति मण्णीतामप्रणय-
नमनुमन्त्रयते ।२५। सर्व्यं जान्वाच्य दक्षिणायावाज्याहुतीर्जुहु-
यादग्मये स्वाहा कामाय स्वाहा लोकाय स्वाहानुमतये स्वा-
हेति ।२६। पञ्चमीमुरसि प्रेतस्यासावै त्वमजायथा अयं तद्-
धि जायतामसौ स्वर्गाय लोकाय स्वाहेति ।२७। ॥३॥

प्रेष्यति युगपदग्नीन्ज्वालयतेति ।१। आहवनीयष्चेतूर्वे प्रा-
ड्मुखात्स्वर्गलोक एनं प्रापदिति विद्याद्रात्स्यत्यसावमुष्ठैवमय-
मसिन्निति पुष्पः ।२। गार्हपत्यष्चेतूर्वे प्राड्मुखादन्तरिक्षलोक
एनं प्रापदिति विद्याद्रात्स्यत्यसावमुष्ठैवमयमसिन्निति पुष्पः
।३। दक्षिणायिष्चेतूर्वे प्राड्मुखान्मनुष्यलोक एनं प्रापदिति वि-
द्याद्रात्स्यत्यसावमुष्ठैवमयमसिन्निति पुष्पः ।४। युगपत्प्राप्तौ प-
रामृष्टिं वदन्ति ।५। तं दह्यमानमनुमन्त्रयते प्रेहि प्रेहि पथिभिः
पूर्व्येभिरिति समानम् ।६। स एर्व्यंविदा दह्यमानः सहैव धूमेन
स्वर्गं लोकमेतीति ह विज्ञायते ।७। उत्तरपुरस्तादाहवनीयस्य
जानुमार्धं गर्तं खात्वावकां शीपाल्मित्यवधापयेत्ततो ह वा
एष निष्क्रम्य सहैव धूमेन स्वर्गं लोकमेतीति ह विज्ञायते ।८।
इमे जीवा वि मृतैरावृत्रन्निति सह्यावृतो व्रजन्त्यनवेक्षमाणाः
।५। यत्रोदकमवहत्रवति तत्राप्य सकृदुन्मज्ज्यैकाञ्जलिमुत्सृज्य
तस्य गोत्रं नाम च गृहीत्वोत्तीर्यान्यानि वासांसि परिधाय सकृ-
देनान्यापीड्योदग्दशानि विसृज्यासत आ नक्षत्रदर्शनात् ।१०।
ज्यादित्यस्य वा ह्रयमाणे प्रविशेयुः ।११। कनिष्ठप्रथमा ज्येष्ठजघ-
न्याः ।१२। प्राक्षागारमष्मानमर्षिं गोमयमक्षतांस्तिलानप उ-

पस्पृशन्ति ।१३। नैतस्यां राच्यामबं पचेरन् ।१४। क्रीतोत्पन्नेन
वा वर्तेरन् ।१५। गिराचमक्षारालवणाशिनः स्युः ।१६। द्वाद-
श्यार्धं वा महागुरुषु दानाध्ययने वर्जयेरन् ।१७। दशाहं सपि-
ण्डेषु ।१८। गुरौ चासपिण्डे ।१९। अप्रत्तासु च स्त्रीषु ।२०। चि-
राचमितरेष्वाचार्येषु ।२१। ज्ञातौ चासपिण्डे ।२२। प्रत्तासु च
स्त्रीषु ।२३। अदन्तजाते ।२४। अपरिजाते च ।२५। एकाहं सब्र-
ह्मचारिणि ।२६। समानयामीये च योषिये ।२७। ॥४॥

संचयनमूर्ध्वं दशम्याः कृष्णपक्षस्यायुजास्वेकनक्षे ।१। अ-
लक्षणे कुम्भे पुमांसमलक्षणायां स्त्रियम् ।२। अयुजो ऽमि-
10 थुनाः प्रवयसः ।३। क्षीरोदकेन शमीशाखया चिः प्रसव्यं परि-
वजन्रोक्षति शीतिके शीतिकावतीति ।४। अकुण्डोपकनिष्ठि-
काभ्यामेकैकमस्थ्यसंहादयन्तो ऽवदध्युः ।५। पादौ पूर्वं शिर उ-
त्तरम् ।६। सुसंचितं संचित्य पवनेन संपूय यच सर्वैत आपो
नाभिस्यन्देरन्नन्या वर्षाभ्यस्तच गर्ते ऽवदध्युरुप सर्पे मातरं भू-
15 मिमेतामिति ।७। उत्तरया पांसूनवकिरेत् ।८। अवकीर्योत्त-
राम् ।९। उत्ते स्तभ्नामीति कपालेनापिधायाधानवेक्षं प्रत्या-
व्रज्याप उपस्पृश्य आह्नमसौ दध्युः ।१०। ॥५॥

गुरुष्वभिमृता अन्यतो वापस्नीयमाणा अमावास्यायां
शान्तिकर्मे कुवीरन् ।१। पुरोदयादमिं सहभसानं सहायतनं द-
20 स्त्रिणा हरेयुः क्रव्यादमिमिं प्र हिणोमि दूरमित्यर्धर्चेन ।२। तं च-
तुष्पथे न्युप्य यच वा चिः प्रसव्यं परियन्ति सव्यैः पाणिभिः
सव्यानूरून्नाघ्रानाः ।३। अथानवेक्षं प्रत्यावव्रज्याप उपस्पृश्य केश-

श्मश्रुलोमनखानि वापयित्नोपकल्पय्यीर्त्तवान्मणिकान्कुम्भा-
नाचमनीयांश्च शमीसुमनोमालिनः शमीमयमिध्मं शमीम-
य्यावरणी परिधीँश्चानडुहं गोमयं चर्म्म च नवनीतमश्मानं च
यावत्यो युवतयस्तावन्ति कुश्रपिण्डूलानि ।४। अग्निवेलाया-
5 मग्निं जनयेदिह्नैवायमितरो जातवेदा इत्यर्धर्च्चेन ।५। तं दीप्-
यमाना आसत आ शान्तरात्रादायुष्मतां कथाः कीर्त्तयन्तो
माङ्गल्यानीतिहासपुराणानीत्याख्यापयमानाः ।६। उपरतेषु
शब्देषु संप्रविष्टेषु वा गृहं निवेशने वा दक्षिणाद्वारपक्षाद्वारन्त-
म्याविच्छिन्नामुदकधारां हरेत्तनु तन्वन्नजसो भानुमन्विही-
10 त्योत्तरसात् ।७। अथाग्निमुपसमाधाय पश्चादस्यानडुहं चर्म्मा-
स्तीर्ये प्राग्यीवमुत्तरलोम तस्मिन्नमात्यानारोहयेदा रोहता-
युज्जैरसं वृणाना इति ।८। इमं जीवेभ्यः परिधिं दधामीति
परिधिं परिदध्यात् ।९। अन्तर्मृत्युं दधतां पर्व्वतेनेत्युत्तरतो
ऽश्मानमग्नेः कृत्वा परं मृत्यो अनु परेहि पन्थामिति चतसृभिः
15 प्रत्यृचं हुत्वा यथाहान्यनुपूर्व्वं भवन्तीत्यमात्यानीक्षेत ।१०। युवत-
यः पृथक्पाणिभ्यां दर्भतरुणकैर्नवनीतेनाङ्गुष्ठोपकनिष्ठिका-
भ्यामक्षिणी आज्य पराच्यो विसृजेयुः ।११। इमा नारीरविधवाः
सुपत्नीरित्यज्ञाना ईक्षेत ।१२। अश्मन्वती रीयते सं रभध्वम्-
त्यश्मानं कर्त्ता प्रथमो ऽभिमृशेत् ।१३। अथापराजितायां दि-
20 श्यवस्थायामिनानडुहेन गोमयेन चाविच्छिन्नया चोदकधार-
यापो हि ष्ठा मयोभुव इति तृचेन परीमे गामनेषतेति परि-
क्रामन्तु जपेत् ।१४। पिङ्गलो ऽनड्वान्परिधेयः स्यादित्युदाहरन्ति

।१५। अथोपविशन्ति यथाभिरंस्यमाना भवन्त्यहतेन वाससा
प्रच्छाद्य ।१६। आसते ऽस्वपन्त आेदयात् ।१७। उदित आादि-
त्ये सौर्याणि स्वस्त्ययनानि च जपित्वानं संस्कृत्याप नः श्रे-
युचद्धमिति प्रत्यूचं हुत्वा ब्राह्मणान्भोजयित्वा स्वस्त्ययनं वा-
चयीत ।१८। गौः कंसो ऽहतं वासश्च दक्षिणा ।१९। ॥६॥

SANSKRIT-ENGLISH VOCABULARY.

1 **a**, *pron. root, see* idam *and* 502.

2 **a**, *negative prefix, see* an.

áṅça, *m.* (that which one gets, *i.e.*) one's portion; *and so, generalized,* portion, part. [√1 aç, 'get.']

aṅçú, *m.* juicy internodium *or* shoot of the Soma-plant; *and so,* shooting ray (of light).

aṅçumánt, *a.* rich in beams, radiant; *as m.* the sun, 16⁴. [aṅçú, 1235b.]

áṅsa, *m.* shoulder. [perhaps, 'the strong' (part), √am, 1197a: cf. ὦμ-ος, Lat. *um-erus,* Goth. *amsa,* 'shoulder.']

a-kasmāt, *adv.* without any "wherefore"; without apparent cause; unexpectedly; accidentally.

akasmād-āgantu, *m.* an accidental arrival, a chance comer.

a-kāra, *m.* the sound *or* letter a. [Whitney, 18.]

a-kāraṇa, *n.* lack of cause; -am, *adv.* causelessly.

a-kīrti, *f.* non-fame, disgrace.

akīrti-kara, *a.* causing disgrace, disgraceful.

á-kṛta, *a.* not done; uncooked.

aktú, *m.* —1. ointment; —2. light, beam of light; —3. night. [for 2, cf. ἀκτίς, 'beam.']

a-kriyamāṇa, *a.* not being accomplished. [√1 kṛ, 'do,' 770c.]

a-krūra, *a.* not harsh.

1 **akṣá**, *n.* for akṣán *at end of cpds* [1315a].

2 **akṣá**, *m.* a die for playing. [named, perhaps, from its 'eyes' (1 akṣá) or 'spots.']

ákṣa, *m.* axle. [cf. ἄξων, Lat. *axis,* AS. *eax,* Eng. *axe* (i.e. 'axle'), and *axle.*]

á-kṣata, *a.* unhurt, uninjured; unbroken; *as m. pl.* unbroken *or* unhusked grains, *esp.* of barley.

akṣata-kesara, *a.* having an uninjured mane.

akṣata-deha, *a.* having an unhurt *or* perfect body.

akṣán [431], *n.* eye. [cf. ὄκ-σον-α, 'have seen,' ὤψ, 'eye'; ὄσσε, ὀκ-je, 'eyes'; Lat. *oc-ulus,* 'eye'; the kinship of AS. *eáge,* Eng. *eye,* remains to be proved: cf. √īkṣ.]

akṣa-priya, *a.* beloved of the dice, *i.e.* lucky at gaming.

a-kṣama, *a.* not equal to a thing; unable, *w. inf.*

a-kṣaya, *a.* imperishable.

akṣayatva, *n.* imperishability. [akṣaya.]

a-kṣára, *a.* imperishable; *as n.* word; syllable; the sacred syllable, om, 60¹⁴; sound, letter, 61⁴.

akṣara-nyāsa, *m.* the commitment to letters, the writing.

a-kṣāra, *a.* not pungent.

akṣārālavaṇa, *n.* that which is not pungent and not salt. [alavaṇa: 1253b.]

akṣārālavaṇāçin, *a.* eating that which is not pungent and not salt, abstaining from seasoned and salted food. [āçin.]

ákṣi [431], *n.* eye; *see* akṣán.

akṣáuhiṇī, *f.* a complete army.

akṣáuhiṇī-pati, *m.* master of an army; general.

a-khila, *a.* without a gap, entire; all.

a-gadá, *a.* not having disease, well, healthy, whole; wholesome; *as m.* medicine.

agāra, *m. n.* house.

agni, *m.* fire; *esp.* a sacred fire; the god of fire, Agni, mediator between men and gods, messenger who carries the sacrifice to them, protector from the terrors and spirits of darkness, and keeper of house and hearth. [perhaps, 'the quickly moving or agile one,' √aj, 1158: cf. Lat. *ignis*, 'fire,' *agilis*, 'agile'; akin, poss., is αἴγλη, 'flashing light.']

agni-kuṇḍa, *n.* round hole in the ground for the sacred fire.

agni-velā, *f.* fire-hour, time for kindling the sacred fire; afternoon.

agni-hotrá, *n.* fire-sacrifice (a burnt-offering of fresh milk).

agnihotra-hávaṇí, *f.* fire-sacrifice ladle.

agny-ādhéya, *n.* placing or setting up of the sacred fire. [acct, 1272.]

ágra, *n.* −1. front; agre, in front, before, in presence of, *w. gen.;* −2. beginning; agre, in the beginning, in the first place, first; −3. tip, end. [perhaps, 'that which goes before, leader,' √aj: cf. ἄγω, 'lead,' στρατ-ηγός, 'army-leader.']

agratás, *adv.* in front [1098c²]; before (one's self); *w.* kṛ, place in front, cause to lead. [agra, 1098b.]

agryá, *a.* foremost, best. [ágra, 1212c.]

aghá, *a.* distressful, harmful; *as n.* harm, trouble, evil; sin; sorrow. [like aṅhú, 'narrow,' and áṅhas, 'distress,' from √aṅgh or aṅh, 'straiten': cf. ἄχος, 'distress'; ἄγχω, Lat. *ango*, 'strangle'; AS. *ange*, 'anxious,' Ger. *enge*, 'narrow,' *Angst*, 'distress': for connection of mgs, cf. Eng. *straiten*, 'to narrow' and 'to distress.']

√ **aghāya** (aghāyáti). harm; plan mischief. [agha, 1059b.]

á-ghoracakṣus, *a.* not evil-eyed.

á-ghnya, *m.* bull (the animal that is 'hard to overcome,' or more exactly, 'not to be slain').

aghnyā, *f.* cow. [formed as a pendant to aghnya.]

aṅká, *m.* −1. the bend at the groin made by taking a sitting position, lap; −2. the bend just above the hip (where babes, sitting astride, are carried by Hindu women — *see* āroha); −3. hook; −4. (*like Eng.* pot-hook) mark, sign. [√añc: for 1, cf. ἀγκών, 'bend in arm or wall or shore'; for

3, cf. ὄγκος, Lat. *uncus*, AS. *ongel*, 'hook'; cf. Eng. *angle*, not a borrowed word.]

√ **aṅkhaya** (aṅkháyati [1056, 1067]). hook on, grapple. [from aṅka, 'hook,' despite the aspiration.]

+ **pari**, clasp, embrace.

√ **aṅg**. move, *in derivs.*

aṅgá, *asseverative particle.* yád aṅgá, just when; té aṅgá, they only.

áṅga, *n.* limb, member; *by synecdoche,* body, person, form. [√aṅg: for mg, cf. aṅgúli, aṅgúṣṭha.]

áṅgana, *n.* court. [orig., perhaps, 'gangway,' √aṅg.]

aṅganá, *f.* a (fair) form, *i.e.* a woman. [áṅga.]

áṅgāra, *m.* coal.

áṅgiras, *m.* −1. *orig., probably,* messenger; *esp.* messenger between gods and men; *by eminence,* Agni; −2. *as pl.* Angirases, a name applied by the Hindus to a certain race among their forefathers (perhaps because their intercourse with the gods was conceived as very intimate), these forefathers being regarded as half divine; −3. *as s.* the (mythical) ancestor of the Angirases.

aṅgúli, *f.* finger. [√aṅg, 1191: for mg, cf. áṅga.]

aṅgúṣṭha, *m.* thumb. [for mg, cf. áṅga.]

√ **ac** or **añc** (ácati, áñcati; akná, añcitá; -ácya). bend. [cf. aṅka and vbl añc.]

+ **ā**, bend.

a-cara, *a.* not moving; *as subst.* plant (as distinguished from animals).

a-cala, *a.* immovable; *as m.* mountain.

a-cit, *a.* not knowing; unwise; foolish.

á-citti, *f.* unwisdom; folly.

a-citvā, *grd.* without piling. [√1 ci.]

a-cintya, *a.* incomprehensible.

áccha, *vbl prefix.* to, unto; hither; *w.* √ 2 naq, yā, vah, vṛt; *often* acchā, 248a.

√ **aj** (ájati, -te). drive. [orig. 'put in motion': cf. Lat. *ago*, 'lead, drive'; ἄγω, 'lead': cf. also agra, ajira, áji.]

+ **ud**, drive out.

ajá, *m.* he-goat. [prob. 'the agile one,' √aj: cf. αἴξ, 'goat.']

a-jára, *a.* not aging; ageless.

ajarámaravat, *adv.* as if ageless and immortal. [ajara-amara, 1107, 1257.]

á-jasra, a. not dying out; perpetual (of fire).

ajá, f. she-goat. [see aja.]

á-jāta, a. unborn.

ajína, m. goat-skin; pelt. [aja: cf. αἴγίς, 'goat-skin, Aegis,' w. αἴξ, 'goat.']

ajirá, a. agile, swift. [√aj, 1188e: cf. Lat. agilis, 'agile.']

√ ajirāya (ajirāyate). be swift; press swiftly onward. [ajira, 1059b.]

a-jña, a. not knowing, ignorant; foolish; as m. fool.

á-jñāta, a. unknown. [√jñā: cf. ἄ-γνωτος, Lat. i-gnotus, Eng. un-couth, 'unknown.']

ajñāta-kulaçíla, a. whose family and character are unknown.

a-jñātvā, grd. without knowing.

a-jñāna, n. ignorance; -āt and -ātas, out of ignorance.

√ añc, see √ac.

añc, as vbl at end of cpds [see 407-9], turning, directed; e.g. úd-añc, directed upward. [for mg, cf. Eng. -ward (in to-ward, etc.), which is akin w. √vṛt, 'turn.']

√ añj or aj (anákti, añkté; ānáñja, ānajé [788]; áñjīt; aktá; aktvā; -áñjya, -ájya). —1. smear; anoint; —2. adorn. [cf. aktu: cf. Lat. ungo, 'anoint.']
+ á, anoint.
+ vi, —1. anoint; —2. adorn; and so, bring to notice; vyàkta: adorned, fair; manifest; —caus. make clear or manifest.
+ sam, —1. anoint; —2. adorn; —3. unite by anointing, 89¹⁹; —4. generalized, unite with, take to one's self (e.g. food), 88¹⁰.

añjali, m. the two hollowed and open hands placed side by side; the hands so placed and raised to the forehead, i.e. a gesture of reverent salutation; a double handful (as measure).

áñjas, adv. quickly, suddenly. [prob. adv. acc. or instr. of an obsolete subst. áñjas, 'a slippery way or a gliding motion,' √añj.]

√ aṭ (áṭati, -te; aṭiṣyáti; aṭitá; aṭitvá). wander about. [cf. √aṭ.]

aṭaní, f. the notched end of a bow.

aṭaví, f. forest. [perhaps, 'roaming-place,' √aṭ.]

aṇḍa, n. egg.

aṇḍa-ja, a. egg-born; as m. bird.

√ aṭ (áṭati, -te; aṭitá). wander about. [cf. √aṭ.]

a-tandrita, a. unwearied.

átas, adv. —1. (as abl. of pron. root a [1098], and synonymous w. asmāt) from it; so 22⁹, sc. pañkāt; ato 'nya, other than it, 68¹²; —2. from this (place), 83¹⁵; —3. from this (time), 96²¹; cf. ūrdhvam; then, 40¹⁶; —4. from this (cause), 35¹⁰; therefore, 27³, etc.; w. correl. yatas, 36³; hence; and so, 39⁴, 42²¹; so then, 73¹². [pron. root a, 502.]

áti, adv. across, beyond, past, over, as vbl prefix; in cpds, to excess, excessive, see 1289b; as prep. beyond, over. [cf. ἔτι, 'further, besides'; Lat. et, 'besides, and.']

atikrama, m. act of overstepping or overcoming. [√kram + ati.]

átithi, m. guest. ['wanderer,' √aṭ.]

ati-durvṛtta, a. excessively wicked.

ati-dūra, a. very far or distant; as n. great distance.

ati-bhāra, m. excessive burden.

ati-lāulya, n. excessive greediness.

ati-vṛṣṭi, f. excessive rain.

á-tiṣṭhant, a. not standing; restless. [√sthā.]

ati-saṃcaya, m. excessive accumulation.

ati-saṃnidhāna, n. excessive nearness.

atīndriya, a. transcending the senses; as n. soul, spirit. [ati + indriya, 1310a.]

atīva, adv. exceedingly; very. [ati + iva.]

a-tyājya, a. not to be abandoned.

aty-ugra, a. extraordinary. ['excessively strong.']

atyugra-puṇyapāpa, a. extraordinarily good and bad; as n. pl. extraordinarily good and bad deeds.

átra (átrā, 248a), adv. —1. (as loc. of pron. root a [1099⁴], and synonymous w. asmin) substantively: in it, 97¹⁰; in this case, 31⁵; in that case, 18¹⁷; on this point, 29²; adjectively: w. antare: in this interim, meantime, 24¹⁹, 45², 50²³, 55⁴; on this occasion, at this juncture, 19¹¹; atra sarasi, in this pool; —2. in this or that (place); here, 25¹⁶; there, 33⁵, 89⁴; in that world (opp. to 'in this world'), 87¹⁷⁹; —3. in that (time), then, 56¹². [pron. root a, 502.]

8

átri, *m.* Afri, name of a famous Rishi.

átha (**áthā**, 248a), *adv. expresses a sequence, temporal or resultant:* then; so; so then; accordingly; thereupon; —1. *temporal: e.g.* **áti drava, áthā · · úpehi**, run past, and then go unto · ·, 83¹⁸; *in apodosis after* **yadā**, 84⁵⋅⁶⋅⁷, 96²²; —2. *resultant: e.g.* **ma-rúdbhiḥ sakhyám te astu, átha jayāsi**, make friends with the Maruts, and then (if thou dost) thou shalt conquer, 82²ɴ.; —3. *very frequent as a simple continuative:* now; so; then; *usually at beginning of sentence (e.g.* 20¹) *or çloka (e.g.* 2⁶); *sometimes within the çloka (e.g.* 3¹⁴); *exceptionally at the end,* 13⁹; *at beginning of section or book,* now, 98¹⁶; here beginneth (*cf.* **íti**), 1¹; *sometimes much attenuated in meaning; often almost equivalent to a capital letter, to mark the beginning of a new clause, e.g.* 94¹⁸; *connecting parts of sentence,* 4¹¹; —4. *pleonastically w.* **tatas**, 13⁹; *mere verse-filler,* 10¹⁹; —5. **átho**, *i.e.* **átha u**, and also, 90¹⁶; —6. *serving as a point d'appui for an enclitic, which may thus precede its word: e.g.* **devo, 'tha vā yakṣas**, a god or a Yaksha, *instead of* **devo, yakṣo vā**, 8¹⁸; *so* 2¹²; *in this use,* **vā : atha vā : : que : atque;** *cf.* 27²¹; *cf.* **vā**; —7. **atha vā**, or rather, 26⁷ɴ. [pron. root **a**, 1101, 502; later form of **ádhā** (which is more common in the Veda): cf. Lat. *at*, 'then, further, but.']

√ **ad** (**átti**; **atsyáti**; **áttum**). eat; consume. [cf. *ēdω*, Lat. *edo*, AS. *etan*, Eng. *eat:* cf. **anna.**]

ád, *vbl.* eating, consuming, *in cpds.*

ada, *a.* eating, *in cpds.* [√**ad.**]

a-daṅṣṭrin, *a.* without tusks *or* large teeth.

á-datta, *a.* not given.

a-dantajáta, *a.* not having teethed. ['not having grown teeth,' for **a-jātadanta.**]

adás [501], *pron.* yon, yonder, that, that there, *in opposition to the one here or just mentioned: e.g.* **asáu**, 22⁷, that one (the traveller—*last mentioned at* 20¹⁹); *so* 31¹⁰; **asáv amútra, ayam asmin**, that one in that world, this one in this, 103⁷; that one (*correl.* **ya**), 7⁶, 37¹¹; *as designation of persons not to be named,* so-and-so, N. or M.;

asáv aham, I am so-and-so, 61¹⁴; 60³¹; 103⁵; *follows at a distance the word to which it refers, thus emphasizing it,* 23¹. [see 501 and 503.]

áditi, *a.* without bond *or* limit; infinite; *as f.* infinity, the endless heaven, 79¹⁹; infinity, *personified as a goddess,* Aditi, 75⁸. [apparently **a + -diti**, acct. 1304a²: **diti**, 'bond,' would be a reg. deriv. of √3 **dā**, 'bind,' but does not occur as such, although there is a word **díti**, q.v., of quite different mg and origin.]

a-dína, *a.* not depressed.

adīnátman, *a.* with cheerful spirit, undaunted. [**átman.**]

á-durmaṅgala, *f.* **-í**, *a.* bringing no bad luck. [for declension, cf. **sumaṅgála, -galí**, and 355b.]

a-dṛṣṭa, *a.* unseen, unnoticed. [√**dṛç.**]

adṛṣṭa-káma, *m.* love for one not yet seen.

a-devá, *m.* non-god, who is no god. [1288a⁴.]

adbhís, *see* 393.

ádbhuta, *a.* wonderful; *as n.* wonder. [despite **anatidbhuta**, prob. from **at(i)-bhūta**, 'transcending what has existed,' 1310a: cf. **ambara.**]

ádbhuta-rūpa, *a.* having wonderful beauty.

adyá, *adv.* to-day; **adya niçi**, in this night (just past), 51⁸; now; **adya yávat**, until now; **adya_árabhya**, from now on. [perhaps from **-a-dyavi**, 'on this day,' 1122f, see **dyu**: cf. Lat. *ho-die*, 'to-day.']

a-dravya, *n.* non-thing, unworthy object.

ádri, *m.* rock; stone; *esp.* Soma-stone (for bruising the Soma); missile stone.

adrivant, *a.* having *or* armed with the hurling-stone.

ádha (**ádhā**, 248a), *Vedic adv. expressing a sequence:* then; so, 79⁸; so then, 89¹⁸; **adha yad**, just then when, 76¹⁴; (then, *i.e.* besides, *i.e.*) and, 77¹⁸, 78⁶. [1104⁸: cf. **átha.**]

a-dhanya, *a.* not rich; poor.

adhamá [525], *a.* lowest; worst. [cf. **adhas** and 474: cf. Lat. *infimus*, 'lowest.']

ádhara [525], *a.* lower. [cf. **adhas** and 474: cf. Lat. *inferus*, 'lower'; Eng. *under*.]

á-dharma, *m.* unrighteousness.

adhaḥ-çāyin, a. lying low, i.e. sleeping on the ground.

adhás, adv. below; down.

adhástāt, adv. below; as prep., w. gen. [1130], under. [adhas, 1100b.]

ádhi, adv. over, besides, in addition, 96¹⁶; as prep. above, over, on; w. instr. (of smú only), away over, 79¹¹; w. abl. from, out of, 103⁴; w. loc.: over, 90⁷; on, 70¹³, 92¹¹.

adhika, a. (like Eng. over in adj. uses) additional; surpassing the usual measure, superior, extraordinary; as n. surplus. [ádhi, 1222a.]

adhika-rūpavant, a. surpassingly or most beautiful.

adhikānurāga, m. superior affection or most affection. [anurāga.]

adhikāra, m. authority; office; duties of office. [√ 1 kṛ + adhi, 'put over or in office.']

ádhijya, a. having the bow-string up or on, i.e. strung. [2 jyā, 1305.]

adhi-pa, m. lord; ruler. ['over-keeper,' 1289a: cf. 354.]

ádhi-pati, m. over-lord; sovereign. [1289a.]

adhi-pā [352], m. lord. ['over-keeper,' 1289a.]

adhiṣṭhāna, n. standing-place; (of the soul) a dwelling-place or manifestation. [√ sthā + adhi.]

adhunā, adv. now.

adho-nivīta, a. having the sacred cord (worn) low. [adhas.]

adhyayana, n. reading; study, esp. of the Veda. [√ i + adhi, 1150. 1a.]

adhyāya, m. reading; study, esp. of the Veda; (like Eng. lesson), lectio, chapter, 56¹⁶, 58¹⁵, etc. [√ i + adhi, 1148. 2.]

adhvará, m. religious or liturgical service; sacrifice, esp. Soma-sacrifice.

√ adhvarya (adhvaryáti). perform sacrifice. [adhvara, 1059d.]

adhvaryú, m. priest, who did the actual work of the sacrifice, and appears in the oldest period as companion of the hotṛ — see ṛtvij. [√ adhvarya, 1178h.]

an, before consonants a, negative prefix. [1121a; acct, 1288a, 1304a: cf. áv-, á-, Lat. in-, Eng. un-.]

√ an (ániti [631]; ána; ániṣus; aniṣyáti; anitá; ánitum; -ánya). breathe, blow; live. [cf. anila, ἄνεμος, Lat. anima, 'current of air'; Goth. an-an, 'breathe.']
+ pra, breathe.

aná, pron. stem, see idam.

an-agha, a. faultless.

anadváh [404], m. bull. ['cart-drawing,' ánas + váh.]

an-adhigata, a. un-studied.

an-anuṣṭhāna, n. non-observance, neglect.

an-antará, —1. a. having no interval; immediately adjoining; -am, adv. immediately afterwards, afterwards; thereupon; —2. as n. non-interval, in sam-.

an-amīvá, a. without sickness or trouble, well; as n. weal. [ámīvā, 1304a.]

an-arghya, a. not to be priced, priceless. anarghyatva, n. pricelessness. [1239.]

an-artha, m. non-advantage; disadvantage.

anala, m. fire.

an-avadyá, a. not un-praiseworthy; blameless, faultless.

anavadyāṅga, f. -ī, a. having a faultless body. [áṅga.]

an-avekṣa, a. without any looking around; -am, adv. without looking around. [avekṣā.]

an-avekṣamāṇa, a. not looking around. [√ īkṣ + ava.]

an-açrú, a. without tears. [áçru, 1304a.]

a-naṣṭa, a. not lost. [√ 1 naç.]

ánaṣṭa-paçu, a. who loses nothing from his herd. [prop. 'having a not lost herd.']

ánas, n. cart for heavy burden. [cf. Lat. onus, 'burden.']

án-āgata, a. not arrived; not (yet) come, impending, future. [√ gam + ā.]

anāgatavant, a. having to do with the future. [1233.]

anāgata-vidhātṛ, m. arranger for the future; Forethought, name of a fish.

án-āgas, a. without sin. [acct, 1304a²].

an-ādhṛṣyá, a. un-approachable. [acct, 1285.]

an-āmayá, a. without disease, healthy; as n. health.

an-āmayitnú, a. not sickening; healing.

8 *

an-āyudhá, a. weaponless; defenceless. [áyudha, 1304a.]

an-āruhya, grd. without going into (danger). [√ruh + ā.]

anila, m. wind. [√an, 1189.]

á-niviçamāna, a. not going to rest. [acct, 1283.]

a-niveçaná, a. having no resting-place, unsettled. [nivéçana, 1304a.]

an-iṣṭa, a. undesired; disagreeable; un-approved, unlawful. [√1 iṣ.]

aniṣṭa-cintana, n. the thinking about something unlawful.

an-iṣṭvā, grd. without sacrificing. [√yaj.]

ánīka, n. —1. face; —2. fig. appearance; —3. of a hatchet (face, i.e.), sharp edge; —4. front, and so, by synecdoche, troop. [so Lat. acies has mgs 3 and 4.]

a-nītijña, a. not knowing discreet conduct.

ánu, prep. after, along, toward; w. acc. along or over; after, i.e. according to.

anugati, f. a going after. [√gam + anu.]

anucará, a. going after; as m. attendant; companion. [√car + anu.]

anu-jīvin, a. living upon, dependent; as m. a dependent. [√jīv + anu.]

ánu-tta, ppl. see √1 dā + anu.

á-nutta, a. un-moved, i.e. invincible. [√nud.]

anuttama, a. most highest; best, most excellent; supreme. [lit. 'most best,' formal superl. to anuttara, which is itself logically a superl.]

an-uttara, a. not having a superior, i.e. best. [for mg, cf. niḥçreyasa.]

án-udita, a. not arisen. [√i + ud.]

an-udyoga, m. non-exertion.

anunaya, m. conciliation. [√nī + anu.]

an-upakārin, a. not doing or unable to do a friendly service.

anu-pūrva, a. following the one preceding, one after another; -ám, adv. in regular order. [1310a.]

ánumati, f. approbation; favor (of gods to the pious); personified, Grace. [√man + anu.]

anumāna, n. the forming of a conception. [√1 mā + anu, 'conceive.']

anurāga, m. affection. [√raj + anu.]

anurodha, m. regard. [√1 rudh + anu.]

anurodhin, a. having (some) regard for. [√1 rudh + anu.]

an-ulbaṇá, a. not lumpy; smooth or perfect (of a weft). [1288a⁴.]

anuvṛtti, f. sequence, and so, continuance. [√vṛt + anu.]

ánu-vrata, a. acting according to the will or command (of another), obedient; devoted to, w. acc. [272], 6¹⁶, 100⁴. [1310a: cf. apavrata.]

anuçaya, m. repentance. [perhaps 'that which lies down after one or follows one to his bed': √çī + anu.]

anuṣṭhāna, n. devotion to, observance. [√sthā + anu.]

anuṣṭheya, grdv. to be accomplished. [see √sthā + anu, and 963a.]

anusaraṇa, n. a going after, a searching. [√sṛ + anu.]

anustaraṇa, a. strewing over, covering over; —f. anustáraṇī (sc. go), a cow, slaughtered at the funeral ceremony, and the pieces of which are used for covering over the corpse, limb by limb. [√stṛ + anu.]

anūcānā, see 807 and 784.

an-ṛta, a. untrue; ánṛta, n. untruth; wrong. [ṛtá, 1288a.]

an-eka, a. not one, i.e. more than one; many.

anekadhā, adv. many times. [1104.]

anekaças, adv. in large numbers. [1106.]

á-nedya, a. not to be blamed; blameless. [acct, 1285a.]

an-enás, a. free from guilt. [énas, 1304a.]

an-oṁkṛta, a. not having om uttered, i.e. unaccompanied by om. [see oṁkṛta.]

ánta, m. —1. vicinity, proximity; —2. border; limit; end. [see ánti: cf. Eng. end.]

antaḥ-pura, n. inner stronghold or citadel; inner apartment of the royal citadel, gynaeceum, harem, 2²¹. [antar, 1289a.]

ántaka, m. ender (death). [ánta, 1222a.]

anta-kara, a. end-making; as m. destroyer.

ántama, *a.* nearest, very near; *as m.* intimate, companion. [see **ánta**, mg 1, and 474: cf. Lat. *intumus*, 'inmost.']

antár, *adv.* inward, inwardly, within; *prep., w. loc.:* between, among, within; along with, 78¹²; cf. **Wi, gam, dhā**. [cf. Lat. *inter*, 'between.']

1 **ántara**, *a.* very near, *only in V. and B.* [see **ánta**, mg 1, and 474.]

2 **ántara**, *a.* inner; *as n.* —1. the interior, middle; **jala_antare**, in the middle of the water = in the water, 50⁷; **vana_antara-saṁcārin**, wandering in the forest, 49¹³; —2. interval—*see* **atra**; —3. distance between two things; the difference, 29⁷; —4. difference, *at end of cpds* [1302c 5]: ···-**antara**, that which has a difference of ··, *i.e.* another ··, 33¹, 38¹², ²³, 43⁶; —5. occasion, juncture, 19¹¹. [**antár**: cf. *ἕντερα*, 'inwards, guts.']

antar-ātman, *m.* the in(-dwelling) soul; heart. [1280.]

antári-kṣa, *n.* the atmosphere, *see* 92⁹ ɴ. ['lying *or* situate in the middle' between heaven and earth: **antar** + **kṣa**: for mg, cf. τὸ μεσηγύ, as used of the aerial space traversed by Iris.]

antarikṣa-ga, *a.* moving in the air; *as m.* bird. [for mg, cf. **khaga**.]

antarikṣa-loká, *m.* atmosphere-world [1280b]; the atmosphere, regarded as a separate world.

antar-gata, *a.* gone within, *i.e.* being within; hidden.

antardhāna, *n.* a hiding; disappearance; *w.* **i**, disappear. [√1dhā + antar, q.v.]

antar-lajjā, *f.* inward shame. [1280.]

antar-vedi, *a.* situate within the sacrificial bed; **-dí**, *adv.* within the sacrificial spot. [1310a.]

ánti, *adv.* opposite, in front, before; near. [see **ánta**: cf. ἀντί, 'opposite,' ἄντα, 'face to face'; Lat. *ante*, 'before'; *anticus*, 'former, ancient'; AS. *and-swaru*, Eng. *an-swer*.]

1 **antiká**, *n.* neighborhood *or* presence; *used like* **samipa**, *q.v.* [**ánti**.]

2 **antika**, *for* **anta** *at end of cpds*, 1222, 1307; **grahaṇa_antika**, having acquisition as its conclusion.

antimá, *a.* last. [**ánti**, 474: for mg ('endmost'?), cf. **ánta** 2, and **antya**.]

ante-vāsin, *m.* pupil. [lit. 'abiding in the vicinity,' 1250c.]

antya, *a.* being at the end, last; lowest; of lowest caste. [**ánta**.]

antya-jāti, *a.* having lowest birth.

antyajātitā, *f.* condition of having lowest birth. [1237.]

antya-strī, *f.* woman of lowest caste.

andhá, *a.* blind; blinding (of darkness).

ándhas, *n.* darkness. [cf. **andhá**.]

ánna, *n.* food; *esp.* rice, *usually* boiled, the chief food of the Hindus; grain. [√ad, 1177a: cf. ἔδαρ, Lat. *esca*, *ₑed-ca*, 'food'; *ador*, 'spelt'; AS. *āta*, Eng. *oat*.]

anna-prāçana, *n.* rice-feeding, the first feeding of an infant with rice.

anna-rasa, *n.* food and drink. [1253b.]

ánnavant, *a.* provided with food. [**ánna**.]

anyá [523], *pron. a.* another, other, else; **anyac ca**, and another thing, *i.e.* again, *see* **ca** 3; other than, different from, *w. abl.*, 3⁴, 24¹⁹, 68¹², 104¹⁴; *otiose*, 2¹²; **yad anyat kiṁ cana**, whatever else, 9¹⁶; **anya** *or* **eka** ·· **anya**, the one ·· the other, 90¹³, 29⁸. [cf. ἔνιοι, 'some'; Goth. *an-þar*, 'other,' Eng. *other*.]

anyatama, *a.* one of several, some one. [**anya**, 525³.]

anyátas, *adv.* from another direction [1098b], otherwise; elsewhere [1098c³], to another place. [**anya**.]

anyáthā, *adv.* otherwise, 18⁹; *w.* **bhū**, become otherwise, suffer change, 17⁵; otherwise than it really is, falsely, 35²⁰; otherwise (*i.e.* if not), 48⁸. [**anya**.]

anya-hrada, *m.* another pool.

anye-dyús, *adv.* on the next day. ['altero die': 1250c.]

anyonya, *pron. a.* one the other, *for* **anyò 'nyá** [175a], *the first part being a crystallized nom. s. m.* [1314c]; *w. value of gen.*, **anyonyam prati hṛcchaya** = **anyasya_anyam prati h.**, love of one towards the other, 2¹⁹. [see **paraspara**.]

anváñc [409c], *a.* directed after, following after, being behind. [**ánu** + **áñc**.]

anvita, *see* √**i** + **anu**.

áp [393], *f. plurale tantum.* water; waters.
[unrelated to Lat. *aqua*, 'water,' Goth.
ahva, 'stream.']

ápa, *prep.* away, forth, off; *opp. of* **úpa**,
see √i, kr. [cf. ảπό, Lat. *ab*, 'from';
Eng. *off*, *of*.]

apakāra, *m.* injury. [√1kr + apa.]

apakārin, *a.* injuring. [do.]

apacāra, *m.* going off; absence. [√car
: apa.]

á-patighnī, *a. f.* not husband-slaying.
[402: acct, 1288a.]

ápatya, *n.* offspring; child; young (of
animals). [ápa, 'off,' 1245b.]

a-pád [391], *a.* footless. [cf. ảποδ-ες,
'halt': 1304a.]

apabhraṣṭa, *a.* fallen off; deviating (from
good grammar); provincial. [√bhraṅç +
apa.]

ápara [525], *pron. a.* hinder, *opp. of* pūrva;
following a former one (pūrva), 86[13];
later; westerly, *opp. to* pūrva — *cf.* prāñc;
a following one, *i.e.* an other; aparam ca,
and another thing, and further, *see* ca 3;
—apari [*cf.* 355b], *f. pl.* the future
(days), the future. [lit. 'remoter,' fr. ápa,
474.]

a-parāñmukha, *a.* not having an averted
face, *i.e.* not turning the back, 5[19].

á-parājita, *a.* unconquered; *w.* diç, the
northeast quarter, 99[22] N. [√ji.]

aparādha, *m.* sin. [√rādh + apa.]

a-parijāta, *a.* not completely grown (of
an embryo), *i.e.* prematurely born, still-
born. [see pari-jāta and ref.]

a-pariṇīya, *grd.* without any leading
around. [√nī.]

á-parimita, *a.* unmeasured, unlimited.
[√1mā.]

ápa-vrata, *a.* disobedient; stubborn.
['away from command,' 1310a: cf. ánu-
vrata.]

apás, *see* ap.

ápas, *n.* work. [perhaps from √⁎ap, 'reach,
take hold of' — see √āp: cf. Lat. *opus*,
'work.']

apāya, *m.* a going away; what takes one
from the mark (*cf.* upāya); danger;
disadvantage; diminution. [√i + apa,
1148. 1a: for mg, cf. Eng. *untoward*.]

a-párá, *a.* boundless. [pārá: acct, 1304a.]

ápi, *indecl.* unto, close upon *or* on; —1.
prep. to, *w.* √gam; —2. *adv.* (thereto, besides, *i.e.*) further, also; *connecting clauses*
(63[23]) *or words* (65[11]); *connecting sentences*,
api ca, and besides, 29[9], *see* ca 3; · · api
· · api, both · · and, 54[23]; · ·, · · ca api,
and, 5[12], 26[5]; · · ca, · · cāpi, both · · and
also, 12[1]; · ·, · · cāiva, · · cāpi, 65[15]; · · cāpi,
· · ca, 3[21], 16[11]; · · cāpi, · · ca, · · ca, 16[6],
60[10]; na · ·, na᎐api · ·, neither · ·, nor · ·,
9[9]; na · ·, na cāpi, 22[13]; na · ·, na · ·, · · api
ca, neither · ·, nor · ·, nor also · ·, 2[13]; · ·,
· · vā, · · vā᎐api, either · ·, or · ·, or even · ·,
62[1]; —3. also, too, *immediately following*
the emphasized word, 6[12], 11[3], 21[18], 24[21];
mām api, me too, 41[20]; —4. even, *imme-*
diately following the emphasized word, and
often marking a circumstance under which a
thing is true where this is not to be expected:
e.g. 2[13], 28[7, 18], 33[19]; tathā᎐api, so even, *i.e.*
nevertheless, 21[11]; *concessively,* although,
29[1], 21[14], 51[1, 5]; *w.* na, not even, 19[15]; *w.*
indefinites, kadā cid api na, not ever at
all, 31[14], 32[5]; —5. but, *immediately follow-*
ing a new subject, after change of subject,
6[15], 28[21], 32[22], 41[17, 20, 21]; —6. at least,
28[9, 11]; —7. *converts an interr. into an indef.*
[507]; *so* ka, 17[11], etc.; katham, 51[1].
[cf. ἐπί, 'on, upon'; perhaps Lat. *op-*, *ob-*,
'unto, on.']

á-pīḍayant, *a.* non-oppressing. [√piḍ.]

a-pūrvá, *a.* having no predecessor; un-
precedented; incomparable. [pūrva:
acct, 1304a.]

apekṣā, *f.* regard; expectation. [√īkṣ +
apa.]

á-praja, *a.* having no offspring, childless.
[prajā, 367b.]

a-prajñāta, *a.* undistinguished *or* not
clearly to be known. [√jñā.]

a-pratarkya, *a.* un-imaginable.

a-pratima, *a.* without match *or* equal;
unqualled. [pratimā, 367b.]

á-pratīta, *a.* not gone against; not with-
stood; invincible. [√i + prati.]

a-pratta, *a.* not given (in marriage).
[√1dā + pra, 1087e.]

á-prayucchant, *a.* not heedless; watchful. [√2yu ⊢ pra, q.v.]

á-priya, a. not dear; disliked; disagreeable.

apsarás, f. one of a class of semi-divine beings, wives of the Gandharvas; an Apsaras, 67^{12} ʀ. [1151. 2d.]

a-buddhimant, a. unwise; foolish.

ábda, m. lit. water-giving; (then, perhaps, rainy season, and so) year. [ap + da, but w. irreg. acct, 1269: for mg, see varṣa.]

a-bhakṣya, a. not to be eaten; as n. that which ought not to be eaten.

á-bhaya, a. dangerless; as n. safety; feeling of safety; superl. greatest safety. [bhayá: acct, 1304a².]

a-bhāva, m. non-existence; absence; lack.

a-bhāvin, a. not about to be, not destined to be.

abhí, adv. to, unto; against; frequent as vbl prefix; as prep. unto, w. acc. [cf. ἀμφί, 'around'; Lat. ambi-, amb-, 'on both sides, around'; AS. ymbe, Ger. um, 'around'; for mg, cf. abhitas.]

abhijña, a. knowing, acquainted with. [√jñā + abhi, 333.]

abhítas, adv. on both sides; on all sides, 101^{10}; around; near. [abhí.]

abhidrohá, m. offense. [√druh + abhi.]

abhidhā́, f. name; cf. ā́khyā. [√1 dhā + abhi, q.v.]

abhidhā́na, n. name; designation. [do.]

abhidhyā́na, n. the thinking upon. [√dhyā + abhi.]

abhiniveça, m. inclination towards. [√viç + abhi-ni.]

abhibhāṣin, a. addressing. [√bhāṣ + abhi, 1183³.]

abhíbhūti, f. superiority; as a. [1157. 2], superior. [√bhū + abhi.]

abhíbhūty-ojas, a. having superior might.

abhímāti, f. hostile plot; concrete, plotter, foe. [√man + abhi, 1157. 1d : ā irreg.]

abhi-mukha, a. having the face towards; facing; turned towards. [1305.]

abhivāda, m. salutation; at 60^{22}, signification. [√vad + abhi.]

abhivādana, n. salutation. [do.]

abhivādin, a. signifying. [do.]

abhivādya, grdv. to be saluted. [do.]

abhi-çiras, a. having the head towards, w. acc. [1305.]

a-bhīta, a. fearless; -vat [1107], fearlessly.

abhīpsu, a. desirous of obtaining, w. acc. [√āp + abhi, 1178f, 1038.]

abhy-adhika, a. additional; more.

abhy-antara, a. situated in the inside [1310a]; as n. interior; interval.

abhy-ātma, a. directed towards one's self [1310a]; -ám, adv. towards one's self [1310d].

abhyāsa, m. study. [√2 as + abhi, q.v.]

abhrá, n. rain-cloud. [cf. ὄμβρος, 'rain'; Lat. imber, 'rain': cf. ámbhas and ambu, 'water.']

abhrāvakāçika, a. (having, i.e.) affording an opportunity for the rain, exposing one's self to the rain. [abhra + avakāça, 1307.]

√ am (ámīti [634]; āmé; āmáyati). press on violently; harm; caus. [1041²], harm; be sick. [cf. aṅsa.]

áma, pron. this; he. [508⁴: cf. amā́.]

a-mantú, a. without intention. [mántu: 1304a.]

a-mára, a. deathless; immortal; as m. an immortal, a god; -vat [1107], adv. like a god. [mará: 1304a² end.]

amarottama, a. chief of gods. [uttama.]

amaropama, a. like a god. [upamā, 367b.]

á-martya, a. immortal.

a-marṣa, m. non-endurance; impatience; anger.

a-mahātman, a. not high-minded.

amā́, adv. at home, chez soi; amā́ kṛ, keep by one. [áma, 1112a and e.]

amātya, m. inmate of the same house, relative. [amā́, 1245b.]

a-māyā, f. no guile; sincerity.

amā-vāsa, m. a dwelling (of the moon) at home (i.e. with the sun).

amāvāsyā, a. of amā́vāsa; f. -ā̀, w. or without rā́tri, the night of amā́vāsa, i.e. night of new moon. [1212d 4.]

a-mithuna, a. not forming pairs (of both sexes).

a-mīmāṅsya, a. not to be called in question.

ámīva, n., but generally -ā, f. plague, distress; as m. tormenting spirit. [√am.]

amīva-cátana, f. -ī, a. driving away disease. [1271.]

amīva-hán [402], a. slaying the tormenting spirits.

amú, pron. root, see adas. [503².]

amútas, adv. from there, opp. of itas; there. [amu.]

amútra, adv. there; in the other world, opp. of iha or asmin (loke). [amú.]

amuyá, adv. so. [amú, 1112a, e end.]

a-mŕta, a. immortal; as subst. an immortal; as n. immortality; the drink of immortality, ἀμβροσία. ['not dead,' mṛtá, 1284a: cf. ἄ-μβροτος, 'immortal.']

amŗtatvá, n. immortality. [amŗta.]

ámbara, n. garment; sky. [prob. 'covering, envelope,' √1 vŗ + anu, for an(u)-vara: cf. adbhuta.]

ambu, n. water. [see abhrá.]

ambu-ja, a. water-born; as n. lotus.

ámbhas, n. water. [see abhrá.]

áya, a. subst. going, a going. [√i, 1148. 1a b.]

áyana, n. a going; place of going, way; course; esp. course (of the sun from one solstice to the other), i.e. half-year. [√i, 1150. 1a.]

áyas, n. metal; iron. [cf. Old Lat. ais, gen. ais-is, Lat. aes, 'metal, bronze'; AS. ār, 'bronze;' Eng. ore; perhaps AS. ísern, íren, Eng. iron, 'ferrum, ferreus.']

ayasmáya, a. iron. [see maya.]

a-yúj, a. not paired; in uneven numbers. [cf. ἄ-ζυξ, 'unyoked.']

a-yujá, a. not paired, uneven. [cf. ἄ-ζυγος, 'unpaired'; also ζυγὰ ἢ ἄζυγα, the game 'even or odd.']

á-yuddha, n. no fight. [1288a.]

a-yoddhŕ, m. non-fighter, coward. [1288a¹.]

ará, m. spoke. [√ŗ, caus. 'fit in.']

árana, a. distant, strange.

aráni, f. piece of wood for kindling fire by attrition.

áranya, n. wilderness, forest. ['strange land,' fr. árana.]

aranya-rájya, n. forest-sovereignty.

aranya-vāsin, a. dwelling in the forest.

aranyāní, f. wilderness. [áranya, cf. 1223b.]

a-rapás, a. without infirmity; whole. [rápas, 1304a.]

áram, adv. so as to fit or suit, ready, at hand, enough; w. kŗ, make ready, serve, 79¹; w. gam, attend upon. [adv. acc. of ara, √ŗ, 1111d: cf. alam.]

á-rāti, f. non-favor; malignity; personified, pl., malign hags. [acct, 1288a.]

arí [343d], a. —1. eager, esp. in one's relations to the gods, and so, pious; —2. greedy; —3. hostile; as m. enemy. [√ŗ, 'go for': cf. árya.]

á-rișta, a. unharmed. [√riș: acct, 1284.]

ariștátāti, f. unharmedness, health. [árișta, 1238.]

aruná, a. ruddy; as m. Aruna, name of a teacher, 95¹¹. [cf. aruṣá.]

a-rundhatí, f. Arundhatī, name of the faint star Alkor in Ursa Major, conceived as consort of the Seven Rishis. [√rudh, 691: acct, 1283a.]

aruṣá, f. áruṣí, a. ruddy. [see 362b²: cf. aruná.]

are, word of address. Ah! [voc. of ari, 1135c: cf. re.]

a-roga, a. not having disease, diseaseless.

arká, m. the sun. [√ŗc, 216.1.]

arghá, m. worth, price. [√arh.]

arghya, a. of price or that may be priced. [argha, 1212.]

√ arc, see √ŗc.

arcís, n. flame. [√ŗc, 1153.]

√ arj, see √2 ŗj.

arjana, n. acquisition. [√2 ŗj, 'get.']

árjuna, a. silver-white. [√3 ŗj, q.v.]

ártha, m. —1. aim, object, purpose, errand, sake; artham and arthe [1302c 4], for the sake of, on account of, for, esp. frequent at end of cpds; —2. (object, i.e.) thing, matter, affair, cause, business; —3. (object, i.e.) advantage, profit (w. instr.), wealth, property; —4. aim, intent, meaning, 59¹⁵. ['that which one goes for,' √ŗ, 1163.]

artha-tattva, n. true state of the matter or case.

√ arthaya (artháyate, -ti). seek for an object. [artha, 1067.]

+ abhi, ask, entreat.
+ pra, desire, sue for.

arthārjana, *n.* acquisition of an object. [arjana.]

arthín, *a.* having an object, desiring, seeking; (begging, *i.e.*) needy. [artha.]

arthya, *a.* wealthy. [artha.]

ardhá, *a.* half; *as m.* the half.

ardharcá, *m.* half-stanza. [ardha + ṛca.]

árdhika, *a.* amounting to half. [ardha.]

árpaṇa, *n.* the sending, consignment, entrusting. [caus. of √ṛ.]

árbuda, *n.* a hundred millions.

arbuda-çikhara, *m.* Million-peaks, name of a mountain.

aryá, *a.* faithful; attached, kindly, 79³. [' going eagerly to,' √ṛ: cf. árya.]

aryamán [426a], *m.* bosom-friend, *esp.* a bridegroom's friend, παρανύμφιος; Aryaman, name of an Aditya (invoked at the wedding, and often with play upon the appellative mg of the word). [aryá.]

arvāk-kālika, *a.* belonging to hither or nearer time, posterior; -tā, *f.* posteriority. [arvāñc (1249a) + kāla, 1222c 2.]

arvā́ñc [409a], *a.* directed hitherwards; *w.* kṛ, bring hither; *w.* nud, thrust hither, *i.e.* downwards.

√ arh (árhati, -te; arháyati). deserve; have a right to; *w. inf.*, be able; *w. inf.*, *as a weak imperative,* 7¹¹; caus. give a right to, presént with.

arha, *a.* deserving; worthy; fit. [√arh.]

a-lakṣaṇá, *a.* without any characteristic mark; without special mark, *i.e.* plain, unornamented. [lakṣaṇá.]

á-lakṣita, *a.* unnoticed. [√lakṣaya.]

a-labhamāna, *a.* not catching.

álam, *adv.* enough; *sometimes equiv. to an adj.,* adequate, fitting, ready; —*w. instr.* enough with, have done with; —*w.* kṛ, make ready, adorn; sv-alaṁkṛta, well adorned; sam-alaṁkṛta, well (sam *intens.*, 1077b) adorned. [later form of áram.]

a-lavaṇa, *a.* not salt.

a-lasá, *a.* not lively; without energy; slothful; tired.

a-lobha, *m.* non-greed; absence of cupidity.

álpa, *a.* small.

alpa-dhī́, *a.* small-minded, of small intelligence.

alpaçás, *adv.* to a small degree. [alpa.]

√ av (ávati; áva; ávīt; aviṣyáti; ūtá; -ā́vya). —1. set a-going; —2. further, favor, wish well; —3. refresh; —4. have pleasure in (*acc.*). [cf. Lat. *avēre,* 'have pleasure in,' *ave,* 'hail.']

+ pra, show forth favor; *then,* be attentive *or* heedful (*as, conversely, in Eng.* attention *has come to mean* 'act of kindness *or* courtesy').

áva, *vbl prefix.* down; off.

ávakā, *f.* grassy swamp-plant, Blyxa octandra Richard.

avakāçá, *m.* —1. open place; —2. (place, *and so*) opportunity. [√kāç + ava.]

avajñā, *f.* contempt. [√jñā + ava: for mg, cf. avamāna.]

avatāra, *m.* descent, *esp.* of supernatural beings to the earth; an epiphany; incarnation, *Anglo-Indian* avatár. [√tṛ + ava.]

ávatta, *see* 1087e.

avadāna, *n.* cutting off. [√2 dā + ava.]

a-vadyá, *a.* un-praiseworthy; *as n.* imperfection. [1285.]

√ avadhīraya (avadhīrayati). despise; reject.

a-vadhyá, *a.* not to be harmed, inviolable. [vádhya, 1285.]

avadhya-bhāva, *m.* inviolability, 35ⁿ¹.

avanata-kāya, *a.* with bent down body, 34¹⁷. [√nam.]

avamāna, *m.* contempt; self-contempt, 50¹⁴. [√man + ava: for mg, cf. avajñā.]

avalambitavya, *grdv.* to be held on to. [√lamb + ava.]

a-vaçá, *a.* not willing *or* submissive; uncontrolled. [váça: acct, 1288a⁴.]

avaçyam, *adv.* necessarily, surely. [fr. an unused adj. a-vaçya, 'unyielding.']

ávas, *n.* furtherance; grace. [√av.]

avás, *adv.* downwards; *w. abl.* [1128], down from. [cf. áva.]

avasá, *n.* refreshment, nourishment. [√av, mg 3.]

avasara, *m.* occasion. [√sṛ + ava: for mg, cf. Lat. *cāsus,* 'occasion,' *w. cadere,* 'fall,' and Ger. *Fall,* 'case, instance,' *w. fallen,* 'fall.']

avasāna, *n.* place of rest. [√sā + ava.]

avasthā́, *f.* state, condition. [√sthā + ava: for mg, cf. Lat. *status* w. *stāre*.]

a-vahant, *a.* not flowing, standing. [√vah, mg 4.]

a-vācya, *a.* not to be spoken to.

avāñc [409a], *a.* directed downwards; *acc. s. n.* avā́k, *adv.* downwards, in depth.

ávi, *m.* sheep; *as f.* ewe. [cf. ὄις, *ὄϜις*, Lat. *ovis*, 'sheep'; Eng. *ewe.*]

a-vicchindant, *a.* not severing. [√chid.]

a-vicchinna, *a.* not severed, continuous. [do.]

a-vijñāya, *grd.* without discerning. [√jñā.]

a-vijñeya, *a.* unknowable. [do.]

a-vidāsin, *a.* not drying up, perennial. [√das.]

á-vidvā́ns, *a.* unwise; *as m.* fool. [acct, 1288a.]

a-vidhavā́, *f.* not widow. [vidhávā: acct, 1288a⁴.]

a-vidhānatas, *adv.* not according to regulation.

a-vipluta, *a.* not dishonored; unsullied. [√plu + vi, q.v.]

a-viveka, *a.* without discrimination.

avivekatā́, *f.* lack of judgment. [1237.]

a-vicañka, *a.* without hesitation, unhesitating. [vicañkā, 334², 1304a.]

a-viṣaya, *m.* a non-province; something out of one's line *or* that one has no business to do; unlawful thing.

a-vṛká, *a.* not harmful; -ám, *adv.* harmlessly, lovingly. [vṛka: acct, 1288a⁴.]

avekṣā́, *f.* a looking around. [√īkṣ + ava, 1149².]

a-vyakta, *a.* not manifest; *as m.* The All-soul, 67¹⁷. [√añj.]

a-vyaya, *a.* imperishable; not subject to change; unbroken. [1288a.]

√ 1 aç, *orig.* añç (açnóti, açnuté; ānáñça, ānaçé [788⁴]; áṣṭa; aṣṭā́; áçitum). reach; attain; obtain, get. [cf. ποδ-ηνεκ-ής, 'reaching to the feet'; ἤν-εγκ-α, 'carried': see also the closely related √2 naç.] + upa, attain to.

√ 2 aç (açnā́ti; áça; áçīt; açiṣyáti; açitā́; áçitum; açitvā́; -ácya). partake of; taste; eat. [a specialization of √1 aç: cf. ἄκ-ολος, 'bit': for mg, cf. bhakṣ.] + pra, partake of; *caus.* feed.

a-çaknuvant, *a.* not being able. [√çak.]

a-çakya, *a.* impossible.

a-çañka, *a.* without hesitation. [çañkā: cf. aviçañka.]

açaná, *n.* food. [√2 aç.]

a-çuci, *a.* impure.

á-çubha, *a.* disagreeable.

á-çeva, *a.* not dear; hostile. [çéva: acct, 1288a.]

a-çeṣa, *a.* without remainder, entire; -tas, *adv.* entirely, without exception.

áçman, *m.* —1. stone; —2. thunderbolt; —3. vault of heaven, 79⁹. [cf. ἄκμων, 'anvil, thunderbolt'; kinship w. Eng. *hammer* uncertain.]

áçmanvant, *a.* stony. [áçman.]

áçru, *n.* tear.

áçva, *m.* horse; áçvā́, *f.* mare, steed. [cf. ἵππος, dialectic ἵκκος, Lat. *equus*, Old Saxon *ĕhu*, AS. *eh, eoh*, 'horse.']

açva-kovida, *a.* well skilled in horses.

açva-medhá, *m.* horse-sacrifice.

açvín, *a.* horsed; *as dual m.* the Açvins, gods of the morning light, 85¹⁵ N. [áçva.]

áçvya, *a.* consisting of horses; of a horse. [açva: cf. ἵππιος, 'of a horse.']

aṣṭā́ [483²], *num.* eight. [cf. ὀκτώ, Lat. *octō*, AS. *eahta*, Eng. *eight*.]

aṣṭamá, *a.* eighth. [aṣṭā́, 487⁶.]

aṣṭa-vidha, *a.* of eight sorts; eight-fold. [vidhā, 1302c 5.]

aṣṭā́ñga, *n.* eight members. [añga, 1312.]

aṣṭā́ñga-pā́ta, *m.* a fall on eight members, *i.e.* on hands, knees, feet, breast, and face, *i.e.* a most profound obeisance.

áṣṭi, *f.* attainment. [√1 aç.]

√ 1 as (ásti [636]; ā́sa). —1. be, exist; be present *or* on hand; take place, happen; asti, ā́sīt, there is, there was, *very frequent at beg. of stories;* —2. be, w. predicate possessive gen., *i.e.* belong to; asti mama, I have; *observe that Skt. has no verb for* 'have'; —3. *most frequent as simple copula; further, w. ppls: e.g.* prāpto 'si, art thou come, didst thou come, 9¹; hantavyo 'smi, occidendus sum, 3²; çepāno 'smi, I have sworn, 97⁷; *redundantly* [303b⁴ *end*]: *e.g.* tathā_anuṣṭhite sati, it being thus performed, 35¹⁷; *so* 37¹³, 39¹⁶,²²; prahṛṣṭaḥ

san, being pleased, 48¹¹; —4. *w. advs:*
tūṣṇīm āsīt, kept silent; evam astu, so
be it; *w.* prādus, *see s.v.;* —5. become,
96¹⁹. [w. **ás-ti, s-ánti**, 'is, are,' cf. *ἐσ-τί,*
'is, exists,' *εἰσί,* Doric *ἐντί, ἐᾶντι,* 'are,'
Lat. *es-t, s-unt,* AS. *is, eis-t, s-ind,* 'is, are,'
Eng. *is;* cognate are *a-m, ar-t, are.*]

√ **2 as** (**ásyati, -te**; **ása**; **asiṣyáti**; **astá**;
ásitum; **asitvā̀**; **-ásya**). throw, cast,
shoot; throw aside. [cf. **así**, 'the bran-
dished' sword; Lat. *ensis*, 'sword'; *ālea,
-aslea,* 'die,' like Ger. *Würfel,* 'die,' fr.
werfen, 'throw.']

+**vy-ati**, throw over, cross.

+**abhi**, throw (one's self) upon, direct
(one's attention) to, study. [for mg, cf.
προσέχειν without *τὸν νοῦν.*]

+**ni**, throw down; deposit; commit.

+**pari-ni**, throw down over, stretch
over.

+**nis**, throw out; root out; destroy.

+**vi**, —1. cast asunder; cast *or* throw
away; —2. break in pieces, 70¹⁴.

+**sam**, cast *or* put together.

a-saṁhrādayant, *a.* not causing to
rattle. [√hrād.]

a-satyasaṁdha, *a.* unfaithful, treach-
erous.

á-sant, *a.* non-existing; *as n.* non-existence.

a-sapiṇḍa, *a.* related more distantly than
in the sixth generation, *see* sapiṇḍa.

a-samartha, *a.* unable.

a-sampatti, *f.* non-success.

a-sambaddha, *a.* un-connected, in-coher-
ent, *w. same fig. mg as in Eng.* [√bandh.]

a-sambandha, *a.* not having relationship.

a-sambhāvya, *a.* unsupposable, impossible.

a-saha, *a.* impatient.

ásu, *m.* vital spirit; vigorous life. [√1 as.]

a-sutṛp, *a.* insatiable. [1288a⁴.]

asu-tṛp, *a.* life-robbing. [vbl of √2 tṛp.]

ásu-nīti, *f.* the leading *or* continuing of
life (in the other world); spirit-life; spirit-
world. [acct, 1274.]

a-sunvá, *a.* not pressing (Soma), *i.e.*
indifferent to the gods, godless. [see
1148. 3b and 716.]

ásura, —1. *a.* spiritual (used of the gods,
and designating esp. the difference between celestial and mundane existence);
—2. *as m.* a spirit of life, a god; ásura
adevá, spirit that is no god, demon, 82⁶;
—3. *later,* demon (45⁶), enemy of the
gods, an Asura, a not-god (as if the word
were a-sura— whence, by popular etymology, the pendant sura, 'god'). [asu-
ra, 1226 (cf. 1188f), and as-u fr. √1 as,
1178b.]

asuryà, *a.* godlike; *as n. pl.* godhead.
[ásura, 1212d4.]

√ **asūya** (**asūyáti**). be impatient.

asūyā̀, *f.* impatience. [√asūya, 1149⁶.]

ásṛj [432], *n.* blood, 24²³. [cf. Cyprian *ἔαρ,*
'blood.']

asā́ú, *see* 501 *and* adas.

ásta, *n.* home; **ástam**, *w.* i, gam, yā, go
home; *esp.* of the sun [*see* 1092b], set.
[prob. √1 as: for mg, cf. bhavana.]

asta-máuna, *a.* having thrown aside *or*
abandoned silence. [√2 as.]

asti, *f.* being. [√1 as.]

asthán [431], *n.* bone. [cf. *ὀστέον,* Lat.
stem ossi-, -osti-, nom. os, 'bone.']

a-sthāvara, *a.* not standing.

ásthi, *see* asthán.

a-spṛçant, *a.* not touching. [√spṛç.]

asmá [494], *pron. stem.* we, us. [cf. *ἡμεῖς,*
Lesbian *ἄμμες,* 'we.']

asmád, *as stem in cpds* [494], our; *as pl.
majestaticus*, my.

asmáka, *a.* of us; our. [**asma**, 516⁴.]

á-svapant, -a. not sleeping. [√svap.]

a-svastha, *a.* not well, ill; not self-contained, not master of one's self.

a-sveda, *a.* free from sweat.

√ **ah** (**áttha, áha, áháthus, -tus, áhús**
[801a]). say; call; áhus, they say. [cf.
Lat. *aio*, 'say,' *ad-ag-ium,* 'saw, proverb,'
nego, 'say no.']

+**pra**, declare to be.

1 áha, *assev. particle.* certainly, of course;
namely. [pron. root a: cf. 1104³ end.]

2 áha, *for* áhan *in cpds.* [1209a, 1315a.]

á-hata, *a.* —1. not beaten; —2. (since
Hindu washermen wet the clothes and
pound them with stones) unwashed, of a
garment, *i.e.* new. [√han.]

áhan, áhar, áhas [430a], n. day (as opp.
to night), e.g. 92[18]; day.

ahám [491], pron. I. [cf. ἐγώ, Lat. ego,
AS. ic, Eng. I: see 491 and ma etc.]

áhar, see áhan.

ahar-niça, n. day and night, νυχθήμερον;
-am, adv. constantly. [niçá: 1253b.]

ahalyá, f. Ahalyā, Gautama's wife.

áhas, see áhan.

a-hastá, a. handless. [hásta, 1304a.]

ahaha, excl. of joy or sorrow. [1135a.]

a-hárya, a. not liable to be stolen.

aháryatva, n. non-liability to be stolen.
[1239.]

áhi, m. serpent; esp. the dragon of the sky,
often identified w. the demon Vritra. [see
under agha: cf. ἔχις, Lat. anguis, 'serpent'; ἔγχελυς, Lat. anguilla, 'eel.']

á-hiṅsá, f. non-injuring (any creature).

áhi-gopá [352], a. having the dragon as
their keeper. [1302[1].]

ahivat, adv. as a dragon. [1107.]

ahi-hátya, n. the slaying of the dragon;
the (victorious) fight with the dragon.
[acct, 1272a, 1213c.]

á-hṛṇāna, a. not being angry. [√2hṛ.]

aho, excl. of astonishment, pleasant or unpleasant. [1135a: euphony, 138f.]

aho-rátrá, n. day and night, νυχθήμερον.
[áhas + rátri, 1253b: see rátra.]

á, adv. —1. hither, unto, as prefix w. verbs
of motion; —2. conjunctively, thereto, besides; ca ·· á, both ·· and, 85[5]; —3. as-
severatively, (up to, i.e.) quite, entirely,
73[20]; —4. as prep., w. abl.: hither from,
all the way from; and then [293c], all the
way to, until, 49[12], 64[14], 103[30], 105[6], 106[2];
as far as, 105[10]. [cf. Lat. ä, 'from,' which
is not akin w. ab, 'from.']

ákará, m. —1. accumulation, abundance;
—2. mine. [√3kṛ + á, q.v.]

√ ákarṇaya (ákarṇayati; ákarṇita;
ákarṇya). listen; give ear to; hear.
[denom. fr. the possessive adj. -ákarṇa,
'having the ear to, i.e. listening.']

ákarṣaka, a. attractive; — f. -iká
[1222d], Pleasanton, as name of a town.
[√kṛṣ + á.]

ákarṣikákhya, a. having the name
ákarṣiká. [ákhyá.]

ákára, m. make; shape; appearance.
[√1kṛ + á: cf. ákṛti.]

ákāravant, a. like the Eng. shapely.
[ákāra.]

ákáçá, in Veda, m.; later, n. free or open
space; sky. [prop. 'outlook, clearness,'
√káç + á.]

ákula, a. —1. bestrewn, covered, filled;
—2. fig. confused; agitated. [√3kṛ + á,
q.v.]

√ ákulaya (ákulayati). confuse; áku-
lita, at one's wit's end. [ákula.]

ákúta, n. intention. [√kū + á.]

ákṛti, f. make; shape; appearance.
[√1kṛ + á, 1157.1d: cf. ákāra.]

ákhú, m. mold-warp; mouse. ['burrower,'
√khā + á, 1178a end.]

ákhyá, f. name; at end of cpds, having ··
as name. [√khyá + á.]

ákhyána, n. tale. [√khyá + á, 1150.]

ágantavya, grdv. see √gam + á.

ágantu, m. arrival; and so, as in Eng.,
person arriving. [√gam + á, 1161.]

ágamana, n. a coming hither; w. punar,
a returning. [√gam + á.]

ágas, n. sin. [orig., perhaps, 'a slip,'
√añj: cf. ágyos, 'guilt': different is ágyos,
see √yaj.]

ághṛṇi, a. glowing, beaming. [√2ghṛ,
'glow,' + á, 1158.]

áṅgirasá, a. descended from Angiras.
[Áṅgiras, 1208a.]

ácamana, n. the rinsing of the mouth.
[√cam + á.]

ácamaníya, m. dish for use in rinsing
the mouth. [ácamana, 1215.]

ácára, m. walk and conversation; conduct;
usage; observance. [√car + á.]

ácáryà, m. teacher, esp. of the Veda.
[perhaps, 'the man of observances,' fr.
ácára, 1212d 4.]

ájarasám, adv. to old age. [from the
phrase á jarás-am.]

ájarasáya, adv. to old age. [dat. (1113)
formed fr. the preceding, as if that were
acc. of ájarasá.]

ájí, m. race; contest; battle. [√aj, 1155.
cf. ἀγ-ών, 'contest.']

ājñā́, f. order; command. [√jñā́ + ā́.]

ā́jya, n. clarified butter (for anointing, etc.); cf. ghṛta. [√añj + ā, see 100⁸⁰: for mg, cf. Eng. noun *smear*, 'ointment,' and verb *smear*.]

ājya-çeṣa, m. n. rest of the clarified butter.

ājyā̀huti, f. oblation of clarified butter. [ā̀huti.]

ā́ñjana, n. ointment. [√añj + ā: cf. Lat. *unguen*, 'ointment.']

ādhyá, a. wealthy; rich. [perhaps fr. arthya.]

ā́t, adv. thereupon; ā́d íd, then indeed. [lit. 'from that,' abl. of ā́, 1114a.]

ātithyá, n. hospitality. [ātithi, 'guest,' 1211.]

ātma, *for* ā́tman *in cpds*, 1249a².

ātmaka, *for* ā́tman *in mg 4 at end of cpds* [1222, 1307]; *e.g.* māra-ā̀tmaka, murder-natured, murderous.

ātmán, m. — 1. breath; — 2. spirit; soul (*cf.* 84⁸ N.), as principle of life and feeling; — 3. self; *very often so used as a simple reflexive pron.* [514]; *e.g.,* myself, 36¹⁶; thyself, 26¹⁵; himself, 4¹⁹; *in genitive:* his, 17¹⁶; her, 46⁵; one's own, 21¹⁸, 58²²; — 4. nature, character, peculiarity; *esp. at end of cpds, see* ātmaka; — 5. the soul κατ' ἐξοχήν, the soul of the universe, 66⁵. [cf. ἀϑτμήν, 'breath'; ἀτμός, 'vapor'; AS. ǽþm, ǽðm, 'breath': for mg, cf. πνεῦμα and Lat. *anima*, 'breath, spirit.']

ātma-pakṣa, m. one's own party.

ātma-prabha, a. having his *or* their own splendor. [prabhā́, 354.]

ātma-bhava, m. the coming into existence of one's self.

ātma-māṅsa, n. one's own flesh.

ātmavát, adv. as one's self. [ātma, *i.e.* ātman: 1107.]

ātma-çakti, f. one's own power.

ātma-çoṇita, n. one's own blood.

ātma-saṁdeha, m. danger of one's self, personal risk.

ātma-hita, n. one's own welfare.

ātmāupamya, n. likeness to one's self, *i.e.* a putting one's self in another's place. [ā̀upamya.]

ā́dara, m. respect, notice, care. [√2 dṛ + ā, 'regard.']

ādā́hana, n. burning-place, place of cremation. [√dah + ā.]

ādā́na, n. receiving. [√1 dā + ā, 'take,' 1150.]

ā́di, m. — 1. in-ception, beginning, 60⁵; ādim ādatte, he makes a beginning; ādāv eva, just before, just now; — 2. *esp. at end of adj. cpds* [*see* 1302c 1]: ·· -ādi, having ·· as the beginning, *i.e.* ·· and so forth; *or, the qualified noun being omitted, and the adj. cpd being used as subst.,* ·· and so forth. [undoubtedly fr. √1 dā + ā, 'take,' 'a taking hold of, *i.e.* beginning,' 1155.2e: for mg, cf. Lat. *in-cipere*, Ger. *an-fangen*, 'take hold of, begin.']

ā́dika, *equiv. to* ādi *in use* 2. [1222, 1307.]

ādityá, m. — 1. son of Aditi, name applied to the gods of the heavenly light, Varuṇa, Mitra, Aryaman, etc.; — 2. Aditya, name of the sun-god, son of Aditi; the sun. [áditi, 1211.]

ādín, a. eating, devouring. [√ad, 1183².]

ā́devana, n. gambling-place, 98¹². [√1 dīv, 'play,' + ā.]

ā́dya, a. first; *equiv. to* ādi *in use* 2. [ādi, 1211.]

ādhipatya, n. sovereignty. [ádhipati, 1211² end.]

ādhṛṣya, grdv. to be ventured against; approachable. [√dhṛṣ + ā, 963d.]

ādheya, n. a placing, *esp.* of the sacred fire. [√1 dhā + ā, 'put,' 1213c.]

ādhvaryava, n. service of sacrificing priest. [adhvaryú, 1208c.]

ānaḍuha, a. of a bull, taurine. [anaḍúh, weak form of anaḍvah, 404; 1208a.]

ā́nana, n. mouth; face. [prop. 'the breather,' √an: cf. ἥνεσ-, 'face,' in προσ-ηνής and ἀπ-ηνής, 'with face turned towards,' 'with face averted': for mg, cf. nayana.]

√ ā́p (āpnóti; ápa; ā́pat; āpsyáti; āptá; ā́ptum; āptvā́; -ápya; āpyáte; ipsati [1030]; āpáyati). reach; win; get; bring upon one's self; — āptá: — 1. having reached; extending over; *and so,* adequate, suitable, fit; — 2. having reached, *i.e.* being near *or* intimate, *and so, as m.,*

a friend; —ī́psitá, whom or what one
desires to obtain, sought for, desired.
[prob. for ā-ap, 108g, see ā́paṣ: cf. ἥπιος,
'approachable, friendly'; Lat. ap-iscor,
'reach,' ap-ere, 'seize, fasten'; ἅπτω (√ἀφ
for ἀπ), 'fasten.']

+abhi, reach to a thing, attain; desíd.
strive to win; caus. cause to reach the
mark, i.e. carry out fully, 96¹².

+ava, come upon, fall in with; obtain,
acquire; take upon one's self; incur.

+pra, reach; arrive; come upon; catch;
win, obtain, get; incur; —prā́pta: reached,
found, caught, obtained; reached, arrived,
having come; —caus. cause to arrive at,
bring to, 53¹⁷; prā́paṇīya, to be brought
to, 53¹⁵.

+vi, reach through, pervade, 66⁹.

ā́paṇa, m. market. [√paṇ + ā́.]

ā́pad, f. misfortune. [lit. 'a getting into'
(trouble), √pad + ā́: for specialization of
mg, cf. ā́rti, and Eng. ac-cident, lit. 'a happening' (of trouble).]

ā́paṣ, see ā́p.

ā́pí, m. friend. ['one who has reached or
stands near another' (cf. ā́pta), √āp: cf.
ἥπιος, s.v. ā́p.]

ā́pta-dakṣiṇa, a. having or accompanied
by suitable presents. [dakṣiṇā́, 334².]

ā́bdika, a. annual; · · -ā́bdika, · · -ennial,
lasting · · years. [abda.]

ā́bharaṇa, n. ornament (jewels, etc.).
['what is worn,' √bhṛ + ā́: for mg, cf.
φάρος, 'garment,' w. φέρω, and Ger. Tracht,
'dress,' w. tragen, 'wear.']

āmá, a. raw. [cf. ὠμός, 'raw'; Lat. am-
ārus, 'bitter.']

āmaya, m. injury; disease. [caus. of √am.]

āmayitnu, a. sickening. [caus. of √am,
1196b.]

āmiṣá, n. flesh. [cf. āmá and āmis.]

āmiṣāçin, a. flesh-eating. [āçin.]

āmis, n. raw flesh; flesh. [cf. āmá.]

āmóda, a. gladdening; as m. fragrance.
[√mud + ā́.]

āyátana, n. foot-hold; resting-place; esp.
place of the sacred fire, fire-place. [√yat
+ ā́.]

āyata-locana, a. having long eyes.
[√yam + ā́.]

ā́yasá, a. metallic, of iron; as n. metal,
iron. [áyas, 1208a.]

āyā́ma, m. like Eng. extent, i.e. length.
[√yam + ā́, 'extend.']

āyú, a. active, lively. [√i, 1178a: prob.
akin are ἠΰς, αἰεί-ς, ἐΰς, 'active, doughty,
mighty,' εὖ-, 'strongly,' εὖ, generalized,
'well': for mg of āyú, cf. the phrase
"full of go."]

ā́yudha, n. weapon. [√yudh + ā́.]

ā́yuṣmant, a. having life or vitality;
long-lived; old. [ā́yus, 1235a.]

ā́yus, n. (activity, liveliness, and so) life;
vitality; personified as a genius, Ayus, 85¹⁸;
period or duration of life; long life; (like
Eng. life, i.e.) living creatures. [√i, 1154,
cf. ā́y-ú: cf. al-ών, Lat. ae-vu-m, AS. ǽw,
ǽ, 'life-time, time'; AS. āwa, ā, Eng. aye,
'ever'; AS. ǽfre, Eng. ev-er.]

āraṇyaka, a. pertaining to the wilderness; as n. forest-treatise (to be read in
the solitude of the wilderness — Whitney,
p. xvi.). [áraṇya, 1222e.]

ārā́dhana, n. the gratifying, propitiation,
service. [√rādh + ā́, caus.]

ārogya, n. lit. diseaseless-ness, i.e. health.
[aroga.]

ārohá, m. the swelling hips or buttocks of
a woman. [prop. 'the seat' on which a
child is carried astride by its mother,
√ruh + ā́, 'get upon, take one's seat
upon': see aṅka and cf. the words of an
ogress, MBh., āruha mama çroṇíṁ, neṣ-
yāmi tvāṁ vihā́yasā, 'get upon my hip,
I will carry thee through the air.']

ārtá, a. visited, esp. by trouble; afflicted;
stricken; distressed. [√ṛ + ā́, q.v.: for
mg, cf. American slang phrase gone for.]

ā́rti, f. a visitation (of evil), i.e. trouble,
misfortune, see 93¹⁵ N. [√ṛ + ā́: for mg.
cf. ā́rta and ā́pad.]

ārdrá, a. wet.

ārdrá-vāsas, a. having wet garments.

ā́rya, a. belonging to the faithful, i.e., as
m. man of one's own tribe, an Aryan, as
designation of a man of the Vedic Indian
tribes; as adj. Aryan; noble; reverend
(used in respectful address). [aryá, 1208f:
cf. Avestan airya, 'Aryan'; New Persian,
irān, 'Persia'; Hdt. vii. 62, οἱ Μῆδοι ἐκα-

λέοντο πέλαι 'Αριοι; Keltic nom. *eriu*, acc. *erinn*, name of Ireland; Eng. *Ir-ish*: cf. **ari, aryá.**]

álasya, *n.* sloth. [**alasa.**]

álasya-vacana, *n.* sloth-dictum, as designation for the ignava ratio *or* fatalist's argument.

álāpá, *m.* talk; conversation. [√lap + á.]

álokana, *n.* the beholding. [√lok + á.]

ává, *pron. stem,* 491.

ávis, *adv.* forth to sight, in view; *w.* kṛ, make visible. [1078.]

ávṛt, *f.* a turning. [√vṛt + á.]

áça, *m.* food. [√2 aç, 'eat.']

áçayá, *m.* lying-place; abode. [√çī + á.]

áçás, *f.* wish, hope. [çaṅs + á.]

áçā, *f.* hope. [younger form of áçás.]

áçā, *f.* region; quarter (of the sky). [specialized from 'place, objective point, that which one reaches,' √1 aç, 'reach.']

áçāvant, *a.* hopeful. [áçā.]

áçín, *a.* eating, in cpds. [√2 aç, 1183³.]

áçis [392], *f.* wish *or* prayer, *esp.* for good. [√çās + á, 639, 225²: cf. praçís.]

áçīr-vāda, *m.* expression of a (good) wish, *i.e.* a benediction. [áçís, cf. 392.]

áçīrvādābhidhānavant, *a.* containing a designation of a benediction. [áçīr-vāda + abhidhāna, 1233.]

áçú, *a.* swift. [cf. ὠκύ-ς, 'swift'; Lat. *ōc-ior,* 'swifter.']

áççarya, *n.* wonder; prodigy.

áçrama, *m.* —1. (place of self-castigation, *i.e.*) hermitage; —2. stadium in a Brahman's religious life (of which there are four: that of the student *or* brahmacārin, that of the householder *or* gṛhastha, that of the hermit *or* vānaprastha, and that of the beggar *or* bhikṣu), *see* 65³ ℵ. [√çram + á.]

áçraya, *m.* that on which anything leans *or* rests; support; refuge; protection; authority. [√çri + á.]

áçraya-bhūta, *a.* having become a protection, *i.e., as m.,* protector. [1273c.]

ás, *excl. of joy or of displeasure.* ah!

√ **ás** (**áste** [628], **ásīna** [619³]; **ásám cakre; ásiṣṭa; ásiṣyáte; ásitá; ásitum; ásitvā; -ásya**). —1. sit; seat one's self; settle down, 98¹; —2. abide; dwell, 85¹⁰; stay;

remain; continue, 64¹⁴; —3. *w. ppl.* [1075c], continue (doing anything), keep on, 32¹⁴,¹⁸. [cf. ἧσ-ται, 'sits'; Lat. *ānus, *ās-nu-s,* 'seat, buttocks'; Old Lat. *āsa,* Lat. *āra,* 'family-seat, hearth, altar.'] +**adhi;** take one's place in, *i.e.* visit, 49¹⁶; get into (shoes), *i.e.* put on, 45¹⁷. +**upa,** sit by (in sign of readiness to serve), wait upon (a command), 92⁴; sit by (expectantly), sit waiting for, 91⁴. +**pary-upa,** sit around, surround, 2⁷.

ásana, *n.* sitting, 4¹²; seat. [√ás.]

ásāra, *m.* (*like Eng. colloq.* a pour, *i.e.*) pouring rain. [√sṛ + á, 'run.']

ásurá, *a.* demonic; *as m.* demon. [**ásura,** 1208f.]

ásecana, *n.* cavity (into which one pours). [√sic + á.]

ásecanavant, *a.* having a cavity, hollow. [**ásecana.**]

áhati, *f.* blow. [√han + á, 1157¹ and 1d.]

áhanás, *a.* swelling, fermenting, foaming.

áhávana, *n.* oblation. [√hu + á.]

áhavanīya, *a.* of *or* for the oblation; *w.* agni, oblation-fire; *as m., without* agni, oblation-fire (the one that receives the oblation), *see* 102² ℵ. [**āhavana,** 1215.]

áhāra, *m.* the taking to one's self (of food), eating; what one takes, *i.e.* food. [√hṛ + á.]

áhāra-dāna, *n.* giving of food.

áhāra-parityāga, *m.* relinquishment of food.

áhārādi, *n.* food and so forth. [**ádi,** 1302c 1.]

áhārārthin, *a.* seeking food. [**arthin.**]

áhitāgni, *a.* having a set *or* established fire; *as m.* one who is keeping alive a sacred fire. [**áhita,** √1 dhā + á, 'set': 1299a.]

áhuti, *f.* oblation, offering (used both of the act and of the thing offered); *cf. the later word* homa. [√hu + á: *w.* -huti, cf. χύ-σι-ς, 'a pouring.']

áhvāna, *n.* call; invitation. [√hū *or* hvā + á.]

ι, *pron. root, see* idam and 502³.

√ **i** (**éti** [612]; **iyáya, īyús** [783b²]; **eṣyáti; itá; étum; itvá; -ítya**). —1. go; go to *or* towards; come; enter; —2. move on, 86¹²; pass; —3. go to, *i.e.* attain (a thing *or* condition); —**iyase** [1021²], goest hither and thither, 90¹⁵; —**imahe** [1021²], (*like Ger.* an-gehen) we approach with prayers, beseech. [w. i-más, *cf.* ῐ-μεν, Lat. *i-mus,* 'we go'; Goth. *i-ddja,* AS. *eode,* 'went'; radically akin, perhaps, is AS. *gān* (stem *gā* for •*ga-i, ga-* being the inseparable prefix), Eng. *go,* Ger. *gehen:* see also **āyú, áyus.**]

⊦**ati,** go beyond *or* past *or* over; overwhelm; transcend; leave behind, get rid of, 68⁹; escape.

⊦**adhi,** come upon, notice; take notice, 87¹⁸; —*middle* **adhīté** [612 note], go over for one's self, repeat, learn, read; *ppl.* **adhīta:** *w. act. mg,* learn-ed, 18⁵; *w. pass. mg,* learned, 21¹⁵; —*caus.* **adhyāpáyati** [1042e], cause to learn, teach.

⊦**upa_adhi,** *in* **upādhyāya.**

⊦**anu,** go along *or* after; accompany; *ppl.* **anvita,** accompanied by, endowed *or* filled *or* connected with.

⊦**sam-anu,** *the same.*

⊦**antar,** go within; retire, withdraw.

⊦**apa,** go off; slink away.

⊦**abhi,** go unto; become embodied in.

⊦**ava,** approach.

⊦**ā,** come near *or* unto *or* hither; *w. the adv.* **punar,** go back.

+**abhy-ā,** approach, go near.

+**upa_ā,** come unto.

⊦**sam-ā,** come near to together; assemble.

⊦**ud,** go up, rise (of the sun).

+**upa,** go unto; fall to the lot of; *ppl.* **upeta,** gone unto, attended by, provided with.

+**sam-upa,** come hither.

+**ni,** go into *or* in; *cf.* **nyāya.**

+**parā,** go away *or* forth; depart.

+**anu-parā,** go forth along (a path).

+**vi-parā,** go away separately.

⊦**pari,** circumambulate; walk round (the fire).

+**pra,** —1. go forward *or* onward, 83¹¹; *esp.* go forth out of this world, *and so (like Eng.* depart), die; **pretya,** after dying, *i.e.* in the other world (*opp. of* iha); **preta,**

dead; —2. come out, stick out, be prominent.

+**prati,** go against, withstand; go back to; recognize, 98¹⁸; **pratīta,** recognized, approved.

+**vi,** go asunder; separate; disperse, 83¹⁵; spread one's self over, *i.e.* pervade, 72²; **vīta,** *at beg. of cpds,* having departed ··. *i.e.* free from ··.

+**sam,** come together; assemble.

icchā, *f.* wish; desire; inclination. [√1**iṣ,** 'seek': *cf.* AS. *Æsce,* 'an asking.']

ij, *vbl.* sacrificing, *in* ṛtv-**íj.** [√**yaj,** 252.]

ijyā, *f.* sacrifice. [√**yaj,** 252.]

itara [523], *pron. a.* other; the other; another; other than, *i.e.* different from, *w. abl.* [pron. root i, 502³: *cf.* Lat. *iterum,* 'another time.']

itás, *adv.* —1. *used like the abl. of a pron.* [1098c²], 24¹⁸; —2. from this (place), from here; here; from this (world), 5³; **itas tatas,** here and there; —3. from this (time), now, 41⁵. [pron. root i, 502³.]

iti, *adv. see* 1102a. —1. in this way, thus; so; **iti devā akurvan,** thus the gods did, 96⁹; —2. *used w. all kinds of quotations made* verbis ipsissimis: **tathā_ity uktvā,** upon saying "Yes," 4²; **sa pṛṣṭavān kāu yuvām iti,** he asked, "Who are ye," 45⁵; **evam astu iti tāu dhāvitāu,** with the words, "So be it," the two ran off, 45¹⁸; *so* RV., 85¹²; *so* MS., 92¹⁵; **ity ākarṇya,** on hearing (so, *i.e.*) the preceding çlokas, 17¹⁶; *cf.* 18¹⁰; —2a. *designating something as that which was, or under the circumstances might have been said or thought or intended or known, sometimes* (46¹⁸) *preceding it, but usually following it:* **martavyam iti,** at the thought, "I must die," 29⁹; **gardabho 'yam iti jñātvā,** recognizing (the fact), "This is an ass," 34²⁰; —2b. *interr. in place of the exact quotation:* **kim iti,** alleging *or* intending what, under what pretext, with what intention, 30⁴, 41⁵; —2c. *used in giving an authority:* **iti dhāraṇā,** so (is) the rule, 62¹⁷; **ity eke,** so some folks (say), 101⁹; —2d. *used in citing a Vedic verse by its first word* (60¹³) *or words* (98²⁰, etc.); —2e. *at the end of a section or book* (*cf.* **atha),** here endeth, 4⁴; —2f. *w. verbs* *of naming, considering, etc., the predicate, marked by* iti, *is nom., sometimes acc.* — *both constructions at* 61 [12]; damayanti̱iti viçrutā, known as *or* named "D.," 6 [3]; —3. *used to include under one head or as in a list several separate objects,* 21 [7], 100 [8], 105 [1]; —4. evam *superfluously added,* 61 [11]; iti *doubled,* 60 [11]; —5. iti ha = iti, 12 [8], 61 [18]. [pron. root i, 1102a: cf. Lat. *iti-dem,* 'just so.']

itihāsá, *m.* story, legend. [agglomeration of iti ha āsa, 'thus, indeed, it was': 1314b.]

ıtthā (*V. only*) *and* itthám, *adv.* in this way; so; kím ta itthā, how does this happen thee? 73 [8]. [adverbs made from the acc. sing. neut., i-d, of the pron. root i, see 1101: cf. Lat. *itā* and *item,* 'so.']

ity-ādi, *at end of possessive adj. cpds used substantively,* that which has " · · ·" as its beginning, *i.e.* " · · ·" and so forth. [see 1302c 1 end.]

íd, *V. pcl.* just; exactly; even; *emphasizing the preceding word and to be rendered by laying emphasis on that word.* [acc. of pron. root i, 1111a: cf. Lat. *i-d,* 'it.']

1 idám [501-2 — *forms made from four stems,* ā *and* anā, i *and* imá, *those from* ā *being often unaccented, see* 74 [9] N.], *pron.* this, this here, *tóde, e.g.* 20 [9], 86 [10], 87 [8]; *contrasted w.* asáu, 'that one,' 103 [7]; asmin loke, in this world, 66 [12]; *without* loke *and contrasted w.* amutra, 103 [8]; idaṁ víçvam bhuvanam, this whole world, 85 [12]; idaṁ sarvam, this entire (world), 63 [21]; so 66 [19]; so idam, tò tár, 56 [13, 17]; iyam pṛthivī, this earth, 10 [10]; iyam *alone,* this earth, 93 [1, 3]; —*refers very often, like* tóde, *to something following (just as* etad *and* taúra *to something preceding), e.g.* 13 [22], 26 [7], 45 [14], 51 [8]; *occasionally refers to something immediately preceding, e.g.* 10 [17], 24 [9], 74 [12], 79 [4]; —*joined w. pronouns:* ko 'yam āyāti, who comes here? 27 [12]; yo 'yaṁ dṛçyate, which is seen here, 46 [17]; mám imam, me here, 76 [16]; *nom. to be rendered* here is *or* are, 56 [1], 4 [21]; imáu vātas, blow hither, 90 [11]. [cf. Lat. *i-d,* Goth. *i-ta,* Ger. *es,* 'it.']

2 idám, *adv.* now, 86 [19]; here, 80 [9], 96 [9]. [1111a: cf. 502.]

idāním, *adv.* now. [pron. root i, 1103b.]

√ idh *or* indh (inddhé [694]; ídhé [783b]; āindhiṣṭa; indhiṣyáti; iddhá; -ídhya). kindle. [cf. *aíth-ō,* 'burn'; Lat. *aed-e-s,* 'fire-place, hearth, dwelling' (cf. *stove* and Ger. *Stube,* 'room'); *aestus,* *aid-tu-s,* 'heat'; AS. *ād,* 'funeral pile'; *āst,* Eng. *oast,* 'kiln for drying hops *or* malt.']
+ sam, kindle, *trans. and intrans.*

idhmá, *m.* fuel. [√idh, 1166: for mg, cf. Eng. *kindlings.*]

idhma-citi, *f.* fuel-pile.

√ in (in-ó-ti, *prop.* i-nó-ti [713]). drive; force; *in* enas. [cf. √inv.]

indra, *m.* Indra, name of a Vedic god; *in the later language,* the best of its kind, chief, prince. [none of the numerous proposed derivations is satisfactory.]

indra-purogama, *a.* having Indra as leader, preceded by Indra. [1302c 2.]

indra-loká, *m.* Indra's world, heaven.

indra-çatru, *a.* having Indra as his conqueror. [1302.]

indra-senā, *f.* Indra's missile weapon; personified as his bride, RV. x. 102.2; *hence,* name of a woman, see 16 [11] N.; — *m.* -a, name of a man, *formed as a mere pendant to the fem.* [indra + 1 senā.]

indrāgní, *m.* Indra and Agni. [indra + agni: acct, 1255b.]

indrā-bṛhaspáti, *m.* Indra and Brihaspati. [acct, 1255a.]

indrāyudha, *n.* Indra's weapon, the rainbow. [āyudha.]

indriyá, *a.* belonging to Indra; *as n.* —1. the quality pertaining especially to Indra, *i.e.* great might, power, 73 [18], 97 [6]; —2. *in general,* one of a man's powers, *i.e.* a sense *or* organ of sense. [indra, 1214b.]

√ indh, see idh.

√ inv (ínvati). drive; send. [secondary root from i, 749b, 716: cf. in.]

imá, *pron. stem, see* idam.

iyacciram, *adv.* so long. [iyant (1249a) + ciram.]

iyant [451], *a.* so great; so much. [fr. pron. root i, 502.]

iras, *n.* ill-will; anger; *assumed as basis of the following denom.* [√ṛ, 'go for' in hostile sense: cf. Lat. *ira,* 'anger.']

9

√ irasya (irasyáti). be evil disposed.
[iras, 1058.]

irasyá, f. ill-will; wrath. [√irasya,
1149⁶: cf. īrgyā.]

íriṇa, n. a run or runlet; gulch; gullied
and so desert land. [√r, 1177b: for mg,
cf. Provincial Eng. run, 'brook.']

iva, encl. pcl. —1. as; like; —2. used to
modify a strong expression, in a manner;
so to speak, 56¹⁶; as it were, 1¹⁰; perhaps;
almost, 34¹³; —3. sometimes (like eva),
just, quite; nacirād iva, right soon.
[pron. root i, 1102b.]

√ 1 iṣ (icchāti [753]; iyéṣa, iṣús [783b];
āíṣīt; eṣiṣyáti; iṣṭá; éṣṭum; -íṣya).
seek; desire; esp. w. inf. [981³]; pass. be
desired; be approved or recognized, and
so pass for, 59¹⁸; iṣṭá, desired, i.e. desirable, 1⁴. [radical mg, 'go, go for,' √2 iṣ
being merely a causative of √1 iṣ: cf.
ἵμερος, ⸱ιμμερος, 'desire'; w. icchā, 'desire,'
cf. A8. ⸱āsce, 'petition,' whence āscian,
Ger. (h)eischen, Eng. ask: icchati for ⸱is-
skati, cf. √vāñch.]
+ anu, seek after.
+ abhi, seek for; ppl. abhíṣṭa, desired,
dear, 21¹⁸.

√ 2 iṣ (iṣáyati [1042a²]; also iṣyati [761c];
iyéṣa, iṣús [783b]; iṣitá; iṣayitum;
-íṣya). send; set in swift motion; impel, 74¹⁹. [caus. of √1 iṣ, q.v.]
+ pra, —1. preṣáyati: send forth; send,
e.g. 9¹⁰; —2. préṣyati: drive forth, impel;
start up (e.g. game); prāíṣam [970a]
āicchan, sought to start up, 93¹⁶; and so
—3. préṣyati: call upon or summon (technical term used of the chief priest's calling
upon another to begin a text or action),
103⁶.

iṣ, f. refreshment; strength; vigor; w. ūrj,
drink and food, like Ger. Kraft und Saft.

iṣá, —1. m. = iṣ [399]; —2. as a. vigorous,
fruitful.

iṣu, m. f. arrow. [√2 iṣ, 'send': cf. lós,
⸱ιοός, 'arrow.']

1 iṣṭá, see √1 iṣ, 'desire.'

2 iṣṭá, —1. offered; —2. as n. offering,
sacrifice, holy work. [√yaj, 252.]

iṣṭaká, f. brick used in the sacred fire-
pile. [2 iṣṭá.]

iṣṭa-lābha, m. acquisition of a desirable
object. [1 iṣṭá.]

iṣṭā-pūrtá, n. what is offered (to the
gods) and bestowed (upon them), i.e. what
a man offers to the gods for his benefit
after death, and so, by metonymy, such fruit
of these offerings as can come to him,
83¹³ n. [2 iṣṭá, 247, 1253b.]

iṣṭi, f. sacrifice (simple offering of butter, fruit, etc.), 101⁶. [√yaj, 252,
1157. 1a.]

ihá, adv. here, opp. of atra (87¹) and
amutra (64⁴); hither, 9²; here on earth,
ici bas, 27²; opp. of pretya (√i), 59²; 58¹¹;
in this book, 17⁶; w. loc. [cf. 1099⁴], iha
samaye, in this case, 41¹⁶, 42¹⁵. [pron.
root i, 1100a.]

————

√ īkṣ (íkṣate; īkṣāṁ cakre; āíkṣiṣṭa;
īkṣiṣyáte; īkṣitá; íkṣitum; īkṣitvā;
-íkṣya; īkṣyáte). look; look at; see;
behold. [desid. of √⸱aç, 'see,' contained in
ak-ṣán, 'eye,' etc., 108g: see akṣán.]
+ apa, look off to (like Ger. es absehen
auf); regard; expect.
+ ava, look after; look after one's self,
i.e. look behind or around.
+ upa, w. two mgs, like Eng. overlook:
—1. look over, i.e. inspect; and —2. (more
commonly) look beyond, i.e. neglect.
+ nis, look out or after; contemplate.
+ pari, look about one; investigate;
consider.
+ vi, look; look on; víkṣita, beheld.
+ sam, look upon; behold; perceive.

íkṣaka, m. beholder; spectator. [√īkṣ,
1181.]

íkṣaṇa, n. a look; glance. [√īkṣ.]

√ īṅkh (íṅkhati, -te; īṅkháyati, -te
[1041²]). move unsteadily.
+ pra, rock or pitch onward.

√ īḍ (īḷe, íḷiṣe, íṭṭe [628, 630]; perf. īḷé;
īḷitá). supplicate; call upon; praise.
[Whitney, 54.]

íḍya, grdv. to be praised. [√īḍ, 963² and
d: pronounced íḷia, Whitney, 54.]

īdṛça, a. of this sort; such. [502 end,
and 518.]

ípsitá, a. desired to be obtained; desired. [desid. of √āp, 1030.]

ím, encl. —1. as acc. s. of pron. root i, him, her, it; him, 79⁷; —2. indef., yá īm, quicunque, RV. x. 125.4; —3. ká īm, who pray? 77¹⁸; —4. to avoid hiatus: between átha and enam, 84⁵·⁶. [see 1111a and 502 end.]

√ ir (írte [628]; irṇá; iráyati, -te; íritá). set one's self in motion; —caus. set in motion; cause to go forth, i.e.: —1. bring into existence; —2. utter (a sound), 14²⁵. [near akin w. √ṛ.]

+ ud, rise up; caus. rouse; send out; utter; announce, 63¹⁶.

+ sam-ud, caus. utter, declare.

+ pra, caus. drive or steer onward (ship).

+ sam, caus. bring together, i.e. into shape or being; create, 75⁶; sameriré, established (as an ordinance), instituerunt, 88⁶ɴ.

īrṣyá, f. ill-will; envy; jealousy. [contracted fr. irasyá, q.v.: cf. çíṛṣ-an and çíras.]

√ íç (íçe [628]; íçiṣyáti). own, be master of, w. gen. [cf. AS. ág-an, 'possess,' Eng. owe, 'possess' (so Shakespere often), 'possess another's property, be in debt'; thence the participial adj. ágen, Eng. adj. own, 'proprius'; thence the denom. ágnian, Eng. verb own; further, to āh, preterito-present of ágan, is formed a secondary past tense, āhte, 'possessed,' Eng. ought, 'possessed' (so Spenser), 'was under obligation.']

íçá, m. master; lord. [√íç.]

íçvará, m. master; lord; prince; rich man, 22³. [√íç, 1171a.]

√iṣ (íṣate; íṣé; íṣitá). hasten from, flee before, w. abl. [if not desid. of √i (108g¹ end), perhaps akin w. √1 iṣ, orig. 'go.']

---

u, Vedic encl. copula. —1. and; also; further; used in one (oftenest the latter) of two clauses or sentences containing things alike or slightly contrasted (e.g. 78¹⁴, 79⁹), esp. in anaphora (e.g. 79⁵, 90⁹); —2. now, straightway, w. verbs present and past and w. imperatives or imperative subjunctives, 71¹⁰, 85¹⁸, 85⁵, 87⁸; often followed by sú, right

soon; —pragṛhya [see 1122a³, 138c] when combined with átha (90¹⁶), úpa (78¹⁴), mā́ (87⁸); for 83⁹ and 84¹¹, see notes; —3. in classical Skt. only w. (atha, kim, and) na, and not, 21¹⁴, 27¹⁷.

u-kāra, m. the sound u. [Whitney, 18.]

uktá, see √vac.

ukti, f. expression; declaration, 53¹⁶. [√vac, 1157. 1a.]

ukthá, n. utterance, esp. of devotion; praise; hymn of praise; invocation. [√vac, 1163a.]

uktha-várdhana, a. strengthening, i.e. refreshing or delighting one's self with hymns of praise. [acct, 1271.]

√ ukṣ [252] or vakṣ (ukṣáti, -te; ā́dkṣīt; ukṣiṣyáti; ukṣitá; -úkṣya). sprinkle; besprinkle; drop, intrans., 75⁷. [secondary form (1042g end) of √ ·uj or ug: cf. ὑγ-ρός, 'wet'; Lat. ūvens (·ugvens) caelum, 'the dropping sky'; w. ukṣán, 'besprinkler, impregnator, bull,' cf. Goth. auhsa, 'bull,' Eng. ox, and for mg, √vṛṣ.]

+ pra, sprinkle before one by way of consecration.

ugrá, a. mighty; exceedingly strong; terrible. [√vaj, 252, 1188; see ójas.]

ugrá-çāsana, a. having a terrible way of ruling; as m. a strict ruler. [1298a.]

√ uc (úcyati [only w. preps]; uvóca [783b]; ūcivā́ṅs [803]; ucitá). be pleased; be wonted; ucitá: —1. with which one is pleased; proper; suitable; —2. accustomed.

uccá, a. lofty; uccā́is, adv. [1112c], high; of sound, loud. [fr. uccá, adv. instr. (1112e) of údañc.]

uccaya, m. heap, pile, collection. [√1 ci + ud, 'heap up.']

uccārá, m. evacuation; excrement. [√car + ud.]

uccāvacá, a. high and low; various; diverse. [ud + ca w. ava + ca, 1314b.]

úcchiṣṭa, ppl. left; as n. leavings, esp. of a sacrifice or of food. [√çiṣ + ud.]

ucchedin, a. destroying. [√chid + ud.]

ujjayinī, f. Oujein, name of a city, Ptolemy's Ὀζήνη. [fem. of ujjayin, 'victorious,' √ji + ud, 1183³: of like mg are Νικό-πολις and Cairo.]

√ uñch (úñchati, uñcháti; úñchitum).
sweep together, glean. [for ●unak, ●vanak,
orig. 'wipe, or whisk, i.e. sweep': cf. AS.
wascan, 'wash,' Eng. wash and whisk.]
+ pra, wash away; wipe out, 23¹.

úñçiṣṭa, same as ucchiṣṭa.

utá, conj. and; also; even; connecting
words, clauses, and sentences; repeated:
uta ·· uta ·· (uta), both ·· and ·· (and);
at beg. of verse, 78¹¹; —uta vā: or even,
87²⁰; or, 84¹⁴ (cf. atha, 6); apy uta, also.

utkarṣa, m. elevation. [√kṛṣ + ud.]

uttamá, a. —1. up-most; highest; best,
esp. at end of cpds; excellent; chief; —2.
(out-most, i.e.) ut-most; extreme; last (see
67⁶ ꜰ.), 99²⁰. [úd, 'up, out,' 473.]

uttamagandhādhya, a. rich in excellent odors, 15¹⁹. [uttama-gandha +
ādhya.]

uttamādhamamadhyama, a. highest
and lowest and midmost; best and worst
and middling.　　[uttama + adhama +
madhyama, 1257.]

úttara [525²], a. upper; higher; —1. being
above, (opp. adhara) 70¹⁸; having the
upper hand, victorious, 81¹¹; —2. northern (on account of the Himālayas, cf.
udañc); ā_uttarasmāt, as far as the
north (side), 105¹⁰; —3. the left (because
in prayer the face is turned eastward:
cf. dakṣiṇa), 99¹²; —4. (like ὕστερος) the
latter (opp. pūrva); later; following,
99¹²; -am, as adv. finally, last, 104¹¹; —5.
as neuter subst. the final element of a
phrase of salutation, 60¹; —6. answer,
retort. [úd, 473: cf. ὕστερος, 'latter';
Eng. comp. ut-ter, 'outer.']

uttaratás, adv. northward; to the north
of; w. gen. [1130], 105¹³. [uttara.]

uttara-dāyaka, a. giving answer; contradicting.

uttara-paçcima, a. north-westerly.

uttara-purastāt, adv. north-east of;
w. gen., 1130.

úttara-loman, a. having the hair above,
with the hairy side up.

uttará, adv. northerly. [úttara, 1112e,
330⁴.]

uttará-patha, n. the northerly way;
the north country.

uttareṇa, adv. northerly; north of, w.
acc. [1129], 102⁵. [uttara, 1112c.]

uttarottara, —1. a. higher and higher
[1260]; -am, as adv. more and more, 24²;
—2. as n. answer to an answer [1264];
wordy talk, 24⁹. [uttara + uttara.]

utthā, see 233a.

utpala, n. a Nymphaea, i.e. water-lily or
lotus. [√paṭ + ud.]

utpādana, n. procreation.　[caus. of
√pad + ud.]

utphulla, a. wide open. [√phal + ud.
958.]

utsavá, m. —1. an undertaking, beginning; —2. feast-day, festival, 25⁴, 49¹⁶.
[√2 su + ud, 'set a-going'; but the development of 2 from 1 is not clear.]

úd, prefix. never used alone; up, up forth,
out. [cf. AS. ūt, Eng. out: see uttara,
uttama.]

√ ud or und (unátti; unná, uttá; -údya).
—1. spring; boil or bubble up; flow; —2.
wet, bathe. [cf. Lat. und-a, 'wave'; w.
ud-an, 'water,' cf. 55-ωp, Eng. wat-er; w.
ud-ra, 'otter,' cf. 55-ρα, 'water-snake,'
Eng. otter.]
+ sam, flow together; wet.

uda, n. water. [√ud.]

udaká [432], n. water. [√ud.]

uda-kumbhá, m. water-jar; jar with
water.

udag-ayaná, n. north-course (of the
sun), or the half-year from the winter to
the summer solstice. [udañc.]

údagdaça, a. having the seams upward.
[udañc + daçā, 'fringe, border, seam.']

udañ-mukha, a. having the face to the
north. [udañc, 1249a, 161.]

údañc [409b], a. directed upward; directed
northward (on account of the Himālayas),
cf. uttara), northerly; in cpds, udak.
1249a. [ud + añc, 407.]

udayá, m. a going up; rising (of the sun).
[√i (1148. 1a) + ud.]

udára, n. belly. [orig., perhaps, 'rising,
swelling,' √ṛ + ud: for mg, cf. the relation
of belly to AS. belgan, 'swell.']

udārá, a. (like Eng. exalted, i.e.) noble,
excellent. [√ṛ + ud, 'rise.']

udāra-carita, a. of noble behavior.

udita, *see* √vad; úd-ita, *see* √i.

údīcī, *see* 407³, 409b.

udumbalá, *a.* brown.

uddiçya, at, towards, *see* √diç.

uddhata, *see* 163 *and* √han.

údbāhuka, *a.* having the arms out *or* extended. [ud + bāhu, 1305, 1307.]

udya, *grdv.* to be spoken *or* pronounced. [√vad, 1213c end, cf. 963c.]

udyama, *m.* raising (of the hands to work); exertion. [√yam + ud.]

udyāna, *n.* —1. a walking out; —2. (place for walking out, *i.e.*) garden, park. [√yā + ud, 1150.]

udyoga, *m.* undertaking; exertion. [√yuj + ud, 216. 1.]

udyogin, *a.* active; energetic. [udyoga.]

udvigna-manas, *a.* having a terrified mind, distressed. [√vij.]

unmatta-darçana, *a.* having a frantic look. [√mad + ud.]

unmārga, *m.* by-way, evil way. [ud + mārga.]

unmārga-gāmin, *a.* going in evil ways.

úpa, —1. *vbl prefix.* to, unto, toward; *opp. of* ápa; —2. *prep., w. acc.,* unto, 81¹⁵; *w. loc.,* in, 77⁵; —3. *in noun cpds* [1289b], *denoting something near, accessory, or subordinate.* [cf. *ὑπό,* Lat. *s-ub,* 'under.']

upakaniṣṭhikā (*sc.* aṅguli), *a. f.* next to the little, *i.e.* the third (finger). [upa (mg 3) + kaniṣṭhaka, 1222d.]

upakartṛ, *m.* one who does kindness; benefactor. [√1 kṛ + upa, q.v.]

upakāra, *m.* friendly service; kindness. [√1 kṛ + upa, q.v.]

upakāraka, *a.* doing friendly service. [upakāra.]

upakārin, *a. the same; as m.* benefactor. [√1 kṛ + upa, q.v.]

upacārá, *m.* a coming to *or* waiting upon; *pregnantly,* (polite) attention; (correct) procedure, *i.e.* duty. [√car + upa.]

upatya, *a.* lying under. [upa, 1245b: cf. *ὑπ-τιο-ς,* 'lying under, supine.']

upatyakā, *f.* land lying at the foot (of a mountain). [upatya.]

upadeça, *m.* a pointing out to, a direction; instruction; advice. [√diç + upa.]

upadeçin, *a.* giving (good) instruction. [√diç + upa.]

upadeṣṭavya, *grdv.* to be taught. [do.]

upanāyana, *n.* investiture. [technical term, see √nī + upa.]

upapṛc, *a.* clinging close to, *w. gen.* [√pṛc + upa.]

upabhṛt, *f.* wooden cup (used in sacrifices), *see* sruc. ['tó-bringer,' √bhṛ (383h) + upa.]

upabhoga, *m.* enjoyment; eating. [√2 bhuj + upa, q.v.]

upamá, *a.* highest. [úpa, 474.]

upamá-çravas, *a.* having highest glory; *as m.* Upamaçravas, *a name like* Μεγιστο-κλῆς *or* Τψι-κλῆς.

upamā, *f.* comparison, image; *and so* likeness, resemblance; *at end of cpds,* having likeness with · ·, like · ·. [√1 mā + upa, 'compare.']

upamārtha, *m.* purpose of an image; -ena, figuratively. [artha.]

upayoga, *m.* ap-plication; use; utility. [√yuj + upa.]

upári, *adv.* above; *as prep., w. gen.* [1130], above; *at end of cpd* [1314f], upon, 30¹⁶. [cf. *ὑπείρ, ὑπέρι,* Lat. *s-uper,* 'over.']

upalā, *f.* upper mill-stone; *cf.* dṛṣad.

upavañcana, *n.* a tottering unto, a faltering approach. [√vañc + upa.]

upavana, *n.* small forest, *i.e.* grove. [upa (mg 3) + vana.]

úpavīta, *ppl.* wound about, *esp.* with the sacred cord; *as n.* [1176a], the being surrounded with the sacred cord; the cord itself. [√vyā + upa, 954c.]

upaveçá, *m.* a sitting down. [√viç + upa.]

úpaveçi, *m.* Upaveçi, name of a man.

upaçama, *m.* stopping; cessation. [√2 çam + upa, 'stop.']

upasaṃgrahaṇa, *n.* the clasping and taking to one's self (the feet of another), *as sign of great respect.* [√grah + upa-sam.]

upasevā, *f.* a serving; a being devoted to. [√sev + upa.]

upasevin, *a.* serving; revering. [√sev + upa.]

upástha, *m.* lap, groin.

upākhyāna, n. subordinate tale; episode, 1¹. [upa (mg 3) + ākhyāna.]

upādāna, n. the taking to one's self; appropriation. [√1 dā + upa_ā, 'take.']

upādhyāya, m. teacher. [√i + apa_adhi.]

upānáh, f. sandal; shoe. ['under-bond,' √nah + upa (247): for mg, cf. ὑπό-δημα, 'sandal.']

upántá, n. proximity to the end; edge; immediate neighborhood. [upa (mg 3) + anta.]

upāya, m. approach; that by which one reaches an aim; means; expedient, 39³; stratagem; advantage, 39⁴. [√i + upa, 1148.1a: for mg, cf. Eng. to-ward, as an adj.]

upáyana, n. approach. [√i + upa, 1150.1a.]

upārá, m. transgression. [√ṛ + upa.]

upekṣá, f. overlooking; neglect. [√īkṣ + upa.]

upoṣita, ppl. having abstained (i.e. from food), having fasted; as n. [1176a], fasting. [√3 vas + upa, q.v.]

√ ubh (ubhnāti, umbhāti [758]; ubdhá; -úbhya). unite; couple. [cf. ubhá.] + apa, bind, fetter.

ubhá, a. both. [cf. ἄμφω, Lat. ambō, AS. nom. fem. neut. bā, Goth. nom. neut. ba, nom. masc. bai, w. dental extension, bajoþs, all meaning 'both,' Eng. bo-th: orig., perhaps, 'couple,' and akin w. √ubh.]

ubháya [525⁴], a. of both sorts; both. [ubhá.]

ubháya-kāma, a. desirous of both.

ubhayátas, adv. from both sides; in both cases. [ubháya, acct!]

ubhayataḥ-sasya, n. having a crop at both times, i.e. bearing two crops a year.

urá-ga, m. serpent. ['breast-going,' ura for uras: for mg, cf. khaga.]

úras, n. breast. [perhaps, 'a cover,' from √1 vṛ, 'cover,' 1151.1b, w. a specialization like that in Eng. chest, 'thorax.']

urú, f. urvī, a. (prop. encompassing, and so, like Eng. capacious) extensive, wide, great; as n. (like Ger. das Weite) the distance. [√1 vṛ, 'encompass,' 1178a: cf. εὐρύ-s, 'wide.']

uru-vyácas, a. having wide embrace, wide extending. [acct, 1298b.]

√ uruṣya (uruṣyáti). to distance, i.e. escape; put another in the distance, i.e. save. [urú, 'the distance,' 1061².]

urū-ṇasá, a. having broad snouts. [urú (247) + nás, 193, 1315c: acct, 1298b.]

ulūkhala, n. a mortar.

úlba and úlva, n. enveloping membrane of an embryo. [for ·ur-vá, √1 vṛ, 'enclose,' 1190· cf. Lat. vol-va, 'covering, womb.']

ulbaṇá, a. lumpy, knotty, thick, massy. [ulba, for ·urva, hence ṇ, 189.]

√ uṣ (óṣati; uvóṣa; āóṣīt; uṣṭá). burn. [for cognates, see the collateral form √1 vas, 'light up,' also uṣás, usrá, etc.: cf. εὔω, 'singe'; αὔω, 'kindle'; Lat. ūr-o, 'burn,' and ustus = uṣṭá-s; AS. ys-le, 'glowing ashes.']

uṣás [415b], f. morning-red; dawn; personified, Dawn. [√1 vas, 'light up, dawn,' 252: cf. ἠώς, Aeolic αὔως, Lat. aurōra, ·ausōs-a, 'dawn'; radically cognate also is Eng. eas-t, 'the point where day breaks': see uṣ and usra.]

úṣṭra, m. camel.

uṣṇá, a. hot. [√uṣ, 1177a.]

usrá, a. bright; of or pertaining to the dawn; as f., usrá, dawn. [√1 vas, 'light up,' 252, 1188, 181a: w. us-rá, cf. Old Germanic Aus-t-rō, a goddess of the (year-dawn, i.e.) spring-light, and AS. Eos-t-ra, the name of whose festival, easter, 'Easter-day,' occurring in April, was transferred to the Christian festival that replaced it; for t between s and r, see under svasṛ: see uṣ and uṣas.]

ūti, f. furtherance, help, blessing; refreshment, food. [√av, 1157.]

údhan, údhar, ádhas [430b], n. udder. [cf. οὖθαρ, Lat. über, AS. úder, Eng. udder.]

ūná, a. lacking. [cf. εὖνις, 'bereft'; AS. wan, 'lacking,' wanian, 'decrease,' Eng. wane.]

ūrú, m. thigh. [prob. 'the thick' of the leg, from urú.]

úrj, *f.* sap; strength; vigor; nourishment. ['*√*varj, 'swell with, be full of': cf. ὀργάω, 'swell with, abound'; Lat. *virga,* 'swelling twig.']

ūrṇa, *n.,* and ūrṇā, *f.* wool. ['cover,' √1vṛ, 'cover' (cf. 712): cf. εἶρος, εὐ-ṛp-os, Lat. *vellus,* Goth. *vulla,* Eng. *wool.*]

úrṇa-mradas, *a.* having the softness of wool, soft as wool.

ūrṇā-stukā, *f.* braid *or* plait of wool.

√ ūrṇu, *see* 712, *and* √1vṛ.

ūrdhvá, *a.* tending upwards; upright; elevated; -am, *as adv.,* upwards; over; beyond; after, *w. abl.* [1128]; ata ūrdhvam, from now on. [cf. Lat. *arduus,* 'lofty.']

ūrdhva-dṛṣṭi, 'a. having an upward gaze. [1298.]

ūrmí, *m.* wave. [lit. 'roller, rolling billow,' √·vṛ, 'roll, turn hither and thither': cf. ἴλλω, εϝι-ϝλ-ω, Lat. *volvo,* 'roll'; Ger. *Welle,* 'wave.']

√ 1ūh (úhati; ūdhīt; ūḍhá, ūhitá; úhitum; -úhya). remove.

√ 2ūh (óhate [745a]; ūhé; ūdhīt, úūhiṣṭa; úhitum; -úhya). notice.

+ api, grasp; understand, 88¹⁰.

√ ṛ (íyarti [643c]; ṛṇóti; ṛchāti [753 end, 608]; āra [788a²]; ārat; ariṣyáti; ṛtá; ṛtvā; -ṭtya; arpáyati [1042d]). move, *as trans. and as intrans.;* — 1. rise, 73¹⁰; come upon *or* unto, reach, attain; — 2. raise (*e.g.* dust); — *caus.* send; put; fasten; fit in. [w. ṛ-ṇó-ti, cf. ὄρ-νυσι, 'rouses'; cf. Lat. *or-ior,* 'rise,' *or-tus,* 'risen'; ὀρ-το, 'rose,' — ár-ta, 3d sing. aor. mid.; w. ṛ-cchá-ti, cf. ἔρ-χε-ται, 'goes,' also ἐλ-θεῖν, 'go'; w. caus., cf. ἀρ-αρίσκω, 'fit,' Lat. *ar-tu-s,* 'well-fitted, close, narrow'; see also ṛtá.]

+ ā, — 1. get into (trouble), 93¹⁵ ɴ.; — 2. (*like the American* go for, 'treat harshly by word *or* deed') visit with trouble; *ppl.* ārta, visited by trouble, distressed.

+ ud, rise; raise.

+ upa, go against, transgress. [for mg, cf. ṛṇá.]

+ nis, (go forth, *i.e.*) dissolve connection with.

+ sam, come together, meet; go along with, 73⁹; — *caus.* send; deliver to; consign, entrust.

ṛkti, *f.* praise, in su-v-ṛkti. [√ṛc.]

ṛg-vedá, *m.* the Rigveda (each stanza of which is called an ṛc in distinction from a yajus and a sāman).

√ ṛc (árcati; ānárca, ānṛcé [788]; arciṣyáti; arcitá; árcitum; arcitvā; -árcya; arcáyati). — 1. beam; — 2. praise; sing (praise); sing (of the winds); honor; — *caus.* [1041²], salute. [cf. arka.]

ṛc, *f.* — 1. hymn of praise; *esp.* a stanza that is spoken, as distinguished from one that is sung (sāman) *or* from a sacrificial formula (yajus); — 2. stanza *or* text to which a certain rite *or* explanation has reference, 98⁵; — 3. the collection of ṛc's, the Rigveda, 57¹⁴, 63⁵. [√ṛc.]

ṛca, *for* ṛc, *at end of cpds* [1209a, 1815c].

√ 1ṛj *or* ṛñj (ṛñjáti, -te; ṛjyati, -te). reach out, *esp.* in a straight direction (*and so, the opp. of* √vṛj, 'bend, turn,' *q.v. and see* ṛjú), stretch out, *intrans.; press* on; *with this root, compare the root* rāj, mg 1. [cf. ὀρέγ-ω, 'reach out'; Lat. *reg-ere,* 'direct'; Eng. *right,* 'straight, not wrong.']

√ 2ṛj (árjati; arjáyati [1041²]; arjitá). reach, *and so,* get *or* obtain. [the same as √1ṛj, but w. another conjugation and w. trans. mg: for mg, cf. Eng. *reach,* intrans., w. *reach,* trans., and Ger. *langen* and *erlangen.*]

√3ṛj, in ṛj-rá, 'ruddy,' árj-una, 'silver-white'; *see also the root* raj *and root* rāj, mg 2. [cf. ἀργ-ός, 'bright'; Lat. *arguo,* 'make clear'; w. rajatá, 'silver,' cf. ἄργυρος, Lat. *argentum,* 'silver.']

ṛjiṣá, *a.* on-rushing. [√1ṛj, 1197b.]

ṛjiṣín, *a.* on-rushing. [ṛjiṣá, 1230a.]

ṛjú, *a.* straight, right, *opp. of* vṛjiná, 'crooked, wrong.' [√1ṛj, 1178a.]

√ ṛñj, *see* √1ṛj.

ṛṇá, *a.* (having gone against *or* transgressed, *and so*) guilty; *as n.* [1176a and 1177], guilt; debt, 25². [√ṛ: cf. Lat. *reus,* 'guilty': for mg, cf. upārá.]

ṛtá, a. fit, right; true; as n. [1176a], — 1.
established order; esp. eternal or divine
order; — 2. order in sacred things, sacred
custom, pious work, 69¹⁵, 74⁹; ṛtasya
yoni or sadana, central place of sacred
work or belief: in this world, the altar,
89⁸; in the other world, the holy of holies,
75⁷; — 3. truth, 98⁸⁹; —ṛtena, rightly.
[prop. 'fitted, made firm,' √ṛ: for form
and mg, cf. Lat. ra-tu-s, 'settled.']

ṛta-sáp [387a], a. following after right,
righteous.

ṛtávan, f. -varī, a. true to established
order (of regularly recurring natural phe-
nomena, e.g. dawn), 75¹¹; true to sacred
law, pious (Manes), 91¹⁰; holy, sacred
(god), 75⁸. [ṛta, 247: for fem., 435,
1171².]

ṛtā-vṛdh, a. rejoicing in right, holy
(Manes). [ṛta, 247.]

ṛtú, m. — 1. a fixed and settled time; esp.
time for sacrificing; — 2. time of year,
i.e. season; — 3. the menses. [√ṛ, 1161a:
cf. ἀρτύ-ω, 'fit together, prepare'; Lat.
artu-s, 'joint.']

ṛté, prep. without; except. [1128 end, 1129
end.]

ṛtv-íj, a. offering at the appointed time;
as m. priest; in the ritual, pl., priests, of
whom there are four, hótṛ, adhvaryú,
brahmán, and udgātṛ. [ṛtú + íj.]

ṛddhi, f. welfare; blessedness. [√ṛdh,
1157.]

√ ṛdh (ṛdhnóti; ānárdha, ānṛdhé [788];
ardhiṣyáte; ṛddhá; ṛdhyáte). thrive;
succeed; prosper, both as intrans. and as
trans. [cf. √edh, rādh: cf. ἄλθομαι, 'get
well.']

+ sam, pass. be prospered, i.e. fulfilled.

√ 1ṛṣ (árṣati; ānárṣa [788]). flow; glide.
[cf. ἄψ-ορρος, 'flowing back,' παλίν-ορσος,
'darting back.']

√ 2ṛṣ (ṛṣáti; ṛṣṭá). push; thrust.

ṛṣi, m. — 1. singer of sacred songs, poet;
priestly singer; regarded by later generations as a patriarchal saint or sage of the
olden time and as occupying a position
given in other lands to the heroes and
patriarchs; one of those inspired poets
who "saw" the Vedas, which were "re-

vealed" to them; — 2. sapta ṛṣayas:
the many Rishis; later, the seven stars of
the Great Bear; — 3. a Rishi, i.e. a person
renowned for piety and wisdom, 100²²; —
see note to 1¹⁴.

ṛṣṭí, f. spear. [√2ṛṣ.]

ṛṣvá, a. lofty.

————————

e, pron. root in éka, etá, ena, evá, evám.

éka [482a], num. — 1. one; only; alone
(by one's self); alone (excluding every
one else); sole; single; solitary; advly
in cpds, solely; — 2. one (of two or more);
the one, followed by anya, dvitīya, para;
eke · · eke, some · · others; eke, some
folks, some; — 3. later, a certain, quidam;
or almost as an indef. article [482a³], a or
an, 20⁸. [pron. root e.]

eka-tatpara, a. solely intent on, 45⁴.

ekatra, adv. in one place. [eka, 1099.]

ekadā, adv. at one time, simultaneously,
at 37⁹; elsewhere, at a certain time, i.e.
once upon a time. [eka, 1103.]

eka-deça, m. a certain place, and so, a
place or spot or part.

eka-nakṣatrá, n. lunar mansion consisting of a single star or one whose name
occurs but once, see 104⁸N. [nákṣatra,
1312.]

éka-patnī, f. wife of only one man,
faithful wife. [acct, 1267a.]

eka-pada, f. -ī, a. having (i.e. taking)
one step.

eka-bhakṣa, m. sole food; at end of
cpds [1298], having · · as sole food, eating
· · alone.

eka-mati, a. having one mind, unanimous.

eka-varṇa, a. having one color, not
brindled.

ekākin, a. solitary. [eka.]

ekāñjali, m. one handful. [añjali.]

ékādaça, num. eleven. [éka + dáça,
476³.]

ekādaçá, a. eleventh. [ékādaça, 487⁷.]

ekānta, m. an end; a retired or secret
spot. [anta.]

ekāpāya, m. diminution by one. [apāya.]

ekārtha, m. one purpose, i.e. one and
the same purpose. [artha.]

ekāhá, m. one day. [2áha.]

ékāika, a. one by itself; one singly; each one singly; every single one. [eka + eka.]

ekāikaçaṣ, adv. one by one; severally. [ekāika, 1106.]

ekona, a. lacking one. [ūna, 477a.]

etá, see etád and cf. 499b with 497.

éta, a. rushing; darting; as m. deer. [√i, 1176c.]

etat-sama, a. equal to this. [1265.]

etat-samīpa, n. presence of this one. [1264.]

etád [499b], pron. this here, prop. referring to something near the speaker (e.g. 18⁶, 19¹¹, 51¹⁰); this; refers almost always to what precedes (e.g. 6⁹, 19³, 51¹⁸, 68⁵), has just happened (e.g. 20¹¹, 25¹³·¹³), or has just been mentioned (e.g. 7⁵, 25¹⁸, 28¹¹), as being nearer the speaker; very seldom — 28⁶, 92¹⁹, 96⁵ — to what follows; joined with other pronouns: w. yad, 94¹⁵; w. tad, 45⁹, 95⁶; w. aham to be supplied, 52⁹. [pron. root e, 499b: in usage, etád : idám : : ταῦτα : τόδε.]

etad-artham, adv. for this purpose; therefore. [499b², 1302c⁴.]

etárhi, adv. nowadays. [etá, 1103c.]

etā-dṛç, a. such; etādṛk, acc. s. n., such as I have, 82¹⁴. [518.]

etā-dṛça, a. such; et. · · yat, such · · that. [518.]

etávant, a. thus much, 12⁹; etāvān · · yena, so great · · that, 21¹⁰. [etá, 517.]

√ edh (édhate; edhām cakre; āidhiṣṭa; edhitá; édhitum).   thrive; prosper. [ident. w. √ṛdh, q.v.: cf. geha w. gṛha.]

ena [500], encl. pron. used only substantively; unemphatic him, her, it, them. [pron. root e.]

énas, n. sin. [perhaps, 'deed of violence,' √in.]

énasvant, a. sinful. [énas.]

enā, adv. in this way; here; pará enā: beyond here; beyond, w. instr., RV.x. 125.8; there; yátra · · enā, whither · · thither. [pron. root a, see idám, and cf. 502² and 1112a.]

eraṇḍa, m. Ricīnus communis, i.e. castoroil plant or Palma Christi.

evá, adv. — 1. in this way; so; in this signification Vedic only, its place being supplied in post-Vedic by evám; yáthā · · evá, as · · so, 86¹³; evá_id, in very truth, 74⁶;

— 2. just, exactly, etc., emphasizing the preceding word; in this sense Vedic (69⁵, 85¹, 87¹, 91⁵) and post-Vedic; requires the most various translations — sometimes mere stress of voice: precisely; no more nor less than; nothing short of; no other than; merely; quite; without exception; andha eva, blind outright; vasudhā_eva, the whole earth; mṛtyur eva, sure death; mūṣika eva kṛtas, was changed back to a simple mouse; cintayann eva, just while he was thinking; uktam eva mayā, just what I told thee; lokāiḥ kiṁcid vaktavyam eva, folks will be sure to say something; eka eva, entirely alone; pumāṅsa eva, only males; — in connection w. pronouns and adverbs: etad eva, this very; tathā_eva, all so, i.e. also; na_eva, by no means; w. very attenuated mg in ca_eva, and also, and eva ca, and also, the latter at end of a çloka, 58¹³. [pron. root e, 1102b: sometimes evá, 248a.]

evaṁ-víd, a. knowing so or such, i.e. well instructed, knowing what's what.

evaṁvidha, a. of such sort, such. [evam (1306) + vidha, 1302c 5.]

evám, adv. in this way; so; post-Vedic, and supplying the place of evá in mg 1; used first w. √ vid: yá evám vidús, who know thus, have this knowledge, 97¹·³; yathā · · evam, as · · so; very frequent w. uktvā or çrutvā, upon saying or hearing this; evam ukta, thus addressed; w. impers. used ppl., 7⁸, 39²⁷; evam astu, so be it; mā_evam, not so! yady evam, if that's the case, 48¹¹; evam, in that case, 11⁴; evam, likewise, 103⁷; refers back (e.g. 28²¹, 52⁸), or forward (e.g. 31⁵, 37⁸, 50⁶); used superfluously w. iti, 61¹³; as equiv. to evaṁvidha, 15⁴. [pron. root e, 1102b.]

evam-bhūta, a. such. [see 1273c.]

eṣo, a Prakrit form for eṣas, 49⁸

───────

āikamatya, n. unanimity. [ekamati, 1211.]

āitihāsika, m. teller of old legends. [iti-hāsa, 1222e 2.]

āindrābārhaspatyá, a. belonging to Indra and Brihaspati. [índrābŕhaspáti, 1204c.]

───────

ókas, n. wonted place; home. [√uc.]

oṁ-kṛta, a. having an uttered om, accompanied by om. [the natural order would require kṛtáum: order inverted to avoid such an undeclinable stem.]

ójas, n. strength; power. [√vaj or uj, 252, cf. ug-rám ój-as, 78⁴: cf. Lat. augus-tus, 'mighty, i.e. august.']

ojo-dá [352], a. strength-giving.

odaná, m. n. grain boiled with milk; porridge. [√ad: for mg, cf. Eng. broth and brew.]

opaçá, m. top-knot; plume. [perhaps for *ava-paça, √2 paç.]

óm, a word of solemn asseveration and reverent acknowledgment, somewhat like ἀμήν; a sacred mystic syllable, uttered at the beg. and end of Veda-reading; cf. praṇava. [origin uncertain.]

óṣadhī, later óṣadhi, f. herb; plant; a simple.

───────

āupamya, n. similitude; likeness. [upamá, 1211.]

áupaveçi, m. patronymic of Aruna. [úpaveçi (or upaveçá?): cf. 1221.]

āuṣadhá, a. consisting of herbs; as n. herbs collectively; simples; medicine. [óṣadhi, 1208d.]

───────

I ká [504], pron. —1. interrogative. who, what; used as subst. (7⁶·⁷) or as adj. (18¹⁷); kim w. instr.: e.g. kiṁ yuddhena, what (is there) with fighting, what's the use of fighting, 45¹⁴; so 17¹⁹, 24⁹; so ko 'rthas, 17¹³; kim w. instr. and gen.: e.g. nírujaḥ kim āuṣadhāis, what has a well man (to do) with medicines, 22⁸; so 32²¹, 51²⁰; ka w. particles: ko nāma, who indeed; ko nu, who pray; ko vā, who possibly, 18¹;

—2. indefinite, both adj. and subst., chiefly in negative clauses and w. the particles [see 507] ca, caná, cid, ápi; —2a. w. má: má kásmāi dhātam abhy āmitríṇe nas, deliver us not over to any foe; —2b. ka ca, some, any, adj. or subst.; kiṁ ca, anything; w. relative, yāç (ca) kāç ca, (and) what soever, 68¹⁰; —2c. w. ca na and cana: ka ca na, also or even not any; esp. after a negative: na taṁ çaknuvanti vyāhartum api, kiṁ ca na, can not even speak to him, not even anything, i.e. can not even speak anything to him, 8¹⁹; so 96²¹; and so (the feeling for the negation in cana in such collocations becoming lost), ka cana means any, anything, cf. cana; w. relative, soever; yat kiṁcana, whatsoever, 9¹⁶; —2d. very often ka cid: any body or thing; certain, 18¹¹; often w. negative: e.g. 9⁹; 24¹¹ (twice with, twice without); kiṁcit kiṁcid, each a little, 27⁹; w. relative, ya ka cid, whosoever, whatsoever, any soever, 21¹¹; kāni kāni cid, any soever, 82¹⁵; —2e. ka api, something, somebody, 17¹¹; some, a or an, a certain, 21²; na ka api: nothing, 39²¹; no, no one, 20¹⁰;

—3. derivs of ka, see 505; —4. exclamatory, at beg. of cpds: cf., e.g., ká-puruṣa, kim-prabhu, ku-dṛṣṭi, ko-vida, and see 506, 1121e; —5. for kim as adv., see kim. [for the stem-forms ka, ki, ku, see 505: cf. Ionic κο-, Attic πο-, in κό-θεν, κῶς, etc., 'whence, how'; τί-s, τί, Lat. qui-s, qui-d, AS. hwā, hwæ-t, Eng. who, wha-t; w. katará, 'which of twain,' cf. κό-τερο-s, Lat. uter, AS. hwœ-ðer, Eng. whe-ther, 'which of twain'; w. ka as indef., cf. τι-s, 'any one.']

2 ka, m. Who, as name of a god, 94¹⁴·¹⁶ N.

kaṁsá, m. metallic vessel; as collective, metallic implements.

kakṣā, f. —1. region of the girth; —2. girdle, cincture; —3. (like French ceinture) circular wall; and so the enclosed court. [cf. kañkaṇa: cf. Lat. cinc-tus, 'girded'; for 1, cf. coxa, 'hip'; for 3, cf. canc-er, 'fence.']

kañkaṇa, n. ring-shaped ornament, bracelet. [cf. kakṣā.]

kañkāla, m. n. skeleton.

kaccid, see kad.

kaccha, m. border; shore; marsh-land; the district Cutch.

kaccha-pa, *m.* tortoise. ['keeping, *i.e.* inhabiting the marsh,' √bl 2 pa.]

kaṭaka, *m. n.* dale.

káṇa, *m.* a small grain (as of dust or rice). [cf. kaniṣṭha.]

káṇṭaka, *m.* thorn.

kaṇṭaki-kṣīrin, *m. pl.* thorn-plants and milk-plants.

kaṇṭakin, *a.* thorny; *as m.* thorn-plant. [kaṇṭaka.]

kathám, *Vedic* **kathá,** *interr. adv.* how? in what way? **katham etat,** how's that? **katham nu,** how indeed? **katham cana,** in any wise soever (*emphasizing a preceding negation*); **katham api,** somehow. [ka, 1101.]

√ **kathaya** (kathayati). tell; talk about; *pass.* be called, pass for. [lit. 'tell the how,' 'τὸ ὅπως λέγειν': denom. fr. **katham,** 1058.]

1 **kathá,** *see* kathám.

2 **kathá,** *f.* −1. story, tale, fable; discussion; −2. *personified,* Story, 56⁹. [prop. 'the how, τὸ ὅπως,' 1 kathá.]

kathá-chala, *n.* cover *or* guise of a fable.

kathá-pīṭha, *n.* pedestal of Kathá, name of the first book of the Kathá-sarit-sāgara. [2 kathá, mg 2.]

kathávatára, *m.* incarnation of Kathá. [2 kathá (mg 2) + avatára.]

kathá-sarit-sāgara, *m.* Story-stream-ocean, title of Soma-deva's collection.

kád, *interr. pcl.* nonne, num; *w.* cid, nonne, num; **kaccid dṛṣṭā,** was she seen? [crystallized acc. s. n. of ka, 1111a.]

kadá, *adv.* when? **na kadá cana,** not at any time soever, never; **kadá cid,** once on a time, one day; **kadá cid api na,** never. [ka, 1103.]

kádru, *a.* brown; **kadrú** [355c], *f.* brown Soma-vessel.

√ **kan** *or* **ká** (caké; ákānīt). be glad. [cf. √kam and √can.]

kánaka, *n.* gold.

kanaka-sútra, *n.* gold cord *or* chain.

kanaka-stambha-rucira, *a.* shining with gold columns.

kaniṣṭha, *a.* smallest; youngest. [cf. the following words and kaṇa and kanyá.]

kaniṣṭhaka, *a.* smallest; *f.* -ikā [1222d], *sc.* aṅguli, the little finger. [kaniṣṭha.]

kaniṣṭha-prathama, *a.* having the youngest as the first.

kánīyāṅs, *a.* smaller; younger. [cf. kaniṣṭha and 467².]

kandara, *n.* cave. [perhaps 'great cleft,' kam (see ka 4) + dara.]

kandarpa, *m.* the god of love. [perhaps 'of great wantonness,' kam (see ka 4) + darpa.]

kanyaká, *f.* girl. [kanyá, 1222b.]

kanyá, *f.* girl; maiden; daughter. [cf. kaniṣṭha.]

kanyá-ratna, *n.* girl-jewel, excellent maiden.

kapaṭa, *m. n.* fraud.

kapaṭa-prabandha, *m.* continued series of frauds; machination, plot.

kaparda, *m.* small shell used as a coin, 80 = 1 paṇa; **-aka,** *m. the same.*

kapála, *n.* −1. cup *or* dish, 102¹³; −2. cover *or* lid, 104¹⁶; −3. cranium. [for mg, cf. Lat. *testa,* 'earthen pot,' w. French *tête,* 'head.']

kapóta, *m.* dove.

kám, *pcl.* −1. *emphasizing the preceding word,* 79¹¹; −2. *interr. pcl.,* 88¹⁰. [ka, 1111a: cf. kád, kim.]

√ **kam** (cakamé; kamiṣyáte; kāntá [955a]; kāmáyate, -tí [1041¹]). wish; will; desire; love. [cf. √kan and √can.]

kamaṇḍalu, *m.* water-jar.

√ **kamp** (kámpate; cakampé; kampitá; kámpitum; -kámpya). tremble *or* shake.

kambalá, *m.* woolen cloth.

kambu, *m.* shell.

kambu-grīva, *m.* Shell-neck (*i.e.* having folds in the neck like a spiral shell), name of a tortoise. [grīvá.]

1 **kará,** −1. *a.* doing; making *or* causing *or* producing, *at end of many cpds*; −2. *as m.* the hand (*lit.* the busy one); −3. *as m. nomen actionis,* the doing, performance, *in* duṣkara, sukara. [√1 kṛ: cf. Lat. *cerus,* 'creator.']

2 **kara,** *m.* ray, beam. [prob. same as 1 kara 2: the rays of the heavenly bodies are conceived as their hands and feet, cf. pāda 4.]

kara-vāri, *n.* water from the hand.

karuṇa, *a.* mournful, pitiable; -ā, *f.* pity.

karuṇā-para, *a.* compassionate. [1302b.]

karkaṭa, *m.* crab; -aka, *the same.*

kárṇa, *m.* ear.

kartá, *m.* (earth-) cut, ditch. [√kṛt: see garta.]

kartṛ́, *m.* doer; accomplisher; officiating priest, 101 ¹¹. [√1 kṛ.]

kartavya, *grdv.* to be done *or* made, *w. the various mgs of* √1 kṛ. [√1 kṛ.]

kartavyatā, *f.* the to-be-done-ness; -tām brūhi, tell me what I must do. [1237.]

karpūra, *m. n.* camphor.

karpūra-paṭa, *m.* Camphor-cloth, name of a certain washerman.

karpūra-vilāsa, *m.* Camphor-joy (*lit.* having pleasure in camphor), name of a washerman.

karma, *for* karman *in cpds,* 1249a².

karma-ceṣṭā, *f.* deed-performance; action.

karma-ja, *a.* deed-born, resulting from the actions of a life.

karma-doṣa, *m.* deed-sin, sinful deed.

kárman, *n.* deed, work, action; sacred work (as sacrifice, ablution); rite, 59¹. [√1 kṛ.]

kárhi, *adv.* when? karhi cid, at any time. [ka, 1103c.]

√ kal (kāláyati). drive. [cf. κέλεται, 'urges on'; βου-κόλος, 'cattle driver'; Lat. *celer,* (like colloq. *driving,* i.e. 'hurrying') 'swift.'] -anu-sam, lead along after.

kala, *a.* dumb; indistinct; -am, *adv.* gently, *and so* pleasantly (of humming).

kalaha, *m.* strife, contention.

kalā, *f.* a small part, *esp.* a sixteenth.

kálpa, *m.* ordinance, precept; manner, way; etena kalpena, in this way.

kalmaṣa, *n.* spot, stain; *fig., as in Eng.,* sin.

kalmaṣa-dhvaṅsa-kārin, *a.* sin-destruction-causing, preventing the commission of crime.

kalya, *a.* well, healthy. [cf. καλός, 'fair': prob. not akin are AS. *hāl,* Eng. *hale, whole.*]

kalyāṇa, *f.* -āṇī [355b], *a.* fair, lovely. [kalya.]

kalyāṇa-kaṭaka, *m. n.* Fair-dale, name of a place.

kaví, *a.* wise, possessed of insight (of gods, *esp.* Agni); *as m.* wise man, seer, sage; poet; *pl.* wise men of eld (whose spirits hover about the sun), 91¹². [prop. 'seer,' √kū, 'see,' for -akū: cf. θυοσκόος, ι-σκοϝο-ι, 'inspecting the sacrifice'; Lat. *cav-ēre,* 'look out, be cautious'; Ger. *schauen,* AS. *sceāwian,* 'look,' Eng. *show,* 'cause to look at.']

kaví-kratu, *a.* having the power *or* insight (krátu) of a wise one; intelligent. [1296.]

√ kas (kásati; kastá; kāsáyati). move. +vi, move asunder; open; bloom; *caus. pass.* be made to bloom.

kásmāt, *adv.* why? wherefore? [ka, 1114a.]

kāṅsya, *a.* brazen; *as n.* brass. [kaṅsá.]

kāka, *m.* crow; —*f.* kākī, crow-hen; *cf.* vāyasa, 'crow.'

√ kāṅkṣ (kāṅkṣati, -te; cakāṅkṣa; kāṅkṣitá). desire, long for. [desid. of √kam, but reduplicated somewhat like an intens. (1002), -kām-ka(m)-s.]

kācá, *m.* glass.

kāca-maṇi, *m.* rock-crystal, quartz. [lit. 'glass-jewel.']

kāñcana, *n.* gold.

kāṇá, *a.* one-eyed; perforated (of the eye), blind.

kāṇa-bhūti, *m.* Kāṇabhūti, name of a Yaksha, *see* 53¹ ᴺ. [lit. 'Blind-luck.']

kāṇḍa, *m. n.* section; joint of a stalk from one knot to another; arrow.

kāntāra, *m. n.* great *or* primeval forest.

kānti, *f.* loveliness. [√kam, 1157, cf. 955a.]

kā-puruṣa, *m.* miserable man, coward. [see 1 kā 4, and 506.]

kāma, *m.* wish, desire, longing; love; *at end of possessive cpds* [1296], having desire for ··, desirous of ··; kāmam, *see s.v.* [√kam.]

kāma-dúh (-dhuk, -duham, -dhugbhis, etc. [155]), —1. *a.* yielding wishes, granting every wish; —2. *as f., sc.* dhenu, the fabulous Wonder-cow. [for 2, cf. the horn of Amalthēa.]

kāmam, *adv.* at will; if you please; **kāmam tu ·· na tu**, if she please, ··, but by no means ··, 64[11]. [**kāma**, 1111b.]

kāmín, *a. subst.* affectionate (spouse). [**kāma**.]

kāminī-sakha, *a.* in the company of his wives. [see **sakha**.]

kāya, *m.* body. [√1ci, 'build,' Whitney 43: for mg, cf. δέμας, 'body, form,' and δέμω, 'build,' and Eng. noun *build*, as used of 'a man's figure.']

kāyika, *a.* corporeal; performed by the body. [**kāya**.]

kāra, *a.* making; *as m.* maker; deed, action; sound. [√1kr.]

kāraṇa, *n.* that which makes *or* occasions; cause, 57[7]; occasion; reason; sake, 10[1]; ground for a judgment, 22[11]. [√1kr.]

kārin, *a.* causing. [do.]

kārú, *m.* praiser, poet, singer. [√2kr, 'mention with praise.']

kārttikeya, *m. metronymic of* Skanda, god of war (so called because he was nourished by the Pleiads, kṛttikās): *cf.* **kumāra** *and* **svāmikumāra**. [kṛttikā, 1216.]

kāryà, *grdv.* to be done, faciendus, *w. the various shades of mg belonging to* √1kr; requiring to be instituted, 4[19]; requiring to be shown; —*as n.* what is to be done; business; work; matter, 4[17]; affair; duty; emergency. [√1kr, 963b.]

kārya-kāla, *m.* time for action.

kārya-hantṛ, *m.* business-destroyer, mar-plot.

kāryākṣama, *a.* unequal to *or* unfit for work. [**akṣama**.]

kālá, *m.* —1. the right *or* proper *or* appointed time; —2. time *in general*; —3. Time, *as* the destroyer, *i.e.* Death.

kāla-pāça, *m.* snare of Death.

kāvya, *n.* poetry; poem. [**kavi**.]

kāvyaçāstra-vinoda, *m.* entertainment with poetry and science. [**kāvya-çāstra**, 1252.]

\ **kāç** (**kāçate**; **cakāçé**; **kāçitá**; -**kāçyà**). be visible; shine.

+ **ava**, be visible, lie open.

+ **ā**, look on.

- **pra**, shine out; become clear.

kāça, *m.* visibility, *in* **sakāça**. [√kāç.]

kāṣṭhá, *n.* stick of wood; log.

kāṣṭha-ccheda, *m.* dearth of wood. [227.]

kāṣṭha-bhārika, *m.* wood-carrier.

kāṣṭhā, *f.* race-course; course; track of the winds and clouds in the sky.

kāṣṭhika, *m.* woodman. [**kāṣṭha**.]

ki, *cf.* 1kā4, *and* 504.

kim-suhṛd, *m.* a bad friend. [see 1kā4, and 506.]

kitavá, *m.* gambler; *f.* -vī, *as a.*, addicted to gaming. [poss. **kim** + **tava**, 'what of thee?' 'what is thy stake?']

kim, —1. *as nom. acc. s. n. to* **kā**, *see* 1kā; —2. *as interr. adv.* [1111a], how? 73[8]· why? 18[10]; —3. *as interr. pcl.:* num; **kim aham ajñas**, am I a fool? 39[11]; an, 78[13], —4. *in connection w. other pcls:* **kiṁ ca**, moreover, *see* ca 3; **kiṁ tu**, however, 20[11]; **kiṁ cana**, somewhat, 46[9]; **kim punar**, how much more (*or* less)? 17[16]. [see under 1kā.]

kim-artha, *a.* having what as object; **kimártham**, *as adv.* why? [1302c4.]

kim-prabhu, *m.* a bad master. [see 1kā4, and 506.]

kim-bhṛtya, *m.* a bad servant. [do.]

kiyad-dūra, *n.* small distance; -re, *as adv.* [1116], a little way. [**kiyant**.]

kíyant [451], *pron. a.* —1. how great? how much? what sort of a? 45[10]; —2. (how great, *in a derogatory sense, i.e.*) not great; small, 46[1]. [1kā or ki, 505, 1172[2].]

kiyámbu, *n.* water-lily, *perhaps.* [cf. ambu.]

kíla, **kílā** [248a], *adv.* indeed, *emphasizing the foregoing word*.

kís, *interr. pcl.* so at 88[10]. [1kā, 504[2]: see 1117: cf. nákis.]

kíṭa, *m.* worm; caterpillar.

kídṛg-vyāpāra, *m.* what business. [**kídṛç**, 145.]

kídṛgvyāpāravant, *a.* having what business. [1233.]

kídṛç, *a.* of what sort? [see 518.]

kiri, *m.* praiser. [√2kr.]

√ **kirtaya** (**kirtáyati** [1056, 1067]; *pass.* **kīrtyáte**). —1. make mention of; tell; —2. repeat; call. [**kīrtí**, 1061[2].]

+ **pari**, tell around, announce.

+ **sam**, announce.

kīrti, *f.* mention; *esp.* good report, fame. [√2 kṛ.]

ku, *see* 1 ká 4, *and* 504.

kukkura, *m.* dog. [younger form of the onomatopoetic **kurkurá**.]

kuṭumba, *n.* household; family; -aka, *the same.*

kuṭṭanī, *f.* bawd.

kuṇḍa, *n.* round vessel; round hole in the ground (for water or sacred fire).

kuṇḍala, *n.* ring, *esp.* ear-ring. [cf. **kuṇḍa** and 1227.]

kútas, *adv.* from what place? whence? wherefore? why? how? 19¹⁷. [1 ká or **ku**, 505.]

kutūhala, *n.* —1. interest felt in something extraordinary; eagerness; -āt, *as adv.* [1114b], eagerly; —2. interest caused by something remarkable, 56¹¹.

kútra, *adv.* where? whither? [1 ka or **ku**, 505.]

ku-dṛṣṭi, *f.* a bad *or* false view; heterodox philosophy. [see 1 ká 4, and 506.]

kunti, *f.* Kuntī, one of the two wives of Pāṇḍu.

√ **kup** (kúpyati; cukópa; kupitá). —1. become moved *or* agitated; boil; *and so* —2. *fig., as in Eng.*, be angry; boil with rage.

+ **pra**, *the same.*

kumārá, *m.* —1. new-born child; boy; youth, 51¹⁰; —2. The Youth, epithet of Skanda, the eternally youthful god of war—*see* **kārttikeya**; —*f.* -rī, girl. [cf. **sukumāra**.]

kumāra-datta, *m.* name of a man. ['given by the god Kumāra.']

kumbhá, *m.* jar; pot; urn. [cf. κύμβη, 'vessel.']

kumbha-kāra, *m.* pot-maker, potter.

kumbhikā, *f.* pitcher. [**kumbha**.]

kúru, *m. as pl.* the Kurus, a people of India; *as sing.* Kuru, the ancestor of that people.

kuru-çrávaṇa, *m.* name of a prince. [lit. 'glory of the Kurus,' like Πυθο-κλῆς: acct, 1271.]

kúla, *n.* —1. herd *or* large number *or* swarm (of quadrupeds, birds, insects); —2. race; family; *and so, as in Eng.*, good family, noble stock. [√3 kṛ, q.v.: cf. **ākula**.]

kula-çīla, *n.* family and character. [1253b.]

kúlāla, *m.* potter.

kú-liça, *m.* axe. [perhaps 'cutting well,' see 1 ká 4, and 506.]

kulīna, *a.* of good family. [**kula**, 1223d.]

kulīra, *m.* crab.

kuçá, *m.* grass; *esp.* the sacred grass, Poa cynosuroides, with long stalks and numerous pointed leaves.

kuça-piñjúla, *n.* tuft *or* bunch of Kuça.

kúçala, —1. *a.* in good condition; equal to *or* fit for a task; able; clever, 46¹⁸; —2. *as n.* welfare, well-being; kuçalaṁ te, hail to thee.

kuçalin, *a.* well; prosperous. [**kuçala** 2.]

kuça-hasta, *a.* having Kuça in the hand. [1308.]

√ **kū** (kuváte). *found only w.* ā, *and perhaps meaning* see, look. [prob. for •akū, see under **kavi**.]

+ **ā**, look forward to, *i.e.* intend. [see **ākūta**.]

kúṭa, —1. *n.* horn; —2. *m. n.* peak. [for mg 2, cf. the Swiss peak-names, *Schreck-horn*, *Wetter-horn*, etc.]

kūpa, *m.* cave, hole; well. [cf. κύπη, 'cave, hut,' Lat. *cŭpa*, 'vat'; 'niche for the dead,' borrowed Eng. *coop*, 'vat,' whence *cooper*.]

kūrmá, *m.* tortoise.

√ 1 kṛ (*Vedic*, kṛṇóti, kṛṇuté [715]; *later*, karóti, kuruté [714]; cakāra, cakré; *V.* ákar, ákṛta [831, 834a]; *later*, ákārṣīt; kariṣyáti; kṛtá; kártum; kṛtvā; -kṛtya; kriyáte; cíkīrṣati; kāráyati, -te). do, make, *in the various meanings and uses of these words; thus*,

—1. perform, 59²¹; accomplish; cause; effect; prepare, 83¹⁵; undertake, 52²; commit, 29¹²; show: *e.g.* honor, 5⁶; familiarity, 9¹⁷; compassion, 21¹⁹; love, 42¹⁸; favor, 52²¹; contempt, 54¹⁸; attend to: an affair, 11⁴; engage in: trade, 46¹¹; a quarrel, 42¹⁹; —2. do something (good *or* bad) for a person (gen.), 3², 9¹⁵; —3. make or procure for another, 82⁴; grant; —middle: get for one's self; assume: human voice, 3¹⁴; take on: form or shape, 48², 49⁶; —4. execute; follow: advice, 40⁷; —5. work over, prepare: food, 68²; —6. accomplish; be good for, 18⁶; —7. make: a sound, 26¹⁷; utter: the syllable om, 60⁸·⁹;

—8. (like Eng. do in don, doff) put in or on; w. loc., 81¹, 43⁶; set, 105¹⁴; w. adverbs: see agratas, amā, āvis, tiras, puras, bahis; —9. make a person (acc.) to be something (acc.), 79¹²; transform into, 40¹³ff.; render, w. factitive predicate acc., 18⁸; w. the predicate in composition [1094]: e.g. sajjī-kṛ, make ready, 34¹⁷; —10. w. adv. in -dhā, divide in parts, 57¹⁰; —11. do, go to work, proceed, 37⁵; pass. impers., 30¹⁸; —12. do, esp. sacred work; with karma, 97²; without karma (like ῥέζειν θεῷ and facere), to sacrifice, 93¹²; —see also kṛta.

—desid. desire to perform; ppl. [1037], cikīrṣita, that which is sought to be done, intention.

—caus. cause to do or make or be done or made; see to it that a thing takes place, 16¹; pass. tena sa praṇāmaṁ kāritas, by him he was caused to make obeisance, 36⁷; caus. equiv. to simple verb, 26⁵.

[cf. αὐτο-κρά-τωρ, 'self-actor, independent'; Κρό-νος, an old harvest-god, 'Perficus, the Completer, Ripener'; Lat. cer-us, 'creator'; κραίνω, 'accomplish'; Lat. creāre, 'create': see kratu: orig. root-form, perhaps, skṛ, 1087d.]

+adhi, put over; put in office.

+apa, put off; injure, opp. of upakṛ.

+aram or alam, see these words.

+ā, bring hither, 74¹⁰; prepare, fashion, make.

+vy-ā, separate, analyse.

+upa, bring something to some one; do a service, act as an auxiliary, opp. of apakṛ. [w. the use of upa, cf. that of sub in subvenire, 'aid.']

+pari, (poss. surround, deck, and so) make ready; adorn.

+pra, —1. carry forward, accomplish; effectuate, cause; —2. mid. set before; put before one, i.e. make the subject of discussion or treatment; w. buddhim, put a plan before one's self, i.e. decide.

+prati, work against, counteract.

+sam, —1. put together; conficere, prepare; —2. treat according to the sacred usages, administer a sacrament to, see saṁskāra; consecrate, 106²; —3. adorn.

√ 2 kṛ (ákārīt; intens. cárkarti). mention with praise.

√ 3 kṛ (kiráti [242]; cakāra, cakré; ákārīt; kariṣyáti; kīrṇá [957b]; -kirya). pour out or scatter abundantly (e.g. hail-stones); cast forth (missiles); strew; cover or fill with. [cf. kula, 'swarm.']

+vy-ati, pass. be scattered in various directions; be brought to confusion. [cf. vyatikara, 'disaster.']

+ava, strew (loose earth); throw in.

+ā, scatter abundantly; cover over, fill; ākirṇa, bestrown, covered. [cf. ākara, 'abundance, mine,' ākula, 'full.']

+sam-ā, bestrew; cover.

kṛcchrá, a. distressful; troublesome; as n. trouble.

kṛcchra-karman, n. hard work; drudgery.

√ kṛt (kṛntáti, -te [758]; cakárta; ákṛtat; kartiṣyáti, kartsyáti; kṛttá; -kṛtya; kṛtyáte). cut; cut off. [cf. kaṭa (for karta, 'cut, depression in the head,' i.e.), 'temple,' and κρότ-αφος, 'temple'; Lat. curt-us, 'docked, short.']

+ud, cut out or off; cut up, butcher.

1 kṛt, vbl in cpds. making; doing; causing; as m. maker. [√1 kṛ, 1147c.]

2 kṛt, a time, in sa-kṛt. [perhaps fr. √1 kṛ, 'a doing, a time': cf. kṛtu, 'a time.']

kṛtá, a. —1. made; done; —2. prepared; —3. attained, —4. well done, and so, good; —5. as n. deed; —6. (perhaps made, i.e. won) and so, the side of the die marked with four spots, the lucky or winning one; —7. the golden age, name of the first yuga, see 58² ℵ. [√1 kṛ.]

kṛta-kṛtya, a. having one's duty done or end attained.

kṛtakṛtyatā, f. condition of having performed one's duty. [1237.]

kṛta-buddhi, a. having a made-up mind, of resolute character.

kṛta-māuna, a. having a kept silence, silent.

kṛta-saṁketa, a. having an agreement made, agreed upon as a rendezvous.

kṛtāñjali, a. having a made gesture of reverence, with reverent gesture. [añjali.]

kṛtānná, n. prepared or cooked food. [anna.]

kṛtāvajña, a. having contempt (done, i.e.) shown to one, disdained. [avajñā.]

kṛti, f. —1. the doing, the production; —2. a production, literary work. [√1 kṛ.]

kṛtu, a doing, a time; only in acc. pl. -kṛtvas, and that at the end of cpds. [√1 kṛ, 1105a.]

kṛte, as prep. on account of, for the sake of, for, w. gen. [1130] or in composition. [loc. of kṛta, lit. 'in the matter of' (cf. mg 5), 1116.]

kṛtti, f. pelt, hide. [√kṛt: for mg, cf. δέρμα, 'hide,' and δείρω, 'flay.']

kṛttikā, f. pl. the Pleiades. [cf. kṛtti: perhaps the constellation was conceived as having the shape of a pelt.]

kṛtya, grdv. to be done; as n. that which ought to be done or is to be done, and so, duty, purpose, end; —f. -ā, action, deed. [√1 kṛ, 963b end.]

kṛtvas, adv. times; see kṛtu.

kṛtsná, a. whole; entire.

√ kṛp (kṛpate [745b]). mourn, lament.

kṛpā, f. pity, compassion. [√kṛp.]

kṛmi, m. worm.

√ kṛç (kṛçyati [761a]; cakárça; kṛçitá). grow lean. [cf. κολοκ-dνος, 'long lank person,' κολοσσός, σκολοκ-jος, 'colossus'; Old Lat. crac-entes, Lat. grac-iles, 'lean, slender.']

kṛçá, a. lean, haggard. [√kṛç, 958.]

√ kṛṣ (kárṣati; kṛṣáti; cakárṣa; ákṛk-ṣat; karṣiṣyáti; krakṣyáti, -te; kṛṣṭá; krāṣṭum; kṛṣṭvá; -kṛṣya). —1. kárṣ-ati: tug, draw, pull; —2. kṛṣáti: draw furrows; plough.

+ā, draw on, attract; draw from (a source).

+ud, pull up, elevate.

+pra, draw forward, place in front.

kṛṣṭí, f. pl. people, folk. [√kṛṣ, mg 2: orig. 'tillages, tilled lands,' then 'settlement, community.']

kṛṣṇá, a. black, dark; w. pakṣa, the dark half of the lunar month, from full to new moon; as m., sc. pakṣa, the dark lunar fortnight.

kṛṣṇa, m. the black antelope.

kṛṣṇa-pakṣa, m. the dark lunar fortnight.

kṛṣṇa-sarpa, m. a very poisonous black Cobra, Colüber Naga.

kṛṣṇājina, n. skin of the black antelope. [ajína.]

√ kṛṣṇāya (kṛṣṇāyáte). blacken. [kṛṣṇá, 1059b.]

√ kḷp (kálpate; cākḷpé [786]; kalpayáte; kḷptá; kalpáyati, -te). be in order; be suitable or serviceable to; help; kḷptá, in order, fixed, settled; —caus. put in order; ordain; arrange; dispose; fix (in the manifold applications of this word as used colloquially). [prob. not akin are Goth. hilpan, Eng. help.]

+upa, caus. prepare; furnish; provide.

+sam, caus. arrange together; determine; will; purpose.

kḷpta-keçanakhaçmaçru, a. having hair and nails and beard in order, i.e. trimmed. [keça-nakha-çmaçru, 1252.]

kḷptānta, having its end prescribed; limited. [anta.]

kéta, m. intention; desire; will. [√cit, 'look, be intent upon.']

ketú, m. brightness; pl. beams. [√cit, 'look, appear, shine': cf. Goth. haidu-s, ('appearance, manner,' i.e.) 'way,' AS. hād, 'way, manner, condition,' Eng. -hood, -head (as in maidenhood, godhead), Ger. -heit: cf. under maya.]

kévala, a. exclusive; excluding all else; alone; —am, adv. only.

kéça, m. hair (of the head); mane. [see kesara.]

keça-pakṣa, m. du. the two sides of the hair of the head; the temples.

keça-çmaçru-loma-nakha, *n. pl.* hair of the head, beard, hair of the body, and nails. [1253a.]

keçānta, *m.* hair-end; long hair hanging down; locks.

keçin, *a.* maned, with flowing mane. [keça.]

késara, *m.* hair; mane. [written also keçara, cf. keça: cf. Lat. *caesaries*, 'hair, mane,' but not Eng. *hair.*]

· kesarāgra, *n.* ends of a mane. [agra.]

kāivarta, *m.* fisher.

koṭara, *n.* hollow of a tree.

koṭṭa, *m.* fort.

ko-daṇḍa, *m.* bow (of an archer). ['good-stick,' see 1kā4, and 506.]

kodaṇḍāṭanī, *f.* the notched end of a bow. [aṭanī.]

kopa, *m.* anger; -āt, *adv.* [1114b], angrily. [√kup.]

kopākula, *a.* full of anger. [ākula.]

kolāhala, *m. n.* uproar, confused cry. [onomatopoetic.]

ko-vida, *a.* well knowing or skilled. [see 1kā4, and 506.]

kāutuka, *n.* curiosity, eagerness; -āt, *adv.* [1114b], eagerly.

kāunteya, *m.* son of Kuntī, *i.e.* king Yudhishthira. [metronymic, 1216.]

kāuravya, *m.* descendant of Kuru, *i.e.* Yudhishthira. [patronymic, 1211: cf. 1208c.]

kāulālá, *n.* pottery. [kūlāla.]

kāuçala, *n.* cleverness; ability. [kúçala.]

krátu, *m.* power, *whether* of body or of mind or of both: — 1. might, 73¹⁷; — 2. will, 75²; understanding, 80⁶ — *cf.* dakṣa; inspiration, insight, *esp.* for sacred songs and acts; — 3. sacred deed, sacrifice, 16⁷; ceremony, *cf.* yajñakratu. [√1kṛ, 'do, effect,' 1161: orig. sense of word in mgs 1 and 2 was prob. 'an effecting, a power to do or carry out': for mg 3, see √1kṛ 12: cf. κρατύς, 'mighty,' AS. *heard*, 'strong, hard,' Eng. *hard.*]

\ kram (krámati [745d], krámate; ca-kráma, cakramé; ákramīt; kramiṣyáti, -te, kraṅsyáte; krāntá [955a]; krámi-tum, krántum; kramitvā, krāntvā; -krámya; kramyáte; kramáyati, krām-

āyati [1042c² mid.]). step; go; go to-wards.

+ ati, step beyond; excel; overcome.

+ sam-ati, excel. [sam intens., 1077b end.]

+ ā, step near to; come upon; attack; overpower.

+ ud, go out; depart (of the vital spirit); *caus.* cause to disembark.

+ abhy-ud, *caus.* cause to step out.

+ upa, step unto; approach, 3¹⁰.

+ nis, go out.

+ parā, step forth; advance boldly; *and so,* show one's strength or courage. [hence parākrama, 'valor': cf. kram + vi.]

+ pari, go around, circumambulate.

+ pra, step forward; set out; start from.

+ vi, move away or on; proceed; attack boldly; *and so,* show one's courage. [hence vikrama, 'valor': cf. kram + parā.]

+ sam, come together; approach; enter (a zodiacal sign, said of the sun).

krámá, *m.* — 1. step; regular progress or order; -eṇa, -āt, gradātim, *cf.* yathākra-mam; — 2. procedure; method; way, 36²¹. [√kram.]

kramaças, *adv.* step by step; gradually; in order. [1106.]

kravyá, *n.* raw flesh; corpse; carrion. [√kru, which perhaps means 'coagulate, become stiff': w. kravís, 'raw flesh,' cf. κρέας, ἐκρέϝας, 'flesh'; w. krū-rá, 'bloody, raw,' cf. Lat. *crū-dus*, 'bloody, raw,' *cruor*, 'blood'; cf. AS. *hrāw*, 'corpse'; Eng. *raw*, Ger. *roh*, 'raw.']

kravya-vāhana, *a.* carrying off the corpses.

kravyād, *a.* consuming corpses. [ád.]

kravyāda, *a. the same.* [ada.]

kriyā, *f.* action; performance; doings; labor, pains. [√1kṛ, 1213d.]

√ krī (krīṇāti, krīṇīté; kreṣyáti; krītá; krétum; krītvā; -krīya). buy, *w. instr.* [281b] *of price.* [perhaps akin w. √1kṛ, and so meaning 'do business, trade.']

+ upa, buy.

+ vi, sell; sell for (*instr.*).

10

√ krīḍ (krī́ḍati, -te; cikrī́ḍa, cikrīḍé; krīḍiṣyáti; krīḍitá; krī́ḍitum; -krī́ḍya). play, sport.

krīḍā́, f. play, sport. [√krīḍ.]

krītotpanna, a. bought or on hand (of food). [utpanna, √pad.]

√ krudh (krú́dhyati, -te [761]; cukródha; ákrudhat; kruddhá; króddhum; kruddhvā́). be angry.

krudh, f. anger.

krúdhmi or krúdhmin, a. wrathful. [√krudh: cf. 1167 and 1231: paroxytone.]

√ kruç (krócati; cukróça; ákrukṣat; kruṣṭá; króṣṭum; -krúçya). cry out; call; howl. [cf. κραυγή, 'cry,' for *κραυκ-η· for γ in place of κ, cf. τήγανον, 'crucible,' w. τήκω, 'melt.']

krūrá, a. bloody; raw; fig. harsh. [see under kravya.]

kroḍá, m. —1. breast, bosom; —2. interior. [for mg 2, cf. garbha 2.]

kródha, m. anger. [√krudh.]

króça, m. call; calling distance; Anglo-Indian a Kos. [√kruç.]

kroçamātrāvasthita, a. stationed at the distance of a Kos. [kroça-mātra + avasthita.]

√ kliç (klíçyate, -ti; cikléça; kliṣṭá; kléṣṭum; -klíçya). be distressed.

kleça, m. pain; trouble. [√kliç.]

kvà, V. kúa, adv. —1. where? whither? kúa babhūvus, what has become of? —2. kva cid: anywhere; in any case, ever, 27 20; w. na, never. [1 ká, 505.]

kṣa, as collateral form of √1 kṣi in kṣa-tra, and as vbl of the same, w. the mg 'abiding, situate,' in antari-kṣa.

kṣaṇa, m. instant; moment; -eṇa, -āt, as advs [1112b, 1114b], instantly. [prob. 'the time of a glance,' a shortened form of īkṣ-aṇa, 'glance': for mg, cf. Eng. "in the twinkling of an eye," and Ger. Augen-blick, 'glance of an eye,' i.e. moment.']

kṣaṇika, f. -ī, a. momentary. [kṣaṇa.]

kṣatá, ppl. of √kṣan.

kṣatrá, n. —1. rule, dominion, power, 86 20; —2. later, the temporal power, imperium (as distinguished from the spiritual power, bráhman, 'sacerdotium') ; the second or princely caste or a member of it. [from kṣa = √1 kṣi 2 : cf. kṣatra-pa, 'governor of a dominion, satrap,' and the borrowed σατρά-πης.]

kṣatra-bandhu, m. one who belongs to the kṣatra or second caste.

kṣatríya, m. —1. ruler, 75 1; —2. one who belongs to the kṣatra or princely caste, a Kshatriya, 57 16 N. [kṣatra, 1214a.]

√ kṣan (kṣaṇóti, kṣaṇuté; ákṣaṇiṣṭa; kṣatá). harm; hurt; break. [closely akin w. √2 kṣi, q.v.]

kṣantavya, grdv. to be put up with or pardoned. [√kṣam, 212.]

kṣapā́, f. night. [cf. σκέπω, 'cover,' ψέφας, 'darkness': for ψ, cf. √kṣar.]

kṣapāha, n. a night and day, νυχθήμερον. [2 aha, 1253b.]

√ kṣam (kṣámate, -ti; cakṣamé; kṣamiṣyáte, kṣaṅsyáte; kṣāntá [955a]; kṣántum; kṣamyáte). —1. be patient; endure; put up with; kṣānta, patient; —2. forgive; pardon.

kṣamá, a. patient; bearing or enduring; and so, equal to a thing, able. [√kṣam.]

kṣamā́, f. patience; long-suffering. [do.]

1 kṣáya, m. dwelling-place. [√1 kṣi.]

2 kṣaya, m. destruction; decay. [√2 kṣi.]

√ kṣar (kṣárati, -te; cakṣāra; ákṣār [890]; kṣaritá). —1. flow; —2. liquefy; melt away; and so, perish. [for akṣar: cf. ψείρω (σσκείρω) = φθείρω, 'destroy,' έ-φθάρ-η, 'perished': for ψ, cf. kṣapā, kṣíti: for φθ, cf. 2 kṣi.]

kṣara, a. perishable. [√kṣar.]

√ kṣā (kṣā́yati [761d1]; kṣāṇá). burn.

kṣārá, a. pungent; saline. [√kṣā: cf. ξηρό-s, 'dry': for mg, cf. Eng. caustic, lit. 'burning,' fig. 'pungent.']

√ 1 kṣi, with two meanings, 'dwell,' and 'rule,' attaching themselves to the stems kṣi and kṣáya respectively; thus,

—1. kṣé-ti, 3d pl. kṣi-y-ánti: abide or while or dwell, esp. in quiet and safety, 79 18; inhabit. [cf. kṣiti, 1 kṣáya, kṣétra, kṣéma 1, 'dwelling-place'; άμφι-κτί-ονες, 'dwelling around,' κτί-σι-ς, 'settlement.']

+ upa, rest on, be dependent on.

—2. kṣáya-ti: pos-sess, be-sitzen; be master of; rule, 71 9. [cf. kṣéma 2, 'possession'; κέ-κτη-μαι, 'am master of,' κτά-ομαι, 'get.']

[cf. the collateral form kṣa: for connection of 1 and 2, cf. the relation of Lat. sedēre, 'sit,' and pos-sidēre, 'be master of,' and of Ger. sitzen, 'sit,' and be-sitzen, 'be master of.']

√ 2 kṣi (kṣiṇā́ti, later kṣiṇóti; ákṣeṣṭa; kṣitá, kṣiṇá; -kṣiya; kṣiyáte; kṣapá-yati [1042e]). destroy; make an end of; exhaust; — pass. wane; kṣiṇa, ruined, lost; — caus. weaken. [cf. φθίνω, φθίνυγ, 'perish, wane,' φθί-μενος, 'dead': for φθ, cf. kṣar: w. the secondary kṣa-n, cf. κτά-μενος, 'slain,' κτείνω, κτεν-jω, 'slay.']
+ apa, pass. be afflicted, suffer loss.

kṣit, vbl. inhabiter or ruler, at end of cpds. [√1 kṣi 1 and 2: see 1147c.]

kṣití, f. dwelling, abode, 79¹³; piece of ground or land; the earth, the ground. [√1 kṣi 1: cf. κτί-σι-s, 'settlement.']

kṣíti, f. destruction. [√2 kṣi: cf. φθί-σι-s = φθίσις, 'decay': for ψ, cf. kṣar.]

√ kṣip (kṣipáti, -te; cikṣépa, cikṣipé kṣepsyáti, -te; kṣiptá; kṣéptum; kṣip-tvā́; -kṣípya; kṣepáyati). dart; cast; throw; caus. cause to fly or burst, 84⁴.
+ ā, —1. throw at; —2. fig. (like Eng. fling, make flings at), deride, put to shame, 8¹⁰; —3. draw towards one's self, call out (a person to vindicate himself), 55⁶.
+ ni, throw down (one's self, one's body).
+ vi-ni, lay down separately or orderly.
+ sam, dash together in a heap; destroy.

kṣipta-laguḍa, a. having the cudgel thrown.

kṣiprá, a. darting; quick; -am, adv. quickly. [√kṣip.]

kṣīrá, n. milk. [prob. √kṣar.]

kṣīrín, a. milky; as m. milk-plant. [kṣīra.]

kṣīrodaka, n. milk and water. [udaka: 1253b.]

√ kṣud (kṣódati, -te; cukṣóda; kṣuṇṇá; -kṣúdya). shatter; stamp upon; grind small.

kṣudrá, a. small. [√kṣud.]

kṣudra-buddhi, m. Small-wit, name of a jackal. [1298.]

kṣud-vyādhi, m. hunger and disease. [kṣudh: 1253a.]

√ kṣudh (kṣúdhyati; kṣudhitá). be hungry; kṣudhitá, hungry.

kṣúdh, f. hunger. [√kṣudh, 383a.]

kṣudhā, f. hunger. [√kṣudh.]

kṣudhārta, a. distressed with hunger. [kṣudhā + ārta.]

kṣétra, n. dwelling-place, 87¹⁷; piece of ground; field. [√1 kṣi 1.]

kṣetra-pati, m. master of a field; farmer.

kṣéma, m. —1. abode; place of rest; security; well-being, 61⁸; —2. possession; kṣeme · · yoge, in possession · · in acquisition, i.e. in the enjoyment of what we have got and in the getting of more. [√1 kṣi 1 and 2: for -kṣe-ma, 1166: cf. Goth. haim-s, 'village'; A.S. hám, Eng. home, and -ham in place-names; perhaps also κώμη (if for κόμη?), 'village.']

———

khá, n. —1. hole; hollow; —2. opening; —3. hole in the hub of a wheel; —4. void space; the sky. [√khan, cf. 333.]

kha-ga, —1. a. moving in the sky, flying; —2. as m. bird. [for mg 2, cf. antarikṣa-ga and kha-gama, 'bird,' ura-ga and bhujaṁ-gama, 'snake,' and turaṁ-ga, 'horse.']

kha-gama, the same.

khaṇḍa, a. broken; as m. a break, section, piece; khaṇḍaka, m. lump-sugar. [hence, prob., through the Persian, Arabic, Italian, and French, the Eng. candy.]

√ khaṇḍaya (khaṇḍayati). break; khaṇḍita, broken (of a command). [khaṇḍa, 1055.]

√ khan or khā (khánati, -te; cakhā́na, cakhnús; ákhān [890]; khaniṣyáti; khātá; khánitum; khanitvā́, khātvā́; -khā́ya; khanyáte, khāyáte; khānáyati). dig; caus. cause to be dug. [if for -kan, cf. Lat. can-ális, 'ditch, canal.']
+ ā, dig, burrow, in ākhu.

khára, a. harsh; as m. ass (so called from his harsh bray), 67¹⁹.

khála, m. —1. threshing-floor; —2. a mean, low-lived fellow. [the tertium

10*

comparationis for 1 and 2 is perhaps 'dirt.']

khálu, *pcl.* —1. now (*continuative*); **atha khalu,** now; —2. indeed (*emphasizing the preceding word*), 55³; —3. to be sure (*concessive*), 98³.

√ khā, *see* khan.

√ khād (khādati; cakhāda; khādiṣyáte; khāditá; khāditum; khāditvā; khādyáte; khādáyati). chew; bite; eat, *esp.* of animals; feed on, 24¹⁶; devour, 21¹¹; khādita, eaten, 23³, etc. [if for •akand or aknd, *cf.* κνίζω, √κνιδ, 'bite, sting,' κνίδη, 'nettle,' but not Eng. *nettle.*]

khāditavya, *grdv.* edendus. [√khād.]

√ khid (khidáti; khinná; -khídya). depress, *but only fig.*
   + ud, pull out.

khilá, —1. *m.* piece of waste land between cultivated fields; a bare spot; —2. a gap.

khu, *a Prakrit form for* khalu.

khe-cara, *a.* moving in the sky. [kha, 1250c.]

khecaratva, *n.* power of flying (by magic). [1239.]

kheda, *m.* depression, sorrow. [√khid.]

kheda-vaça, *a.* having depression as one's controlling influence, under the dominion of sorrow.

√ khyā (khyáti; cakhyáu; ākhyat [847]; khyāsyáti; khyātá; khyátum; -khyáya; khyāyáte; khyāpáyati, -te [1042d]). *simple verb only in pass. and caus.* — *pass.* be well known; be talked of; — *caus.* make known. [orig. mg, perhaps, 'shine, appear *or* look (intrans.), see (trans.)'.]
   + abhí, look at; behold, 78¹³.
   + ā, —1. show, tell; narrate, 55¹⁹; —2. designate, name; —*caus.: act.* tell; *mid.* have told to one's self, 105⁷.
   + praty-ā, (*lit.* show back, *i.e.*) turn away, repulse, reject, 9³⁰; refuse. [the Ger. *zurück-weisen* has just the same mgs.]
   + vy-ā, show to discriminately, *i.e.* explain.
   + sam, tell together, *i.e.* reckon up.
   + pari-sam, reckon up completely, 58⁶.

khyāti, *f.* the being well known; fame; khyātim gam, become famous. [√khyā.]

---

ga, *vbl.* going, *in many cpds; situate, e.g. in* madhyaga; *as m. nomen actionis, the* going, *in* durga, suga. [√gam, cf. 333.]

gagaṇa, *n.* sky.

gáṅgā, *f.* the Ganges. [fr. √gam — gā, w. intens. reduplication, 1002b.]

gaja, *m.* elephant.

gaja-yūtha, *m.* herd of elephants.

gajendra, *m.* a great elephant. [*see* indra.]

gaṇá, *m.* —1. troop, (of Maruts) 90¹⁸; crowd, (of friends) 3³; host (of stars); flock, (of birds) 3⁵; —2. *pl.* troop-deities, inferior deities which regularly appear not singly, but in troops, 67¹³; *esp.* those that compose the retinue of Çiva; *then, as sing.,* a single one of Çiva's attendants, a Gana, 55³⁰; —3. a number.

gaṇanā, *f.* a numbering, calculation, taking into account. [√gaṇaya.]

√ gaṇaya (gaṇayati). number, calculate. [gaṇa, 1055.]

gaṇita, *ppl.* calculated; *as n.* [1176a], calculation, arithmetic. [√gaṇaya.]

gatá, *ppl.* —1. gone, 2²¹; departed; *w. inf.* snātuṁ gata, gone to bathe, 44¹; *so* 41¹; —2. *often at beg. of cpds, see these;* —3. gone to: *w. acc.* 5⁵, 15³⁰; *w.* prati *and acc.,* 23¹⁵; —4. (having arrived at, *i.e.*) situated in: *w. acc.,* 62¹⁵; *w. loc.,* 5¹⁴; *in cpd, e.g.* svahasta-gata, situated on my own hand; —5. gone to a condition, *see* √gam 4; attained to, (fame) 56¹³; -conditioned, *in* durgata, sugata. [√gam, 954d.]

gata-prāṇa, *a.* whose breath is gone, dead.

gata-saṁkalpa, *a.* whose purpose *or* will for the moment is gone, purposeless. [1299.]

gatānugati, *f.* the going after him who has gone (before), the following in the old ruts. [anugati.]

gatānugatika, *a.* addicted to following in the old ruts. [gatānugati, 1222a.]

gatāsu, *a.* whose life is gone. [asu.]

gáti, f. —1. a going, way of going, ability to go; —2. progress, 18¹⁸; eventus, issue, 20¹³; —3. way of escape, refuge, 52¹⁵; —4. the way or course esp. of the soul through different bodies, metempsychosis; and so, a condition of the soul during these transmigrations, a man's lot or fate, 53¹³, 65¹⁰, 66⁶, 66²¹ ff. [√gam, 1157: cf. βά-σι-ς, 'going, power to go.']

√ gad (gádati; jagáda; gadiṣyáte; gadit́; gáditum; -gádya). speak.
+ ni, say.

gada, m. disease.

gantavya, grdv. eundum, used impers. [√gam.]

gandhá, m. smell; pl., w. çubha, perfumes.

gandharvá, m. —1. orig., perhaps, the deity of the moon, the Gandharva; —2. in Epos, pl. Gandharvas, heavenly singers belonging to Indra's court; as sing. one of these, a Gandharva.

gabhīrá (V., later) gambhīrá, a. deep.

√ gam (gácchati, -te [747, 608]; jagáma, jagmé; V. ágan [833], later ágamat; gamiṣyáti, -te; gatá; gántum; gatvá; -gátya, -gámya; gamyáte; jígamiṣati; gamáyati, -te). —1. go, move; go to, 3⁶; go towards; go away, 28¹⁷, 36⁶; come; w. pratīpam, go wrong; —2. go by, pass (intrans.): of time, 20³; of days, 29¹²; —3. come unto, i.e. arrive at, w. acc., 3⁷, 84⁷; reach, w. loc., 69⁸; come into, w. loc., 71⁶; get at, 95¹⁹; —4. go to a state or condition: w. pañcatvam, go to dissolution, i.e. die, 32²¹, etc.; so to destruction, 29⁶; despondency, 44¹⁸; w. nijām gatim, (went) to his own proper condition, i.e. became a Yaksha once more, 53¹²; —5. manasā gam, (go with the mind, i.e.) perceive, 15¹⁰.

[cf. βαίνω (*βανjω, ογϝεμjω), 'go'; Lat. vénio, *gvémio, 'come'; AS. cum-an, Eng. come; for the kw which is to be expected in Germanic as answering to the old gv, cf. Ger. be-quem, Old Eng. cwēme, 'convenient, fit, pleasant': cf. gáccha and βάσκε, 'go thou'; gatá-s, 'gone,' and βατό-s, '(gone over, i.e.) passable'; gáti-s and βάσι-s, 'a going': see also √gā.]

+ adhi, —1. go to; attain; —2. get at, learn, study, read — cf. √i + adhi.
+ anu, go after, follow.
+ antar, go within, enter.
+ api, go unto, join, 91⁵ ff.
+ abhi, go unto, 1¹⁴; go.
+ aram, see s.v.
+ ava, come down.
+ ā, —1. go to, 6¹⁰; come to; come hither, 5²², 10²³; —2. return (52²²), usually w. punar, 4³, etc.; —ágata: —1. arrived, come, 7⁹; w. inf. çrotum ágata, come to hear, 28⁵; so 27¹⁶; arrived (as guest), 28⁷; —2. returned, 24¹⁷; —3. having gone to a condition, e.g. death, 46³; —ágantavyam, grdv., as impers. pass. w. anena, this one will come hither; —desid. desire to return, 101⁵.
+ abhy-ā, come unto, visit; abhyā́gata, as subst. guest.
+ upa_ā, approach.
+ sam-upa_ā, go to together.
+ sam-ā, assemble; meet, 61⁶.
+ ud, go out, proceed from.
+ upa, go unto, approach.
+ nis, proceed from (abl.), 51¹¹; nirgata, departed.
+ prati, come back, return.
+ vi, go asunder; vigata, gone, vanished.
+ sam, mid. come together, meet; unite one's self with; and so, come to enjoy; —caus. assemble, as trans.

gama, a. going, at end of cpds. [√gam.]

gambhīrá, a. deep; cf. gabhīrá.

garut, n. wing.

garútmant, a. winged; as m. bird. [for mg, cf. pakṣin.]

√ garj (gárjati; jagárja; garjitá; garjitvá; -gárjya). roar.

garjana, n. roar.

gárta, m. (earth-)cut, ditch. [younger form of kartá, q.v.]

gardabhá, m. ass; -ī, f. she-ass. [1199.]

gárbha, m. —1. uterus concipiens, the conceiving womb; abde garbhād ekādaçe, in the eleventh year from (the womb, i.e.) conception; —2. (as in Milton's Earth's inmost womb) the interior, inside, 34⁵, 43²,cf. kroḍa; at end of cpds, having ·· in the interior, containing ··, cf.

padmagarbha; —3. conceptum, fruit of the womb; garbhaṁ dadhānās, conceiving fruit, 92[11]; embryo, 46[5], 93[7]; scion; and so —4. a new-born child. [√grabh, 'concipere': with garbha in mg 1, cf. δελφύς and δολφός, 'womb,' ἀ-δελφός and ἀ-δελφε-ιό-s (= sa-garbh-ya-s), 'of the same womb, i.e. brother'; in mg 3, cf. βρέφος, 'embryo,' and Eng. calf in mooncalf: in mg 4, cf. Goth. kalbo, Eng. calf.]

garbhavant, a., in fem. only, pregnant. [garbha 3: see 1233.]

garbha-stha, a. being in the womb, unborn.

√ garh (gárhate; jagarhé; garhitá; gárhitum; -gárhya). blame, reproach; garhita, despised.

√ gal (gálati; galitá). —1. drip; —2. fall; galita, fallen out, gone (claws, teeth, eyes). [hence jala, 'water': cf. √βαλ in intrans. mg, e.g. ποταμὸς εἰς ἅλα βάλλων, 'river flowing into the sea'; Ger. quellen, 'flow, spring,' Quelle, 'fountain.']

gava, equiv. of go, 'bull, cow, beeve,' in cpds. [see 1209a.]

gávyūti, f. pasture-land; generalized, territory, abiding-place. [lit. 'having food for cattle,' gó + ūtí, see go 4: the y is euphonic, cf. 258.]

√ gā (jígāti; ágāt). go; come. [collateral form of gam, q.v.: w. jígāti, cf. Laconic βίβāτι, 'strides'; w. ágāt, cf. ἔβη, 'went.']

+ abhi, go unto; w. çramam, become weary.

gātú, m. —1. motion, movement, course; —2. progress; equiv. to the Eng. -fare in wel-fare (for mg, cf. verb fare, 'get on, go') — see sugātuyā; —3. (place of recourse, i.e.) refuge, abiding-place, 83[5]. [√gā, 'go,' 1161.]

gátra, n. —1. (means of moving, i.e.) a limb of the body; —2. by synecdoche, the body. [√gā, 'move,' 1185a.]

gāmin, a. going, going upon, going to. [√gam, 1183[3].]

gárbha, a. relating to the embryo or to pregnancy (of sacrifices). [garbha, 1208f.]

gárbhika, a. relating to the womb, prenatal. [garbha, 1222e 2.]

gárhapatya, —1. a. pertaining to the householder; as m., sc. agni, the householder's fire, 102[3]N.; —2. as n. the being head of the house, 89[6]; the housekeeping, 89[11]. [gṛhápati, 1211.]

gír [392], f. —1. invocation, praise, 74[11]; —2. sing. and pl. speech, words, 87[16], 49[8]; —3. voice, 3[14]. [√1 gṛ, 242[1,2].]

giri, m. mountain, 55[5].

√ gu (intens. jóguve [1007[3]]). cause to sound, proclaim. [cf. γόος, βοή, 'cry'; Lat. bovāre, 'howl.']

guṇá, m. —1. a single thread of a cord; a string; esp. bow-string; —2. quality; adscititious quality, as distinguished from the real nature (svabhāva, 'ingenium'), 22[20]; —3. as philosophical technical term, one of the three pervading qualities of all nature, to wit, sattva, 'goodness,' rajas, 'passion,' and tamas, 'darkness,' 66[5]ff.; —4. as specialization of mg 2, a good quality, virtue, 14[12], etc.; excellence. [for play on mgs 1 and 4, see nirguṇa and 18[5].]

guṇa-deva, m. Guṇadeva, a pupil of Guṇāḍhya. [lit. 'having virtue as his god,' 1302.]

guṇavant, a. virtuous, 18[4]; excellent, 3[22]. [1233.]

guṇaçālin, a. possessing virtues, excellent. [see çālin.]

guṇāḍhya, m. Guṇāḍhya, see 53[3]N. [lit. 'rich in virtue,' āḍhya.]

guṇānvita, a. endowed with excellence; (of an asterism) lucky. [anvita, √i.]

guṇin, a. virtuous, excellent. [guṇa.]

√ gup (jugópa; gopāyáti; gupitá, guptá; gópitum, góptum; gupyáte; júgupsate, -ti). keep; guard; desid. seek to keep one's self from, i.e. shun, detest; ppl. jugupsita, detested, inspiring aversion, 59[11]. [prob. a secondary root, originating in the denom. verb-stem gopaya: see this and go-pa.]

gurú, a. —1. heavy; and so —2. fig. (like Eng. weighty), important; —3. worthy of honor, 28[13]; —4. as m. the one to be honored κατ' ἐξοχήν, the teacher or Guru, 60[4]ff.; loc. gurāu: in the house of the Guru, 61[23]; in case of a Guru, 104[4]. [cf.

the comp. gárīyāṅs: cf. βαρύς, Lat. gravis,
•garu-i-s, Goth. kaurus, 'heavy.']

√ guh (gúhati [745c]; jugúha [793f],
juguhé; ághukṣat [916, 155]; gūḍhá
[222³]; gúhitum; -gúhya). hide; gūḷhá,
hidden, 76¹⁵.
　+ apa, hide (trans.) away from, w. abl.,
85¹⁴; put away, get rid of, 77¹.

gúh, f. hiding-place; instr. gúhā: used as
adv. gúhā [1112e], in secret. [√guh.]

gúhā, f. hiding-place; cavern. [do.]

gúhya, grdv. cēlandus; secret, hidden.
[do.]

guhyaka, m. one of a class of demigods,
who, like the Yakshas, wait on Kubera,
god of wealth, and, dwelling in mountain
caverns (gúhā), keep his treasures. [so
named from their living in caverns or
hidden places: 1222.]

√ 1 gṛ (gṛṇáti, gṛṇīté; jagára; gariṣyáti;
gīrṇá [957b]; -gírya). — 1. invoke, call;
—2. salute, praise; —3. speak out, say.
[cf. gír, 'speech, voice'; γῆρυς, 'speech,
voice'; Doric γάρυεν, 'speak'; Lat. garrio,
'talk'; Eng. call.]
　+ sam, chime in with, agree.

√ 2 gṛ (giráti; jagára; ágārīt; gīrṇá
[957b]; -gírya). swallow. [cf. βορά,
'food,' βι-βρώ-σκω, 'eat,' δημο-βόρ-ο-s,
'folk-devouring'; Lat. carni-vōr-us, 'flesh-
eating,' de-vorāre, 'swallow down, devour.']
　+ ni, swallow down; devour (the sun in
an eclipse), 76¹⁴ — see √ gras.

√ 3 gṛ (aor. ájīgar [867]; intens. jágarti
[1006]; caus. jāgaráyati). — 1. intens. be
awake; wake, intrans.; jāgṛhi [1011], be
thou watchful, have a care for, w. dat.,
89¹¹; wake up, intrans., 30¹⁶; —2. caus.
wake, trans., 30⁶. [for the history of the
word, see 1020: for 1, cf. ἐ-γρή-γορ-α, 'am
awake,' ἔ-γρ-ετο, 'awoke' (intrans.); for
2, cf. ἐγείρω, 'wake' (trans.).]

gṛ́tsa, a. clever; wise.

√ gṛdh (gṛ́dhyati; jagárdha; ágṛdhat;
gardhiṣyáti; gṛddhá; gṛddhvā́). —1.
take long strides; —2. be eager or greedy
for. [for •ghṛdh: cf. Eng. greedy.]

gṛ́dhra, —1. a. greedy; —2. m. vulture.
[√gṛdh, 1188a: the Ger. offers an exact

parallel: Geier, 'vulture,' is prop. 'the
greedy (bird),' from Gier, 'greediness.']

gṛdhra-kūṭa, m. Vulture-peak, a mountain in Magadha.

gṛhá, in V., m.; later, m. in pl.; otherwise,
n. house, 28⁷, 79¹⁵; w. mṛnmaya, house
of earth, the grave; gṛhaṁ gam, go home,
52¹⁶; so 40⁸, 68¹⁷; as pl. the house as consisting of various rooms and buildings,
89¹¹; mansions, 87⁷. ['that which receives one,' √grah: cf. geha.]

gṛhá-pati, m. master of the house. [acct,
1267a.]

gṛhá-patnī, f. mistress of the house.
[do.]

gṛha-stha, a. abiding in a house; as m.
householder or Brahman in the second
stage of his religious life, see āçrama.

gṛhāçrama, m. house-stage, second stage
in a Brahman's life, see āçrama.

gehá, n. house. [ident. w. gṛhá: cf. the
ident. √ṛdh and edh.]

gó [361c], m. f. — 1. a beef in its old sense
of bull or cow; pl. beeves, kine, cattle;
the Vedic type or symbol of all welfare
and blessing and riches (e.g. 80¹⁶), like
"milk and honey" with the Hebrews; —2.
beef in the derived and now usual sense of
flesh; pl. pieces of flesh, 84¹⁶; —3. (the
milch cow of kings, i.e.) the earth, 63⁷;
—4. observe that gavyūti, gotra, gopa,
gopati, gomaya, and many other cpds of
go lose their special reference to cattle and
take a more general mg. [cf. βοῦς, stem
βοϝ, 'a beef, ox, cow'; Lat. bos, stem bov,
'ox, cow'; AS. cū, Eng. cow.]

go-ghná, a. kine-killing; as m. cow-
slayer.

gótama, m. Gotama, a Vedic seer of the
tribe of Angiras.

gotrá, n. —1. cow-stall, cattle-pen; —2.
perhaps, pen of cattle, and so —3. group
in general (see go4); —4. esp. family, 19¹⁶;
—5. family name, 103¹⁸, see nāman 2.
[from go: mgs 2 and 3 are not authenticated by the literature.]

gotra-ja, a. born in the family; as m. a
relative.

go-pá, m. —1. cow-keeper, cow-herd; —2.
keeper in general (see go4). [2 pa.]

gó-pati, *m.* −1. lord of kine; −2. lord *in general* (*see* go 4). [acct, 1267a.]

√ gopaya (gopayati, -te). be keeper, keep. [gopa, 1055.]

go-pá [351], *m.* −1. cow-keeper; −2. keeper *in general* (*see* go 4), 85¹⁶; protector, 69¹⁵. [2 pā.]

√ gopāya (gopāyáti, -te). be keeper; keep, 91¹³. [gopā, 1055.]

gomáya, −1. *a.* bovine; *as n.* −2. cow-dung, 103²²; − 3. dung *in general* (*see* go 4); *w.* ānaḍuha, dung of a steer, 105ᴬ²⁰. [see maya.]

go-yukta, *a.* yoked with cattle; *w.* cakra, wagon drawn by cattle. [√yuj.]

go-rakṣaka, *m.* cattle-keeper, cow-herd.

gó-ṣakhi [343a], *a.* having cattle as companions, rich in cattle. [sákhi, 186.]

go-ṣṭhá, *m.* cow-stall, byre. [stha, 186.]

gāuṇika, *f.* -ī, *a.* standing in relation to the three guṇa's, *see* guṇa 3. [guṇa, 1222e 2.]

gāutamá, *m.* *patronymic from Gotama;* Gautama, name of various men. [gótama, 1208f.]

√ grath *or* granth (grathnā́ti; granthiṣyáti; grathitá; -gráthya). −1. string together, connect; −2. put together, *i.e.* com-pose (a literary work). [for mgs, cf. Lat. *com-pŏnere*, 'put together, compose'; also *serere*, 'connect, entwine,' *w. sermo*, 'discourse.']

grantha, *m.* −1. (a string of words, *i.e.*) verse *or* couplet, 53⁶, etc; −2. a composition, book, work, 17⁵. [√granth: for mgs, see under grath, and for 1, cf. Lat. *serere w. series,* 'row, string.']

granthín, *a. subst.* having books, bookish, book-reader. [grantha.]

√ grabh, *in Rigveda; later,* grah.

−*from* grabh : gṛbhṇā́ti, gṛbhṇīté; jagrábha, jagṛbhé; ágrabhīt, ágrabhiṣṭa [900]; gṛbhītá; gṛbhītvā́; -gfbhya.

−*from* grah: gṛhṇā́ti; jagrā́ha, jagṛhé; ágrahīt, ágrahiṣṭa [900]; grahīṣyáti, -te; gṛhītá; gráhītum; gṛhītvā́; -gṛ́hya; gṛhyáte; grāháyati, -te.

−1. grasp; seize with the hand; hold; take; *w.* hástam *or* pāṇím, take the hand (of the bride at the wedding), 89⁵; take

hold on (*loc.*), 14¹⁶; gṛhītá keçeṣu, seized by the hair; *used* of a rabbit taking, *i.e.* leading with him a lion, 33⁴; −2. take possession of, take, 46²²; get, 44⁵; −3. receive, accept, 20¹⁰, 56¹; −4. of fluids, take in the ladle, 94¹; −5. of names, take upon the lips, mention, 64¹⁵, 103¹⁹; −6. *fig., as in Eng.,* grasp, *i.e.* perceive, know; −7. get, learn; −*caus.* cause to learn. [see under garbha: connection w. Eng. *gripe,* Ger. *greifen,* exceedingly doubtful.]

† pari, −1. hold on both sides; *and so* −2. become master of; master, overcome, surpass.

+ prati, take hold of, 59²²; accept.

+ vi, −1. hold asunder; separate; make a division; *and so* −2. quarrel; fight.

+ sam, hold together, clasp.

+ upa-sam, clasp with the hands.

√ gras (grásate; jagrasé; ágrasīt; grasiṣyáte; grastá; grasitvā́; grasyáte; grāsáyati). −1. swallow; devour, 10¹⁰; −2. of the demon Rāhu, who swallows, *i.e.* eclipses sun and moon, 23¹. [perhaps akin w. √2 gṛ, 'swallow.']

√ grah, *see* grabh.

grahá, *m.* seizure (with a claw, *i.e.*), bite. [√grah.]

gráhaṇa, *n.* the grasping, *i.e.* acquisition. [√grah 6, 7.]

grabhá, *a. subst.* grasping, grasper. [√grabh.]

grāma, *m.* −1. inhabited place, hamlet, village, *see* 98¹⁶ ɴ.; −2. the inhabitants, community.

grāma-kāma, *a.* having desire for the village, fond of abiding in the village.

grā́van, *m.* stone; *esp.* stone for pressing the Soma.

grāhá, *a. subst.* grasping, grasper, *in cpds.* [√grah.]

grāhyà, *grdv.* to be grasped; perceivable. [do.]

grīvā́, *f.* nape of the neck; neck. [for *gaᵉrvā*: cf. Aeolic δέρρα, •δερϝα, Epic δειρή, 'throat, neck.']

grīṣmá, *m.* summer.

gha, *form of* ghan, *i.e.* han, *in cpds.* [1143c, 333.]

ghaṭa, m. a jar.

ghaná, m. —1. slayer; —2. slaughter; —3. a compacted mass, lump; —4. cloud. [√ghan, i.e. han: cf. φόνο-s, 'slaughter.']

gharmá, m. warmth, heat. [√2ghṛ: cf. θερμό-s, for *φορμός, Lat. *formus,* 'warm.']

√ ghuṣ (ghóṣati, -te; jughóṣa; ghuṣṭá; -ghúṣya; ghoṣáyati). sound; make a noise.

√ 1ghṛ (jígharti; ghṛtá; ghāráyati). be-sprinkle; be-drop; drip (*trans.*); ghṛtá, *see s.v.*

+praty-abhi, *caus.* sprinkle over repeatedly.

+vy-ā́, sprinkle here and there.

√ 2ghṛ, glow, be warm, *in* ā́-ghṛṇi, 'glowing,' *and* gharma, *q.v.*

ghṛtá, n. —1. butter, clarified and then hardened, *Anglo-Indian* ghee, much used for culinary (*cf.* 68[1]) and religious (*cf.* 88[11]) purposes: *cf.* ā́jya, 'butter in a melted state'; —2. butter *or* fat *in general,* also as symbol of fruitfulness and abundance. [√1ghṛ, 'drip,' 1176a: for mg, cf. Eng. *dripping,* 'fat which falls in drops from meat in roasting.']

ghṛta-paçu, m. sacrificial beast made of ghee.

ghṛta-çcút, a. dripping with (ghee, *i.e.*) fatness.

ghorá, a. awful; dreadful; horrid.

ghora-cakṣus, a. having an evil eye.

ghorākṛti, a. having an awful form. [ākṛti.]

ghóṣa, m. noise. [√ghuṣ.]

ghna, a. killing; destroying; removing. [√ghan, i.e. han: see 216.9.]

ghnya, *grdv.* to be slain, *in* aghnya. [do.]

√ ghrā (jíghrati [749a]; jaghrāú; ghrātá; -ghrā́ya; ghrāyáte; ghrāpáyati [1042d]). smell; snuff at.

---

ca, *encl. conj.* and, also, τε, que; —1a. *is found, esp. in the older literature, with both parts to be connected* (*e.g.* 71[5,7], 97[7,11]; *so* 13[5], 16[11], 17[3], 19[19], 38[7], 9[3]); *or only with the latter, as is oftenest the case in the later language* (*e.g.* 2[1,7], 3[8], 8[8]; 82[6], 84[16]; 98[16]); —1b. *in case of three or more parts to be*

connected, ca occurs: with the last only (*e.g.* *three parts,* 13[2], 17[3], 31[16], 44[6]; 71[8], 72[10], 83[15]; 106[5]; *four parts,* 2[3], 17[7], 28[10]; *five parts,* 2[5], 21[5], 25[3]); *with the last two* (7[6,7], 22[5], 37[15], 45[7]; 77[13]); *sometimes after each,* (29[3,4]); *very rarely after the first of a series* (26[6]; 21[23]); *various irregular combinations on page 67 passim; see also* 21[20] N.;

—2. *variously combined:* w. eva (*e.g.* 13[21]; 9[16], 11[9], 14[15]; 5[9], 12[5], 14[2,6,20], 15[15], 25[4]; 30[16]), *and* w. api (*see examples under* api); · · ca, · · tathā, · · ca, both · ·, likewise · ·, and, 10[6,9]; · · ca, · · ā, both · ·, and · ·, 85[5]; sa ca, *often at beg. of clause* (*e.g.* 24[23]; *so* 34[16]; 41[7]); —3. anyac ca, api ca, kim ca, tathā ca, *joining two proverbs of like drift,* moreover, further, likewise;

—4. *otiose,* 6[9]; —5. *connecting things contrasted:* but, 8[16], 17[20], 18[2,3], 19[2]; *and yet,* 1[13], 3[20]; —6. (*even, concessively, i.e.*) though, 26[13]; —7. (*like Eng.* and *or* an, *and Icelandic* enda, 'moreover,' 'if') if— *see* ced; —8. w. *interrogatives, rendering them indef., see* ka, kim.

[*cf.* τε, 'and'; Lat. *que,* 'and'; Goth. *-h* and Ger. *-ch* in *ni-h* and *no-ch,* the exact equivalents of Lat. *ne-que,* 'and not, nor': for ca8, cf. *-τε* and *-κα* in *πο-τε* and Doric *πο-κα,* 'at any time'; Lat. *quis-que,* 'any, each.']

cakrá, n. —1. wheel; chariot-wheel, wagon-wheel; —2. *by synecdoche,* wagon, *in* piṭha-cakra. [prob. reduplicated form, ca-kra, fr. √kṛ or *kl, 'roll,' cf. κυλίω, 'roll': w. ca-krá, cf. κύ-κλος, *skFe-κλος,* AS. *hweohl, hweól,* Eng. *wheel.*]

√ cakṣ (cáṣṭe [628]; cacakṣé; cáṣṭum; -cákṣya). —1. appear; —2. look upon, behold; —3. (cause to appear, *i.e.*) announce, tell. [reduplicated form of √kāç, see 675 and 108g[1] end.]

+ā, —1. look on; —2. show, tell, 63[1].

+vi, appear far and wide, shine.

+sam, look upon, consider.

cákṣas, —1. *perhaps adj.* beholding, *see* 1296[3] end; —2. n. look; eye. [√cakṣ.]

cakṣuḥ-piḍā, f. eye-ache.

cákṣuṣmant, a. possessing eyes. [1235.]

cákṣus, n. eye. [√cakṣ, 1154.]

cañcala, a. moving to and fro; trembling. [√cal, 1148.4, w. intens. reduplication, cf. 1002b: cf. κίγ-καλ-ος, 'wag-tail'; Lat. *quer-quer-us*, 'shaking with fever chills.']

cañcu, f. beak, bill.

caṇaka, m. chick-pea.

cáṇḍa, a. impetuous; wrathful.

caṇḍāla, m. a Chandāla or man of the most despised class of society (born of Çūdra father and Brahman mother). [cf. caṇḍa.]

√ cat (cátant; cattá; caus. cātáyati). get off; hide; caus. drive away.

catasṛ, fem. to catúr.

catúr [482d], num. four. [w. catvâras, cf. τέτταρες, Lat. quattuor, Goth. fidvor, AS. feōwer, Eng. four.]

catur-akṣá, a. four-eyed. [see 1300b.]

caturthá, f. -î, a. fourth; -am, adv. the fourth time. [catúr, 487⁵.]

catur-yuga, n. the four ages. [1312.]

catur-varga, m. group of four.

cátur-vidha, a. of four kinds; four-fold. [vidhā, 1302c 5.]

cátuṣṭaya, a. of four; as n. a collection of four, a quaternion. [catúr, 178: 1245a.]

catuṣ-pathá, m. n. place where four ways meet, quadrivium. [catúr, 178, 187: 1312.]

cátuṣ-pad, a. quadruped; as n. s. collectively, the four-footed beasts. [catúr, 178: 1300.]

catuṣ-pada, f. -î, a. having (taken) four steps.

catvara, m. n. quadrivium. [catúr.]

catvār, strong form of catur, q.v.

√ can (ácanīt). be glad in; gladden. [collateral form of √kan: cf. √kan, kāma, cāru.]

caná, adv., immediately following the emphasized word. —1. not even; svápnaç caná, not even sleep, 79¹; —2. w. preceding negation, even; ná devānām áti vratám, çatâtmā caná, jīvati, not beyond the decree of the gods, (not) even if hundred-lived, does one live, 88²; hence, the feeling for the negation in cana in such collocations becoming faint, —3. even, at all, w. interrogatives, emphasizing their indefinite sense; na kim cana, not any thing even

or at all, 8¹⁹; see esp. 1 ká 2c, also katham, kadâ, and kim. [cf. Lat. *-quam* and *-cun-* in quisquam, quicunque, 'any one'; Goth. *-hun* in ni hvas-hun, 'not any one.']

candrá, a. shining, shimmering; as m. the moon; the moon-god. [for çcandrá, q.v.]

candrámas, m. the moon; the moon-god. [orig. a descriptive cpd, stem candra-más (383d 6), nom. candra-mâs, and so with long ā throughout, but transferred to the ás-declension (cf. 418).]

candrá-varṇa, a. of shining hue.

√ cam, sip, only with ā.

+ ā (ācāmati [745d]; ācacāma; ācānta [955a]; ācāmya; ācāmayati). sip (water), i.e. rinse the mouth.

camasá, m. beaker; cup, made of wood, square, and with handle. [√cam, cf 1197.]

campaka, m. Michelia Champaka, a tree with strong-smelling yellow blossom.

campakavant, a. abounding in Champaka trees; as f. Champakavatî, name of a forest. [1233.]

√ car (cárati, -te; cacāra, cerús, ceré; ácārīt, ácariṣṭa; cariṣyáti; caritá; cáritum; caritvâ; -cârya; caryáte; cárā-yati, -te). —1. move, 77¹²; go; wander; wander about; used of men, beasts, waters, heavenly bodies; —2. (like Eng. proceed —cf. Lat. prō-cēdere, 'go on') act; w. ppl. [1075b], go on, i.e. keep on (doing a thing), 96¹¹; —3. (like Eng. go about, i.e.) undertake, set about; bhāikṣam car, go begging, beg; undergo (troubles), 88¹¹; perform (a vow, duty); observe (silence); commit (offense or injustice), 80², 63¹; sasyam car, feed on corn, 34¹⁸; carita, see s.v. [cf. περι-τελ-λομένων ἐνιαυτῶν, 'as years go round,' and περι-πλ-ομένων ἐνιαυτῶν, 'as years went round,' with τ before a palatal and π before a non-palatal; also πόλ-ος, Milton's 'turning sphere': see also car + ud, and the younger collateral form cal, and under cañcala: akin is also √kal.]

+ anu, move along after, follow.

+ apa, go off, be absent.

+ abhi, go against, trespass against; esp be unfaithful (of a wife).

+ **ā**, — 1. move unto, approach, 86³; —2. go to (an undertaking), set about; *and so*, do, 10⁶, 64¹¹, 66¹⁴; practice (virtue); perform (vow); follow (rule); —3. proceed, conduct one's self, *cf.* **ācāra**, 'cónduct.'

+ **ud-ā**, rise up out of (*abl.*), 77¹⁴, of the moon.

+ **sam-ā**, proceed; do; perpetrate.

+ **ud**, go up, rise, of the sun; *caus.* cause to go out, evacuate, *cf.* **uccāra**, 'evacuation.' [cf. sū́ryam uc-cárantam w. ἥλιον ἀνα-τέλλοντα, 'the rising sun.']

+ **upa**, — 1. come to; —2. come to, *esp.* in order to serve, *and so*, attend, wait upon politely; —3. proceed with, undertake.

+ **parā**, move away from, 86³.

+ **vi**, move in different directions, spread over; of waters, overwhelm; wander about; *caus.* cause to go hither and thither in thought, balance, ponder.

+ **sam**, go, walk, wander.

cara, *a.* moving; *as subst.* animal (as distinguished from plant). [√car.]

cáraṇa, —1. *m. n.* foot; —2. *as n.* a wandering. [√car: for 1, cf. **nayana**.]

caritá, —1. *ppl.* done; —2. *as n. sing.* [1176a], (*like Ger.* Wandel *and Eng.* walk) behavior; proceedings; deeds. [√car.]

carita-vrata, *a.* having his (marital) duty performed.

carcā, *f.* a going over, repetition (of a word in a school-boy's Veda-recitation); a troubling one's self about. [perhaps fr. √car.]

cárman, *n.* skin; pelt.

carya, *grdv.* to be accomplished; —*f.* -**ā**, (*like Eng.* walk) way of life; a performing, busying one's self with. [√car.]

√ **carv** (**carvitá**, **cūrṇá**; **cárvitum**). chew, crush with the teeth.

carṣaṇí, *a.* active, busy; *as f. pl.* busy mortals, men, folk. [√car, 1159b end.]

√ **cal** (**cálati**; **cacála**, **celús**; **caliṣyáti**; **calitá**; **cálitum**). move; start off. [younger form of √car, q.v.: cf. κέλ-ευθος, Lat. *cal-lis*, 'path.']

cala, *a.* moving. [√cal.]

cāṇḍālá, *m.* a Chandāla. [see **caṇḍāla** and 1208f.]

cātana, *a.* driving away. [√cat, caus.]

cāturmāsyá, *n.* a sacrifice to be made every four months, *i.e.* at the beginning of each of the three seasons. [catur + māsa, 1211.]

cāndrāyaṇa, *n.* *with or without* vrata, the Chāndrāyana observance *or* lunar penance, 65⁶ N. [lit. 'connected *or* according with the moon's course,' candra + ayana.]

cāraṇa, *m.* wanderer; *esp.* wandering player *or* singer. [caraṇa.]

cārin, *a.* moving; observing; busying one's self with. [√car.]

cāru, *a.* gladsome; dear; pleasant; fair. [√can, q.v., 1192: cf. Lat. *cā-rus*, 'dear.']

cāru-hāsin, *a.* sweetly laughing.

√ 1 **ci** (**cinóti**, **cinuté**; **cikyé** [787]; **ácet**; **ceṣyáti**, -**te**; **citá**; **cétum**; **citvā́**; -**cítya**; **cī́yáte**). — 1. arrange in order; pile up; build; construct, *esp.* the sacrificial altar; *active, if the priest builds for others; middle, if the sacrificer builds for himself;* — 2. gather together, collect; get possession of.

+ **ud**, heap up, collect.

+ **sam**, gather together, collect; accumulate.

√ 2 **ci** (**cáyati**, -**te**). — 1. hate; —2. avenge, take vengeance on, punish. [cf. Arcadian ἀνυτελω, Attic ἀπο-τίνω, 'pay off,' ἀποτίνομαι, 'get paid to myself, take vengeance, punish,' ποινή, 'penalty.']

√ 3 **ci** (**cikéti**; **cikáya**, **cikyús** [787]; **ácet**; **ceṣyáti**; **cétum**; -**cítya**; **cī́yáte**). — 1 notice, observe; —2. look, investigate. [cf. √cit.]

+ **nis**, (search out, *i.e.*) ascertain; determine; consider as certain *or* settled.

+ **vi-nis**, (look out this way and that, *i.e.*) ponder, consider, 13¹⁹.

+ **pari**, investigate thoroughly, find out.

cikitú, *prob. f.* understanding. [√cit, 1178c.]

cikitvit, *adv.* with understanding. [cikitú, 1109.]

√ **cit** (**cétati**, -**te**; **cikéta**, **cikité**; **ácait**; **cittá**; **cetáyati**, -**te**). — 1. look at, notice; observe; consider; —2. be intent upon, intend; —3. understand, know; *perfect*, **cikéta**, has understood, knows; **cikitvā́ṅs**,

wise; — *caus.* make to know, instruct.
[extension of √3ci: the √cit shows an
intrans. aspect, 'be noticeable *or* bright,'
in ketu: cf. √cint.]
+ **pra**, know.

cít, *vbl.* knowing. [√cit, 383a.]

cíti, *f.* pile. [√1 ci.]

cittá, *n.* notice; thought; mind. [lit.
'noticed,' √cit, see 1176a.]

citta-pramāthin, *a.* disturbing the
mind.

citti, *f.* understanding; wisdom. [√cit.]

citrá, *a.* —1. noticeable, excellent; —2.
clear; bright; bright-colored; of sounds,
clear, *i.e.* loud; — 3. variegated, 10⁸;
varied; —4. *as n.* a bright-colored thing,
a picture. [√cit, 1188.]

citrá-çravas, *a.* whose praise is loud *or*
whose fame is excellent.

citra-stha, *a.* being in a picture;
painted.

citrāṅga, *m.* Dapple-coat, name of a deer.
['having a variegated *or* mottled body':
áṅga.]

cid, *encl. pcl.* —1. *emphasizes, sometimes
very gently, the preceding word:* even,
78¹⁰,¹⁵; just, 74², 79⁴; yáç cid, what
very ones, 70¹⁶; at least, 79¹⁴; —2. *gen-
eralizes a pron.:* yé cid ·· táṅç cid, whatsoever ··, unto all those, 91¹⁰; *so far
Vedic;* —3. *in classical Skt., very common
w. an interr., rendering it indef.:* kaç cid,
a certain; na kā cid, not any; *see* ka,
kad, kadā, karhi, kva. [acc. s. n. of
pron. root **ka**, **ki** (505), w. palatalization:
1111a.]

\ **cint** (cintáyati, -te; cintayām āsa;
cintayiṣyáti; cintitá; cintayitvā; -cint-
ya). —1. think, reflect, have a certain
thought; —2. set one's thoughts upon,
think upon *or* of, consider, turn one's attention to; —3. call attention to; make
an observation, 35⁹. [younger form of
√cit: cf. 255 and 240.]
+ **vi**, reflect.
+ **sam**, think to one's self.

cintana, *n.* a thinking upon. [√cint.]

cintā, *f.* —1. thought; —2. *esp. (like
μέριμνα),* anxious *or* sad thought; sorrow;
—3. plans, 43². [√cint.]

cintā-para, *a.* having sad thought as
one's chief thing, sunk in sad thought.
[1302b.]

cintāviṣa-ghna, *a.* destroying the poison of sorrow.

cintitopasthita, *a.* which approached
as soon as thought of. [lit. 'thought of
and (immediately) at hand,' cintita +
upasthita, 1257.]

cintya, *grdv.* to be thought of, comprehensible. [√cint.]

cirá, *a.* long, of time; -am, -āt, *as adverbs*
[1111c, 1114c], long, for a long time.

cira-mitra, *n.* an old friend.

cīt-kāra, *m.* the sound cīt, *i.e.* the bray-
ing of an ass. [cīt, onomatopoetic.]

cīra, *n.* strip of bark *or* cloth; rag.

\ **cud** (códati, -te; ácodīt; codáyati,
-te). drive on; speed; excite; *caus. the
same.*
+ **pra**, *caus.* drive on; further; inspire.

\ **cur** (coráyati). steal.

curā, *f.* theft. [√cur.]

cūḍā, *f.* tuft of hair left on the crown
of a child's head after the ceremony of
tonsure.

cūḍā-karman, *n.* ceremony of tonsure,
59¹⁹.

cūrṇa, *m. n.* meal, powder. [√carv: for
mg, cf. piṣṭa.]

\ **cūrṇaya** (cūrṇayati). powder, crush
fine; crush; smash. [cūrṇa, 1055.]

\ **cṛt** (cṛtáti; cacárta; cṛttá; -cṛtya).
fasten together.
+ **pra**, loosen, untie.

cétana, *a.* noticing; cetanā, *f.* consciousness; mind. [√cit.]

cétas, *n.* consciousness; mind; heart.
[√cit.]

céd, *adv. never at beg. of sentence, clause,
or half-verse.* if; *apodosis, if it follows,
marked by* tad (37⁴), tatas (52⁵), *or not
marked* (32²¹, etc.), *or marked by* na, *if
negative* (18⁹); na ced, if not, 52⁸; no ced,
*forms a shortened but complete clause, and if
not,* 27¹⁷. [ca + id, 1133⁵: see ca7.]

\ **ceṣṭ** (céṣṭati, -te; cicéṣṭa; ceṣṭitá;
céṣṭitum; ceṣṭitvā). move the limbs;
bestir one's self; be active; act.

ceṣṭā, *f.* activity; performance. [√ceṣṭ.]

ceṣṭita, *ppl.* performed; *as n. s.* [1176a], deeds. [√ceṣṭ.]

códana, *n.* an impelling; order; precept. [√cud.]

cāuḍa, *n.* ceremony of tonsure. [cūḍā.]

cāura, *m.* thief. [curá.]

√ cyu (cyávati, -te; cucyuvé; ácyoṣṭa; cyoṣyáte; cyutá; cyávitam; cyāváyati). —1. move, bestir one's self; —2. go off, disappear; —3. come to nought, 68¹²; —4. fall (from, *abl.*), 51⁹; —5. set agoing, undertake, mōlíri, 74³. [akin, perhaps, are ἰ-σσυα, 'impelled,' and δορυ-σσόος, 'lance-brandishing.']

┼ pra, *caus.* move *or* lead onward.

────────

√ 1 chad (channá; chādáyati; chādayám cakre; chādítá; chādayitvā; -chādya). cover; cover over.

┼ā, cover over; conceal, 25¹⁰.

┼ pari, envelope, cover over.

┼ pra, cover; clothe one's self with (*instr.*).

√ 2 chad *or* chand (chántti; cacchánda; áochān [890²]; chadáyati [mgs 1, 2]; chandáyati [mg 3]; chandayám āsa; chandítá). —1. appear, seem; —2. seem good to, please; —3. (please a person, *acc.*, with a thing, *instr., i.e.*) offer a person, *acc.*, a thing, *instr.* [prob. ident. w. √ccand.]

chanda, *m.* pleasure; will. [√2chad.]

chala, *m. n.* (*perhaps* cover, *i.e.*) guise, disguise; pretence, deceit. [perhaps fr. √1chad.]

chāga, *m.* goat. [for *skāga: cf. Germanic skēpo-, for *skēqo-, Ger. *Schaf*, AS. *sceáp*, Eng. *sheep*.]

chāyā, *f.* shade; shadow; image. [cf. σκιά, 'shadow.']

chāyā-dvitíya, *a.* having one's shadow as second, accompanied by one's shadow. [1302b.]

\ chid (chinátti; cicchéda; ácchāitsīt; chetsyáti; chinná; chéttum; chittvá; -chídya; chidyáte). —1. cut off; hew down; sever; cut in two; nibble; —2. divide. [cf. σχίζω, √σχιδ, 'split'; Lat. *scindo, scidi*, 'cut'; AS. *sceádan*, 'divide,'

Eng. water-*shed*, 'the divide between two valleys.']

┼ ud, —1. cut out; —2. destroy; —*pass.* be cut off, fail, be lacking.

┼ vi, cut asunder; sever.

chidrá, *n.* hole; defect; weak spot. [√chid.]

chucchundari, *m.* musk-rat.

cheda, *m.* cut; cutting off; failure, dearth [√chid.]

────────

já, *vbl.* born; born from; occasioned *or* produced by; *only in cpds.* [√jan, 333 : cf. jā, the older form, 354.]

jágat [450d], *a.* movable; *as n.* all that moves, men and beasts. [√gam: cf. 383b² end.]

jaghána, *m. n.* the hinder parts, the buttocks.

jaghanyà, *a.* hindermost; last; lowest *or* worst. [jaghana, 1212d4.]

jáṅgama, *a.* movable; *as subst.* all that moves, *equiv. to the ancient* jágat. [√gam, 1148.4, cf. 1002b.]

jáṅghā, *f.* lower half of the leg, from knee to ankle; shin. [prob. fr. √1hā, 'move,' 1148.4, cf. 1002b.]

jaṭā, *f.* matted hair; tangled locks.

jaṭhára, *n.* belly; womb. [akin are Goth. *kilþei*, 'womb,' AS. *cild*, Eng. *child*.]

√ jan (jáyate [772]; jajána, jajñé [794d]; ájaniṣṭa; janiṣyáti, -te; játá; janáyati, -te; ájījanat). *see* 761b end, *and* 772. —1. *transitive*, janáyati *and active forms:* beget; bring forth; generate *or* produce; —2. *intransitive*, jáyate *and middle forms:* be born; be produced; come into being; be born again, 18¹; be, 86³; jajñé, natus est, ortus est; jajñānās, children ; *for* játa, *see s.v.* [cf. γε-γον-ός, 'born,' ἐ-γέν-ετο, 'became'; Lat. *genui*, 'begat'; AS. *cennan*, 'beget, bring forth'; AS. *cynn*, Eng. *kin*, 'race, family'; AS. *cyn-ing*, Eng. *king*, 'the man of (noble) kin' — for mg, cf. kulína w. kula 2 : cf. also jana and jani.]

┼ abhi, *pass.* be born unto, be destined unto from birth.

+ **ā**, *caus.* cause to be born for some one, *w. dat.*

+ **upa**, *mid.* be born, arise.

+ **pra**, *mid.* be born; *caus.* procreate.

+ **sam**, *mid.* be produced; **saṃjāta**, having arisen.

jána, *m.* creature; man; person; *in pl.* (*e.g.* 40[16]), *and collectively in sing.* (*e.g.* 77[11]), folks; a people *or* race *or* tribe; **dāivya jána**, heavenly race, the gods. [√jan: cf. γένος, Lat. *genus*, Eng. *kin*, 'race.']

jana-padá, *m.* (tribe-place, *i.e.*) district; community.

jáni [343c], *f.* woman; wife. [√jan: cf. γυνή, Eng. *quean*, 'woman': for mg, cf. **jāyā**.]

janítra, *n.* origin. [√jan, 1185d.]

janitvá, *n.* wifehood. [jani.]

jániman, *n.* production, creation. [√jan, 1168.2a.]

jánī, *f.* *same as* jani.

janús, *n.* origin; ingenium, nature; creation. [√jan, 1154[2].]

jantú, *m.* creature; man. [√jan.]

jánman, *n.* birth; production; creature, 72[2]. [√jan.]

√ **jap** (**jápati**; **jajápa**; **ájapīt**; **japiṣyáti**; **japitá**, **japtá**; **jápitum**; **japitvā**, **japtvā**). say in under-tone; mutter.

jamád-agni, *m.* Jamadagni, a Rishi, friend of Viçvamitra, and foe of Vasishtha. [jamant, unclear: see 1309[4].]

jambuka, *m.* jackal.

jara, *a.* growing old, aging. [√jṛ.]

jarád-aṣṭi, *a.* long-lived. [jarant, see 1299b end.]

jarad-gava, *m.* Old-bull, name of a vulture. [jarant.]

jarad-dāsa, *m.* old slave *or* servant. [jarant.]

járant, *ppl.* aging; old. [√jṛ: cf. γέροντ-α, 'old man.']

jarás, *f.* the growing old; old age. [√jṛ: cf. γῆρας, 'old age.']

jaritṛ́, *m.* invoker; singer.

jalá, *n.* water. [see √gal.]

jala-dhara, *m.* rain-cloud. [lit. 'water-holder.']

jalāçaya, *m.* water-abode; lake. [āçaya.]

√ **jas** (**jásyati**; **jajāsa**; **jāsáyati**). be exhausted *or* tired to death; *caus.* exhaust; quench.

jasra, *a.* dying out. [√jas.]

jā [352], *vbl.* born, *at end of cpds.* [√jan *or* jā: cf. **já**, later form of **jā**.]

√ **jāgṛ**, *same as* √3 gṛ, *see* 1020.

jātá, *ppl.* born; grown; come into being, present; *at beg. of cpds:* arisen, existing, manifest; produced, aroused; *as n.* a living being; birth. [√jan, 955b.]

jāta-karman, *n.* birth-ceremony.

jāta-rūpa, *a.* having native beauty; splendid; -**pá**, *n.* gold.

jāta-víçvāsa, *a.* having arisen confidence, inspired with confidence.

jātá-vedas, *m.* Jātavedas, epithet of Agni. [perhaps, 'having knowledge of all beings, *i.e.* of gods and men,' or, better, 'having all beings *or* things as his possession.']

jāta-saṃkalpa, *a.* having a purpose *or* desire arisen, feeling a passion for another.

jātāmarṣa, *a.* having anger aroused, vexed. [amarṣa.]

jātāvamāna, *a.* having arisen contempt, filled with self-contempt. [avamāna.]

jāti, *f.* birth; position *or* rank. [√jan, 1157[1].]

jāti-mātra, *n.* mere rank. [see mātrā 2, and 1302c 3.]

jātu, *adv.* at all, ever; na jātu, not at all. [√jan, 1111d: development of mg unclear.]

jāterṣya, *a.* having jealousy aroused, jealous. [īrṣyā.]

jánu, *n.* knee. [cf. γόνυ, Lat. *genu*, Eng. *knee*, whence *kneel*.]

jāmadagnya, *a.* of Jamadagni; *as subst.* descendant of J. [jamádagni, 1211.]

jāyā, *f.* wife. [√jan: for mg, cf. jani.]

jārá, *m.* paramour.

jāla, *n.* net.

√ **1 ji** (**jáyati**, -te; **jigāya**, **jigyé** [787]; **ájāiṣīt**, **ájeṣṭa**; **jayiṣyáti**, -te; **jeṣyáti**, -te; **jitá**; **jétum**; **jitvā**; -**jítya**). overpower; conquer; win (battles); win by conquest. [cf. βία, 'force,' βιάω, 'to force'; Lat. *vis*, *ǫvis*, 'force': cf. √jyā.]

+ **ud**, conquer; be victorious.

+ **parā**, *pass.* be conquered.

+ **vi**, *mid.* be victor; conquer (conquests); subdue.

√ **2ji** (jinóti). enliven; quicken; *hence* [716], √jinv. [for •gvi: cf. βίος, 'life': see also √jīv.]

jijñāsā, *f.* investigation. ['effort to find out,' fr. desid. of √jñā, 1149⁴.]

jitápsaras, *a.* having the Apsarases conquered, surpassing the Apsarases. [apsaras.]

jitendriya, *a.* having the senses conquered, having the passions subdued. [indriya.]

√ **jinv** (jínvati; jijínva; jinvişyáti; jinvitá). be lively, hasten; *trans.* quicken; speed onward. [secondary root fr. √2ji, see 716.]

jívri, *a.* old. [for jírvi, √jṛ, 1193².]

jihvá, *f.* tongue.

jihvágra, *n.* tip of the tongue. [agra.]

jīmúta, *m.* thunder-cloud.

jīrá, *a.* quick. [√2ji, 1188: cf. √jyā.]

jīrá-dānu, *a.* having swift drops, swift dripping, *i.e.* well watered.

√ **jīv** (jívati, -te; jijíva, jijīvé; ájīvīt; jīvişyáti, -te; jīvitá; jívitum; jīvitvá; -jívya; jīváyati). live; be alive; *caus.* make alive. [see √2ji: cf. Lat. *vīv-ere,* 'live'; AS. *cwicu,* 'alive,' Eng. *quick,* 'alive, lively.']

+ **anu**, live after, be dependent on, live upon.

jīvá, *a.* living; *as m.* the principle of life, the individual soul, 66⁴. [√jīv: cf. Lat. *vīvus,* 'alive.']

jívana, *n.* existence. [√jīv.]

jīvana-hetu, *m.* cause of existence, *i.e.* means of subsistence.

jīva-pati *or* -patnī, *a. f.* having one's husband yet alive.

jīva-praja, *a.* having one's children yet alive. [prajā.]

jīva-loká, *m.* the world of the living (as distinguished from that of the Manes), 86¹³, 23¹³.

jīvitá, *ppl.* alive; *as n.* [1176a], life. [√jīv.]

jīvitavya, *grdv.* vivendum; *as n. impers.,* see 999. [√jīv.]

jīvitāçā, *f.* the wish for life, hope to save one's life. [āçā.]

jīvin, *a.* living. [√jīv.]

√ **juş** (juşáte, -ti; jujóşa, jujuşé; ájoşişţa; juşţá). taste, *esp.* with pleasure; relish; take pleasure in *or* accept graciously. [cf. γεύομαι, 'taste'; Lat. *gus-tus,* 'taste'; AS. *ceósan,* Eng. *choose.*]

júşţa, *a.* acceptable. [ppl. of √juş, w. accent altered as in dhūrta.]

juhū [356], *f.* sacrificial ladle for pouring the melted butter into the fire, cf. srúc. [√hu, 1147b².]

√ **jū** (junáti [728]; jūjáva [786⁴]; jūtá). speed, *intrans. and trans.;* incite, inspire; further, assist to. [cf. √2ji.]

√ **jṛ** (*V.* járati; *later,* jíryati, -te; jajára; ájārīt; jīrṇá [957b]). decay; grow frail *or* worn out *or* old. [cf. járant, 'old,' and γέροντ-α, 'old man'; jarás and γῆρας, 'old age.']

jógū [352], *a.* loudly singing; praising. [fr. intens. of √gu, 1147b², 1002a.]

jóşas, *n.* pleasure. [√juş.]

jña, *vbl.* knowing, *at end of cpds.* [√jñā, 333.]

√ **jñā** (jānáti, jānīté [730]; jajñáu, jajñé; ájñāsīt [911], ájñāsta; jñāsyáti, -te; jñātá; jñātum; jñātvá; -jñāya; jñāyáte; jñāpáyati, -te, jñapáyati, -te [1042d³]; jñaptá). know; have knowledge of a person *or* thing; recognize; become aware of; learn; notice. [cf. ἰ-γνω, Lat. *co-gnóvit,* 'knew'; AS. *cann,* 'have learned, *i.e.* know, am able,' Eng. *can;* AS. *ge-cnáwan,* Eng. *know.*]

+ **sam-anu**, wholly acquiesce in; approve; give leave; dismiss.

+ **abhi**, recognize; know.

+ **praty-abhi**, recognize.

+ **ava**, look down upon; despise.

+ **ā**, attend to, notice; *caus.* command.

+ **pari**, carefully observe; find out.

+ **pra**, know; *esp.* know one's way *or* bearings *or* how to go to work; prajñāta, clearly to be known, well known.

+ **prati**, recognize, allow; promise; affirm.

+ **vi**, distinguish; understand; know; recognize; consider as; observe; find out; —*pass.* vijñāyate, *in stating a dogma, is* well known *or* recognized (by good author-

ities); —*caus.* make any one know *or* understand; make a representation to, with
a request *or* question *or* proposal; memo-
rialize; interrogate.

jñāti, *m.* kinsman; relative. [√jan: cf.
κασί-γνητος, 'brother-born.']

jñāna, *n.* knowledge; wisdom; *esp.* knowledge of the higher truths of religion and
philosophy. [√jñā, 1150.]

jñānin, *a.* wise; possessing jñāna; understanding (what one reads), 68¹⁵. [jñāna.]

jñeya, *grdv.* to be known *or* considered as.
[jñā.]

√ jyā *or* ji *or* jī (jināti; jijyāú [785];
ájyāsīt; jyāsyáti; jītá). *Bías;* overpower. [cf. 1 jyā, 'power,' and √1ji,
'overpower.']

1 jyā, *f.* superior power; *βία;* force. [√jyā:
cf. *βία,* 'force.']

2 jyā, *f.* bow-string. [cf. *βιός,* 'bow.']

jyáyāns, *a.* stronger *or* superior; older.
[comp. of jyā, 'being strong *or* superior,'
the vbl of √jyā, 470².³.]

√ jyut (jyótati; -jyótya). light. [fr.
√dyut.]

jyeṣṭha, *later* jyeṣṭhá, *a.* best; principal;
first; oldest. [superl. of jyā, the vbl of
√jyā, 470³: see jyáyāns.]

jyeṣṭha-prathama, *a.* having the oldest as the first.

jyotiṣ-kṛt, *a.* light-making. [jyotis:
187.]

jyótiṣmant, *a.* full of light; light.
[jyotis: 184b.]

jyótis, *n.* light (of sun, dawn, etc.); *as pl.*
the heavenly bodies; stars. [√jyut.]

jyótsnā, *f.* moonlight. [jyotis: cf. 1195.]

jráyas, *n.* stretch; expanse. [√jri.]

√ jri (jráyati). *perhaps,* go, stride; *used
only w.* upa, stretch out to.

√ jval (jválati, -te; jajvála; ájválīt;
jvaliṣyáti; jvalitá; -jválya; jválāyati,
jvalāyati, -te). burn bright; flame; *caus.*
kindle, make to flame.

+ pra, *caus.* kindle.

———

jhaṭ-iti, *adv.* with a jhaṭ, as quick as one
could say "boo." [jhaṭ, onomatopoetic:
see 1102a² mid.]

jhalla, *m.* a cudgel-fighting athlete (descended from outcast Kshatriyas).

———

†hio, *a Prakrit form for* sthito.

———

√ ḍhāuk (ḍhāúkate; dudhāuké; ḍhāuk-
itá; ḍhāukáyati). approach; *caus.* bring
near.

+ upa, bring to; provide.

———

tá [495], *pron.* he, she, it, they; that, those;
both subst. and adj., 1¹⁵, 3⁴·⁹; —1. *correl.
of* ya, *which usually precedes* [512], 3¹⁴,
9¹⁸, 10⁵, 22⁵, 29¹⁶, 32¹⁰, 70¹⁶, 77¹³; *but sa*
·· ya, 17²¹, 33¹⁶, 73⁹; *otiose,* 18²⁰, 20¹⁴;
—2. *in connection w. a pron. of the 1st or 2d
pers.: e.g.* tám tvā ·· ímahe, thee, who
art such a one (as aforesaid), we beseech,
i.e. therefore we beseech thee, 76¹²; *cf.*
82⁹; tébhyo nas ·· brūhi, to us, who are
these (unsuccessful ones —*just described*),
tell thou, *i.e.* do thou tell us then, 96¹²;
*similarly, w. a verb in the 1st or 2d pers.,
whose subject is not expressed,* 69¹⁷, 73²,
76¹², ¹⁷, 83¹, 95¹³, 99⁴, 100⁴; —3. *w. other
pronouns:* tasya ·· etasya, of this, 95⁶;
yat tad ·· tad, what (was) that ··, that,
57⁷; ya ta, whoever, anybody, 18⁴; ya
ya ·· ta ta, whoever ·· that, 13¹²; *cf.* 45¹²;
—4. *attenuated in mg* (*like the Greek* ὁ) *to a
simple article:* te devās, the gods, 92¹⁴;
sa bhīmas, Bhīma, 1¹⁵. [w. sa, sā, tad,
cf. ὁ, ἡ, τό, Goth. sa, so, þata, AS. se, seó,
ðæt, 'he, she, it,' Eng. *that;* cf. also Lat.
is-tud, 'that.']

√ takṣ (tákṣati; tatákṣa, tatakṣé; átakṣ-
īt; taṣṭá; -tákṣya). hew; work (wood);
make (of wood or other material); fashion.
[cf. tákṣ-an and τέκτ-ων, 'carpenter';
ἔ-τεκ-ον, 'produced'; Lat. tignum, 'log':
cf. √tvakṣ and toka.]

taj-jīvana, *n.* his subsistence. [tad.]

√ taḍ (táḍáyati; táḍayām āsa; táḍitá;
-táḍya). beat.

+ pari, strike; pelt.

tatá, *m.* father. [cf. τέττα, Lat. *tata,*
'papa': Eng. *dad,* though of similar
make, has of course no direct connection.]

tátas, adv. −1. (as abl. of pron. root ta
[1098], and synonymous w. tasmât) out of
it, 36¹²; −2. from that (place), from
there, 103¹⁵; thence; there; itas tatas,
here and there, hither and thither, 25¹¹,
29¹⁴·¹⁷; −3. from that (time), thereupon,
2²²; then, very often, e.g. 11¹¹, 20¹¹, 56¹⁷;
correl. w. yad, 92¹⁸; w. yadā, 37⁹; w. ced,
52⁵; tataḥ prabhṛti, from then on, 4⁷,
32¹⁷; −4. therefore; −5. otiose, 47¹¹;
5²·¹¹, 11¹⁶; then, w. otiose tadā, 3¹, 4⁶.
[pron. root ta, 497, 1098.]

tat-kṣaṇa, m. that moment; -am, adv.
in that moment, straightway. [tad.]

tat-tīra, n. its bank. [tad.]

tattva, n. (that-ness, i.e.) essence, real
condition or state of a thing. [tad.]

tattva-jña, a. knowing the essence or
the truth or what's what.

tat-para, a. having that as highest object; given over to, intent upon. [tad.]

tat-pārçva, n. his side. [tad.]

tat-prahṛṣṭa, a. pleased with that.
[tad.]

tátra, adv. −1. (as synonymous w. loc. of
tad in all numbers and genders) in or among
or on this or these or them, 13⁷, 21⁶, 38¹¹,
57⁷³; in this matter, 37⁵; herein, 98³;
−2. there, often, e.g. 2⁶, 5⁶; thither, 6⁶,
11¹⁴, etc.; correl. w. yatra, 24⁴; −3. on
that occasion, in that case, then, 4¹, 14²²,
40¹. [pron. root ta, 497, 1099.]

tatra-stha, a. abiding there.

tat-saṁnidhāna, n. his presence.
[tad.]

tat-sapatnī, f. her co-wife. [tad.]

tat-samīpe, adv. near him. [tad: see
samīpa.]

tat-sahacārin, a. accompanying him.
[tad.]

táthā, adv. −1. so, thus, 11⁴, 24¹⁶; in
this way, 99³⁰; w. yathā, yathā regularly
preceding: yathā · · tathā: as · · so, 21¹⁶,
61⁶, 77¹³; in order that · · thus, 30¹⁶, 37⁷;
but tathā · · yathā, so · · as, 22¹², 43³⁹;
yathā yathā · · tathā tathā, to what
degree · · to that degree, the more · ·
the more, 48¹⁴; yathā tathā, in one way
or another, 62⁹; −2. particle of assent, so
be it, yes, 4¹, 8⁶, 48¹², 94⁵; that is so, 52¹⁶;

−3. so, in like manner, 19⁸; or, simply
conjunctive, also, likewise, 10⁶, 12¹², etc.;
tathā_eva, just so (cf. Middle Eng. al so,
i.e.), likewise, also, 1¹¹, 7¹⁰; tathā ca, 18³⁹,
see ca3; −4. tathā_api, so even, even
under those circumstances, nevertheless,
21¹¹. [pron. root ta, 497, 1101.]

táthā-vidha, a. of such sort, in such
condition. [tathā (1306) + vidhā, 1302c 5.]

tád, −1. as nom. acc. s. n. to ta, see ta; used
also in cpds and derivatives, see 497; −2.
as adv. there; yatra · · tad, where · · there,
103¹⁶; −3. then, in that case, 27¹⁷, 36⁵;
ced · · tad, if · · then, 37⁵; so yadi · · tad,
37¹²; tad · · yad, then · · when, 71⁹; simply continuative: tat ko vṛtras, who then
is V., 97¹⁹; so 24¹; −4. in this way, i.e.
therefore, accordingly, 18⁶, 19¹⁴·²², 27¹⁴,
etc.; yad · · tad, since · · therefore, 17⁶;
so yatas · · tad, 37⁷. [cf. 495.]

tad-aṅga, n. his person.

tad-anantara, a. immediately adjoining that; -am, adv. [1311], immediately
after that; thereupon.

tad-abhimukha, a. turned towards
him; -am, adv. [1311], towards him.

tad-abhivādin, a. signifying that.

tad-ardhika, a. amounting to or lasting
half of that.

tadā, adv. at that time; then, 2³⁹; in that
case; often otiose in Epos, 3⁷; so after
tatas, 3¹, 4⁹; yadā · · tadā, when · · then,
26¹⁷; yadā yadā · · tadā tadā, whenso-
ever · · then, 31¹¹; yadi · · tadā, if · · then,
25⁹. [pron. root ta, 497, 1103.]

tad-ākṛti, a. having the appearance of
them (i.e. of Piçāchas).

tad-ājñā, f. his (the moon-god's) command.

tadāhāra-vartman, n. the way of that
food. [tad-āhāra.]

tad-īpsita, a. desired by those two.

tadīya, a. pertaining to him, her, it, or
them; such. [tad, 497.]

tad-upadeça, m. his advice.

tad-gṛha, n. his house.

tad-bhaya, m. fear of it or them.

tad-bhāṣā, f. that language.

tad-rasa, m. the essence of it.

tad-vacana, n. his words.

11

tad-vat, *adv.* in this way, so; likewise. [tad: 1107.]

tad-víd, *a.* knowing that; *as m.* connoisseur *or* judge.

tad-vṛkṣa, *m.* that tree.

tad-vṛddhi, *f.* the interest of them.

√ **1 tan** (tanóti, tanuté; tatāna, tené [794e]; átānīt; taṅsyáte; tatá; tántum; tatvā; -tátya; tāyáte [772]). — 1. stretch, *trans. and intrans.;* extend, reach; spread over; —2. continue, endure, 79[18]; —3. stretch (a weft *or* a line); continue (the line of a family); —4. *metaphorically,* of sacrifice and supplication (which are compared with a weft), perform, make. [cf. τάνυμαι, 'stretch'; Lat. *tenēre,* 'hold,' *tendere,* 'stretch'; AS. *þenian,* Ger. *dehnen,* 'stretch': see also tanu.]

+ **ā**, spread over; overspread (*esp.* with light), beshine; stretch (a bow).

+ **pari**, stretch around; surround; envelope.

+ **vi**, stretch out; spread out, cover; vitata, stretched, hung, dependent, 92[11].

+ **sam**, hold together, *intrans.;.* bind together; make continuous; saṁtata, (*just like Lat.* con-tinens) uninterrupted.

√ **2 tan** (tányati). resound. [cf. τόνος, 'tone'; Lat. *tonare,* 'thunder'; AS. noun *þunor,* 'thunder,' whence denom. verb *þunrian,* Eng. *thunder;* AS. *þunres dœg,* Eng. *Thurs-day,* 'day sacred to the Old Germanic god of the thunder-storm, þonar *or* Thor': see tanyatú, 'thunder.']

tanú, *f.* [344[2]] tanu, tanū, tanvī, *a.* thin, tenuis, slender; — tanu *or* tanú [decl. 356], *as subst. f.* body, 56[3], 89[18]; person; one's own person, self, *used like* ātman [514] *as reflexive pron.,* 73[12], 78[12]; outward form *or* manifestation, 84[11]. [prop. 'stretched out, thin,' √1 tan: cf. τα␣␣-, 'extended, long,' in cpds; Lat. *tenuis,* Eng. *thin,* Ger. *dünn,* 'thin.']

tanu-trāṇa, *n.* body-cover, 84[11].

tanu-madhya, *a.* having a slender middle, *i.e.* slender-waisted.

tanū-tyáj, *a.* abandoning the body, risking life, brave.

tantí, *f.* cord; *esp.* a long line to which calves are tethered by means of short ropes; tantī, *the same.* [√1 tan.]

tántu, *m.* thread, 89[1]; *metaphorically,* of the thread, *i.e.* course, of a sacrifice. [√1 tan.]

tántra, *n.* thread; warp of a web; *fig.* fundamental doctrine; division of a work. [√1 tan.]

√ **tand** (tándate). relax, grow weary.

tandrā, *f.* fatigue. [√tand, 1188c.]

tandrita, *a.* wearied, *only w. a-.* [tandrā, 1176b.]

tannimittam, -ena, *see* nimitta. [tad.]

tanyatú, *m.* thunder. [√2 tan.]

√ **tap** (tápati, -te; tatāpa, tepé [794e]; átāpsīt; tapsyáti; taptá; táptum; taptvā; -tápya; tapyáte, tápyate [761b]). —1. be warm; burn, *intrans.;* —2. heat; make glowing; burn, *trans.;* —3. *fig.* (*like* √cuc), distress, pain; —4. *pass.* suffer; suffer voluntarily, castigate one's self, do penance. [cf. Lat. *tepēre,* AS. *þefian,* 'be warm.']

+ **upa**, heat; become sick; sicken, *used impers., w. acc. of the person,* 101[3].

+ **sam**, heat; pain.

tapaḥ-prabhāva, *m.* efficacy of devotion.

tápas, *n.* —1. heat, fire; —2. voluntary suffering (*see* tap 3, 4), self-castigation, self-torture (64[21]), mortification, asceticism, devotion. [√tap.]

tápasvant, *a.* full of devotion; pious. [1233a.]

tapasvín, *a. the same.* [1232.]

tapo-já, *a.* asceticism-born, whose element is asceticism. [tapas.]

√ **tam** (tāmyati, -te [763]; tatāma; átamat; tāntá [955a]). become darkened, of the eye; become powerless, deadened, stupefied, numb, *or* inactive. [orig. mg, prob., 'be dark,' see tamas: cf. tāmisrā, 'darkness,' Lat. *tenebrae, ‹temsrae,* 'darkness,' Old High Ger. *dinstar,* 'dark'; Old High Ger. *dēmar,* 'dusk,' Ger. *dämmern,* 'become twilight,' but not Eng. *dim.*]

támas, *n.* —1. darkness; —2. spiritual darkness, infatuation; —3. darkness *as* one of the three pervading qualities of all existence, *see* guṇa 3. [√tam.]

tamo-niṣṭha, *a.* resting *or* founded on darkness.

tamo-nuda, a. darkness-dispelling.

tamo-bhūta, a. dark, enveloped in darkness. [lit. 'become darkness,' tamas: 1273c.]

tára, m. crossing, passage. [√tṛ.]

taram-ga, m. wave; wave as subdivision of a work entitled "ocean," 56¹³, cf. 45¹ⁿ. [lit. 'which goes crossing the water': taram, grd of √tṛ, 995, cf. 1250a.]

taráṇi, a. pressing onward. [√tṛ, 1159b.]

taru, m. tree. [prob. a modern form of dāru, q.v.]

taru-koṭara, n. tree-hollow.

táruṇa, a. young; tender; -ka, n. sprout. [cf. τέρην, 'tender, fine.']

taru-tale, under the tree, see tala.

√ tark (tarkáyati [1041²]; tarkayām āsa; tarkayiṣyáti; tarkitá; tarkáyitum; tarkayitvā; -tárkya). —1. think over, 13¹⁶; reflect, 13¹³; —2. form an idea of. [orig. mg, 'turn,' and so (like Lat. volvere animo), 'turn over or revolve in one's mind': cf. tarku, 'spindle'; τρέπ-ω, Lat. torqueo, 'turn'; Old High Ger. drāhsil, 'turner,' Ger. drechseln, 'turn.']
+ pra, form a conception of.

tárhi, adv. at that time; then; yadi·· tarhi, if··then. [pron. root ta, 497, 1103c.]

tala, m. n. —1. surface; -tale, at end of cpd, equiv. simply to on, 6¹⁷, 46¹¹; —2. the surface or place under an object, e.g. a tree; -tale, at end of cpd, equiv. simply to under, 34¹, 43²; —3. sometimes otiose in cpds, e.g. nabhas-tala, sky-surface, i.e. sky.

tálpa, m. couch; bed. [for ⁕star-pa, √stṛ, 1201² end: for mg, see under stṛ.]

talpa-çívan, f. -varī, a. lying on beds. [1169.2¹.]

taviṣá, a. powerful. [√tu, 1197b.]

táskara, m. robber.

tásmāt, adv. from this (cause), hence; therefore; yad·· tasmāt, since··therefore. [pron. root ta, 1114a.]

tā́ta, m. used in voc. s., to a father, but generally to a junior or an inferior, my dear. [cf. tata.]

tādítnā, adv. then. [perhaps instr. (1112d) of ⁕tādítna, and this fr. ⁕tadi-tna, 'of that time,' and this fr. ⁕tadi (1245e), correl. of yadi.]

tā́dṛç, a. such. [see 518: for declension, see dṛç.]

tā́dṛça, a. such. [see 518.]

tápasá, m. ascetic. [tápas.]

tā́masa, a. dark; pertaining to darkness or the guṇa called tamas. [támas.]

tāyú, m. thief. [cf. stāyú.]

tārā, f. star. [form of transition to the a-declension (399) from tṛ, see under stṛ.]

tāvac-chata, f. -ī, a. having or embracing so many hundreds. [tāvant (1249a) + çata.]

tāvat-kṛtvas, adv. so many times. [tāvant, 1249a.]

tā́vant [457], —1. adj. so great; so much; so many, 105⁴; extending so far, 101⁹; lasting so long, 58⁹; correl. w. yāvant, 101⁹, 105⁴; —2. tāvat, as adv. so much; so far; to such an extent, 95¹⁶; so long; for a while, 19¹; yāvat·· tāvat: as long as ·· so long, 15⁴, 32³, 40¹⁶; when··then, 44¹⁵; just as··then, 22⁷; tāvat··yāvat, so long··as, 19³, 42³; —3. at once; now, 24²⁰, 34⁶, 53¹⁷; —3a. w. 1st pers. pres. ind., first, before doing any thing else, at once, 20¹⁸, 23⁶, 38¹¹; —3b. w. imperative: at once, 24²³; tāvat·· tatas or paçcāt, first ·· then or afterwards, 27¹⁸, 38⁴; —4. concessively, iha samaye, tāvat, in this case, one must admit, 41¹⁰; —5. emphasizing, like eva, what precedes, 30⁴, 25⁷. [pron. root ta, 517.]

tigmá, a. sharp. [√tij, 216.5.]

√ tij (tejáyati; tejayām āsa; tejitá). be sharp. [orig. ⁕stig: cf. στίζω, 'prick,' στίγ-μα, 'prick'; Lat. in-stigāre, 'prick on'; Eng. stick, 'to pierce.']

títhi, m. f. a lunar day (of which there are 15 in a half-lunation).

tirás, —1. prep. through; across; —2. as adv. crossways, sideways; aside; w. kṛ [171³, 1078⁴], put aside, treat disrespectfully, scold. [√tṛ, 'cross': cf. Lat. trans, 'across.']

tiras-kā́ra, m. a scolding. [√kṛ + tiras: 171³.]

tiryaktva, n. condition of a beast. [tiryak, middle stem of tiryañc, 1249a: 1239.]

11 ⁕

tiryáñc [409d], — 1. a. directed across; horizontal; — 2. as subst. m.n. beast (going horizontally, as opposed to man, who walks upright — ūrdhva); — 3. acc. s. n. tiryak, as adv. across. [tiras or tir, w. añc, 409d: tir, like tiras, is akin w. √tṛ.]

tilá, m. — 1. the sesame plant, Sesamum indicum; — 2. its seed, which is eaten, and furnishes good oil.

tisṛ, fem. to tri, see 482c.

tíra, n. shore or bank. [prop. 'place of crossing or going into the water,' √tṛ.]

√ tu (távīti [633]; tūtáva [786⁴]). have power; be strong. [orig. 'swell, grow': cf. τύ-λη, 'swelling, lump,' Corcyraean τῦμο-s, 'mound'; AS. þúma, 'the big (finger),' Eng. thumb; further, túm-ra, 'fat, strong'; Lat. tum-ulus, 'mound,' tum-or, 'swelling.']

tú, pcl. never at beg. of sentence. —1. w. imperative, pray; —2. in sooth, 78¹⁰; —3. but, 8¹³, 26¹³, 34¹⁰, etc.; on the other hand, 20⁴; tu ·· tu, on the one hand ·· on the other, 2¹⁴·¹⁷; so ·· , ·· tu, ·· tu, 60³; na tv eva tu, but by no means, 63¹⁰, 64³; kámaṁ tu ·· na tu, see kámam; kiṁ tu, nevertheless, 39⁵; —4. used loosely: as equiv. to ca, 58¹; often as a mere expletive [1122a⁴], e.g. 4⁹, 64¹³⁵.

tu, pron. root of 2nd pers, see tvad.

túc, f. progeny. [cf. toka.]

√ tud (tudáti; tutóda; tunná). strike; push. [cf. Τύδεύς, 'The Hammer, Martel'; Lat. tundo, tu-tud-i, 'strike, struck'; Goth. stautan, Ger. stossen, 'strike.']
+ **ā**, strike at, pick at.

√ tur (turáti, -te). press onward swiftly. [subsidiary form of √tṛ (242) and allied w. √tvar.]

1 turá, a. —1. swift, esp. of horses; -am, as adv. swiftly, in turaṁga; —2. quick, ready, willing, 78¹⁷. [√tur.]

2 turá, a. strong, mighty, 78⁹. [√tu, 1188.]

turaṁga, m. horse. ['swiftly going,' turam + ga, see 1 tura: for mg, cf. khaga.]

turíya, a. fourth. [for ·ktur-ia: catúr, 487⁵, 1215.]

√ tul (toláyati; tolayám āsa; tolayiṣyáti; tolitá; -tólya). —1. raise up; —2. esp. raise up a thing so as to find its weight; weigh ; —3. counterpoise ; —4. equal. [orig. mg, 'bear, i.e. hold up': in the cognates, the mg 'bear, i.e. endure' appears: cf. Lat. tul-i, 'endured'; Goth. þul-an, Eng. thole, 'endure'; Ger. Ge-dul-d, 'endurance'; also ἔ-τλη-ν, 'bore,' πολύ-τλᾶ-s, 'much enduring'; Lat. lātus, ·tlā-tus, 'borne.']

tulá, f. balance; weight; equality. [√tul: cf. Anglo-Indian tola, about 180 grains troy: cf. τάλαντον, 'balance, weight.']

tulya, a. keeping the balance with; equal to; like. [tulá, 1212d 4 end.]

tulyákṛti, a. having like appearance; alike. [ákṛti.]

tuví, a. in cpds. mighty; much; many. [√tu, 1155.]

tuvi-bádhá, a. distressing many (enemies) or besetting (them) sore.

túviṣmant, a. mighty. [tuvis.]

tuvis, n. in derivs. might. [√tu, 1153.]

√ tuṣ (túṣyati, -te; tutóṣa; tuṣṭá; tóṣ-ṭum; -túṣya; toṣáyati). become quiet; be satisfied or pleased; caus. satisfy; gratify.
+ **sam**, caus. satisfy.

tuṣṭi, f. satisfaction. [√tuṣ.]

tūṣṇím, adv. silently, in silence. [prob. fr. an obsolete ·tūṣṇa, 'silent,' √tuṣ, 1111d.]

√ tṛ (tárati, -te; tiráti, -te; tatára, terús [794e]; átārīt; tariṣyáti, -te; tīrṇá; tártum; tīrtvá; -tírya; tāráyati). —1. cross over (a water, the sky); —2. get across or to the end; get through, escape; survive. [cf. τέρμων, Lat. terminus, 'boundary': see √trā and tiras: for treatment of root-vowel, see 242.]
+ **ava**, descend, esp. from heaven to earth; come down, esp. of divine beings who become incarnate as men; alight; betake one's self to; caus. take down or off.
+ **ud**, come up out of the water.
+ **abhy-ud**, come out of the water unto, cross the water unto, 89⁴.
+ **pra**, take to the water; start on.
+ **vi**, cross through; traverse.

tṛ, m. star, see stṛ.

tṛcá, m. n. strophe of three stanzas. [tri + ṛc, 243, 1315c.]

tṛ́ṇa, n. grass. [cf. (θρόνα=) τρόνα, 'flowers, herbs'; Eng. thorn; Ger. Dorn, 'thorn.']

tṛtíya, a. third. [fr. tri, through trita, 243, 487⁴: cf. τρί-τος, Lat. ter-tius, Eng. thir-d, Ger. dri-tte, 'third.']

√ tṛd (tṛṇátti, tṛntté; tatárda, tatṛdé; tṛṇṇá; -tṛ́dya). split; bore; open.
    + anu, bore after (waters), release, make flow.

√ 1 tṛp (tṛ́pyati, -te [761a]; tatárpa; átṛp-at; trapsyáti; tṛptá; -tṛ́pya; tarpáyati). be satisfied; become content; — caus. satisfy, please; nourish. [cf. τέρπω, 'satisfy, please,' τρέφω, 'nourish.']
    + ā, become content or glad.

√ 2 tṛp, steal, not actually occurring in vbl forms, but rendered probable by the deriv. tṛpu, 'thief,' the cpds asu- and paçu-tṛp, and by the Avestan √tṛf, 'steal.'

√ tṛṣ (tṛ́ṣyati; tatárṣa; átṛṣat; tṛṣitá; tarṣáyati). be thirsty. [cf. τέρσ-ομαι, 'become dry'; Lat. torret, stors-et, 'grows dry, scorches'; Eng. noun thirst; Ger. dorr-et, 'grows dry'; also Lat. terra, sters-a, 'the dry (land).']

tṛṣā́, f. thirst. [√tṛṣ.]

tṛ́ṣṇā, f. thirst. [√tṛṣ, 1177a.]

téjas, n. —1. sharpness, edge; —2. tip of flame or ray; gleaming splendor, 1⁸; fire; —3. (splendor, i.e.) beauty of person, 8¹⁰ff.; —4. (like Eng. fire, i.e.) energy, vigor, power; —5. moral or magic power, 11²³; influence, dignity, 95⁸; majesty, 1⁶, 2⁴. [√tij: observe that ἀκμή has mgs 1 and 4.]

téna, adv. in that way, 47¹⁷; so; therefore, 18⁷, etc.; yatas or yad or yena · · tena, for the reason that · ·, therefore, 30⁸, 57⁶, 64⁹. [pron. root ta, 1112a: of like derivation and mg is τῷ.]

tāilá, n. sesame oil. [tilá, 1208f¹ end.]

toká, n. creation, progeny. ·[cf. √takṣ and √tvakṣ, and túc.]

toraṇa, n. arched portal; arch. ['passage,' √tur, subsidiary form of √tṛ, 'cross, pass.']

tyá [499a], pron. that; that well-known (like Lat. ille).

tyakta-jívita, a. having life set aside, risking one's life, brave.

tyaktajívita-yodhin, a. bravely fighting. [1279.]

√ tyaj (tyájati, -te; tatyája, tatyajé; átyākṣīt; tyakṣyáti, -te; tyaktá; tyák-tum; tyaktvá; -tyájya; tyajyáte; tyáj-áyati). —1. withdraw from; leave in the lurch; abandon (dove, goat, tree); —2. renounce (passions, use of a language); relinquish (exertion); lay aside (a certain form, an earthly body); set aside, i.e. risk (life). [cf. σέβομαι, 'shrink back from in awe, revere.']
    + pari, leave to one's fate (a jackal); abandon; leave (one's party); relinquish or give up (play, food, affairs); pari-tyakta, (abandoned by, i.e.) separated from, 66³.

tyáj, vbl. abandoning, w. tanū-. [√tyaj.]

tyájya, grdv. to be abandoned. [√tyaj, 963c.]

trayá, a. triple, threefold, 57¹³; as n. triad, triplet, τριάς. [tri, 489⁴.]

√ tras (trásati; tatrása, tatrasús, treṣús [794c²]; átrāsīt; trasiṣyáti; trastá). tremble; fear. [cf. τρέω, τρέσ-σε, 'tremble, trembled'; Lat. terreo, 'affright'; a-trastas and ά-τρεστος, 'unterrified.']

trasádasyu, m. Trasadasyu, a generous prince, the favorite of the gods, and descended from Purukutsa. [perhaps for trasád-dasyu, 'affrighting the evil beings,' see 1309⁴· √tras.]

√ trā (trā́ti, trā́te [628]; trā́yate [761c]; tatré; átrāsta; trāsyáte; trātá; trā́-tum; trātvā́). protect; rescue; rescue from, w. abl. [collateral form of √tṛ ('get through or across'), w. a caus. mg, 'bring through or across (trouble).']

trātṛ́, m. protector, saviour. [√trā.]

trāsa, m. terror. [√tras.]

trāsadasyava, m. descendant of Trasadasyu, 87¹². [trasádasyu, 1208c.]

tri [482c], num. three. [cf. τρεῖς, τρία, Lat. trēs, tria, Eng. three, Ger. drei, 'three.']

triṅçát [485], f. thirty. [cf. tri.]

trikadruka, m. pl. perhaps designation of certain Soma-vessels, three in number. [cf. tri and kadrū.]

tri-kāla, n. the three times, present, past and future. [kāla, masc.: 1312.]

trikāla-jña, a. knowing present, past, and future; omniscient.

tri-daçá [declined like kāma, 330], m. pl. the three times ten, the thirty, a name in round numbers for the 33 deities (12 Adityas, 8 Vasus, 11 Rudras, 2 Açvins), i.e. the gods. [tri + daça, 477c : cf. triñçat.]

tridaçeçvara, m. pl. lords of the gods, i.e. the four chief gods, Indra, Agni, Varuna, and Yama. [īçvara.]

tri-divá, n. the triple or third i.e. highest heaven. [div, 1315c : 1312³.]

tri-dhátu, a. having three parts, tri-partite, threefold. [acct, 1800c.]

tri-pada, f. -ī, a. having (taken) three steps.

tri-rātrá, n. space of three nights, tri-noctium. [rátri, 1315b, 1312⁴⁴: cf. the Eng. usage in sen-night, fort-night.]

tri-vidyā, f. the three sciences, i.e. Vedas. [1312³.]

tri-vidha, a. of three sorts, threefold. [vidhā, 1302c5 : acct, 1800c.]

tri-vṛt, a. threefold, tri-partite. ['turning thrice, with three turns.']

tri-veda, in cpds and derivs. the three Vedas. [1312³.]

tri-savaṇa, a. pertaining to the three Soma-pressings; -am, adv. at morning, noon, and evening. [savana.]

tris, adv. thrice. [see tri: cf. τρίς, Lat. ter, -ters, 'thrice': Eng. thrice is a gen. form, cognate in root only.]

trāividya, n. study of the three Vedas. [trividyā.]

trāivedika, a. relating to the three Vedas. [triveda, 1222e2.]

try-adhiṣṭhāna, a. having three mani-festations.

tvá, pron. stem of 2d pers., see tvad.

√ tvakṣ, work, principally in derivs., and ident. w. takṣ.

tvác, f. skin.

tvaj-jāra, m. thy paramour. [tvad, 494.]

tvát, abl. of tva, and used in place of tva in cpds : by Hindus written tvad, q.v. [494.]

tvat-kṛte, for the sake of thee. [1314f, 1130: tvat represents the stem tva, and in gen. relation.]

tvad [491], so-called stem [494] of 2d pers. pron. thou; see tvat. [w. the real root tu, cf. Doric τύ, Lat. tū, AS. ðū, Eng. thou, Ger. du, 'thou.']

√ tvar (tvárate; tatvaré; tūrṇá [cf. 957b], tvaritá; tvaráyati). hasten; tvarita, having hastened, in haste. [see √tur, tṛ.]

tvarā, f. haste. [√tvar.]

tváṣṭṛ, m. — 1. wright, workman, 75⁶; — 2. Twashtar, the artificer of the gods (70²), former of fruit of the womb, giver of growth and long life (86¹⁵), father of Saranyū (85¹²). [√tvakṣ, 221.]

tvávant, a. like thee. [tva, 517.]

tvāṣṭrá, m. descendant of Twashtar. [tvaṣṭṛ.]

───────

dā, vbl. giving, in cpds. [√1dā, 333, 354.]

√ danç or daç (dáçati [746]; dadánça; daçiṣyáti; daṣṭá; danṣṭvā; -dáçya). bite. [cf. δάκνω, 'bite'; Goth. tahjan, 'rend, tear.']

dança, m. gad-fly. [√danç.]

dáṇṣṭra, m. large tooth; tusk; fang. [√danç, 1185b.]

daṇṣṭrin, a. having tusks or large teeth. [dáṇṣṭra.]

√ dakṣ (dákṣati, -te; dadakṣé; dakṣiṣyáte). act. suit; mid. be able or dexterous or strong. [cf. dakṣa and dakṣiṇa.]

dákṣa, a. able, dexterous, strong; as m. ability, faculty, strength, power; esp. spiritual power, will; dakṣa and kratu, will and understanding (as faculties of the manas, 'soul'). [√dakṣ: cf. δεξιός, 'clever, right,' and dakṣiṇa.]

dákṣiṇa, a. — 1. clever, able; and so — 2. (as opp. to awkward, gauche), right, of the hand, hasta, e.g. 102¹¹; so pāṇi, 60⁵; foot, pāda, 60⁵; side, párçva, 102¹²; — 3. southern (because in prayer the face is turned eastward : cf. uttara3), 105⁶; sc. agni, southern fire, 102³ɴ.; — 4. as f., dakṣiṇā, sc. go, the able, i.e. fruitful cow, milch cow; milch cow as the customary reward for conducting a sacrifice; then, — 5. in general, any reward or present for the sacrificing priest, see 106⁶; so 95³,²; — see also adv. dakṣiṇā. [√dakṣ: cf. δεξιός, Lat. dexter, 'clever, right'; Goth.

taiḣsva, 'right hand': from **dakṣiṇa** in mg 3, comes *Deccan*, name of the country south of Hindustan, lit. 'the South.']

dakṣiṇa-paçcima, *a*. southwesterly.

dakṣiṇa-pūrva [525⁴], *a*. southeasterly.

dakṣiṇā, *adv*. southerly; toward the south. [**dákṣiṇa**: acct, 1112e.]

dakṣiṇāgní, *m*. the southern fire, 103², *cf*. 102²ⁿ.

dakṣiṇāpara [525²], *a*. southwesterly. [**dakṣiṇa** + apara.]

dakṣiṇā-pravaṇa, *a*. sloping to the south. [**dakṣiṇā**, adv.]

dakṣiṇābhimúkha, *a*. facing southerly. [**dakṣiṇā** (adv.) + abhimukha.]

dakṣiṇāyana, *n*. south-course (of the sun), *or* the half-year from the summer to the winter solstice. [**dakṣiṇa** + ayana.]

dakṣiṇāraṇya, *n*. the southern forest (a forest in the Deccan). [**dakṣiṇa** + araṇya.]

dákṣiṇāvant, *a*. abounding in gifts to the priests, *i.e.* (from the point of view of the priests) pious. [**dákṣiṇā**: see **dakṣiṇā**δ.]

dagdhá, *a*. — 1. burned; — 2. pained, tortured; — 3. wretched, good-for-nothing, cursed, damned. [ppl. of √dah: for mg 2, cf. √çuc.]

dagdhodara, *n*. one's cursed belly. [dagdha + udara.]

daṇḍá, *m*. stick; staff (of Brahman), 59²³; mace, 97⁸; rod as symbol of dominion and punishment. [cf. δένδρον, 'tree.']

daṇḍa-bhaya, *m*. fear of the rod.

daṇḍín, *a*. bearing a staff; *as m*. warder. [daṇḍa.]

dattá, *a*. given; *as m*. (a son) given (by his parents to others for adoption); *common at end of proper names, esp. of Vaiçyas*. [ppl. of √1 dā, 955c.]

dadṛh, *a*. firm; **dadhṛk**, *acc. s. n.*, *as adv*. firmly. [√dṛh.]

dadhán [481], *n*. sour milk; curds. [orig., perhaps, 'milk,' fr. √2 dhā.]

dádhi, *supplementary stem to* **dadhan**.

dadhi-karṇa, *m*. Curd-ear, name of a cat. ['having curd-ears, *i.e.* ears as white as curds.']

dadhṛk, *see* **dadṛh**.

dánt [396], *m*. tooth. [cf. ὀδόντα, Lat. *dentem*, Goth. *tunþus*, AS. *tōð*, Eng. *tooth*, Old High Ger. *zand*, Ger. *Zahn*, 'tooth.']

dánta, *m*. tooth. [dant, 399.]

√ **dabh** *or* **dambh** (**dábhati**; **dadábha**, **dadámbha**, **debhús**; **ádabhat**; **dabdhá**; **dábdhum**). harm with guile; hurt; deceive.

dábha, *m*. deception. [√dabh.]

√ **dam** (**dámyati** [763]; **dāntá** [955a]; **damitvá**; -**dámya**; **damáyati**). — 1. be tame; — 2. tame; conquer; become master; control. [cf. δαμάω, Lat. *domāre*, 'tame'; Eng. *tame*, Ger. *zahm*, 'tame.']

dám, *n*. house. [cf. δῶ, 'house': see under **dáma**.]

dáma, *m. n*. house, home. [cf. δόμος, Lat. *domus*, 'house, home': it is not certain whether **dáma** comes from √dam and so means lit. 'the place where one is master, one's *Gebiet*,' or whether it is to be connected w. δέμω, 'build': in the latter case, it would mean lit., like Ger. *Bau*, 'a building,' and should be connected w. AS. *timber*, *stem-ra*, 'building-material, a building,' Eng. *timber*, 'building-material,' Ger. *Zimmer*, 'building-material, a building, a room.']

damá, — 1. *a*. conquering, *at end of cpds*; *as m*. — 2. Dama, *i.e.* Victor, name of a son of Bhima; — 3. self-control. [√dam: cf. ἱππό-δαμος, 'Horse-tamer,' etc.]

damana, — 1. *a*. conquering, *at end of cpds*; — 2. *as m*. Damana, *i.e.* Vincent, name of a priestly sage, and of a son of Bhima. [√dam: cf. Lat. *dominus*, 'master.']

damayantī, *f*. Damayantī, *i.e.* Victoria, name of Bhima's daughter. ['conquering (men),' fr. √dam, 1043.5.]

dám-pati, *m*. master of the house; *as dual*, master and mistress, man and wife; pair. [acct, 1267a.]

dambha, *m*. deception. [√dabh.]

√ **day** (**dáyate**; **dayám āsa**; **dayitá**). — 1. part; allot; — 2. take part in; sympathize with; have tender feeling for; love; — **dayita**, loved, dear; *as f*., -**tā**, wife. [for 1, cf. κρέα δαίετο, 'parted, carved the meat'; for 2, cf. δαίεται ἦτορ, 'heart is divided *or* takes part in (?), *i.e* sympathizes.']

dayā́, *f.* sympathy; compassion. [√day.].

dayālú, *a.* compassionate. [dayā, 1227³.]

dayāvant, *a.* compassionate. [dayā.]

dayita, *see* √day.

dara, *m.* cleft, hole. [√1 dṛ.]

daridra, *a.* wandering about; mendicant; poor; *as m.* poor man. [fr. intens. of √1 drā, 'run about,' 1147b³: for mg, cf. Eng. *tramp,* in its American sense of 'vagrant beggar.']

darpa, *m.* wildness; wantonness; impudence; pride. [√dṛp.]

darbhá, *m.* grass-tuft; grass used at sacrificial ceremonies, *esp.* Kuça-grass, Poa cynosuroides. [√dṛbh.]

darça, *m.* sight; the moon when just becoming visible; the new moon; the day *or* festival of new moon. [√dṛç.]

darçaka, *a.* —1. seeing; —2. (*fr. caus.*) showing, making clear. [dṛç.]

darçatá, *a.* to be seen; visible. [√dṛç, 1176e.]

dárçana, *a.* seeing; *as n.* the beholding, sight; the becoming visible, 103²⁰; appearance, 4¹⁰. [√dṛç.]

darça-pūrṇa-māsá, *dual m.* new and full moon; the days and the festivals of new and full moon.

dáça [483⁴], *num.* ten. [cf. δέκα, Lat. *decem,* Goth. *taihun,* Eng. *ten,* Ger. *zehn,* 'ten'; Eng. *-teen* in *six-teen,* etc.]

daçamá, *f.* -í, *a.* tenth; daçamí, *sc.* tithi, tenth day of a lunar half-month. [daça, 487⁴.]

daça-çata, *n.* ten hundred; a thousand.

dáçaçākha, *a.* having ten branches, *i.e.* fingers. [dáça + çā́kha: acct, 1300a.]

daçā́, *f.* the threads projecting at the end of a weft, fringe; lamp-wick; *fig.* wick of life, course of life; time of life.

daçāhá, *m.* space of ten days. [dáça + 2 áha, 1312⁴.]

√ das (dásyati; dadā́sa; ádasat; dastá; dāsáyati). suffer lack. [cf. √dās, dasyu: also δέω, 'lack.']

+ vi, become exhausted.

dásyu, *m.* demon, foe of gods and men. [cf. √das, dāsá.]

√ dah (dáhati, -te; dadā́ha, dehé; ádhāk-ṣīt; dhakṣyáti; dagdhá; dágdhum;

dagdhvā́; -dáhya; dahyáte). —1. burn with fire; burn; —2. *pass.:* be burned; be pained *or* tortured; —3. dagdha, *see s.v.* [for -dhagh: cf. Goth. *dags,* AS. *dæg,* Eng. *day,* Old High Ger. *tak,* 'day.']

+ ā, *in* ādahana.

+ vi, injure by burning, 84¹⁷.

+ sam, consume.

√ 1 dā (dádāti, dádati [668]; dadā́u, dadé; ádāt, ádita [884]; dā́syáti, -te; dattá [955c], -tta [1087e]; dā́tum; dattvā́; -dáya; dīyáte [770b]; dítsati [1030]; dāpáyati). give; bestow; grant; impart; *w. acc. of thing and dat. or gen.,* later also *loc., of person,* 1¹⁷, 23⁷⁰, 21¹⁷; varaṁ dā, grant a wish; çápaṁ dā, (give, *i.e.*) pronounce a curse; sāubhāgyaṁ dā, (give, *i.e.*) wish conjugal felicity; dā, (give, *i.e.*) sell, *w. instr. of price,* 47⁴; uttaraṁ dā, make answer; çrā́ddhaṁ dā, perform a çrā́ddha, 44³, 104¹⁷; punar dā, give back; — *desid.* desire *or* be ready to give. [cf. δίδωμι, Lat. *dā-re,* 'give.']

+ anu, (*like Ger.* nach-geben, 'yield,' *and so*) grant, admit; *ppl.* ánutta [1087e], admitted.

+ ā, take (*opp. of* give), 28¹⁷; grasp, 70⁸; ādāya, having taken, *equiv. to* with.

+ upa-ā, receive, appropriate.

+ pari, deliver over; commit; entrust.

+ pra, give; grant; impart (sciences); *ppl. f.* práttā [1087e], given in marriage, married.

√ 2 dā (dyáti [761d 3]; dadé; ádāt, ádita [884]; diná [957a], -tta [1087e]; -dáya; dīyáte). cut. [cf. √day, dāya.]

+ ava, cut off, *esp.* a part of the sacrificial cake; *ppl.* avatta [1087e], *as subst.* that which is cut off.

+ sam-ava, cut in pieces and collect them; *ppl.* samávatta, *as subst.* gathered pieces.

√ 3 dā (dyáti [761d 3]; dítá [954c]; -dáya; dīyáte). bind. [cf. δέω, δίδημι, 'bind.']

dā, *vbl.* giving, *in cpds.* [√1 dā.]

dātavya, *grdv.* dandus. [√1 dā.]

dātṛ, *m.* giver; *as a.* [375²], generous, 21⁴, 48³. [√1 dā.]

dāna, *n.* giving, imparting; gift. [√1 dā, 1150: cf. Lat. *dōnum,* 'gift.']

dāna-dharma, *m.* the virtuous practice of alms-giving.

dānavá, *m.* child of Dānu, a Dānava, one of a class of demons, foes of the gods; Titan. [1 dā́nu, 1208c.]

1 dā́nu, *f.* Dānu, name of a demon, 70[16].

2 dā́nu, *n.* dripping fluid, drop, dew.

dānta, *a.* tamed, mild; subdued (as to one's passions); *as subst.* Dānta, name of a son of Bhīma. [ppl. of √dam, 955a.]

1 dā́man, *n.* a giving, gift. [√1 dā, 1168.]

2 dā́man, *n.* bond. [√3 dā, 1168.]

dāmbhika, *a. subst.* deceitful, deceiver. [dambha.]

1 dāya, *a.* giving. [√1 dā.]

2 dāyá, *m.* portion, inheritance. [√2 dā: cf. δαίς, 'portion, meal.']

dāyaka, *a.* giving. [1 dāya.]

dāra [264[2]], *m. pl.* wife.

dāridrya, *n.* poverty. [daridra.]

dāru, *n.* wood; log *or* billet of wood; stick. [see the equiv. drú and táru: cf. δόρυ, 'wood, beam, shaft'; δρῦς, 'tree, oak'; Goth. *triu*, 'wood, tree'; Eng. *tree*, 'tree' (so Wyclif), 'a large woody plant' (usual mg), 'a wooden bar' (in whiffle-*tree*).]

dāruṇa, *a.* hard; dreadful.

√ dáç (dáçati; dadáça, dāçvā́ṅs [790b]). grant, offer; *esp.* serve *or* honor a god with offerings; dāçvā́ṅs, *as subst.* a pious servant of a god, 69[11]. [w. dadáça, cf. δέδωκα, 'granted, gave'; ἔ-δωκ-α is an imperfect indicative without thematic vowel, corresponding to •á-dáç-am; but both Greek forms became connected in the popular mind with δίδωμι, 'give.']

√ dās (*only with* abhi, abhidā́sati). bear ill-will to; try to harm. [cf. √das, dasyu, dā́sa.]

dāsá, *m.* −1. foe; *esp.* supernatural foe, evil demon; −2. (*in opp. to* ā́rya) foe of the gods, infidel; *used like* Caffre *and* Giaour; −3. (subdued foe, *i.e.*) servant, slave, 79[2]; −dāsī, *f.* female slave. [√dās: cf. √das, dasyu.]

dāsá-patnī, *a. f.* having the demon for their master. [acct, 1251b, 1295.]

díti, *f.* Diti, name of a deity without definite character, a mere pendant to aditi as sura to asura, and formed by popular etymology as sura from asura. [see aditi and daitya.]

didíkṣu, *a.* desirous to see. [fr. desid. of √dṛç, 1178f: acct!]

didyú, *m.* missile. [see √1 dīv or dyū, and 1147b[2].]

didhiṣú, *a.* desirous to win; *as m.* suitor; husband; *esp.* second husband. [fr. desid. of √1 dhā, 1178f, 1028d.]

dīna, −1. *perhaps adj.* clear, *in* su-dīna; −2. *as n.* day. [perhaps ppl. of √dī or di, 'shine', w. shifted acct.]

dina-traya, *n.* day-triad, tríduum, space of three days.

√ div: *there is no verbal root div in Sanskrit: cf. noun div and √1 and 2 dīv or dīū.*

dív [361d], *m.* −1. sky, heaven, *e.g.* 72[2]; −1a. Heaven, *personified as* Father, *e.g.* RV.vi.51.5; −1b. duhitā́ divás, of the Dawn, daughter of the sky *or* of Heaven, 75[16]; −2. day, *e.g.* 70[6], 79[13]; −3. *observe that* dív *is sometimes fem. in Veda, so* 92[1.8], RV.x.125.7.

[w. gen. div-ás, cf. the genitives Διός, •Διϝ-ός, Lat. *Jōv-is*, and AS. *Tiw-es* in *Tiwes dæg*, Eng. *Tues-day*: (Tiw corresponds to the old Germanic *Tiu*, no longer a god of the sky or bright day, but rather a god of battle or fighting, the chief occupation of our early forefathers:) w. nom. dyāús, cf. Ζεύς, •Δjηύς: w. voc. dyāùs pítar, cf. Ζεῦ πάτερ, Lat *Jū-piter*, 'Heaven Father': w. dúhitar divas, cf. Θύγατερ Διός, ἄμβροτ' Ἀθάνα, Oedipus Rex 159: cf. also δῖος, 'heavenly'; Lat. nom. *Diovi-s*, 'god of heaven,' *Jōv-em*, 'Jove'; *sub dio*, 'under the sky'; Eng. *Tewes-ley*, 'Tiw's lea,' a place in Surrey.]

divá, *n.* heaven; day, *in* divé-dive, day by day. [dív, 1209a.]

divā́, *adv.* by day. [fr. the instr. div-ā́, w. shifted acct, 1112e.]

divāukas, *m.* caelicola, god. ['having heaven as a dwelling': diva + okas.]

divyá, *a.* heavenly; divine. [dív.]

√ díç (diçáti; didéça; ádikṣat, ádiṣṭa [883]; dekṣyáti; diṣṭá; déṣṭum; -díçya; diçyáte; deçáyati). point; direct; show. [cf. δείκνυμι, 'show'; Lat. *dico*, 'show, tell'; AS. *tǣh*, Ger. *zieh*, 'pointed out (as

guilty), accused'; Ger. *zeigen*, 'show';
also AS. *tāh-te*, *tǣh-te*, Eng. *taught*, 'showed,
instructed'; AS. *tācn*, Eng. *token*.]

+ **apa**, show; make a false show of.

+ **vy-apa**, make a false show of.

+ **ā**, point out to, give a direction to,
direct.

+ **sam-ā**, point out to, direct; command.

+ **ud**, point out; aim towards; uddiçya,
w. acc., with an aiming towards, *equiv. to
the prep.* at, 26²¹.

+ **upa**, show to, teach, instruct; give advice to, advise.

+ **pra**, point out, designate; direct.

diç, *f. just like Eng.* point, *i.e.* cardinal
point, quarter of the heaven (N., E., S.,
W.); **aṣṭāu diças**, eight regions (N., E.,
S., W., and NE., SE., SW., NW.), 57¹².
[√diç, 'to point.']

√ **dih** (dégdhi; didihé; digdhá; -díhya).
—1. stroke, touch lightly; —2. smear;
—3. besmear, pollute. [for *dhigh*: cf.
θιγγον, 'touched'; Lat. *fingo*, 'form, fashion, *esp.* with the hand in soft material';
Goth. *daigs*, 'moulded mass of clay or
bread-paste'; Old Eng. *dāg*, Eng. *dough*.]

+ **sam**, *pass.* (be plastered together, be
indistinct, *and so*) be uncertain, doubtful.

√ **dī** (dídeti [676]; dīdāya [786³], dīdi-
vāṅs). shine, glance, gleam.

√ **dīkṣ** (dīkṣate; didīkṣa, didīkṣé; ádīkṣ-
iṣṭa; dīkṣiṣyáte; dīkṣitá; dīkṣitvá;
-dīkṣya). consecrate one's self, *esp.* for
performing the Soma-sacrifice. [perhaps
desid. of √dakṣ, 'make one's self suitable
or ready': 108g.]

dīti, *f.* glance, flame, *actually occurring only
in* su-dīti. [√dī, 1157.1a.]

dīdivi, *a.* shining. [√dī, 1193.]

dīná, *a.* scanty; cast down, sad; wretched.

dīnátā, *f.* scantiness; smallness. [dīna.]

dīnāra, *m.* denarius, name of a certain
gold coin. [borrowed fr. Lat. *dēnārius*, a
silver coin worth ten *asses*.]

√ **dīp** (dípyate; didīpé; dīptá; -dīpya;
dédīpti; dīpáyati, -te). blaze; flame;
caus. kindle; *intens.* blaze brightly; *fig.* be
radiant. [cf. √dī.]

+ **ud**, blaze up; *caus.* cause to blaze up.

dīrghá, *a.* long, in space *and* in time;
-am, *as adv.*; —comp. drāghīyāṅs, *superl.*
drāghiṣṭha. [√drāgh: cf. δολιχός, 'long.']

dīrgha-karṇa, *m.* Long-ear, name of a
cat.

dīrgha-rāva, *m.* Long-yell *or* Far-howl,
name of a jackal. (Their howling is both
long-continued and far-reaching.)

dīrgha-varṇa, *m.* a long vowel.

dīrghavarṇānta, *a.* having a long
vowel as final. [anta.]

√ 1 **dīv** (dívyati; didéva [240²]; ádevīt;
deviṣyáti; dyūtá; dévitum; -dívya).
dice; play. [prop. dīu, see 765¹ and ²:
orig., perhaps, 'throw,' cf. didyu.]

+ **ā**, in ādevana.

√ 2 **dīv** (dévati [240²]; dyūná [957a];
dévitum; deváyati, -te). lament. [prop.
dīu, see 765¹ and ².]

+ **pari**, moan, bemoan; *caus. the same.*

duḥkhá, *a.* miserable; *as n.* misery, pain,
sorrow. [cf. sukha.]

duḥkhita, *a.* pained. [duḥkha, 1176b.]

ducchúnā, *f.* calamity; harm. [dus ‖
çuna, 'mis-fortune, ill-luck,' 168³.]

√ **ducchunāya** (ducchunāyáte). seek to
harm. [ducchunā, 1058.]

dur-, *the form taken by* dus *before sonants.*

dur-atikrama, *a.* hard to overcome.
['having a hard conquest,' cf. 1304b.]

dur-ātman, *a.* evil-minded; bad.

dur-gá, *a.* whose going is hard, hard to
go through or to, impassable; *as n.* difficult place; danger.

dur-gata, *a.* ill-conditioned; unfortunate.

dur-jana, *m.* evil person; scoundrel.

dur-dānta, *a.* overcome with difficulty;
as m. Hard-to-tame (Δυσνίκητος), name of
a lion.

dur-nivāra, *a.* whose warding-off is hard;
hard to get rid of.

dur-bala, *a.* of (poor, *i.e.*) little strength;
feeble.

durbuddhi, *a.* of (bad, *i.e.*) small wit;
foolish.

dur-bhága, *a.* ill-portioned, ill-favored;
-ā, *f.* ugly woman. [acct, 1304b.]

dur-bhikṣa, *a.* (time) having its alms-
getting hard, *i.e.* in which alms-getting is
hard; *as n.* famine. [bhikṣā.]

dur-maṅgala, a. of bad luck, bringing bad luck.

dur-matí, f. ill-will.

dur-máda, a. badly intoxicated; drunken. [acct, 1304b.]

dur-vijñeya, a. hard to distinguish.

dur-vipāka, m. evil issue (of one's destiny).

dur-vṛtta, a. of evil life, wicked.

√ dul (doláyati; dolitá). heave upwards; swing. [cf. √tul.]

dúvas, n. gift; oblation; worship. [√1dū.]

duvás, n. perhaps same as dúvas, but see 74¹⁰ ɴ.

√ duvasya (duvasyáti). reward with a gift; honor or worship (a god) with an offering. [dúvas.]
+ ā, perhaps bring or entice hither by worship, but see 74¹⁰ ɴ.

√ duṣ (dúṣyati; ádoṣīt; duṣṭá; dūṣáyati [1042a¹]). spoil. [see dus.]

duṣ-kara, a. whose performance is hard, hard to be performed. [dus.]

duṣ-kṛtá, n. evil deed; sin. [dus.]

duṣṭa, a. spoiled; bad, morally; cross. [ppl. of √duṣ.]

dus, inseparable prefix, characterizing a thing as evil, bad, hard; forming w. action-nouns cpds w. the same mg as if compounded w. a future pass. ppl., e.g. duṣ-kara, 'having its doing hard, i.e. difficult to be done.' [cf. √duṣ: also δυς-, 'mis-'. see 225².]

dus-tara, a. having its crossing hard, hard to cross.

√ duh (dógdhi, dugdhé; dudóha, duduhé; ádhukṣat, -ata [918]; dhokṣyáte; dugdhá; dógdhum; dugdhvá; doháyati). —1. milk; then, generalized —2. get the good out of a thing; —3. extract; —4. give milk; —5. in general, give or yield any good thing, 80¹⁶; —caus., like simple, milk, extract. [for mg 2, cf. ἀμέλγεσθαί τινα, 'milk a person dry.']
+ nis, milk out of; extract from.

dúh, vbl. yielding, in kāma-duh. [√duh.]

duhitṛ [373²], f. daughter. [derivation uncertain, 1182d: cf. θυγάτηρ, Goth. dauhtar, Eng. daughter, Ger. Tochter, 'daughter.']

√ 1dū, subsidiary form of √1dā, in dúvas, duvasya. [cf. √sthā and gā w. their equiv. collateral forms sthū and gū.]

√ 2dū, go to a distance, in dūtá and dūrá. [cf. δεύομαι, 'am at a distance from something, fall short of.']

dūḍábha, a. hard to deceive. ['whose deceiving is hard': for dusdabha, i.e. dus + dabha, 199b².]

dūtá, m. messenger; ambassador, envoy. [√2dū, 1176a.]

dūrá, a. far; as n. the distance; —case-forms as adverbs: -am, to a distance, far away; -e, in the distance, afar; at or from a distance; -āt, from afar. [√2dū, 1188.]

dūrī-kṛ (dūrīkaroti). put far away; send off. [dūra, 1094.]

dūrvā, f. millet-grass, Panicum Dactylon.

dūḷábha, same as dūḍábha, Whitney 54.

√ 1dṛ (dṛṇáti; dadára, dadré; ádārṣīt; dīrṇá; -dīrya; dīryáte; dárdarti [1002b]; daráyati, dāráyati). burst, trans. and intrans.; —caus. and intens.: split; tear, w. gen. [cf. δέρω, δείρω, 'flay'; AS. teran, Eng. tear, Ger. zerren, 'tear, rend.']

√ 2dṛ (driyáte; ádṛta; dṛtá; -dṛtya). used only w. ā, see 773. [cf. √δελ in δερδίλλω, 'glance at'; AS. tilian, 'be intent upon, attend to, esp. the earth, i.e. till (the soil),' Eng. till; Ger. zielen, 'aim at'; AS. eorð-tilia, 'earth-tiller.']
+ ā, (look at, i.e.) regard; pass. be regarded, i.e. respected.

dṛdhá, see √dṛh and 224a.

dṛti, m. bag of leather; bellows. [√1dṛ: for mg, cf. δέρμα, 'skin bag or bottle.']

√ dṛp (dṛpyati; ádṛpat; darpiṣyáti, drapsyáti; dṛptá; darpáyati). be crazed, wild, proud, insolent, or arrogant.

√ dṛbh (dṛbháti; dṛbdhá). make into tufts.

√ dṛç (dadárça, dadṛçé; ádrākṣīt, ádṛṣṭa; drakṣyáti, -te; dṛṣṭá; dráṣṭum; dṛṣṭvá; -dṛçya; dṛçyáte; didṛkṣate; darçáyati). see; behold; —pass. be seen; be or become visible; appear; —caus. cause (a person, acc., 83²) to see (a thing, acc., 33⁶, 35⁷, 36⁷); show (w. gen. 63²); w. ātmānam, show one's self, appear, pretend to be (e.g. frightened, 41⁴). [present forms supplied by √1 paç, q.v.: w. dadárça, cf. δέδορκε, 'saw': cf. Goth. *ga-tarh-jan*, 'make a show of.']

+ prati, *pass.* appear óver against one or before one's eyes.

+ vi, *pass.* be seen far and wide.

+ sam, behold; *caus.* show; *w.* ātmānam, show one's self, appear, pretend to be (*e.g.* dead).

dṛ́ç [218², dṛk, dṛçam, dṛgbhyām], — 1. *vbl.* seeing, looking ; — 2. *as f.* the seeing ; dṛçé, *as inf.* [970a], for beholding ; — 3. *in cpds* [518], look, appearance. [√dṛç.]

dṛ́ça, m. the seeing; *in cpds* [518], look, appearance. [do.]

dṛçí, *f.* the seeing; dṛçáye, *as inf.* [970f], for beholding. [do.]

dṛ́çya, *grdv.* to be seen; worthy to be seen, splendid. [√dṛç, 963d.]

dṛṣád, *f.* stone; *esp.* nether mill-stone.

dṛṣad-upalá, *dual f.* the nether and the upper mill-stone. [1253a, 1258.]

dṛṣṭá, *ppl. of* √dṛç, *q.v.*

dṛṣṭa-pūrva, *a.* seen previously. [equiv. to pūrvaṁ dṛṣṭa, see 1291.]

dṛ́ṣṭi, *f.* — 1. seeing ; — 2. sense of sight ; — 3. glance, look ; — 4. view. [√dṛç: cf. δέρξις, 'sense of sight.']

√dṛh (dṛṁhati, -te [mg 1, *cf.* 758] ; dṛ́hyati, -te [mg 2, *see* 767]; ádṛṁhīt; dṛḍhá [224a]; dṛṁháyati). — 1. *act.* make firm *or* steady *or* enduring ; establish ; *mid.* be firm ; dṛḍhá [1176a], firm ; — 2. be firm ; — 3. *caus.* make stable. [cf. Old Lat. *forc-tis*, Lat. *fortis*, 'strong.']

dṛḷhá, *same as* dṛḍhá, √dṛh, Whitney 54.

déya, *grdv.* to be given *or* granted. [√dā, 963a.]

devá, *f.* devī, — 1. *a.* heavenly, 74¹⁴·¹⁶·¹⁸, 92⁷; *as subst.* — 2. god, goddess; — 2a. *pl.* the gods (in later times reckoned as 33, *cf.* tridaça); — 2b. víçve devā́s, all the gods; *also* all-gods (a term comprehending into a class all the separate gods, *cf.* All-saints, *and see* viçvádeva); — 2c. devī, The Goddess, *i.e.* Çiva's wife, Durgā ; — 2d. -deva, *at end of Brahman-names*, having ··as god, *so, e.g.*, guṇadeva; — 3. *m.* manuṣya-deva, god among men, *i.e.* a Brahman, *see* 95¹; similarly, — 4. *m.* king, 19¹¹, 50⁴, 51⁴·⁷·¹⁴;

so used of a lion (32¹⁵) *or even* of a jackal (36⁷¹); *f.* queen. [perhaps fr. the noun dív (1209i): cf. Lat. *deus*, 'god': the alleged root div, 'shine,' has no existence.]

devá-kāma, *a.* having love for the gods. [acct, 1293³, 1295.]

devátā, *f.* godhead *or* divinity, *both as abstract and as concrete*; devátā, *instr.*, with divinity (*collective*), *i.e.* among deities, 73³⁰ [1237.]

devatvá, *n.* divinity, *abstract only.* [1239.]

deva-dūtá, *m.* messenger of the gods.

deva-dáivatya, *a.* having the gods as divinity, (of hymns) addressed to the gods.

deva-pati, *m.* lord of the gods, *i.e.* Indra.

deva-pána, *a.* serving the gods for drinking. [lit. 'god-drenching, *i.e.* gotttränkend': acct, 1271, 1251c.]

deva-yána, *n.* path of the gods, on which the intercourse between gods and men takes place. [acct, 1271, 1251c.]

devara, *m.* husband's brother. [devṛ́, 1209a.]

deva-rájá, *m.* king of the gods, *i.e.* Indra. [rájan, 1315a.]

deva-liṅga, *n.* god-characteristic, mark by which a god may be distinguished from a man.

deva-çarman, *m.* Devaçarman *or* God's-joy, name of a certain Brahman. [of like mg is Θεό-χαρις.]

deva-saṁnidhi, *m.* presence of the gods.

devá-hūti, *f.* invocation of the gods. [acct, 1274.]

devī, *see* devá.

devī-kṛta, *a.* made by Durgā.

devī-koṭṭa, *m.* Goddess-fort, name of a town.

devī-vinirmita, *a.* laid out by Durgā. [√1 mā.]

devṛ́ [369³], *m.* husband's brother. [cf. δαήρ, Lat. *lēvir*, 'husband's brother.']

deça, *m.* — 1. (point, *i.e.*) place, 41¹³; — 2. country, 24⁵, *see* 98¹⁶ ɴ.; — 3. place, *pregnantly, as in Eng., i.e.* proper place, 22⁵; — 4. *as in Eng.*, place *or* region of the body, *see* muṣka-, skandha-. [√diç, 'point.']

deça-bhāṣā, *f.* dialect of the country.

deṣṭṛ, m. pointer, guide, instructor; f. déṣṭrī, Instructress, as a deity, 90⁹. [√diç, 1182: cf. •δεικτηρ in δεικτήριος, 'pertaining to one who shows.']

deha, m. n. body; mentioned w. manas and vāc, 65⁹. [√dih, 'stroke lightly so as to mould or form,' and so, prob. 'the figure, form, shape,' like the Lat. figūra, 'shape, form,' from the cognate √fig, fingo: see √dih.]

dehin, a. connected with the body, 65¹¹; as m. a living being, man. [deha, 1230.]

daitya, m. descendant of Diti, q.v.; a Daitya or demon. [díti, 1211.]

daitya-dānava-mardana, m. Daitya-and-Dānava-crusher, epithet of Indra.

daiva, a. of the gods, 57¹¹; coming from the gods; divine; as n. divine appointment, i.e. fate, 18¹⁸, etc. [devá, 1208f.]

daivata, a. pertaining to a divinity; as n. —1. a divinity or, collectively, the divinities, esp. that or those celebrated in any Vedic hymn; —2. idol, 62¹⁸. [devatā, 1208e.]

daivatya, at end of cpds, having ·· as divinity, addressed to ··, 63⁵. [devatā, 1211.]

daivika, a. of the gods; divine. [deva, 1222e.]

daívya, a. of the gods; divine. [devá, 1211.]

dola, m. a swinging; f. dolā, a dooly (Anglo-Indian term), a little bamboo chair slung on four men's shoulders. [√dul.]

√ dolāya (dolāyate). swing like a dooly; waver. [dolā.]

dolāyamāna-mati, a. having a wavering mind. [√dolāya.]

1 doṣa, m. —1. fault, defect; bad condition, 55⁵; —2. sin, transgression, fault, 11⁸, 18¹¹, 65¹¹; doṣam avāp, incur a transgression, 68⁴; —3. harm; evil consequence; doṣeṇa, doṣāt, by or as a bad consequence of, by, faute de, 23²¹, 35⁷. [√duṣ.]

2 doṣa, m. evening, dark; f. doṣā, evening, dark.

doṣā-vastṛ, m. illuminer of the darkness; or, as adj. [cf. 375⁸], lighting up in the dark.

dāutya, n. message. [dūtá, 1211.]

dyāvā-pṛthivī, dual f. heaven and earth. [dív + pṛthivī, 1255 and a².]

dyú, same as div, 361d.

√ dyut (dyótate; didyuté; ádyutat; dyotiṣyáti; dyuttá; -dyútya). gleam; lighten; shine. [akin w. noun dív, q.v.: cf. also √jyut.]
+ vi, lighten.

dyuti, f. sheen, 19⁷; lustre; dignity. [√dyut.]

dyumánt, a. heavenly, bright, splendid. [dyú.]

dyūtá, n. gambling. [√1 dív, 1176a.]

dyó, same as div, 361d.

dráviṇa, n. movable property (as opp. to house and field), wealth. [√dru, 1177b.]

dravya, n. —1. property; —2. in general, thing, object; —3. esp. worthy object. [√dru: see draviṇa.]

draṣṭavya, grdv. to be seen. [√dṛç.]

√ 1 drā (dráti; dadrāú; ádrāsīt; intens. [1002c, 1024²] daridrāti). run; intens. run about, run hither and thither. [cf. δι-δρά-σκω, 'run': see √dru.]
+ apa, run off. [cf. ἀπο-δρᾶναι, 'run off.']

√ 2 drā (dráti; dráyate; dadrāú; ádrāsīt; drāsyáti; drāṇá). sleep. [cf. ἔδραθον, 'slept'; Lat. dormire, 'sleep.']
+ ni, go to sleep; sleep.

√ drāgh, only in derivs. drag, draw; draw out; extend; lengthen. [poss. for •dhragh (cf. √dhraj), and akin w. Eng. drag: but see dīrghá.]

drāghīyāṅs, a. longer, as comp. to dīrghá. [√drāgh, 467.]

√ dru (drávati, -te; dudráva, dudruvé; ádudruvat [868]; droṣyáti; drutá; drótum; drutvá; -drútya). hasten; run; run away, flee, 94⁷. [ident. w. √dram, 'run,' and w. √1 drā, q.v.: cf. ἔδραμε and ἔδρα, 'ran.']
+ ati, run past or by; escape.
+ ā, run unto, make an attack, charge, 94⁴·⁶.
+ upa, run unto.
+ sam-upa, run unto, rush at, 3¹¹.

drú, m. n. wood. [see dáru.]

drugdhá, see √druh.

druta, *ppl.* having hastened [952²]; -am,
as *adv.* hastily, rapidly; quickly; immediately. [√dru.]

druma, *m.* tree. [drú: cf. δρῦμός, 'a wood.']

√ **drumāya (drumāyate)**. pass for a tree.
[druma, 1058, 1059b.]

√ **druh (drúhyati ; dudróha ; ádruhat;**
dhrokṣyáti; drugdhá; drógdhum; -drúh-
ya). hurt (by deceit, wile, magic); strive
to harm; *ppl.* drugdhá: as *m.* one who
has striven to harm, hurtful foe; as *n.*
misdeed. [if for •dhrugh, cf. Old High
Ger. *triukan*, Ger. *be-trügen*, 'deceive so as
to harm.']
+ **abhi**, offend against.

dvá [482b], *num.* two. [cf. δύο, Lat. *duo*,
Eng. *two*.]

dvaṁdvá, *n.* pair; quarrel. [dvam-dvam
is the repeated nom. s. n. of dva: cf.
1252¹.]

dvayá, *a.* twofold; of two sorts; as *n.*
couple, pair. [dvá: cf. δοιός, 'double.']

dvádaça [483⁴], *cardinal.* twelve. [dvá
+ dáça, 476²: cf. δυώδεκα, Lat. *duōdecim*,
'twelve.']

dvádaçá, *f.* -í, *ordinal.* twelfth; dvá-
daçí (*sc.* tithi), twelfth day of a lunar
half month, 59⁹. [dvádaça, 487⁷.]

dvádaça-rátra, *n.* space of twelve
nights. [dvádaça + rátri, 1315b, 1312⁵·⁶.]

dvádaça-sahasra, *cardinal, n.* twelve
thousand. [481.]

dvádaçasáhasra, *a.* consisting of twelve
thousand. [dvádaça-sahasra, 1204c.]

dvár [388c], *f.* door. [perhaps 'the clos-
ure,' fr. √dvṛ, 'close,' for •dhvṛ: cf. θύρα,
'door'; Lat. *foris*, nom. s., 'door'; Eng.
door.]

dvára, *n.* door. [dvár, q.v.. 399.]

dvára-pakṣa, *m.* side of the door.

dvi, *form of* dva *in composition and derivation.* [475⁶.]

dvi-já, *a.* twice-born; as *m.* member of
one of the three upper castes, re-born by
virtue of investiture (*see* √nī + upa), 60²,
58²⁰, 59⁴, 62⁷; *in a narrower sense*, a Brahman, 21¹⁴, 43⁴, 55⁹, 64¹⁶.

dvi-jánman, *a.* having double birth; as
m. same as dvija; man of one of the three
upper castes, 59¹. [acct, 1300c.]

dvi-játi, *a. and as m. same as* dvijan-
man; man of one of the three upper
castes, 59¹⁹.

dvijottama, *m.* the highest of the twice-
born, *i.e.* a Brahman. [dvija + uttama.]

dvitá, *a.* second. [dvi.]

dvitá, *adv.* just so; so also; equally.

dvitíya, *a.* second. [dvitá, 487⁴, 1215d.]

dvidhá, *adv.* in two parts, in twain. [1104.]

dvi-pád [391], *a.* having two feet; as *m.*
the two-footed one, man, 16²; as *n. sing.*
that which is two-footed, *collectively*, men,
90¹·³, 92². [cf. δίποδα, Lat. *bipedem*, 'bi-
ped.']

dvi-pada, *f.* -í, *a.* having (taken) two
steps.

dvi-pravrājin, *f.* -ní, *a. in f.* going
after two (men), unchaste, 98¹⁶.

√ **dviṣ (dvéṣṭi, dviṣṭé; didvéṣa; ádvikṣat,
-ata; dviṣṭá; dvéṣṭum). hate; show
hatred; be hostile. [cf. ὀ-δύσ-αντο, 'became wroth,' w. prothetic *o*.]

dviṣ, *vbl.* hating, *in cpds*; as *f.* hate; as *m.*
concrete, hater, foe. [√dviṣ.]

dvis, *adv.* twice. [see dvi, dva: cf. δίς,
Lat. *bis*, •dvis, 'twice': the radically cognate Eng. *twice* is a gen. form.]

dvípá, *m.* island.

dvípi-carman, *n.* tiger-skin. [dvípin.]

dvípin, *a.* having islands *or* island-like
spots; as *m.* leopard; tiger. [dvípa.]

√ **dvṛ**, cover, close, *in derivs*. [see dvár.]

dvedhá, *adv.* in two, in two kinds. [for
•dvayadhá, fr. dvaya, 1104².]

dvéṣa, *m.* hatred. [√dviṣ.]

dvéṣas, *n.* hatred ; *concrete*, hater, foe.
[√dviṣ.]

_____

dha, *vbl.* bestowing, granting, *in* vasu-dha
[√1 dhā, 333.]

√ **dhan (dadhánti).** set in motion. [cf
√dhanv.]

dhána, *n.* —1. the prize of the contest ;
not only the reward put up for the victor,
but also the booty taken from the foe —
Vedic; so w. √ji, win booty by conquest,
81²; *then*, —2. *in general*, wealth, riches,
property, money. [√dhā, 'put': cf. θέμα,
'thing put up as a prize,' and for the mg
also Ger. *Ein-satz*, 'stakes.']

dhanu, *m.* bow. [fr. dhanus, a transfer to the u-declension.]

dhanus-kāṇḍa, *n.* bow and arrow. [dhanus: see 1253b.]

dhānus, *n.* bow. [√dhan, 1154.]

dhānya, *a.* wealthy; fortunate. [dhana.]

√ dhanv (dhánvati; dadhanvé; ádhan-vīt). set in motion; run. [secondary form of √dhan.]

dhánvan, *n.* bow. [√dhan, 1169.1a.]

dhanvin, *a. subst.* having a bow, bow-man. [dhanvan, 1230b.]

√ dham *or* dhmā (dhámati[750]; dadhmāú; ádhmāsīt; dhamiṣyáti; dhamitá, dhmā-tá; -dhmáya). blow; breathe out; blow (pipe, shell, bag-pipe, bellows). [see 108g and 750.]

+ ā, blow up; ādhmāta, *fig.* puffed up.

dhara, *a.* holding; bearing; keeping; wearing. [√dhṛ.]

dhárma, *m.* — 1. custom, 98¹⁶; usage, 99¹¹; right; duty, 28⁵; virtue, 21⁷, 10¹², 15¹⁷, 29¹; (virtue, *i.e.*) good works, 29⁵, 63¹¹; correct course of conduct, 11³; dharme, in a question of right, 21¹⁴; — 1a. dharmeṇa, *adv.:* as was right, 14¹⁷; dutifully, 16⁵; — 2. law; prescription, rule; the law (as a system), 28⁵, 58¹⁶·¹⁹; — 3. *personified,* Virtue, 67¹¹, 48⁴.

[a post-Vedic word, taking the place of V. dhárman: dharma is fr. √dhṛ (1166b), perhaps in mg 6, and thus designating ancient custom or right as 'that which holds its own, which persists or endures'; but it may come fr. √dhṛ in mg 1, so that dharma is 'that which is established or settled'; in the latter case, cf., for the mg, θέμις, 'that which is established as custom or law,' w. τίθημι, 'set, establish,' and Ger. *Ge-setz,* 'law,' w. *setzen,* 'set.']

dharma-jña, *a.* knowing the law *or* one's duty *or* what is right.

dharma-jñāna, *n.* knowledge of the law.

dharmatas, *adv.* in a way which starts from dharma, *i.e.* in accordance with good usage, 59¹⁹; by rights, 61¹⁶. [dharma, 1098c³.]

dhárman, *n.* established ordinance; stead-fast decree (*e.g.* of a god), 80¹⁰; dhár-maṇā, according to the established order of things, in a way that accords with nature, 84⁶. [√dhṛ, 1168.1c: see under dharma.]

dharma-mūla, *n.* the root *or* foundation of the law.

dharma-vid [391], *a.* knowing the law *or* one's duty, 1¹⁵; acquainted with good usage, 61¹⁰.

dharma-çāstra, *n.* authoritative *or* ca-nonical compend of dharma, 58¹⁸; law-book; law-shaster.

dharmātman, *a.* having virtue *or* right as one's nature; just. [ātman.]

√ dhav (dhávate). run. [see under √dhū, and cf. θέω, √θεϝ, 'run.']

dhavala, *a.* dazzlingly white. [√2dhāv. 'rinse,' 1189, 1188.]

√ 1dhā (dádhāti, dhatté [668]; dadhāú, dadhé; ádhāt, ádhita [884]; dhāsyáti, -te; *V.* -dhita, *later* hitá [954c]; dhātum; dhitvā; -dhāya; dhīyáte; dídhiṣati, dhítsati; dhāpáyati [1042d]).

— 1. put, 86¹⁰; set; lay, 39¹⁴; — 2. put in a place, bring to, *w.* tatra, 85¹⁹; *w. loc.,* 89⁶, 95⁵; *w. dat.,* 83¹; — 3. put upon, di-rect towards; dharme dhā manas, set the heart on virtue, 66⁷; — 4. put something for a person (*dat.*), *i.e.* bestow upon him, grant him, 84¹, RV.x.125.2; — 5. put in a position, *i.e.* appoint, constitute, *w. double acc.,* 88¹²; — 6. make, cause, produce; — 7. hold, keep, 86⁶·⁹;, — 8. *mid.* take to one's self, receive, obtain, win; *esp.* gar-bhaṁ dhā, conceive fruit in the womb, 92¹³; — 9. *mid.* assume, 19⁷; maintain; — 10. hita, *see s.v.;* — 11. *desid. act.* desire to grant; *mid.* desire to win.

[The original meaning of the root is 'put'; but, from the proethnic period, a secondary development in the line ('set,' 'establish,' and so) 'make,' 'do,' is clear. The secondary mg has even won the more prominent place in Germanic and Slavic.

For the primary mg, cf. τίθημι, 'put' (the parallelism of its mgs is remarkable — θέσαν λίθον, 'they set a stone'; θέσθαι υἱόν, 'conceive a son,' etc., etc.); Lat. *ab-de-re,* 'put off *or* away,' and *con-de-re,* 'put together, construct, establish'; Eng. do, 'put,' in the contract forms *doff, don, dup;* Ger. *weg-thun,* 'do away *or* put away.'

For the secondary mg, cf. θεῖναί τινα βασιλέα, 'make one a king'; AS. *dōn hine tō cyninge,* 'make him a king'; Lat. *fīo,* 'am made'; Eng. *do, deed;* Ger. *thun,* 'do'; Slavic *dě-lo,* 'deed': observe that *fī-eri,* 'become,' is to *fă-c-ere,* 'make,' as *i-re* (√*ja*), 'go,' is to *jă-c-ere,* 'make to go, throw.']

+**antar,** −1. put into the interior of a thing; *and so* −2. hide, conceal.

+**api,** put close upon; cover (a jar with its lid); **ápihita,** closed up. [cf. ἐπιτίθημι, 'put upon.']

+**abhi,** put on; put a name upon, designate; address; speak to, 43¹⁰; say, 42²⁰; **abhihitam,** (it was) said, 38¹³.

+**ava,** put down in; *esp.* duck (*trans.*) into the water; **ávahita,** fallen into the water; *caus.* cause to be laid in.

+**ā,** −1. put *or* lay *or* set in *or* on, *w. loc.,* 77¹, 79¹², 88¹³, 90⁵, 102²¹; −2. put on (wood on the fire), 82¹³; −3. *mid.* set for one's self on (the hearth a sacred fire), 95¹²; −4. *mid.* put on one's self, take on, 74⁶; −5. take, *i.e.* take away, 87¹⁰.

+**vy-ā,** *pass.* be separated; be uncomfortable *or* sick.

+**sam-ā,** put upon; *w.* **manas,** concentrate the mind upon one thing; **samāhita,** intent, eager, 1¹³.

+**upa-sam-ā,** set together (wood) unto (an already burning fire), put (fuel) on, 100¹⁶, 105¹⁰.

+**upa,** put on (*esp.* a brick *or* stone on the sacred fire-altar *or* enclosure), 96⁸ ff.

+**ni,** lay down, 87⁵; set down (sacred fire), 85⁶; *w.* **kriyām,** put labor upon (*loc.*), take pains with, 19¹⁴; **nihita,** put down, lying low, 70¹⁹.

sam-ni, lay down together; put together; *pass.* be near together; **samnihita,** near, impending, 25¹³.

+**pari,** put around; *esp.* put (part of a sacrificial fence) around (an altar), 105¹²; put around one's self, put on, (garments) 103¹⁹, (shoes) 45¹¹; clothe.

+**puras,** *see s.v.*

+**pra,** set forward. [cf. **pradhana, pradhāna.**]

+**vi,** −1. part, mete out, distribute; −2. spread abroad, RV. x. 125.3; −3. (*like Lat.* dis-pōnere) arrange, determine; prescribe, 59⁷; **vihita,** ordained, 14⁴; −4. lay out, make, build; prepare, 54¹⁸; −5. accomplish, 56¹²; make, do (*in a great variety of applications*); **vadham vidhā,** do slaughter, slay, 32¹⁴; **pūjām vidhā,** do *or* show honor, 28¹³; **pravṛttim vidhā,** make an advance into, *w. loc.,* expose one's self to, 20¹²; **upāyam vidhā,** employ an expedient, 39²; **kim vidheyam,** what's to be done, 31⁵; **tathā vidhīyatām,** so let it be done, 11⁴; **yathā ··, tan mayā vidheyam,** I must take such a course, that··, 37⁶; *cf.* 38⁷².

+**çrad,** *see* çrad.

+**sam,** put together, unite; embroil in, *w. loc.,* 73¹⁴.

√ 2**dhā** (dháyati [761d 2]; dadhāú; ádhāt; dhāsyáti; dhītá; dhātum; -dhíya; dhītvā). suck; drink, 63¹. [cf. dadhi, dhenu: also θήσατο, 'sucked'; γαλα-θηνός, 'milk-sucking'; θη-λή, 'breast'; Lat. *fē-lare,* 'suck'; Goth. dadd-jan, 'give suck.']

1 **dhā,** *in cpds. as* vbl. bestowing, granting; *as subst.* place. [√1**dhā,** 'place, grant.']

2 **dhā,** *in cpds. as subst.* drink. [√2**dhā,** 'drink.']

dhātu, *m.* layer, *as* part of a composite whole. [√1**dhā,** 'put, lay.']

dhātṛ, *m.* establisher; creator; Dhātar, *as* name of a deity, 90⁹ ɴ. [√1**dhā.**]

dhāna, *a.* holding, containing. [√1**dhā,** 115Ⅱ.]

dhānā, *f. pl.* corns, *i.e.* grain.

dhānyà, *a.* cereal (*adj.*); *as* ɴ. cereal (*noun*), grain. [**dhānā.**]

dhāraṇa, *a.* holding; *as n.* a holding, keeping; wearing, 14¹¹; -ā, *f.* established ordinance; rule, 62¹⁷. [√**dhṛ.**]

dhārā, *f.* stream, jet. [√1**dhāv,** 'run, pour.']

dhārāsāra, *m. pl.* stream-pourings, violent pourings. [**āsāra.**]

dhārin, *a.* holding; possessing, 22²³; retaining, 68¹⁴. [√**dhṛ.**]

dhā́rmika, a. righteous; virtuous. [dharma.]

√ 1 dhā́v (dhávati, -te; ádhāvīt; dhāviṣyáti; dhāvitá; dhāvitvā́; -dhávya). run (of fluids), stream, pour; run (of animate beings). [see under √dhū.]
+ anu, run after.
+ upa, run unto.
+ sam-upa, run on unto, 3¹³.
+ pra, run forth, flow; run.

√ 2 dhā́v (dhávati, -te; dadhā́vé; ádhāviṣṭa; dhāutá; dhāutvā́; -dhávya). rinse.

dhi, vbl. containing, granting, in cpds. [√1 dhā́, 1155.2e.]

dhik, excl. fie! w. acc.

√ dhī (dídheti [676]; dīdhā́ya [786³]; dhītá). think. [see √dhyā.]
+ anu, think over.

dhī́ [351], f. —1. thought; dhiyā́-dhiyā́, with each thought, every time it occurs to one; —2. (like Ger. An-dacht, lit. 'thinking upon,' and then 'devotion') religious thought, devotion, 69¹³, 74¹⁹, 82¹⁷; observe that matí, mánas, maniṣā́, mántra, and mánman show this same specialization of mg; prayer, 74¹⁵; —3. intelligence, insight, mind, 89¹; understanding, skill. [√dhī.]

1 dhītí, f. perhaps draught, see 82⁷ ɴ. [√2 dhā́, 'drink,' 1157.1a.]

2 dhītí, f. —1. thought; —2. devotion; —3. skill. [√dhī: for 2, cf. dhī 2.]

dhī́mant, a. gifted with understanding, wise. [dhī.]

1 dhī́ra, a. wise, 78⁴·¹⁰. [√dhī, 1188a.]

2 dhī́ra, a. firm; resolute, 48². [√dhṛ: cf. Lat. fir-mus, 'firm.']

dhī́vara, m. —1. a very clever or skilful man; —2. a fisher. [dhī́, 1171.]

dhúni, a. shaking, stormily moved, boisterous, wild. [fr. quasi-root dhun of dhunóti, √dhū.]

√ dhū (dhūnóti, dhūnuté; later, dhunóti, -nuté [see 711]; dudhā́va, dudhuvé; ádhūṣṭa [887a]; dhaviṣyáti; dhūtá, later dhutá; dhūtvā́; -dhúya). —1. move quickly hither and thither; shake; —2. fan (a fire); —3. shake off.

[orig. 'move violently, agitate': cf. θύω, θύω, 'rush on'; θῡμός, 'agitation, anger, passion, spirit': θύω, 'sacrifice,' is poss akin w. √dhū as a generalization of mg 2: closely akin w. √dhū is √1 dhā́v, 'run,' and also √dhav, 'run' (cf. θέω, √θεϝ, 'run'): see also under dhūma.]
+ ava, shake down; mid. shake off from one's self.

dhūmá, m. smoke; vapor. [cf. Lat. fūmus, 'smoke': smoke has no such "swift eddying motion" as to make it easy to connect these names for it w. √dhū, q.v.; but on this connection their identification w. θῡμός should seem to depend: more prob. is the explanation of dhūmá as 'the enveloping or blackening,' fr. √1 dhvan, as vāma fr. √van.]

dhūmaka, m. smoke, at end of cpds [1307] for dhūma; f. -ikā [1222d], the same.

dhūrta, a. subst. shrewd, sly, cunning; rogue. [ppl. of √dhvṛ, 'harm by deceit' (cf. 957b³): according to the grammarians, dhūrta, w. acct altered as in júṣṭa: for a somewhat analogous development of mg, cf. Middle Eng. schrewen, 'curse,' whence schrew-ed, 'cursed, bad,' Eng. shrewd, 'bad, artful.']

dhūrta-traya, n. rogue-triad, trio of swindlers.

dhūsara, a. dusted over, dusty, dust-colored, gray. [√dhvaṅs, dhvas, 1188d: cf. 181a.]

√ dhṛ (dādhā́ra [786], dadhré; ádhṛta; dhariṣyáti, -te; dhṛtá; dhā́rtum; dhṛtvā́; -dhṛtya; dhāráyati; ádīdharat). mgs of caus. forms ident. [1041²] w. those of simple forms; hold, in its various mgs, trans. and intrans.;

trans. —1. hold, bear, support, 33¹¹, 39³, 75⁴·⁷, 87⁹, 92¹; make firm, 92¹⁰; carry, 62¹²; wear; —2. hold fast, 22¹⁰, 33¹; hold in check, bear, withstand, 2³⁰, 8¹²; —3. keep (a cat), 31⁹; —4. set or lay or place in or on, w. loc., 33¹¹, 41²¹; —5. hold or make sure or ordain for some one (dat.); mid. be ordained for some one (dat.), belong of right to, 75³;

intrans. —6. mid. hold, i.e. remain, continue; w. this mg, even in the active, 15⁵.

[cf. θρό-νος, 'support, seat,' θρᾶ-νος, 'bench,' θρή-σασθαι, 'sit'; Lat. frē-tus,

12

'held or supported by (hence w. abl.), relying on,' frē-num, 'holder, bridle.']
+ava, caus. −1. set down, fix; −2. (like Eng. hold) assume as certain, 44¹⁴.

√ dhṛṣ (dhṛṣṇóti; dadhárṣa; ádhṛṣat; dhṛṣitá, dhṛṣṭá; -dhṛṣya; dharṣáyati). be bold or courageous; dare; venture; 74²; −caus. venture on some one or something; offend; overpower; dharṣitá, overcome. [cf. θρασ-ύς, 'bold'; Lat. fastus, 'pride'; Goth. ga-dars, AS. dearr, Eng. he dare (all 3d persons sing. of a preterito-present); AS. dors-te, Eng. durs-t.]
+ā, venture against.
+prati, hold out against, withstand, 82⁵.

dhṛṣṇú, a. daring; courageous, doughty, 78⁷; bold, 84¹⁷. [√dhṛṣ, 1162.]

dhenú, f. milch cow; cow. [√2 dhā, 'suck,' 1162.]

dheya, n. the giving. [√1 dhā, mg 4, 'bestow, give': 1213c.]

dhāirya, n. firmness; earnest or resolute bearing. [2 dhīra, 1211.]

√ dhmā, see √dham.

√ dhyā (dhyáti, dhyáyati [761d 1]; dadhyáu; ádhyāsīt [911]; dhyāsyáti; dhyātá; dhyātvá; -dhyáya). think upon; meditate. [see √dhī and 108g.]
+abhi, set the mind on something; sink one's self in thought, 57¹.

dhyāna, n. meditation. [√dhyā, 1150.]

dhyāna-para, a. having meditation as highest object, absorbed in contemplation. [1302b.]

√ dhraj (dhrájati; ádhrājīt). draw onward, advance, intrans. [see √drāgh, of which this is poss. a collateral form.]

√ dhru, collateral form of √dhvṛ.

dhrúti, f. a deceiving; infatuation. [√dhru.]

dhruvá, a. −1. holding or continuing, i.e. remaining fixed in place; as m. the pole-star, 100⁵; −2. of abodes certain, safe, 79¹⁶. [√dhṛ in mg 6: see 1190.]

dhruvá, f. sacrificial ladle, 102¹³, see sruc. [lit. 'holder,' √dhṛ in mg 1: see 1190.]

√ dhvaṅs or dhvas (dhváṅsati, -te; dadhváṅsa, dadhvasé; ádhvasat; dhvastá; -dhvásya). −1. fall to dust, perish; dhvasta, exhausted, hurt, impaired; −2. vanish, be off; −3. only in ppl. dhvasta, bestrewn, covered over, esp. with dust. [cf. Eng. dus-t; prob. also AS. dwǣs and dysig, 'foolish,' Eng. dizzy, Old High Ger. tusic, 'foolish.']

dhvaṅsá, m. the perishing; destruction. [√dhvaṅs.]

√ 1 dhvan (ádhvanīt; dhvāntá; dhvanáyati). −1. cover one's self; dhvānta, dark; −2. become extinguished; −caus. −1. envelope, cover over; −2. blacken. [perhaps akin w. √dhvaṅs: see dhūma: cf. AS. dunn, Eng. dun, 'dark, brownish-black.']

√ 2 dhvan (dhvánati; dadhvāna; dhvāntá [955a]). sound, resound. [cf. Old Eng. dune, Eng. din.]

dhvaní, m. sound. [√2 dhvan.]

√ dhvṛ (dhvárati). bend or make crooked; cause to fall; harm by deceit. [see dhūrta and dhruti: cf. AS. dwellan, 'lead astray, cause to delay,' Eng. dwell, intrans., 'delay, linger, abide'; Eng. dwaul, 'wander, rave,' dwale, 'stupefying potion'; Dutch dwaal-licht, 'ignis fatuus'; Goth. dvals, 'foolish'; Eng. dull, dol-t; Ger. toll, 'mad.']

na [491], encl. pron. root of 1st person, see ahám. [w. nas, 'us,' cf. vá, 'we two,' Lat. nōs, 'us.']

ná, adv. −1. not [1122b], 3²; −1a. in connected sentences or clauses: repeated simply: 97⁸, octies; 62¹⁴,¹⁵, quinquies: 63¹³,¹⁴, 71⁴, ter; 4¹³, 17¹⁸, 74¹, 80¹⁷, bis: with ca: na · ·, na · · ca, na ca · ·, 62¹⁶; na · ·, na ca · ·, na · ·, 63¹; with api: see api 2; with u, 21¹⁴; −1b. not repeated, but replaced by api ca or vā_api (see these), 2¹², 63⁴; −1c. combinations: na ca, 8¹⁶; na · · ca, 13⁷, 62¹⁶; nāiva, 22¹⁹, 23¹⁹, 96¹⁰; na vāi, 92¹⁵; na vā, 96¹²; na tu, 64¹³; na tv eva tu, see tu; na ha, 95¹⁷; na_iva, not exactly, 93⁵; −1d. tantamount to a- in negative cpds [1122b⁴], as nacira, nā-

tidūra, nādhīta, etc.; —1e. *at beg. of adversative clause: with adversative conj.*, 34 [10]; *without*, 22 [20], 41 [13], 92 [16]; —1f. *in emphatic litotes*, 21 [9]; —1g. *substantive verb to be supplied*, 32 [5] (asti); —1h. na *precedes* ced, *if it belongs to the protasis*, 63 [9]; *if it immediately follows* ced, *it must be joined to the apodosis*, 18 [9]; —1i. *for prohibitive negative, see* mā́; —1j. ná, 'not,' *coalesces metrically in Veda w. following initial vowel, e.g.* 70 [13], 71 [4], 83 [9];
—2. *like* [*see* 1122d *and* d [2]], *in this sense Vedic only*, 70 [15, 18], 71 [7, 9], etc.; ná, 'like,' *does not coalesce metrically in Veda w. following initial vowel.*

[cf. νη, Lat. ne̅-, negative prefix in νη-κερδές, 'gain-less,' ne̅-fas, 'not right, wrong'; AS. and Old Eng. ne, 'not'; AS. nä (ne + ä), 'not ever, never, no,' Eng. no,' Eng. na- in nathless, AS. nä þe læs, 'not the less'; Eng. n- in n-ever, n-aught, etc.]

nákis, *indecl. subst. pron.* —1. no one, 78 [1], 73 [20] ?; —2. nothing, 73 [20] ?; —3. *even as adv.* [*see* 1117], never, 75 [11]. [ná + kís, *see* 504 [2] *end.*]

nakulá, *m.* Viverra ichneumon, an animal like the polecat, often domesticated, and a bitter foe of serpents and mice.

nákta, *n.* night; -am [1111b], by night. [cf. νύξ, stem νυκτ, Lat. nox, stem nocti, Eng. *night.*]

√ nakṣ (nákṣati, -te; nanákṣa, nanakṣé). attain unto; *w.* dyā́m, mount up to heaven. [collateral form of √2 naç, 'attain.']

nákṣatra, *n.* —1. sīdus, heavenly body, *in Veda*, of sun as well as of stars; star, 13 [8], 71 [12]; *sing. collectively*, 78 [11]; constellation; —2. asterism of the lunar zodiac, 59 [10]. [perhaps the stars are they that 'mount up' to heaven, cf. √nakṣ w. dyā́m.]

nakhá, *m. n.* nail (on fingers or toes); claw; talon. [cf. ὄνυξ, stem ὄ-νυχ, Lat. unguis, 'nail, claw'; AS. nægel, Eng. *nail.*]

nakhín, *a.* having claws; *as m.* beast with claws. [nakha.]

nágara, *n.,* and -rī, *f.* town, city.

nagaropānta, *n.* neighborhood of the town. [upānta.]

na-cira, *a.* not long; -āt, *adv.* [1114c], soon. [1122b [4].]

naṭa, *m.* dancer, mime, actor (these form a very despised caste). [√nṛt.]

naḍá *or* naḷá, *m.* reed. [Whitney 54: cf. 2 nadá and nala.]

√ nad (nádati; nanā́da, nedé; naditá; -nádya). sound; roar; bellow. [see 1 nadá and nadī.]

1 nadá, *m.* the bellower, *i.e.* bull. [√nad.]

2 nadá, *m.* reed, rush. [cf. naḍá.]

nadī, *f.* roaring stream; river. [√nad: cf. Nḗda, Nḗdων, names of streams.]

nánāndṛ [369 [2]], *f.* husband's sister.

√ nand (nándati, -te; nanánda; nandiṣyáte; nanditá; -nándya). be glad.
+ abhi, be glad in; greet joyfully.

nandana, *a.* gladdening; causing joy; *as m.* son, 21 [17]; *as n.* Nandana, *or* Elysium, the pleasure ground of the gods, *esp.* of Indra, 49 [18]. [caus. of √nand.]

nandi, *m.* The Gladsome One, euphemistic epithet of the dreadful god, Çiva-Rudra. [√nand: cf. çiva.]

nandi-deva, *m.* Nandideva, name of a Brahman. ['having Çiva as his god.']

nápāt, náptṛ [370], *m.* —1. *in Veda*, descendant *in general;* son; grandson, 87 [18]; —2. *in Skt.*, grandson, 63 [9]. [declension: in Veda, nápāt, nápātam, náptrā, náptṛbhis, etc.; in Skt., náptā, náptāram, náptrā, náptṛbhis, etc.: see 1182d: cf. νέποδες, 'young ones'; Lat. nepōtem, 'grandson'; AS. nefa, 'son's son *or* brother's son' — supplanted by Old French neveu (Eng. *nephew*), which in Old Eng. meant 'son's son' as well as 'brother's son.']

napti [356], *f.* daughter, 72 [6]; granddaughter. [*f.* to nápāt: acct, 355b.]

√ nabh (nábhate). burst; tear.

nábhas, *n.* —1. mist, clouds; —2. atmosphere, sky. [cf. νέφος, νεφέλη, 'cloud, mist'; Lat. nūbes, 'cloud,' nebula, 'mist'; AS. nifol, 'misty, gloomy'; Ger. Nebel, 'mist': for mg 2, cf. Ger. Wolken and AS. wolcnu, 'clouds,' w. Eng. welkin, 'sky.']

nabhas-tala, *n.* sky-surface, *i.e.* sky, *see* tala.

√ nam (námati, -te; nanā́ma, nemé [794e]; ánaṅsīt; naṅsyáti; natá [954d]; nāmi-

tum, nántum; natvá; -námya; namá-
yati). bow (intrans.), bend one's self; aim
at a person (gen.) with (instr.), 73 ¹⁵; nata,
bowed down, bending over, 68 ¹⁹ ɴ.; —caus.
cause to bow, subdue; namyate, is subdued, 31 ⁶.
+ ava, bow down, 34 ¹⁷.
+ á, bow down to.
+ ud, raise one's self up, arise.
+ sam-ud, rise.
+ nis, bend out; contort one's self.
+ pra, make obeisance before (acc.).

námas, n. bow, obeisance; adoration (by
gesture or word); reverence; used also
like the Lat. gloria in the Gloria patri.
[√nam.]

namas-kārá, m. a making of namas;
adoration. [171².]

namas-kr (see √1kr). do homage, 9 ¹⁴.
[171², 1092a.]

√ namasya (namasyáti). pay reverence.
[namas, 1063, 1058.]

námuci, m. Namuchi, name of a demon,
foe of Indra, 81 ¹⁶, 97 ⁶.

nayana, n. eye. ['leader, organ of sense
that leads,' √nī, 1150. 1a : for mg, cf.
ānana, gātra, caraṇa, netra.]

nára, m. man, 3 ²¹, etc.; at 57 ⁵, the primal
man or spirit. [transition-stem fr. nr,
1209a.]

nara-nārī, f. man and woman. [1253a.]

nara-pati, m. lord of men; king.

nara-vāhana, a. subst. having men as
his team, drawn by men; epithet and
name of Kuvera, god of wealth; name
of a king, successor of Cālivāhana.

naravāhana-datta, m. Naravāhanadat-
ta, name of a son of king Udayana.

naravāhanadatta-carita, n. adventures of N.

naravāhanadattacaritamaya, f. -ī, a.
containing the adventures of N. [1225:
see maya.]

nara-vyāghra, m. man-tiger, i.e. brave
and noble man. [cf. naraçārdūla : 1280b.]

nara-çārdūla, m. man-tiger, i.e. best
among men. [cf. naravyāghra: 1280b.]

nara-çreṣṭha, a. subst. best of men.

nara-sūnu, f. daughter of the primal
man or spirit.

narādhipa, m. lord of men, i.e. king
prince. [adhipa.]

nareçvara, m. lord of men, i.e. king,
prince. [íçvara.]

narottama, a. subst. best of men. [ut-
tama.]

narmada, a. granting or causing fun;
making gladness; f. -dā, Narmadā (called
also Revā), the modern Nerbudda river.
[narman + da.]

narman, n. fun.

nala, m. reed; Nala, name of a prince of
Nishadha. [cf. naḍá, Vedic naḍá.]

nalopākhyāna, n. Nala-episode, 1 ¹.
[upākhyāna.]

1 náva, a. new; of an earthen dish, (fresh,
i.e.) unburned. [prob. fr. nú, 'now,' q.v.:
cf. véos, Lat. novus, Ger. neu, Eng. new.]

2 náva [483⁴], num. nine. [cf. ἐννέα, Lat.
novem, Ger. neun, Eng. nine.]

navatí [485], f. ninety. [2 náva.]

náva-nīta, n. fresh butter. [perhaps
'fresh-brought,' as we say 'bring the butter, i.e. make it come,' in churning.]

návedas, a. perhaps well-knowing, cogni-
zant of (gen.). [apparently fr. an affirma-
tive particle na-, and vedas: see 1296 ³
end.]

√ 1naç (náçyati; nanáça, neçús; ánaçat;
nañksyáti [936]; naṣṭá; nāçáyati). be
missing; get lost; vanish; perish, be
ruined. [cf. νεκ-ρός, 'dead'; Lat. nex,
'death'; nocēre, 'harm.']
+ vi, get lost; perish; caus. cause to disappear; bring to nought, 81 ²⁰.

√ 2naç (náçati, -te; nanáça; ánat [833]).
attain; reach, come up to, 74 ¹; w. acchā,
draw hither, 76 ¹¹. [see √1 aç, 'reach': cf.
Lat. nac-tus sum, 'am having reached';
AS. neāh, comp. neār, superl. neāhst, Eng.
nigh, near (as comp., Macbeth ii.3.146),
next; AS. ge-neah, 'it reaches, es reicht, it
suffices'; ge-nōh, Eng. e-nough.]
+ pra, reach to, hit; fall upon, 78 ⁶.

nās [397], f. nose. [nom. dual, nāsā: cf.
Lat. nas-turcium, 'nose-teaser, nasturtium';
nār-es, 'nostrils'; AS. nosu, Eng. nose;
nos-tril, 'nose-thrill, nose-hole.']

nas [491], encl. pron. form of 1st pers. [cf.
νώ, 'we two'; Lat. nōs, 'us.']

nasa, *for* nás *in cpds* [1815c].

√ nah (náhyati [761c]; naddhá [223⁸];
-náhya). bind; join. [despite naddha (a
poss. false formation), and Avestan naзda
(Morphologische Untersuchungen, iii. 144),
probably for ₋nagh: cf. Lat. nec-t-ere,
'bind.']
+ u p a, tie on, lace.

nahí, *adv.* not, to be sure; nahí me ásti,
to be sure, I have no · ·. [ná + hí, 1122a
and b⁴: acct of verb, 595d.]

náhuṣa, *m.* Nahusha, name of an ancient
king. [perhaps 'neighbor,' from náhus,
and in that case a transfer-form (1209b).]

náhus, *m.* neighbor. [√nah.]

náka, *m.* vault of heaven, firmament.

nátidúra, *a.* not very far. [na + ati-
dúra, 1122b⁴.]

√ nāth (náthate; náthitá; náthitum;
-náthya). turn with supplication to.

nāthá, *n.* a refuge; *as m.* protector;
lord. [√nāth.]

nádhīta, *a.* un-learnéd. [na + adhīta,
√i: 1122b⁴.]

nábhi, *f.* — 1. navel; — 2. nave *or* hub.
[cf. ὀμφ-αλός, Lat. umb-ilicus, AS. naf-ela,
Eng. navel; also AS. naf-u, Eng. nave.]

nábhi-vardhana, *n.* the cutting of the
navel(-string).

náma-dhéya, *n.* the name-giving, naming, 59⁹; name, 17⁹, 60²². [náman.]

náman, *n.* — 1. distinguishing characteristic; form; — 2. name, 13⁸, 60²¹ᵇ, 78⁴,
61⁹; náma grah, (take *i.e.*) mention the
name, 64¹³; personal name (*e.g.* devadatta), as distinguished from the gotra
or 'family name' (*e.g.* kā́çyapa, 'descendant of Kaçyapa'), 103¹⁹ N.; *at end of
cpds*, having · · as name, named · ·, *so* 11
times, e.g. 19¹¹; — 3. náma, *adv.* [1111b],
by name, *so* 19 *times, e.g.* 1³, 60²¹ᵇ, 94¹⁶;
also námná, 56⁶; *w. interrogatives*, pray,
54¹⁶. [origin unknown: cf. ὄ-νομα, Lat.
nōmen, Eng. name.]

nárá, — 1. *a.* human; — 2. *as m.* man;
— nári, *f.* woman, 1⁹, 86¹⁶, etc.; wife.
[nṛ, 1208b: for mg 2, cf. mánava.]

nárada, *m.* Nárada, name of an ancient
devarṣi (*see note to* 1¹⁴), who often appears
on the earth to bring news from the gods,

and returns to heaven with reports from
men.

nārāyaṇá, *m.* Nārāyana, son of the primal man. [simply a patronymic of nara,
see 1219.]

nává, *f.* ship. [transfer-form (1209, 399)
fr. náu, náv.]

náça, *m.* loss; destruction. [√naç, 'be
missing.']

nása, *dual f.* the two nostrils, the nose.
[transfer-form (399) fr. nás, strong nás.]

násika, *f.* nostril; *dual*, the two nostrils;
the nose. [nása, 1222c 1.]

nástika, *a. subst.* atheist, infidel, not be-
lieving the Vedas and Puránas. [fr.
na + asti, 'there is not,' 1314b.]

náhuṣa, *m.* descendant of Nahusha, patronymic of Yayāti. [náhuṣa, 1208 and f.]

ní, *prep.* down; in, into. [cf. ἐνί, 'in';
Eng. ne-ther, be-nea-th.]

nikaṭa, *a.* near; *as n.* neighborhood;
presence. [1245g.]

nikhila, *a.* entire; all. [perhaps for
niḥ-khila, 'without a gap,' nis + khila:
1305² end.]

nijá, *a.* own; belonging to our party, 24⁸;
nijo ripus, foe in one's own camp, 37¹⁵;
often used as reflexive possessive pron., my
own, his own, our own, etc., — *or rather*,
my (47¹⁷), his (50¹⁴, 53¹², 56⁴⁸), etc.
[perhaps 'in-born,' fr. ni + ja.]

ninyá, *a.* inner; hidden, 70²⁰; *as n.* secret,
78³. [ni.]

nítya, *a.* — 1. own (*Vedic*), 79¹⁸; — 2. constant; eternal, 57⁷; -am, *adv.* constantly,
always, 17¹⁶, 64¹⁹. [in mg 1, fr. ni, 'in,'
1245b, and so signifying 'inward, not
alien.']

nítya-kála, *m.* uninterrupted time; -am,
adv. always, under all circumstances, 60⁶.

nítya-snáyin, *a.* constantly making
sacred ablutions. [1279.]

√ nid *or* nind (níndati; nin(́nda; ánindít;
ninditá; -níndya). blame; reproach.
[cf. ὄνειδος, 'reproach.']

nidrá, *f.* sleep. [√2 drā, 'sleep,' + ni.]

nidhána, *m. n.* end; death, 5¹⁹. [perhaps
fr. √dhā + ni, 'put down *or* out of the
way,' 'make an end of.']

√ nind, *see* nid.

nindaka, a. subst. scoffer. [√nid, nind.]

nibandhana, n. a binding, ligation, 59³; that on which a thing is fastened or rests or depends, condition, means, 46⁷. [√bandh + ni.]

nibhṛta, a. (borne down, lowered, i.e.) hidden; -am, adv. secretly. [√bhṛ + ni.]

nimajjana, n. bathing. [√majj + ni.]

nimitta, n. mark (for shooting at); sign, token; occasion or cause; -am, -ena, adverbially, because of; tannimittam, -ena, because of this, on account of this.

nimeṣá, m. closing or winking of the eyes. [√miṣ + ni.]

niyoga, m. a fastening on; injunction, and so, commission; business, 30⁶. [√yuj + ni: for mg, cf. alicui injungere laborem, 'fasten or impose a task on a person.']

nir, for nis before sonants [174]; see nis.

nir-antara, a. without interval or free space; completely filled, 53¹⁰; continuous; uninterrupted, 56¹².

nir-apāya, a. without failure or danger; infallible or safe.

nir-apekṣa, a. without regard or expectation; regardless, 52²⁰; not expecting anything from another, independent, 31¹⁷. [apekṣā, 334¹.]

nir-āmiṣāçin, a. not meat-eating. [see nis 3.]

nir-āhāra, a. without food, abstaining from food.

nir-ukta, a. spoken out; loud; clear; as n. explanation; etymological interpretation of a word; esp. Nirukta, title of a commentary to the nighaṇṭavas or Vedic Glossary. [√vac + nis.]

nír-ṛti, f. dissolution; destruction. [√ṛ + nis, 1157. 1d.]

nir-guṇa, a. without a string, 18⁵; void of good qualities, 18⁵; worthless, bad.

nir-ṇāmá, m. contortion, sinuosity. [√nam + nis.]

nir-dhana, a. without money.

nir-buddhi, a. without wit, stupid.

nir-bhara, a. — 1. without measure, much; -am, adv. very; -am prasupta, fast asleep; — 2. full of.

nir-mala, a. without impurity; pure; clear.

nir-lakṣya, a. not to be perceived, avoiding notice. [see nis 3.]

nir-vaṅça, a. without family; alone in the world.

nir-vāta, a. windless; sheltered.

nir-viçeṣa, a. without distinction; undistinguished; alike; like.

nirviçeṣākṛti, a. having like appearance, looking just alike. [ākṛti.]

nivāra, m. the warding off. [√1 vṛ, 'cover,' + ni.]

nivīta, ppl. hung, i.e. draped, with hangings, esp. with the sacred cord; as n. [1176a], the wearing the sacred cord about the neck; the sacred cord itself. [√vyā + ni.]

nivṛtta, ppl. — 1. turned away; esp. of an action which is turned away, i.e. not directed (to any ulterior purpose or object), free from hope of reward in this world or the next, disinterested, opp. of pravṛtta, q.v.; — 2. having turned away from, and so abstaining from, 29⁸. [√vṛt + ni.]

nivéçana, n. a going in and settling down to rest; resting-place; sleeping-place, bed, 105⁸; dwelling, 8⁶. [√viç + ni: for mg, cf. bhavana.]

niç [397], f. night. [cf. nákta.]

niçā, f. night. [cf. níç, nákta.]

niçcaya, m. (ascertainment, determination, i.e.) a fixed opinion or a firm resolve. [poss. fr. √3 ci, 'notice, look,' + nis; but better, perhaps, fr. √1 ci + nis, and so, 'an un-piling, i.e. discrimination, determination.']

niçcala, a. not moving. [nis + cala: see nis 3.]

niçcita, ppl. determined, decided; -am, adv. decidedly, surely. [see under niçcaya.]

niḥçreyasa, a. without a superior, i.e. best; as n. final beatitude. [nis + çreyasa: acct, 1305⁸.]

niḥçvāsa, m. breathing out, expiration; sigh. [√çvas + nis.]

niḥçvāsa-parama, a. having sighs as chief thing, much addicted to sighing. [1302b.]

niṣadha, m. pl. the Nishadhans, name of

a people; Nishadha, name of a country, 1⁷ N., 4².

niṣadhādhipa, m. ruler or king of the Nishadhans. [adhipa.]

niṣūdana, m. finisher (in its colloquial sense), one who makes an end of, destroyer. [√sūd + ni.]

niṣeka, m. an injecting, esp. of semen, impregnation; the ceremony performed upon impregnation. [√sic + ni.]

niṣevin, a. devoting one's self to; cohabiting with, 67²². [√sev + ni.]

niṣkramaṇa, n. the stepping out; esp. the first going out with a child. [√kram -·nis.]

niṣṭha, a. resting upon. [√sthā + ni, 333.]

niṣphala, a. fruitless, 63¹⁰; vain, 68¹¹. [nis + phala.]

nis, adv. prep. — 1. out, forth; — 2. in cpds [1305² end], having · · away, without · ·, e.g. nirantara; — 3. in cpds, not, e.g. niçcala.

√ nī (náyati, -te; nināya [800b], ninyé; ánāiṣīt, áneṣṭa [882]; neṣyáti, -te; nītá; nétum; nītvā; -nīya; nīyáte; nāyáyati [1042b]). lead, 24¹⁵; guide; conduct, 85³⁰; carry, 39¹⁹, etc.; carry off, 36¹⁵, 43¹⁷; vyāghratāṁ nī, bring to tiger-ness, change into a tiger; vaçaṁ nī, bring into one's power.

+ anu, (draw along toward one, i.e.) try to win or conciliate by friendly words.

+ abhi, bring hither to.

+ ā, bring to, 29¹⁴; bring, 31⁹; bring (one liquid) into (another, loc.), mix, 101¹⁴; raus. cause to be fetched, 50⁵.

+ ud, bring up; rescue (as a drowning man from the water), 90¹⁰.

+ upa, take unto one's self, of the teacher who receives a youth of one of the three free castes as pupil, and at the same time invests him with the sacramental cord, thus conferring spiritual rebirth, and making him a full member of his caste; see upanāyana; upanīta, invested with the sacramental cord.

+ pari, lead around (a cow, steer), 91¹⁴, 105²²; esp. lead a bride around the fire (as wedding ceremony), page 99.

+ pra, — 1. bring forward; — 2. as liturgical terminus technicus, convey the sacrificial fire and water to their places on and near the altar; praṇītās (sc. āpas), holy water; — 3. bring forward (one's feelings), i.e. come out with or manifest one's affection, 9¹⁵.

+ vi, lead; guide; train; discipline.

nī [352], vbl. bringing, in vaçanī. [√nī.]

nícā, a. low, not high;. morally and socially low. [inorganic transfer-form (1209a) fr. níc-ā, q.v.]

nícā, adv. down, low. [adverbially accented instr. — instead of níc-ā, 1112e — fr. ny-ăñc.]

nícā-vayas [418], a. whose strength is low; exhausted. [1306.]

nīḍá, Vedic nīḷá, m. n. — 1. (place for settling down, i.e.) resting-place; — 2. esp. bird's nest. [for ni-zd-a, i.e. ni-s(a)d-a — 198b³ — √sad + ni: cf. Lat. nidus, Ger. Nest, Eng. nest: for ḷ, see Whitney 54.]

nīḍa-garbha, m. nest-interior.

nīti, f. — 1. cónduct, esp. right and sagacious conduct; the knowledge of all that governs virtuous and discreet and statesman-like behavior; political and social ethics; — 2. leading. [√nī, 'condúct.']

nīti-jñá, a. knowing how to conduct one's self discreetly.

nīti-vidyā, f. knowledge of nīti or political and social ethics, esp. as it concerns princes.

nīti-çāstra, n. doctrine or science of political and social ethics.

nītha, m. a leading; nīthá, n. (way, and so, like the German Weise) a musical air, song. [√nī, 1163a.]

nīrá, n. water.

nīrasa, a. sapless, dried up; tasteless; insipid, 54¹¹. [nis + rasa, 174, 179.]

nīruj, a. without disease; healthy, 22³. [nis + rúj, 174, 179.]

nīla, a. dark-colored, esp. dark blue; as n. indigo; nīlī, f. indigo. [hence, through the Arabic an-nīl, for al-nīl, 'the indigoplant,' come Eng. anil and aniline.]

nīla-paṭa, m. dark garment.

nīla-varṇa, a. blue-colóred.

nīlasaṁdhāna-bhāṇḍa, n. vat for the mixing, i.e. preparing of indigo.

nīlībhāṇḍa-svāmin, m. indigo-vat-proprietor.

nīvāra, m. wild rice; sing. the plant; pl. the grains.

nīḷá, see nīḍá.

√ nu (návate; nunáva; ánūṣṭa; nutá; -nútya). cry aloud; shout; exult; praise. + pra, murmur; hum; esp. utter the sacred syllable om.

nú, adv. —1a. now, at once, temporal; —1b. now, continuative; adhā nu, so now, 79⁵; —1c. now, introductory, 70¹; —1d. so then, in encouraging or summoning; —1e. now, pray, in questions, 5²¹, 7¹⁸, 51²⁰, 74⁶, 78¹¹; —2. asseverative: nakír nu, surely no one or nothing, 73³⁰; mā nú, in order that surely not, 86¹⁰; —3. w. relatives: yā nu, whatsoever, 74²; yān nu, i.e. yát nu, as long soever as, 79¹⁵. [in V. often nū́: cf. vó, vū́r, Lat. nun-c, Ger. nu, nun, AS. nu, nū, Eng. now: see also náva, nútana, nūnám.]

√ nud (nudáti, -te; nunóda, nunudé; ánutta [881]; notsyáti, -te; nuttá, nun-ná; -núdya). push; thrust. + parā, thrust away; move from its place. + pra, push forward; set in motion. + vi, drive asunder or away; turn away, esp. from cares, like the Eng. di-vert; amuse. [for mg, cf. also dis-port and s-port.]

nuda, a. dispelling, in cpds. [√nud.]

nútana, a. of now; recent; young. [nú, 1245e.]

nūnám, adv. now. [nú, 1109.]

nṛ [370, 371⁵,⁹,¹⁰], m. man; hero; used also of gods: of the Maruts, 74⁴, 77¹⁸. [cf. ἀνήρ, stem ἀνερ, 'man'; Old Lat. nero, stem nerōn, 'manly, strong'; Lat. Nero.]

nṛ-cákṣas, a. men-beholding. [1296⁸.]

√ nṛt (nṛtyati, -te; nanárta; ánartīt; nartiṣyáti; nṛttá; nártitum; nart-itvā́). dance.

nṛti, f. dance. [√nṛt, 1155. 1.]

nṛ-pa, m. protector of men, i.e. prince, king.

nṛ-páti, m. lord of men, i.e. prince, king. [acct, 1267a.]

nṛmṇá, n. virtus, manliness, courage, strength. [fr. nṛ (1224c), as virtus fr. vir.]

nṛ-çaṅsa, a. man-cursing; malicious.

netavya, grdv. to be carried. [√nī.]

netra, n. eye. ['leader,' √nī, 1185a: for mg, cf. nayana.]

néd, adv. lest, in order that not, w. accented verb (595d) in the subjunctive (581c), 84¹⁷. [ná + íd, 1111a².]

nedya, grdv. to be blamed. [√nid, 963d.]

nemi, f. felly, rim. [nam, 1155.]

nāirukta, a. pertaining to the Nirukta; as m. an etymologist. [nirukta, 1208f.]

nāiṣadha, a. pertaining to Nishadha; as m. prince of the Nishadhans, i.e. Nala. [niṣadha, 1208f.]

nó, adv. and not, 21¹⁴; no ced, and if not, see ced. [ná + u.]

nāu, see 491.

nāú [361a], f. boat; ship. [cf. vaûs, Lat. návis, 'ship'; perhaps AS. naca, 'skiff': perhaps 'the swimmer,' √snū, cf. √snā.]

nyag-ródha, m. Ficus indica, banyan tree. ['downwards-growing': nyañc (1249a) + rodha.]

nyàñc [409b], a. directed downwards. [ni + añc, 407.]

nyāyá, m. —1. (that to which a thing goes back, i.e.) rule, norm; —2. (that in which a thing goes, i.e.) way; —3. esp. the right way, propriety. [√i + ni, 1148. 2.]

nyāyya, a. regular, normal, right; -am, adv. rightly; properly. [nyāyá, 1211.]

nyāsa, m. a putting down, commitment. [√2 as + ni, 'throw down.']

1 pā, vbl. drinking, in cpds. [√1 pā, 333.]

2 pā, vbl. keeping, keeper, in cpds. [√2 pā, 333.]

pakṣá, m. —1. wing, 93²; —2. side, of a door or of the hair of the head; —3. half, esp. of a lunar month, 27¹, 57¹⁹, cf. kṛṣṇa-, çukla-; —4. side, i.e. party, 37¹⁵.

pakṣa-bala, n. strength of wing.

pakṣin, a. winged, 92¹⁹; as m. bird, 2²³. [pakṣa.]

pakṣimṛgatā, *f.* condition of bird or of beast. [fr. pakṣin + mṛga: 1237, 1252.]

pakṣi-çāvaka, *m.* young of a bird; birdling. [pakṣin.]

páṅka, *n.* mud, mire.

paṅktí, *f.* set or series or row of five; row in general. [páñca, 1157.4.]

paṅkti-krama, *m.* order of a row; -eṇa, in a row, 89¹⁴.

√ **pac** (pácati, -te; papáca, pecé [794e]; ápākṣīt; pakṣyáti, -te; páktum; paktvá). cook, by baking or boiling or roasting; ripen. [cf. πέσσω, 'cook'; πέπ-ων, 'ripe'; Lat. coquo, 'cook'; borrowed AS. noun cōc, Eng. cook.]

+ **vi**, cook thoroughly; pass. be brought to maturity; ripen (of an action), i.e. come to its consequences or issue.

páñca [483²], *num.* five. [cf. πέντε, Aeolic πέμπε, Lat. quinque, Goth. fimf, AS. fíf, Eng. five.]

pañca-tantra, *n.* Panchatantra, name of a collection of fables. ['having five divisions or books.']

pañca-tapas, *a.* having five fires, of an ascetic who sits between four fires, one at each cardinal point, and with the burning sun above.

pañcatva, *n.* fiveness; esp. dissolution of the body into the five elements (earth, water, fire, air, ether, see bhūta and 66⁸ɴ.), i.e. death; w. gam, die. [pañca, 1239.]

páñca-pada, *f.* -ī, *a.* having (taken) five steps. [acct. 1300.]

pañcamá, *f.* -ī, *a.* fifth. [pañca, 487⁶.]

páñca-yāma, *a.* having five courses. [acct. 1300.]

pañca-çīrṣa, *a.* five-headed. [çīrṣan, 1315a.]

√ **paṭ** (páṭáyati, etc.). split, slit.

+ **ud**, open out.

paṭa, *m.* woven stuff; cloth; garment.

paṭala, *n.* veil; cover. [cf. paṭa.]

paṭu, *a.* —1. sharp; and so —2. fig. (nearly like Eng. sharp), clever.

√ **paṭh** (páṭhati; papáṭha; paṭhitá; paṭhitvá; páṭháyati). read aloud, 54²³, 55⁹; recite, 17¹¹; repeat to one's self, study, 22¹¹; caus. teach to talk, 19¹⁵.

√ **paṇ** (páṇati, -te; paṇitá). —1. bargain; buy; —2. bet, wage, stake, play. [prob. for ᵒpaln: cf. πέρνημι and πωλέω, 'sell'; Ger. feil, 'for sale, venal.']

+ **ā**, in āpaṇa, 'market.'

+ **vi**, sell.

paṇa, *m.* —1. bargain, stipulation, 45¹⁴; —2. wage, gage, prize; —3. a certain coin, 47¹⁶. [√paṇ.]

paṇi, *m.* —1. bargainer, who gives nought without return; chafferer, haggler, and so —2. niggard; esp. one who is stingy towards the gods, an impious person; —3. a malicious demon. [√paṇ.]

paṇḍitá, *a.* learned; as *m.* learned man, Anglo-Indian pandit.

paṇḍita-sabhā, *f.* assembly of pandits.

páṇya, *grdv.* to be bargained for or bartered; as *n.* article of trade. [√paṇ, 963.]

√ **pat** (pátati, -te; papáta, petús [794e]; ápaptat; patiṣyáti; patitá; pátitum; patitvá; -pátya; pátáyati, -te). —1. fly; move swiftly through the air; —2. descend, let one's self down; cast one's self at, 26⁸; —3. fall down, tumble down, 34⁶, 40²·⁵; fall (morally), fall from one's caste; fall down (dead); —4. fall upon, be directed to, 13⁸; —5. fall or get into, 22⁵·⁹; —caus. cause to fly; hurl (a curse), 49¹¹. [cf. πέτομαι, 'fly'; πί-πτω, 'fall'; Lat. peto, 'fall upon, make for, seek': see also pattra.]

+ **anu**, fly after, pursue.

+ **ud**, fly up.

+ **sam-ud**, fly or spring up together, 3⁶, 8¹⁴.

+ **ni**, fly down; light, 3⁸; tumble into, 36¹³; caus. cause to fall; kill, 32¹¹, 33¹⁷.

+ **sam-ni**, fall together, 90²⁰; come together; caus. bring together or convene, 9¹⁹.

+ **parā**, fly off, 93¹.

pátatra, *n.* wing. [√pat, 1185d.]

patatrín, *a.* winged; as *m.* bird. [patatra.]

pátana, *n.* fall. [√pat.]

páti [343b], *m.* —1. master, possessor; lord; ruler, 4¹; —2. then (like Eng. lord), husband, 9⁷, 89⁵, 86¹⁹, 64¹³. [cf. πόσις, 'husband'; Lat. impos, stem im-pot, 'not master of'; Goth. *faþs* in *bruþ-faþ-s*, 'bride-groom.']

pati-ghni, *a. f.* husband-slaying. [for-mally a fem. to pati-han, 402.]

patitvá, *n.* condition of spouse; wedlock. [pati.]

pati-loká, *m.* husband's place, abode of the husband in the future life.

pati-sthāna, *n.* husband's place.

patisthānīya, *a.* belonging to *or* in the husband's place; *as m.* husband's representative. [patisthāna, 1215.]

páttra, *n.* — 1. feather; wing; — 2. (plumage of a tree, *i.e.*) leaf — *for mg, cf.* parṇa; — 3. a leaf for writing on; a written leaf, 54¹⁹. [√pat: cf. πτερόν, 'wing'; Lat. *penna* and Old Lat. *pesna* (for *petna*), 'wing'; Ger. *Fed-er,* Eng. *feath-er.*]

pattra-çāka, *n.* leaf-vegetable, a vege-table consisting chiefly of leaves.

pátnī, *f.* — 1. mistress, lady; — 2. *then* (*like Eng.* lady), wife. [fem. to páti, just as πότνια, 'lady,' is to πόσις.]

patsutaḥ-çí [352], *a.* lying at the feet.

patsutás, *adv.* at the feet. [fr. patsú, loc. pl. of pád, 1098b.]

path [433], *same as* panthan.

patha, *for* path *in cpds* [1315c].

pathí [433], *same as* panthan.

pathi-rákṣi, *a.* guarding the paths. [panthan, 1249a: acct, 1276.]

pathyà, *a.* (pertaining to the way, course, *or* progress of a thing, *and so*) suitable, wholesome; pathyà, *f.* pathway. [path, 1212d 1.]

√ **pad** (pádyate; papáda, pedé [794e]; ápatta [882]; patsyáte, -ti; panná [957d]; páttum; -pádya; pādáyati). — 1. go, step, tread, *only w.* prepositions *and in derivatives;* — 2. fall, sink down (from fatigue), perish. [connection be-tween 1 and 2 not clear: uncompounded verb very rare: see under pád and padá.]

+ **ā**, come unto; get into (a condition); *esp.* get in trouble.

+ **vy-ā**, fall away, perish; *caus.* destroy; kill.

+ **ud**, go forth *or* out of; come into existence; be produced; utpannam an-nam, food (not cooked for the occasion, but) already on hand, 104¹; utpanne kārye, when the emergency has arisen, 38¹⁴; — *caus.* engender, 23⁸; produce; get, 42¹⁷.

+ **praty-ud**, *in ppl.* pratyutpanna, ready *or* on hand to meet an emergency.

+ **upa**, fall upon; happen, take place, 100¹⁰; come to, get at, reach; upapanna, (having gotten at [962²], *i.e.*) in posses-sion of, endowed with, 1⁴, 2⁸.

+ **prati**, — 1. step to; enter upon, 66¹⁸; — 2. get into (a condition), 49¹⁵; get at, acquire, attain, 98¹⁰; get back again, 60¹⁷; — 3. go to meet, *and so* (*like the Lat.* ac-cēdere), accede, yield; say yes to; con-sent, 48¹².

+ **vi**, fall asunder, 93⁹; come to nought, get into trouble.

+ **sam,** — 1. turn out well, succeed, prosper; — 2. become, 45¹³, 47¹⁸; — 3. fall together, be united with; sampanna, en-dowed with, 2¹⁰.

pád [391], *m.* foot. [√pad: cf. πόδ-α, Lat. pĕd-em, Eng. *foot.*]

padá, *n.* — 1. step, 17²¹, 99²²; — 2. foot-step; — 3. foot, 86⁶; — 4. standing-place, stead, place; home, 56⁴; station, position, 41¹. [√pad: cf. πέδον, 'ground'; Lat. *op-pedum, op-pidum,* 'town, (on *or* over the field)'; *peda*, 'footprint'; AS. *fœt,* 'step, going, journey,' whence *fetian,* 'go for,' Eng. *fetch.*]

padma, *m. n.* lotus, Nelumbium speciosum (not the plant, but the flower, which closes at evening).

padma-garbha, *a.* containing lotuses; Lotus-filled, name of a lake. [see garbha 2.]

padma-rāga, *a.* having the color of a lotus; *as m.* ruby. [1296.]

pánthan [433], *m.* road, path, way. [cf. πάτος, 'path'; Lat. *pont-em,* 'path, bridge': Eng. *path* and Ger. *Pfad,* if they belong here at all, must be regarded as very early borrowings, fr. the Greek πάτος, or poss. from the Scythian.]

pánthā [433⁵], *same as* panthan.

páyas, *n.* milk. [√pī.]

payo-mukha, a. having milk on the face or surface. [payas, 1303.]

pára [525⁴], a. −1. far, distant, more distant, further off, 86⁴; −2. following, later, future; −3. being beyond, surpassing, summus; chief, 68⁷; best, 36¹⁰; utmost, 1¹³; greatest, 44¹⁷; highest, 103¹¹; at end of cpds [1302b], having · · as chief thing, given over to · ·, devoted to · ·; −4. a. and subst. other, 64¹³; eka · · para, the one · · the other, 53¹⁹; another, 30²²; strange, hostile; stranger, 24⁸; foe, 29¹⁰, 37¹⁹. [√2 pṛ, 'bring across'; cf. πέρα, 'beyond'; Lat. peren-die, 'the day after,' i.e. 'day after to-morrow'; Eng. far and fore.]

para-dāra, m. pl. another's wife.
para-dravya, n. pl. another's property.
para-pakṣa, m. party of the foe.
para-patnī, f. wife of a stranger.

param, adv. beyond; w. abl. [1128], after, 60²⁰. [pára, 1111c.]

paramá [525³], a. −1. farthest, extreme, last; of heaven, highest, 83¹³; so 85³; −2. chiefest, 29¹; supreme; most excellent, 15¹⁷; at end of cpds [1302b], having · · as supreme object, devoted to · ·; −3. advly in cpds, before an adj. [1279], highly, exceedingly. [pára, 474.]

parama-çobhana, a. exceedingly beautiful.

paramāñganā, f. most excellent woman. [añganā.]

parameçvara, m. supreme lord. [īçvara.]

parame-ṣṭhín, a. standing in the highest place; supreme, as epithet of Prajāpati. [parame (1250c) + sthin, 186.]

para-loka, m. the other or future world.

parás, adv. far; in the distance; beyond; w. advly used instr. [1127] enā, beyond here, i.e. beyond, RV. x. 125. 8. [see pára.]

parástāt, adv. beyond; afterwards, at the end. [parás, 1100b.]

paras-para, one another; parasparam and parasparatas, adv. with one another; mutually. [an agglomeration (1314c) of paras (nom. s. m. of para) and para: the

syntactical forms sometimes correspond to the logical relation of the two parts — so, e.g., in parasparaṁ nindanti, 'they scold, the one the other' — but have come to be stereotyped and used often where the logical relation would require other caseforms: cf. anyonya.]

parasparādin, a. devouring one another. [ādin.]

párā, adv. to a distance, away, forth. [cf. παρά, w. gen., 'away from, from beside'; Lat. per- in per-īre and Ger. ver- in ver-gehen, 'pass away, perish'; Eng. for- in for-bear 'hold off from.']

parākrama, m. s. and pl. bold advance; courage; strength. [√kram + párā.]

parāñ-mukha, a. having the face averted; turning the back upon, avoiding. [parāñc, 1249a, 217, 161.]

párāñc [409a], f. párācī, a. directed away; averted; turning the back. [parā + añc, 407.]

parārtha, m. the sake of others; -am, -e, adv. for others. [artha, 1302c4.]

parāvát, f. the distance. [parā, 383d 1, 1245f.]

pári, adv. around; prep. w. abl.: from around, 87⁵; from, 75¹⁵. [cf. περί, 'around.']

parigha, m. iron bar for locking a gate. [√han + pari, 1143c, 333: for mg, cf. Ger. Schlag, 'coach-door,' and schlagen, 'strike': force of prep. unclear.]

parighopama, a. like iron bars. [upamā, 334².]

pari-jana, m. the surrounding folk, περίπολοι; retinue. [1289a.]

pari-jāta, a. completely grown. [1289a.]

pariṇeya, grdv. to be led around. [√nī + pari.]

parityāga, m. relinquishment. [√tyaj + pari.]

paridevita, n. lament. [√2 div, 'lament,' + pari, 1176a.]

paridhí, m. (a put-around, i.e.) enclosure, fence, protection, 86¹⁰; in the language of the sacrifice, the three green sticks laid about the altar fire and supposed to hold it together, 105¹³,⁸. [√1 dhā, 'put,' + pari, 1155. 2e.]

paripanthín, a. besetting the path; as m. waylayer. [pari + panthan, 1310a and c end.]

paribhú [352], a. being around, encompassing. [√bhū + pari, 323.]

pari-vatsará, m. a full year. [1289.]

parivartin, a. turning round, circling, constantly returning into itself. [√vṛt + pari.]

parivāra, m. that which surrounds, i.e. retinue. [√1 vṛ, 'cover,' + pari.]

pariçrit, f. (encloser, i.e.) one of the little stones by which the sacrificial altar is surrounded. [√çri + pari, 'enclose': 383b.]

parisamkhyā, f. complete tale or enumeration; sum. [√khyā + pari-sam.]

paruṣá, a. knotty, rough, harsh. [parus, 1209b.]

párus, n. knot; joint, of a plant or of the body. [perhaps 'a fullness,' √1 pṛ, 'fill': cf. párvan.]

parókṣa, a. beyond the eye, out of sight, invisible; -e, adv. [1116], behind one's back. [for paro 'kṣa, i.e. parás + akṣá, 'eye': 1310a.]

parokṣārtha, m. invisible thing, the invisible. [artha.]

parkaṭī, f. waved-leaved fig-tree, Ficus infectoria.

parṇá, n. -1. wing; plume, feather; -2. leaf — for mg, cf. pattra. [√spṛ (1177a), see under √sphur: cf. Lithuanian spárna, 'wing'; Ger. Farn, Eng. fern, so called (like πτερίς, 'fern,' — cf. πτερόν, 'feather,') from its feathery fronds.]

paryālocana, n. deliberation; -ā, f. plan, consilium. [√loc + pary-ā, 1150. 2a².]

párvata, -1. a. consisting of knots or ragged masses, used of a mountain, giri; as m. -2. mountain, 27⁶, 92¹⁹; hill; -3. cloud-mountain, 70²; -4. rock or bowlder, 86¹¹; -5. Parvata, name of a Rishi, companion of Nārada (q.v.), 5⁹. [fr. párvan, cf. 1245c: cf. Παρβασία (σπαρϝατια), sc. πόλις, i.e. 'Hil-ton.']

parvata-kandara, n. mountain-cave.

parvata-çikhara, m. n. hill-top.

parvatopatyakā, f. mountain-lowland, lowland by a mountain range. [upat-yakā.]

párvan, n. knot, joint. ['fullness,' √1 pṛ, 'fill,' 1169. 1a: cf. párus.]

párçu, f. rib; sickle.

√ palāy (pálāyate; palāyām cakre; ápalāyiṣṭa; palāyiṣyáti, -te; pálāyita; palāyitum; palāyya). flee; depart, cease, 40¹⁹. [quasi-root fr. √i, 'go,' + parā, 'away,' see 1087c and c²: quite different is √pālaya, 'protect.']

palāyana, n. flight. [√palāy.]

pávana, n. instrument for purifying; winnowing-fan. [√pū, 1150.]

√ 1 paç, orig. spaç (páçyati, -te; in Veda: paspaçé; áspaṣṭa [834c]; spaṣṭá; later: dadárça, etc.). -1. see; -2. perceive; behold; -3. look; -4. look on, 39⁷; gaze, 13⁷; -5. (see, i.e.) experience, 20¹⁶, 35¹; -6. look upon, 21²³, 40¹⁵; consider as; -7. see with the spiritual eye (as seers and poets), 94⁹. [for the initial s, see the perfect and vi-spaṣṭa: cf. σκέπτομαι, 'look about'; Lat. specio, 'behold'; Ger. spähen, 'spy,' Old High Ger. spehôn, whence, through Old French espier, the Eng. espy, and shortened spy.]

+ anu, look along or spy out (e.g. a path for some one, i.e.), disclose or show, 83⁷.

+ vi, see in places apart, distinguish, see clearly; vispaṣṭa, clear.

√ 2 paç, fasten, bind, in derivs, see paçú, pāça. [cf. πάσσαλος, σπαπ-jαλος, 'peg'; Lat. pac-iscor, 'bind myself, agree'; pax, 'agreement, peace'; pang-ere, 'make fast,' pac-tum, 'agreed upon'; Goth. fah-an, AS. fón, sfōh-an, 'fasten on, take hold of'; Eng. verb fang, 'seize,' noun fang, 'seizing-tooth'; connection of fing-er ('grasper, holder'?), doubtful: cf. also Goth. fagrs, 'fitting,' AS. fægr, Eng. fair; AS. ge-fēgan, Eng. fay, Ger. fügen, 'fit together,' trans., and Eng. fadge, 'fit together or agree,' intrans.]

paçú, m. cattle, 90² — a single head or a herd; domestic animal (opp. to mṛga, 'wild beast'), 67²; esp. beast for sacrifice, 101⁶. [prop. 'tethered (beasts),' √2 paç, 'fasten': cf. Lat. pec-u, Ger. Vieh, 'cattle,' AS. feoh, 'cattle, property,' Eng. fee, orig. 'property,' then 'payment.']

paçu-ghna, a. slaying cattle; as m. cattle-slayer.

paçu-tṛp, a. cattle-stealing. [vbl of √2 tṛp.]

paçu-bandhá, m. animal sacrifice. ['binding of beast' to sacrificial post.]

paçumánt, a. rich in cattle. [paçu, 1235 and b.]

paçu-roman, n. a hair of an animal.

paçu-vadha, m. slaughter of animals.

paçcá, a. hinder; later; west; paçcát, as adv. [1114c]: −1. behind; after, 39²³; −2. later, afterwards, 29¹⁷, 38⁴; thereupon, 36¹³, 39¹⁷, 40¹²; paçcát, as prep. w. gen. [1130]: −3. after, 51²; −4. to the west of, 98¹⁷, 100¹⁷, 105¹⁰. [paçcá is an inorganic transfer-stem (1209a) fr. paçcá, q.v.]

paçcá, adv. behind; later; west. [adverbially accented instr. — instead of páçc-ā, i.e. pás-(a)c-ā, 1112e — fr. ●pás-añc (407): with pas cf. Lat. pos-terus, 'later,' etc.]

paçcát, see paçca.

paçcima, a. last, 52¹⁶; westerly. [paçca: cf. 1224a and b.]

√ 1 pā (píbati, -te [671, 749]; papáu, papé; ápāt; pāsyáti, -te; pītá [954c]; pátum; pītvá; -pā́ya, -píya). drink. [cf. πέ-πω-κα, 'have drunk'; Πῖ-σα, 'The Burn, The Fountain'; Lat. pō-tus, 'drunk'; bibo, ●pi-b-o, 'drink.']

√ 2 pā (páti; ápāsīt; pátum). protect; keep; for so-called caus., see pālaya. [cf. πέ-πā-μαι, 'have kept, possess'; πῶ-υ, 'herd'; Lat. pa-sc-o, 'keep, pasture'; see go-pá.]

+ pari, protect around.

1 pā, vbl. drinking, in cpds. [√1 pā.]

2 pā, vbl. keeping, keeper, in cpds. [√2 pā.]

pāṅsú, m. pl. dust.

pāka, a. −1. of a calf, young; −2. simple. [lit. 'sucking,' √1 pā, 'drink.']

pāka-dū́rvā, f. young millet-grass. [pāka + dū́rvā: acct, 1280².]

pāṭala, a. pale red; as m. Bignonia suaveolens.

pāṭali, f. Bignonia suaveolens or trumpet-flower. [cf. pāṭala.]

pāṭali-putra, n. Pāṭaliputra, capital of Magadha, at the old confluence of the Sone (çoṇa) and Ganges, the Παλίβοθρα of Ptolemy, 17⁹ ɴ.

pāṭavá, n. sharpness; cleverness. [paṭu, q.v.: 1208c.]

pāṇí, m. hand. [prob. for ●palni: cf. παλάμη, Lat. palma, AS. folm, 'palm, hand': radically akin is AS. fēl-an, Eng. feel.]

pāṇi-grāha, m. hand-grasper, i.e. (see 89⁵ɴ.) husband.

pāṇḍava, m. descendant of Pāṇḍu. [pāṇ-ḍu, 1208c.]

pāṇḍitya, n. learning, erudition. [paṇ-ḍitá.]

pāṇḍú, a. whitish, pale; as m. Pāṇḍu, name of a prince of the Lunar Race.

pāṇḍu-nandana, m. son of Pāṇḍu.

pāṇḍu-varṇa, a. pale-colored.

pāta, m. fall. [√pat.]

pātaka, a. causing one to fall (from caste); as n. crime. [fr. caus. of √pat.]

pātra, n. −1. instrument of drinking, cup; vessel; −2. in general, utensil (cf. bhāṇḍa), 102¹¹; −3. fig., as in Eng. sthāna 5), a fit vessel or worthy person, 22⁵; pātrī [364], f. sacrificial vessel. [√1 pā, 'drink,' 1185a: cf. 362b².]

pāda, m. −1. foot; leg, 26¹⁸; −2. limb of a quadruped, i.e. quarter (as, conversely, in Eng., quarter means 'fourth part of a quadruped, including a leg'); then quarter (of anything); −3. esp. quarter of a (four-versed) stanza, verse; then verse (even of a three-versed stanza), 60¹²; −4. (foot of a heavenly body, i.e.) ray, beam — see 2 kara. [transition-stem (399) fr. pád, acc. pád-am, to which, as if it were páda-m, is formed the nom. páda-s, etc.]

pāda-pa, m. plant, esp. tree. [lit. 'drinking with its foot, i.e. root.']

pāda-rajas, n. foot-dust.

pādika, a. amounting to or lasting one fourth (of a time). [pāda.]

pādukā, f. shoe, slipper. [cf. pád, 'foot.']

pāna, −1. n. the drinking (esp. of strong drink); −2. perhaps as vbl adj. drenching, i.e. tränkend. [√1 pā, 'drink,' 1150.]

pānīya, *grdv.* to be drunk, for drinking; *as n.* drink; water. [√1 pā, 'drink,' 965: prop. fr. pāna, 1215b.]

pānīya-varṣa, *m.* water-rain, downpour of water.

pántha, *m.* wayfarer; viätor. [pánthan, 1208a² end.]

pāpá, *a.* bad; evil; *as m.* bad fellow, 46¹⁹; *as n.* trouble; harm, 26³; evil (deed), 27².

pāpa-karman, *a.* of evil deeds; *as m.* villain.

pāpa-çīla, *a.* having evil as one's nature, prone to evil.

pāpīyáṅs, *a.* worse; very bad. [pāpa, 466.]

pāpmán, *m.* evil; sin, 93¹¹. [cf. pāpa.]

pārá, *n.* the further bank *or* bound. [√2 pṛ, 'bring across.']

pārameçvara, *a.* of the supreme lord (Çiva). [parameçvara.]

pāruṣya, *n.* harshness, *esp.* of speech. [paruṣá.]

pārthiva, *a.* of *or* belonging to the earth; *as m.* king. [pṛthivī, 1208d.]

pārthiva-sutā, *f.* king's daughter.

pārthivendra, *m.* most excellent of kings. [indra.]

pārçvá, *n.* — 1. side; *and so* — 2. *as in Eng.,* immediate neighborhood. [párçu, 'rib,' 1208c: so French côté, 'side or ribbed part,' Medieval Lat. costatum, fr. Lat. costa, 'rib.']

pāla, *m.* protector. [√2 pā, 'protect,' 1189.]

√ pālaya (pāláyati). be protector; protect; keep. [pāla, 1042f: acct, 1067: quite different is √palāy, 'go away.'] + pari, protect around.

pāvaká, *a.* pure; clear; bright. [√pū, 1181b and a: cf. çvāpada.]

pāvana, *a.* purifying; freeing from sin. [√pū, 1150b.]

pāça, *m.* bond; snare; trap. [√2 paç, 'fasten.']

√ pi, *same as* pī.

piṅga, *a.* reddish brown.

piṅgalá, *a.* reddish brown. [piṅga, 1227.]

piñjūla, *n.* tuft of stalks; grass.

piṇḍa, *m.* — 1. lump; ball; lump (of earth), 98⁵; — 2. *esp.* lump *or* cake of meal offered to the Manes; — 3. mouthful, 65⁵; piṇḍī, *f.* meal-cake.

pitāmahá, *m.* father's father, grandfather; great father. [pitā (nom. s. of pitṛ) + maha, 1314c and d.]

pitṛ́ [373], *m.* — 1. father; — 2. *pl.* father and his brothers.(*cf.* French parent, 'relative'), 61¹⁷; — 3. *pl.* the fathers, spirits of the forefathers, the Manes, 67¹⁶, 83¹³, etc. [origin unknown, see 1182d: cf. πατήρ, Lat. pater, Eng. father.]

pitṛtas, *adv.* on the father's side. [pitṛ, 1098b.]

pitṛ-mitra, *n.* father's friend.

pitṛ-yajñá, *m.* sacrifice to the Manes. [yajñá.]

pitṛvya, *m.* father's brother, patruus. [pitṛ, 1228c: cf. πάτρως, Lat. patruus, AS. fædera, 'father's brother.']

pítrya, *a.* of one's father; of (our) fathers, 78¹³; of *or* belonging to *or* sacred to the Manes. [pitṛ́, 1212b: cf. πάτριος, Lat. patrius, 'of one's father.']

√ pin v (pínvati; pipínva; pinvitá). cause to swell *or* stream. [√pī or pi: 749, 749b, 716.]

pipāsá, *f.* desire to drink, thirst. [fr. desid. (1026) of √1 pā, 'drink': 1149⁴.]

pipīlá, *m.* ant. [perhaps for •pipíḍa, 'pressed in *or* constricted in the middle,' √piḍ.]

√ piç (piñçáti, -te [758]; pipéça, pipiçé; piṣṭá). adorn. [cf. ποικίλος, AS. fáh, 'many-colored'; Lat. pic-tor, 'painter.']

piçáṅga, *a.* reddish brown. [√piç.]

piçácá, *m.* one of a class of demons (*perhaps* personifications of the ignis fatuus); goblin.

píçuna, *a.* backbiting, slanderous. [cf. πικρός, 'bitter.']

√ piṣ (pináṣṭi; pipéṣa, pipiṣé; ápiṣat pekṣyáti; piṣṭá; péṣṭum; piṣṭvā; -piṣya). crush; grind, 47⁵; mill. [cf. Lat. pinsere, pisere, 'crush': of doubtful kinship is πτίσσω, 'pound, husk.'] + sam, crush together *or* to pieces.

piṣṭá, *ppl.* milled; *as n.* meal. [√piṣ: for the mgs. cf. piṣ, piṣṭa, and molere, mola, with mill, meal.]

piṣṭa-paçu, m. effigy of a sacrificial beast made of meal.

√ pī or pyā (pyáyate [761d1]; pīpáya [786⁸], pipyús; ápyāsīt; pītá, pīná). swell; overflow. [hence pī-van, π῁-ον, 'fat.']

pīṭha, n. −1. seat; −2. pedestal (of an image of a god).

pīṭha-cakra, n. seat-wagon; wagon with a seat.

√ pīḍ (pīḍáyati [1041²]; pīḍayám āsa; pīḍitá; pīḍayitum; pīḍayitvā; -pīḍya). press; oppress, pain. [for ∘piṣd, ∘pisd, 198b⁸: cf. √pis.] + ā, press out, 103²⁰.

pīḍā, f. pain, ache. [√pīḍ, 1149³.]

pīná, a. thick, brawny. ['swollen,' ppl. of √pī, 957a.]

pívas, n. fat. [√pī: cf. πῖαρ, i.e. πῖ-Ϝαρ, 'fat.']

púṁs, same as púmāṁs.

puṭa, m. n. fold; cavity; nose (of a basket). [for ∘plṭa: cf. -πλασιος, ∘πλ͂γϳος, in δι-πλάσιος or δι-παλτος, Eng. two-fold.]

púnya, a. prosperous; happy; lucky, faustus, auspicious, 12¹⁸, 59¹˙¹⁰; right, good; as n. good work; sing. collectively, good works, 28¹⁷; merit (from good works). [perhaps fr. √puṣ.]

púṇya-gandha, a. of good or pleasant smell.

puṇya-pāpa, n. pl. good and bad deeds. [1253a.]

puṇya-çloka, a. of good fame; as m. Puṇyaçloka, epithet of Nala.

puttikā, f. white ant. ['the doll-like insect': for putrikā.]

putrá, m. −1. son; child, 98²⁰; −2. whelp; −3. shortened form for Putraka as proper name.

putraka, m. −1. little son (as term of endearment), boy; −2. Putraka, otherwise Putra, name of the founder of Pāṭaliputra-pura, 45²; − putrikā, f. [1222d], daughter; doll (of wood or lac). [putra.]

putra-dāra, n. son and wife. [1253b.]

púnar, adv. −1. back; home; w. ā-gam, go back, 4³, 41¹⁸; so ā_i, 83¹⁴; w. vac, reply, 19¹⁹; −2. again, 8⁸, 40²⁰; anew; punaḥ punar, again and again, 2¹⁷;

punar, equiv. to punaḥ punar, 4¹⁸; −3. continuative, again, further, 29¹¹; moreover, 16⁸, 57²¹; besides or in turn, 10¹⁰; kim punas tu, but what besides, how much more, a fortiori, 17¹⁵; longer, 84⁸; −4. but, 46²˙¹⁹; on the other hand, 20¹⁷. [cf. the similarly connected notions of iteration and opposition shown by πάλιν, Eng. again and against, Ger. wieder and wider.]

punar-garbhavatī, a. f. again pregnant.

punar-janman, n. re-birth.

punaḥ-sará, a. coming back (as a ghost from the other world — exactly like the French revenant), and so ghostly, uncanny. [punar, 178.]

púmāṁs [394], m. man; a male, 59⁷; opp. of strī, e.g. 104⁹; pumāṁsaḥ putrās, male children, 98²⁰.

1 púr, f. fullness. [√1 pṛ, 'fill.']

2 púr [392], f. stronghold; castle; fortified town. [cf. πόλις, 'city.']

pura, n. stronghold; fortified town; city. [2 púr, 399.]

púramdhi, −1. a. courageous, highspirited, exalted; −2. as m. perhaps as name of a god, Purandhi; −3. as f. exaltation.

purás, adv. in front, forward, before; at first, 54¹⁸; compounded [1078⁵] esp. w. kṛ and dhā: w. kṛ, put in front, appoint; w. dhā, put in front or in charge, esp. of the priestly duties. [see pra: cf. πάρος, 'before.']

puras-kārya, grdv. to be appointed or commissioned, praeficiendus. [see puras + kṛ: also 963b and 171⁸.]

purástāt, adv. −1. before; in the front, 85¹⁸; −2. previously, afore, 98⁵, 101¹¹˙¹²; −3. before, i.e. (see prāñc) eastward; −4. prep. w. gen. [1130], before, in the presence of, 20¹. [puras, 1100b.]

puraḥ-sará, a. going before; as m. forerunner; at end of cpds [1302c2], having ·· as forerunner, i.e. accompanied by··; ··-puraḥsaram, adv. with ·· or after ···.

purā, adv. formerly, 46², 79¹⁴; once upon a time, 38⁹, 48²⁰; prep. w. abl. [1128], before, 95¹⁷, 104¹⁹. [see prā.]

purāṇá, a. former, belonging to old times; as n. things of the past; tale of old times, λόγος and μῦθος. [purā, 1245d.]

púriṣa, n. crumbling earth, as opp. to fluids; rubble; loose earth. ['fillings or heaps,' fr. √1 pṛ, in the sense 'fill, i.e. heap': 1197b.]

purú, a. much, many. [√1 pṛ, 'fill,' q.v.: cf. πολύ, AS. fela, 'much, many.']

purutrá, adv. in many places. [puru, 1009.]

púruṣa, m. −1. man; −2. (as in Eng., man, i.e.) servant; −3. the personal and life-giving principle in man and other beings, soul, spirit; then −4. personified as The Supreme Spirit, Soul of the Universe, 57⁸.

puruṣa-kārá, m. deed of a man, human effort, as opp. to dāiva, 'fate.'

puruṣa-siṅha, m. man-lion, stout-hearted man.

purúcí, a. f. many, abundant; long. [formally fem. to a stem ●puru-ác, 'directed or reaching in many ways, abundant': cf. 407.]

puro-gama, a. going before; as m. leader; at end of cpds [1302c 2], having ·· as leader, accompanied by ··. [puras.]

puro-gavá, m. fore-bull, and so, generalized (see g6 4), leader; purogavī, f. leader. [puras.]

puró-hita, ppl. set before or in charge (esp. of priestly service); as m. priest, house-priest of a prince. [see puras with dhā.]

pulkasa, m. one of a despised mixed caste.

√ puṣ (púṣyati, -te; pupóṣa; ápuṣat; puṣṭá). −1. thrive; bloom; −2. trans. cause to thrive; develop; unfold, display, 78⁴.

puṣka, bloom, a word assumed as probable on account of púṣpa, 'bloom,' púṣkara, 'lotus blossom,' and puṣkalá. [√puṣ, 1186².]

puṣkalá, a. abundant. [prob. 'blooming,' fr. ●puṣka, 1227.]

puṣṭá, ppl. having thrived; strong; fat. [√puṣ, 955².]

puṣṭáṅga, a. fat-limbed. [áṅga.]

puṣṭi, f. thrifty growth; prosperity [√puṣ.]

púṣpa, n. bloom; flower. [poss. for ●puṣka, q.v.: cf. 1201² end.]

puṣpa-danta, m. Pushpadanta or Flower-tooth, name of an attendant of Çiva, see 53³ ɴ.

puṣpámoda, m. fragrance of flowers. [ámoda.]

pustaka, m. n. manuscript; book.

√ pū (punáti, punīté; pávate; pupáva; ápāvīt; pūtá; -púya). −1. make clear or bright; purify; καθαίρειν; pūtá, pure; −2. mid. clear itself, flow clear. [cf. πῦ-ρ, Eng. fire (τὸ πῦρ καθαίρει): w. pūtá, cf. Lat. pūtus, 'clear,' pūrus, 'pure.']
+ sam, purify, clean.

pū, vbl. purifying, in cpds.

pūga, m. betel-palm, Areca Catechu; as n. betel nut.

√ pūj (pūjáyati, -te; pūjayiṣyáti; pūjitá; -pújya). honor.
+ abhi, do honor to.

pūjanīya, grdv. to be honored. [√pūj, 965.]

pūjā, f. honor.

pūjya, grdv. to be honored. [√pūj, 963d.]

pūrṇá, ppl. filled; full. [√1 pṛ, 'fill,' 957b: cf. Goth. fulls, Eng. full.]

pūrṇá-māsa, m. full moon and the full-moon sacrifice.

pūrtá, ppl. filled; bestowed, fulfilled; as n. [1176a], fulfilment; reward; merit. [√1 pṛ, 'fill,' 242.]

pū́rva [525⁴], a. being before in place or time: −1. east (cf. prāñc); −2. prior; preceding, 86¹²; pūrva ·· uttara, former ·· latter, 21⁸; ancient, 57⁶; of old time, 69⁸, 83¹⁰; first spoken, 60³; w. past pass. ppl. [1291]: dṛṣṭa-pūrva, seen before; pūrvam, adv. before; beforehand, 60⁹; previously, already, 7²¹, 25¹⁷; in former times, 48¹; long ago, 46⁸; first, 103⁶; pūrvam ·· uttaram, first ·· last, 104¹²; −3. at end of cpds, (having ·· as preceding thing, i.e.) accompanied by ··, or simply with ··, 8²¹. [connected w. puras and pra.]

pūrvaka, f. [1222d] -ikā, a. — 1. preceding; — 2. *used like* pūrva 3. [pūrva, 1222c and 1307.]

pūrva-janman, n. former birth, previous state of existence.

pūrvākṣara, a. with the preceding letter. [akṣara.]

pūrvyá, a. ancient. [pūrva, 1212c.]

pūṣán [426a], m. Pūshan, a Vedic divinity, keeper of flocks and herds, and bringer of prosperity. [√puṣ, 1160c.]

√ 1 pṛ (pṛṇáti; pūryate; pūrṇá [957b]; *pass.* pūryáte; pūráyati, -te; etc.). fill; bestow abundantly; sate; pūryate, becomes sated [*see* 761b]; *caus.* [1041²], fill; make a thing (*acc.*) full of (*gen.*), 102¹⁸. [for treatment of root-vowel, see 242: cf. -πί-πλη-μι, Lat. *plēre*, 'fill'; *po-pul-us*, 'folk'; Eng. *fol-k* (doubtful): see also pūrṇá and √prā.]

+ pra, *intrans.* prapūryate, becomes sated.

+ sam, *intrans.* sampūryate, becomes full; sampūrṇa, full.

√ 2 pṛ (píparti; pāráyati, -te; etc.). pass, *trans.*; bring across. [cf. περάω, 'pass over, cross'; πόρος, 'passage, *i.e.* ford, ferry, bridge'; Lat. *por-ta*, 'gate'; Eng. *fare*, 'get on'; *ferry*, *for-d*; Avestan *peretu*, 'bridge,' and Εὐ-φράτης, 'the well-bridged (stream)'; also Βόσ-πορος and *Ox-ford*.]

+ ati, bring across.

√ 3 pṛ (pṛṇóti; pṛtá; priyate; pāráyati). be busy; *only w.* ā, *see* 773.

+ ā, *in* ápṛta, busied.

+ vy-ā, *in* vyápriyate, is busied.

√ pṛc (pṛṇákti, pṛṅkté; papárca; áprāk-ṣīt, áprkta [882]; pṛktá; pṛcyáte). fill; mix; put in connection with. [perhaps connected w. √1 pṛ, 'fill.']

+ upa, put one's self close to, be near.

pṛt, f. fight, battle.

pṛtanā, f. battle. [cf. pṛt.]

√ pṛtanāya (pṛtanāyáti). fight; *present ppl.* fighting; *as subst.* enemy. [pṛtanā, 1060.]

√ pṛtanya (pṛtanyáti). fight; attack; *present ppl.* fighting; *as subst.* enemy. [pṛtanā, 1059d.]

√ pṛth, *collateral form of* prath, *in derivs.*

pṛthá, m. the flat of the hand, πλατεῖα. [√prath, 241.]

pṛthak, adv. separately, 105¹⁶; severally, 65⁴; for one's self, 64⁸. [perhaps 'directed widely (apart)': cf. pṛth and see 1111d.]

pṛthivī, f. the earth *as* the wide and broad. [fem. to pṛthú, 344², and standing for pṛthvī, as the metre shows it is to be pronounced at 92¹⁰: for mg, cf. mah-í, s.v. máh.]

pṛthivī-kṣit, a. earth-ruling; *as* m. prince.

pṛthivī-pati, m. lord of the earth, king.

pṛthivī-pāla, m. keeper of the earth, king.

pṛthú, f. pṛthvi, a. wide, broad. [√prath, 241: cf. πλατύς, 'wide'; akin are Old Eng. *flaþe*, Ger. Fladen, 'broad, thin cake,' Old High Ger. acc. s. *fladon*, 'sacrificial cake,' whence, through French *flan*, 'flat cake,' comes the Eng. *flawn*, 'flat custard or pie': √prath has no connection w. AS. *bräd*, Eng. *broad*.]

pṛçni, a. speckled; dapple, *esp.* of kine; *as* f. Pṛçni, mother of the Maruts. [cf. περκνός, 'dark colored'; Old High Ger. *forhana*, whence Ger. Forelle, 'trout.']

pṛṣad-ājyá, n. speckled butter, ghee clotted with curds. [pṛṣant.]

pṛṣant, a. speckled. [450c.]

pṛṣṭhá, n. — 1. back, of an animal; — 2. the upper side, surface; — 3. top, of a hill or palace. [cf. Ger. First, 'ridge of a house'; AS. *fīrst-hróf*, 'ridge-pole': observe that νῶτος has mgs 1, 2, and 3, that Lat. *tergum* has mgs 1 and 2, and that Eng. *ridge* has mgs 1 and 3.]

pṛṣṭhatás, adv. a tergo, from behind; with the back, with averted face, 30¹⁷. [1098c⁸.]

pṛṣṭha-māṅsa, n. back-flesh; *w.* khād, *in double sense*, bite the back-flesh *and* back-bite.

peya, n. a drinking. [√1 pā, 'drink,' 1213c.]

pāiçāca, f. -ī, a. of the goblins. [piçācá, 1208f.]

pāiçunya, n. slander. [píçuna, 1208f.]

13

póṣa, m. thriving, development; welfare.
  [√puṣ.]
páuṁsya, n. manliness; manly deed.
  [puṁs, 1211².]
páuruṣá, n. manliness; manly deed.
  [púruṣa, 1208f.]
√ pyā (pyáyate [761d 1]; ápyāsīt [882];
  pyātá). swell; overflow. [a collateral
  form of √pī, q.v.]
  + ā, become full of or rich in.
prá,. prep. forward, onward, forth, fore.
  [cf. πρό, 'before'; Lat. prŏ, later prō,
  'before'; Eng. fore: see also the following articles, and purás, purá, and púrva.]
prakaraṇa, n. treatment; discussion;
  subject of discussion, what's being talked
  about. [√1 kṛ, 'do, put,' + pra.]
prakarṣa, m. (preference, advantage,
  i.e.) superiority.   [√kṛṣ, 'draw,' + pra:
  for mg, cf. Eng. pre-ference; also Ger.
  Vor-zug, 'preference, advantage,' with
  vor-ziehen, 'draw forward, prefer.']
prakāçá, a. shining out, clear; open;
  -am, adv. openly, aloud. [√kāç + pra.]
prakṛti, f. that which one pre-supposes
  (voraus-setzt), i.e. the original or natural
  form or condition; nature. [√1 kṛ, 'do,
  set,' + pra.]
prakopa, m. a boiling with rage; anger.
  [√kup + pra.]
prage, adv. early in the morning.
pracṛtta-çikha,   a. with loosened
  braids or flowing hair. [çikhā.]
prácetas, a. knowing, wise. [√cit +
  pra, cf. 1151. 2b.]
√ prach (pṛcháti, -te; papráccha [794c];
  ápprākṣīt; prakṣyáti; pṛṣṭá; práṣṭum;
  pṛṣṭvā; -pṛchya). ask; ask after, in-
  quire about; ask some one (acc.) about
  something (acc.), 61⁷. [true root-form
  praç (see 220, 241, and √vṛçc), orig.
  •pṛk: cf. θεο-πρόπ-ος, 'asking the gods';
  Lat. prec-es, 'prayers,' proc-us, 'suitor';
  Old High Ger. frāh-ēn, Ger. frag-en, 'ask':
  pṛcháti is a sk-formation (•pṛk-sketi),
  cf. Lat. poscit, •porc-scit, Old High Ger.
  forskōt, •forh-skōt, 'asks for,' Ger. forscht,
  'inquires into.']
  + pari, ask.
  + vi, find out by inquiry.

+ sam, mid. consult with, converse or
  talk with.
prajá, f. – 1. procreation; – 2. offspring,
  children, descendants; – 3. creatures,
  57¹; esp. – 4. folk, subjects, of a prince,
  16⁸. [√jan or jā + pra, 1147.]
prajá-kāmá, m. desire for offspring.
  [prajá + kāma, 1264: acct, 1267.]
prajá-kāma, a. possessing prajākāmá,
  i.e. desirous of offspring, 93⁶, 1¹². [1296,
  1295.]
prajá-pati, m. – 1. lord of creatures;
  – 2. genius presiding over procreation,
  89¹⁹; – 3. lord of creatures, i.e. creator
  or Prajāpati, 60¹⁰, see note.   [acct,
  1267a.]
prajārthe, adv. for the sake of offspring.
  [artha, 1116, 1302c 4.]
prajñá, f. understanding. [√jñā + pra.]
prajñāta, ppl. well-known.   [√jñā +
  pra.]
praṇaya, m. manifestation of one's affection. [√nī + pra: for ṇ, see 192a.]
praṇayana, n. – 1. a fetching; – 2.
  means for fetching, vessel. [do.]
praṇava, m. the sacred syllable om.
  [√nu + pra, q.v.]
praṇāma, m. bow, reverent salutation.
  [√nam + pra.]
práṇīta, ppl. see √nī + pra; -ās, f. pl.
  holy water.
praṇīta-praṇayana, n. the fetching
  of the holy water. [1250e.]
pratarám, adv. further, longer. [pra,
  473², 1111c: cf. πρότερον, 'before.']
práti, prep. in reversed direction, back to,
  back against, against, in return; – 1. to,
  towards, w. acc., 2¹⁹, 23¹⁴; – 2. with
  reference to, in respect to, w. acc., 4⁷.¹⁷,
  13²⁰; – 3. over against, i.e. like; ÷4. in
  cpds [1313a]: before; on, w. idea of constant repetition; at; (back-, i.e.) reflected;
  see the following words. [cf. προτί, 'to';
  Lat. por- (•port) in por-rigere, 'reach out
  to.']
pratijñā, f. promise. [√jñā + prati.]
prati-dinam, adv. on (each) day, daily.
  [1313a, 1310a and d: cf. pratyaham.]
pratipatti, f. the acquiring. [√pad +
  prati.]

prati-bimba, *n.* reflected disk (of sun or moon in the water); image.

pratimā̆, *f.* match; image; likeness. [√1 mā̆ + prati, 'make (so as to be a match) against': for mg, cf. Eng. *counterfeit*, 'imitated,' fr. French *contre-fait*, whose elements go back to Lat. *contra* and *facere*.]

pratimā́na, *n.* that which is made *or* put over against, a match, equal. [√1 mā̆ + prati.]

pratiṣṭhā̆, *f.* stead; standing-place; *then* (*like Eng.* standing), position, *i.e.* celebrity. [√sthā̆ + prati.]

pratiṣṭhā́na, *n.* stead; *then* (*like Ger.* Stadt, 'place, town'), The Town, name of a town on the Godāvari, the Παίθανα of the Greeks. [√sthā̆ + prati, 1150: cf. *Hampstead.*]

pratihastaka, *m.* proxy. ['person at one's hand,' prati + hasta, 1310a, 1222c.]

pratīkāra, *m.* counter-action, remedy. [√1 kṛ, 'do, act,' + prati, 'against': 1087b.]

pratīcīna, *a.* backward; being behind; following, *i.e.* future. [pratyañc, 1223d.]

pratīta, *ppl. see* √i + prati.

pratīpá, *a.* (against the stream, *i.e.*) contrary; -ám, *adv.* contrarily, frowardly. [prati + ap, 1310a, 1315c, cf. samīpa: for mgs, cf. Eng. *contrary.*]

prátta, *see* 1087e.

pratyakṣa, *a.* before the eyes, plainly visible; -e, *adv.* before one's face. [prati + akṣa, 1310a.]

pratyakṣa-darçana, *n.* a seeing before one's eyes; the ability to see any one (*e.g.* a god) bodily, 15¹³.

pratyag-dakṣiṇa, *adv.* (west-southerly, *i.e.*) southwesterly. [pratyañc, 1249a.]

pratyañ-mukha, *a.* having the face westward, turned to the west. [pratyañc, 1249a, 161: 1306.]

pratyáñc [408], *f.* [410] pratīcī, *a.* —1. (directed back, *i.e.*) turned backwards; moving in reverse direction *or* away, 87¹¹; —2. turned westward (*see* prāñc), westerly; —3. (being to-ward, *i.e.*) with the face towards, *w. acc.*, 71¹³. [prati + añc, 407: see añc.]

praty-abhivādana, *n.* return-salutation, Gegen-gruss. [1289b.]

praty-aham, *adv.* on (each) day, daily. [1313a, 1310a and d: 1315a: cf. pratidinam.]

pratyākhyāna, *n.* refusal. [√khyā + praty-ā.]

pratyutthāna, *n.* rising up to meet (a person), respectful reception. [√sthā̆ + praty-ud, 233a.]

pratyutpanna-mati, *a.* having wits ready to meet an emergency; *as m.* Ready-wit, name of a fish. [√pad + praty-ud.]

pratyṛcam, *adv.* at *or* with each stanza. [prati + ṛc, 1313a, 1310a and d: 1315c.]

√ **prath** (práthate, -ti; paprathé; áprathiṣṭa; prathitá; pratháyati; ápaprathat). broaden, *intrans.*; *caus.* broaden, *trans.*; spread out, 78¹¹. [see under pṛthu.]

  + **vi**, *caus.* spread out wide, 75⁸.

prathamá, *a.* first; primal; -am, *adv.* at first. [lit. 'fore-most,' for ⚬pra-tama, superl. of pra, 487², 473².]

prathama-jā́ [352], *a.* first-born. [1286.]

prada, *a.* giving; furnishing. [√1 dā + pra, 333.]

pra-dakṣiṇa, —1. *a.* moving to the right; —2. -ám, *adv.* to the right, so that the right side is towards an object (a sign of respect), 60¹, 99¹; *w.* kṛ, put (an object) to the right; —3. *adj.* standing on the right, 62¹⁹. [perhaps the use as adv. (mg 2) is the primary one, lit. 'forward to the right.']

pradā́na, *n.* a giving. [√1 dā + pra.]

pradíç, *f.* intermediate region (between the cardinal points — *see* díç). [pra + díç, 'fore-point.']

pradeça, *m.* direction; *and so,* place. [√diç + pra.]

pradóṣa, *m.* evening, nightfall. ['fore-dark,' pra + doṣa.]

pradhána, *n.* prize of the contest; the contest therefor; battle. [√1 dhā + pra: cf. dhana.]

pradhāna, *n.* (that which is put forward) the important *or* chief thing; *at end of cpds* [1302], having ·· as chief thing, devoted to ··. [√1 dhā + pra.]

13*

prá-patha, m. (forth-path, i.e.) onward way, 85 18 ; journey in the distance or distant journey, 86 2.

prabandha, m. uninterrupted connection; continued series. [√bandh + pra.]

prabhavá, m. origin; at end of cpd [1302], having · · as origin, originating with · ·. [√bhū + pra.]

prabhā́, f. splendor; radiant beauty. [√bhā + pra.]

prabhāta, ppl. begun to be light; as n. [1176a], day-break. [√bhā + pra.]

prabhā́va, m. superior might, of gods, of ascetics, of asceticism. [√bhū + pra.]

prabhú, a. being before or superior to others; as m. ruler; master; lord; husband, 52 14. [later form (354) for Vedic prabhū́: √bhū + pra.]

prabhutva, n. lordship, power. [1239.]

prábhṛti, f. — 1. lit. a carrying forward or on, i.e. continuance; used esp. at end of cpds [1296], having continuance from · ·, i.e. continuing from · ·; — 2. then in such cpds used in acc. s. n. adverbially [1311], continuing from · ·, beginning with · ·, from · ·; — 3. then as an adv. uncompounded, prabhṛti, w. abl., from · · on; tataḥ prabhṛti, from then on. [√bhṛ + pra, 1157. 1d.]

pramada, m. pleasure. [√mad + pra.]

pramada-vana, n. pleasure-grove (of a prince).

pramadā-vana, n. pleasure-grove (of the wives of a prince). [a quasi feminine to the preceding.]

pramā́ṇa, n. measure, extent (57 28), scale, standard; something by which to judge, 54 11 ; norm, rule of action, 21 21 ; authority, 12 10, 19 22. [√1 mā, 'measure,' + pra, 192a: hence, through the Persian farmān, the borrowed Eng. firman, 'an authority or decree,' esp. of the Sublime Porte.]

√ pramāṇaya (pramāṇayati). regard as an authority; take a person (acc.) as authority in a matter (loc.). [pramāṇa, 1058.]

pramāṇābhāva, m. lack of anything to judge by. [abhāva.]

pramāthin, a. stirring; agitating [√math + pra, 1183 8.]

pramṛṣṭa-maṇi, m. polished or bright gem. [√mṛj + pra.]

pramṛṣṭamaṇi-kuṇḍala, a. possessing bright-gem ear-rings.

prayatna, m. effort, pains; -ena, -āt, adv. carefully. [√yat + pra, 1177a.]

prayā́ṇa, n. a going forth (from home), journey. [√yā + pra, 1150, 192c.]

prayotṛ́, m. remover. [√2 yu, 'keep off,' + pra.]

pralaya, m. dissolution; esp. dissolution of the universe. [√lī + pra.]

pralāpá, m. unintelligible or childish or lamenting talk; chatter. [√lap · pra.]

pravaṇá, a. prone; sloping. [pra, 1170 (cf. 383d 1): cf. πρηνής, Doric πρᾱνός, Lat. prōnus, 'inclined forward.']

pravát, f. slope, of a mountain; height, 83 7. [pra, 383d 1.]

prá-vayas, a. having (forward, i.e.) advanced age; aged. [1305 2.]

pravartaka, a. causing to roll onward (as a wheel), setting in motion, promoting; as m. promoter, prompter. [caus. of √vṛt + pra.]

pravāda, m. a saying or an on dit. [√vad + pra.]

pravibhāga, m. division. [√bhaj · pra-vi.]

praviṇa, a. clever.

praviṇatā, f. cleverness. [praviṇa.]

pravṛtta, ppl. — 1. having turned forward; directed forward (to a specific object), esp. of an act performed with a view to the attainment of some advantage, i.e. interested, opp. of nivṛtta, q.v.; — 2. engaged in. [√vṛt + pra.]

pravṛtti, f. a moving forward or taking an active step, 20 15 ; advance into or exposure of one's self to (danger, loc.), 20 12. [√vṛt + pra.]

pravṛddha, ppl. grown up, great. [√vṛdh + pra.]

praveça, m. entrance. [√viç + pra.]

pravrājin, a. going forth or after, in cpd dvi-. [√vraj + pra, 1183 8 : for mg, cf. (γυνὴ) περίδρομος, 'lewd woman.']

praçíṣ [392], f. command. [√çās + pra, 639, 225¹·²: cf. āçíṣ.]

praçraya, m. respectful demeanor. ['an inclining forward,' fr. √çri + pra.]

pra-savya, a. moving to the left; -am, adv. to the left — cf. pradakṣiṇam.

prasāda, m. grace; favor; prasādaṁ kṛ, do favor, be gracious. [√sad + pra, q.v.]

prásiti, f. continuation; extended path (of life, for example). [√sā + pra, 250.]

prasiddhi, f. success; celebrity; a being known; ato me çaçāṅka iti prasiddhis, therefore I am known as "Ç.", 36⁸; cf. prasiddha. [√2 sidh, 'succeed,' + pra.]

prastará, m. — 1. stramentum, straw; — 2. rock, 33¹⁰. [√stṛ, 'strew,' + pra: for mg 1, cf. Eng. straw w. strew: connection of mg 2 unclear.]

prastāva, m. beginning, introduction. [√stu + pra, 1148. 2.]

prastuta-yajña, a. having one's sacrifice begun; as m. Prastutayajna, name of a Brahman. [√stu + pra.]

prastha, m. n. table-land on a mountain. ['that which stands forth from the surrounding country,' fr. √sthā (333) + pra.]

prá-svādas, a. (lit. having advanced agreeableness, i.e.) highly pleasing. [1305².]

prahara, m. a stroke (on a gong, announcing the lapse of a watch), and so a watch (of about three hours). [√1 hṛ + pra.]

prahartavya, grdv. to be struck; impers. one must strike. [do.]

prahṛṣṭa-manas, a. having a delighted heart. [√hṛṣ + pra.]

√ prā (práti; paprāú; áprās [889]; prā-tá). fill. [Vedic collateral form of √1 pṛ, 'fill,' q.v.: cf. πλή-ρης, Lat. plē-nus, 'full.'] + ā, fill.

prák, see prāñc.

prákṛta, a. natural; usual; common; vulgar; as n. the vulgar (language), language of the vulgus, the Prākrit. [prakṛti, 1208d: for mg, cf. Ger. deutsch, Old High Ger. diut-isk, '(language) of the people (diot), i.e. German' (as contrasted with the Latin of the Church and with the neighboring Romance tongues); cf. also ἡ κοινή (sc. διάλεκτος), 'the Common (dialect),' as opp. to Doric, etc.]

prāg-grīva, a. having the neck directed eastward. [prāñc (1249a) ; grīvā.]

prāg-dakṣiṇā, adv. east-southerly, south-easterly. [prāñc, 1249a.]

prāṅgaṇa, n. fore-court, Vor-hof; court-yard. [pra + aṅgana, 1289a, 193.]

prāṅ-mukha, f. -ī, a. having the face directed eastward. [prāñc, 1249a, 149, 161.]

prājñá, a. wise; as m. wise man. [prajñā, 1208e.]

prāñc [408], f. prācí, a. — 1. directed forwards; w. verb of motion, onward, 86⁹; — 2. east, eastern (since the Hindus, in naming the cardinal points, began with the east, as we do with the north, and conceived it as before them, as we do the north); prācī diç, the eastern quarter, 101⁸; — 3. prák, acc. s. n. as adv. before: (in place) before one's face, 26⁸; (in time) formerly, 20²⁰, 51⁷; (in order) before, w. abl. [1128], 59⁷. [pra + añc, 407.]

prāñjali, a. having an añjali (q.v.) before one, i.e. in a posture of reverent salutation. [pra + añjali, 1305.]

prāṇá, m. breath; vital breath, 60¹⁶; vital spirit, 63²¹; then (like Eng. breath), life; esp. in pl. prāṇās, life, 15⁵, 21¹⁸, 29⁸. [√an + pra, 192b.]

prāṇín, a. having life; as m. living being. [prāṇa, 1230.]

prātár, adv. — 1. early in the morning; then — 2. (like the Ger. morgen and Eng. morrow) on the next morning, on the morrow, to-morrow. [pra, 1109: cf. πρω-ΐ, Ger. früh, 'early.']

prādús, adv. forth to view; w. as [1078⁶], be visible, appear, reveal one's self.

prāntara, n. a long and lonely road. ['an advanced interval or long distance,' pra + antara, 1289.]

prāpaṇīya, grdv. to be brought to. [caus. of √āp + pra, 965, 192c.]

prāpta-kāla, m. arrived time, favorable moment. [√āp + pra.]

prāpta-yāuvana, a. possessing attained adolescence, having reached a marriageable age. [see 1308.]

prāptavya, *grdv.* to be obtained, about to be got. [√āp + pra, 964.]

prā́pti, *f.* a reaching, arriving at. [√āp + pra.]

prāyá, *m.* —1. a going forth *or* out; —2. that which sticks out *or* is prominent; the principal part of a thing; the most part; *at end of cpds* [1302], having ·· for the most part, having ·· for its predominant characteristic, like ··, 22[16]. [√i + pra, 1148. 1a.]

prāyaças, *adv.* for the most part. [prāya, 1106.]

prāyas, *adv.* for the most part, almost, 50[22]. [prop. acc. s. n. (1111d) of a neuter noun ●prāyas, 'that which is predominant' (see prāya), √i + pra, 1151. 1.]

prāví, *a.* attentive, heedful, zealous. [√av + pra, 1156[8], 355b end.]

prāçana, *n.* —1. the eating; —2. the giving of food, feeding. [in mg 1, fr. √2aç, 'eat,' + pra; in mg 2, fr. caus. of the same.]

prāçitṛ́, *m.* eater. [√2aç, 'eat,' + pra, 1182a.]

prāçitrá, *n.* the portion of ghee to be eaten by a Brahman at a sacrifice. ['that which belongs to the prāçitṛ,' 1208b.]

prāçitra-háraṇa, *n.* vessel for holding the prāçitra. ['prāçitra-holding,' 1271.]

prāsāda, *m.* lofty seat; building on high foundations, palace, 20[1]. [√sad + pra, perhaps in the sense 'sit forward *or* in a conspicuous place': see 1087b.]

priyá, *a.* —1a. dear, 79[16]; beloved of, *w. gen.* (296b), 84[18]; —1b. priyā́, *f.* the beloved, the wife, 32[6], 33[10]; —2a. desired, pleasant; agreeable, 58[22]; priyaṁ kṛ, do a favor, 3[2]; —2b. *as n.* that which is desired, one's wish, 89[17]; —3. (*like Homeric* φίλος) to which one is attached *or* wonted, 76[5], 86[8]; own, 78[9]; wonted; —4a. loving, devoted to; —4b. *as m.* friend. [√prī, q.v., 1148. 3 : cf. πρᾷος, 'gentle'; Goth. *freis,* acc. s. m. *frijana,* AS. *fri,* Ger. *frei,* Eng. *free:* although the modern mg 'free' is common also to the Goth. and AS. words, yet the orig. mg

must have been 'loving *or* loved, kindly treated, spared' (and so 'free'), as is shown by the Goth. abstract *frija-þva,* AS. *freōd,* 'love': for mg 1b, cf. AS. *freō,* 'woman': cf. also Old High Ger. *Fria,* 'The Loving One,' in *friā tag,* Eng. *Fri-day,* 'dies Veneris.']

priya-vādín, *a.* saying pleasant things.

priyā́priyá, *n.* comfort and discomfort. [apriya: 1253b.]

√ prī (prīṇā́ti, prīṇīté; prīyate; pipráya, pipriyé; ápraiṣīt; prītá; prītvā́). —1a. prīṇā́ti, gladden, show favor to, propitiate; —1b. prīṇā́ti, have pleasure in; —1c. prīṇīté, be glad *or* content; —2. prīyate, be glad *or* content; have pleasure in; love, be favorably inclined to; —3. prītá : glad, pleased, satisfied; loved, dear. [cf. Goth. *frijon,* 'love'; *frijonds,* AS. *freōnd,* 'loving, *i.e.* friend,' Eng. *friend;* also AS. *freo-þo,* 'a sparing *or* indulgence, favor, grace, peace,' Ger. *Friede,* 'peace'; Goth. *Friþa-reiks,* Eng. *Frede-rick,* 'grace-ruler, gracious prince': see also under priyá.]

prīti, *f.* —1. pleasure; prītyā, with pleasure, gladly; —2. friendship. [√prī.]

prīti-vacas, *n.* friendship-talk, friendly words.

preṅkhá, *a.* rocking, pitching; *as m. n.* unsteady boat, skiff. [√iṅkh + pra.]

préta, *ppl.* gone onward, *i.e.* departed, dead; *as m.* ·—1. dead man; —2. ghost. [√i + pra.]

prétya, *grd.* after dying, *i.e.* in the other world (*opp. to* iha). [√i + pra, 992.]

préṣṭha, *a.* very pleasant. [√prī, 470[4]: serves as superl. to priya.]

preṣya, *grdv.* to be sent; *as m.* servant. [√2iṣ, 'send,' + pra.]

praiṣyá, *n.* servitude. [preṣya, 1208f.]

próṣṭha, *m.* bench *or* couch. ·

proṣṭhe-çayá, *a.* lying on a couch. [1250c, 1270.]

plavá, *a.* swimming; *as m.* swimmer, name of a kind of duck. [√plu: cf. πλόος, ●πλοϜος, 'a sailing.']

√ plu (plávate, -ti; puplāva, pupluvé; áploṣṭa; ploṣyáti, -te; plutá; -plútya, -plúya). float through water *or* air:

—1. swim; —2. bathe; —3. sail; —4. hover; fly; —5. fly off; hasten away; —6. spring; —pluta, floating, and so (see Whitney 78), protracted, of a vowel.

[cf. πλέω, «πλεΈω, 'float, sail'; Lat. *pluere*, 'rain': for mg of *pluere*, cf. the Eng. intrans. *float*, 'swim,' w. trans. *float*, 'cover with water,' and the intrans. *bathe* w. trans. *bathe:*

closely connected w. √plu is the extended form plud_as seen in Lithuanian *plud-iti*, 'swim, float': w. this, cf. AS. *fleót-an*, 'swim or float about,' Eng. verb *fleet*, 'float, sail, hasten,' Ger. *fliessen*, sometimes 'swim,' but usually 'flow'; further, AS. *fleót*, 'raft, ship, fleet,' Eng. *fleet*, 'ships'; also AS. *flota*, 'ship,' Eng. *float*, 'a thing that swims on the surface of a fluid, e.g. a raft' (verb *float* is a denom. of this), Ger. *Floss*, 'raft'; finally Eng. *fleet*, 'streamlet or bay,' whence *The Fleet*, as name of a small affluent of the Thames at London and of a famous prison thereon, and *Fleet Street*, which crossed The Fleet.]

+ ā, bathe, *intrans.*

+ sam-ā, —1. bathe, *intrans.;* —2. bathe, *trans.;* inundate; suffuse, 10 [19].

+ ud, spring up.

+ upa, hover unto.

+ vi, float asunder; drift in different directions; be dispersed; be lost; be ruined or dishonored.

√ phal (phálati; paphála; phalitá; phullá [958]). burst, split, *intrans.* [prob. for •spal, of which √sphaṭ (i.e. •sphalt), 'split, break,' is an extension: cf. Ger. *spalten*, Eng. *split*.]

+ ud, burst out or open; utphulla [958], expanded, wide open.

√ phala (phalati). bear fruit; fruit; phalitám, *impersonally*, it is fruited, fruit is borne (by a thing, *instr.*), 24 [20]. [denom. of phála, 1054.]

phála, n. —1. fruit; —2. *then (like Eng. fruit)*, the good or evil consequences of human deeds; result; reward or punishment. [perhaps 'the ripe and bursting fruit,' fr. √phal.]

phálavant, a. fruitful; yielding good results. [phála, 1233a.]

phulla, a. burst open, expanded, blooming. [see √phal and 958.]

phullotpala, a. having blooming lotuses; as n. Blooming-lotus, name of a lake. [utpala.]

phéna, m. foam.

√ baṅh or bah (bādhá [223³]; *caus.* baṅháyate). be thick, firm, strong; *caus.* make strong. [perhaps for •bhagh: see bahú and bāhú.]

baka, m. heron, Ardea nivea.

baka-mūrkha, m. heron-fool, fool of a heron. [1280b.]

baddha-maṇḍala, a. having constructed-circles, i.e. ranged in circles. [√bandh.]

√ bandh (badhnáti, badhnīté [730]; babándha, bedhé; bandhiṣyáti, bhantsyáti; baddhá; bándhitum, bánddhum, báddhum; baddhvá; -bádhya). —1. bind; fasten; catch; *esp.* bind (a victim for the gods, *i.e.*), sacrifice; —baddha: bound; caught; fastened; —2. bind together, join; *and then (w. a specialization of mg like that seen in the Eng. joiner)*, construct, *e.g.* a bridge; compose (verses, cf. Lat. serere). [for •bhandh: cf. πενθ-ερός, 'connection (by marriage)'; πεῖσμα, •πενθμα, 'rope'; Lat. *of-fend-ix*, 'knot'; *fīd-es*, 'string'; *foed-us*, 'league'; Eng. *bind, band:* for mgs, cf. Eng. *connection* and *league* w. Lat. *con-nectere* and *ligāre*, 'bind together.']

+ ni, —1. bind; fasten; —2. (bind down together, put down connectedly, *i.e.*) put into written form, write down, 53 [6].

+ pra, bind on; connect onward, form an advancing connection, form a continued series.

+ sam, bind together, con-nect; sambaddha, con-nected, co-herent (w. the same fig. mg as in Eng.).

bandhá, m. —1. a binding; *esp.* a binding to the sacrificial post (see bandh 1), sacrifice; —2. band, string. [√bandh: cf. Eng. *band.*]

bándhana, *a.* binding; *as n.* bond *or* bonds. [√bandh.]

bándhu, *m.* —1. connection *or* relationship; —2. (*concrete, as in Eng.*) a connection, relative; friend; one who belongs to (a certain caste, *for example*). [√bandh, 1178.]

barbara, *a.* stammering, balbutiens; *as m.* —1. *pl.* foreigners, οἱ βάρβαροι, name applied by Aryans to non-Aryan folks (*as Welsh and Wälsch by English and Germans to folks that speak a strange tongue*); —2. *sing.* a man of lowest origin; a wretched wight, wretch, 30¹⁰. [cf. βάρβαρος, 'foreign, outlandish'; Lat. *balbus*, 'stammering,' whence Spanish *bobo*, 'blockhead,' Eng. *booby.*]

barha, *m. n.* tail-feather. [prop. 'pluckings,' √1 bṛh, 'pluck': cf. the no less arbitrary specialization of mg in Eng. *pluck*, 'that which is plucked out after killing a beast, its liver, lights, heart,' and, fig., 'courage.']

barhiṇa, *m.* peacock, 68². [transition-stem fr. **barhin**, 1223f, 1209c.]

barhin, *m.* (having tail-feathers, *i.e.* the tail-feathered bird κατ' ἐξοχήν,) the peacock. [barha.]

barhís, *n.* grass *or* straw of Kuça-grass, spread over the sacrificial ground to serve as a place for the oblations and as a seat for gods and offerers. [prop. 'that which is torn up, vulsum, pluckings,' √1 bṛh, 'tear, pluck': for mg, cf. Eng. *hay*, 'cuttings,' from *hew*, 'cut.']

bála, *n.* —1. might, power, strength, force; **balāt**, forcibly; —2. *then, as in Eng.*, force (for making war); forces, troops, 5⁴. [for *vala: cf. Lat. *valēre*, 'be strong, well.']

bala-dá [352], *a.* strength-giving. [1269.]

bálavant, *a.* powerful. [1233a.]

balādhika, *a.* superior in strength. [adhika: 1265.]

balānvita, *a.* connected with power; suggestive of power. [anv-ita, √i.]

balí, *m.* —1. of-fering, tribute; —2. *esp.* portion of a daily meal *or* sacrifice offered as tribute to gods, semi-divine beings, men, animals, *esp.* birds, and even inanimate objects, 65². [perhaps fr. √bhṛ;

if so, cf., for the mg, φόρος, 'tribute,' w φέρω, 'bear, bring.']

balín, *a.* mighty, 1⁸. [bála, 1230a.]

báliṣṭha, *a.* most mighty; very strong. [balin, 468².]

balonmatta, *a.* frenzied *or* crazed with power. [unmatta, √mad + ud.]

√ bah, see **baṅh**.

bahiṣ-kārya, *grdv.* to be put outside, to be banished. [bahis and kṛ, 'do, put,' 1078⁷.]

bahiṣ-kṛta, *ppl.* put out, expelled. [bahis and kṛ, 'do, put,' 1078⁷.]

bahiḥ-paridhi, *adv.* outside the enclosure (*see* paridhi). [1310a.]

bahís, *adv.* [1111d], outside; *as prep.* outside of, *w. abl.* [1128].

bahú, *a.* much, many; **bahu man**, consider as much, think much of, esteem. [√baṅh or bah: cf. παχύς, 'thick.']

bahudhá, *adv.* many times. [bahu, 1104.]

bahumāna, *m.* esteem, respect. [√man + bahu.]

bahumāna-puraḥsaram, *adv.* with respect. [1302c 2, 1311.]

bahulá, *a.* —1. thick; —2. abundant; much. [in mg 1, perhaps directly fr. √bah, 1189, and in mg 2, fr. bahu, 1227.]

bahulāuṣadhika, *a.* having abundant herbs. [oṣadhi, 1307.]

√ bādh (**bádhate**; babādhé; ábādhiṣṭa; bādhiṣyáti, -te; bādhitá; bádhitum; -bádhya). press hard; distress; beset. [see √vadh: cf. Lat. *de-fend-ere*, 'press or ward off'; *of-fend-ere*, 'press hard upon, hurt.']

+ ni, press down heavily.

bādhá, *a.* distressing; *as m.* distress. [√bādh.]

bándhava, *m.* (having connection *or* relationship, *i.e.*) a relative; friend. [bándhu, 1208c.]

bāla, *a.* young, not grown; *as subst. m. and f.* —1. child (*distinguished from* yuvan, 'young man,' 28¹²); boy; girl; —2. *applied to a grown person* (*cf. Eng.* childish, puerile), child *or* booby, *w. double* mg, 61²¹.

bālaka, *a.* young; *as m.* child. [bāla.]

bālāpatya, n. young offspring, of men and of animals. [apatya.]

bāṣpa, m. tears.

bāṣpākula, a. agitated by tears. [ākula.]

bāhú, m. arm; esp. fore-arm; of beasts, the fore-leg, esp. the upper part thereof, 101¹⁹. [for ⸱bhāghú: cf. πῆχυς, Doric πᾶχυς, ⸱φαχυς, 'fore-arm'; AS. bóg, 'arm' and 'arm of a tree, i.e. branch,' Eng. bough, 'arm of a tree,' Ger. Bug, 'shoulder, hip'; also Dutch boeg, Eng. bow, 'shoulder of a ship,' bow-sprit, 'bow-spar.']

bāhu-yuddha, n. arm-fight, wrestling.

bāhulya, n. abundance; commonness, state of being usual; concretely, usual order of things; -āt, from or in accordance with the usual order of things, in all probability, 24²¹. [bahula, 1211.]

bāhya, a. being outside, external; at end of cpds, equiv. to Eng. extra- at beg. of cpds. [bahís, 1211: cf. 1208a² end.]

biḍāla, m. cat.

bimba, m. n. disk of sun or moon.

bíla, n. cleft; hollow. [perhaps fr. √bil or bid, collateral forms of bhid, 'cleave.']

bíja, n. seed, of plants and animals.

buddhá, ppl. awakened; illuminé; enlightened; —esp., as m. The Enlightened One, epithet of Gautama of the Çākya tribe. [√budh: for budh-ta (160), the formal equivalent of -πνθ-το- in ἄπυστος, 'not having learned.']

buddhi, f. —1. insight, understanding, intellect; mind, 13¹³; wit, wits; —2. mind in the sense of opinion (as in Eng.); belief; at end of cpds: vyāghra-buddhyā, with tiger-belief, (mistakenly) thinking that it was a tiger, 34¹⁵; —3. mind in the sense of purpose, resolve (as in Eng.); buddhim kṛ, make up one's mind, 58¹²; buddhim pra-kṛ, mid., put a plan before one's self, decide, 9¹¹. [√budh, 1157: for budh-ti (160), the formal equivalent of πύστις, πνθ-τι-ς, 'an inquiring.']

buddhi-jīvin, a. living by one's mind, employing one's intelligence, intelligent.

buddhimant, a. possessing understanding; intelligent.

√ budh (bódhati, -te; búdhyate; bubódha, bubudhé; ábuddha [160]; bhotsyáti,

-te; buddhá; bóddhum; buddhvá; -búdhya). —1. be awake; —2. come to consciousness; hence —3. notice; give heed to, w. gen., 76¹²; —4. notice, i.e. perceive; and so, become acquainted with; understand; —5. rarely, (like Eng. remember a person, i.e.) presént a person with a thing (instr.); —caus. —6a. cause to notice or understand; —6b. teach; announce to.

[for ⸱bhudh, orig. 'be awake,' cf. Church Slavonic bŭd-ěti, 'be awake': the cognate words of the related languages agree closely in form, but show considerable diversity of mgs: mg 4 mediates the transition to the idea of the Greek √πνθ, ⸱φνθ, in πνθίσθαι, 'find out': mgs 5 and 6 form the bridge to the principal Germanic mgs, 'offer' and 'command': cf. Goth. ana-biud-an, (prob. 'give notice to,' and so) 'command,' AS. beód-an, 'announce, offer, command,' Eng. bid, 'announce, offer in words, offer in general, esp. at an auction, declare, proclaim, command, invite,' Ger. biet-en, 'offer'; (from an entirely different root is Eng. bid, AS. biddan, Ger. bitten, 'pray,' as in bid beads, 'pray prayers'); cf. also Eng. noun bode, 'announcement,' whence denom. verb bode, 'foretell': for mg 5, observe the analogy of Ger. Jemand bedenken, 'remember or take notice of a person esp. in one's will, i.e. make a bequest to.']

+ ni, attend to, 58¹; understand, know, 7⁹.

+ pra, come forth (from sleep) to consciousness; awake, intrans.

+ prati, awake, intrans.; awake, trans., 76⁸.

budha, a. awake; intelligent; wise; as m. wise man. [√budh.]

bubhukṣā, f. desire to eat, hunger. [fr. desid. of √2 bhuj, 'frui,' 1149⁴.]

√ 1 bṛh, collateral form of √ vṛh, 'pluck,' q.v.

√ 2 bṛh (bṛ́hati, -te; babárha; bṛḍhá; caus. bṛṃháyati, -te). be thick, great, strong, in bṛhánt, q.v.; caus. make great, strengthen.

bṛh, f. prayer, conceived as a swelling and filling of the heart in devotion. [√2 bṛh.]

bṛhat-kathā, f. Great-Story, title of a collection of stories ascribed to Gunādhya (guṇādhya), and abridged by Soma-deva under the name Kathāsaritsāgara. [bṛhant, 1249a, 1279.]

bṛhád-açva, a. possessing great or powerful horses; as m. Brihadaçva, name of the sage who narrates the story of Nala to Yudhishthira. [bṛhánt (1249a) + áçva, 1298: cf. •Meydλ-ιττος, which is similarly compounded and of like meaning.]

bṛhánt [450a], a. great; mighty; lofty. [present ppl. of √2 bṛh, 'be great.']

bṛ́has-páti, m. Brihaspati, name of a divinity in which the activity of the pious in their relations towards the gods is per-sonified, the mediator between gods and men, and the type of the priest and of the priestly dignity; later, god of wisdom and eloquence. ['lord of prayer,' bṛ́h-as + páti: for cpd, see 1250 and d, and 1267d; for acct, Whitney 94b; for eu-phony, 171².]

bāijika, a. pertaining to the semen; of guilt, inherited from one's father. [bīja, 1222e and e2.]

brahma-cárya, n. life of holiness (bráhman), walk and conversation of a Brahman student (brahmán), esp. cha-tity; religious studentship, the first of the four periods of a Brahman's life, see āçrama. [bráhman (1249a²) or brahmán (probably both) + carya, equiv. of caryā: acct, 1272, 1213c.]

brahma-cārín, a. (busying one's self with, i.e.) studying sacred knowledge; as m. Brahman student, 65⁸; as adj. esp. observing chastity, 64¹⁴, 100²¹. [bráh-man, 1249a².]

brahmaṇyà, a. pertaining or attached to the holy life and study (bráhman), i.e. pious; attached or friendly to Brahmans (brahmán). [1212d 1.]

brahma-dāya, m. sacred-word heritage, heritage consisting of the sacred word. [bráhman, 1249a².]

brahmadāya-hara, a. receiving the sacred word as a heritage.

brahma-dviṣ, a. devotion-hating, god-less. [bráhman, 1249a²: acct, 1269.]

bráhman, n. —1. devotion (conceived as a swelling and filling of the soul with adoration for the gods), worship, in gen-eral, any pious expression in the worship of the gods; hymn of praise, praise, 73⁶·¹⁰, 74⁴·¹¹; prayer, 76¹⁵; —2. sacred word, word of God (opp. to the profane), 60⁸; —3. divine science, 57¹⁵; sacred learning, theology, theosophy; —4. holy life, i.e. chastity; —5. the (impersonal) spirit that pervades the universe. [√2 bṛh, 1168.1c: bráhman (n.) is to brahmán (m.) as prayer ('supplication') is to pray-er ('supplicant').]

brahmán, m. —1. pray-er, 76¹⁸; wor-shipper; priest, 88⁹, RV. x. 125.5; pray-er by profession, Brahman; —2. the imper-sonal universe-pervading spirit (bráhman 5), personified as a god, i.e. Brahmán, the Supreme All-soul, 57⁴·⁸; in the theological system, the Creator of the world, 67¹⁷. [√2 bṛh, see bráhman.]

brahmarṣi, m. priest-sage, priestly sage, see 1¹⁴ N. [brahmán (1249a²) + ṛṣi, 127, 1280b.]

brahmavarcasá, n. pre-eminence in sacred learning or holiness. [for brah-mavarcas, which occurs only in derivs. brahmán (1249a²) + várcas, 1315c.]

brahmavarcasvin, a. eminent in divine knowledge. ['possessing brahma-varcasa,' q.v.: 1232.]

brahma-vedin, a. knowing divine knowledge. [bráhman, 1249a².]

brahma-hán [402], a. Brahman-slaying; as m. murderer of a Brahman. [brah-man, 1249a².]

bráhmá, f. -ī, a. —1. pertaining to bráh-man, divine; holy, 59⁶; spiritual, 61¹⁵; —2. pertaining to brahmán, in both its senses, i.e.: —2a. of Brahmans; —2b. of Brahmán or (anglicized) Brahma, the Creator, 57²⁸, 58⁹. [bráhman and brah-mán, 1208a² end.]

bráhmaṇá, m. (having to do with bráh-man or prayer and praise and divine science, i.e.) priest, 84¹⁵; theologian, Brahman, 57¹⁶; —f. bráhmaṇī, woman of the priestly caste, Brahmanee. [bráh-man, w. usual shift of acct, 1208a.]

brâhmaṇa, n. (of a brahmán, of a priest or Brahman, i.e.) the dictum of a priest on matters of faith and cultus; esp. a Brāhmana, as designation of one of a class of Vedic writings which contain these dicta. [brahmán, w. usual shift of acct, 1208a.]

brâhmaṇa-vâda, m. a statement of the Brāhmaṇas. [brâhmaṇa.]

√ brū (brávīti [632], brūté: the second clause of 632 should read "before the initial consonant of an ending"). —1. act. say; w. dat. of person and acc. of thing, 10²¹, 96¹⁴; w. acc. of person and either oratio recta (12⁵, 60⁷·²³, 98¹¹) or else acc. of thing (95¹⁸); speak to, w. acc. of person, 3¹⁴; speak of, w. acc. of person, 11¹⁸; say, i.e. announce, tell; w. vacas, ἔπος εἰπεῖν, 10¹⁸; w. punar, answer, 8⁸; —2. middle, brūté (used esp. to introduce oratio recta and without designation of the person addressed), says, inquit, 20¹⁸, 28¹, 30⁵·¹⁰·¹², 35¹⁸.

+ apa, remove (the thought or recollection of a thing or person, acc., from a person, abl.) by speaking, i.e. try to console a person (abl.) for the loss of a thing or person (acc.), 92¹⁴. [this locution is apparently like the Eng. colloq. phrase "I'll talk it (his opinion) out of him."]

+ pra, tell forth, proclaim, 75¹⁸; announce, 88⁷; then (like the Eng. tell of, bad and colloquial tell on), inform against, betray, 93¹⁷.

+ prati, speak back to (acc.), answer.

———

√ bhakṣ (bhákṣati, -te; bhakṣitá; bhákṣitum; -bhákṣya; bhakṣáyati [1041²]). (partake, enjoy, i.e.) eat; consume; devour. [old desid. of √bhaj, 108g end: cf. bhíkṣ, and for mg, √2 aç, 'eat.']

bhakṣá, m. the enjoying, eating or drinking; food; at end of adj. cpds, having ·· as food, living on ·. [√bhakṣ.]

bhakṣaka, m. eater. [√bhakṣ: see 1181a end.]

bhakṣitavya, grdv. to be eaten. [√bhakṣ, 964².]

bhakṣin, a. eating. [√bhakṣ, 1183⁸.]

bhakṣya, grdv. to be eaten, eatable; as n. proper food. [√bhakṣ, 963.]

bhága, m. —1. (he who deals out, i.e.) dispenser; rich or kind master; lord, frequent epithet of Savitar — so 74¹⁷; —2. esp. Bhaga, name of an Aditya, from whom welfare is expected and who brings about love and institutes marriage, 89⁶: —3. portion; lot (w. dur-, su-); fortune; esp. (as in Eng.), good fortune, happy lot; —4. loveliness. [√bhaj, 216.1: —1. cf. Old Persian baga, 'God'; Βαγαῖος· Ζεὺς Φρύγιος; Slavonic bogŭ, 'God'; for mg, cf. Eng. lord, AS. hláf-ord (⤳hláf-weard?), 'loaf-ward, loaf-keeper'; —3. for mg, cf. the relation of μόρος, 'lot, fate,' to ἔμ-μορ-ε, 'gat a share.']

bhágavant, a. —1. fortunate, possessing a happy lot, blessed; then —2. (like Eng. blessed) heavenly, august, lordly, applied to Indra, Brahma, The Self-existent, the Wood-deity, Sun, Moon, Earth, etc.; used, esp. in voc., as a form of address, so 94⁸, 26⁴. [bhága.]

bhagín, a. fortunate; happy; splendid; —bhaginī, f. sister (the happy one — so far forth as she has a brother). [bhága.]

bhagiratha, m. Bhagīratha, name of an ancient king, who brought the Ganges down from heaven. [perhaps fr. bhagin + ratha, 'having a splendid chariot.']

bhagna, see 957c.

bhagna-bhâṇḍa, a. having broken pots or [1308] who broke the pots.

bhagnâça, a. having broken hopes, disappointed. [âçá, 334².]

bhaṅgá, m. a breaking. [√bhañj, 216.1.]

√ bhaj (bhájati, -te; babhája, bhejé [794e]; ábhākṣīt, ábhakta [883]; bhajiṣyáti, -te; bhaktá; bháktum; bhaktvá; -bhájya; caus. bhājáyati). —1. deal out; apportion; divide; then (as Eng. share means both 'give a part of' and 'have a part of') —2. middle, have as one's part, receive; have or take part in; —3. give one's self up to; —4. (choose as one's part, i.e.) declare one's self for, prefer, 15³; —5. betake one's self to; turn to; go to, 20¹⁰, —6. belong to, be attached to; revere;

love, 9²⁰; —caus. cause to have a share, w. acc. of person and gen. of thing, 83⁵.

[cf. φαγ-εῖν, 'get one's portion, eat,' w. a specialization of mg like those seen in Eng. partake and take as used with the implied object food or drink, in bhaktá, 'thing divided, portion, food,' and in bhakṣ: akin are the names of the two food-trees yielding eatable nuts (acorns, buck-mast), φᾱγός, φηγός, 'oak,' Lat. fāgus, 'beech,' AS bōc, Eng. buck-, 'beech-,' in buck-mast, 'beech-nuts,' and buck-wheat (so called from the likeness of the kernels to beech-nuts), AS. bēce, Eng. beech: with bōc, 'beech,' is ident. bōc, 'book,' orig. 'runes scratched on branches of a fruit-bearing tree,' see Tacitus, Germania, x.; such a branch was called by a name which became in Old High Ger. puah-stap or buoh-stab, and meant orig. 'beech-staff'; but the word came to be used for the significant thing on the branch, 'the rune or letter,' AS bōc-stæf, Ger. Buch-stabe.]

+ ā, act., sometimes mid., deal out to, give a person (acc.) a share in a thing (loc.).

+ vi, part asunder; divide.

+ pra-vi, divide.

+ sam-vi, —1. divide a thing (acc.) with a person (instr.); give a share; —2. present a person (acc.) with a thing (instr.).

ⵏ bhañj (bhanákti; babháñja; ábhāṅkṣīt; bhaṅkṣyáti; bhagná [957c]; bhaṅktvā́; -bhájya). break. [opinions are divided as to whether ⵏⵏbhañj, 2 bhuj, and bhām (see these) orig. began w. bhr-; cf giri-bhrāj, 'breaking forth from the mountains': if bhañj does stand for ⵏbhrañj, then Lat. frangere, 'break,' nau-frag-a, 'ship-breaking' (tempestas), and Ger brechen, Eng. break are akin.]

bhaṭṭāra, m. lord. [a transition-stem (399) fr. bhartṛ: corresponding to the strong acc. s. form bhartār-am, taken as if it were bhartāra-m, is made the nom. s. bhartāra-s, etc.; both transition to the a-declension and assimilation of rt to ṭṭ are regular in Prakrit.]

bhaṭṭāraka, m. lord, applied to gods and learned men. [bhaṭṭāra, 1222c 1.]

bhaṭṭāraka-vāra, m. lord's day, Sunday.

bhadrá, a. —1. praiseworthy, pleasing; gladsome, 76⁴, 90¹⁷; —2. good, happy, 84⁸; voc. f., good lady, 9¹⁰; bhadram, adv., w. kṛ or ā-car, do well, 22¹⁷, 23¹⁹; —3. favorable, auspicious, 86⁸; —as n., sing. and pl., welfare, prosperity, 20¹⁶; w. kṛ, grant welfare to a person (dat.), bless, 69¹¹. [ⵏbhand, 1188a.]

bhadra-kṛt, a. granting welfare; blessing. [1269.]

ⵏ bhand (bhándate). receive jubilant praise.

bhándiṣṭha, a. most loudly or best praising.

bhayá, n. —1. fear, anxiety; in composition w. the thing feared, 10¹², 31⁹, 46⁸; fear of a thing (abl.), 40¹⁴; bhayāt, from fear, 20¹⁰, 36⁴, 41¹⁷; then, as conversely in Eng., fear (orig. 'danger,' so Job 39. 22) has come to mean 'anxiety,' —2. danger, peril, 25¹⁹, 42⁵·⁴. [ⵏbhī, 1148. 1a: for mg 2, cf. samdeha.]

bhayā́rta, a. stricken with fear. [ārta.]

bhārá, m. —1. a bearing, carrying; —2. burden; weight, 50¹; —3. mass, quantity; —4. (w. specialization as in Lat. pondus, 'weight,' then also 'pound') a particular quantity or measure, in nir-. [ⵏbhṛ: cf. φωσ-φόρο-s, Lat. luci-fer(u-s), 'light-bringing'; AS. horn-bora, 'hornbearing, trumpeter': for mgs 2–4, cf. Eng. weigh, orig. 'bear up, lift,' as in weigh anchor, AS. wegan, 'carry, bear,' and weight, 'burden,' then 'mass,' then 'definite mass.']

bharatá, a. to be supported or maintained; esp. to be kept alive by the care of men, as epithet of the god Agni; as m. Bharata, name of a patriarchal hero. [ⵏbhṛ, 1176e.]

bhárgas, n. radiant light; glory. [ⵏbhṛj or bhrāj, q.v., 216. 1⁸: cf. φλέγος, n., 'flame'; Lat. fulgur, 'lightning.']

bhartṛ, m. —1. bearer; —2. supporter, maintainer; lord; husband, 10²¹. [ⵏbhṛ, 1182b: cf. Lat. fertor, 'bearer.']

bhavá, m. the coming into existence. [ⵏbhū.]

bhavat-pūrva, *a.* having bhavant as first *or* preceding; -am, *adv.* [1311], in a way having bhavant first, *i.e.* with the voc. s. f. of bhavant at the beginning of one's begging formula.

bhavadāhārārtham, *adv.* for your food. ['in a way having your food as object,' 1311, 1302c4 : bhavant + āhāra and artha.]

bhavaduttaram, *adv.* with bhavant as last (word of one's begging formula). [acc. s. n. of adj. ₀bhavad-uttara, 1311.]

bhavana, *n.* dwelling, abode, house. [prop. 'an existing,' then 'place of existing,' √bhū, 1150.1a . so Eng. *dwelling* and *abode* and Lat. *man-sio* meant 'a waiting, an abiding,' and then 'abiding-place, maison': cf. also mandira and asta.]

bhávant [456], *a.* lordly; *—used in respectful address as substitute* [514] *for pronoun of the second person, and translatable by* your honor, thou (*e.g.* 6²³), ye (*e.g.* 7⁶, 12¹⁰); *used in the pl. of a single person to express greater courtesy*, 19²², 28⁴·⁵; *used in the voc. s. m.* (bhavas, *contracted*) bhos, *f.* bhavati, *as word of address,* (lord, master, mister,) sir, lady. [prob. a contraction of bhágavant: cf. 61¹⁰ ɴ.]

bhavan-madhya, *a.* having bhavant as middle (word); -am, *adv.* [1311], with the voc. s. f. of bhavant as the middle (word of one's begging formula).

bhavitavyà, *grdv.* deserving to become, destined to be, about to be; *impers.* [999], mayā bhavitavyam, *sc.* asti, I must be, 23¹³; bhavitavyam, it must be, 27¹⁴. [√bhū, 964.]

√ **bhas** (bábhasti [678]; bhasitá). chew, bite; crush; devour, consume; bhasita, consumed to ashes. [cf. φάμ-μη, ₀φασ-μη, 'barley-groats': w. the 3d pl. bá-ps-ati cf. the collateral form psā and ψá-μα-θos, 'sand.']

bhásman, *n.* ashes. ['consumed': see √bhas.]

√ **bhā** (bháti; babhāú; bhāsyáti; bhātá). be bright, shine; appear. [cf. φη-μί, Lat. *fā-ri*, 'make appear, reveal, say'; Eng. *ban*, 'public proclamation, manda-

tory *or* prohibitory,' 'notice (of marriage),' etc.: cf. √√bhāṣ, bhās.]

+ **ā**, shine upon; illumine.

+ **ud**, shine out, become manifest, 56²⁰.

+ **nis**, shine forth from (*abl.*), *fig.*

+ **pra**, shine forth; begin to be light (of the night).

+ **vi**, shine far and wide.

bhāgá, *m.* part: —1. allotted part, 96²⁰; share, 84¹⁰; lot; *esp.* happy lot; —2. *in post-Vedic,* portion (*not* lot), 64²²; —3. place, spot (*cf. Eng.* parts, 'regions'). [√bhaj.]

bhāga-dhéya, *n.* (bestowal *or* allotment of a part, *i.e.*) portion, 88⁷; *esp.* bestowal of a goodly lot, blessing, 82⁴. [1213c.]

bhāgaças, *adv.* part by part; gradually. [bhāga, 1106.]

bhāgīratha, *a.* of Bhagiratha; -ī, *f.* the stream (nadī) of Bh., the Ganges. [bhagīratha, 1208f.]

bhāgya, *n.* lot; fate; *esp.* happy lot; luck; bhāgyena, luckily. [bhāga, 1211.]

bhājana, *n.* vessel, dish. [lit. 'receiver,' √bhaj, mg 2: 1150.1b.]

bhāṇḍa, *n.* —1. vessel, pot; vat; dish; —2. *generalized* (*like* pātra), utensil; wares *or* ware.

bhāṇḍa-mūlya, *n.* capital consisting of wares; stock in trade.

bhānú, *m.* light; beam. [√bhā, 1162.]

√ **bhām** (bhāmitá). rage, be angry. [orig., perhaps, 'be agitated,' and so, a Prakritic form of bhram, q.v.: for loss of r, see under √bhañj.]

bhāma, *m.* rage, fury. [√bhām.]

bhārá, *m.* burden. [√bhṛ.]

bhárata, *a.* descended from Bharata; *as m.* descendant from Bharata, epithet of Yudhishthira, to whom Brihadaçva tells the story of Nala. [bharatá, 1208f.]

bhārika, *m.* carrier. [bhāra.]

bhāryà, *grdv.* to be supported *or* maintained; -ā, *f.* wife. [√bhṛ, 963b.]

bhāryātva, *n.* condition of being wife *or* (among animals) mate. [bhāryā.]

bhāva, *m.* —1. the becoming, 61²; existence, 15¹⁸; being; *in cpds,* used as equiv. *to the suffix* tva *or* tā, condition of being··, 35²¹, 49¹² ; —2. (way of being, *i.e.*) condition; — 3. (way of being, *i.e.*) nature; — 4. natural disposition; feeling; — 5. feelings; heart, 30[18]; — 6. the existent; existent thing, 66[9]. [√bhū, 1148. 2.]

bhāvin, *a.* becoming, coming into existence; about to be, destined to be, 18[9]; future, 38[18]; -inī, *f.* a beautiful woman. [√bhū, 1183[8] end.]

√ bhāṣ (bhāṣate; babhāṣé; ábhāṣiṣṭa; bhāṣitá; bhāṣitum; bhāṣitvā; -bhāṣya). speak; talk; say. [perhaps for *bhāsk, a sk-formation fr. √bhā: 182a.]

+abhi, speak unto, address, *w. acc.;* speak, *without object.*

+prati, speak back, answer.

bhāṣā, *f.* speech, language. [√bhāṣ.]

bhāṣita, *ppl.* spoken; *as n.* [1176a], what is spoken, the words. [√bhāṣ.]

√ bhās (bhāsati, -te; babhāsé; bhāsitá). shine. [cf. √bhā.]

+prati, shine over against, make a show, appear well.

bhās, *n.* light. [√bhās: but cf. 1151.1c[2].]

bhās-kará, *m.* the sun. [‘light-making’: 171[5].]

√ bhikṣ (bhíkṣate; bibhíkṣé; bhikṣiṣyé; bhíkṣitum; bhikṣitvā). desire to have a share for one’s self, wish for; *then (like the Eng.* desire, ‘express a wish for’), request; beg; *esp.* go begging for food. [old desid. of √bhaj, 108g[1] end: cf. bhakṣ.]

bhikṣā, *f.* — 1. the act of begging, begging; — 2. that which is got by begging, alms. [√bhikṣ, 1149[4]: w. the relation of 1 to 2, cf. that of Eng. *getting,* ‘act of getting,’ *to getting,* ‘that which is got.’]

√ bhid (bhinátti, bhintté; bibhéda, bibhidé; ábhet [832]; bhetsyáti, -te; bhinná [957d]; bhéttum; bhittvā; -bhídya). cleave, cut asunder; break in twain, 102[14]; smite sore (in battle), 81[5]; pound, bruise, crush (as a reed), 70[15]; pierce. [orig. ‘split, crush’: cf. Lat. *findo,* ‘cleave,’ perfect *fidi*; Ger. *beissen,* Eng. *bite;* also *bit,* ‘morsel,’ and *bit,* ‘part of a bridle’; *bitter,* used of a sword, w. a trace of the orig. mg, Beówulf, 2705; caus. *bait,* in *bait a bear,* ‘make dogs bite him,’ and *bait a horse,* ‘let him eat.’]

+pra, split forth *or* open.

+vi, split asunder; break to pieces, destroy.

bhiyás, *m.* fear. [√bhī, 1151. 2c.]

√ bhiṣaj (bhiṣákti). heal.

bhiṣáj, *a.* healing; *as m.* healer. [√bhiṣaj, 1147.]

√ bhī (*V.* bháyate; *V. and later,* bibhéti; bibhāya; ábhaiṣīt; bheṣyáti; bhītá; bhétum; *caus.* bhīṣáyate [1042f]). fear; be afraid of (*abl.*); bhīta, having feared, frightened; *caus.* affright. [w. bi-bhé-ti, cf. Old High Ger. *bi-bē-t,* ‘trembles,’ whose *bi-* is syllable of reduplication, Ger. *bebt,* AS. *beofað,* ‘trembles’: the connection of these words with φέ-β-ομαι, ‘am afeard, flee in fright,’ and φόβος, ‘fear,’ is still a moot-point.]

bhī [351], *f.* fear. [√bhī, 348. 1.]

bhītá, *ppl.* feared; *as n.* [1176a], fear.

bhīmá, *a.* fearful, terrible; *as m.* Bhīma, name of a Vidarbhan king. [√bhī, 1166b.]

bhīma-parākramá, *m.* terrible strength *or* courage. [1264, 1267.]

bhīmá-parākrama, *a.* possessing bhīma-parākramá, 1[11], 2[8]. [1293.]

bhīma-çāsana, *n.* command *or* summons of Bhīma. [1264, 1267.]

bhīrú, *a.* timid. [√bhī, 1192.]

√ 1 bhuj (bhujáti; bhugná; -bhújya). bend; turn; make crooked. [so far as the meaning goes, the following words may well be taken as cognate: φυγ-εῖν, Lat. *fug-ere,* ‘turn about, flee’; AS. *būg-an,* ‘bend, turn about’ (intrans.), sometimes also ‘flee,’ Eng. verb *bow* (as in *bow down*), ‘bend’; AS. *boga,* Eng. *bow,* ‘arcus,’ *el-bow, rain-bow;* Ger. *bieg-sam,* ‘pliable,’ Old Eng. *būh-sum,* ‘pliable, yielding,’ Eng. *buxom,* ‘lithe, lively, vigorous’: but the Germanic *g* raises phonetic difficulties which are not yet satisfactorily cleared up.]

√ 2 bhuj (bhunákti, bhuṅkté; bubhója, bubhujé; ábhujat; bhokṣyáti, -te; bhuktá; bhóktum; bhuktvā). — 1. enjoy; *in Veda,* (have use with, *i.e.*) have the use of a thing (*and so w. instr.*); — 2. *in later Skt.* (*like Ger.* geniessen, *cf. also* bhoga *and* bhojana), enjoy *esp.* food,

w. acc.; —3. without object, take one's
meal; *then* —4. enjoy (things that are
not food), *w. acc.,* 10⁹; —5. reap the fruit
(of sin) at the hands of a person (*gen.*),
79¹⁷; —6. *caus.* cause to take food, feed.
[if for •bhruj (but this is doubtful — see
√bhañj), then cf. Lat. *frui, •frugvi,* 'have
use with' (a thing, hence instr.-abl.),
'enjoy'; *frug-es,* 'fruit'; AS. *brūcan,*
'enjoy' (food or drink), 'use,' Eng. *brook,*
orig. 'use,' now 'put up with.']

+**anu,** reap the fruit (of good *or* evil
deeds).

+**upa,** —1. enjoy, *esp.* (enjoy food, *i.e.*)
eat; —2. reap the fruit (of good *or* evil
deeds).

bhujaṁ-gama, m. serpent. ['going
with bending *or* with crooking': bhujam,
grd of √1bhuj, 995: for mg, cf. **khaga.**]

√ **bhur** (bhuráti). make short and quick
motions, twitch, jerk, kick, struggle, stir.
[cf. φύρω, 'stir around, mingle'; φλύω,
'bubble'; Lat. *fur-ere,* 'be agitated, rage';
de-fru-tum, 'boiled off'; Eng. *brew,* 'boil';
bro-th, 'bouillon.']

bhuraṇa, a. (*like the Eng.* stirring, *i.e.*)
both —1. moving quickly *and* —2. active,
busy. [√bhur, 1150. 2c.]

√ **bhuraṇya** (bhuraṇyáti). be stirring,
busy. [bhuraṇa, 1059d.]

bhúvana, n. —1. being, existence; —2.
world; —3. *with* víçva: *sing.,* tout le
monde; *pl.,* all beings. [√bhū, 1150.
2c.]

bhuvana-traya, n. world-triad, *i.e.*
heaven and atmosphere and earth.

bhúvas, *the second of the so-called "utterances"* (*see* **vyāhṛti**), bhuvas!, *interpreted
as* air *or* atmosphere, *on account of its
position between* bhūr *and* svar. [prob.
nothing more than the voc. pl. of **bhú,**
'O ye spaces.']

√ **bhū** (bhávati, -te; babhúva [789a];
ábhūt; bhaviṣyáti, -te; bhūtá; bhá-
vitum; bhūtvá; -bháya; *caus.* bhāvá-
yati, -te). become, 93⁸, 40²¹, 57⁸, 67²¹,
3¹⁷; come into being, 92¹⁷; arise, happen,
take place; exist; *very often to be rendered simply by* be, 2¹⁶, 3¹⁸,²², 7¹;
—pūrvam abhúd rájā, once there was a

king, 48¹; **tathā bhavatu,** so be it, 27¹⁴;
so 32¹⁷; **prāñjalir bhūtvā,** (having become prāñjali, *i.e.*) assuming suppliant
posture, 13²²; —*w. possessive gen.,* become
(the property) of a person; **ādhipatyaṁ
tasya babhūva,** lordship became his, he
attained lordship, 37¹; *seldom w. dat.,*
96²⁰; —*imperative,* bhavatu: (be it, *i.e.*)
good; enough; what's the use of talking,
30¹⁶, 42²; the thing is clear, 23⁷, 31⁵;
tad bhavatu, never mind that, 34⁶;
—bhūta, *see s.v.;* —*in self-explaining
periphrases w. ppls,* 49¹⁹, 52¹⁷, 99²¹;
—*desid.* búbhūṣati [1027], desire to be,
70¹⁴. [w. ábhūt cf. ἔφυ, 'became, grew';
cf. Lat. *fu-it,* 'was'; Old Lat. *fu-at,* 'may
be'; AS. *beōm, 'am';* Eng. *be.*]

+**anu,** —1. (*perhaps* be along after,
and so) come up with, attain; —2. experience; enjoy, 24⁹; —3. (experience,
i.e.) make practical acquaintance with,
come to understand; perceive; hear, 4²¹.

+**abhi,** be against [1077⁸], oppress,
and so overpower.

+**ud,** arise up, make itself perceptible.

+**pari,** —1. be around, surround, encompass; —2. (*like the Eng.* colloq. get
around, *i.e.*) get the better of, prove
superior to; be superior to, *and so* —3.
treat with contempt, 37⁵.

+**pra,** —1. come forth into being;
arise; —2. be before (others), have the
power; have power, be strong.

+**vi,** (become asunder, *i.e.*) expand, develop; pervade; —*caus.* cause to expand
or open; discover; **vibhāvita,** discovered,
found out.

+**sam,** —1. (unite [*intrans.*] together,
and so take form, *i.e.*) be shapen *in its
old sense,* be created; be born, 97²; come
into being; become; originate; **sam-
bhūta,** sprung from, 19¹²; —2. exist,
39²; be, 39⁵; **sambabhūva,** am, RV.
x. 125. 8; —3. happen, 20¹²; occur; pass
current, 52⁷; —*caus.* —1. (cause to be
together, bring into form, *i.e.*) make,
accomplish; —2. honor, 30¹²; —3. (bring
together, *and so, like* Eng. con-jecture)
suppose. [development of caus. mg 2
unclear.]

+**abhi-sam**, (*lit.* become unto, *i.e.*) attain (*e.g.* a condition) by a process of change, enter into (*e.g.* wifehood), 86¹⁹; be born unto (immortality), 97⁸.

bhū [351-2], *a. at end of cpds,* becoming, being, existent; *as f.* —1. a becoming, being; —2. the place (*for mg, cf.* **bhavana**) of being, the world, space; *pl.* worlds, spaces (*cf.* **bhuvas**); —3. the earth, as distinguished from heaven and atmosphere; **bhuvi**, on earth; —4. the land, lands. [√bhū, 347.]

bhūtá, *ppl.* —1. become, been, *i.e.* past; real; —2. having become, being, *used in composition w. its predicate as a grammatical device to give the predicate an adj. form w. number and gender* [1273c], 6⁷, 19⁴, 29⁴, 56¹⁵; —3. *as n.* (that which has become, *i.e.*) a being, divine (90¹⁹) *or* human *or* other; creature *in general,* 21¹⁵ˑ²², 57¹⁸, 63¹²; created thing, 58¹⁰; world, 91¹⁶; —4. *as m. n.* uncanny being, ghost, goblin, 55¹⁹; —5. *as n.* element; **pañca bhūtáni**, five elements (earth, water, fire, air, ether, of which the body is composed and into which it is dissolved), 66⁵, 68⁹; *so* 66¹ˑ³. [√bhū: cf. φῠ-τό-ν, 'plant, creature.']

bhūta-grāma, *m. sing. and pl.* community of creatures.

bhūta-bhāṣā, *f.* language of the goblins *or* Piçāchas.

bhū-tala, *n.* earth-surface, ground, earth. [*cf.* **tala**.]

bhūti, *f.* being, *esp.* well-being. [√bhū: *cf.* φύσις, 'a being, nature.']

bhū-pa, *m.* protector of the earth *or* land, king, prince.

bhū-pati, *m.* lord of the land, king, prince.

bhū-bhāga, *m.* spot of the earth, place.

bhūman, *n.* earth; world. [√bhū, 1168. 1d: for mg, cf. bhū.]

bhūmi, *f.* —1. earth, 57¹¹; ground, 43¹³; —2. land; —3. place, 23¹⁴; *esp.* fit place, proper vessel (*cf.* **sthāna, pātra**), 21⁵, 28⁵. [√bhū, 1167: for mg, cf. bhū.]

bhūmi-pati, *m.* lord of the land, king, prince.

bhūmi-bhāga, *m.* spot of ground.

bhūmi-ṣṭha, *a.* standing on the ground. [**sthā**.]

bhūyāṅs, *a.* more; greater. ['becoming in a higher degree, increasing,' √bhū, 470².]

bhūr, *the first of the three "utterances"* (*see* **vyāhṛti**), bhūr!, O earth. [crystallized voc. sing. of **bhū**.]

bhūri, *a.* abundant; much. [√bhū, 1191: cf. **bhūyāṅs**.]

bhūri-kāla, *m.* long time.

bhūri-sthātra, *a.* having many stations, being in many places.

bhūrṇi, *a.* stirring, *and so* vigilant, jealous (of a god). [√bhur, 1158.2, 245b.]

√**bhūṣ** (bhū́ṣati; bhūṣáyati [1041²]). —1. **bhū́ṣati**, be busy for; —2. **bhūṣáyati**, (make ready for, *i.e.*) adorn.

bhūṣaṇa, *n.* ornament. [√bhūṣ, mg 2: 1150.]

√**bhṛ** (bíbharti [645]; bhárati, -te; *V.* jabhára, jabhré [789b]; *later,* babhā́ra; ábhārṣīt; bhariṣyáti; bhṛtá; bhártum; -bhṛ́tya). bear (*cf. the various senses of* bear *in Eng.*): *thus,* —1. hold, *and so* possess; —2. bear (in the womb); abharat, she bare, 85¹⁵; —3. endure; —4. carry, convey; —5. (bear, *i.e.*, as in *Latimer*) win; —6. bring (as an offering, *cf.* of-fer), 69¹⁴, 82¹⁴; *w.* **ū́dhar**, offer the breast, suckle, 78⁸; —7. (bear, *i.e.*) support; *and so* (*like Eng.* support), furnish sustenance to, 22²; maintain, RV. x. 125.1; *so also,* keep (on hire); —8. wear (*as Ger.* tragen *means* 'bear' *and* 'wear'); *w.* **nakhāni**, wear the nails, keep them untrimmed, 64¹⁹. [*cf.* φέρω, Lat. fero, Eng. bear, 'bear' in its various mgs, Ger. ge-bären, 'bring forth': AS. bear-n, Eng. bairn, 'child,' is an old ppl., lit. 'that which is borne *or* born'; cf. also φώρ, Lat. fūr, 'carrier off, thief': see also under the derivs, **bhara, bhartṛ**, and **bhṛti**; cf. **bhāra** and the following.]

+**apa**, carry off, take away, ἀποφέρω.

+**ava**, bear down (an assailing weapon), ward off.

+**ā**, bear unto, bring to.

+**upa**, bring unto.

+**ni**, *only in ppl.,* **nibhṛta**, (borne down, lowered, *i.e.*) hidden.

+ **pra**, *act. mid.* bring forward; offer; prabhṛta, brought forward, made ready. [cf. προφέρω, Lat. *prŏfero*, 'bring forward.']

√ **bhṛjj** (bhṛjjáti; bhṛṣṭá; bhṛṣṭvā). roast; parch, *esp.* grain. [cf. φρύγω, Lat. *frigere*, 'roast': akin w. √bhrāj.]

bhṛtí, *f.* the supporting, maintenance. [√bhṛ, 1157.1a : cf. Ger. *Ge-bur-t*, Eng. *bir-th*.]

bhṛtya, *m.* (one who is to be maintained, *i.e.*) servant. [grdv. of √bhṛ, 963b.]

bhṛça, *a.* powerful.

bhṛça-duḥkhita, *a.* (powerfully, *i.e.*) exceedingly pained.

bhetavya, *grdv.* to be feared; bhetavyam, *impers.* [999], timendum est, one should fear, 42³; na bhetavyam, never fear. [√bhī, 964.]

bhedá, *m.* fissure, split, breach; a creating of divisions. [√bhid.]

bheṣajá, *f.* -í, *a.* healing; *as n.* healing (*subst.*). [bhiṣáj, 1209i.]

bhāikṣa, *n.* begging; bhāikṣaṁ car, go a-begging. [bhikṣá, 1208e.]

bhāima, *a.* descended from Bhīma; *f.* -í, Bhīma's daughter, Damayantī. [bhīmá, 1208f.]

bhāirava, *a.* fearful, *i.e.* awful; *as m.* Terrible, name of a hunter. [bhīrú, 1208c.]

bho, *see* 176a (in 2d ed., see 174b).

bhóga, *m.* enjoyment; use; *esp.* use of food, *i.e.* eating. [√2 bhuj, 'enjoy,' 216. 1.]

bhogin, *a.* enjoying *or* having enjoyment; *esp.* enjoying food, well-fed. [not directly fr. √2 bhuj, but fr. bhoga, on account of the g, 1230c end.]

bhójana, *n.* the enjoying, *esp.* of food; the eating; *then* (*like Eng.* eating), food. [√2 bhuj, 'enjoy,' 1150.1a.]

bhojyà, *grdv.* to be eaten; *as n.* food, supply of food. [√2 bhuj, 'enjoy, eat,' 963d.]

bhobhavat-pūrvaka, *a.* accompanied [1302c2] by bhos or bhavant; -am, *adv.* [1311], with bhos or bhavant.

bho-bhāva, *m.* the becoming bhos; *w.* nāmnām, the becoming bhos of names,

i.e. the use of bhos instead of a person's real name.

bhos, *excl. of address.* thou, sir!, O!, ho!, halloo!; *often repeated, e.g.* 6²³. [for origin, see bhavant: for euphonic combination, see 176a (in 2d ed., see 174b).]

bhoḥ-çabda, *m.* the word bhos.

√ **bhraṅç** *or* bhraç (bhráncate; bhráçyati [767]; ábhraçat; bhraṣṭá). fall.

+ **apa**, fall off; *see* apabhraṣṭa.

bhraṅça, *m.* fall; ruin; loss. [√bhraṅç.]

√ **bhram** (bhrámati, -te; bhrámyati, -te [763]; babhráma; bhramiṣyáti; bhrāntá [955a]; bhrámitum, bhrāntum; bhrāntvā; -bhrámya, -bhrámya). — 1. move unsteadily *or* without aim; wander; roam, 36¹², 23⁶; flutter, of insects, etc.; — 2. move in a circle, rotate; — 3. *fig.* be wandering (of the mind); be agitated *or* confused.

[the orig. meanings seem to have included irregular and aimless and rotary motion as applied to water, wind, and fire, and also to have been transferred to the sound thereof: cf. the derivs bhṛmi, 'whirlwind,' bhramá, 'whirling flame' and 'whirlpool,' and bhramara, 'bee': cf. βρέμ-ειν, 'rage,' 'roar' (of storm and wave), βρόμος, 'rage, roar'; Lat. *frem-ere*, 'rage, roar'; Ger. *brummen*, 'hum, rumble'; AS. *brim*, 'surf, surge,' Eng. *brim*, 'place of surf, edge, margin'; Old Eng. *brim*, 'flame, fire,' preserved in Eng. *brimstone*, 'fire-stone': see also √bhām.]

+ **pari**, wander around.

+ **sam**, be much confused; sambhrānta, agitated, perplexed, in a flutter.

√ **bhrāj** (bhrājate, -ti; babhrāja; ábhrāṭ [890 *or* 833?]; bhrājiṣyáte). shine; be radiant; flame; *fig.* be radiant (with beauty *or* glory). [cf. φλέγ-ω, 'flame, burn'; φλέγ-μα, 'flame'; Lat. *flam-ma*, *flag-ma*, 'flame'; *fulg-ēre*, 'shine, lighten'; AS. *blāc*, 'shining, splendid' (of fires and flames), then 'white' (of the dead), Eng. *bleak*, 'pale'; *bleach*, 'whiten.']

+ **vi**, shine.

bhrātṛ [373], *m.* brother. [origin unknown, cf. 1182d: cf. φρά-τηρ, 'brother, *esp.* one of a brotherhood *or* clan,' and

14

so, 'clansman'; Lat. *frā-ter*, 'brother'; Eng. *brother*.]

bhrātṛ-sthāna, a. (having, *i.e.*) taking the brother's place; *as m.* representative of a brother.

bhruva, for bhrū *at end of cpds*, 1315c.

bhrū [351], *f.* brow. [cf. ὀ-φρύ-s, 'eyebrow'; AS. *brū*, 'eye-lid'; Eng. *brow*.]

---

ma [491], *pron. root, see* **ahám**. [cf. μέ, Lat. *me*, AS. *mē*, Eng. *me*.]

√ **maṅh** (máṅhate). make great *or* abundant a thing (*acc.*) for a person (*dat.*), grant abundantly to. [for ♦magh, cf. magha: orig. 'be great,' and trans. 'make great *or* high,' and essentially ident. w. √mah: see under √mah: for mg, cf. Lat. *largus*, 'large, liberal,' w. *largīri*, 'give liberally,' and Eng. *large* with *largess*.]

máṅhiṣṭha, a. granting most abundantly, most generous. [√maṅh, 467.]

ma-kāra, m. the letter m. [Whitney 18.]

makhá, a. jocund. [cf. √mah.]

magádha, m. *pl.* Magadhans, name of a people; Magadha, name of their country, Southern Behar.

magadha-deça, m. the land of Magadha.

√ **magh**, *see* **maṅh**.

maghá, n. liberal gift; bounty. [√magh, *i.e.* maṅh.]

maghávan [428], a. —1. abounding in liberal gifts, generous; *esp., as m.*, generous (patron), designation of the rich lord who institutes a sacrifice and pays the priests, 88[1]—*cf.* **sūri**; *applied in particular to* Indra, *as* Rewarder (of priests and singers), 70[6], 71[5], 73[20], 75[10]; —2. *in the Epos*, The Generous One, standing epithet of Indra, 5[11]. [maghá, 1234.]

maṅgalá, n. —1. welfare, luck; —2. anything lucky, auspicious, *or* of good omen; —3. old *or* traditional usage, 59[18].

maṅgalya, a. lucky, auspicious, of good omen. [maṅgalá, 1212d 4.]

mac-chiṣya, m. pupil of me, my pupil. [mad + çiṣya, 159, 203.]

√ **majj** (májjati, -te; mamájja; ámajjīt; maṅkṣyáti, -te; majjiṣyáti; magná

[957c]; májjitum; -májya). sink under; dip one's self; dive; duck *or* sub-merge, *intrans.* [perhaps orig. ♦maagh, 'get into': cf. madgu, 'duck'; Lat. *merg-ere*, 'duck'; *merg-us*, 'diver' bird: for the phonetic relations, cf. majjan, Avestan maega, Church Slavonic *mozgŭ*, AS. mearg, Eng. *marrow*, Ger. *Mark*, all meaning 'marrow,' and, as meaning originally 'the inmost part *or* pith,' prob. from this root: see rajju.]

+ **ud**, e-merge.

+ **ni**, sink down; dip one's self, bathe.

majjāo, *Prakrit for* mārjāra-s ('cat') *and for* maj-jāra-s ('my paramour').

maṭhara, a. *perhaps* persistent; *as m.* Mathara, name of a man.

maṇí, m. —1. pearl; jewel; —2. water-jar.

maṇika, m. large water-jar. [maṇi.]

maṇḍapa, m. n. open hall *or* pavilion.

maṇḍapikā, f. small shed *or* shop. [maṇḍapa, 1222 and d.]

máṇḍala, n. disk, circle, ring.

maṇḍūka, m. frog; f. maṇḍūkī [355b], female frog.

matí, f. —1. (thinking upon, *i.e., like the* Ger. An-dacht, *see* dhī 2) devotion; pious hymn *or* song of praise, 73[10], 79[6]; —2. thought; thoughts, 49[2]; purpose, 73[6]; mind; intention; —3. opinion; —4. understanding, 19[9]; intelligence. [√man, q.v.: cf. Lat. *mens*, stem *men-ti*, 'mind'; AS. *ge-myn-d*, 'mind,' Eng. *mind*.]

mati-prakarṣa, m. wit-superiority, *i.e.* a fine dodge.

mátsya, m. fish. ['the lively one,' √mad.]

√ **math** *or* **manth** (mathnáti, mathnīté; mánthati; máthati [746]; mamátha, mamathús, mamanthús, methús; ámathīt; mathiṣyáti, -te, manthiṣyáti; mathitá; máthitum; mathitvá; -máthya). —1. stir *or* whirl; w. agnim, produce fire by whirling the stick of attrition in a dry piece of wood; —2. shake, agitate, distress.

+ **pra**, agitate.

√ **mad** (mádati; mádyati; mamáda; ámādīt; maditá, mattá; máditum; mādáyati, -te). −1. bubble, undulate, of water, and as a type of joyousness; apām ūrmir madann iva stomas, praise (joyous) as a bubbling water-wave, 81[10]; boil, be agitated; −2. *fig.* be (pleasantly excited, *i.e.*) glad; rejoice; *w. instr.*, 83[12]; be exhilarated *or* intoxicated with joy; −3. *esp.*, as describing the life of the gods and the blessed, be in bliss; *w. cognate acc.*, 83[18]; −4. *trans.* gladden, rejoice, 75[12]; intoxicate; **matta**, drunk; −*caus.* −1. *act.* gladden; −2. *mid.* take delight, 84[19].

[the rather rare physical mg (1) is prob. the orig. one, w. a transfer to fig. use, as in Eng. *bubble over with joy or mirth:* cf. μαδ-*δω*, 'be moist'; Lat. *mad-ēre*, 'be soaked, full, drunk'; mat-ta-s (mg 4) and Lat *mat-tu-s*, 'drunk': see the collateral form √1 mand, and √mud.]

+ **ud**, be out (of one's senses) with excitement; be frantic.

+ **pra**, take pleasure.

mad, *so-called stem of 1st pers. pron.*, 494.

máda, *m.* excitement, inspiration, intoxication, 81[4]; *pl.* intoxicating drinks, *esp.* Soma-draughts, 81[11]. [√mad.]

madíya, *a.* mine. [mad, 494[8], 1215d.]

madgú, *m.* a water-fowl. ['diver,' √majj, q.v.]

mádhu, *a.* sweet; *as n.* sweet food and drink: *esp.* Soma; milk and its products; *oftenest* honey, 26[18]. [cf. μέθυ, 'wine'; AS *medu*, Eng. *mead*.]

madhura, *a.* sweet; of speeches, honeyed. [mádhu, 1226a.]

mádhya, −1. *as n.* middle; *w.* nabhasas, middle of heaven, mid-heaven; madhye: in the middle, 57[12]; *w. gen.* [1130] *or at end of cpd*, in the midst of · ·, in · ·, 18[7], 2[9]; −2. *m. n.* (the middle, *i.e.*) the waist; −3. *as adj., used like* Lat. medius: samudram madhyam, in medium mare. [cf. μέσσος, ομεθ-jo-s, Lat. medius, Goth. *midjis*, AS *mid*, Eng. *mid-*, 'middle.']

madhya-ga, *a.* situated in the middle of, tarrying among.

madhya-cārin, *a.* moving in the middle of (*w. gen.*, 1816[2]), *i.e.* moving among.

madhyamá, −1. midmost, situated between; −2. of middling quality, size, etc.; −3. *as m. n.* the middle (of the body), waist; −4. *as n.* the middle (of anything). [mádhya, 474: cf. 525[8].]

√ **man** (mányate; mené [794e]; ámaṅsta; maṅsyáte, -ti; matá; mántum; matvá; -mánya, -mátya; *desid.* mímāṅsate). be minded: −1. think, believe, imagine, 34[18], 43[16]; conjecture; yadi nányathā manyase, if thou art not otherwise minded, if thou art agreed, 25[8]; manye, *inserted parenthetically*, methinks, 51[13]; expect, 52[11]; −2. consider something (*acc.*) as something (*acc.*), 13[12], 37[7], 55[20], 79[8]; prāptakālam amanyata, considered (*sc.* it) an arrived time, thought that the time had come, 13[20]; bahu man, consider as much, esteem, honor; −3. think fit *or* right, 10[16]; −4. think upon, set the heart on, 3[4]; −5. have in mind *or* view, 88[6]; −*caus.*, see **mānaya**; −*desid.* consider, examine, call in question. [cf. μέ-μον-α, 'mind, *i.e.* fix the thoughts on, wish, strive' (see man 4); Lat. me-min-i, 'keep in mind'; AS. preterito-present man, 'am mindful,' and the indirectly connected *mēnan*, Eng. mean, 'have in mind, intend.']

+ **anu**, (be minded after another, *i.e.*) follow another in opinion, assent, approve; consent; give leave, *w. acc. of person*, 49[4]; permit, 62[6].

+ **abhi**, −1. put one's mind upon, desire; abhimata, desired, agreeable; −2. have intentions against [1077[8]], plot against.

+ **ava**, (mind, *i.e.* regard downwards, *i.e.*) regarder de haut en bas, look down upon, *like the* Lat. de-spicere, despise, treat with contempt.

mánas, *n.* mind, *in its widest sense as applied to the* powers of conception, will, and emotion: thus, −1. the intellect; the thoughts, 8[16], 10[6], 66[7]; understanding, 82[17]; mind, 10[16], 15[10], 65[12, 13]; −2. reflection; excogitation; *perhaps* the thing excogitated, praise, *or* (*like* dhí 2) devotion, 73[7]; −3. wish, inclination towards; −4. desire; −5. feelings; disposition;

14*

heart, 78[7]. [√man: cf. μένος, 'mind, spirit'; Lat. *Miner-va*, the goddess 'gifted with understanding.']

maniṣā́, *f.* —1. thought; understanding; *instr.* maniṣā́, *adv.* wisely; —2. expression of thought and wisdom in saw, prayer, and hymn (*cf.* dhī 2). [√man, 1197b.]

maniṣín, *a.* —1. having understanding, wise; —2. prayerful, devout. [maniṣā́, 1230a.]

mánu, *m.* —1. man; *collectively* (*as in Eng., and like Hebrew* adam), man, mankind, 73[19]; —2. (*like Hebrew* Adam) The Man κατ' ἐξοχήν, Manu, father of mankind; Manu, as originator of prayer, praise, and sacrifice, 89[2]; Manu, as type of piety and majesty, 1[10]; Manu, suppositititious author of the law-book of the Mānavas. [cf. Goth. *manna,* Ger. *Mann,* AS. *man,* Eng. *man:* the noun is generalized to a quasi pronoun in AS. *man,* Ger. *man,* like Lat. *homo* in French *on,* but retains a distinct form as noun in Ger. *Mann* (as *homo* does in French *homme*): cf. also *Mannus,* mythical ancestor of the West-Germans (Tacitus, Germania, ii.): perhaps related are Μίνω-ς and Μίνως, mythical Greek forefathers: the derivation of mánu fr. √man, 'think,' is unobjectionable so far as the form goes (1178b), but the usual explanation of manu as 'the thinker' defies common sense.]

manu-ja, *m.* man. [prop. adj., 'Manuborn, sprung from Manu,' 1265.]

manujendra, *m.* (prince of men, *i.e.*) prince, king, 1[5]. [manuja + indra, 1264.]

manuṣyà, —1. *a.* human; —2. *as m.* man. [manus, 1212d 1: cf. mā́nuṣa: for mg 2, see mānava.]

manuṣyatvá, *n.* condition of being man. [manuṣya, 1239.]

manuṣya-devá, *m.* human god [1280[1]] *or* man-god [1280b] *or* god among men [1264], *i.e.* Brahman, 95[1].

manuṣya-loká, *m.* world of men.

mánus, *m.* man. [cf. mánu and 1154.]

mano-ratha, *m.* wish. [lit. 'heart's joy,' manas + 2 ratha.]

mano-hara, *a.* (heart-taking, *i.e.*) captivating.

mántu, *m.* counsel, *i.e.* deliberation; *then* (*like Eng.* counsel), result of deliberation, plan, intent. [√man, 1161a.]

mántra, *m.* —1. thought; *esp.* thought as uttered in formal address, in prayer *or* song of praise (*see* dhī 2), *or* in pious text; —2. *usual designation of* the hymns and texts of the Vedas; —3. *later* (when these Vedic texts came to be used as magic formulas), spell, charm; —4. *like* mántu, deliberation, plan. [√man, 1185b: for mg 3, cf. Lat. *carmen,* 'solemn utterance' (see √çaṅs), then 'magic spell,' whence Eng. *charm.*]

mantra-da, *a.* giving, *i.e.* imparting the sacred texts, *i.e., as m.,* Veda-teacher.

√ mantraya (mantráyate [1067]). —1. speak with solemn *or* formal utterance; —2. deliberate. [denom. of mantra — see its various mgs.]

+ anu, follow with a mantra, accompany with a sacred text, *like Lat.* prosequi vocibus.

+ abhi, address a spell unto; charm *or* cónjure.

+ ā́, speak unto; *esp.* bid farewell to, 56[5].

+ ni, invite. [for mg, cf. (under √budh) Eng. *bid,* 'make formal announcement of,' and then 'invite.']

+ sam-ni, invite together, 4[20].

mantravant, *a.* accompanied by sacred texts. [mantra, 1233.]

mantra-varṇa, *m.* the wording of a sacred text.

√ 1 mand (mándati; mamánda; ámandīt). gladden, 74[4]. [collateral form of √mad.]

√ 2 mand *or* mad (mamátti; mádati). tarry, loiter. [amplification of ●man, 'remain,' the congener of μέν-ειν, Lat. *man-ēre,* 'remain.']

manda, *a.* —1. tarrying, slow; —2. (sluggish, *and so*) weak; insignificant; little; —3. (*like Eng. colloq.* slow) stupid. [√2mand, 'tarry.']

manda-bhā́gya, *a.* having little luck, unlucky.

mandara, *m.* Mandara, a sacred mountain.

mandādara, *a.* having little regard for (*w. loc.,* 303a), careless about. [manda + ādara.]

mandāra, *m. n.* —1. coral tree, Erythrina indica; —2. *m. used, perhaps, as name of a man,* Mandāra.

mandira, *n.* dwelling; house; palace. [√2 mand, 'tarry,' 1188e: prop. 'a waiting, an abiding,' and then 'abiding-place, mansion': cf. μάνδ-ρα, 'fold, stable,' later 'monastery': for mg, observe that Lat. *mansio,* stem *man-si-on-* (fr. *man-ēre,* 'tarry'), meant first 'a tarrying,' and then 'a stopping-place, mansion,' French 'maison'; see also bhavana.]

manmatha, *m.* love; the god of love. ['the agitator, distresser,' intensive formation fr. √math or manth, 1148.4, 1002b.]

mánman, *n.* thought; *esp.* (*like* dhī2) An-dacht, devotion, prayer *or* praise. [√man, 1168.1a.]

man-māṅsa, *n.* my flesh. [mad, 494.]

manyú, *m.* —1. mood, *i.e.* temper of mind; *then* —2. (*like Eng.* mood) anger, heat of temper. [√man, 1165a.]

māma, *see* 491 *and* ma.

maya, —1. *called a derivative suffix* (*see* 1225, 161³), *but really a nomen actionis meaning* formation, make, *used as final element of a cpd,* having ·· as its make, made of ··, consisting of ··, containing ·· in itself; —2. *nomen agentis,* maker, former; *esp.* Maya, The Former, name of an Asura, artificer of the Daityas, and skilled in all magic, 45⁶. [fr. mi, weak form (cf. 954c, 250) of √1mā, 'measure, arrange, form,' 1148.1a and b: so the Eng. deriv. suffix *-hood, -head,* Ger. *-heit,* was once an independent noun, see under ketu.]

máyas, *n.* invigoration, refreshment, cheer, gladness, joy. [prop. 'a building up,' fr. √1mi, 'establish,' or fr. the weak form mi (cf. 954c, 250) of the kindred and partly equivalent √1mā, 'measure, arrange, form, build,' 1151.1a.]

mayo-bhū [352], *a.* being for *or* conducing to mayas, *i.e.* refreshing, gladdening.

mara, *m.* death. [√mṛ, 'die.']

marakata, *n.* smáragd *or* emerald. [cf. σμάραγδος, whence Lat. *smaragdus,* Old French *esmeralde,* French *émeraude.*]

maraṇa, *n.* death. [√1mṛ, 'die.']

márīci, *f.* —1. mote *or* speck in the air, illuminated by the sun; —2. *later,* beam of light. [cf. marút.]

marīci-mālā, *f.* garland of rays.

marīcimālin, *a.* having a garland of rays. [marīcimālā, 1230a.]

marú, *m.* a waste; desert. [perhaps 'the dead and barren' part, whether of land or water, √1mṛ, 'die': cf. 'Αμφί-μαρος, son of Poseidon; Lat. *mare,* 'sea'; AS. *mere,* 'sea, lake, swamp,' Eng. *mere,* 'lake, pool,' *Winder-mere, mer-maid;* AS. *mōr,* Eng. *moor,* 'marshy waste, heath.']

marút, *m. pl.* the Maruts *or* gods of the storm-wind, Indra's companions, *selections* xxxv., xlii., xlvii., lxvii. [perhaps 'the flashing ones,' as gods of the thunderstorm, and connected w. a √•mar seen in μαρ-μαίρ-ω, 'flash.']

maru-sthalī, *f.* desert-land, desert.

martavya, *grdv.* moriendum; *impersonally, see* 999. [√1mṛ, 'die,' 964.]

mártya, *m. like Eng.* a mortal, *i.e.* a man; *as a.* mortal.

mardana, *m.* crusher; *fig., as in Eng.,* subduer. [√mṛd, 1150.1a.]

marma-jña, *a.* knowing the weak spots. [marman.]

márman, *n.* mortal part, vulnerable *or* weak spot, *lit. and fig.* [cf. √1mṛ, 'die.']

márya, *m.* man, *esp.* young man; *pl.* (*like Eng.* men, Ger. Mannen), servants, attendants, henchmen.

marṣa, *m.* patient endurance. [√mṛṣ.]

mála, *n. m.* smut; impurity, physical and moral. [cf. μέλ-αν, 'dark'; Lat. *mălu-s,* 'bad.']

malla, *m.* —1. *pl.* the Mallas, a people; —2. professional boxer and wrestler; one who engages in the παγκράτιον, pancratiast.

maçáka, *m.* biting and stinging insect, gnat.

maṣī, *f.* —1. bone-black; —2. ink, made of lac *or* of almond-charcoal boiled in cow's urine.

maṣy-abhāva, m. lack of ink.

√ mah (máhate; māmahé [786]; mahitá;
mahitvá; caus. maháyati, -te). orig. be
great or high, and so −1. mid. be glad,
rejoice; then (trans. make great or high,
and so) −2. act. elate; gladden; exalt
(mid.), 74⁸; −3. esteem highly, honor.
[for ∗magh, cf. magha, also √manh:
for orig. mg, cf. participial adj. mahánt,
'great': for mgs 1 and 2, cf. American
colloq. use of high as 'high in spirit,
elated, esp. intoxicated':
　—with orig. √∗magh in the mgs 'be
great, mighty, i.e. powerful or able,' trans.
'make able, help,' cf. μοχ-λόs, 'helping-
bar, lever'; μηχ-avh, 'means'; Goth. mag,
AS. mæg, 'am able,' Eng. may:
　—with the collateral form ∗mag, whose
deaspiration is prob. Indo-European, cf.
μέγ-as, Lat. mag-nus, AS. mic-el, Eng.
mickle, 'great.']

máh, f. mahí, a. great; mighty, 78⁸;
strong; —mahí, as subst. the great, i.e. the
earth; for mg, cf. pṛthivī. [cf. √mah:
see 400².]

mahá, a. great. [√mah.]

mahánt [450b], f. mahatí, −1. a. great
(in space, time, quantity, or quality, and
so), large, long, mighty, important; significant, 6¹¹; as m. great or noble man,
19²¹, 36¹⁰; −2. m. (sc. ātman), the intellect, 66⁹, 67¹⁷. [orig. ppl. of √mah, q.v.]

maharṣi, m. great Rishi. [mahá + ṛṣi.]

máhas, n. greatness; might; glory; gladness; mahobhis, adv.: with power, 79¹²;
joyfully, 73¹⁸. [√mah, see its various mgs.]

mahá, used as prior member of a cpd, instead
of mahánt, 1249b, 355a. [√mah.]

mahā-kathā, f. great tale.

mahā-kavi, m. great poet.

mahā-kula, n. (great, i.e.) noble family.

mahā-guru, a. exceedingly reverend
[1279]; as m. person worthy of unusual
honor.

mahā-tapas, a. (having, i.e.) practising
great austerity; as m. Great-penance, name
of a sage.

mahātman, a. having a (great, i.e.) noble
nature, noble; magn-animus. [mahá +
ātman.]

mahā-dhana, a. having great wealth,
very rich.

mahā-paṅka, m. n. (great, i.e.) deep
mire.

mahā-paṇḍita, a. exceedingly learned
[1279].

mahāparādha, m. great crime. [mahá
+ aparādha.]

mahā-prājña, a. very wise [1279].

mahā-bāhu, a. great-armed [1294], i.e.
stout-armed.

mahā-bhūta, n. grosser element, i.e.
earth, air, fire, water, or ether (as distinguished from a subtile element or rudimentary atoms).

mahā-manas, a. great-minded.

mahā-muni, m. great sage.

mahā-yajña, m. great sacrifice, 59⁶ ᴍ.

mahā-yaças, a. having great glory,
famous.

mahā-rājá, m. great prince. [rājan.
1315a.]

mahā-rāva, m. great howl.

mahā-vikrama, a. having great might
or courage; as m. Great-might, name of a
lion.

mahā-virá, m. great hero.

mahā-vratá, n. great vow. [1267.]

mahā-vrata, a. having a mahāvratá,
having undertaken a great vow. [1295.]

mahā-siṅha, m. great lion.

máhi, a. great. [√mah.]

mahitvá, n. greatness, might. [1239.]

mahimán, m. might; instr. mahiná, see
425e. [√mah, 1168. 2b.]

mahiṣa, a. mighty; mahiṣo mṛgas, the
powerful beast, i.e. buffalo, RV.; as m.,
without mṛga, buffalo, 55⁸; —máhiṣī, f.
[acct, cf. 362b²], the powerful one, as designation: of a woman of high rank; of the
first wife of a king, 1¹⁸; sometimes of any
queen of a king, 50¹. [√mah, 1197b.]

mahí, see under máh.

mahī-kṣit, m. earth-ruler, king.

mahī-pati, m. earth-lord, king.

mahī-pāla, m. earth-protector, king.

√ mahiya (mahīyáte). be glad, happy,
blessed. [prop. 'be great, high,' denom.
of mahi (1061), with the modification of
mg mentioned under √mah, q.v.]

mahendrá, *m.* −1. Great-Indra; −2. great chief, 10¹⁵ (*w. mg* 1 *also*). [mahā + indra.]

mahendratva, *n.* the name *or* dignity of Great-Indra. [1239.]

maheçvara, *m.* great lord; *esp., as pl., designation of* the four lokapālās, Indra, Yama, Agni, and Varuna. [mahā + īçvara.]

mahāujas, *a.* having great strength, mighty. [mahā + ojas.]

√ 1 mā (mimīte [660−3]; mamāú, mamé; ámāsta; mitá [954c]; mātum; mitvā; -māya). −1. measure; −2. measure with, compare; −3. mete out; −4. arrange, form; build; make, 72². [for 1, cf. *μέ-τρον*, 'measure'; Lat. *ni-mi-us*, 'not to be measured, excessive'; for 4, cf. *μά-pŋ* and Lat. *mā-nu-s*, 'former, *i.e.* hand'; *εὐ-μαφής*, 'handy, easy': see also the collateral form √1 mi, 'build, set up,' and under mātṛ and mās.]

+anu, (form after, *i.e.*) re-create in imagination, conceive.

+upa, measure with, compare.

+nis, fashion *or* make out of (*abl.*); construct.

+vi-nis, lay out (garden).

+pari, measure around, limit.

+pra, measure.

+prati, make (so as to be a match) against, *cf.* pratimā.

+vi, measure out; *then* (*like Eng.* measure), pass over, traverse (the sky).

√ 2 mā *or* mī (mimāti [660−3]; mimáya). bellow.

+vi, bellow *or* cry aloud.

mā, *adv. and conj.* not, *mostly in prohibitions* [1122b]: −1. *regularly w. subjunctive, i.e. augmentless form of a past tense* [579−80], 76¹⁸, etc.; in order that not, 53⁷; −2. *w. imperative,* 22², 35¹¹, 50⁴; −3. *rarely w. optative,* 79¹⁷; −4. *w.* evam, not so, 38⁵; −5. *w.* u, mo, see u. [cf. *μή,* Elian *μά,* 'not, that not.']

māṅs *and* māṅsá [397], *n.* meat, flesh; *used also in pl.* [cf. Church Slavonic *męso,* Prussian *mensa,* 'flesh': cf. 64⁷ɴ.]

māṅsatva, *n.* the being meat, the etymological meaning of māṅsa. [1239.]

māṅsa-ruci, *a.* having pleasure in meat, greedy for meat.

māṅsa-lubdha, *a.* desirous of meat. [√lubh.]

maṅgalya, *a.* bringing happiness, pleasant. [maṅgalá.]

māciram, *adv.* (not long, *i.e.*) shortly, straightway. [mā + ciram, 1122b⁴.]

māthara, *m.* Māthara, name of a man. [maṭhara, 1208f.]

māṇava, *m.* boy, youngster. [not akin w. manu, 'man': perhaps for ∗malnava: cf. Prussian *malnyx,* 'child.']

māṇavaka, *m.* manikin, dwarf. [māṇava, 1222b.]

mātariçvan, *m.* Mātariçvan, mystic name of Agni.

mātula, *m.* mother's brother. [mātṛ, 1227²: cf. *μήτρως,* Doric *μάτρως,* 'mother's brother.']

mātṛ [373], *f.* mother; applied also to the earth, the Dawn, the sticks of attrition (82⁹). [perhaps 'the one who metes out' food to the household, or else 'the former' of the child in the womb, √1 mā, 'measure *or* mete,' 'form,' 1182d: cf. *μήτηρ,* Doric *μάτηρ,* Lat. *māter,* AS. *mōder,* Eng. *mother;* also *μαῖα,* 'mother.']

mātṛtas, *adv.* from the mother, on the mother's side. [mātṛ, 1098b.]

mātṛvat, *adv.* as one's mother.

mātrā, *f.* −1. measure; *at end of adj. cpds* [see 1302c 3], having ·· as its measure, so and so long *or* high *or* large, etc.: jānu-mātra, knee-deep; vyāma-mātra, a fathom broad; −2. the full measure, *i.e.* limit; *at end of adj. cpds,* having ·· as its limit, not more than ··; *and then, these adj. cpds being used substantively* (1247 III⁴), ·· merely, ·· only, mere ·', 27²⁰, 50⁹; *such a cpd as first member of another cpd,* 34⁸, 37⁶; *hence* −3. *from this frequent use of* mātrā *at end of cpds in the form* mātra (334²), *the quasistem,* mātra, *n.* measure, *i.e.* height, depth, length, breadth, distance (43¹²). [√1 mā, 'measure,' 1185c: cf. *μέ-τρον,* 'measure.']

māda, *m.* revelry. [√mad.]

1 **māna**, *m. n.* —1. opinion; —2. (*like the Eng.* opinion) estimation, *esp.* good esteem; —3. honor. [√man, 1148.2.]

2 **māna**, *m. like the Eng.* building, *and so* structure, castle. [√1 mā, 'make, build,' 1150.1a.]

3 **māna**, *m.* —1. *like the obs. Eng.* maker, ποιητής, poet; —2. as name of Agastya's father, Māna. [do.]

māna-da, *a.* (giving, *i.e.*) showing honor (to others); *as m.* honor-giver, *address of a woman to her lover.*

√ **mānaya** (mānáyati). honor. [denom. of 1 māna: cf. 1067.]

mānavá, —1. *a.* human; descended from man *or* Manu (*see* manu); —2. *as m.* one of the sons of men, a man; —3. *m.* Mānava, name of a school of the Yajurveda. [mánu, 1208c: for mgs 1 and 2, observe that Old High Ger. *mennisch*, though prop. an adj. fr. *man*, 'homo,' and meaning 'humanus,' is used also as a subst. meaning 'man,' and used in its Ger. form *Mensch*, 'man,' as subst. only: cf. also nāra, manuṣya, mānuṣa.]

mānava-dharmaçāstra, *n.* law-book of the Mānavas *or* Mānava-school.

mānasá, *a.* sprung from the mind; of the mind. [mánas, 1208a.]

mánuṣa, *f.* -ī, *a.* pertaining to man, human; *as m.* man (*cf.* mānava). [mánus, 1208a end: cf. manuṣya.]

mānuṣa-dáivika, *a.* of men and of gods. [1257.]

māndāryá, *a.* descended from Mandāra; *as m.* descendant of M. [mandāra, 1211.]

mānyá, *a.* descended from a poet *or* from Māna; *as m.* the poet's son *or* Māna's son. [3 māna, 1211.]

māma, *a. lit.* of mine; *voc. s. m., as word of address of a dog to an ass,* uncle. [mama (491), 1208f.]

māyā́, *f.* —1. (a working, *and so*) a power; *esp., in Veda,* supernatural *or* wonderful power; wile; —2. *later,* trick; illusion. [√1 mā, 'make, *i.e.* have effect, work,' 1149, cf. 258.]

māyā-kapota, *m.* illusion-pigeon.

māyākapota-vapus [418], *a.* having the form of a phantom-pigeon.

māyín, *a.* wily. [māyā́.]

māyobhavya, *n.* gladness, happiness. [mayobhū́, 1211, cf. 1208c.]

māra, *m.* a killing, murder. [√1 mṛ, 'die.']

mārakata, *f.* -ī, *a.* smarágdine, emerald (*adj.*). [marakata, 1208f.]

māraṇa, *n.* a killing; *w.* pra̲_āp, incur killing, get killed. [caus. of √1 mṛ, 'die,' 1150.1b.]

mārātmaka, *a.* having murder as one's nature, murderous. [māra + ātmaka, 1302.]

mārga, *a.* of *or* pertaining to game *or* deer; *as m.* track of wild animals, slot; then, in general, track, way, path. [mṛga, 1208f.]

mārja, *adj. subst.* cleaning, a cleaner, *in cpds.* [√mṛj, 627 1.2.]

mārjāra, *m.* cat. ['the cleaner,' so called from its habit of cleaning itself often: fr. mārja: formed like karmāra, 1226b.]

mālava, *m.* Malwa, name of a country in west-central India.

mālava-viṣaya, *m.* the land of Malwa.

mālā, *f.* crown, wreath, garland.

mālin, *a.* crowned, wreathed. [mālā.]

mālya, *n.* crown, wreath. [mālā, 1210.]

mās [397], *m.* —1. moon, *see* candra-mās; then (*as in Eng.*), a moon, *i.e.* month. ['the measurer,' √1 mā, 1151.1c²: cf. μή-νη, 'moon'; Lat. *Mēna*, 'menstruationis dea'; Goth. *mena*, AS. *mōna*, Eng. *moon*; AS. *mōnan dæg*, 'dies Lunae,' Eng. *Monday*; also μήν, stem μενς, Lat. *mens-i-s*, 'month'; AS. *mōnað*, prop. 'a lunation,' Eng. *month*.]

māsa, *m.* —1. moon, *see* pūrṇa-māsa; —2. month. [transition-stem fr. mā́s, 399.]

māsa-traya, *n.* month-triad, three months.

māsa-ṣaṭka, *n.* month-hexade, six months.

māhina, *a.* glad, blithe. [√mah, 1177b.]

√ 1 **mi** (minóti, minuté; mimāya; mitá; -mítya). build; establish; set up (a post, pillar). [collateral form (250a) of √1 mā, 'make, build,' q.v.: cf. mit and Lat. *mē-ta*. 'post'; *mū-rus*, 'wall.']

√ 2 mi or mī (mināti, mīnāti; mimáya, mimyé; ámeṣṭa; meṣyáte; mitá; -mīya). minish, lessen; minish, bring low; bring to nought. [cf. μι-ρό-ω, Lat. mi-nu-o, 'lessen'; AS. positive min, 'small'; Old High Ger. comp. minniro, ▪minv-iro, Middle High Ger. minre, Ger. minder, 'less'; μείων, ▪μη-ίων, 'less'; Lat. min-or, 'less'; per-mi-t-ie-s, 'ruin': fr. AS. min comes perhaps Eng. minnow, 'very small fish.'] + pra, bring to nought; pass. come to nought, perish.

√ migh, see mih.

mit, f. post, pillar, prop. [√1 mi, 'set up,' 383b⁸: for mg, cf. Eng. post, Lat. postis, with pōnere, 'set up.']

mitrá, −1. m. friend, comrade (Vedic only); esp. −2. Mitra, name of an Aditya; −3. n. friendship (rare and Vedic only); −4. n. friend (commonest meaning and gender).

mitrabandhu-hīna, a. destitute of friends and relatives. [1265, 1252.]

mitra-lābha, m. Friend-acquisition, as title of the first book of the Hitopadeça.

mitrātithi, m. Mitrātithi, name of a man. ['having Mitra as his guest' or else 'guest of M.': the mg of the cpd depends on its accent (see 1302¹ and 1267¹), and this is not known: mitrá + átithi.]

mitrá-váruṇā, nom. du. m. Mitra and Varuna. [see 1255 and a, and Whitney 94a.]

√ mith (méthati; mimótha; mithitá; mithitvá). −1. meet together as friends, associate with, pair; −2. meet as rivals, dispute, wrangle, altercari. [observe that Eng. meet is just such a vox media and means both 'harmonize' and 'have a conflict.']

mithás, adv. together, mutually, among each other; in turns. [√mith, 1111d.]

mithu, a. wrong; false; used only in the adv. acc. s. n. míthu (1111d), and instr. s. f. mithuyá (1112e), wrongly, falsely. [√mith: for mg, observe that Ger. verkehren means both 'to turn the wrong way' and 'to associate with,' whence Verkehr, 'intercourse,' and verkehrt, 'wrong.']

mithuná, −1. a. paired, forming a pair; − 2. m., later n. pair (consisting of a male and female), pair of children; pair (of anything). [√mith, 1177c.]

mithuyá, adv. falsely. [see míthu: acct!]

mithyá, adv. wrongly, falsely. [younger form of mithuyá.]

mithyopacāra, m. false service or simulated kindness. [mithyā + upacāra, 1279, mithyā being used as a quasi-adj.]

√ mil (milāti; miméla; miliṣyáti; militá; militvá; -mílya). meet; assemble. [cf. Lat. mille, 'assemblage, host, thousand,' pl. mil-ia, whence the borrowed Eng. mile, 'a thousand (paces), mīlia passuum'; perhaps mil-it-es, 'going in companies or troops' and so, like Eng. troops, 'soldiers.']

√ miç, mix, in the desid. mimikṣ (see 1033), and the deriv. miçra or miçla. [cf. μίγνυμι, ▪μιχ-νυ-μι, Lat. misceo, ▪mic-sc-eo, 'mix'; Old High Ger. misken, Ger. mischen, Lat. miscian, ▪mih-sc-ian, whence Eng. mix for misk (like ax, formerly good English for ask); also Eng. mash, 'mixture' esp. of grains, whence verb mash, 'mix, and esp. make into a confused mass by crushing.']

miçrá, a. mixed. [√miç, 1188.]

miçrībháva, m. the becoming mixed, the mingling (intrans.). [miçrībhū.]

miçrībhāva-karman, n. mingling-action, process of becoming mixed.

miçrībhū, become mixed. [miçra, 1094.]

miçla, same as miçra. [1189.]

√ miṣ (miṣáti; miméṣa; ámīmiṣat; miṣitá; -míṣya). open the eyes, have the eyes open.

+ ni, close the eyes; fall asleep; wink.

√ mih or migh (méhati; ámikṣat; mekṣyáti; mídhá [222³]). make water. [fr. migh (223³) come ppl. méghamāna, and noun meghá, 'cloud': cf. ὀ-μιχ-έω, Lat. ming-ere, AS. mig-an, 'make water': orig. mg, 'pour out,' whence on the one hand 'mingere' and on the other 'rain, drip, drop' (cf. noun míh); then, fig. 'drop fatness, bestow richly' (see under mídhvāṅs).]

mih, *f.* mist. [√mih: cf. *ὀ-μίχ-λη*, 'mist';
AS. *mist, emig-st,* Eng. *mist.*]

mīdhvāṅs, *a.* bestowing richly, bountiful.
[said to be perfect ppl. of √mih, 222²,
790b, 803².]

mīmāṅsya, *grdv.* to be called in question.
[fr. desid. of √man, 1028e, 963.]

mīlhúṣe, *see* mīdhvāṅs *and* Whitney 54.

mukta-çāpa, *a.* having a laid aside
curse, leaving his curse behind him.
[√muc.]

múkha, *n.* —1. mouth, 39⁸, 40¹⁰, 51¹²;
jaws, 18²⁸; —2. visage, countenance,
face, 13⁸; snout *or* face of an animal,
44¹²; at end of cpds, esp. w. an adj.
[1298a], *or adjectively used prep.* [1305],
or adv. [1306] *denoting direction:* udañ-
mukha, having a northward face, turning
northward; abhi-mukha, having the face
towards; —3. *(like Eng.* face*)* surface,
25²¹; —4. *(like Eng.* head, *and like* chief
from caput*)* the head, *i.e.* chief, best,
most excellent, 51²³.

múkhya, *a.* (at the mouth *or* front, *and
so*) chief, most excellent. [múkha, cf.
ṇg 4: 1212a.]

√muc (muñcáti, -te [758]; mumóca, mu-
mucé; ámucat; mokṣyáti, -te; muktá;
móktum; muktvá; -múcya; mocáyati,
-te [1041²]). release; free; let go; let
loose, 34¹⁴; lay aside; release *esp.* from
the bonds of sin (93¹³) *or* existence; (let
go, *i.e.* emit *or*) utter, *e.g.* sounds; shed
(tears); discharge (phlegm, urine, ordure,
smells). [orig. mg, 'to free *or* clear':
specialized in Greek and Latin — 'to clear
the nose, to snot': cf. *ἀπο-μύσσω, ἀ-μυκ-jω,*
Lat. *e-mung-o,* 'snot'; *μυκ-τήρ,* 'snout,
nose'; Lat. *mūc-us,* 'snot': for mg, cf.
relation of snout to the cognate verbs *snot*
and *snite.*]

+ nis, let out; release.

+ pra, let go forth from, release from,
w. abl.

+ vi, loosen, *e.g.* a bond (acc.) from (abl.),
79¹⁸; untie; free; *pass.* be freed *or* separated from, be deprived of, *w. abl., but
also w. instr.* (283²). [for last mg, cf.
Eng. *loose* with *lose.*]

múñja, *m.* sedge; *esp.* Saccharum Munja.

√mud (módate; mumudé; modiṣyáte;
muditá). be glad, rejoice; mudita, glad,
happy. [cf. √mad and √1mand.]

+ ā, *in* āmoda.

múni, *m.* —1. pressure, the pressing onward, impetus, 78⁷; — 2. a man driven on
by inward pressure *or* impulse, person in
a (religious) ecstasy, enthusiast; *later*
—3. *any* distinguished sage *or* seer *or*
ascetic, *esp.* one who has taken a vow of
silence (*cf.* máuna); hermit, 40⁹, etc.

mumūrṣu, *a.* wishing to die, about to die,
moribund. [fr. desid. of √1mr, 1028b,
1178f.]

√muṣ (muṣṇáti; mumóṣa; ámoṣīt; muṣ-
itá; muṣitvá; -múṣya). rob; steal. [cf.
múṣ, 'the thief, *i.e.* mouse'; *μῦς,* 'mouse,'
and from the shape, 'muscle'; Lat. *mūs,*
'mouse,' whence diminutive *mus-culus,*
'muscle'; AS. *mūs,* 'mouse' and 'muscle,'
Eng. *mouse;* Ger. *Maus,* 'mouse' (whence
denom. *mausen,* 'steal,' in which we are
brought back again to the orig. mg of
the primitive), and also 'muscle of the
thumb'; further, *μυῖα, ϵμυσια,* Lat. *mus-ca,*
'fly': see also muṣka.]

muṣká, *m.* —1. testicle; —2. pudenda
muliebria. [from noun muṣ, *i.e.* (383a²)
múṣ, 'mouse': for mgs, see under √muṣ:
cf. *μύσ-χον· τὸ ἀνδρεῖον καὶ γυναικεῖον μόριον:*
w. muṣka, cf. also Persian *mushk,* Eng.
musk, 'perfume got from a bag behind
the navel of the musk-deer.']

muṣka-deça, *m.* region of the testes,
groin.

muṣṭí, *m. f.* fist.

músala, *m. n.* pestle. [181c.]

√muh (múhyati, -te; mumóha, mumuhé;
ámuhat; mohiṣyáti; mugdhá, mūḍhá).
be confused; err; lose one's senses;
mūḍha, foolish, *and as subst.,* fool, simple-
ton. [cf. Lat. *mūg-er,* 'false player.']

múhus, *adv.* suddenly; in a moment;
muhur muhus, at one moment — at
another, *i.e.* repeatedly. ['in a bewilder-
ing way,' √muh, 1111d.]

muhūrtá, *m. n.* —1. moment; —2. thir-
tieth of a day, an hour (of 48 minutes),
59¹⁰. [muhus.]

mūḍha, *see* √muh.

mū́tra, *n.* urine.

mūrkhā́, *a.* stupid, foolish; *as* m. fool.
[√mūrch, mg 3.]

mūrkha-çata, *n.* fool-hundred.

√mūrch (mū́rchati; mumū́rcha; mūr-
chitá, mūrtá [220²]). become rigid:
— 1. coagulate, acquire consistency; *and
so* — 2. take shape, be formed; — 3. (become stiff, numb, torpid, *and so*) become
stupid, senseless. [for mg 3, cf. Eng.
torpid, 'numb,' and then 'dull, stupid':
see mūrti and mūrkha.]

mū́rti, *f.* firm body, definite shape, em-
bodiment. [√mūrch, 220².]

mū́rtimant, *a.* having bodily form, incarnate. [mūrti, 1235.]

mūrdhán, *m.* forehead, skull; head;
oftenest figuratively, highest part; mūrdhni, at the head.

mū́la, *n.* root; *fig.* (*like* Eng. root), that
from which a thing grows or proceeds,
root, basis; capital.

mūlya, *n.* price, 47⁸˙¹¹; capital, 46¹⁴.
[properly, perhaps, adj. 'pertaining to
the root, radical, basal,' and then, as
subst., 'basis' of a transaction: fr. mūla,
q.v.]

mū́ṣ, *m. f.* mouse. ['the thief,' √muṣ,
q.v.: see 383a².]

mūṣaka, *m.* thief; mouse, 46¹⁷; Mousey,
as name of a man, 47²¹. [√muṣ, q.v.]

mūṣakākhyā, *f.* the name Mousey.
[ākhyā: 1280b.]

mūṣika, *m.* mouse, rat. [√muṣ, q.v.]

mūṣika-nirviçeṣa, *a.* undistinguished
from a mouse.

√ 1 mṛ (mriyáte [773]; mamā́ra; amṛta;
mariṣyáti; mṛtá; mártum; mṛtvā́).
die; mṛtá, dead. [w. mṛtá, cf. βροτός,
ἄμβροτος, 'mortal'; cf. φλὸξ ἐ-μαρ-άν-θη,
'flame died away'; Lat. *mor-i,* 'die';
mors, stem *mor-ti-,* 'death'; Goth. maur-
þr, AS. morðor, Eng. *murther, murder:*
see amṛta.]

+ abhi, (*lit.* die against, *i.e.*) affect un-
pleasantly by dying; guruṇā_abhimṛta,
(affected by a teacher by dying, *i.e.*)
bereaved by the death of a teacher.

√ 2 mṛ (mṛṇā́ti; mṛṇáti [731]; mūrṇā́.)
crush; smash. [cf. μάρ-να-μαι, 'fight,'

used of "bruisers," Odyssey 18.31; μύλ-η,
'mill'; Lat. *mol-a,* 'mill'; Eng. *meal* (for
mg, cf. piṣṭa); AS. *mol-de,* Eng. *mol-d,*
'fine earth' (for mg, cf. mṛd): cf. also
√mṛd.]

√ 3 mṛ, *exists perhaps in* marut. [cf. μαρ-
μαίρω, ϲμαρ-μαρ-ju, 'flash'; Lat. *mar-mor,*
'marble.']

mṛgá, *m.* — 1. (*like AS.* deōr) wild animal,
beast of the forest, *as opp. to* paçu,
'cattle,' 67²; *then* — 2. (*w. the same specialization of mg as in Eng.* deer) animal
of the genus Cervus, deer, gazelle. [per-
haps 'the ranger, rover,' √mṛj, q.v.: for
2, observe the use of *deer* in the more
general sense in King Lear, iii.4.128,
"rats and such small deer."]

√ mṛj (mā́rṣṭi [627]; mamā́rja; āmārjīt,
ámārkṣīt; mārkṣyáte; mṛṣṭá; mā́rṣṭum;
mṛṣṭvā́; -mṛ́jya; *also* mā́rjitum, mār-
jitvā́, -mā́rjya). rub off; wipe away;
clean; polish.

[original meaning 'move hither and
thither over': then, on the one hand,
— 1. 'range, rove, streifen,' as in Avestan
merḗgh, and Skt. mṛga; and, on the
other, — 2. 'go over with the hand, *i.e.*
rub, wipe, strip (a tree, a cow), milk':
for 2, cf. ὁ-μόργ-νυμι, 'wipe off'; ἀ-μέργ-ω,
'strip off, pluck'; ἀ-μέλγ-ειν, Lat. *mulg-
ēre,* 'to milk'; AS. noun *meolc,* Eng.
milk.]

+ apa, wipe away; *also fig.,* of guilt.
[cf. ἀπομόργνυμι, 'wipe away.']

+ pra, wipe off, polish.

√ mṛd (mṛlā́ti, mṛláyati [1041²]). be
gracious; forgive. [for ḷ, see Whitney
54.]

mṛlīká, *n.* grace, mercy. [√mṛd, 1186⁴,
Whitney 54.]

mṛtá, *ppl.* dead; *as n.* [1176a], death.
[√1 mṛ, 'die.']

mṛtavat, *adv.* as if dead. [mṛta,
1107.]

mṛtyú, *m.* death. [√1 mṛ, 'die,' 1165a:
see 95¹⁶.]

√ mṛd (mṛdnā́ti; má̄rdati, -te; mamā́rda;
mardiṣyáte; mṛditá; má̄rditum;
mṛditvā́; -mṛ́dya). press or rub hard,
squeeze, crush, smash, destroy.

[extension of √2 mṛ, 'crush': cf. ἀ-μαλδ-
ύνω, 'destroy' e.g. a wall: w. mṛdú, 'soft,
weak,' cf. Lat. *mollis, ∗molvis, ∗moldv-i-s,
'soft, weak,' and βραδύς, ∗μραδυ-s, 'slow'
(for mg, cf. Ger. *weich*, 'soft,' w. Eng.
weak, and Lat. *lēn-is*, 'soft,' w. *len-tus*,
'slow'):

with √mṛd in hima-mardana, 'melting
of the snow,' we might compare μέλδω,
'melt,' Eng. *melt*; but the *s* of the collateral form *smelt* makes this doubtful:
see also mradas.]

+ vi, destroy.

mṛd, *f.* earth; loam; clay; mound of
earth, 62¹⁸. [prop. 'crumbled earth,'
√mṛd: similar specializations of mg are
frequent: thus AS. *mol-de*, 'crumbling
earth, dust,' Eng. *mol-d*, come fr. a √mal,
the cognate of √2 mṛ, 'crush, crumble';
Ger. *Grand*, 'sand,' is fr. the same root
as Eng. *grind*; Ger. *Scholle*, 'clod,' and
zer-schellen, 'break to pieces,' go back to
the same root; logá and loṣṭá, 'clod,'
are deriv of √ruj, 'break.']

mṛdú, *a.* soft; weak. [√mṛd, q.v.]

mṛnmáya, *a.* made of earth; w. gṛha,
house of clay, the grave. [mṛd + maya:
see maya.]

√ mṛç (mṛçáti, -te; mamárça, mamṛçé;
ámṛkṣat; mṛṣṭá; márṣṭum; -mṛçya).
—1. touch, mulcêre, stroke; grasp, take
hold of; —2. take hold of mentally,
consider. [cf. the Hesychian βρακεῖν,
√∗μρακ, 'grasp, understand'; Lat. *mulc-
ēre*, 'stroke.']

+ abhi, touch.

√ mṛṣ (mṛṣyati, -ti; mamárṣa, mamṛṣé;
ámarṣiṣṭa; -mṛṣya; *caus.* marṣáyati).
—1. forget, 92¹⁶; —2. (*like Eng.* not
mind) disregard, treat as of no consequence, bear patiently.

meka, a setting up, *in* su-méka. [√1 mi,
'establish.']

mékhalā, *f.* girdle, *see* 59³ ⁿ.

meghá, *m.* cloud. [√mih, *see* mih.]

médas, *n.* fat. [√mid or med (761a),
médyati, 'be fat.']

médha, *m.* —1. juice of meat, broth;
—2. sap and strength, essential part, *esp.*
of the sacrificial victim; —3. sacrificial

victim; animal sacrifice. [cf. √mid
under médas.]

medhas, wisdom, *in* su-medhas. [equiv.
of medhā.]

medhā, *f.* wisdom.

melaka, *m.* assembly; w. kṛ, assemble.
[√mil, 1181.]

modaka, *m.* small round comfit, sweet-
meat. [prop. 'gladdener,' √mud, 1181:
so Eng. *cheer* and *refreshment* are applied
esp. to eatables.]

mauñjá, *a.* made of Munja-grass; —*f.*
-ī, *sc.* mekhalā, girdle of Munja-grass.
[múñja, 1208f.]

mauñji-nibandhana, *n.* ligation of
the Munja-girdle.

mauná, *n.* silence. [múni, 1208d.]

mna, *uncertain verbal.* minded; *assumed
on account of* sumná. [√mnā.]

√ mnā (mánati; ámnāsīt; mnātá). *collateral form of* √man, 'be minded,' 108g.
[see √man: cf. μι-μνή-σκω, 'keep in
mind.']

√ myakṣ (myákṣati; mimyákṣa [785];
ámyak). be fixed in *or* on; be present.

+ sam, keep together, 73⁴.

mradas, *n.* softness. [√mrad, collateral
form of √mṛd, q.v.]

√ mlā (mláyati; mamlāú; ámlāsīt;
mlāná). wither. [collateral form of
√1 mṛ, 'die,' and so 'perish, decay,
fade.']

mlāna-sraj, *a.* having a withered garland.

√ mluc (mlócati; mumlóca; mluktá).
go.

+ apa, go off, retire; apamlukta, retired, hidden.

mlecchá, *m.* barbarian. [√mlech.]

√ mlech (mlécchati). speak unintelligibly
or barbarously. [root ∗mlēk: mlécchati
is for ∗mlēk-sketi, like prócchati, q.v., for
∗pṛksketi: cf. ἀ-μ(β)λακ-εῖν, √μλακ, 'err,
miss'; βλάξ, βλακ-ός, 'stupid.']

---

yá [500], *relative pron.* —1. who, which;
sometimes following its correlative: 7⁶, 17¹⁸,
29⁵, 30¹⁶, 33¹⁶, 52⁷, 73⁹, 78¹⁰, 79⁷;
evambhūto vidvān, yas ·· samarthas,

tam doctus · · qui possit, 19⁴; —2. but much oftener preceding its correlative: ya · · ta, 77¹², 69⁷, 3¹³, 17¹³, 21²³, 22⁴, 30¹¹, 32¹⁰; yāni · · eṣām, 74³; yac ca ucyate · ·, etad ālasyavacanam, and (what is said, i.e.) as for the saying · ·, that is [fatalists'] sloth-talk, 18⁸˙¹¹;

—3. converting the subject or object of a verb into a substantive clause:— sometimes, perhaps, merely for metre: 29³, 38⁷, 58⁶; but often for emphasis: 9¹³, 56¹⁹, 57⁷; yé pakṣā́ āsaṅs, té jīmūtā́ abhavan, what were wings, those became clouds, for té pakṣā́ abhavan jīmūtās, 93³; ayáṁ yó hótā, kír u sá yamásya, who this priest [is], is he also that of Yama, 88¹⁰; so yad, even w. words of different gender and number, as, prajā́pater vā́ etáj jyeṣṭhám tokám, yát párvatās, of P. that [was] the first creation, what the mountains are, 92¹⁹; so 95¹⁵, 97¹;

—4. which, what, as adj. pron. agreeing w. incorporated antecedent: ná asmāi vidyút siṣedha, ná yā́m míham ákirad dhrādúniṁ ca, not for him did the lightning avail, not what mist he scattered abroad, and hail, 71⁴; so 71²⁰ to 72², 74⁴, 79⁹ ?, 83³, 88⁷; as subst. pron., the antecedent not being expressed, 74¹˙², 78¹⁸;

—5. ya in special connections: ya ya [511], whoever, whichever, whatever, whosoever, etc., 13¹², 45¹³; so ya ka ca, 68¹⁰; ya ka cid, 60²², 68¹²; ya ka cana, 9¹⁶; ya ka cid, anyone soever, no matter who, quilibet, 21¹¹; so ya ta, 18⁴; —6. two or more relatives in the same clause: yo 'tti yasya yadā mānsam, when (who) someone eats the flesh of (whom) someone, 29⁷; so 37¹¹, 66¹³; —7. ya, if anybody, si quis (really an anacoluthon): so 79¹⁶; —8. ya, and · · he, 74¹⁵; —9. for further illustration, see 512, 511; for derivatives, 510; for influence on the accent of the verb, 595; cf. yad, yasmāt, yāt, yena.

[orig. and primarily a demonstrative (like Eng. that and Ger. der): cf. ṓs, 'he,' in ꜣ ꝺ' ṓs, 'said he'; ṓs, 'so,' in oꝰꝺ' ṓs, 'not even sṓ'; —secondarily a relative (like Eng. that and Ger. der): cf. ṓs, ꜣ or ꜣ, ꝺ for ꝺꝺ, 'who, which'; hence yát,

with which cf. ṓs, 'as'; —but these comparisons are rejected in toto by some.]

√ yakṣ (yákṣate). perhaps an extended form of ·yah (·yagh), 'stir, move quickly': and so, on the one hand, pursue, esp. pursue avengingly, avenge, and on the other, dart swiftly (as a suddenly appearing light). [see the following three words and √·yah: kinship of Ger. jag-en, 'pursue, hunt,' is doubted.]

yakṣá, n. spirit or sprite or ghost; as m. a Yaksha, one of a class of fabulous genii, attendants of Kubera. [perhaps 'a restless one,' √yakṣ: for connection of mgs of root and deriv., cf. the converse relation of Eng. spirit or sprite to sprightly, 'brisk, stirring,' and cf. Scott's "restless sprite."]

yakṣín, a. avenging. [√yakṣ.]

yákṣma, m. disease. [perhaps, the sin-avenging Varuna's 'avenger,' √yakṣ, 1166.]

√ yaj (yájati, -te; iyā́ja, ījé [784¹]; áyākṣīt, áyaṣṭa; yakṣyáti, -te; iṣṭá; yáṣṭum; iṣṭvā́; caus. yājáyati). honor a god (acc.), 99¹²; worship; worship with prayer and oblation (instr.); and so consecrate, hallow, offer; sacrifice; in Veda, active, when one honors or sacrifices (e.g., as a paid priest) on account of another, and middle, when one sacrifices on one's own account; yájamāna, as m. one who institutes or performs a sacrifice and pays the expenses of it; —caus. cause or help or teach a person (acc.) to worship with a certain sacrifice (instr.); serve a person as sacrificing priest. [cf. ἅγ-ος, 'worship, sacred awe, expiatory sacrifice'; ἅζομαι, ·ἅγ-jομαι, 'stand in awe of,' e.g. gods; ἁγ-νός, 'worshipped, hallowed'; w. yaj-ya, 'colendus,' cf. ἅγ-ιος, 'to be worshipped, holy': different is ἅγος, see āgas.]

+ ā, get as result of sacrifice a thing (acc.) for a person (dat.), einem etwas er-opfern.

yájatra, a. venerable, holy. [√yaj, 1185d.]

yájīyāṅs, a. excellently sacrificing, right cunning in the art of sacrifice. [√yaj, 1184, 468.]

yajur-vedá, *m.* the Veda of sacrificial texts, Yajurveda. [see yajus.]

yájuṣmant, *a.* (possessing, *i.e.*) accompanied by sacrificial texts; —*f.* -matī (*sc.* iṣṭakā), Yajushmatī, name applied to certain bricks used in building the sacred fire-pile, and so called because each was laid with the recitation of a special text of its own. [yajus, 1235.]

yájus, *n.* —1. sacred awe; worship; —2. sacrificial text, as distinguished from stanza (ṛc) and chant (sāman); —3. the collection of such texts, the Yajur-veda. [√yaj, 1154.]

yajñá, *m.* worship, devotion (*so in Veda*); *later, esp.* act of worship, sacrifice, offering (*these the prevailing mgs*). [√yaj, 1177a, 201.]

yajña-kratú, *m.* sacrifice-ceremony, *i.e.* rite. [1280b.]

yajña-cchāga, *m.* sacrifice-goat. [chāga, 227.]

yajña-pātrá, *n.* sacrificial utensil. ·

yajñārtham, *adv.* for a sacrifice. [artham, 1302c4.]

yajñíya, *a.* —1. worthy of worship or sacrifice, reverend, holy, divine; —2. active or skillful in sacrifice, pious; *as m.* offerer. [yajña, 1214.]

yajñopavītá, *a.* the sacrifice-cord, sacred cord worn over the left shoulder. [upavīta.]

yájvan, *m.* worshipper, sacrificer. [√yaj, 1169.1a.]

√yat (**yátati**, -te; **yeté**; **áyatiṣṭa**; **yatiṣyáti**, -te; **yatitá**, **yattá**; **yátitum**; -**yátya**). —1. *act.* join, *trans.*; —2. *mid.* join, *intrans.*; range one's self in order, proceed in rows, 86¹⁴; —3. *mid.* try to join, strive after; take pains; —4. *caus.* (cause to attain, *i.e.*) requite with reward or punishment. [perhaps orig. 'reach out after' and akin w. √yam.]
+ **ā**, reach to, attain, get a foot-hold.
+ **pra**, (reach out, *i.e.*) make effort, take pains.

yátas, *adv.* from what (time *or* place *or* reason): —1. where, 6¹⁴; —2. because, for, 28²², 38⁵; *esp. common as introducing a proverb or the first (only) of a series of* proverbs *motivating a preceding statement or action*, *e.g.* 19⁷; **yatas · · tena**, since · · therefore, 30⁷; *so* **yatas · · atas**, 36²; **yatas · · tad**, 37⁶; *cf.* **tatas**. [pron. root ya, 510, 1098.]

1 **yáti** [519], *pron.* as many, quot. [pron. root ya, 510, 1157.4.]

2 **yáti**, *m.* ascetic, man who has restrained his passions and abandoned the world; *see* āçrama *and* 65³ᴺ. ['striver, one who takes pains, one who castigates himself,' √yat, 1155: its mg was perhaps shaded towards that of 'restrainer' by a popular connection of the word with √yam, 1157¹, cf. 954d.]

yatna, *m.* a striving after; effort; pains; *w.* kṛ: take pains; bestow effort upon (*loc.*), have a thing (*loc.*) at heart, 1¹⁸; **yatne kṛte**, pains having been taken. [√yat, 1177.]

yátra, *adv.* where, *e.g.* 11¹⁰; whither; —*correl. w.* tatra, 24⁴, 85¹⁹; *w.* enā, 83¹⁰; **yatra yatra**, where soever; **catuṣpathe, yatra vā**, at a quadrivium, or somewhere (else), 104²¹. [pron. root ya, 510, 1099.]

yáthā, *rel. adv. and conj.* —1. in which way, as; *sometimes following its correlative:* **tathā · · yathā**, 22¹⁴, 43²⁰, 44²⁰; **evam · · yathā**, 37⁸; —2. *but much oftener preceding its correlative:* **teṣāṁ saṁ hanmo akṣāṇi, yathā_idaṁ harmiaṁ, tathā**, of them we close the eyes, as (we close) this house, so, 77¹²; *so* 61⁶, 27¹⁴, 21¹⁶·¹⁸, etc.; **yathā · · evam**, 18¹⁸, 95⁷·⁹; **yathā · · eva** (*Vedic*), 86¹²·¹²;

—3. *correlative omitted:* **buddhiṁ prakuruṣva, yathā_icchasi**, decide (so), as thou wishest, 9¹¹; 5²⁰, etc.; *so with verbs of saying, etc.:* **tad brūhi, yathā · · upadadhāma**, this tell us (*viz.* the way) in which we are to put on · ·, 96¹⁴; *so* 88⁶·⁷;

—4. *without finite verb, as mere particle of comparison*, as, like, *e.g.* 6¹⁹; *so enclitic at end of a* pāda, 71¹²·¹⁸, 87¹¹, 1⁶, 2⁹, 31¹, 43⁴; *in solemn declarations:* **yathā · ·, tena satyena**, as surely as · ·, so, 13²³ff.;

—5. *combinations* (*cf.* ya 5); **yathā yathā · · tathā tathā**, according as · · so, the more · · the more, 48¹²; **yathā tathā**, in some way or other (*cf.* ya 5 end), at any rate, 62⁹;

—6. in order that, so that, ut, (so) that : *in Veda, w. subjunctive,* 88¹⁴, 89⁵·¹⁰·¹², 90¹⁹; *later, w. opt.,* 14⁹; *w. fut. ind.,* 3⁴; *w. pres. ind.,* yathā svāmī jāgarti, tathā mayā kartavyam, I must act so, that the master wakes, 30¹⁶; *so* 37⁵·⁷, 38²², 39¹; —7. that, *w. verbs of saying, knowing, etc.,* 30⁷; —*for influence on accent of verb, see* 595. [pron. root ya, 510, 1101: cf. article ya.]

yathā-kartavya, *a.* requiring to be done under given circumstances ; *as n.* the proper course of action, 41¹¹.

yathākāmám, *adv.* according to wish, agreeably, 16²; in an easy-going way, slowly, 49¹⁴. [yathā + kāma, 1313b.]

yathā-kārya, – yathākartavya.

yathākramam, *adv.* according to order, in regular series. [yathā + krama, 1313b.]

yathāgata, *a.* on which one came; -am, *adv.* by the way by which one came. [yathā + āgata, √gam, 1313b.]

yathāṅgám, *adv.* limb after limb *or* limb on limb; membrātim. [yathā + aṅga, 1313b.]

yathātatham, *adv.* as it really is, accurately. [yathā + tathā, 1313b, 1314a.]

yathābhimata, *a.* as desired, that one likes. [yathā + abhimata, √man.]

yathābhimata-deça, *m.* desired place, place that one likes. [1280¹.]

yathāyogyam, *adv.* as is fit, according to propriety. [yathā + yogya, 1313b.]

yathārtha, *a.* according to the thing *or* fact, true; *as n.* the pure truth. [yathā + artha.]

yathārha, *a.* according to that which is fit; -am, *adv.* suitably, according to one's dignity. [yathā + arha, 1313b.]

yathāvat, *adv.* according to *le comment, comme il faut,* duly. [yathā, 1107.]

yathāvidhi, *adv.* according to prescription *or* rule. [yathā + vidhi, 1313b.]

yathā-vṛtta, *a.* as happened; -am, *w. verb of telling :* either the actual occurrence *or* circumstances (*as nom. or acc. s. n.*), *or* as it really happened (*as adv.,* 1313b).

yathāçraddhám, *adv.* according to inclination, as you will. [yathā + çraddhā, 1313b, 334².]

yathepsita, *a.* as desired ; -am, *adv.* according to one's wish. [yathā + īpsita, √āp.]

yathokta, *a.* as (afore-)said ; -am, *adv.* as aforesaid. [yathā + ukta.]

yád, —1. *as nom. acc. s. n.* to ya, *see* ya; *used in cpds and derivs, see* 510; —2. *as conjunctive adv.* that; tan na bhadram kṛtam, yad viçvāsaḥ kṛtas, therefore it was not well done (herein), that trust was reposed, 22¹⁷; ninyā ciketa, pṛçnir yad ūdho jabhāra,- he knoweth the secret, that P. offered her udder, 78⁸; *introducing oratio recta,* 38¹; yad · ·, tad, as for the fact that · ·, therein, 36¹; *so* 94¹⁶; yad vái tad abruvan, as for the fact that they said thát, indeed, 96²⁸;

—3. *in causal connections : like Eng. that* (*i.e.* on account of which), 78¹⁶; yad · · tad, since · · therefore, 17⁵; yad · · tasmāt, inasmuch as · · therefore, 15³; since (*i.e.* considering that), 79¹⁴; *purpose:* in order that, 78⁹, 72¹²·¹⁴; *result:* that, 71⁶·⁷; etādṛçā dharmajñā, yan mām hantum udyatās, so understanding the law, as to undertake to slay me, 28⁶;

—4. *temporal:* as, 86⁶; tad · · yad, then · · when, 71²; yad · · tatas, when · · then, 92¹²; so yad · · tādītnā, 70⁷; *correl. often lacking:* yad · ·, · ·, when · ·, (*sc.* then), 75¹²; so 80⁸, 81¹⁷; while, 71⁵; —*hence, the temporal use passing insensibly* (*cf.* yad vaçāma, when *or* if we will, 73¹⁷, *and Eng.* when *w.* Ger. wenn) *into the conditional,* — 5. if, 80⁹·¹⁰·¹¹; —yad *placed within the dependent clause,* 78⁸ (*quoted under* 2), 79¹⁴; —*for influence on acct of verb, see* 595. [pron. root ya, 510, 1111a.]

yadā, *adv.* when; yadā · · tadā *or* tatas, when · · then; yadā · · atha, *Vedic,* 84⁴·⁵·⁷; yadā yadā, quandocunque, *see* tadā. [pron. root ya, 1103a.]

yádi, *adv.* if ; —1. *w. pres. ind. in protasis: apodosis has pres. ind.,* 20¹⁷, 37¹², 42¹⁴, 43⁷, 65²⁸, 99⁸²; *has fut.,* 39²⁰, 44⁴; *has im-*

perative, 10[16]; *has no finite verb*, 18[17], 25[8], 28[9], 40[1]; —2. *w. fut. in protasis and apodosis*, 9[20], 11[8]; —3. *w. pres. opt. in protasis and apodosis*, 3[17], 98[20]; —4. *w. no finite verb in protasis: apodosis has imperative*, 32[17], 48[11], 84[9]; *has no finite verb*, 27[18], 28[12], 63[9]; —*alternative conditions*: · · **vā**, **yadi vā** · ·, · · **vā**, *whether* · ·, *or* · ·, *or* · ·, 28[12]; —*apodosis introduced by* **tadā** (*e.g.* 25[8]), **tad** (37[12]), **tarhi** (32[17]), *or without adv.* (*e.g.* 3[17]). [pron. root **ya**, 1103d.]

yadbhaviṣya, *a.* who says **yad bhaviṣyati**, (tad) bhaviṣyati *or* "What will be, will be"; *as m.* fatalist; Yadbhavishya *or* Whatwillb', name of a fish. [1314b.]

√ **yam** (yácchati, -te [747]; yayáma, yemé; áyāṁsīt, áyaṁsta; yaṁsyáti; yatá; yáṁtum; yamitvá; -yámya). hold; hold up, sustain, support; hold back, restrain; hold out, offer, grant, furnish; show (the teeth), 77[4]. [cf. *ǵṇḷa*, 'restraint, *i.e.* punishment.']

+ **ā**, hold out, *i.e.* extend, *and so* (*like Eng.* extend), lengthen; **áyata**, extended, long.

+ **ud**, —1. raise (the arms, weapons), 35[20]; —2. (*like Eng.* take up, *i.e.*) undertake *or* set about (a thing); **udyata**, having undertaken, *w. inf.*, 28[6].

+ **sam-ud**, *like* ud-yam [1077b]: —1. raise; —2. set about; **samudyata**, having set about, *w. inf.*, 40[2]).

+ **upa**, hold on to, take hold of; *esp.*, *middle*, take to wife, marry, 98[8].

+ **ni**, hold, restrain; **niyata**, having restricted one's self (to a certain thing), all intent upon one definite object.

+ **pra**, hold *or* reach out, offer, give; give in marriage (as a father his daughter), 98[7].

+ **prati-pra**, offer in turn, pass (food), *w. gen.*, 100[2]).

+ **vi**, hold asunder, stretch out.

+ **sam**, hold together, co-hibēre, hold in check; **saṁyata**, restrained.

yáma, —1. *a.* holding, restraining; —2. *m.* (holder, *i.e.*) bridle. [√yam.]

yamá, —1. *a.* paired, twin, geminus; *as m.* a twin; —2. The Twin, Yama, who, with his sister Yamī, constituted the first human pair, *selection* lxiii.; honored as father of mankind (*cf. also* **manu**) and as king of the spirits of the departed fathers (**pitaras**), *see* 83[8]ɴ.; *in later times*, regarded as the 'Restrainer' (√yam) or 'Punisher,' and ruler of death and of the dead in the under-world, 7[11]; —yamí, *f.* Yamī, twin sister of Yama. [so *Thomas*, Hebrew *t'om*, means 'twin.']

yamá-rājan, *a.* having Yamá as their king; *as m.* subject of Yama. [1302a.]

yayáti, *m.* Yayāti, a patriarch of the olden time, son of Nahusha. [perhaps 'The Striver,' √yat, cf. 1155.2c: or from √yā, 1157.1c.]

yáva, *m. orig. prob.* any grain *or* corn, yielding flour; *later*, barley-corn, barley. [cf. *ǵeid*, *ǵaF-id*, 'corn.']

yava-madhyama, *a.* having a barley-corn middle, *i.e.* big in the middle and small at the ends, like a crescendo-diminuendo sign; *as n.* the Yavamadhyama, name of a cāndrāyaṇa or lunar penance. [1297, 1280b.]

yáviṣṭha, *a.* youngest; *esp.* of a fire just born of the sticks of attrition *or* just set on the altar. [superl. to yúvan, q.v., but from the simpler •yu, 468.]

yáviṣṭhya, *a.* = yaviṣṭha, *but always at the end of a pāda and as diiambus.*

yávīyāṁs, *a.* younger. [comp. to yúvan, q.v., but from the simpler •yu, 468.]

yáças, *n.* fame, honor. [1151.2a.]

yaçás, *a.* honored, splendid. [1151.2a.]

yaṣṭí, *f.* staff. [perhaps 'a support,' fr. yacch, quasi-root of the present system of yam: cf. 220, 1157.]

√ **yah**, stir, move quickly, *inferred fr.* yakṣ, q.v., *and* yahva, 'continually moving, restless.'

√ **yā** (yáti; yayáu; áyāsīt [911]; yāsyáti; yātá; yātum; yātvá; -yáya). —1. go, 39[1]; **yátas**, *avasitasya*, of him that journeys (and) of him that rests, 71[8]; *w.* **astam**, 62[14], *see* astam; —2. go to, *w. acc.*, 43[17], 91[6]; *w. dat.* 49[14]; —3. go to, *i.e.* attain to (a condition): *e.g.* **devatvaṁ yā**, attain to godhead, *i.e.* become divine,

19²¹; *so* 17²², etc.; —4. yātu, let it go,
no matter, 44⁸.

[collateral form of √i, 'go,' 108g:
hence yāna, 'passage, way,' w. which cf.
Lat. *jānus*, 'passage, archway,' and the
god thereof *Jānus:* fr. √yā comes also
yā-ma, 'period *or* watch of the night';
ṣ-pa, 'time, season,' Eng. *year*, show a
development of mg like that of yāma,
q.v., but their connection w. √yā is
doubtful (see 2 vāra).]

+ anu, go after, follow.

+ ā, come hither *or* to *or* on.

+ sam-ā, come hither together; assemble; samāyāta, come.

+ ud, go forth *or* out.

+ upa, go *or* attain unto.

+ pra, go forth; set out.

√ yāc (yācati, -te; yayācé; áyāciṣṭa;
yāciṣyé; yācitá; yācitum; yācitvā;
-yācya). make a request; ask a person
(*acc.*) for a thing (*acc.*), 46¹⁴; ask a
thing (*acc.*) of a person (*abl.*), 55²¹.

yāt, *adv.* as; *temporally*, so long as, 79¹⁸.
[abl. of pron. root ya, 1114a, 510: see
under ya.]

yātanā, *f.* requital; *esp.* punishment,
pains of hell. [√yat, 1150.]

yātṛ, *m.* avenger. ['pursuer,' √yā, 1182.]

yāna, *m.* way; *as n.* wagon. [√yā, 1150.]

yāmá, *f.* -ī, *a.* of *or* coming from Yama.
[yamá, 1208f.]

yāma, *m.* —1. course *or* going, 78⁵; —2. *as
in Eng.*, course (of a feast); —3. watch
of the night. [√yā, 1166: for mg 2, cf.
περί-οδος, 'way around, circuit, course at
dinner,' and Ger. *Gang*, 'course': for
mg 3, cf. περίοδος, 'time of circuit.']

yāvant [517], —1. *a.* as great, 101⁹; as
many, 64⁴, 105⁴; as much; *preceding its
correl.* tāvant; —2. yāvat, *adv.* as long,
while; tāvat · · yāvat, so long · as,
19², 42⁸; yāvat · · tāvat: as long
as · ·, so long, 15⁵, 32², 40¹⁸; as soon
as *or* the moment that · ·, then, 44¹⁸,
22⁷; —3. yāvat, *as quasi-prep. w. acc.:*
during; up to (in space *or* time); sarpa-
vivaraṁ yāvat, as far as the serpent's
hole, 39¹⁸; adya yāvat, until to-day,
24². [pron. root ya, 517: cf. tāvant.]

yāvayád-dveṣas, *a.* driving away foes.
[√2 yu, 'keep off': see 1309.]

√ 1 yu (yāúti [626], 3rd pl. yuvánti, mid.
yuté; yuváti, -te; *finite forms Vedic
only;* yutá; -yūya). fasten, hold fast;
draw towards one, attract; join, unite.

+ sam, unite; saṁyuta, connected with,
i.e. having reference to, 59¹⁴.

√ 2 yu (yuyóti; yúcchati [608²]; áyāuṣīt;
yutá; -yūya; *caus.* yāváyati). repel,
keep off *or* separate, *trans.*; *sometimes*
keep off *or* separate, *intrans.*; *a Vedic
word.*

+ pra, remove; prayucchant, removing
(*intrans.*), moving away, *and so (like Eng.*
absent), heedless.

yu, *root of 2d pers. pronoun, cf.* 494. [cf.
ὑμεῖς, Lesbian ὕμμες, 'ye': kinship of
Eng. *ye*, doubtful.]

yukti, *f.* —1. a yoking, harnessing;
—2. yoke, team. [√yuj, 1157, 219: cf.
ζεῦξις, *ζευγ-σι-ς, 'a yoking.']

yugá, *n.* —1. yoke; —2. couple, pair;
—3. *esp. w.* mánuṣa, a human generation
(*as that which is united by common
descent), γένος ἀνθρώπων; —4. *and so, in
a temporal sense, an age of the world, see*
58¹ₙ. [√yuj, q.v., 216. 1: cf. yugma.]

yugapat-prāpti, *f.* simultaneous reaching *or* arriving at. [1279 and a.]

yugapad, *adv.* simultaneously. [apparently acc. s. n. of an adj. ·yuga-pad,
'pair-footed, even-footed, side by side,' a
possessive form (1801) of a descriptive
cpd (1280b) ·yuga-pad, 'pair-foot.']

yugmá, *a.* paired, even; *as n.* pair,
couple. [√yuj, 1166, 216. 5: for mg, cf.
couple, Lat. *cōpula*, ·co-ap-ula, √ap + co-,
'fit or join together.']

√ yuj (yunákti, yuṅkté; yuyója, yuyujé;
áyukta; yokṣyáti, -te; yuktá; yóktum;
yuktvā; -yújya; yojáyati). —1. yoke;
harness; make ready for draught, *used*
of wagon (101¹⁷) as well as of steed (72⁶);
then, generalized, —2. make ready, set to
work, apply; use, *e.g.* the Soma-press-
stones, 76¹⁸; yukta, engaged upon (*loc.*),
busied with, 62¹¹; —3. unite; *middle*,
unite one's self with (*instr.*); yujāná, in
company with, 73¹²; —4. *passive*, be

15

united with (*instr.*), *i.e.* become possessed of, 60¹⁵; **yukta**: possessed of (*instr.*), 1¹²; having · ·, *at end of cpd,* 65¹²; — 5. *pass.* be joined *or* made ready, *and so* be fitted, suited; **yukta**, fit, suitable, right, proper, 23¹⁰; **yuktam**, *adv.* fitly, rightly, etc., 36²; — 6. yojayati [1041²], apply'; lay on, 102¹¹. [cf. *ζεύγ-νυμι,* Lat. *jung-o,* 'yoke, harness, join'; w. yugá, 'yoke,' cf. *ζυγόν,* Lat. *jugum,* Ger. *Joch,* Eng. *yoke :* for euphony, see 219.]

+ **ud,** *mid.* make one's self ready, set to work, exert one's self.

+ **upa,** *mid.* harness, put tó, 78¹⁸; apply, use.

+ **ni,** *mid.* — 1. fasten to; — 2. put (a task) upon, commission; — *caus.* [1041²], set, lay, *e.g.* snares, 24¹⁷. [for mg 2, cf. niyoga; also Eng. *en-join* w. its Lat. predecessor *in-jungere.*]

+ **pra,** apply, use; *w.* **namaskáram,** employ, *i.e.* do adoration.

+ **sam,** join together, unite; **samyukta,** *at end of cpd :* joined with, *i.e.* endowed with, 34⁴; connected with, *i.e.* having reference to, 59¹²·¹⁴.

yúj [389, 219, 386b], — 1. *a.* yoked together; *as m.* yoke-fellow, *and so* comrade, 88⁸; — 2. *a.* paired, even. [√yuj: see ayuj and ayuja.]

yújya, *a.* united, combined. [√yuj, 1213e.]

yuddhá, *ppl.* fought; *as n.* [1176a], fight, battle, contest. [√yudh, 1176, 160.]

yuddha-varṇa, *m.* a sort of battle; a battle, so to speak.

√ **yudh** (yúdhyate; yuyudhé; áyuddha; yotsyáte; yuddhá; yóddhum; -yúdhya). fight. [cf. *ὑσμίνη, ὑσ-μίνη,* 'battle.']

+ **á,** fight against.

yúdh, *f.* fight. [√yudh.]

yudhi-ṣṭhira, *m.* Yudhishthira, son of Pāndu and Kuntī, to whom Brihadaçva tells the story of Nala; *see* 1¹⁴ⁿ. [' firm in battle,' yudh-i (1250c) + sthira.]

√ **yup** (yuyópa; yupitá; yopáyati[1041²]). set up an obstacle, block *or* bar the way; hinder, thwart, 80¹⁰; obstruct *or* clog, *see* 86⁶ⁿ.

yuvá, *pron. stem,* 2d *pers. dual,* 491.

yuvati, *serving as a feminine to* **yúvan.** young woman; maiden. [1157.3 end: perhaps pres. ppl. of √1 yu, ' attract.']

yúvan [427], *a.* young; *as subst.* young man (*distinguished from* bāla, ' child,' 28¹²); youth (used even of youthful gods). [perhaps fr. √1 yu, ' attract,' suffix an, not van, 1160: see yavīyāṅs, yaviṣṭha, yuvati: cf. Lat. *juven-i-s,* ' young'; w. *juven-cu-s,* ' young,' cf. Germanic *-yuvunga, yunga,* Eng. *young;* also Old Eng. *yung-þe,* Spenser's *youngth,* Eng. *youth.*]

yuṣmá, see 491.

yūthá, *m. n.* herd. [prop. ' a union,' √1 yu, ' unite,' 1163: for mg, cf. also Ger. *Bande,* ' gang *or* set of men,' and Eng. *band,* ' company,' both indirectly fr. the root of *bind.*]

yūtha-nátha, *m.* protector *or* leader of the herd.

yūtha-pa, *m.* keeper *or* protector of the herd; *esp.* the elephant that leads the herd.

yūtha-pati, *m.* lord of the herd; *esp.* the elephant that leads the herd.

yūnas, *see* 427.

yūyám, *see* 491.

yena, *adv.* — 1. wherefore, 6²; — 2. **yena · · tena,** because · · therefore, 64⁹; — 3. that, ut, *introducing a result and corresponding to a 'such' or 'so' expressed* (21¹⁰) *or implied* (11⁸). [pron. root ya, 1112a.]

yéṣṭha, *pronounced* yaíṣṭha, *a.* (best going, *i.e.*) swiftest. [√yā, 470³, 468.]

yóga, *m.* — 1. a setting to work; use; appliance (act of applying); — 2. appliance (thing applied), *and so* means; *esp.* supernatural means, magic, 56⁸; — 3. (the applying one's self to a thing, *and so*) pursuit *or* acquisition (of a thing), *cf.* kṣema; — 4. connection, relation; -yogát, *at end of cpd,* from connection with · ·, *i.e.* in consequence of · ·. [√yuj, 216.1.]

yógya, *a.* of use, suited for use, fit, fitting. [yóga, 1212a.]

yoddhṛ, *m.* fighter. [√yudh, 1182, 160.]

yodhin, *a. at end of cpds,* fighting. [√yudh, 1183³.]

yóni, *m.f.* — 1. lap; womb *or* birth-place; — 2. place of origin; origin, 93⁴; — 3. birth-place, *i.e.* home; place of abiding; place, 86¹⁷, 89⁸, RV. x.125.7; — 4. (*like Eng.* origin *or* birth) family, race; form of existence (as man, Brahman, beast, etc., in the system of transmigrations) as this form is determined by birth, 67²⁰. ['the holder' of the born or unborn babe, √1yu, 'hold,' 1158.2²: cf. the analogous metaphors in Lat. *con-cipere*, 'take, hold, conceive'; and in *volva*, 'cover, envelope,' and so 'womb,' fr. a root cognate with 1vṛ, 'cover.']

yonitas, *adv.* from birth, by blood. [yoni, 1098b.]

yoṣit, *f.* young woman, maiden. [perhaps 'the attractive one,' fr. √1yu, 'attract,' 1200a, 383.3 (through the intermediate form yó-ṣā, 1197, of the same mg): cf. yuvatí.]

yāuvaná, *n.* youth, period between childhood and maturity, adolescence (of man or maid). [yúvan, 1208a.]

yāuvana-daçá, *f.* time of youth.

√ **raṅh** (ráṅhati, -te). — 1. make to run; hasten, *trans.*; — 2. *mid.* run; hasten, *intrans.* [for *raṅgh*: cf. the forms laṅgh and raghú, and see under laghú.]

raktá, *ppl.* colored; *esp.* red; *as n.* blood. [√rañj, 954a.]

√ **1rakṣ** (rákṣati, -te; rarákṣa; árakṣīt; rakṣitá; rákṣitum; -rákṣya). de-fend, protect; keep, *i.e. both* retain *and* maintain; take care of (as a sovereign), *i.e.* govern; guard, ward; save. [a desid. extension of √·rak or ark: cf. ἀλέξ-ω, 'ward off,' which bears a similar relation to √ἀλκ or ἀρκ in ἔλ-αλκ-ε, 'warded off,' ἀρκ-έω, 'ward off, protect'; cf. also Lat. *arc-eo*, 'ward off,' *arx*, 'stronghold of defence, citadel'; AS. *ealh-stede*, 'defence-stead, strong-hold'; *ealgian*, 'protect': for the two chief mgs of √rakṣ, cf. Lat. *de-fendere*, 'ward off, protect.']

+ **pari**, protect around; save.

√ **2rakṣ**, harm, *in* rakṣas. [perhaps only another aspect of 1rakṣ, 'ward off,' *i.e.* 'beat away.']

rakṣaka, *m.* keeper; warder; protector. [√1rakṣ, 1181.]

rákṣaṇa, *n.* protection; preservation. [√1rakṣ, 1150.]

rákṣas, *n.* — 1. harm; — 2. *concrete*, harmer, name of nocturnal demons who disturb sacrifices and harm the pious. [√2rakṣ, 1151.2a.]

rakṣā, *f.* protection; watch. [√1rakṣ, 1149.]

rakṣi, *a.* guarding, *at end of cpds.* [√1rakṣ, 1155.]

rakṣitṛ, *m.* protector; watcher. [√1rakṣ, 1182a.]

raghú, — 1. *a.* running, darting, swift; *as m.* runner; — 2. *m.* Raghu (The Runner, Δρομεύς), name of an ancient king. [√raṅh, q.v.: older form of laghú, q.v.]

raṅga, *m.* — 1. color; — 2. theatre, amphitheatre. [√raj *or* rañj, 216.1: connection of mg 2 unclear.]

√ **raj** *or* **rañj** (rájyati, -te; raktá; -rájya; *caus.* rañjáyati). — 1. be colored; *esp.* be red; raktá: red; dyed; *as n.* blood; — 2. *fig.* be affected with a strong feeling (*cf.* raj + vi); *esp.* be delighted with, have pleasure in, be in love with; — *caus.* — 1. color; redden; — 2. delight, please, make happy.

[orig. 'be bright *or* white' (whence rajaka); then 'glow, be red': see the ident. √3rj and its cognates ἀργυφος, etc.; and cf. √βρy in aor. βέξαι, 'dye,' and βεγεύς, 'dyer': w. this root may be connected the root rāj in its mgs given under 2.]

+ **anu**, — 1. be colored after, take the tinge of; — 2. feel affection towards.

+ **vi**, — 1. lose color; — 2. be cold *or* indifferent towards (*loc.*), 45⁸. [for mg 2, cf. the senses of the simple verb: the metaphor may be either 'not glowing,' and so, as in Eng., 'cold,' or else 'colorless,' and so, 'indifferent.']

rajaka, *m.* washerman, who is also a dyer of clothes. ['whitener' *or* else 'dyer,' √raj, 1181.]

rájas, *n.* — 1. atmosphere, air, region of clouds, vapors, and gloom, clearly distinguished from heaven (dyāus, 72²) or

15*

the ethereal spaces of heaven (rocanā́ divás, 81⁸, or svàr), "where the light dwelleth," these being beyond the **rájas**, just as the *alθήp* is beyond the *άήp*; *used loosely in pl.*, the skies, 71⁷; the sky conceived as divided into an upper and a lower stratum, *and so dual*, rajasī́, 75⁴·¹²; *so far Vedic*; —2. *post-Vedic: like the Greek άήp*, the thick air, mist, gloom, darkness; —3. dust, *e.g.* 14¹³; —4. *in the philosophical system*, darkness (*cf.* 2), the second of the three qualities (*see* guṇa), soul-darkening passion (popularly connected with rāga, 'passion'), 66⁴·¹⁶. [since the orig. mg, as indicated by usage, is 'the cloudy (region), region of gloom and dark' as distinguished from the everlasting light beyond, the word is prob. to be derived fr. √raj in the sense 'be (colored, *i.e.*) not clear': cognate are *ἔ-ρεβος*, 'darkness, Erebus,' and Goth. *riqis*, neut., 'darkness': for connection of mgs 2 and 3, *cf.* Ger. *Dunst*, 'vapor,' and Eng. *dust*.]

rájju, *f.* cord; rope. [√•rasg, 'plait': *cf.* Lithuanian *rezgis*, 'plaited work, basket'; Lat. *restis*, •*resctis*, •*rezg-ti-s*, 'rope': see √majj.]

√ rañj, *see* raj.

ráṇa, *m.* pleasure, gladness. [√ran.]

raṇvá, *a.* pleasant, lovely. [√ran, 1190.]

ráti, *f.* —1. rest, quiet; —2. comfort, pleasure. [√ram, 1157, *cf.* 954d.]

rátna, *n.* —1. gift; blessing, riches, treasure, *as something* bestowed *or* given (*cf.* ratna-dhá́); *so far Vedic*; —2. *post-Vedic*: precious stone, jewel, pearl; *fig.*, *as in Eng.*, jewel, *i.e.* the most excellent of its kind. [√1rā, 'bestow.']

ratna-dhá́ [352], *a.* bestowing blessings.

1 rátha, *m.* wagon, *esp.* the two-wheeled battle-wagon (lighter and swifter than the anas, 'dray'); car *or* chariot of gods (72⁴·⁶, 89¹¹) as well as of men (87¹⁴). [√ṛ, 'move,' 1163: for mg, *cf.* Lat. *currus*, 'chariot,' and *currere*, 'run.']

2 rátha, *m.* pleasure, joy. [√ram, 1163, cf. 954d.]

√ ran (ráṇati; raráṇa; áraṇīt). be pleased; *Vedic*. [ident. w. √ram.]

rápas, *n.* bodily injury; disease.

√ rabh (rábhate; rebhé; árabdha; rapsyáte; rabdhá; rábdhum; -rábhya). grasp; take hold of. [prob. a collateral form of √grabh, and ident. w. labh, see these: *cf.* τὰ λάφ-υρα, 'spoils, booty'; εἴ-ληφ-α, 'took'; Lat. *lab-or*, 'undertaking, labor'; perhaps ἤλφ-ον, 'gat, earned.']

+ā́, —1. take hold upon; touch, RV. x.125.8; —2. take hold of, *i.e.* undertake, 14⁶; *w.* yatnam, undertake an effort, *i.e.* exert one's self, 11²; —3. (*like Ger.* an-fangen *and Lat.* in-cipere) begin; ārabhya: *w. abl.*, beginning from • •, *or simply* from • •, 39¹³; *w.* adya, from to-day on, 36¹⁹.

+anv-ā́, take hold of from behind, hold on to.

+sam-anv-ā́, hold on to each other (said of several); sam-anv-ārabdha, touching.

+sam-ā́, undertake (*see* ā́-rabh) together.

+sam, take hold of each other (for dance, battle, etc.), hold together; take hold (of a thing) together.

√ ram (rámati, -te; rarā́ma, remé; áramāīt, áraṁsta; raṁsyáte; ratá; rámtum; raṁtvā́; -rámya; rāmáyati). —1. *act.* stop, *trans.* —2. *mid.* stop, *intrans.*; rest; abide; stay gladly with; —3. *mid.* (rest, take one's ease *or* comfort, *and so*) find pleasure in; rata, *w. loc.*, or at end of cpds, taking pleasure in, devoted to; —4. *caus.* bring to a stand-still, stay, 73⁷. [*cf.* ἤ-ρέμ-α, 'quietly'; Goth. rimis, 'quiet'; ἔραμαι, ἔραται, •ὅṃ-μαι, •ὅṃ-ται, 'love, loves'; ἐ-ρατό-ς, 'lovely,' formally ident. w. ratá: for mgs 2 and 3, cf. √2çam.]

+abhi, *mid.*—1. stop, *intrans.*; —2. find pleasure; please, *intrans.*, 106¹.

+ā́, *act.* stop, *trans.*

+upa, stop; uparata, ceased, (of sounds) hushed.

+vi, *act.* stop, *intrans.*; pause.

ramaṇíya, *grdv.* enjoyable, pleasant. [√ram, 965, 1215.]

ramyà, *grdv.* enjoyable, pleasant. [√ram, 963.]

rayí, *m.* wealth, treasure. [prop. 'bestowal' (cf. 76¹¹), fr. ri, a weaker form of √1 rā, 'bestow,' 1155. 1: cf. **ratna** and **rāi**.]

ravi, *m.* the sun.

raçaná, *f.* cord; strap; rein. [cf. **raçmi**.]

raçmí, *m.* —1. line, cord; —2. *fig.* (line, *i.e.*) ray, of light; beam. [so Eng. *ray* involves a metaphor, its Lat. predecessor *radius* meaning orig. 'staff' and then 'spoke': cf. **raçaná** and **rāçi**.]

rása, *m.* —1a. the sap *or* juice of plants (36¹⁸), *and esp.* of fruits; fruit-syrup, 68¹; —1b. *fig.* the best *or* finest *or* strongest part of a thing, its essence *or* flos, 44⁷, 83⁸; —1c. sap, *generalized*, fluid, liquid; drink, 15¹⁷; —2a. taste (*regarded as* the chief characteristic of a liquid); —2b. taste, *i.e.* relish for, 97⁶; —2c. object of one's taste, *esp.* that which pleases one's taste, *e.g.* the beauties (of a story), 56¹¹.

rasá, *f.* —1. moisture; —2. Rasā, a mythical stream supposed to flow round the earth and atmosphere. [cf. **rása**.]

rasika, *a.* tasty; *as m.* connoisseur. [rasa, 1222.]

√ rah (rahitá; ráhitum). leave, give up, abandon.

　+ **vi**, abandon, separate from, *in* viraha.

rahas, *n.* solitude; lonely place; *as adv.* [1111b], secretly. [√rah.]

√ 1 rā (rárāte; rarāú, raré; árāsta; rātá). give, grant, bestow. · [see **rāí**: cf. rayí.]

√ 2 rā (ráyati [761 d 1]). bark; bark at. [cf. Lat. *in-ri-re*, 'growl at.']

rākṣasa, *a.* demoniacal; *as m.* a demoniacal one, a Rakshas. [rákṣas, q.v., 1208a.]

rága, *m.* —1. coloring, color; —2. affection, feeling, passion. [√raj, 216. 1.]

rághava, *m.* descendant of Raghu, *i.e.* Rāma. [raghú, 1208c.]

√ rāj (rájati, -te; rarāja, rejé [794e²]; árājīt).

　—1. direct; rule; be first; be master *or* king of, *w. gen.*;

　—2. shine; be illustrious; distinguish one's self; —*caus.* cause to shine.

[orig., perhaps, two distinct roots, but no longer distinguished in form, and with the two sets of mgs partly coincident: w. rāj 1, cf. √1 rj, 'reach out'; w. rāj 2, cf. √3 rj, 'be bright,' and √raj: see under rājan.]

　+ **vi**, —1. become master of, master (*gen.*), 81¹¹; —2. shine out; —*caus.* adorn, 12¹⁷.

rāj [*nom.* rā́ṭ], *m.* king. [√rāj.]

rāja, *at end of cpds for* rājan, 1249a².

rāja-kula, *n.* —1. royal family; *in pl.*, equivalent *to* princes; —2. (*as conversely in Eng.*, The Sublime Porte, *lit.* 'the high gate,' *is used for* the Turkish government) the royal palace. [1280b.]

rāja-dvāra, *n.* king's door, door of the royal palace.

rājan, *m.* —1. king, prince, 1⁸, etc.; applied also to Varuna, 83¹², 75⁸, 76¹⁷, 78¹⁹, 80¹; to Indra, 71⁶; to Yama, 83¹² ⁸, 84²⁰; —2. *equiv. to* rājanya, a kṣatriya *or* man of the military caste, 59¹⁸ ²²; —3. *at end of cpds: regularly* rāja; *sometimes* rājan, 6⁸, 84²⁰. [√rāj, 1160c: cf. Lat. *rēg-em*, 'king'; Keltic stem *rig-*, 'king': from the Keltic was borrowed very early the Germanic *rik-*, 'ruler'; of this, Goth. *reiki*, AS. *rice*, 'dominion,' are derivs; so also Goth. *reiks*, AS. *rīce*, 'powerful,' Eng. *rich : rice*, 'dominion,' lives in Eng. *bishop-ric*.]

rājanyà, *a.* royal, princely; *as m.* one of royal race, a noble, *oldest designation of* a man of the second caste; *see* **kṣatriya**. [rájan, 1212d 1.]

rāja-putrá, *m.* king's son, prince. [acct, 1267.]

rāja-putra, *a.* having princes as sons; -trā, *f.* mother of princes. [1302: acct, 1295.]

rāja-puruṣa, *m.* king's man, servant of a king, royal official.

rājasa, *f.* -ī, *a.* pertaining to the second of the three qualities (*see* rajas 4), passionate, *as terminus technicus*. [rajas, 1208a.]

rājendra, *m.* best *or* chief of kings. [rāja + indra.]

rājñī, *f.* queen, princess, *Anglo-Indian* rannee; ruler. [rájan, 1156.]

rājya, n. kingship. [ráj, 1211.]

rātí, a. ready to give or bless; gracious; as f. grace. [√1 rā, 'give.']

rātra, n. for rātri at end of cpds. [1315b.]

rātrī, later rātri, f. night. [perhaps fr. √ram, 'rest.']

√ rādh (rādhnóti; rādhyate [761a], -ti; rarādha; árātsīt; rātsyáti; rāddhá; rāddhvā; -rādhya; rādháyati). —1. be - successful; prosper, have luck; be happy, 103⁷; —2. trans. make successful or happy; gratify; —caus. accomplish; make happy, satisfy. [akin w. √ṛdh.]
　+ apa, —1. hit away (from the mark), miss (the mark), fail; —2. be at fault, be to blame; offend, sin; aparāddha, guilty, to blame, 33¹. [for 1, cf. the simple verb, 'succeed,' i.e. 'make a hit': for 2, cf. the relation of Eng. fail and fault.]
　+ ā, caus. make happy, satisfy.

rādhas, n. gracious gift, blessing. [√rādh, 'gratify': for mg, cf. French gratification, 'gift.']

rāmá, a. dark; as m. Rāma, hero of the epos Rāmāyana; cf. rāghava.

rāyas-poṣa, m. development, i.e. increase of wealth. [gen. s. of rāi, 1250d: 171².]

rāva, m. cry; yell; howl. [√ru, 1148.2.]

rāçí, m. troop, host; heap. [perhaps akin w. raçmí, q.v.: for connection of mg, cf. Eng. line and French cordon, as applied to soldiers.]

rāṣṭrá, n. kingdom; sovereignty. [√rāj 1: see 219⁵, 1185a.]

rāṣṭrī, f. directrix, sovereign. [√rāj 1: see 219⁵, 1182².]

rāṣṭríya, a. belonging to the sovereignty; as m. sovereign, ruler. [rāṣṭra, 1215.]

rāhú, m. The Seizer, Rāhu, who is supposed to seize and swallow sun and moon, and thus cause eclipses. [prob. fr. √rabh, 1178².]

√ ri or rī (riṇāti; ríyate [761c]). —1. act. cause to run or stream, let loose; —2. mid. flow; run; dissolve. [cf. Lat. ri-vus, 'stream, brook'; provincial Eng. run, 'brook,' as in Bull Run; Ger. rinnen, Eng. run: see also √lī + pra.]

√ ric (riṇákti; ricyate [761b]; riréca, ririóe; áraikṣīt, árikta; rekṣyáti; riktá; pass. ricyáte; caus. recáyati). —1. leave; —2. let go, let free; —3. very rarely (like Eng. colloq. part with), sell.
　[w. riṇákti cf. Lat. linquit, 'leaves': cf. ἔ-λιπ-ε, 'left'; Lat. lic-et, 'it is left, i.e. permitted' (Eng. leave means 'permission'); AS. leōn, ⌞lih-an, Ger. leih-en, 'leave a thing to a person for a time, einem etwas überlassen, i.e. lend'; AS. lǣn, 'gift, loan,' Eng. noun loan, whence denom. verb loan; fr. lǣn comes lǣnan, 'give, loan,' Old Eng. lēn-en, preterit lēn-de, whose d has become part of the root in Eng. lend (though good usage has not sanctioned the precisely similar blunder in drown-ed-ed).]
　+ ati, mid. (through pass. sense be left over) surpass; predominate; —caus. cause to be in surplus; overdo, 96¹².

√ rip (rirépa; riptá). —1. smear; stick; smear, and so —2. as in Eng., defile; —3. (with the same metaphor as in the Ger. an-schmieren) cheat, impose upon. [the old form of √lip: see under √lip.]

ripú, m. impostor, cheat; later foe. [√rip, 1178b.]

riprá, n. defilement; impurity. [√rip, 1188c.]

ripra-vāhá, a. carrying off or removing impurity. [acct, 1270.]

√ riç (riçáti, -te; riṣṭá). —1. pull; —2. pull or bite off, crop. [older form of √liç.]

√ riṣ (réṣati; riṣyati, -te [761a]; riṣṭá; caus. reṣáyati; árīriṣat). be hurt; receive harm; caus. harm.

√ rī, see ri.

√ ru (rāúti [626]; ruváti; rurāva; árāvīt; rutá; rótum). cry; yell; howl; hum, 26⁹. [cf. ὠ-ρύ-ομαι, 'howl'; Lat. raucus, 'screaming, hoarse'; AS. rȳn, 'a roaring.']

rukmá, m. ornament of gold; as n. gold. [√ ruc, 1166, 216.5.]

√ ruc (rócate, -ti; rurucé, ruróca; árucat, árociṣṭa; rociṣyáte; rucitá; rócitum). —1. shine; be bright or resplendent; —2. appear in splendor; —3. appear beautiful or good, please. [cf. ἀμφι-λύκ-η, 'twilight'; λευκ-ός, 'bright'; Lat. *lūx, lūmen*, for *luc-s*, *luc-men*, 'light'; *lūna*, *luc-na*, 'moon'; AS. *leōh-t*, Eng. *light*; cf. also Lat. *lūc-us* (*a lucendo*, after all!), 'a clearing (Eng. of U.S.) *or* Lichtung (Ger.) *or* glade *or* grove'; AS. *leāh*, Eng. *lea*, 'field, meadow'; *-ley* in *Brom-ley*, 'broom-field,' and *-loo* in *Water-loo*.]

+ **prati**, appear good unto, please, 74⁶.

rúci, *f.* pleasure. [√ruc, 216.2.]

rucira, *a.* splendid; beautiful.

rucirānana, *a.* fair-faced. [ānana: 1298.]

√ **ruj** (rujáti; rurója; rugṇá; ruktvá; -rújya). — 1. break, break to pieces; — 2. injure, pain. [cf. λυγ-ρός, 'painful, sad'; Lat. *lūg-eo*, 'grieve'.]

rúj, *f.* pain, disease. [√ruj: for mg, cf. Ger. *Ge-brechen*, 'infirmity,' w. *brechen*, 'break'; also roga.]

rujáná, *f.* perhaps breach, cleft, rift (of the clouds). [√ruj.]

√ **rud** (róditi [631], rudánti; ruróda; rodiṣyáti; rudita; róditum; ruditvá; -rudya). — 1. cry, weep; — 2. weep for, lament. [cf. Lat. *rud-ere*, 'roar'; AS. *reōt-an*, 'weep.']

rudrá, *a.* connected by Hindus w. √rud, 'cry,' *and so* howling, roaring, terrible, applied to Agni and other gods; *true meaning uncertain;* — *as m.* — 1a. *sing. in the Veda*: Rudra, leader of the Maruts *or* Storm-gods, 77¹⁸, RV. x.125.6; — 1b. *in pl.* The Rudras, a class of storm-gods, RV. x.125.1; — 2. *sing.* Rudra, *received into the Hindu Trinity in the later mythology, and known by the name Çiva, q.v.*

√ **1 rudh** (ruṇáddhi, runddhé; ruródha, rurudhé; árāutaīt, áruddha; rotsyáti, -te; ruddhá; róddhum; ruddhvá; -rúdhya). — 1. hold back; obstruct; hold; — 2. keep off; hinder; suppress; — 3. shut up; close.

+ **anu**, *as pass., or mid. intrans., i.e. as of the yá- or ya-class*, anurudhyate, *also* -ti, be held to, keep one's self to; be devoted to, practice, 10¹³; have regard for.

+ **ava**, — 1. hold off; — 2. *mid.* (hold apart for one's self, lay up, *and so*)

obtain; — *desid. mid.* desire to obtain, 96¹¹.

+ **ni**, hold; stop; shut up.

+ **vi**, hinder *or* disturb.

√ **2 rudh** (ródhati). grow. [collateral form of √ruh, q.v.: cf. Lat. *rud-is*, fem., 'rod, staff': for mg, cf. w. √rudh and Ger. *wachsen*, 'grow,' the nouns **vī-rudh** and *Ge-wächs*, 'a growth, *i.e.* plant': kinship of Eng. *rod*, 'a growing shoot, rod, measure of length,' older *rood*, 'measure of length or surface,' is improbable on account of the ō of AS. *rōd*.]

√ **ruṣ** (róṣati; rúṣyati; ruṣitá, ruṣṭá). be cross or angry. [cf. λύσσα, ♦λυσ-ja, 'rage.']

rúṣ (rut, rudbhyām], *f.* anger. [√ruṣ.]

√ **ruh** (róhati, -te; ruróha, ruruhé; áruhat, árukṣat; rokṣyáti, -te; rúḍhá; ródhum; rūḍhvá; -rúhya; rúrukṣati; roháyati, *later* ropáyati [1042e]). — 1. rise, mount up, climb; — 2. spring up, grow up; — 3. grow, develop, thrive; — *caus.* — 1. raise; — 2. place upon. [see √2 rudh: for euphony, see 222³.]

+ **adhi**, *caus.* cause (*e.g.* one's body, *acc.*) to rise to (*e.g.* the balance, *acc.*), *i.e.* put (one's body) upon (the balance), 48¹⁵.

+ **ā**, mount *or* get upon (a stone); seat one's self upon; climb (tree); ascend to (the head, hill-top, life, place); embark upon (boat, ship); *fig.* get into (danger); — *caus.* cause to get upon (stone, pelt) *or* into (wagon, boat), *w. acc. of person and acc. or loc.* (105¹¹) *of thing;* — *desid.* desire to climb up to.

rūpá, *n.* — 1. outward look *or* appearance, *as well* color *as* form *or* shape; *Lat.* forma; form, 48¹⁷, 77², 96¹²; rūpaṁ kṛ, assume a form, 14⁸, 49⁶; (reflected) image, 62¹⁷; — 2. (*like Lat. forma, and Eng.* shape *in* shape-ly) good form, *i.e.* beauty, 2⁴, etc.; — 3. appearance, characteristic mark, peculiarity. [cf. varpas: see also varcas.]

√ **rūpaya** (rūpáyati [*cf.* 1056, 1067]). *used esp. in theatrical language* (to have the look *or* appearance of, *i.e.*) act. [rūpá, 1058.]

+ ni, —1. *like Eng.* look into — *tentatively, i.e.:* investigate, 20[18]; seek, 29[17]; search, 33[12]; —2. look into — *successfully, i.e.:* find out, 44[17]; discover, 26[10]; —3. act, *see simple verb.*

rūpa-jitāpsaras, *a.* surpassing the Apsarases in beauty.

rūpavant, *a.   like Eng.* shape-ly *and Lat.* formosus; beautiful, handsome, 1[4]. [rūpa, 1233.]

rūpa-sampad, *f.* beauty of form, *i.e.* beauty.

rūpa-sampanna, *a.* endowed with beauty, beautiful. [√pad.]

re, *word of address.* O; ho. [cf. are.]

√ rej (rējati, -te). —1. *act.* shake, *trans.;* —2. *mid.* shake, *intrans.;* tremble. [perhaps akin w. √λιγ in ἐ-λέ-λιξε, 'caused to tremble, shook.']

reṇú, *m.* dust. [perhaps connected w. √ri, 'dissolve, go to pieces,' just as Ger. *Staub,* 'dust,' w. *stieben,* 'fly asunder': 1162.]

revā, *f.* Revā, a river, the same as the Narmadā, *q.v.*

rāí [361b], *m., rarely f.* possessions; wealth; prosperity. [stem strictly rā: prop. 'bestowal,' √1rā, see 361b and rayí: w. acc. rā-m, cf. Lat. nom. *rē-s,* 'property.']

roká, *m.* brightness, light. [√ruc.]

róga, *m.* infirmity, disease. [√ruj, 216.1: for mg, see noun rúj.]

rocaná, *a.* shining, light; *as n.* light; the place of the light, ethereal space *or* spaces, 71[17], 81[4.8]; *see* rájas *for further description.* [√ruc, 1150.]

rociṣṇú, *a.* shining, bright; *fig.* blooming. [√ruc, 1194a: or rather perhaps fr. rocís, 1194c.]

rocís, *n.* brightness. [√ruc, 1153.]

ródasī, *dual f.* the two worlds, *i.e.* heaven and earth.

rodha, *a.* growing. [√2rudh, 'grow.']

ropaya, *see* 1042e end.

róman, *n.* hair on the body of men and beasts (usually excluding that of the head and beard and that of the mane and tail); *later* loman, *q.v.*

romānta, *m.   loc.* -e, in hair-vicinity, *i.e.* on the hairy side (of the hand). [roman (1249a[2]) + anta.]

rāukma, *a.* golden, adorned with gold. [rukmá, 1208f.]

———

lakṣá, *n.* —1. *rarely,* mark, token; —2. a hundred thousand, an Anglo-Indian lac; —3. *(like Eng.* mark) mark which is aimed at. [√lag, 'be fastened to,' 1197a: for mg 1, cf. connection of Eng. verb *tag,* 'fasten,' w. noun *tag,* 'attachment, appendage,' and so, esp. as used in modern shops, 'a mark *or* label-tag'; for 2, cf. the specialization of Eng. *marc or* mark as 'a weight' (of gold or silver) and as 'a money of account'; also that of Eng. *token* as 'a coin' and as 'ten quires printed on both sides.']

lakṣaṇá, *n.* —1. mark, token; characteristic; attribute, 66[11]; character, 101[12]; essential characteristic, 41[14]; special mark; *esp.* lucky mark, mark of excellence, 62[7], 98[7.8]; mark *in the sense of* determinant *at* 58[23]; —2. *(like Eng.* designation) name, 57[14]; —3. form, kind, 65[12]. [fr. the denom. lakṣaya (1150.2a), or rather fr. the simpler but very rare form of the same denom. (1054), √lakṣa.]

√ lakṣaya (lakṣáyati [1056]). mark, note, notice. [lakṣa, 1053: so Lat. *notare* fr. *nota.*]

+ upa, mark, notice; see; *pass.* appear.

lakṣasaṁkhya, *a.* having lacs (*see* lakṣa) as their number, numbered by hundred-thousands. [lakṣa + saṁkhyā.]

lakṣmí [363[2]], *f.* —1. mark, sign; —2. *with or without* pāpī, bad sign *or* omen, something ominous, bad luck; —3. *oftenest* a good sign, *in the older language usually with* puṇyā; good luck; prosperity, 18[14]; wealth, 46[2]; (royal) splendor, 51[19]. [fr. lakṣ (1167), the quasi-root of lak-ṣa, which is a deriv. of √lag: for connection of mg 1 w. √lag, see lakṣa: as for 2 and 3, observe that Eng. *luck* sometimes means 'bad luck,' but oftener 'good luck.']

lakṣya, *grdv.* to be noticed *or* seen; to be looked upon *or* considered as, 41[14]. [derivation like that of lakṣaṇa.]

√ **lag** (lágati; lagiṣyáti; lagná [957c]; lagitvá; -lágya). attach *or* fasten one's self to; lagna, attached to, put upon. [cf. **lakṣa, lakṣmī, liṅga.**]

laguḍa, *m.* cudgel.

laghú, *younger form of* raghú, *a.* —1. swift, quick; —2. light, *i.e.* not heavy; —3. (light, *i.e.*) insignificant; small; contemptible; low.

[for derivation, see **raghú** and **√raṅh**: cf. *ἐ-λαχύ-ς,* 'small,' *ἐλάχιστος,* 'smallest'; Lithuanian *lèngvas,* 'light'; Lat. *lĕvis, ᵈlenhu-i-s* ?, '1. swift, 2. light, not heavy, 3. insignificant, small' (mgs quite parallel w. those of laghu); AS. *lung-re,* 'quickly'; Eng. *lungs,* 'lights': kinship of AS. *leōh-t,* Eng. *light,* 'not heavy,' *lights,* 'lungs,' not certain: for connection of mgs 1 and 2, observe that *swift* and *light,* just as *slow* and *heavy,* name qualities naturally associated: for *light,* 'not dark,' see √ruc.]

laghu-krama, *a.* having a quick step; -am, *adv.* [1311], quickly.

laghu-cetas, *a.* small-minded.

√ **laṅgh** (laṅgháyati; laṅghitá; -láṅghya). spring over. [see √raṅh, and under laghú.]

√ **lajj** (lajjáte; lalajjé; lajjitá; lájjitum). be ashamed.
+ **vi,** be ashamed.

lajjá, *f.* shame. [√lajj, 1149.]

lajjávant, *a.* having shame; embarrassed. [1233.]

√ **lap** (lápati; lalápa; lapiṣyáti; lapitá, laptá; láptum; -lápya). chatter; talk; lament. [cf. *ὀ-λοφ-ύ-ς,* 'a lamenting'; *ὀλοφύρομαι,* 'lament'; perhaps Lat. *lā-menta,* 'laments.']
+ **ā,** talk to, converse with.
+ **pra,** talk out heedlessly *or* lamentingly.
+ **vi,** utter unintelligible *or* lamenting tones.
+ **sam,** talk with; *caus.* (cause to talk with one, *i.e.*) address, 26 ¹.

√ **labh,** *younger form of* rabh (lábhate; lebhé; álabdha; lapsyáte; labdhá; labdhvá; -lábhya). —1. catch; seize; —2. receive; get. [see under √rabh.]

+ **pra,** —1. seize; take; —2. dupe; fool. [for 2, cf. Eng. colloq. *take in,* 'gull,' and *catch,* 'ensnare.']
+ **vi-pra,** fool, 37 ⁶. [see √labh + pra.]

√ **lamb** (lámbate; lalambé; lambiṣyáti; lambitá; lámbitum; -lámbya). —1. hang down; —2. sink; —3. hang upon, hold on to; cling to; *and so* —4. (*like* Eng. stick) tarry, lag. [younger form of √ramb, 'hang down limp': cf. *λοβ-ός,* 'lobe *or* pendent part' (of ear, liver); Lat. *lāb-i,* 'sink, fall'; *limbus,* 'fringe, border'; AS. *læppa,* 'loosely hanging portion,' Eng. *lap* (of coat, apron); Eng. *limp,* 'hanging loosely, flaccid'; *lop-ears,* 'hanging' ears (of a rabbit).]
+ **ava,** —1. hang down; —2. sink; —3. hang upon, hold on to.
+ **vi,** lag, loiter. [see √lamb 4: for mg, cf. also Eng. *hang,* in *hang fire.*]

√ **lal** (lálati, -te; lalitá). sport, dally, play; behave in an artless and unconstrained manner; lalita, *see s.v.*

laláṭa, *n.* forehead.

lalita, *a.* artless, naive; lovely. [prop. 'unconstrainedly behaved,' ppl. of √lal, 952 ²: so Eng. *behaved* has rather adjectival than verbal coloring.]

lavaṇá, *n.* salt, *esp.* sea-salt; *as a.* salt.

√ **las** (lásati; lalása; lasitá). gleam, glance. [orig. 'glance,' but, like Eng. *glance,* with the subsidiary notion (see lasa), 'move quickly hither and thither,' and so, 'play' (see the cpds w. preps.): conversely, Eng. *dull* means 'slow,' and then, 'not glancing': cf. Lat. *lasc-īvus* (through ᵈlas-cu-s), 'wanton.']
+ **ud,** —1. glance; —2. play; —3. be overjoyed, 24 ²⁸.
+ **vi,** —1. glance; —2. play; —3. be joyful *or* wanton.

lasa, *a.* moving quickly hither and thither; lively. [√las.]

lájá, *m. pl.* parched *or* roasted grain. [perhaps akin w. √bhrjj.]

lábha, *m.* the getting, acquisition. [√labh.]

√ **likh** (likháti; lilékha; álekhīt; likhiṣyáti; likhitá; likhitvá; -líkhya). —1. scratch; furrow; slit; draw a line; —2. write; write down; delineate. [younger form of √rikh : cf. *é-peík-ω*, 'furrow' (χθόνα, 'ground') ; *é-péχ-θω*, 'tear, rend'; Lat. *rīma, »ric-ma*, 'slit, crack': for mgs, observe that Eng. *write* is fr. the same root as Ger. *ritzen*, 'scratch.']

liṅga, n. mark (by which one knows or recognizes a thing), Kenn-zeichen, characteristic. [connected w. √lag in the same way as lakṣa, q.v.]

liṅga-dhāraṇa, n. the wearing of one's characteristic marks.

√ lip (limpáti, -te [758]; lilépa; álipat, álipta; liptá; -lípya). — 1. besmear or rub over a thing (acc.) with a thing (instr.); — 2. smear a thing (acc.) over or on a thing (loc.); stick (trans.) on to; pass. stick or stick to, intrans.

[younger form of √rip: orig. mg 'smear, stick': cf. *τὸ λίπος*, 'grease'; *á-λείφ-ω*, 'anoint'; Lat. *lippus*, 'bleareyed'; *λῖπαρός*, 'greasy, shiny':

further akin are the following words, but with curious divarication of mg: *λῖπαρέω*, like Eng. *stick to*, i.e. 'persist'; AS. *be-líf-an*, Goth. *bi-leib-an*, Ger. *b-leib-en*, (lit. 'stick,' i.e.) 'remain'; AS. *libban*, Eng. *live*, Ger. *leben*, 'be remaining or surviving, superstitem esse'; AS. *líf*, Eng. *life*; finally AS. *lǽf-an*, Eng. *leave*, 'cause to remain.']

+ anu, smear over, cover with.

+ vi, besmear.

lipi, f. — 1. a rubbing over; — 2. writing. [√lip, 1155. 1.]

√ liç (liçáte ; liliçé ; áleçiṣta ; liṣṭá). tear, break. [younger form of √riç.]

liça, tearing, breaking, and so cutting, in ku-liça. [√liç.]

√ lī (láyate; líyate; lilyé; áleṣṭa; līná; -líya). — 1. cling to; — 2. stick; — 3. (stay, i.e.) of birds and insects, light upon, sit upon; — 4. slip into; disappear.

+ ni, — 1. cling to; — 2. light upon (of birds); — 3. slip into; disappear; hide.

+ pra, go to dissolution. [cf. √ri.]

līlā, f. — 1. play; — 2. (like Eng. child's play) action that can be done without serious effort; līlayā, without any trouble.

√ luṭh (luṭháti; lulóṭha; luṭhitá). roll.

√ lup (lumpáti [758]; lulópa; luptá; lóptum; luptvá; -lúpya). — 1. break; harm; — 2. attack; pounce upon; — 3. rob, plunder. [younger form of √rup: cf. Lat. *rumpere*, 'break'; AS. *reóf-an*, 'break'; *reáf*, 'spoil of battle, booty, armor, etc., esp.* clothing, garments,' Ger. *Raub*, 'robbery, booty'; AS. *reáfian*, 'despoil, rob,' whence Eng. *reave*, ppl. *reft*, and *be-reave*: fr. Old High Ger. *roubōn*, 'rob,' through Old French *rober*, 'rob,' comes French *dé-rober*, Eng. *rob*, and fr. Old High Ger. *roub*, 'robbery, booty, esp.* pillaged garment,' in like manner, French *robe*, 'garment,' Eng. *robe*.]

lubdhaka, m. hunter. [lubdha, √lubh.]

√ lubh (lúbhyati; lulóbha, lulubhé; lubdhá; lóbdhum). — 1. go astray; — 2. be lustful; have strong desire; lubdha, longing for. [cf. *ἡ λίψ, »λιφ-s*, 'longing'; *λίπ-τ-ομαι*, 'long for'; Lat. *lub-et, lib-et*, 'is desired or agreeable'; *libens*, 'willing, glad'; *libido*, 'desire'; AS. *leóf*, 'dear,' Eng. *lief*, 'dear, gladly'; Ger. *lieb*, 'dear'; also Eng. *love*.]

√ lul (lólati; lulitá). move hither and thither.

√ lū (lunáti [728]; luláva; lūná). cut (e.g. grass, hair); cut off; gnaw off. [cf. *λύ-ω*, 'separate, i.e.* loose'; Lat. *so-lū-tus*, 'loosed.']

lekha, m. a writing; letter. [√likh.]

√ lok (lókate; luloké; lókitum; caus. lokáyati [1056]; lokitá; -lókya; only caus. forms are in common use, and these only with ava, ā, and vi). get a look at; behold; — caus. [1041²] — 1. look, look on; — 2. get a look at, behold. [on account of the guttural k, prob. a secondary root fr. roká (√ruc, 216. 1): for connection of mg, cf. *λευκ-ós*, 'bright,' and *λεύσσω, »λευκ-jω*, 'see'; Lat. *lūmen*, 'light,' then 'eye' (see under √ruc); also locana: no connection w. Eng. *look*.]

+ ava, caus. — 1. look; — 2. look at or upon; — 3. behold, see, perceive.

+ ā, caus. — 1. look at; — 2. see, perceive.

+ **vi**, *caus.* −1. look; −2. look at, inspect, 25⁶; −3. behold.

loká, *perhaps a younger form of* **ulóká** (*which appears regularly in the oldest texts, but divided as* **u loká**, 84¹¹), *m.* −1. open space; free room; place, 83¹⁵; −2a. the vast space; the world, 103⁸; any imaginary world *or* worlds, 15¹⁶; *cf.* **antarikṣa-, indra-, jīva-, pati-, para-, manuṣya-, svarga-loka**; −2b. *used of heaven:* **svargo lokas**, the world situate in the light, 103⁵.¹⁴.¹⁶; *so* **sukṛtām ulokas**, the world of the righteous, 84¹¹; *later,* **sukṛtasya lokas**, world of virtue, 89⁸; *so* 5²⁰; −2c. *of earth:* **loke kṛtsne**, in the whole earth, 5¹⁵; **asmin · · loke**, in this world (*cf.* **iha**), 66¹²; *in same sense,* **loke**, 57⁸, 63⁷; −2d. *with senses merging imperceptibly into those given under 3, e.g.,* in the world *or* among men, 26², 36⁸, 47²¹; −3. (*like Eng.* world *and French* monde) people; folks; men *or* mankind; *sing.* 6⁷, 21¹³; *pl.* 2⁵.¹⁴, 39¹⁹, 57¹⁵. [etymology uncertain: no connection with Lat. *locus*, Old Lat. *stlocus,* 'place.']

loka-kṛt, *a.* world-making, world-creating. [1269.]

loka-pālá, *m. pl.* world-protectors, either four in number (regents of the four quarters of the world), or eight (regents of the cardinal points and four points mid-way between).

loka-pravāda, *m.* world-saying, common saying.

lokam-pṛṇá, *a.* world-filling; *f.* -**á** (*sc.* **iṣṭaká**), Lokampṛṇá, name applied to the common bricks used in building the sacred fire-pile, and so called because all laid with the recitation of the one general formula, **lokám pṛṇa**, 'fill thou the world.' [1314b: for **pṛṇa**, √1pṛ, see 731.]

logá, *m.* clod (of earth). [√ruj, 'break,' 216.1: for mg, see under **mṛd**.]

√ **loc** (locayati; locitá; -lócya). *used only with* **ā**. [derived fr. √ruc; just how, is unclear: see √lok.]

+ **ā**, −1. *rarely*, cause to appear *or* be seen; −2. *usually*, bring to one's own sight *or* mind, consider, reflect; **matsyāir**

ālocitam (*impers.*, 999), the fishes reflected; ity ālocya, thus reflecting.

+ **pary-ā**, *see* loc + ā; reflect, deliberate.

+ **sam-ā**, *see* loc + ā; reflect.

locana, −1. *a.* enlightening; −2. *as n.* eye, *usual mg.* [√loc: for mg, cf. *lūmen*, under √lok.]

lobha, *m.* strong desire; greed, avarice. [√lubh.]

lobha-viraha, *m.* freedom from avarice.

lóman, *n.* hair on the body of men and beasts (usually excluding that of the head and beard and that of mane and tail). [prop. 'clippings, shearings,' √lū, 'cut,' 1168. 1a: cf. roman.]

lola, *a.* −1. moving hither and thither, uneasy; *and so* −2. anxious for, desirous of; greedy. [√lul.]

loṣṭá, *m. n.* clod (of earth). [√ruj, cf. 222⁴: for mg, see under **mṛd**.]

lohá, *a.* reddish; coppery; *as m. n.* reddish metal, copper. [cf. **lóhita, róhita**, and **rudhirá**, all meaning 'red': with the last, cf. *ĕ-pvθ-pós*, Lat. *ruber, rūfus*, Eng. *ruddy, red*.]

lohāyasá, *n.* coppery metal, any metal alloyed with copper. [**ávasá**.]

láulya, *n.* greediness. [lola, 1211.]

láuhāyasa, *a.* metallic; *as n.* metallic ware. [lohāyasa, 1208f.]

vaṅçá, *m.* −1. cane *or* stock *or* stem, *esp.* of the bamboo; −2. (*like Eng.* stock, *and* stem [*rarely*], *and Ger.* Stamm) lineage, family, race.

vaṅça-viçuddha, *a.* −1. made of perfectly clear *or* unblemished bamboo; −2. of pure lineage. [lit. 'vaṅça-pure, pure in its *or* his vaṅça,' 1265: √çudh.]

√ **vak** (vāvakré [786, 798a]). roll. [akin w. √vañc, q.v.]

vaktavyà, *grdv.* to be said *or* spoken; *see* 999 end. [√vac, 964.]

vakrá, *a.* −1. crooked; −2. *fig.* (*nearly like Eng.* crooked) disingenuous, ambiguous. [√vak, 1188.]

vakṣáṇā, *f. pl.* belly; bellies (of cloud-mountains).

√ **vac** (**vákti**; **uváca, úcús** [784, 800e]; **ávocat** [847 end, 854]; **vakṣyáti, -te**; **uktá**; **váktum**; **uktvá**; **-úcya**; **ucyáte**; **vācáyati**). say or speak (*w. acc. of person*, 10²²; *or w. acc. of person and acc. of thing*, 7¹⁹); announce *or* tell, 66¹⁹, 98¹⁷; name *or* call, 58⁷; **punar uváca**, replied, 19¹⁹; **ity uktvā**, with saying so, *i.e.* with the words " · · ," saying " · · ," 4²; so saying, 19²³, etc.;

— **uktá**, —1. spoken, said; *impers. pass.* [999 mid.], **kākena uktam**, the crow said, 24¹⁸, etc.; **uktam**, *introducing a proverb*, 't is said, 19⁹, 20¹⁵, etc.; —2. spoken unto; **evam ukta**, thus addressed, 3⁵, etc.

— *caus.* —1. *mid.* cause *or* ask (*e.g.* the Brahmans) to pronounce for one's self (*e.g.* a benediction), 101², 106⁴; —2. cause (a written leaf) to speak, *i.e.* read, 54²⁰.

[cf. ὄσσα, ⊕ϝoκ-ja, 'voice, rumor'; Lat. *vŏc-āre*, 'call'; Ger. *er-wäh-nen*, 'mention': w. **vác-as**, 'word,' cf. ϝϵπος, stem ⊕ϝϵπ-ϵσ, 'word,' w. labialization: w. **ávocam**, ⊕a-va-uc-am, cf. ϵϵιπον, ⊕ϵ-ϝϵ-ιπ-ον, 'said': w. nom. **vák**, ⊕**vák-s**, stem **vác**, 'voice,' cf. Lat. *vox*, ⊕*vŏc-s*, 'voice,' and ὄψ, for ⊕ὄψ, i.e. ϝoπ-s, 'voice.']

+ **anu**, —1. repeat *or* say (sacrificial prayers, etc.) for some one (*gen.*); —2. *mid.* say after (the teacher), *i.e.* learn, study; **anūcāná**, *perf. mid. ppl.*, who studies, studied, learn-ed.

+ **abhy-anu**, say with regard to *or* with reference to something; describe (an occurrence) in (metrical and Vedic) words.

+ **nis**, speak out *or* clearly; explain.

+ **pra**, —1. tell forth, proclaim; tell, announce, mention; *and so* —2. (*as conversely* laudāre, 'praise,' *comes to mean* 'mention') praise; —3. tell of, *colloq.* tell on, *i.e.* betray, 93¹⁸; —4. say, 45⁹; —5. declare to be; name, 57⁵.

+ **prati**, say in return, answer.

+ **sam**, say together.

vacana, *n.* —1. speech; words, 9¹⁸, etc.; dictum; —2. (*like Lat.* e-dictum *and Eng.* edict *and* word) command; injunction, 26¹⁸. [√vac, 1150.]

vácas, *n.* —1. speech, 4⁶, etc.; words; word; counsel; —2. language, 54¹¹; —3. (*like Eng.* word) order; request, 53⁴. [√vac, 1151.1a: cf. ϝϵπος, 'word.']

√ **vaj** (**vājáyati**). *probable root, with the meaning* be strong *or* lively, *inferred from* **ugrá, ójas, vájra, vája**; *see these words;* **vájáyant**, hastening, 75⁹; *cf.* √**vājaya**. [cf. ὑγ-ιής, 'strong, healthy'; AS. *wac-ol*, 'awake'; Eng. *wake*, 'not to sleep'; perhaps Lat. *vig-ēre*, 'be lively or strong,' *vig-il*, 'awake.']

vájra, *m.* Indra's thunderbolt, 70⁸, 88¹⁶. [orig., perhaps, a mere epithet, 'The Mighty' (√vaj), like *Miölnir*, 'The Crusher,' name of Thor's hammer.]

vájra-bāhu, *a.* having the thunderbolt on his arm (of Indra), lightning-armed. [1303.]

vajrín, *a.* having the thunderbolt (of Indra). [vajra, 1230.]

√ **vañc** (**váñcati**; **vañcáyati**; **vañcitá**). totter; go crookedly; *caus.* (cause to go astray, *i.e.*) mislead, deceive; cheat. [cf. Lat. *vacillare*, 'totter, be unsteady'; AS. *wōh*, 'crooked, wrong,' whence Eng. *woo*, 'incline to one's self, court.']

+ **upa**, totter unto.

vañcaka, *m.* deceiver. [√vañc, caus.]

vañcayitavya, *grdv.* to be deceived; *as n.* a to-be-practised deceit, *w. objective gen.* (296b beg.), 26². [√vañc.]

vaṭa, *m.* Ficus indica; *cf.* nyag-rodha.

vaṇik-putra, *m.* merchant's son. [vaṇij.]

vaṇíj, *m.* merchant. [√paṇ, 383.5.]

√ **vat** (**vátati**; **vātáyati**). *only with* api. understand; *caus.* cause to understand *or* know, reveal, inspire (devotion). [cf. Lat. *vāt-es*, 'wise seer': see under **vāta**.]

vatsá, *m.* young; *esp.* young of a cow, calf. [prop. 'yearling,' from a not quotable ⊕**vatas**, 'year': with ⊕**vatas**, cf. ϝϵτος, 'year,' Lat. *vetus-* in *vetus-tu-s*, 'bejahrt, in years, old': akin are Lat. *vit-u-lu-s*, 'yearling, *i.e.* calf,' and Eng. *weth-er:* for mg, cf. χίμαρος, 'goat,' prop. 'winter-ling' (see hima): see vatsara.]

vatsará, *m.* year; *personified*, 67¹⁵. [cf. vatsa; also pari- and sam-vatsara.]

√ vad (vádati, -te; uváda, ūdé [784]; ávādīt, ávadiṣṭa; vadiṣyáti, -te; uditá; vāditum; uditvā́; -údya; vādáyati). —1. speak, 95⁷·⁹; say, 20¹⁹, etc.; speak to, w. acc., or w. loc. (4¹); —2. communicate; announce, RV. x. 125.5; speak of; uditá, stated (authoritatively), 58¹⁶; —3. tell, i.e. foretell, predict, 103¹²; —4. designate as, 55⁶; name.
  ⊦abhi, speak to, salute; signify, in the derivs abhivādin, abhivāda; caus. speak to; salute.
  ⊦praty-abhi, caus. mid. salute in return.
  ⊦ā, speak to; vidatham ā-vad, give orders to (the household), rule (as master or mistress).
  ⊦pra, —1. speak forth; say; —2. declare to be.
  ⊦vi, mid. contradict.
  ⊦sam, mid. talk or take counsel with one's self.
vádana, n. —1. mouth; —2. face. ['organ of speaking,' √vad, 1150: for mg, cf. nayana.]
vaditavya, grdv. to be spoken. [√vad.]
vadya, grdv. to be spoken of, worthy of (favorable) notice, and so praiseworthy. [√vad, 963⁸c.]
√ vadh (ávadhīt, ávadhiṣṭa; vadhiṣyáti, -te). —1. strike; harm; —2. (just as AS. sleán meant first 'strike' and then 'slay, i.e. kill') slay, kill. [see √bādh: cf. ὠθ-έω, 'push': see vadhar.]
vadhá, m. —1. murderer; —2. weapon of death, esp. Indra's bolt; —3. slaying, slaughter. [√vadh.]
vádhar, n. weapon of death, i.e. Indra's bolt. [√vadh.]
vadhasná, only in instr. pl. weapons of death, i.e. Indra's bolts. [vadhá, 1195.]
vadhū́, f. —1. bride; —2. woman. [prop. 'the one fetched home' by the bridegroom, √vah, q.v.]
vadhū-vastra, n. bride's garment.
vádhya, grdv. —1. to be struck, i.e. punished, 27²¹; to be harmed; —2. to be slain, 27¹⁸. [√vadh, 963⁸c.]

vádhri, a. whose testicles have been crushed; emasculated, opp. of vṛṣan. [√vadh, 1191.]
√ van (vanóti, vanuté; vavā́na, vavné; vātá). —1. hold dear, love; desire, seek, beseech, 79¹⁹; —2. get; —3. win. [cf. Lat. ven-ia, 'favor'; Ven-us, 'The Lovely One'; AS. winnan, 'exert one's self, strive,' Eng. win, 'gain by striving'; AS. wén, 'hope, expectation, supposition,' whence wén-an, Eng. ween, 'suppose': see √vāñch.]
vána, n. wood; forest.
vanánā, f. desire. [√van, 1150. 2b².]
vánanvant, a. having desire, desiring. [perhaps fr. vanánā, 1233, w. irreg. loss of final ā: both mg and derivation are doubtful.]
vana-prastha, m. n. forest-plateau, wooded table-land. [1280b.]
vana-vā́sa, m. the living in a wood; -tas, owing to (his) forest-life.
vánas-páti, m. tree. ['lord of the wood': see 1267 and a and d: perhaps vanas stands for vanar, a subsidiary form of vana, cf. 171².]
√ vand (vándate; vavandé; vanditá; vánditum; vanditvā́; -vándya). —1. praise; —2. salute reverentially. [orig. ident. w. √vad, 108g.]
  ⊦abhi, make reverent salutation unto; salute.
vanditṛ, m. praiser. [√vand.]
√ 1 vap (vápati, -te; uptá; -úpya; vāpáyati). shear (hair, beard); trim (nails); caus. cause to be clipped, or simply [1041²], clip.
√ 2 vap (vápati, -te; uvápa, ūpé [784, 800c]; ávāpsīt; vapsyáti; uptá; uptvā́; -úpya). —1. strew; scatter, esp. seed, sow; —2. (like χόω) throw or heap up, i.e. dam up.
  ⊦apa, cast away; fig. destroy.
  ⊦abhi, bestrew.
  ⊦ā, throw upon, strew.
  ⊦ni, throw down.
  ⊦nis, throw out, esp. deal out (from a larger mass) an oblation to a god, dat.; offer.
vapā́, f. caul, omentum.

vápus, *a.* —1. wondrous, admirabilis; —2. (*like Eng.* admirable) exciting wonder mixed with approbation, *esp.* wondrous fair;

—*as n.* —1. a wonder; wonderful appearance; **vapur dṛçaye**, a wonder to see, θαῦμα ἰδέσθαι, 79⁹; —2. beautiful appearance; beauty, 8⁸; —3. appearance; form, 48³·⁴. [for 2 and 3, cf. the converse transition of mg in **rūpa**, 1, 2.]

vayám, we, *see* 491. [cf. Ger. *wi-r*, Eng. *we.*]

1 **váyas**, *n.* —1. fowl, *collective*; —2. bird. [see **ví**, 'bird.']

2 **váyas**, *n.* food, meal. [prop. 'enjoyment,' √1 **vī**, 'enjoy': for analogies, see √2 **bhuj**, 'enjoy,' and √1 **vī**.]

3 **váyas**, *n.* —1. strength, of body and of mind; health; —2. the time of strength, youth; marriageable age, 2⁶; —3. *generalized*, any age or period of life; years (of life). [akin w. **vī-ra**, q.v.]

vayá, *f.* strengthening.

1 **vára**, *m.* choice; wish; a thing to be chosen as gift *or* reward, *and so* gift, reward; **varaṁ vṛ**, wish a wish, make a condition, 94¹; **varaṁ dā**, give a choice, grant a wish, 1¹⁷; **práti váram** *or* **váram ā**, according to one's wish. [√2 **vṛ**, 'choose': cf. Eng. *well*, lit. 'according to one's wish.']

2 **vara**, *a.* (*like Eng.* choice *or* select) most excellent *or* fair, best, *w. gen. or loc.*, 16², 3²¹; *w. abl.*, most excellent as distinguished from · ·, *i.e.* better than · ·, 68¹⁴; **varam** · ·, **na ca** · ·, the best thing is · ·, and not · ·, *i.e.* · · is better than · ·, 17²⁰. [√2 **vṛ**, 'choose': for mg, cf. AS. *cyst*, 'a choice,' and then 'the best,' with *ceōsan*, 'choose.']

varaṇa, *n.* a choosing. [√2 **vṛ**, 'choose.']

vara-varṇa, *m.* most fair complexion.

varavarṇin, *a.* having a fair complexion; -**inī**, *f.* fair-faced woman. [**varavarṇa**, 1230.]

varáṅganā, *f.* most excellent woman. [**aṅganā**.]

varároha, *a.* having fair hips *or* buttocks; καλλίπυγος. [**āroha**.]

varāhá, *m.* boar.

várivas, *n.* breadth; *fig.* freedom from constraint, ease, gladness, *w.* **kṛ**. [belonging to **urú**, 'broad': see 1173⁸, 467².]

várīyāṁs, *a.* very broad, wide extended. [√1 **vṛ**, 'cover, extend over': see 467² and 1173⁸.]

váruṇa, *m.* The Encompasser (of the Universe), Varuṇa, name of an Aditya; *orig.* the supreme god of the Veda (*see selection* xxxvii. *and notes*), and so called king as well as god, 83¹²; omniscient judge who punishes sin and sends sickness and death, *selections* xliii., xliv., xlv.; *later*, god of the waters, 7¹⁰. [a personification of the 'all-embracing' heaven, √1 **vṛ**, 'cover, encompass,' 1177c: cf. οὐρανός, 'heaven,' and Οὐρανός, 'Heaven,' personified as a god.]

varūtha, *n.* cover; *and so, as in Eng.*, protection. [√1 **vṛ**, 'cover,' 1163c.]

varūthyà, *a.* protecting. [**varūtha**, 1212d 4.]

váreṇya, *grdv.* to be desired; *and so*, longed for, excellent. [√2 **vṛ**, 'choose,' 1217¹·²·⁸, 966b.]

varga, *m.* group. [√**vṛj**, 'separate,' 216.1: for mg, cf. Eng. *division*, 'a separating into parts,' and then 'the part separated, group.']

várcas, *n.* vitality, vigor; the illuminating power in fire and the sun; *and so*, splendor; *fig.* glory. [perhaps akin with **ruc**: cf. **varpas** with **rūpa**.]

várṇa, *m.* —1. outside; external appearance; color, 36¹⁹, 37⁶, etc.; complexion; —2. (color, *and so, as in Eng.*) kind, species, sort, 98²; —3. (sort of men, *i.e.*) caste, 28¹⁸; —4. letter; sound; vowel, 59¹⁶; syllable; word, 98⁸. [√1 **vṛ**, 'cover,' 1177a: for mg 1, cf. Eng. *coating*, and *coat* (of paint), and Lat. *color*, prop. 'cover *or* coating,' cognate w. *oc-cul-ere*, 'cover over.']

√ **varṇaya** (**varṇayati**). —1. color, paint; —2. *fig.* (*like Eng.* paint), depict describe; tell about; *pass.* 12⁸. [**varṇa**, 1058.]

vartana, *n. prop.* an existing, *and so* (*like Eng.* living), means of subsistence. [√**vṛt**, mgs 3, 5: cf. **vṛtti**.]

vartí, m. restrainer, stayer. [√1 vṛ, 'cover,' mg 3, 'restrain': 1182.]

vártman, n. wheel-track; path, 43⁸; vartmanā, at end of cpds: by way of, 39¹⁴; or simply through; ākāça-vartmanā, through the air, 39¹. [√vṛt, 1168. 1a.]

vártra, a. warding off, holding back; as n. a water-stop, dam, weir. [√1 vṛ, 'cover,' q.v.]

1 várdhana, a. −1. increasing, trans.; as m. increaser; − 2. delighting in. [√1 vṛdh, 'increase,' q.v.]

2 vardhana, n. the cutting. [√2 vṛdh, 'cut.']

várpas, n. assumed appearance; image, form. [akin with rūpá: cf. varcas.]

várman, n. énvelope; coat of armor; protection; at end of Kshatriya-names, 59¹⁸ɴ. [√1 vṛ, 'envélop,' 1168. 1a.]

varṣá, n. −1. rain; −2. (rainy-season, i.e.) year; −varṣá, f. pl. −1. the rains, i.e. the rainy season; −2. very rarely, rain-water, 104¹⁴. [√vṛṣ: cf. ἔ-ερσαι, 'rain-drops': for mg 2 of varṣa, cf. Eng. "girl of sixteen summers," "man of seventy winters," abda and çarad.]

varṣa-karman, n. the action of raining.

varṣa-ṣaṭka, n. year-hexade, period of six years.

varṣmán, m. height; top; crown of the head. [see 1168. 1c² and 2b.]

valá, m. prop. an encloser, and so −1. (enclosure, i.e.) cave; −2. personified, Vala, name of a demon who shuts up the heavenly waters to withhold them from man and is slain by Indra, 81⁵⁷. [√1 vṛ, 'enclose.']

vala-vṛtra, m. Vala and Vritra. [1252.]

valavṛtra-niṣūdana, m. destroyer of Vala and Vritra, i.e. Indra. [1264.]

valavṛtra-han [402], a. slaying Vala and Vritra; as m. slayer of Vala and Vritra, i.e. Indra. [1269.]

valmíka, m. ant-hill.

vavrí, m. prop. cover, and so −1. place of hiding or refuge; −2. corporeal tegument (of the soul), i.e. body. [√1 vṛ, 'cover,' 1155. 2c.]

√ vaç (váṣṭi, uçánti [638]; uváça [784]). −1. will, 73¹⁷; −2. desire, long for; −ppls, pres. uçánt, perf. vāvaçāná [786]: willing or (when qualifying subject of verb) gladly, 83⁴, 85⁶; longing, 78⁹; −3. (like Eng. will in its rare or obsolete sense 'order') order, command. [cf. ἑκών, stem ϝεκ-οντ, 'willing.']

váça, a. willing, submissive; as m. −1. will; −2. command; and so controlling power or influence. [√vaç.]

vaça-ni [352], a. bringing into one's power; as m. controller.

vaçá, f. −1. cow, esp. farrow cow; −2. female elephant, Elephanten-kuh. [perhaps 'the lowing' beast, fr. √vāç: cf. Lat. vacca, 'cow': usual name for 'cow' is gó.]

vaçín, a. having command or control; as subst. m. or f. master, mistress. [vaça.]

vaçī-kṛ, make submissive, enthrall, ensnare. [vaça and √1 kṛ, 'make,' 1094.]

vaçya, grdv. to be commanded or ordered, and so obedient, submissive, yielding. [vaç, 963⁸ c.]

vas, encl. pron. you, 491. [cf. Lat. vōs, 'ye, you.']

√ 1 vas (uccháti [753, 608]; uvása [784]; vatsyáti [167]; uṣṭá). grow bright; light up (of the breaking day), dawn. [for cognates, Lat. us-tu-s, 'burned,' east, Easter, etc., see the collateral form uṣ, 'burn,' and the derivs uṣas, usra, vasanta, vasu, vāsara: cf. also ἦμαρ, ϝεσμαρ, 'day'; ἔαρ, ϝεσ-αρ, Lat. vēr, vve-er, vves-er, 'dawn of the year-light, i.e. spring'; Ves-uv-ius, 'the burning' mountain.]

+ vi, shine abroad, 75¹⁵; light up, 97¹⁸.

√ 2 vas (váste [628]; vavasé; ávasiṣṭa; vatsyáti; vasitá; vásitum; vasitvá; -vásya). put on (as a garment), clothe one's self in. [cf. ἕννυμι, ϝεσ-νυ-μι, 'put on'; ἔ-εσ-το, 'had on'; εἷμα, 'garment'; Lat. ves-tis, 'garment'; Goth. ga-vas-jan, 'clothe'; AS. wer-ian, Eng. wear.]

√ 3 vas (vásati; uvása [784]; ávātsīt [167]; vatsyáti; uṣitá; vástum; uṣitvá; -úṣya; vāsáyati). stay in a place; esp.

stay over night, 38², 100⁸ (*with* rātrīm); dwell, abide; live. [cf. ἄστυ, ⚹Ϝασ-τυ, 'dwelling-place, town'; Lat. *ver-na*, 'one who lives in the house, *i.e.* slave' or 'one who dwells in the land, *i.e.* native,' like Eng. *domestic*, 'servant,' and *domestic*, 'not foreign'; AS. *wes-an*, 'be'; Eng. *was, were*.]

+ ā, take up one's abode in (a place), occupy; enter upon, 62⁸.

+ ud, *caus.* (cause to abide out, *i.e.*) remove from its place, 97¹⁴?.

+ upa, —1. stay with; wait; —2. (*with a specialization of mg like that in Eng.* abs-tain, 'hold off, *esp.* from 'food or drink') wait, *and so* stop (eating), fast.

+ ni, dwell (of men and of beasts).

+ prati, have one's dwelling.

√ 4 vas (vāsáyati; vāsitá). cut. [cf. Lat. *vōmis, ⚹vos-mis, vōmer,* 'plow-share, colter.']

+ ud, cut away *or* off, 97¹⁴?.

vasantá, *m.* spring. ['the dawning *or* lighting-up' year-time, √1 vas, 1172ᵃ·⁴: see 1 vas: cf. ἔαρ, ⚹Ϝεσ-αρ, Lat. *vēr, ⚹ve-er, ⚹ves-er,* 'spring.']

vásiṣṭha, *a.* most excellent, best; —*as m.* Vasishtha, name of one of the most famous Vedic seers, 78¹⁹ x. [formed as superl. to vasu, fr. √1 vas as a verbal (467), the verbal having the same transferred sense as the adj. vasu, q.v.]

vásu, *a.* excellent, good; —1. *as m.* good (of gods), 76¹¹; —2. *as m. pl.* The Good Ones, the Vasus, a class of gods, RV. x. 125.1; —3. *as n. sing. and pl.* good, goods, wealth. [prop. 'shining, *i.e.* splendid,' √1 vas, 'shine,' but w. a transfer of mg like that in the Eng. *splendid* as used by the vulgar for 'excellent': connection w. ἠΰς, ἐΰς, 'good,' and *εὖ*, 'well,' is improbable, see āyu.]

vasu-dhá [352], *a.* yielding good; vasu-dhā [364], *f.* the earth; the land.

vasudhādhipa, *m.* (lord of the earth, *i.e.*) king, prince. [adhipa.]

vasuṁ-dhara, *a.* holding good *or* treasures; —ā, *f.* the earth. [vásum + dhara, 1250a: we should expect vasu (acc. s. neuter, or stem), not vasu-m (masculine!), 341.]

vasu-çravas, *a. perhaps* [1298a] having good fame, *or else* [1297 and 1280b] having wealth-fame, *i.e.* famed for wealth.

vasu-sampūrṇa, *a.* treasure-filled. [√1 pṛ, 'fill.']

√ vasūya (vasūyáti). crave good. [denom. of vasu, 1058¹, 1061.]

vasūyá, *f.* desire for good; longing. [√vasūya, 1149⁶.]

vastṛ, *m.* illuminer; *or, as adj.*, lighting up. [√1 vas, 'shine,' 1182, 375⁸.]

vástra, *n.* garment, piece of clothing; cloth. [√2 vas, 'clothe,' 1185a.]

vastra-veṣṭita, *a.* covered with clothes, well dressed.

vastrānta, *m.* border of a garment. [anta.]

√ vah (váhati, -te; uvāha, ūhé; ávākṣīt; vakṣyáti; ūḍhá [222]; vóḍhum; ūḍhvá; -ūhya; uhyáte). —1. conduct, 84¹¹; carry, *esp.* the oblation, 85¹, 93¹⁴, 94¹; bring with team, 73¹¹, 81¹⁴, *or* car, 72⁴, 87¹⁴; draw (wagon), guide (horses); —2. *intrans.* travel; proceed (in a wagon); —3. *pass.* be borne along; —4. flow, carry with itself (of water); —5. (*like Ger.* heimführen) bring home to the groom's house, wed; —6. carry, 43¹¹·¹⁶, 52⁹; bear, 26⁴; carry far and wide, *i.e.* spread (a poem, fragrance), 54⁵.

[for ⚹vagh: cf. ὄχος, ⚹Ϝοχος, 'wagon'; ὀχέομαι, 'ride'; Lat. *veh-ere*, 'carry'; *vehiculum*, 'wagon'; AS. *weg-an*, 'carry, bear,' whence Eng. *weigh*, 'lift' (as in *weigh anchor*), 'find weight of by lifting' (cf. bhara); AS. *wægn* or *wēn,* Eng. *wain,* Dutch *wagen* (whence the borrowed Eng. *wagon*), 'that which is drawn, *i.e.* wagon'; further, Lat. *vi-a, ve-a, ⚹veh-ia,* 'that which is to be travelled over, way'; AS. *weg,* Eng. *way,* 'that which carries' one to a place.]

+ ā, bring hither *or* to.

+ ud, —1. bear *or* bring up; —2. *esp.* lead out (a bride from her father's house), wed.

+ pari, —1. lead about; —2. *esp.* lead about (the bride *or* the wedding procession), wed.

+ pra, carry onward.

⁻ **vi**, lead away, *esp.* the bride from her parents' house, *and so* wed, marry; *mid.* get married.

⁺ **sam**, carry together; carry.

váh, *vbl.* carrying, drawing, *in cpds.* [√vah.]

vahatú, *m.* wedding procession; wedding. [√vah, 1161c.]

vahyá, *n.* portable bed, litter. [√vah, 1213: for mg, cf. Eng. *bier* and verb *bear*.]

vahye-çayá, *a.* lying on litters. [vahya, 1250c: acct, 1270.]

√ 1 **vā** (**váti**; **vavāú**; **ávāsit** [882]; **vāsyáti**; **vātá**; **vātum**; **vāpáyati** [1042d]). blow. [cf. ἄημι, ἀ-Fη-μι, 'blow'; Goth. *ra-ian*, Ger. *weh-en*, AS. *wāwan*, 'blow'; *aṹ-ρα*, 'breeze'; ἀήρ, *ἀέηρ*, 'air'; Lat. *rentu-s* (a participial form which has made a transition to the vowel-declension — cf. **vasanta** and 1172ᵇ⁴), 'wind,' Eng. *wind*; AS. *we-der*, Eng. *wea-ther*, 'wind (e.g. in *weather-cock*), condition of the air': see **vāta** and **vāyú**, 'wind.']

⁚ **ā**, blow hither.

. - **nis**, −1. (blow out, *intransitively, i.e.*) go out, be extinguished; −2. *intrans.* (blow till one gets one's breath, *and so*) cool off; −*caus.* −1. extinguish; −2. cool off, *transitively, i.e.* refresh.

+ **parā**, blow away.

⁚ **pra**, blow *or* move forward, *intrans.*

+ **vi**, blow asunder, *i.e.* scatter to the winds.

√ 2 **vā** (**váyati** [761d2]; **uváya** [784²]; **vayiṣyáti**; **utá**; **ótum**; **ūyáte**). weave, interweave, *both lit., and also (like Lat. serere)*, *fig.*, of hymns and songs; plait. [orig. idea perhaps 'wind' *or* 'plait': root-forms are **u**, **vā**, and **vi**: cf. *iréa*, *ἐFίτεA*, 'willow'; *οἶσος*, 'osier'; Lat. *vi-ēre*, 'plait'; *vī-men*, 'plaited work'; *οἴνη*, 'vine'; *οἶνος*, 'wine'; Lat. *vīnum*, 'wine'; *vi-tis*, 'vine,' Eng. *withy* or *withe*, 'pliant twig,' Ger. *Weide*, 'withe, willow.']

vā, *enclitic particle, following its word.* −1. or; ‥ **vā**, ‥ **vā**, 50¹⁷, 64¹⁰, 96¹²·²³, 97¹⁸·¹⁹; ‥, ‥ **vā**, 77⁶, 24⁶, 59⁹·²⁷, 64¹⁸, 97²·ª·¹⁵, 104²¹; *similarly*, 35⁶, 59¹⁵, 84⁹; ‥, ‥, ‥ **vā**, 20⁴, 91⁹; −*further :* ‥

vā, yadi **vā** ‥ ˙, ‥ **vā**, 28¹²; ‥, ‥ **vā**, ‥ **vā_api**, 62²; ‥, ‥ (**vā** *omitted*), **vā**, ‥ **vā**, 61²³, 62¹; *finally*, ‥ **na**, ‥ **vā_api**, ‥ **ca**, neither ‥, nor ‥, nor ‥, 63⁴; −**atha vā**, *see* atha 6; uta **vā**, *see* uta; −2. **vā**, *for* eva, 59¹⁰ N.; −3. *with interrogatives:* kiṁ **vā**, what possibly, 17¹⁹; *so* 18¹. [cf. Lat. *-ve*, 'or.']

vākya, *n.* −1. speech, words; −2. *as technical term*, periphrasis, *e.g.* vīrasenasya sutas *for* vīrasena-sutas. [√vac.]

vāg-doṣát, by *or* as a bad consequence of his voice, *i.e.* because he was fool enough to let his voice be heard. [vāc: see doṣa.]

vāghát [*like* dāsat, 444³], *m.* the pledging one, *i.e.* institutor of a sacrifice, not the priest, but the yajamāna. [perhaps akin are *εὔχ-ομαι*, Lat. *vovēre*, *-vogv-ere*, 'vow.']

vāṅmáya, *a.* consisting of voice *or* utterance. [vāc: see 1225² and maya.]

vāc [391], *f.* −1. speech, voice, word, utterance, sound; vācaṁ vy-ā-hṛ, utter words, 3¹, *and* vācaṁ vad, speak words, 94⁹, verb-phrases, *used like a simple verb of speaking, and construed w. the acc. of the person (see* 274b); perhaps (utterance, *i.e.*) sacred text, 91³; −2. *personified*, The Word, Vāch, Λόγος. [√vac, q.v.]

vācaṁ-yamá, *a.* restraining *or* holding one's voice, silent. [1250a, 1270¹ and b.]

vācaka, *a.* speaking; *as m.* speaker. [√vac, 1181.]

vācika, *a.* verbal, consisting of words. [vāc, 1222e.]

vācya, *grdv.* −1. to be spoken; −2. to be spoken to. [√vac, 1213a.]

vāja, *m.* −1. swiftness; courage, *esp.* of the horse; −2. race, struggle; −3. prize of race *or* contest; booty; reward *in general;* treasure, good. [prob. akin w. √vaj, q.v.: orig. 'strength and liveliness,' 'that in which strength and courage show themselves,' and then 'the result of quick and brave struggle.']

√ **vājaya** (*only in ppl.,* vājayánt). crave treasure; seek good, 74¹⁶; *cf.* √vaj. [denom. of **vāja**, 1058.]

16

√ **vāñch** (vā́ñchati; vāñchitá). wish. [for
◦vānak, orig. inchoative (cf. √ 1 iṣ) to
√van, q.v.: cf. Ger. *Wunsch*, 'a wish';
AS. *wūsc*, 'a wish'; whence verb *wȳscan*,
'wish,' whence Eng. verb *wish*, whence
noun *wish*.]

vāṇijya, n. merchant's business, trade.
[vaṇíj, 1211.]

vā́ta, m. —1. wind; air; —2. Vāta, god
of the wind.   [√ 1 vā, 'blow': acct,
1176c: cf. Icelandic *Ōδ-inn*, AS. *Wōd-en*,
Old High Ger. *Wuot-an*, names of the
highest Germanic god, Odin: the name
still lives in the Eng. *Wednes-day*, AS.
Wōdn-es dæg: some connect *Wōden* w.
√ vat, 'inspire, excite.']

vā́ta-svanas, a. having the roar of the
wind, *i.e.* blustering, exhibiting noisy
violence, tumultuous.

vātāikabhakṣa, a. having wind as sole
food, *i.e.* fasting.   [vāta + ekabhakṣa.]

vā́da, m. speech, expression, statement.
[√ vad.]

vāda-yuddha, n. speech-fight, *i.e.* controversy.

vādayuddha-pradhāna, a. devoted to
controversy; *as m.* eminent controver-
sialist.]

vādin, a. speaking. [√ vad, 1183[8].]

vānaprastha, m. a Brahman of the
third order, who has passed through the
stages of student and householder (*see*
āçrama) and dwells in the woods, 65[8] N.;
hermit. [vanaprastha: for mg, cf.
ἐρημίτης, Eng. *hermit*, and ἐρημία, 'solitude, desert.']

vānara, m. monkey, ape.

vāpī, f. oblong pond; lake.   [√ 2 vap,
'heap up, dam up,' and so, perhaps, orig.
'a dam' (cf. χῶμα, 'dam,' from χόω,
'throw or heap up'), and then, by metonymy, 'the pond made by the dam.']

vāpī-jala, n. lake-water. [perhaps the
first element is here to be taken in its orig.
sense of 'dam,' so that the whole means
prop. 'dam-water,' and so 'pond-water.']

vām, *see* 491.

vāmá, a. lovely, pleasant; *as n.* a lovely
thing, a joy.   [√ van: cf. dhūma and
√ 1 dhvan.]

vāyasá, m. —1. bird; —2. *esp.* crow;
-sī, f. crow-hen. [1 váyas, 'bird,' 1208a.]

vāyú, m. wind. [√ 1 vā, 'blow,' 1165.]

vā́r, n. water. [cf. οὖρ-ο-ν, orig. 'water,'
and so, as in Eng., 'urine'; Lat. *ūrīnāri*,
'stay under water'; *ūr-īna*, 'urine'; *Ur-ia*,
'Water-town,' a port in Apulia; prob.
akin is AS. *wær*, 'sea.']

1 **vāra**, m. tail-hair, *esp.* of a horse.
[prob. akin w. οὐρή, 'tail.']

2 **vāra**, m. —1. choice treasure; —2.
moment chosen or determined for any
thing, appointed time, turn; —3. time
(*as used with numerals*); vāram vāram,
time and again; —4. the time or turn
(of one of the planets which rule in succession the days of the week), *and so*,
day of the week, day. [√ 2 vṛ, 'choose':
identified by some w. ápa, 'time, season,'
see under √ yā.]

vāraṇá, a. warding off (those that attack
it), *and so* strong or ungovernable (of
wild beasts); *as m.* elephant.   [√ 1 vṛ,
'cover, ward off,' 1150. 1b.]

vārānasī, f. Vārānasī, the modern
Benares.

vāri, n. water. [see vā́r.]

vāri-stha, a. situated in the water, *i.e.*
(of the sun's disk) reflected in the water.

vā́vá, *particle, emphasizing the word which
it follows.* surely, just.   [for double
acct, see Whitney 94.]

√ **vāç** (vā́çyate [761c]; vavā́çé; ávi-
vaçat [861]; vāçitá; vāçitvā). bleat;
low; cry (of birds).   [see vaçā, Lat.
vacca, 'cow,' and vā́çrá.]

vāçrá, a. lowing (of kine).   [√ vāç,
1188a.]

vāsá, m. —1. *prop.* a staying over night;
—2. an abiding, 32[5]; —3. abiding-place,
23[30].   [√ 3 vas, 'dwell': for mg, cf.
bhavana.]

vāsa-bhūmi, f. dwelling-place.

vāsará, —1. *in Veda, as adj.* of the
dawn; ἠέριος; —2. *in classical Skt.,
neuter, used as subst., also masculine,* (*prop.*
time of dawn, as distinguished from
night, *and so*) day *in general*. [*prop.* a
secondary deriv. (1188d) fr. an obsolete
◦vas-ar, 'dawn,' √ 1 vas, 'dawn': see

1 vas: and for the form vas-ar, cf. *tap* and *rēr*, there given, and ah-ar, ūdh-ar, 430.]

vāsa-veçman, *n.* chamber for spending the night, sleeping-room.

vāsas, *n.* garment. [√2 vas, 'clothe.']

'vāsin, *a.* dwelling. [√3 vas, 'dwell,' 1183⁸.]

vāstavya, *a.* belonging to an abode; *as m.* inhabitant. [vāstu, 1212d 2.]

vāstu, *m. n.* dwelling. [√3 vas, 'dwell,' 1161a.]

vāstos-páti, *m.* lord *or* Genius of the dwelling, 77²ɴ. [vāstos, gen. of vāstu (1250d) + páti: acct, 1267a and d.]

vāhá, *a.* carrying; carrying off. [√vah.]

vāhana, *a.* carrying off; *as n.* —1. beast of burden, 56⁸; beast for riding; team; vehicle; —2. the carrying, 34¹⁸. [√vah, 1150. 1b.]

1 ví [343e], *m.* bird. [cf. οἰωνός, οἰ̄Fɪ-ωνος, Lat. *avi-s*, 'bird.']

2 ví, *preposition.* apart, asunder, away, out; *denoting intensity in descriptive cpds* (1289), *cf.* vicitra, vibudha; *denoting separation or non-agreement in possessive cpds* (1305), *cf.* vimanas, *etc.; similarly in the prepositional cpd* (1310a), vipriya.

viṅçati [485], *f.* twenty. [cf. εἴκοσι, Boeotian Fίκατι, Lat. *viginti*, 'twenty.']

vikaṭa, *a.* —1. exceeding the usual measure; *and so* —2. (*like Eng.* enormous) monstrous, hideous; —*as m.* Hideous, name of a gander. [cf. 1245g.]

vikramá, *m.* a stepping out, appearance; *esp.* bold *or* courageous advance, courage, might. [√kram + vi.]

vigata-samkalpa, *a.* with vanished purpose, purposeless. [√gam + vi: 1299.]

vigulpha, *a.* abundant. [origin unclear.]

vigraha, *m.* —1. separation; *and so* —2. division; *and so* —3. discord, quarrel, war. [√grah + vi.]

√ vic (vinákti; viktá; véktum; -vícya). separate, *esp.* grain from chaff by winnowing; separate, *in general.*

+ vi, separate out *or* apart; vivikta, isolated, *and so* lonely.

vicakṣaṇá, *a.* appearing far and wide, conspicuous; *or*, far-seeing. [√cakṣ + vi.]

vi-citra, *a.* —1. very variegated; —2. differently colored, varied; —3. (full of variety and surprises, *and so*) entertaining, beautiful. [in mg 1, vi- has perhaps intensive force; in 2, perhaps variative.]

√ vij (vijáte; vivijé; ávikta [834c]; vijiṣyáti; vigná). move with a quick darting motion, ἀίσσειν; (*like Eng.* start) move suddenly from fear. [cf. AS. *wic-an*, 'give way'; Eng. *weak*, 'yielding, soft, feeble.']

+ ud, start up; be affrighted; udvigna, terrified.

vijayá, *m.* victory; *personified*, Victory, name of a rabbit. [√ji + vi.]

víjiti, *f.* conquest. [√ji + vi.]

vijitendriya, *a.* having the organs of sense subdued. [vijita + indriya.]

vijñéya, *grdv.* to be known *or* considered as. [√jñā + vi, 963³ a.]

viṇ-mūtra, *n.* faeces and urine. [viṣ, 226b, 161: for cpd, 1253b.]

vitatha, *a.* false. ['differing from the so,' vi + tathā, 1314a.]

vitathābhiniveça, *m.* inclination towards that which is false. [abhiniveça.]

vítasti, *f.* a span, about nine inches *or* twelve fingers. [prob. fr. √tan + vi, and so 'a stretch' from the tip of the thumb to that of little finger: for mg, cf. Eng. noun *span* and verb *span*, 'extend over,' and see vyāma.]

vitāna, *m. n.* —1. spreading out, extension; —2. canopy. [√tan + vi: for mg 2, cf. Eng. *expanse* (of heaven) and *expand*.]

vittá, *ppl.* gotten; *as n.* (*like Lat.* quaestus) gettings, that which is got, property. [√2 vid, 'get.']

√ 1 vid (vétti; véda [790a]; ávedīt; vediṣyáti, -te; vetsyáti, -te; viditá; véditum, véttum; viditvá; -vidya; vedáyati). —1. know; understand; perceive; ya evam veda, who knoweth thus, who hath this knowledge, *frequent formula in the Brāhmaṇas*, 97³; vidyāt, one should know, it should be known *or* understood; —2. recognize as; nalam mām viddhi,

16*

recognize me as N., know that I am N.;
—3. notice; be mindful of, 75 ¹³; bethink
one's self, 94 ⁶⋅¹⁰; —4. believe; assume;
consider a person (acc.) to be · · (acc.),
43 ¹⁹; —ppl. vidvǎ́ṅs, see s.v.

[with véda, vidmá, cf. οἶδα, ἴδμεν, AS.
ic wät, wě witon, 'I know, we know'; Eng.
I wot, gerund to wit, noun wit, 'understanding': cf. also εἶδον, ᵉἴδον, 'saw';
Lat. vidēre, 'see'; AS. witan, 'see';
whence wit-ga, 'seer, soothsayer, wizard'
(Icelandic vit-ki, 'wizard'), wicca, 'wizard,'
wicce, 'witch,' Eng. witch, masc. and fem.:
véda is an old preterito-present, 'have
seen or perceived,' and so, 'know'—see
√2 vid: the forms of the other tense-
systems are comparatively modern.]
+ anu, know along, i.e. from one end to
the other, know thoroughly.
+ ni, caus. cause to know; do to wit;
announce; communicate.
√ 2 vid (vindáti, -te [758]; vivéda, vividé;
ávidat, ávidata; vetsyáti, -te; vittá;
véttum; vittvǎ́; -vidya). —1. find,
4 ¹², etc.; get, 74 ¹³; obtain (children),
100 ⁶⋅⁹; —2. get hold of, 80 ⁷; —3. pass.
vidyáte: is found; later, equiv. to there is,
there exists; ppl. vidǎ́na [619³], found,
73 ²⁰; —ppl. vittá, see s.v.

[orig. ident. w. √1 vid, of which this is
only another aspect, namely that of 'seeing esp. an object looked for, i.e. of
finding': see 1 vid.]
+ anu, find.

vid, vbl. knowing, at end of cpds. [√1 vid.]
vida, a. knowing, at end of cpds. [do.]
vidatra, a. noticing, in cpds. [√1 vid,
1185d.]
vidátha, n. directions, orders. [prop.
'knowledge given, i.e. instructions,'
√1 vid, 1163b.]
vidarbha, —1. m. pl. the Vidarbhans,
Vidarbha, name of a people, and of their
country, which was south of the Vindhya
mountains, and is now called Berar; —2.
m. sing. Vidarbha, i.e. a king of Vidarbha,
4 ³. [for mg 2, cf. "Norway, uncle of
young Fortinbras," Hamlet, i. 2. 28.]
vidarbha-nagarī, f. city or capital
of Vidarbha, i.e. Kundina (kuṇḍina).

[vidarbha- does not stand in the relation of a gen. of appellation: see 295 ¹.]
vidarbha-pati, m. lord or king of
Vidarbha.
vidarbha-rǎjan, m. king of Vidarbha.
vidǎsin, a. becoming exhausted, drying
up. [√das + vi, 1183 ³.]
vidyǎ́, f. —1. knowledge; a discipline or
science; esp. trayī vidyǎ, the triple
science or knowledge of the holy word, as
hymn, sacrificial formula, and chant, or
the Rigveda, Yajurveda, and Sāmaveda;
—2. esp. the science κατ' ἐξοχήν, i.e. magic;
a magic formula, spell. [√1 vid, 1213d:
for mg 2, observe the equally arbitrary
specialization in Eng. spell, which in AS.
meant 'a saying.']
vidyǎ-dhara, a. keeping or possessed of
knowledge or the magic art; as m. a Vid-
yādhara, one of a class of genii, who are
attendants on Çiva, and reputed to be
magicians.
vidyǎ-mada, m. knowledge-intoxication,
i.e. infatuated pride in one's learning.
vidyǎvayo-vṛddha, a. grown old in
knowledge and years, distinguished for
learning and age. [vidyǎ + 3 vayas,
1252.]
vidyút, —1. a. lightening; and so, as in
Eng., —2. f. lightning. [√dyut + vi,
'lighten.']
vidvaj-jana, m. wise man. [vidvǎ́ṅs,
1249a, 202.]
vidvǎ́ṅs [461], ppl. knowing; wise, 17 ¹⁶,
etc.; learned; tvaṣṭǎ vidvǎ́n, a cunning
workman (cf. Eng. cunning and Old Eng.
cunnen, 'know'), 75 ⁶. [√1 vid, 'know,'
790a, 803 ².]
√ 1 vidh (vidháti). worship a god (dat.)
with (instr.); honor (acc.) with (instr.).
[cf. vedhas.]
√ 2 vidh (vindháte). lack or be without a
thing (instr.), viduṣī; be bereft or alone.
[see vidhavǎ.]
√ 3 vidh, see √vyadh.
vidh, vbl. boring through, wounding, at
end of cpds. [√3 vidh or vyadh, 252, cf.
785.]
vidhávǎ, f. widow. [√2 vidh, 'be bereft,'
1190: cf. ἠ-ίθεος, 'youth without a wife

bachelor'; Lat. *viduus, vidua*, 'widower, widow'; AS. *widwe, wuduwe*, Eng. *widow*.]

vidhā́, *f.* proportion, measure; way; *and so* kind, sort; *esp. at end of cpds* [*see* 1302c 5]: *e.g.* **tri-vidha**, of three kinds, three-fold. [prop. 'dis-position, arrangement, order, method,' see √1 dhā + vi.]

vidhātavya, *grdv.* to be shown. [√1 dhā + vi, mg 5.]

vidhātṛ, *m.* dis-poser, arranger. [√1 dhā + vi.]

vidhā́na, *n.* a dis-position, ordering, ordinance; **vidhānatas**, according to (established) ordinance. [√1 dhā + vi, 1150.]

vidhi, *m.* — 1. a dis-position, ordinance, prescription, rule (65⁷), method; — 2. (method, *i.e.*) way, 38²⁸; procedure; — 3. (the supreme disposition *or* ordaining, *i.e.*) destiny, fate. [√1 dhā + vi, 1155. 2e; 345²: for mg 3, cf. Lat. *destināre*, 'establish, ordain,' and Eng. *destiny*.]

vidhivat, *adv.* according to rule; *equiv. to* Lat. rite. [**vidhi**, 1107.]

vidhú, *a.* lonely (of the moon that wanders alone among the star-hosts); *as m.* moon. [prob. fr. √2 vidh, 1178.]

vidhura, *a.* — 1. alone, bereft; — 2. suffering lack, miserable; — 3. disagreeable; *as n.* trouble. [prob. fr. √2 vidh, through the intermediate **vidhu**, 1188f.]

vidhura-darçana, *n.* sight of adversity.

vidheya, *grdv.* to be done. [see √1 dhā + vi, mg 5: also 963ª a.]

vinayá, *m.* — 1. training, breeding, *i.e.* formation of manners; *and so* — 2. *transferred* (*like the Eng.* breeding), manners, good breeding, politeness. [√nī + vi.]

vinā́, *prep.* without, *w. instr. or acc.* [1127, 1129.]

vinīti, *f.* (good breeding, *esp.*) modesty. [√nī + vi: see **vinaya**.]

vinoda, *m.* *exactly like Eng.* di-version; amusement. [see √nud + vi.]

√ vind, *see* √2 vid.

vindhya, *m.* Vindhya, name of the mountain-range crossing the Indian peninsula and separating Hindustan from the Deccan.

vindhyāṭavī, *f.* the Vindhya-forest. [**aṭavī**.]

√ vip (vépate; vivipé; ávepiṣṭa; vepáyati). be in trembling agitation; tremble *or* shake; *caus.* shake, *trans.* [cf. Lat. *vibrāre*, 'shake, brandish,' from *•vib-ru-s*, *•vip-ru-s*, 'shaking'; AS. *wǽfre* (formed like *•vip-ru-s*), 'moving this way and that,' whence Eng. *waver*; Eng. frequentative *whiffle*, 'veer about, blow in gusts'; *whiffle-tree*, so called from its constant jerky motion (-*tree* means 'wooden bar,' see **dāru**).]

vipaṇa, *m.* trading-place, shop; -ī, *f.* shop. [√paṇ + vi, 1156.]

vipatti, *f.* a coming to nought, destruction. [√pad + vi, 1157.]

vipad, *f.* misfortune, trouble. [√pad + vi, 383a.]

vipāka, *m.* the ripening, *esp.* of the fruit of good *or* bad deeds, *and so* the consequences; the issue, *in general.* [√pac + vi, 216. 1.]

vipra, — 1. *a.* agitated, inspired; *as subst.* he who gives utterance to pious emotion at the altar, poet, singer, 74¹¹·¹⁸; — 2. *a.* (inspired, *i.e.*) gifted with superior insight, wise, of a god, 79¹ª·¹⁷; — 3. *as m.* a Brahman, 60¹⁵, etc. [√vip, 1188a: mg 3 is to be taken directly from 1.]

vipriya, *a.* not dear, unpleasant; *as n.* something disagreeable, an offense. [2 vi + priya, see vi and 1310a end.]

vi-budha, *a.* very wise (vi- *is intensive*, 1289); *as m.* a god.

vibudhānucara, *m.* attendant of a god. [**anucara**.]

vibudheçvara, *m.* a lord of the gods. [**īçvara**.]

vibhava, *m.* — 1. development *or* growth; — 2. (the result of growth, *i.e.*) power, *and so* lordship, majesty, high position; — 3. *sing. and pl.* (*like Ger.* Vermögen) property, possessions. [√bhū + vi: cf. **vibhu** and **vibhūti**.]

vibhā́van, *f.* -varī, *a.* shining far and wide. [√bhā + vi, 1169. 1b and 2², 1171b.]

vibhīdaka, *m. n.* the large tree Terminalia Bellerica; one of the nuts of this tree, which were used for dicing; a die, dice. [perhaps 'the destroyer,' fr. √bhid

+ **vi**: if so, we must suppose that the name was first given to the die as the die, and applied secondarily to nut and tree.]

vibhú, *a.* —1. pervading, far-reaching; unlimited, 74²; —2. powerful, mighty, of Indra, 5¹². ¹⁵; *as subst.* lord *or* ruler. [√bhū + vi, 354: for 2, cf. **vibhava** 1 and 2, and **vibhúti**.]

víbhūti, *f.* —1. development *or* growth; —2. (the result of growth, *i.e.*) power, *esp.* of a lord *or* ruler. [√bhū + vi, 1157d: cf. **vibhava** and **vibhu**.]

vi-manas, *a.* (having an away-removed mind *or* heart, *i.e.*) out of one's senses *or* disheartened. [1305.]

vimarda, *m.* destruction; (of sleep) disturbance. [√mṛd + vi.]

vimāna, *a.* traversing, *esp.* the sky; *as m. n.* a palatial car of the gods that moves through the air, sky-chariot. [√1 mā + vi, 'measure,' q.v.: 1150.]

vi-mukha, *a.* having the face away; vimukhā́ yānti, they go (with averted faces, *i.e.*) homewards. [1305.]

vi-rajas, *a.* having dust away, dustless, pure. [1305.]

viraha, *m.* —1. abandonment, separation from; —2. absence, freedom from. [√rah + vi.]

virāma, *m.* stop, end, pause. [√ram+vi.]

virodhin, *a.* hindering, disturbing. [√rudh + vi, 1183ᵉ.]

vilāsa, *m.* joy. [√las + vi.]

vivará, *m. n.* opening; hole (of creatures that live in the ground). [√1 vṛ + vi, 'uncover, open.']

vi-varṇa, *a.* having the color away, colorless, pale. [1305.]

vivarṇa-vadana, *a.* pale-faced. [1298a.]

vivásvan, *a.* lighting up; vivásvabhis, *as adv.* [1112c], so that it lights up; *as n.*, *perhaps*, flash, spark. [√1 vas + vi, 'light up,' 1169b.]

vívasvant, *a.* lighting up; *as m.* Vivasvant, name of a god of the dawning daylight *or* morning-sun, father of the twins Yama and Yamī and of the Açvins, 85¹³. ¹⁴. [√1 vas + vi, 'light up,' see 1233e.]

vivāhá, *m.* fetching home of the bride, wedding, marriage. [√vah + vi.]

vivāha-catuṣṭaya, *n.* marriage-quaternion, *i.e.* the marrying of four wives.

vivāhāgni, *m.* wedding-fire. [agni.]

vividha, *a.* having different kinds, *i.e.* of different sorts, various. [2 vi + vidhā, 334², 1305.]

vivṛddhi, *f.* growth; increase in size; increase. [√vṛdh + vi, 1157.1d.]

viveka, *m.* —1. a separating apart; —2. discrimination, discernment, good judgment [√vic + vi, 216.1: for mg 2, cf. *discrimination* w. Lat. *discrimināre*, 'separate,' fr. *discrimen* of the same root as *discernere*, 'separate'; cf. also *discernment* with *discernere*.]

√ **viç** (viçáti, -te; vivéça, viviçé; ávikṣat; vekṣyáti, -te; viṣṭá; véṣṭum; -víçya; veçáyati). settle down; go in; go into, enter. [with veçá, 'house,' cf. οἶκος, 'house' (analogous to *entry* from *enter*); Lat. *vicus*, 'settlement, village,' whence the borrowed AS. *wic*, 'village'; Goth. *weihs*, 'village'; Lat. *villa*, *vic(u)la*, 'small settlement, farm': see further **víç** and **veçá**.]

+ **ā**, go into, enter; pervade, RV. x. 125.6; **āviṣṭa**: *actively*, having entered; *passively*, entered by, filled with; —*caus.* cause to go into, put into, communicate.

+ **upa**, settle down upon; sit down; upaviṣṭa, seated.

+ **ni**, *mid.* go in; go home (to house *or* nest); settle down to rest.

+ **abhi-ni**, settle down to; be inclined towards, *fig.*, *as in Eng.*; be bent upon.

+ **pra**, enter, get into; *w. acc.*, 85²; *w. loc.*, 18²³; *without expressed object*: enter, 8⁴; go in, 33¹⁴; go home, 103²¹; penetrate, pierce; —*caus.* cause to enter.

+ **sam-pra**, go in; *w.* gṛham, go home; *w.* niveçanam, go to bed; enter, *w. loc.*

+ **sam**, enter together, *i.e.* make their appearance together *or* come hither together, 86¹⁶; —*caus.* cause to enter upon, put *or* set upon.

víç (víṭ, víçam, viḍbhís [218ᵃ]), *f.* —1. a settlement, *i.e.* dwelling-place; *and so* house; —2. a settlement, *i.e.* the com-

munity, clan, folk; **viçãm patis**, lord of
peoples, *i.e. simply* prince; tribe *or* host
(of gods), 71¹⁸, 78⁴; −3. the folk, as
distinguished from the Brahmans and
Kshatriyas, the third caste, later called
vãiçya; a man of the third caste, 59²³.
[√viç, q.v.: cf. Δωριέες τριχά-ικ-ες, 'three-
tribed Dorians'; also Keltic *vic* in *Ordo-
vic-es*, people of North Wales, and *Lemo-
vic-es*, people of modern Limoges.]
viçaṅkã, *f.* hesitation.   [√çaṅk + vi,
1149.]
viçãkha, *a.* having spread-asunder
branches, *i.e.* forked; -e, *dual f.* Viçãkhe,
name of an asterism.   [2 vi + çãkhã,
1305, 334².]
viçãkhila, *m.* Viçãkhila, name of a merchant.   [viçãkha, 1227: perhaps named
after the asterism because various green-
grocer's commodities belonged to it.]
viçãlã, *a.* capacious, spreading, broad.
viçiṣṭatã, *f.* condition of being distinguished, distinction, superiority. [viçiṣṭa,
1237: see çiṣ + vi.]
viçeṣa, *m.* −1. that which separates *or*
distinguishes one thing from another,
distinction *or* difference; *and so* −2. (*like
Eng.* distinction) eminence, excellence;
viçeṣeṇa, *as adv.* [1112b], to an eminent
degree, *i.e.* very much, especially, *like
French* par excellence.   [√çiṣ + vi.]
viçeṣatas, *adv.* −1. *at end of a cpd*,
according to the difference of · ·, 66²³;
−2. (*like* viçeṣeṇa, *see above*) especially.
[viçeṣa, 1098b.]
viç-pãti, *m.* master of the house.
[euphony, 218⁵; acct, 1267a: cf. Old
Prussian *wais-patti-n*, 'house-mistress';
Lithuanian *vèsz-pat-s*, 'lord.']
viçrabdham, *see* √çrambh.
viçrambha, *m.* confidence. [√çrambh
+ vi.]
viçrambhãlãpa, *m.* confidence-talk,
familiar conversation.   [ãlãpa.]
viçva [524], *pron. adj.* −1a. all, every;
every one; *common in Veda, but replaced
in the Brãhmana and later by* sarva, *q.v.;*
−1b. viçve devãs: all the gods, 82¹; *or*
the All-gods (as a class, *see* deva 2b),
88⁴·⁸, 90⁸; − 1c. viçvam, *as n.* The All,

τὸ πᾶν, 92¹²; −2. *sometimes*, entire, whole;
so 71¹⁷.
viçvã-cakṣas, *a.* all-beholding.   [see
1296⁸: acct, 1298c.]
viçvãtas, *adv.* from *or* on all sides,
everywhere. [viçva, 1098b: acct, 1298c.]
viçvãto-mukha, *a.* having a face on
all sides, whose face is turned every-
whither. [1306.]
viçvã-darçata, *a.* to be seen by all,
all-conspicuous. [acct, 1273, 1298c.]
viçvã-deva, *m. pl.* the All-gods (*see*
deva 2b), RV. x. 125. 1.   [viçva + devã:
acct, 1280a, 1298c.]
viçvã-bheṣaja, *a.* all-healing. [viçva
+ bheṣajã: acct, 1280a, 1298c.]
viçvã-çcandra, *a.* all-sparkling. [viçva
+ çcandrã: acct, 1280a, 1298c.]
viçva-sṛj, *a.* all-creating; *as m. pl.* All-
creators, name of certain creative beings.
viçvãd, *a.* all-consuming. [viçva + ãd.]
viçvãyu, *assumed as stem of* viçvãyos,
75¹, *prop. a form of transition to the u-
declension of the stem* viçvãyus, *and meaning either* friendly to all, all-friendly (*if
taken with* mama, *i.e.* varuṇasya), *or else*
all living creatures (*if taken with* rãṣṭram,
'lordship over'); *see* viçvãyus 1 *and* 2.
viçvãyus, −1. *a.* belonging to *or* appearing to all life *or* living creatures, *i.e.
either* friendly to all *or* all-known (applied
to gods), *or else* dwelling in all (of the
Genius of Life), 85¹⁸; −2. *as n.* all-life,
i.e. all living creatures, men and beasts.
[viçva + ãyus, acct, 1280a, 1298c: for
mg 1, see 1294².]
viçvãsa, *m.* confidence. [√çvas + vi.]
viçvãsa-kãraṇa, *n.* reason for confidence.
viçvãsa-bhũmi, *f.* proper vessel for
confidence, one who may safely be
trusted.
viçvãhã, *adv.* always, for evermore.
[viçva, see 1100a and cf. 1104²·⁸: acct,
cf. 1298c.]
√ **viṣ** (viveṣṭi; viveṣa; vekṣyãti, -te;
viṣṭã; -viṣya). work, be active, accomplish.
viṣ (viṭ, viṣam, viḍbhis), *f.* excrement,
faeces.

viṣá, *n.* poison. [prop. 'the potent *or* overpowering,' √viṣ: no less arbitrary is the specialization in Eng. *poison*, fr. Lat. *potionem*, 'draught': cf. *lós*, *ϝloσos*, Lat. *virus*, 'poison.']

viṣa-kumbha, *m.* jar of poison.

viṣaya, *m.* —1. *prop.* working, *and so* sphere of activity *or* influence; —2. one's department *or* line *or* peculiar province; *and so, generalized* —3. province, field, domain, empire, country; —4. field of activity of one of the sense-organs (*e.g.*, sound is the viṣaya of the ear), *a mere specialization of* mg 1; object of sense, pleasure of sense; —5. object *in general.* [√viṣ: but the formation of the stem is not clear.]

viṣāda, *m.* despondency, dejection. [√sad + vi.]

viṣu, *adv.* on both sides.

viṣuvat-saṁkrānti, *f.* equinox-passage (of the sun from one zodiacal sign to the next); the time of equinox-passage, the equinox. [viṣuvant.]

viṣuvánt, —1. *a.* having *or* taking part on both sides, *i.e.* keeping *or* being in the middle; —2. *m.* middle day (*e.g.* of a long sacrifice); —3. *m. n. esp.* middle day between the solstices, the vernal *or* autumnal equinox. [viṣu, 1233c and b end.]

√ **viṣṭ** (véṣṭate; viṣṭitá; -véṣṭya; veṣṭáyati). wind one's self about; *caus.* wind around, envelope, wrap up, dress.

víṣṇu, *m.* Vishnu, name of a god, whose chief work in the Veda is the measuring of the sky in three paces, and who became one of the Hindu Trinity, and extremely important in the later sectarian development of India; *cf.* brahmán 2 *and* çivá. [prob. 'the mighty worker,' √viṣ, 1162.]

viṣṇu-çarman, *m.* Vishnuçarman, name of a sage. ['having V. as his protection' *or* else 'the delight of V.': the mg of the cpd depends on its accent (see 1302[1] and 1267[1]), and this is not known.]

viṣṇuçarma-nāman, *a.* possessing viṣṇuçarman as name, named V. [1249a[2].]

viṣvañc [408], *a.* directed in both ways *or* parted asunder. [viṣu + añc, 407.]

visárjana, *n.* the letting go; evacuation. [√sṛj + vi.]

vispaṣṭa, *see* √1 paç + vi.

vispaṣṭārtha, *a.* having clear *or* intelligible meaning. [artha.]

vismaya, *m.* astonishment. [√smi + vi.]

vismayānvita, *a.* filled with astonishment. [anvita, √i + anu.]

vi-hasta, *a.* —1. having the hands away, handless; *and so* —2. (*like Eng.* unhandy) awkward; *and so* —3. perplexed, confounded. [1305.]

vihárin, *a.* wandering about. [√1 hṛ + vi, 1183[s].]

√ **1 vī** (véti; viváya, vivyé; vītá). —1. seek eagerly; —2. accept gladly; enjoy; —3. strive to get; —4. fall upon.

[cf. Lat. *vēnāri*, 'hunt,' a denom. of *•vē-na*, 'hunt'; AS. *wā-ð*, 'hunt'; Old High Ger. *weida*, '1. the seeking, *esp.* of food, *i.e.* hunting, fishing, *and then* 2. place for getting food, pasture, *and* 3. food, fodder'; *weida* appears w. mg 1 in Ger. *Waid-mann*, 'hunter' (also as family name, *Weidmann*, 'Hunter'), and w. mgs 2 and 3 in *Weide*, 'pasture, food': perhaps 2 váyas, 'food,' q.v., comes fr. √vī in mg 1, 'seek for, hunt,' and in this case the development of mg is like that of *weida* 3 and like that of Lat. *vēnātiōn-em*, 'hunting, game,' whence Eng. *venison*.]

+ **upa**, seek after.

√ **2 vī**, *see* vyā.

vīṇá, *f.* lute.

vīta, *see* √i + vi; *also referable to roots* vī *and* vyā.

vīta-darpa, *a.* having one's pride departed; humbled. [√i + vi.]

vīta-rāga, *a.* having one's passions departed, *i.e.* having conquered one's passions. [do.]

vīrá, *m.* —1. man; *esp.* man of might, hero; *in pl.* Männer; —2. hero, applied to gods; —3. *pl.* (*like Eng.* men) retainers, Mannen, 86[5]. [cognate with 3 vayas, 'strength': cf. Lat. *vir*, AS. *wer*, 'manly *or* heroic man'; Eng. *were-wolf*, 'man-wolf.']

√ **vīraya** (vīráyate [1067]). be a hero, show one's self brave. [vīra, 1058.]

vīrávant, *a.* having *or* rich in men *or* heroic sons. [vīrá, 1233a.]

vīra-sū [352], *a.* bringing forth heroes (as sons).

vīrásena, *a.* possessing a vīrasenā *or* hero-army; *as subst. m.* Vīrasena, king of Nishadha, *like the Greek* Ἡρό-στρατος *in formation and mg.* [vīra-senā, 334², 1297: acct, 1295.]

vīrasena-suta, *m.* Vīrasena's son, 1⁸. [1264.]

vīra-senā, *f.* hero-army, army of heroes. [vīrá + sénā, 1280b: acct, 1280².]

vīryà, *n.* —1. manliness, courage; strength; —2. *concrete*, heroic deed. [vīrá, 1212 d 4.]

vīhasta, *for* vihasta, *q.v.*, 52¹². [see 1087 b.]

√ **1 vṛ** (vṛṇóti, vṛṇuté; vavára, vavré; ávārīt; vṛtá; váritum, vártum; vṛtvá; -vṛtya; vāráyati). —1. cover, enclose, encompass; surround, *i.e.* guard, 11²¹; —2. *offensively*, keep in, hold back *or* captive; vṛtá, pent up, 75¹⁴; —3. *defensively*, hold back, keep in check (75¹¹), ward off, hinder, restrain; — *caus.* [1041²], keep back, hinder, stop.

[cf. ἐ-ελ-μένος, 'enclosed' and 'held in check,' referred to εἴλω, Aeolic ἔλλω, ⁕Fελ-νω; εἶλαρ, ⁕Fελ-αρ, 'cover, defense'; Lat. ver-ēri, 'be on one's guard, fear'; vellus, '(cover, *i.e.*) pelt, fleece'; vallum, 'defense, palisaded rampart, wall,' whence the borrowed Eng. *wall*; Eng. *ware, wary,* 'on one's guard, cautious'; Ger. *wehren,* 'check, ward off'; *Wehre,* 'defense'; with vártra, 'stopping,' and then 'a dam,' cf Ger. *Wehr,* AS. *wer,* Eng. *weir,* '(water-) stop, dam': for other cognates, see **uru, ūrṇa, varuṇa:** cf. the derivs **vala, vṛtra, varūtha, varṇa,** etc.]

+ **anu,** cover over.

+ **apa,** uncover, open. [*cf.* the relation of Ger. *decken,* 'cover,' and *auf-decken,* 'uncover.']

+ **abhi,** cover.

+ **ā,** cover; —ávṛta: covered, 33²⁰; concealed; encompassed, surrounded, 3⁹;

(covered with, *i.e.*) filled with, provided with, 66¹.

+ **sam-ā,** cover; **samāvṛta,** surrounded.

+ **ni,** keep down, suppress, ward off; *caus.* [1041²], stop, 98⁴.

+ **nis,** *in ppl.* nirvṛta, pleased, contented, free from care. [prop. 'uncovered, not covered over, *i.e.* not dark *or* gloomy,' and so 'clear, bright': cf. √1 vṛ + vi, which shows a similar metaphor.]

+ **pari,** surround.

+ **pra,** cover.

+ **sam-pra,** *mid.* cover completely.

+ **vi,** uncover, open; make open *or* clear, illume. [cf. √1 vṛ + nis.]

+ **sam,** —1. cover over; —2. keep together *or* in order, *and so* put in order, gather up, 26²⁰.

√ **2 vṛ** (vṛṇīté; vavré; ávṛta; variṣyáte; vṛtá; váritum [254⁸]; varitvá; *caus.* varáyati, -te [1042b⁸]). choose; prefer; desire, wish; choose for one's self, make one's portion, 70⁵, 86¹⁴; varaṁ vṛ, wish a wish, make a condition, 94¹; —*caus.* [1041²], choose.

[cf. Lat. *volo,* 'will'; Old Eng. *wol, wul,* 'will,' still living in *I won't,* 'I wol not'; Ger. *Wahl,* 'choice, selection,' whence *wählen,* 'select,' Chaucerian *wail,* 'select'; Ger. *wohl,* Eng. *well,* 'according to one's wish' (see under 1 vara): perhaps akin are βούλομαι, ⁕βόλομαι, Epic βόλομαι, 'will,' and βέλ-τερος, 'choicer, better,' but this is disputed.]

+ **ā,** choose, desire.

vṛka, —1. *a.* tearing, harming, *in* a-vṛka; —2. *m.* (the tearer, *i.e.*) wolf. [√⁕vṛk *or* ⁕vrak, simpler form of √vraçc: cf. λύκος, ⁕Fλύκος, Church Slavonic *vlŭkŭ,* Lat. *lupus,* Eng. *wolf.*]

vṛkka, *dual m.* the kidneys.

vṛkṣá, *m.* tree. ['that which is felled.' √⁕vṛk (1197) *or* ⁕vrak, simpler form of √vraçc: for mg, cf. **barhís.**]

vṛkṣa-traya, *n.* tree-triad, three trees.

vṛkṣatraya-tale, under three (separate) trees, *see* tala.

vṛkṣopari, on the tree. [upari: *see* 1314f.]

√ **vṛj** (vṛṇákti, vṛṅkté; vavárja; ávark
[832]; varkṣyáti, -te; vṛktá; -vṛjya;
varjáyati). — 1. turn; twist off; — 2.
turn or set aside; — 3. (turn aside, i.e.)
di-vert or keep away or alienate something
from some one;
— caus. [1041²] — 1. (set aside, i.e.)
abandon, shun; avoid, 25²¹, 104⁸; — 2.
(set aside, take out, and so, like ex-cípere)
except; varjayitvā, with an excepting,
i.e. with exception of, 54²²; leave out,
exclude, separate.
[orig. 'bring out of its original direction
or position, by bending or diverting or
keeping in' (in this last sense, cf. vṛjána,
'enclosure,' and ἐ-έργ-νν, 'shut in'), and
so the opposite of √1ṛj, 'stretch or reach
straight out,' q.v.: cf. also Lat. vergere,
'bend, turn'; Eng. wrick, 'to twist,' and
wriggle; prob. cognate is wring, 'twist';
also Eng. wrong, 'twisted, crooked' (as in
wrong-nosed, Wyclif), 'bad,' which shows
the same metaphor as vṛjina and French-
Eng. tort, from Lat. torquēre, 'twist.']

vṛjána, n. enclosure, esp. enclosed settlement, and so, either dwelling-place (74¹³)
or the dwellers. [√vṛj, q.v.: 1150.2c.]

vṛjiná, a. crooked, wrong, opp. of ṛju,
'straight, right.' [√vṛj, 1177b: for the
mg, see √vṛj.]

√ **vṛt** (vártate, -ti; vavárta, vāvṛté [786];
ávṛtat; vartiṣyáti, -te; vartsyáti, -te;
vṛttá; vártitum; -vṛtya; vartáyati,
-te). — 1. turn or roll or move as does a
wheel; in general, move or come from
(abl.), 76¹⁴; — 2. (like Eng. take its
course) go on, take place; happen; ekā́-
pāyena vṛt, go with a diminution-by-one,
i.e. decrease by one, 58⁵; — 3. (move
one's self about in a place, and so) abide,
exist, be, be present; mūrdhni vṛt, stand
at the head, be chief in importance, 22²¹;
— 4. be in a certain condition, case, occupation; be concerned with (loc.), 10⁵;
— 5. live; live by (instr.), i.e. live upon,
104²; — 6. proceed, behave; — 7. attenuated in mg from sense 3 to that of a simple
copula, be, 51⁴; — vṛttá, see s.v.
[cf. Lat. vert-ere, 'turn'; AS. weorðan,
'become,' Eng. worth, 'become, be to' (in

wo worth the day), Ger. werden, 'become';
for transition of mg in Eng. and Ger., cf.
Eng. turn, which also means 'become' (as
in turn traitor): — cf. also Eng. -ward, as
in go south-ward, i.e. 'turned to the south,'
fly up-ward, i.e. 'directed up,' etc. (see
añc); also Ger. Wirt-el, 'spindle-ring';
Church Slavonic vret-eno, 'spindle':
— further akin is, prob., AS. wriðan,
'twist,' whence come: Eng. writhe; AS.
wreð, 'a twisted band,' Eng. wreath; wrist,
earlier hand-wrist, ←wrið-st, 'hand-turner':
— with vṛttá, cf. Lat. versus, 'turned,'
whence versāre, 'turn much': for mgs
3–6 of vṛt, cf. Lat. versāri, whose senses
are quite parallel, and the Eng. phrase
"in whom we live and move and have our
being."]

+ **anu**, roll after; follow; and so, continue.

+ **ā**, act. turn hither (trans.), 73⁵; so at
74¹¹ (sc. rátham vas, 'your car'); mid.
turn (intrans.), roll back, 63⁸.

+ **upa ā**, turn hither unto, 93¹⁹.

+ **abhi-pary-ā**, turn around unto.

+ **vy-ā**, turn away, intrans.; separate
from or part with (instr.), 86⁸, 96²³.

+ **sam-ā**, turn back to meet; go home,
used esp. of a religious preceptor's pupil
who has finished his studies.

+ **ud**, turn out (centrifugally), intrans.,
fly asunder; caus. burst asunder or open.

+ **ni**, — 1. turn back; — 2. flee; — 3.
turn away; — 4. turn from, abstain; — nivṛtta, see s.v.

+ **prati-ni**, turn back from (abl.).

+ **nis**, roll out, intrans., and so (with a
metaphor like that in the Eng. e-volve itself
and Ger. sich ent-wickeln) develop, come
into being, 92¹⁸; caus. e-volve from, i.e.
create from (abl.), 57¹⁶.

+ **pari**, turn around; move in a circle.

+ **pra**, — 1. turn or move forward; — 2.
set out; — 3. begin, set about; — 4. engage in; — pravṛtta, see s.v.; — caus. set
in motion.

+ **vi**, turn away; part with (instr.), 88⁸;
caus. whirl about, trans.

+ **sam**, unite, intrans., and so take shape,
form itself, come into being.

vṛt, *vbl.* turning, *in cpds.* [√vṛt.]

vṛttá, *ppl.* −1. happened (√vṛt 2); tad vṛttam, that took place ; −2. existing (vṛt 3); −*as n.* −1. thing happened, occurrence (vṛt 2); −2. life, behavior (vṛt 5, 6).

vṛttānta, *m.* occurrence, adventures, story. [anta: force of anta not clear.]

vṛtti, *f.* prop. an existing, *and so (like Eng.* living) means of subsistence, support. [√vṛt 3, 5: cf. vartana.]

vṛtti-nibandhana, *n.* means of support.

vṛttāujas, *a.* possessing existing strength, *i.e.* mighty. [ojas.]

vṛtrá, −1. *n.* that which wards off or holds in check, *i.e.* the enemy, 75¹⁴; −2. *m.* coverer, encloser; *personified*, Vritra, demon of drought and darkness, principal personification of the malign power that covers *or* darkens the sky and encompasses (70¹⁶) *or* withholds the heavenly waters, *selections* xxxii. *and* lxvii.; slain by Indra, 73¹⁸; *see* 82¹ *and* 97¹⁹. [√1 vṛ, 'cover,' 1185b.]

vṛtratára, *comparative to* vṛtra (*see* 473¹). the arch-withholder. [acct irregular, 471, 1242a².]

vṛtrá-putra, *a.* having Vritra as son; −ā, *f.* the mother of V. [1302.]

vṛthā, *adv.* at will, at pleasure; for pleasure, *i.e.* not for the sake of the gods. [√2 vṛ, 'choose, will,' 1101.]

vṛthā-paçughna, *a.* slaying cattle for pleasure; *as m.* one who slays cattle for pleasure, *i.e.* not for sacrifice. [1279.]

vṛddhá, *ppl.* −1. grown, become great; increased (of wealth), 42¹⁶; −2. *as adj.* grown up, *opp. of* young; old, aged; *as subst.* old man, 28¹²; −3. (grown great, *and so, like Lat.* altus) eminent, distinguished. [√vṛdh, 160.]

vṛddhatva, *n.* condition of being old, old age. [1239.]

vṛddhi, *f.* −1. growth, increase; −2. interest (on money lent), 46²⁰; −3. the (second) increment of a vowel, see 235−6. [√vṛdh, 1157. 1a, 160.]

√ vṛdh (várdhati, -te; vavárdha, vavṛdhé; ávṛdhat, ávardhiṣṭa; vartsyáti; vṛddhá; várdhitum; vardháyati, -te). *act. trans.:* −1. elevate, make to grow, make greater, strengthen; −2. *fig.* elevate inwardly, excite pleasantly, cheer, inspire (*cf. the metaphor in slang Eng.* high, 'slightly intoxicated'), *used* of the effects which the homage and sacrifices of men are supposed to have on the gods;

−*mid. intrans.:* −3. grow, 24⁸; thrive, 69¹⁶; vardhate, he thrives, *i.e.* it goes well with him, 65³; grow strong *or* greater *or* mighty, 81², 82⁸; increase, 8¹¹, 60¹⁹; −4. *fig.* be pleasantly excited, take delight in; be inspired;

−*caus.* −1. make to grow; make strong; bring up (a child), 46⁸; increase, *trans.,* 64²¹; −2. *fig.* excite pleasantly, cheer, inspire; − *distinction between the physical and fig. mgs not always to be made,* so 80¹⁹.

[cf. βλάστη, *ᴇϝʟᴀθ-τη, 'growth, a shoot,' βλαστάνω, 'grow'; ὀρθός, *ᴠᴏʀθᴏs, 'upright'; Lat. *verb-er*, 'a shoot, rod'; *verbēna*, '(sacred) twig.']

+pra, grow on, grow up; pravṛddha, (*like Lat.* altus) exalted.

+vi, grow, increase, 2¹⁹.

+sam, grow; *caus.* make to grow; bring up; nourish, feed.

vṛdh, *vbl.* being pleased, rejoicing. [√vṛdh.]

√ vṛṣ (várṣati, -te; vavárṣa, vavṛṣé; ávarṣit; varṣiṣyáti, -te; vṛṣṭá; várṣitum; vṛṣṭvá, -vṛṣya). rain; várṣati [303b], ὕοντος, while it is raining. [orig., perhaps, more general,· 'to pour down,' esp. either the fructifying water of heaven (masc.) upon the earth (fem.), or semen of the bull or male animal upon the female: with varṣa, 'rain,' cf. ἔ-ερσαι, 'rain-drops'; with vṛṣan and vṛṣabha, 'bull,' cf. Lat. *verres*, *ᴠᴇʀs-es*, 'boar,' so named from his great generative power, just as the sow (see sū) from her fecundity.]

vṛṣa, *used only at end of cpds* [1315a] *in Veda, but later independently, instead of* vṛṣan.

vṛṣan [426b], *adj. and subst.* describing *or denoting* all that was distinguished for

its strength and virility: —1. man, as
opposed to a castrated person, 70 14; —2.
of animals: stallion; bull; boar; —3. of
gods: manly, mighty, great; of Indra,
74 5; of the Maruts, 73 5; of the Sun or
Sun-horse, 79 7. [√vṛṣ, q.v., 1160c: cf.
ἄρσην, stem *Fαρσεν, 'male.']

vṛṣabhá, *essentially the same as* vṛṣan,
q.v.: esp. —1. bull; *with* sahasra-çṛṅga,
the thousand-horned steer, *i.e.* the sun *or*
(77 14) the moon; —2. bull, as type of
greatness and might; most mighty one,
of Indra, 73 16. [√vṛṣ, 1199.]

vṛṣalá, *m. prop.* manikin, *i.e.* little man,
and so, as term of contempt, a low person,
esp. a Çūdra. [vṛṣa, 1227.]

√ vṛṣasya (vṛṣasyáti). desire the male,
be lustful. [vṛṣa, 1059e, 1058.]

√ vṛṣāya (vṛṣāyáte). act as a vṛṣa, *i.e.:*
show one's manly strength *or* courage;
be lustful; *or simply,* be eager. [vṛṣa,
1059b, 1058.]

vṛṣṭi, *f.* rain. [√vṛṣ, 1157.]

√ vṛh *or* bṛh (vṛháti; vavárha; ávṛkṣat;
vṛḍhá [224a]; -vṛhya). pluck, tear.

veṇu, *m.* reed, *esp.* bamboo-reed.

véda, *m.* —1. understanding, knowledge;
—2. *esp.* the sacred knowledge, handed
down in triple form of ṛc, yajus, and
sāman, *see these, and cf.* (trayī) vidyā;
—*later,* the well-known collections called
Rigveda, Yajurveda, and Sāmaveda
(63 5. 6), the holy scriptures, held to be a
revelation and so called çruti, 58 18.
[√1 vid.]

vedá, *m.* tuft of strong grass (kuça *or*
muñja) tied so as to form a broom, 62 18.

veda-traya, *n.* the three Vedas.

veda-nindaka, *m.* one who scoffs at
the Veda, infidel.

veda-puṇya, *n.* Veda-merit, sanctity
acquired by Veda-study.

veda-bāhya, *a.* being outside of the
Veda, *i.e.* extra-Vedic, differing from *or*
conflicting with the Veda. [1265, veda-
being in an abl. relation.]

veda-víd [391], *a.* Veda-knowing. [1269.]

1 védas, *n.* knowledge; *possibly adj.,*
knowing, *cf.* na-vedas. [√1 vid, 'know':
cf. 1151.2a, b.]

2 védas, *n.* (*like Lat.* quaestus) gettings,
property, *cf.* vitta. [√2 vid, 'get.']

vedādhyayana, *n.* Veda-study, scrip-
ture-reading. [adhyayana.]

védi, *f.* sacrificial bed, *i.e.* a spot of ground
excavated two or three inches and covered
with straw and serving as a kind of altar.

vedin, *a.* knowing. [√1 vid, 1183 3.]

vedi-puriṣa, *n.* loose earth of the vedi.

vedhás, *subst. adj.* —1. worshipper of the
gods, worshipping, pious, devoted; —2.
generalized, faithful, true, *used of* Indra,
75 13. [√1 vidh, 'worship a god,' 1151.
2 b.]

vélā, *f.* —1. end-point, limit; —2. *esp.*
limit of time, point of time, hour.

veçá, *m.* —1. settler; neighbor. —2. (settlement, *i.e.*) dwelling, house. [√viç: cf.
οἶκος, 'house,' Old Lat. *veicus,* Lat. *vicus,*
'houses, quarter of a town, village': hence
the borrowed AS. *wic,* 'town,' as in *Eofor-
wic,* Eng. *York,* prop. 'Eber-stadt' *or*
'Boar-town,' and perhaps in *Nor-wich,*
'Nor-ton.']

véçman, *n.* (settlement, *i.e.*) dwelling,
house, abode, chamber. [√viç, 1168.1a.]

vāí, *postpositive particle, emphasizing the
preceding word, e.g.* 3 17, 96 18; *rare in
the* saṃhitā, 90 20, 103 4 (*in a quoted* mantra); *excessively common in the* brāhmaṇa
(92 14. 19, 93 6, 94 6. 13. 18, 95 6. 15) *and* Epos
(7 6, etc.); *in* brāhmaṇa *often marking
the preceding word as the first of its clause*
(*cf.* atha, *near end of* mg 3): *so* 94 6, 95 12,
96 12, *and in the examples just given; often
used, esp. in* Epos, *as a mere expletive*
[*see* 1122a 4], *so at end of a* pāda, 3 9, 10 9,
68 9.

vāicitrya, *n.* variety, diversity. [vici-
tra, 1211.]

vāiṇavá, *f.* -ī, *a.* of reed, *esp.* of bamboo.
[veṇu, 1208c.]

vāidarbha, *f.* -ī, *a.* belonging to Vidarbha; *as m.* the Vidarbhan, *i.e.* king of
V.; *as f.* the princess of V., *i.e.* Damayantī, 8 7, etc. [vidarbha, 1208f.]

vāidika, *a.* Vedic, prescribed by *or* conformable to the Vedas. [veda, 1222e 2.]

vāidyá, —1. *a.* having to do with science,
learned; *and so* —2. *as m.* (*with a* tran-

sition like that from Lat. doctor, 'teacher, learned man,' *to Chaucer's* doctour of phisik) physician, doctor. [vidyā́, 1211.]

vāimānika, *a.* riding in a sky-traversing car called **vimāna,** *q.v.* [vimāna, 1222e 2.]

vāivasvatá, *a.* descended from Vivasvant; *as m.* son of V., *i.e.* Yama. [vívasvant, 1208 and a and a².]

vāíçya, *adj. subst.* man of the víç or folk or third caste, 57¹⁶. [víç, 1211.]

voc, *quasi-root, see* 854 *and* √vac.

vyáṅsa, *a.* having the shoulders apart, *i.e.* broad-shouldered; *as m.* Viansa, Broad-shoulder, name of a demon, slain by Indra. [vi + aṅsa, 1305.]

√ **vyac** (vivyakti [682]; vivyā́ca [785]). embrace, encompass, extend around. [cf. 1087f², 108g.]

vyácas, *n.* compass, extent.

vyatikara, *m.* a mixing, confusing; confusion, disaster. [√3 kṛ, 'scatter,' + vi.]

√ **vyath** (vyáthate; vivyathé [785]; ávyathiṣṭa; vyathitá). — 1. move to and fro, rock, reel; — 2. *fig. (like Eng.* be restless) be disturbed in mind, be pained.

vyáthā, *f.* feeling of painful unrest, discomfort, sorrow.

√ **vyadh** *or* **vidh** (vídhyati; vivyādha [785]; vetsyáti; viddhá; véddhum; viddhvā́; -vídhya). bore through, pierce, hit (with a weapon). [akin w. √vadh: cf. Lat. *di-vid-ere,* 'part asunder, divide.']

vyapadeça, *m.* the making a false show of, an unauthorized referring to *or* using the name of (a person of high position). [√diç + vy-apa.]

vyaya, *a.* going asunder *or* to pieces, perishing, *w. a-.* [√i + vi, 1148. 1b.]

vyálkaçā, *f.* Vialkaçā, a certain plant.

vyavasāya, *m.* determination, resolve. [√sā + vy-ava.]

vyavasāyin, *a.* determined, resolute. [vyavasāya.]

vyavahāra, *m.* — 1. procedure, conduct, way of acting; — 2. (way of acting with others, *i.e.*) intercourse, 24¹². [√1 hṛ + vy-ava.]

vyasana, *n. prop.* a throwing one's self away (upon a thing), *and so* — 1. passionate devotion to a thing (whether good or bad, *e.g.* alms-giving, scripture-study, gambling); hobby; — 2. an overpowering passion, *esp.* for something bad; vice, 20⁴; — 3. (a throwing one's self away, *i.e.*) misfortune, adversity, 25ᵃ⁴. [√2 as + vi.]

√ **vyā** *or* **vī** (vyáyati, -te [761d 2]; vivyāya [785], vivyé; vītá; -víya). *mid.* envelope *or* hide one's self. [orig. 'wind around' as with robe or girdle, and so a a doublet of √vi, i.e. √2 vā, 'weave,' q.v.]

+ **upa,** hang about, *esp.* wind the sacred cord over the left shoulder and under the right arm; upavīta, *see s.v.*

+ **ni,** wind about, hang (*e.g.* garland, cord) about (*e.g.* neck, shoulders); nivīta, *see s.v.*

+ **pari,** *act.* envelope around *or* completely; *mid.* wind something as cover around one's self, envelope one's self in; *perhaps in sense of act.,* 84¹⁶.

vyākaraṇa, *n.* the putting asunder, *and so* analysis, grammar. [√1 kṛ, 'do, put,' + vy-ā.]

vyākhyātṛ, *m.* explainer. [√khyā + vy-ā.]

vyāghrá, *m.* tiger; *like* çārdūla *and* siṅha, as type of noble manliness, *in cpds, see* nara-vyāghra. [perhaps fr. √1 ghṛ, 'besprinkle,' + vy-ā, 'the sprinkled *or* spotted one.']

vyāghra-carman, *n.* tiger-skin.

vyāghratā, *f.* tigerhood, condition of being a tiger. [1237.]

vyādha, *m.* hunter. [√vyadh.]

vyādhi, *m.* disease. [√1 dhā, 'put,' + vy-ā, 1155. 2e.]

vyādhita, *a.* diseased. [vyādhi, see 1176b.]

vyāpāda, *m.* destruction. [√pad + vy-ā.]

vyāpādayitavya, *grdv.* to be destroyed *or* killed. [caus. of √pad + vy-ā.]

vyāpāra, *m.* — 1. business, *i.e.* occupation; — 2. (*as in Eng.*) business, *i.e.* concern, 30⁴; — 3. activity, exertion. [√3 pṛ + vy-ā, 'be busied.']

vyāpāra-çata, *n.* exertion-hundred, a hundred attempts.

vyāmá, m. *prop.* a stretch-out, the distance covered by the stretched-out arms, a fathom, about six feet. [for vi-yāma, √ yam + vi: for mg, cf. the precisely parallel Eng. *fathom* w. AS. *fæðm*, 'the extended arms'; ὀργυιά, 'fathom,' and ὀρέγω, 'stretch'; French *toise*, Medieval Lat. *tesa*, 'fathom,' from Lat. *tensa*, ppl. of *tendere*, 'stretch.']

vyāma-mātra, a. having a fathom as its measure, *see* mātrā. [mātrā, 334².]

vyāhṛti, f. — 1. utterance; — 2. *esp.* one of the three sacred and mystical exclamations, bhūr, bhúvas, and svàr, *which see*. [√ 1 hṛ + vy-ā.]

vyòman, n. heaven, sky.

√ vraj (vrájati; vavrāja; ávrājīt; vrajiṣyáti; vrajitá; vrájitum; vrajitvā; -vrájya). march, proceed, go.
+ ā, come hither, go unto.
+ praty-ā, march *or* go back.
+ pari, march round about; wander around.
+ pra, march forth; go unto; wander; *esp.* leave one's house to wander about as an ascetic, 65².

vratá, n. — 1. will; devānām áti vratam, beyond the will of the gods, 88² — *cf.* ὑπὲρ Διὸς αἶσαν; decree, command *or* Gebot, statute; *and so* — 2. (*as Eng.* command *is applied to the forces under one's command*) that over which one exercises command, domain, Gebiet; — *further, directly from the root again* — 3. choice, determination; firm resolution, 14⁶; — 4. *esp.* resolve (to keep a religious or ascetic observance); vow *or* holy work (*e.g.* of chastity, fasting, etc.), 28²³, 59⁶, 61²³, 64⁸, 65⁸; — 5. religious duty, duty *in general.* [√ 2 vṛ, 'will, choose': for mg 2, observe that Ger. *Gebiet* formerly meant 'command' and now means 'domain.']

√ vraçç (vṛçcáti; vṛkṇá [957c]; vṛṣṭvā; -vṛ́çcya). hew off; fell (a tree); cut to pieces. [orig. form is vṛk, as in vṛk-a, vṛk-ṇá, vṛk-ṣá, which see: vṛçç is prop. only a quasi-root of the present stem vṛçça, for ●vṛk-ska, formed like the present of √ prach and mlech, which see: see 221² and cf. 220.]
+ vi, cut asunder *or* to pieces.

√ çaṅs (çáṅsati, -te; çaçáṅsa, çaçaṅsé; áçaṅsīt; çaṅsiṣyáti; çastá; çastvā; -çásya). *orig.* say in a loud and solemn way, *and so:* — 1. recite, *esp.* a sacred hymn *or* text to a god by way of praise; *and so* — 2. *generalized*, praise; çasta, *see s.v.;* — 3. *rarely*, make a solemn wish, whether blessing *or* curse (*see* çaṅsa), *like* imprecāri; — 4. announce; communicate, 52¹⁸. [cf. Lat. *carmen*, ●cas-men, 'an utterance in solemn, measured, *or* melodious way, *i.e.* song, oracle, magic charm'; *Camēna*, ●casmenja, name of the goddess of song; *cens-ēre*, 'declare, pass judgment on'; AS. *herian*, 'praise.']
+ ā, — 1. wish, *esp. in the noun* āçás *or* āçā́, 'wish,' *q.v.; and so* — 2. hope in, put one's trust in (*acc.*); — 3. pronounce a blessing upon, wish good to (*acc.*), 101⁴. [mg 1 may be a mere specialization of the mg 'speak solemnly unto' (cf. √ çaṅs + ā), and mg 2 a further development of mg 1; for mg 3, cf. the simple verb, mg 3.]
+ pra, tell forth; praise, 2¹⁶. [cf. simple verb.]

çáṅsa, m. — 1. solemn utterance; — 2. imprecatio, blessing *or* curse; *as adj.* — 3. cursing. [√ çaṅs.]

√ çak (A. çaknóti; çaçáka, çekús [794e]; áçakat; çakṣyáti, -te; çaktá; — *pass.* çakyáte, çakitá).
— B. *desid.* çíkṣate [1030, 108g¹ end]; *caus. of desid.* çikṣáyati; *pass. of desid. and of caus. of desid.* çikṣyáte, çikṣitá).
— A. *simple verb:* — 1. be strong; be able, 8¹⁹; *in pass.:* impersonally, it is possible; *with infin.* [988], be able, by the instrumentality of some person *or* thing (*instr.*), to become the object of an action; mayā nītiṁ grāhayituṁ çakyante, they are able to be caused by me to get hold of nīti, 19¹⁸; — 2. *rarely* (be strong for a person, *i.e.*) be serviceable *or* helpful, help, w. *dat.*;

—B. *desiderative:* —1. *desid. to* A. 1, (strive to be able, *i.e.*) practice; learn; *caus.* cause a person (*acc.*) to learn a thing (*acc.*), 51²², 52⁸; *pass. of caus.:* çikṣita, caused to learn *or* taught a thing (*acc.*), 46¹⁰; *without noun*, taught, 52⁵; çikṣyamāṇa, instructed, 51¹⁷; —2. *desid. to* A. 2, be willing to help; aid; (of gods) bestow blessing upon (*dat.*), 80¹³; grant, give.

[cf. Lat. *cac-ula*, 'servant' (like *help* as sometimes used in America for 'servant'); w. çagmā́, ●çak-ma, 'helpful, friendly,' cf. Lat. *cōmis*, ●*coc-mi-s*, 'friendly': prob. akin is Ger. *be-hag-en*, AS. *on-hag-ian*, 'suit, please' (cf. çak, A. 2).]

+ u p a, (bring unto one's self by giving, *i.e.*) attract, 76¹⁸. [for mg, see the uncompounded verb, B. 2.]

çákala, —1. *m. n.* chip; piece; —2. *n.* half (of an egg-shell).

çakuná, *m.* bird.

çákti, *f.* ability, power.

çakya, *a.* —1. possible, practicable, 33¹⁶; *common with the infinitive:* çakya *being used* —2. *impersonally;* or —3. *in agreement with the subject, in which case the inf.* [988] *is to be translated as a passive,* 29¹⁰. [√çak, 1213.]

çakrá, —1. *a.* powerful, mighty, standing epithet of Indra; —2. *as m.* The Mighty One, *i.e.* Indra (*just as we use* The Almighty *as a name for* 'God'). [√çak, 1188a.]

√ çañk (çáñkate; ●çañkiṣṭa; çañkitá; çáñkitum; -çáñkya). —1. be anxious *or* suspicious; —2. hesitate.

+ v i, hesitate.

çañkā́, *f.* hesitation. [√çañk, 1149³.]

çácī, *f.* —1. might *or* help (*esp.* of the helping deeds of Indra); —2. Çachī *or* Might, as wife of Indra (*derived from the misunderstood* çacī-pati, *q.v.*), 2⁷. [√çac, collateral form of çak.]

çácī-páti, *m.* —1. *Vedic*, lord of might *or* of help, epithet of Indra, 80¹³; —2. *later* (páti, *q.v., being misunderstood as* 'husband'), husband of Might *or* Çachī, name of Indra, 15¹⁴, 49⁴. [acct, 1267a and d, Whitney 94b.]

çaṭha, *a.* false.

√ çat (çātáyati; çātitá). cut in pieces; make to fall off.

çatá [485²], *n.* hundred; *also as expression of* a large number; *for construction, see* 486b. [cf. ●-κατόν, 'one-hundred'; Lat. *centum*, AS. *hund*, neut., 'hundred'; Eng. *hund-red*.]

çatátman, *a.* having a hundred lives. [çatá + ātmán: acct, 1300a.]

çátru, *m.* —1. (victor, *i.e.*) victorious opponent; —2. foe, enemy, *in general.*

[if mg 1 is the orig. mg, we may take the word fr. √çad and as standing for ●çat-tru, 1185e, 232:

if mg 2 is the orig. mg, we may analyse thus, çat-ru (1192), and compare Church Slavonic *kot-ora*, Irish *cath*, 'battle'; AS. *heaðo* in cpds, as *heaðo-weorc*, 'battle-work,' Old High Ger. *had-u* in names, as *Hadu-brant*, 'Battle-flame,' *Hadu-wich*, 'Battle-strife,' Ger. *Hedwig*; Ger. *Hader*, 'strife'; cf. also the Keltic proper name *Catu-rig-es* (*rig* under rājan), 'The Battle-kings.']

çatru-nandana, *a.* causing joy to one's enemies.

çatru-saṃkaṭa, *m.* danger from the foe.

√ çad (çācáda, çáçadé [786]). distinguish one's self; get the upper hand, prevail; *Vedic only.* [cf. κεκασμένος, Doric κε-καδμένος, 'distinguished.']

çanakáis, *adv.* quietly; gently; slowly. [instr. (1112c) of an unused stem ●çanaka, diminutive to ●çana, see çanáis.]

çanáis, *adv.* quietly; gently; slowly; gradually. [instr. (1112c) of an unused stem ●çana, which is prob. connected w. √2çam, 'be quiet.']

çáṃtāti, *f.* benefit. [çám, 1238.]

√ çap (çápati, -te; çaçápa, çepé; çapiṣyáte; çaptá; çápitum; çapitvā́). —1. curse, *usually act.*, 93¹⁷; —2. mid. (curse one's self, *i.e.*) assert with an oath, swear, vow, w. *dat. of person*, 97⁷.

çapátha, *m.* curse; oath. [√çap, 1163b.]

çabála, *a.* brinded.

çábda, *m.* —1. sound; cry; noise; çabdaṃ kr̥, make a noise, raise one's voice; —2. word, 50⁹, 61¹.

çabda-çāstra, n. word-theory, word-compendium, i.e. grammar.

√ 1çam (çámyati; çaçamé; áçamişţa; çamitá). get weary by working, work. [cf. κάμ-νω, 'get weary by working.']

√ 2çam (çámyati [763]; çaçáma, çemús; áçamat; çāntá [955a]; çamáyati). be quiet or still or content; stop; for these senses, cf. √ram; çāntá, see s.v.; caus. quiet, still; euphemistically, kill.
+upa, be quiet; stop.
+pra, come to rest; stop; go out; praçānta, extinguished.

√ 3çam (çamnīté). harm.

√ 4çam (çānta; -çámya; çamáyati, çāmáyati). used only with ni. observe; perceive; hear.

çám [384²], n. welfare; happiness; blessing.

çáma, a word of doubtful mg at 718: perhaps tame (cf. √2çam, caus.) or industrious (cf. √1çam).

çamayitŗ, m. slayer. [√2çam, caus.]

çamí, f. a fabaceous plant, either Prosōpis spicigera or Mimōsa Suma; a tree from which the sticks of attrition (araņí) were taken.

çamīmáya, f. -ī, a. of or made of Çamī-wood. [see maya.]

çamī-çākhā, f. Çamī-branch.

çamī-sumanas, f. Çamī-flower.

çamīsumano-mālā, f. garland of Çamī-flowers.

çámyā, f. staff, 102¹⁵.

çaya, a. lying, sleeping, at end of cpds. [√çī, 1148. 1a.]

çayana, n. a lying, sleeping. [√çī, 1150. 1a.]

çayanīya, −1. a. serving for lying; −2. n. bed, couch. [çayana, 1215.]

çayyā, f. −1. bed; −2. a lying, sleeping. [√çī, 1213d, cf. 963⁸b.]

çará, m. −1. reed, esp. of the Saccharum Sara, used for arrows; −2. arrow. [observe that Lat. arundo means 'reed' and 'arrow.']

çaraņá, −1. a. protecting, affording refuge, 877; as n. −2. shed, that gives cover from the rain; καλιά, hut; −3. protection; refuge, 50¹⁷.

[çaraņá presupposes a root •çŗ or •çĮ, 'cover, protect'; w. such a root agree well in form and mg as derivs, çárīra, çárman, and çālā, see these:
further agree as cognates καλιά, 'hut, barn'; AS. heal, Eng. hall; κάλ-υξ, 'husk, pod'; Ger. Hülle, 'covering'; Eng. hull, 'covering' of grain; AS. hel-m, 'protector' (used of God and Christ), 'head-protector, helmet,' Ger. Helm, Eng helm; Lat. oc-cul-ere, 'cover'; color, 'color' (see varņa); cēl-āre, Ger. hehl-en, Chaucer's hel-en, later hele, 'conceal'; further, κ°λύπ-τ-ω, 'cover,' and the ident. κρύπ-τ-ω, 'hide.']

çaraņāgata, a. come for refuge, seeking protection with any one. [āgata.]

çarád, f. autumn; pl. poetic for years (cf. varşa).

çarāva, m. n. flat earthen dish.

çárīra, n. the body, as distinguished from the vital breath or from the immortal soul (so 96²¹· ²², 29⁶) and from the soft viscera and inward fluid secretions, of which things the body, or the firm red flesh with the bones, forms as it were the hollow cover (57¹), tegument, or Hülle; used also in pl., 84⁹; body in general; mŗtam çarīram, corpse, 63¹⁷; so 84⁴. [prop. 'the corporeal tegument' of the soul, √•çŗ, 'cover' (1188e²), see under çaraņa: for mg, cf. the cognate Ger. Hülle (under çaraņa) in sterbliche Hülle, 'mortal envelope, i.e. body': cf. 97¹⁸ ɴ.]

çarīra-ja, a. (born of, i.e.) performed by the body.

çarīrāntakara, m. destroyer of the bodies. [anta-kara.]

çáru, f. missile, either spear or arrow. [cf. çara.]

çarkara, m. brown sugar. [fr. the Prakrit form sakkara comes on the one hand, through Arabic sokkar and Medieval Lat. zucara, the Eng. sugar, and on the other σάκχαρον, Lat. saccharum, all borrowed words: cf. khaņda.]

√ çardh (çárdhati). be strong or defiant.

çárdha, m. troop, host. [cf. Ger. Herde, Eng. herd.]

çárman, n. —1. cover; protection; shelter; refuge; —2. comfort, joy; —3. common at the end of Brahman-names, 19¹¹, 42¹¹, 59¹³ɴ. [see under çaraṇa.]

çarmavant, a. containing (the stem) çarman. [1233.]

çarvá, m. Çarva, name of an arrow-slaying god; later, a common name for the god Çiva. [çáru, 1209, cf. 1209g.]

çarvara, a. variegated; f. çárvarī, the night (as variegated with stars). [cf. çabala.]

çarva-varman, a. having Çiva as his protection; as m. Çarvavarman, name of a man.

çalá, m. —1. staff; —2. prickle (of a hedge-hog). [cf. çará.]

çalyá, m. n. point of spear or arrow; thorn; prickle. [cf. çalá, çará: cf. κῆλον, 'missile.']

çályaka, m. hedge-hog. [cf. çalya.]

çávas, n. superior might; heroic power; also pl. [√çū, 1151.1a.]

çáviṣṭha, a. most mighty. [√çū, 468.]

çaçá, m. hare; the Hindu sees, not "a man in the moon," but rather, a hare or a gazelle. [for ✶çasa (see √çus and çvaçura): cf. Ger. Hase, Eng. hare.]

çaçaka, m. hare, rabbit. [çaça, 1222b.]

çaçáṅka, m. the moon. [prop., adj., 'having a rabbit as its mark,' çaça (q.v.) + aṅka, 1302a.]

çaçin, m. the moon. [prop., adj., 'having the (picture of a) rabbit,' çaça, 1230.]

çáçvant, a. ever repeating or renewing itself.

√ ças (çásati; çaçása; çasiṣyáti; çastá; -çásya). cut to pieces; slaughter. [see çastra.]

çastá, a. praised, esteemed as good or lucky; equiv. to happy, cheerful, 52¹¹. [prop. ppl. of √çaṅs.]

çastrá, n. knife; sword; weapon. ['instrument of cutting,' √ças, 1185: ças-tra is ident. in form and mg w. the Lat. stem ✶cas-tro, which appears in the denom. castrāre, prop. 'cut,' and so, like Eng. cut, 'castrate.']

çastra-páṇi, a. having a sword in the hand. [1303.]

çastra-vṛtti, a. having weapons as one's means of subsistence, living by military service. [1302a.]

çáka, n. an edible herb; vegetable food.

çákhā, f. branch.

çátayitṛ, m. one who cuts in pieces, destroyer, 97¹⁹. [caus. of √çat, 1182c.]

çāntá, a. quiet; still; stopped. [ppl. of √2 çam, 'be quiet.']

çānti, f. a ceasing, stopping; esp. the absence of the evil results of some word or thing of evil omen. [√2 çam, 'be quiet,' cf. 955a.]

çānti-karman, n. a ceremony for averting the results of something ominous.

çāpa, m. curse. [√çap.]

çāpādi, a. having the curse as its first; as n. curse and so forth. [1302c 1.]

çāpādi-ceṣṭita, n. curse-and-so-forth doings, i.e. adventures including the curse et cetera. [1280b.]

çāpānta, m. end of the curse or period during which the curse has effect. [anta.]

çāyin, a. lying, sleeping. [√çī, 1183³.]

çārīrá, a. corporeal, of the body. [çárīra, 1208f.]

çārdūlá, m. tiger; at end of cpds, like vyāghra, the best of · ·.

çálā, f. hut; house; room; stable. [see under çaraṇa: cf. the derivs καλιά and Eng. hall, there given.]

çālin, a. —1. possessing a house; —2. at end of cpds, attenuated in mg so as to signify merely possessing · ·. [çálā.]

çālmalī, f. Salmalia malabarica, the silk-cotton tree.

çáva, m. the young of an animal. [see √çū.]

çávaka, m. the young of an animal. [çáva.]

çáçvatá, a. continual; eternal. [çáçvant, 1208a, a¹.]

√ çās or çiṣ (Vedic, çásti, çáste [639]; Vedic and Epic, çásati; çaçása; áçiṣat [854³]; çāsiṣyáti, -te; çāsitá, çāstá, çiṣṭá [954e]; çāsitum, çāstum; çāsitvá; -çásya, -çíṣya). —1. chasten, correct; —2. instruct, teach; direct; —3. (like Eng. direct) give order to, rule, govern.

17

[perhaps reduplicated form of çaṅs, 675: for the weak form çiṣ, cf. 639.]

+ ā, mid. wish or pray for, cf. āçis and √çaṅs + ā; make supplication, 73[11].

+ pra, instruct; direct; command, cf. simple verb, and praçis.

çā́sana, n. — 1. government, way of ruling; — 2. command. [√çās.]

çā́sitṛ, m. teacher. [√çās.]

çāstrá, n. — 1. instruction; — 2. rule; theory; compendium (of an art or science); a scientific or canonical work; science, 17[18]. [√çās.]

√ çikṣ, see 1030 and √çak.

çikhara, — 1. a. peaked; — 2. m. n. peak. [çikhā, 1226.]

çikhā́, f. — 1. tuft or braid of hair; — 2. (like Eng. crest) top in general, peak.

çithirá, a. loose; flaccid; unsteady, 93[2]; opp. of dṛḍha, 'firm, hard.' [perhaps fr. √çrath, 1188e: for loss of r, cf. √bhām.]

çibi, m. Çibi, name of a king.

çíras, n. head. [cf. κάρα, 'head'; Lat. cerebrum, *ceres-ru-m, 'brain': w. the collateral form çīrṣán, q.v., cf. Ger. Hirn, Old High Ger. hirni, ʒhirsni, 'brain': akin is also κρανίον, 'skull.']

çirīṣa, m. the tree Acacia Sirissa; as n. the blossom.

çiro-mukha, n. head and face. [1253b.]

çilā́, f. stone; crag.

çilā-bhāva, m. condition of being stone; -am āp, turn into stone.

çilī, f. the beam under a door.

çilī-mukha, m. Block-snout, name of a hare.

çiloccaya, m. crag-pile, i.e. craggy hill. [uccaya.]

çivá, — 1. a. kind, 90[2]; friendly; gracious; agreeable, lovely; opp. of ghora; — 2. m. The Friendly One, name euphemistically applied to the horrible god Rudra, who under this name (Çiva) becomes the third person of the Hindu Trinity. [for mg 2, cf. Ἐὑμενῖδες, 'The Gracious Ones, i.e. the Furies,' and nandi.]

çíçu, m. young; child. [see √çū, and 1147b and b[2].]

√ 1çiṣ (çinásti; çiçiṣé; áçiṣat; çekṣyáti, -te; çiṣṭá; çiṣṭvā́; -çíṣya). leave, leave remaining.

+ ud, leave remaining.

+ vi, (leave apart or by itself, i.e.) separate, distinguish; viçiṣṭa, (separated, and so, like Eng. distinguished) eminent, excellent.

√ 2çiṣ, subsidiary form to √çās, q.v.

çiṣya, grdv. to be taught; as m. pupil. [√çās, weak form çiṣ.]

√ 1çī (çéte [see 628–9]; çiçyé; áçayiṣṭa; çayiṣyáte, -ti; çeṣyáte, -ti; çayitá; çáyitum; çayitvā́; -çáyya). — 1. lie still; lie; — 2. sleep. [w. çé-te, cf. κεῖ-ται, 'lies': cf. also κοί-τη, 'bed.']

+ adhi, lie in or on; dwell in.

+ anu, lie down after another.

+ ā, lie in.

+ upa, lie by.

+ sam, be undecided or in doubt. [lit. 'lie together': metaphor unclear.]

√ 2çī, simpler form of √çyā, q.v.

çī́, vbl. lying. [√çī.]

çītá, a. cold; as n. cold. [ppl. of √çyā or 2çī.]

çītaka, f. çītikā, a. cool. [çīta: cf. 1222d.]

çītala, a. cool. [çīta, 1227.]

çītārta, a. distressed with the cold. [ārta.]

çītikāvant, a. cool. [as if from fem. of çītaka: 1233, cf. b.]

çīpāla, m. n. Blyxa octandra, a common water-plant.

çīrṣán, n. head. [çīrṣ-án is to çíras (q.v.), as īrṣ-yā́ is to iras-yā́, see these.]

çī́la, n. — 1. natural or acquired way of being; character, 23[20]; habit or habits, 58[14]; in composition [1302] with that to which one is inclined or accustomed, 21[4], 60[18]; — 2. (character, i.e., as in Eng.) good character, 98[7].

çī́van, a. lying. [√1çī, 1169.1a.]

çúka, m. parrot. [prop. 'the bright one,' on account of its gaudy colors, √çuc: cf. 216.1, 1[2].]

çukavat, adv. like a parrot. [çuka, 1107.]

çukrá, a. clear, bright, 76⁹. [√çuc, 1188a, 216.7.] -

çuklá, —1. a. clear; bright; white; *with* pakṣa, the bright lunar half-month, from new to full moon; —2. *as m.* (*sc.* pakṣa), the bright lunar fortnight, 65⁵. [see 1189 and ².]

çukla-pakṣa, *m.* fortnight of the waxing moon.

çuklapakṣādi, a. having the bright lunar fortnight first, beginning with the bright lunar fortnight. [ādi, 1302c 1.]

çuklāmbara, a. having a white garment. [ambara.]

√ çuc (çócati, -te; çuçóca; áçocīt; çociṣyáti; çócitum; çocitvá). —1. flame, light, beam; glow, burn; —2. *fig.* suffer burning pain; grieve; grieve at (*loc.*), 66¹³; — *intens.* flame brightly. [for mg 2, cf. √tap, dagdha and √dah.]

+ apa, *intens.* [1002a], drive away by flaming brightly, 72⁸.

+ abhi, burn, *trans.*

+ ā, bring hither by flaming, 72⁸.

çúci, a. —1. flaming, beaming; *fig.* beaming (of a smile); light, bright; —2. *fig.* clear, pure; holy (of a god), 80⁵; honorable (in business), 25²; pure (in a ritual sense), 62¹⁰. [√çuc, 1155. 2a, 216. 2.]

çuci-smita, a. having a beaming smile, bright-smiling.

çuddhá, a. pure. [ppl. of √çudh, 160.]

çuddha-mati, a. pure-minded.

çudh *or* çundh (çúndhati, -te; çúdhyati; çuddhá). —1. çúndhati, -te: *act.* purify; *mid.* become pure; —2. çúdhyati, become pure.   [orig., perhaps, 'to clear,' and akin w. √çcand, q.v.]

+ vi, víçudhyati, become entirely pure; viçuddha, perfectly clear.

çuná, a. grown, prosperous, fortunate; *as n.* [*cf.* 1176a], growth, prosperity; luck. [perhaps fr. √çū, 1177a.]

√ çundh, see çudh.

çundhyú, *f.* -yū [355c], a. pure; unblemished; fair. [√çundh, 1165b.]

√ 1 çubh *or* çumbh (çúmbhate). glide along lightly; move onward, 73⁹. [perhaps akin w. κοῦφος, 'light, nimble.']

√ 2 çubh *or* çumbh (çóbhate; çúmbhate;

çumbháti; çuçubhé; çobhiṣyáti). *act.* adorn; *mid.* adorn one's self, 73¹²; look beautiful, appear to advantage, shine (*fig.*).

1 çúbh, *f.* a gliding onward, *esp.* through the sky; onward progress; so, *perhaps*, 78⁵; course, 73⁴; *dat., infinitivally* [982], so as to glide onward, 79¹¹. [√1 çubh.]

2 çúbh, *f.* beauty; so, *perhaps*, 78⁵. [√2 çubh.]

çubha, a. —1. fair, 9¹¹; beautiful, agreeable to the eyes, 15¹³, 45¹³, 62¹³; —2. agreeable (to other senses than the eyes); çubhān gandhān, perfumes; —3. agreeable *in general*, 20¹³; —4. of good quality, 64¹²; —5. fortunate, auspicious, 12¹ᵇ. [√2 çubh, 'adorn.']

çubhānana, a. fair-faced. [ānana.]

çubhāçubha, a. agreeable and disagreeable, agreeable or disagreeable; good and bad, good or bad, *in ethical sense*, 65¹⁹. [açubha, 1257.]

çubhāçubha-phala, a. having agreeable or disagreeable fruit, resulting in weal or woe.

çubhrá, a. beautiful; clear (of sounds). [√2 çubh, 'adorn,' 1188a.]

√ çuṣ (çúṣyati; -çúṣya). be dry, dry up. [for *suṣ* (see çaça), as shown by Avestan √hush, 'dry': cf. αὔω, 'dry'; Syracusan σαυ-κός, 'dry'; AS. seārian, 'dry up,' denom. of seār, Eng. sear.]

çúṣka, a. dry. [√çuṣ, 1186²: see 958.]

çúṣma, *m.* —1. whistling, 73⁵, 78⁷; —2. exhalation, *i.e.* (fragrant) odor (of the Soma), 73¹⁰; —3. (exhalation, breath, and so, like Eng. spirit) courage, impetuosity, 82⁴. [√çvas, 252, 1166.]

√ çū *or* çvā *or* çvi (çváyati; çúçāva [786⁴]; çūná [957a]; çváyitum). swell; be greater *or* superior *or* victorious.

[orig. sense of root, 'swell,' but with two diverse ramifications:

—1. negatively, 'be swollen, *i.e.* hollow, empty'; cf. çūna, 'vacuum'; κύ-αρ, 'hole'; Lat. *cavus*, 'hollow'; *caelum*, *scav-i-lu-m*, 'heaven's hollow vault'; κοῖλος, 'hollow';

—2. positively, 'be swollen, *i.e.* full, strong'; with special reference: (*a*) to

17*

the womb and its fruit; cf. çi-çu and
çāva, 'young'; κύω, 'be pregnant'; Lat.
in-ciens, 'pregnant'; (b) to strength and
growth in general; cf. çūra, 'man of
might'; çavas, çaviṣṭha, çuna; κῦρος,
'might'; κῦμα, 'swell, billow.']

çūdrá, m. a man of the fourth caste, a
Çūdra.

çúna, n. emptiness. [√çū, 1177a.]

çūra, a. mighty, bold; as m. man of might,
hero. [√çū, 1188c: çūra is parallel w.
•κυ-ρο-s, 'mighty,' whence τὸ κῦρ-os,
'might' (cf. αἰσχ-ρό-s w. τὸ αἰσχ-os).]

çū́rpa, n. a plaited basket for winnowing
grain.

√ 1çṛ (çṛṇāti; çaçré; áçarīt; çariṣyáti,
-te; çūrṇá [957b]; -çīrya; çīryáte).
crush; break; tear. [cf. Eng. har-m,
which answers to a Skt. •çar-ma.]
+ vi, pass. be broken to pieces; perish,
60⁹.
+ sam, break (a bow); like zusammen-
brechen.

√ 2çṛ, see çrā, 'boil.'

çṛñga, n. horn.

çṛñgín, a. horned; as m. horned beast.

çṛtá, see √çrā.

çéva, a. kind; dear. [cf. çivá.]

çéṣa, —1. m. n. rest, remainder, 68¹⁷;
çéṣe, like Ger. im Uebrigen, for the rest,
12¹⁰; —2. a. remaining, 55¹⁵. [√1çiṣ,
'leave.']

çéṣas, n. offspring. ['those whom one
leaves behind him, one's relicts,' √1çiṣ,
'leave.']

çóka, m. pain, grief. [√çuc, 216.1.]

çoka-ja, a. grief-born; çokajaṁ vāri,
grief-born water, i.e. tears, 10¹⁹.

çokārta, a. sorrow-stricken. [ārta.]

çociṣ-keça, a. having flame-locks, with
locks of flame. [çociṣ, 187: 1297, cf.
1280b.]

çóciṣṭha, a. most or bright flaming.
[√çuc, 468.]

çocís, n. flame; beam; heat. [√çuc,
1153.]

çóṇa, —1. a. red, deep-red; —2. m. Sone
or Red River, affluent of the Ganges.
[prop. 'flame-colored'. cf. ἴ-καυ-σα,
'burned,' καῦ-μα, 'heat.']

çoṇita, n. blood; also pl. [çóṇa, 1176d.]

çobhaná, a. beautiful. [√2çubh, 'adorn,'
1150.2a.]

çóbhiṣṭha, a. most swiftly moving onward or most beautiful, 78⁵, according as
the word is referred to √1çubh or to
√2çubh — see these. [468.]

√ çcand (intens. ppl. cániçcadat [1002c]).
shine, glance. [for •ṣkandh: cf. ξανθ-ός,
'gold-yellow'; καθαρός, Doric κοθ-αρός,
'clear, clean, pure'; κάνθ-αρος, 'coal';
Lat. cand-ēre, 'glow.']

çcandrá, a. shining. [√çcand, 1188a: cf.
viçvá-çcandra, and candrá.]

√ çcut (çcótati; cuçóta; áçuçcutat;
çcutitá). drip.

çcút, vbl. dripping. [√çcut.]

çmaçāná, n. the place for burning the
corpses and for burying the bones,
cemetery.

çmáçru, n. beard.

√ çyā or çī (çyáyati, -te [761d1]; çītá,
çīná, çyāná; çīyáte). freeze; coagulate.

çyená, m. eagle; falcon; hawk. [cf.
i-κτῖνο-s, 'kite.']

√ çrath (çrathnīté; çaçráthe; áçiçrathat;
çrathitá). become loose.

çrád, indecl. meaning perhaps orig. heart;
used w. dhā ('grant, give,' see √1dhā 4)
and dat. of person, thus, çrád asmāi
dhatta, (your) heart to him give ye, i.e.
trust ye him, have faith in him, RV. ii.
12.5; ppl. çrad-dadhat, trusting, trustful,
26²; cf. 1079².

[cf. καρδία, κῆρ, •κηρδ, Lat. cor, gen.
cord-is, Lithuanian szirdis, Ger. Herz, Eng.
heart: further, w. çrad-dhā, cf. Lat.
crēdere, •cred-dere, 'trust': — the regular
Skt. word for 'heart' is hṛd, and this can
not be connected w. the above words,
since they require in the Skt. an initial ç,
•çṛd or çrad.]

çraddhā́, f. trust, faith; desire. [see
çrád: 1147.]

çraddhivá, a. credible. [çraddhā́,
1228a.]

√ çram (çrāmyati [763]; çaçráma; áçra-
mīt; çrāntá; -çrāmya). be weary;
take pains; esp. castigate one's self,
96¹⁰.

+ ā, *in* āçrama, 'hermitage.'

+ pari, weary one's self exceedingly; pariçrānta, tired of, disgusted with.

çráma, *m.* weariness. [√çram.]

√ çrambh (çrámbhate; çrabdhá; -çrábh-ya). *used only with* vi. put confidence in; viçrabdha: confiding, 26⁸; -am, *adv.* confidently, without distrust *or* hesitation, 9¹⁷.

çrávaṇa, —1. *m.* ear; —2. *n.* hearing; —3. *n.* fame. [√çru, 1150. 1a: for mg 3, cf. çravas and esp. under √çru.]

çrávas, *n.* —1. sounds; *esp.* loud praise, 91¹⁵; —2. glory, 74⁶; fame. [√çru, 'hear,' 1151. 1a: the precise equiv. of κλέος, stem κλεϝ-ες, 'fame': for mg, see √çru.]

√ çrā *or* çrī *or* çr̄ *or* çir (çṛiṇāti, çṛiṇīté; çiçriyé; çrātá, çrītá, çṛtá, çīrtá). cook; boil; çṛtá, cooked, done.

çráddha, *n.* an oblation to the Manes, accompanied by a funeral meal and gifts to Brahmans. [çraddhā, 1208e: according to the Scholiast, 'a thing of trust,' because the gift for the Manes is as a matter of fact entrusted to Brahmans.]

çrāntá, *ppl.* wearied; *as n.* [1176a], weariness. [√çram, 955a.]

çrāntāgata, *a.* wearied and arrived, *i.e.* arriving wearied. [āgata: 1257.]

√ çri (çráyati, -te; çiçráya, çiçriyé; áçi-çriyat; çrayiṣyáti, -te; çritá; çráyitum; çrayitvā; -çritya). —1. *act.* lean, *trans.;* lay against *or* on; rest on, *trans.* —2. *mid.* lean upon, *intrans.;* rest upon, *or, simply,* be lying *or* situated upon, 70⁹; —3. *mid., act.* betake one's self to, *esp.* for help *or* protection, 48⁶. [cf. κλί-νω, 'lean'; κε-κλί-αται, 'rest on'; Lat. clināre, 'lean'; AS. hlinian, Eng. lean; κλι-τός, 'incline,' slope, hill'; Lat. cli-vus, 'hill'; AS. hlǣw, hlāw, Eng. -law, -low, 'hill,' in Mood-law, Lud-low; κλῖ-μαξ, 'ladder'; AS. hlǣ-der, Eng. ladder.]

+ ā, lean upon, *intrans.;* seek support and protection with *or* from; āçrita: depending upon (another); *as m.* a dependent *or* subordinate, 30¹⁸.

+ upa, *mid.* lean against; brace one's

self, 87⁶; upaçrita, (leaned upon, *equiv. to*) laid upon *or* in, *w. loc.,* 79⁴.

+ pari, *act.* lay about; enclose.

+ pra, lean forward.

çrī [351], *f.* —1. beautiful appearance; beauty, 78⁵, 2⁴, 8⁸; —2. welfare; —3. *personified,* Çrī, goddess of beauty and welfare, 2¹⁰; —4. *as honorific prefix to proper names,* the famous *or* glorious ·, 54¹. [cf. çreyāṅs, çreṣṭha.]

√ çru (çṛṇóti, çṛṇuté [243]; çuçráva, çu-çruvé; áçrāuṣit; çroṣyáti, -te; çrutá; çrótum; çrutvā; -çrútya; çrūyáte; çúçrūṣate; çrāváyati). —1. *act.* hear, 86⁶; know by hearing; *w. gen. of person,* 6²; listen; give heed to, 25¹⁴; hear (a teacher), *i.e.* learn, study; çuçruvāṅs, having studied, *i.e.* learned, 94¹⁸; —2. *mid., in Veda, with pass. sense,* be heard of (as subject of talk), *i.e., like Lat.* cluere, be called, be famed as, 75¹⁴;

—3. *pass.:* be heard; çrutá: heard; heard of, 2¹²; *impers.:* çrūyatām, let it be heard, *i.e.* hear ye; evaṁ çrūyate. thus it is heard, there is this saying, 31⁶; çrutam mayā, I've heard (your story), 33⁹; —4. *caus.* cause (hearers, *acc.*) to hear (a thing), *i.e.* proclaim to; recite to, 54²⁰; —5. *desid.* be willing to hear, *and so (cf. Eng.* obedient *and Lat.* ob-oediens *with* audīre), obey, 64⁹.

[with çru-dhí, 'hear thou,' cf. κλῦ-θι, 'hear thou'; Lat. clu-ere, 'be called'; cluens, cliens, 'who hears *or* obeys, *i.e.* a dependent'; with çru-tá, 'heard, heard of,' cf. κλυ-τός, 'famed,' Lat. in-clu-tus, inclitus, 'famed,' Old High Ger. hlu-do in Hludo-wīg, 'Loud-battle,' Ger. lau-t, AS. hlū-d, Eng. lou-d;

with the subsidiary form çruṣ, as in çruṣ-ṭi, 'a listening to, compliance,' cf. AS. hlos-nian, 'listen,' hlyst, 'the hearing,' whence hlyst-an, Eng. listen: —for the mg 'famed' of çruta, etc., cf. çravaṇa, çravas, and çloka.]

+ prati, answer, say yes to; make a promise to (*gen.*). [prop., like Eng. hear, 'give a hearing in return to what is said,' i.e. 'not turn a deaf ear to,' and so 'answer.']

+ **vi**, *pass.* be heard of far and wide, be famous; **viçruta**, known as, named, 6⁸.

+ **sam**, −1. hear; −2. *like Eng.* hear, accede to the request of, make a promise to (*loc.*). [cf. çru + prati.]

çrutá, *ppl.* heard; heard of; *as n.* that which is heard from the teacher, that which is learned; learning. [√çru.]

çrutavant, *a.* possessing learning, learn-ed. [çruta.]

çrúti, *f.* −1. a hearing; −2. ear; −3. the thing heard; sound; −4. report, hearsay; −5. utterance; *esp.* a sacred utterance handed down by tradition, a religious prescription, a sacred text, the Veda, 58¹⁸ ɴ.; −6. learning; *prob. incorrect for* çruta. [√çru, 1157.1a.]

çrutimant, *a.* possessing learning; *prob. incorrect for* çrutavant, *q.v.* [çruti.]

çrútya, *a.* worthy to be heard (of a hymn), goodly. [√çru, 1213a.]

çreyas, *for* çreyas (çreyãs) *in cpds,* 1315c.

çréyãns, *a.* fairer; more beautiful *or* excellent; better; *as n.* (the better, *i.e.*) welfare, prosperity, 35¹. [from an unused root çrī corresponding to the noun çrī, 470⁴: cf. κρείων, ' superior, ruler.']

çréstha, *a.* fairest; most excellent; best: *w. gen.,* 1¹⁰; *w. loc.,* 58¹⁰; *at end of cpd,* 11⁹; best as distinguished from (*abl.*), *equiv. to* better than, 68¹⁴. [see çreyãs.]

çráisthya, *n.* supremacy, precedence. [çréstha, 1211² end.]

çrótra, *n.* ear; hearing. [√çru, 1185a.]

çrótriya, *a.* studied, learned (in sacred tradition); *as m.* a Brahman versed in sacred lore. [çrotra, 1214c: for mg, cf. √çru, mg 1, and çrutá, s.v.]

çlaksná, *a.* slippery; smooth. [cf. 1195.]

√ **çlãgh** (çlághate; çaçlãghé; çlághitá). −1. have confidence in; −2. talk confidently; brag, praise one's self; −3. praise.

çlãghya, *grdv.* to be praised, praiseworthy; honorable. [√çlãgh.]

çlóka, *m.* −1. (thing heard, *i.e.*) sound; −2. fame, *for mg, cf.* √çru; −3. strophe;

later, esp. the anustubh-strophe, the epic çloka, in which, for example, the story of Nala is composed. [√çru, 1186⁸.]

√ **çvañc** (çvañcate). open itself; receive in open arms (as a maid her lover).

+ **ud**, open itself out, open, 87⁴.

çván [427], *m.* dog. [cf. κύων, Lat. *can-i-s,* AS. *hun-d,* Eng. *hound,* ' dog.']

çváçura, *m.* father-in-law. [for ◦svá-çura: cf. ἑκυρός, Lat. *socer, socerus,* Church Slavonic *swekrŭ,* AS. *sweor, ◦sweohor,* Ger. *Schwäher,* ' father-in-law ': for ç in place of s, cf. çaça and √çus.]

çvaçrú [355c], *f.* mother-in-law. [çváçura, 355c: cf. ἑκυρά, Lat. fem. *socrus,* AS. *sweger,* Ger. *Schwieger,* ' mother-in law.']

√ **çvas** (çvásiti [631]; çvásati; çaçvãsa; çvasisyáti; çvasitá, çvastá; çvásitum; -çvásya; çvãsáyati). −1. blow, bluster, whistle, snort; −2. breathe; −3. sigh. [cf. AS. *hweós,* preterit to *hwêsan,* Eng. *wheeze.*]

+ **ã**, get one's breath, become quiet; *caus.* quiet, comfort.

+ **nis**, breathe out, sigh.

+ **pra**, blow forth.

+ **abhi-pra**, blow forth upon, *acc.,* 94⁷.

+ **vi**, have confidence, be unsuspecting; *caus.* inspire confidence.

çvás, *adv.* to-morrow, on the next day; çvah çvas [1260²], from day to day.

çvasátha, *m.* a snorting. [√çvas, 1163b.]

çvástana, *a.* of the morrow; *as n.* the morrow, 92¹⁷. [çvás, 1245e.]

çvápada, *m.* a beast of prey, 84¹⁴. [to be pronounced çvapãda (cf. pãvaka, 1181a): prop., perhaps, ' having the feet of a dog,' çvan + pãda.]

çvãvidh [*nom.* -vít], *m.* porcupine. [çván + vidh, ' dog-wounding.']

satka, −1. *a.* consisting of six; −2. *as n.* a whole consisting of six, a hexade. [sas, 1222a, 226b.]

sát-triñçat [485], *f.* six and thirty. [sas.]

ṣáṭ-pada, f. -ī, a. having (taken) six
steps. [ṣaṣ: 1300a.]

ṣaṇ-mā́sa, n. semester, six months.
[ṣaṣ: prop. 'that which has six months,'
see 1312.]

ṣáṣ [483³], num. six. [see 182b², 146⁸:
cf. *ī̆ḱ, Lat. sex, Eng. six.]

ṣaṣṭí, f. sixty. [ṣaṣ, 1157. 4.]

ṣaṣṭhá, a. sixth. [ṣaṣ, 487⁶: cf. ἕκ-τος,
Lat. sex-tus, AS. six-ta, Eng. six-th.]

---

1 sá, pron. see ta and 495.

2 sa, inseparable prefix denoting similarity,
community, or connection — numerous examples on the pages following; esp. common
w. an adj. value in possessive cpds [see
1304c], having an accompanying ··,
with ··. [1121b: prob. ident. ultimately
w. 3 sa.]

3 sa, one, in sa-kṛt, sa-hasra. [for *sm
(vocalic m), root *sem: cf. εἷς, *σεμ-ς,
μία, *σμ-ια, 'one'; ἑ-κατόν, 'one-hundred';
ἁ-πλόος, 'one-fold'; Lat. sem-el, 'once';
sim-plex, 'one-fold'; ἄ-λοχος, 'having one
(i.e. one and the same) bed, spouse';
ὁ-πατρος, 'having one (i.e. one and the
same) father'; ἀ-δελφός, see under garbha.]

sámyatendriya, a. having restrained
senses, self-controlled, 1⁹. [sáṁyata
(√yam, 1085a) + indriyá, 1298.]

saṁyama, m. restraint, control, 68⁶.
[√yam + sam.]

saṁvatsará, m. year. [sam + vatsara,
q.v.]

saṁçaya, m. — 1. doubt; na saṁçayas,
(there is) no doubt; — 2. danger, 20¹⁶.
[√çi + sam.]

saṁsád, f. like Lat. consessus, a sitting
together and those who sit together, i.e.
assembly. [√sad + sam.]

saṁsarga, m. mixture, union; contact.
[√sṛj + sam, 216. 1.]

saṁsārá, m. the wandering of the soul
from one existence to another, metempsychosis; transmigration, 66¹⁸; the cycle
or round of existence, 18¹. [√sṛ + sam.]

saṁskārá, m. — 1. a working over, a
preparing or purification; esp. a technical
proceeding with a thing; an adorning or
adornment, 17⁵; — 2. a domestic religious
rite to be performed upon or observed by
every member of the three upper castes,
prop. his preparation or purification; sacrament, consecration, 59²ɴ.; — 3. impression; an impression produced on the
mind or a disposition formed in the mind
by something past (e.g. deeds of a former
existence, a past conversation, etc.), but
which has ceased to work on the mind,
40⁴. [√1 kṛ, 'do,' + sam, 1087d.]

saṁskṛta, ppl. — 1. prepared; adorned,
fine, cultivated; as n. the cultivated language, as opposed to the low vernaculars,
Sanskrit, 52⁶. [√1 kṛ, 'do,' + sam, 1087d.]

sáṁhita, ppl. put together; -ā, f. a
putting together; a text whose sounds
and words are put together according to
grammatical rules. [√1 dhā + sam, 954c.]

sa-kacchapa, a. having tortoises along
with them, i.e. along with tortoises.
[1304c.]

sakala, a. having its parts together, i.e.
all, entire; as n. everything, one's entire
property, 46⁴. [sa + kalā, 1304c, 334².]

sakāça, m. presence; tasya sakāçaṁ
gam, go to the presence of him, i.e. go to
him; -sakāçe, at end of cpd, in the presence of ··, before ··, 3⁸. [sa + kāça:
orig., perhaps, 'having visibility, present,'
and then 'presence.']

sakṛt, adv. for one time, a single time,
once. [3 sa + 2 kṛt.]

sa-kopa, a. angry; -am, angrily. [2 sa,
1304c.]

sáktu, m. coarsely ground parched grains,
grits, esp. barley grits.

sakha, for sakhi at end of cpds [1302],
having ·· as attendant, accompanied by
··. [1315b.]

sákhi [343a], m. attendant, companion,
82¹; comrade; friend, 23¹⁶, etc.; in connection with a fem., 75¹⁸,¹⁹, 100⁴. [√sac:
for mg, cf. ἑτ-έτης and soc-ius, under
√sac.]

sakhī [364], f. female companion, friend
(of a woman). [sákhi: cf. 362b².]

sakhī-gaṇa, m. (friend-crowd, i.e.)
friends.

sakhī-jana, m. (friend-persons, *collectively*, *i.e.*) friends.

sakhyá, n. friendship. [sákhi, 1212c.]

sá-gaṇa, a. with (their) troops (of attendants). [2 sa.]

ságara, m. —1. the atmosphere, Luftmeer; —2. Sagara, name of a mythical prince.

saṁkaṭa, —1. a. narrow, strait; —2. m. Slender, name of a gander, 37²⁰; —3. n. narrow passage, a strait; —4. *fig.*, *like* Eng. strait, a difficulty, 52¹⁴; danger, 25⁴. [cf. 1245g.]

saṁkalpá, m. a decision of the mind; the will *or* wish *or* purpose proceeding from such decision, a definite intention. [√kḷp + sam, 1148.1, 236.]

saṁketa, m. agreement; *esp.* a meeting agreed upon with a lover, a rendezvous. [prop. 'co-intention,' sam + keta.]

saṁkrānti, f. an entering, *esp.* entering of the sun upon a new zodiacal sign. [√kram + sam, cf. 1157¹ w. 955a.]

saṁkhyā, f. the tale *or* number. [√khyā + sam.]

saṅga, m. —1. a sticking to *or* hanging upon; —2. *fig.* an attachment (of the mind) to anything, desire for a thing; saṅge, in case of desire, 64²; *pl.* lusts. [√sañj, 216.1.]

saṁgamá, m. a coming together, union. [√gam + sam.]

saṁgámana, f. -ī, a. *subst.* causing to assemble, gatherer. [caus. of √gam + sam.]

saṁgará, m. agreement, promise. [√1 gṛ + sam, 'chime in with.']

saṁgha, m. (a combination, *i.e.*) company, crowd. [√han + sam, 333, cf. 216.9 and 402.]

√ **sac** (síṣakti; sácate; saçcús, saçciré [794d²]). —1. be with, be united with; be together, have intercourse together; 79¹⁴; —2. accompany a person (acc.) to a thing (dat.), *i.e.* help him to it, 69¹⁸; —3. be attached to; *fig.* follow (a commandment), 75²; follow up, *i.e.* attend to, 82¹⁷.

[orig. 'accompany,' *i.e.* 1. 'go at the side of, with help *or* favor,' and 2. 'go after, seek, follow': cf. ἕπ-ομαι, 'accompany,' ἑ-σπ-όμην, 'followed'; Lat. *sequ-or*, 'follow'; sec-*undus*, 'following, second'; also ἕπ-έτης, 'attendant,' Lat. *soc-ius*, 'comrade': further, AS. seōn, *seh(w)on*, Eng. *see*, Ger. *seh-en*, '(seek, look for, follow with the eyes, *i.e.*) see.']

saciva, m. attendant, supporter. [√sac, 1190, with union-vowel i.]

sa-jóṣas, a. (of like pleasure, *i.e.*) unanimous, harmonious; kindly disposed, 86¹⁵. [1304c³.]

sajja, a. —1. *as used* of a bow, having its string on, strung, ready for use (the string being wound around the bow when this is not in use); —2. *generalized*, ready, *as used* of persons and things. [for sajya, q.v., with assimilation as in sajyate, sajjate—see √sañj.]

sajjī-kṛ (-karoti). —1. make strung, string (a bow); —2. make ready, 34¹⁷. [sajja, 1094.]

sajya, a. having its string on, strung. [2 sa + 2 jyā, 'bow-string.']

saṁcaya, m. a piling together, accumulation, *esp.* of wealth; supply (of food). [√1 ci, 'pile up,' + sam.]

saṁcayana, n. the gathering (of the bones of the dead). [do.]

saṁcayavant, a. possessing an accumulation (of wealth), rich; *with* arthāis, rich with money, *i.e.* having capital. [saṁcaya.]

saṁcārin, a. wandering. [√car + sam, 1183³.]

saṁciti, f. a piling; pile. [√1 ci, 'pile up,' + sam.]

√ **sañj** *or* **saj** (sájati; sasáñja; ásāṅkṣit; saktá; sáktum; -sájya; *pass.* sajyáte *or* sajjate). stick to, be attached to; saktá, attached (of a glance), immovable. [cf. Lat. *seg-nis*, 'sticking, *i.e.* slow, lazy.']

+ **pra**, be attached to; prasakta, addicted to.

satata, only in acc. s. neut., -am, *as adv.* continuously, constantly, always. [for saṁtata, see √tan + sam: for mg, cf. Lat. *con-tinens*, 'con-tinuous.']

sat-kṛ, *see* sant 6.

satkāra, *m.* good treatment, *esp.* kind reception of a guest, hospitality. [satkṛ.]

sáttama, *a.* best. [sant, 471.]

sattvá, —1. *n.* condition of being, being-ness, being, existence, essent-ia; —2. *n.* condition of being good, absolutely good being, goodness, the highest of the three qualities (*see* guṇa), 66⁸ ᴺ.; —3. *m. n.* a living being, creature, 28¹⁴, 48². [formed from sant (1239), just as the artificial Lat. *essent-ia*, 'being-ness, that on which a thing depends for being what it is,' from *essens*, a quasi-ppl. of *esse*.]

sátpati, *m.* strong ruler; master. [sánt + páti, 1280, cf. 1267a.]

satyá, —1. *a.* real; true; existing in reality, 45¹²; truthful, trusty, faithful, 69⁹; —2. *n.* the real; the true; reality; truth, 95⁶ end of line; truthfulness, 21⁶, 95⁵ near mid. of line; faithfulness, 69¹²; yathā · ·, tena satyena, as · ·, by this truth, as truly as · ·, so truly, 14¹ff.; —3. *n.* vow, promise, oath; satyam brū, swear, 10²¹, 15⁶; satyaṁ cikīrṣamāṇas, desiring to keep his promise, 8¹²; —4. satyam, *adv.* truly, indeed, 49¹⁰. [sánt, 1212c: radically akin w. ἐτεό-s, 'true,' but of different formation, since the Cyprian shows that ἐτεός stands for ἐϜετεϜο-s.]

satyá-rādhas, *a.* having real blessings, bestowing real blessings. [1298.]

satya-vādín, *a.* truth-speaking, truth-ful. [1275.]

satya-vratá, *n.* vow of truthfulness. [1264, acct 1267.]

satyávrata, *a.* having, *i.e.* keeping a satyavratá, always truthful, 6²⁰. [1296, acct 1295.]

satya-saṁgara, *a.* having, *i.e.* keep-ing a true agreement, *i.e.* true to his promise.

satyásaṁdha, *a.* having, *i.e.* keeping a true agreement, *i.e.* faithful. [satya + saṁdhā.]

satvara, *a.* with haste; -am, *adv.* quick-ly, immediately. [2sa + tvarā.]

sat-saṁnidhāna, *n.* a being near to the good, intercourse with the good. [sant.]

√ sad (sídati, -te [748]; sasāda, sedús [794e]; ásadat; satsyáti; sattá, sanná; sáttum; -sádya; sādáyati, -te). —1. sit; seat one's self; —2. settle down, sink beneath a burden; be overcome; get into trouble; be in a desperate pre-dicament, 18⁷; despair; not know what to do, be unable to help one's self; —*caus.* set. [w. sīdāmi, *·*si-zd-ámi, si-sᵈd-āmi, cf. ἵζω, *·*σι-zδ-ω, *·*σι-σᵈδ-ω, 'sit,' Lat. *sīd-ere*, 'settle down'; cf. also *sed-ēre*, 'sit'; Eng. *sit*, caus. *set*; sad-as, ἴδ-os, ἴδ-pa, Lat. *sella*, *·sed-la*, AS. *set-l*, Eng. *settle*, 'a seat.']

+ava, sink down, get into trouble, be in distress.

+ā, —1. sit upon; —2. lie in wait for, 89¹²; —3. get to, reach (a place); āsan-na: approached; near, neighboring, 33¹⁰; —*caus.* —1. set upon; —2. get to, arrive at, reach; find, obtain, gain, 23¹¹, 46²; —3. āsādya, *often so attenuated in mg as to be equiv. to a mere preposition:* nimittaṁ kiṁcid āsādya, (having obtained some cause or other, *i.e.*) by or in consequence of some cause or other, *cf.* √diç + ud.

+ni, —1. sit down; take one's seat, *esp.* of the hotṛ at the sacrifice, 88⁶·⁸; —2. *act. and mid.* set, install as, *trans.!*, 82¹²; —*caus. act. and mid.* set, install as, 88¹⁷.

+pra, be favorable *or* gracious; pra-sanna, kindly disposed, 1¹⁷; —*caus.* make kindly disposed, propitiate, 36⁶. [behind the mg 'be gracious' lies doubtless the physical mg 'settle forward, incline to-wards, *e.g.* a suppliant.']

+vi, sink, *used* (*like the Eng.* be de-pressed) of the spirits, be dejected; de-spond, 35¹¹; come to grief, 31¹; viṣaṇṇa, dejected.

+sam, sit together.

sadadí, *adv.* always, 93⁵. [cf. sadā.]

sádana, *n.* seat; *generalized, like Eng.* seat *and Lat.* sēdes, place (75⁷), dwelling. [√sad.]

sádas, *n.* seat. [√sad: cf. ἴδos, 'seat.']

sadasat, *n.* existence and non-existence. [sat + asat, the subst. used neuter stems of sant and asant, 1252.]

sadasad-ātmaka, *a.* having existence and non-existence as its nature, whose nature it is to exist and also not to exist at the same time. [**sadasat.**]

sádā, *adv.* always. [cf. 1103a³.]

sad-ācāra, *m.* the conduct *or* practices of the good. [**sant.**]

sa-dṛ́ça, *a.* of like appearance; equal, *used* (296b) *w. gen.* [518.]

sadyás, *adv.* on the same day; immediately. [see 1122f.]

sadha, *adv. equiv. of* 1 **sahá,** *see* 1104³.

sadha-mā́da, *m.* co-revelry, συμπόσιον, common feast; **sadhamādam mad,** revel in bliss with, *w. instr.* [1290.]

sadhá-stha, *n.* (*orig., perhaps,* co-place, *i.e.* place of union, *but generalized to the simple mg of*) place.

sána, *a.* old. [orig. 'of long standing, long continued': cf. ἕνο-ς, 'old'; Lat. *sen-ex,* 'old man'; Goth. *sin-ista,* 'oldest'; AS. *sin-ceald,* 'perpetually *or* extremely cold'; AS. and Old Eng. *sin-grēne,* 'evergreen,' Eng. *sen-green,* '(extremely green, *i.e.*) house-leek': from a not quotable Goth. *sina-skalks,* Medieval Lat. *siniscalcus,* 'oldest house-servant,' through intermediate Romance forms, comes Eng. *seneschal;* Ger. *Sünd-flut,* 'sin-flood,' is a popular interpretation of Old High Ger. *sin-vluot,* 'the long-continued flood, the Noachian deluge.']

sánā, *adv.* of old, always. [instr. of **sána,** 1112c, not a.]

sanā́t, *adv.* from of old, always, forever. [**sána,** acct 1114d.]

sanātána, *a.* everlasting, eternal. [**sanā,** 1245e.]

sá-nīḷa, *a.* having a common nest *or* origin, affiliated, united. [1304c.]

sánemi, *adv.* always. [perhaps from **sana.**]

sánt, −1. *ppl.* being; *otiose,* 24¹⁶, *see* √1 **as;** existing; −2. *a.* real, genuine; true, good; −3. of people, good, noble, excellent, 19⁶·²⁷, 28¹¹; −4. **satí,** *f.* a true, good, virtuous wife (*hence Anglo-Indian* Suttee); −5. *n.* the existent; existence; −6. **sat-kṛ,** make good, treat well, receive kindly.

[present ppl. of √1 **as,** 'be,' q.v.: cf. ἐών, stem ἐοντ, 'being'; Lat. *absens,* stem *ab-sent,* 'being off'; *sons,* stem *sont,* 'the real doer,' 'the guilty one'; Danish *sand,* AS. *sōð,* 'true,' Eng. *sooth,* 'true, truth': for mg 2, cf. the mg of **satya,** of τὸν ἐόντα λόγον, 'the true story,' and of Eng. *sooth.*]

sáṁtati, *f.* −1. continuation; −2. *esp.* continuation of one's race *or* family, *i.e.* offspring.

saṁtāpá, *m.* −1. heat; −2. pain, sorrow. [√ tap + sam.]

saṁtāpavant, *a.* sorrowful. [1233.]

saṁdṛ́ç, *f.* a beholding; sight. [√ dṛç + sam.]

saṁdehá, *m.* −1. doubt; -āt, from (by reason of) uncertainty [291²]; −2. danger, 20¹⁵. [√ dih + sam: for mg 2, cf. bhaya.]

saṁdhā́, *f.* −1. covenant, agreement; −2. promise. [√ 1 dhā, 'put,' + sam: for mg 1, cf. συνθήκη, 'covenant,' and συντίθημι, the counterpart of **saṁdadhā́mi.**]

saṁdhā́na, *n.* a putting together, σύνθεσις, mixing. [√ 1 dhā, 'put,' + sam: paroxytone, 1150. 1c.]

saṁdhí, *m.* −1. a putting together, σύνθεσις; −2. *like* **saṁdhā́,** compact, alliance, 41¹³; peace, 17⁷; −3. the putting together of sounds in word and sentence (*see* Whitney 109b²), euphonic combination, 50⁹; −4. junction (of day and night), *i.e.* morning *or* evening twilight. [√ 1 dhā, 'put,' + sam, 1155. 2e.]

sáṁdhya, *a.* pertaining to **saṁdhi** *or* junction; **saṁdhyā́,** *f.* −1. time of junction (of day and night), morning *or* evening twilight; *du.* morning and evening twilight; −2. morning twilight (of a yuga), 58³. [**saṁdhí,** cf. 1212b.]

saṁdhyāṅça, *m.* (*lit.* twilight-portion) evening twilight of a yuga. [**aṅça.**]

saṁdhyā-samaya, *m.* twilight-time, evening.

saṁnidhā́na, *n.* (a putting down together, juxta-position, approximation, *and so*) a being near; contiguity; presence; neighborhood, 40⁹. [√ 1 dhā, 'put,' + sam-ni, 1150: cf. **saṁnidhi.**]

saṁnidhi, m. presence. [√1 dhā, 'put,' + sam-ni, 1155. 2e : for mg, cf. saṁnidhāna.]

√ sap (sápati, -te; sepús). follow after; be attached or devoted to. [identified by some with √sac.]

sáp, vbl. following after, in cpds. [√sap.]

sapátnī, a. f. having a common husband; as subst. one of two or more wives of the same man, co-wife, fellow-wife, concubine. [sa + pati, but in the fem. form, since the masc. would not be used: 1304c: cf. supatnī.]

√ saparya (saparyáti). pay devotion to, worship. [denom. of a not quotable •sapar, 'devotion,' from √sap.]

sa-piṇḍa, a. subst. having the piṇḍa (q.v.) in common, said of persons who have a common ancestor not more than six generations back to whom they offer a piṇḍa together, persons related in the sixth generation. [1304c.]

saptá [483⁴], num. seven, 53⁶, 99²³; also, as a favorite sacred number, the expression of an indefinite plurality, e.g. 71⁸, 72⁴·⁶. [cf. ἑπτά, Lat. septem, AS. seofon, Eng. seven.]

saptakathāmaya, f. -ī, a. consisting of seven narrations. [sapta-kathā: see maya.]

saptá-tantu, a. having seven courses.

saptá-pada, f. -ī, a. — 1. being for seven, i.e. many or all, steps (see 1294²), i.e. being at every step, constant; — 2. having (taken) seven steps; see 100⁴ ɴ. [1300 a.]

sa-praçraya, a. with respectful demeanor; -am, adv. respectfully.

sa-phala, a. fruitful, fruit-bearing.

sá-bandhu, a. having a friend.

sa-bāṣpa, a. tearful.

sa-brahmacārin, m. fellow-student.

sa-bhaya, a. fearful; -am, adv. in terror.

sabhā, f. house or hall for public meetings, esp. gambling-house; assembly, 19³; society, 19¹. [orig., perhaps, 'family': cf. Goth. sibja, 'relationship,' AS. sibb, 'relationship, related'; Old Eng. god-sib, 'related in God,' i.e. 'a sponsor in baptism,'

Eng. gossip, 'sponsor, familiar friend, tattler'; Ger. Sipp, masc., 'relative,' Sippe, fem., 'relationship, kindred.']

sabhārya, a. having his wife with him, i.e. with his wife, 1¹⁷. [2 sa + bhāryā, 1304c, 334².]

sám, prep. along, with, together. [cf. 2 sa.]

1 sama [525⁴], encl. pron. any; every, 76¹²; cf. samaha. [cf. ἀμό-θεν, 'from some place or other'; οὐδ-αμός, 'not any'; οὐδ-αμῶς, 'in not any wise'; AS. sum, 'some one,' Eng. some.]

2 samá, a. — 1. even; — 2. like, 63¹⁷; equal, 48¹⁰; w. gen. (296b), 3¹⁶; -am, adv. equally with, along with, with, w. instr., 29⁶, 26⁵; — 3. like or equal (to the usual), i.e. not distinguished, common, mediocre, 19¹⁰. [cf. ἅμα, Doric ἅμά, 'at the same time'; ὁμός, 'one and the same, common'; ὁμα-λός, 'even, equal'; Lat. simi-lis, 'like'; AS. same, 'in like manner'; Eng. same.]

samátā, f. equality; mediocrity, 19¹⁰. [2 sama, 1237.]

samád, f. fight, contest. [sam, 383d⁴: cf. ὁμαδ-ο-ς, 'confused voices of men, din of battle, throng.']

sam-adhika, a. having a surplus with it; māsatrayaṁ samadhikam, three months and more. [1305.]

sam-anantara, a. with a non-interval, immediately adjoining; -am, adv. immediately thereupon. [1305.]

samayá, m. — 1. (a coming together, i.e., like Eng. con-vention) agreement; — 2. (like Eng. juncture) a point of time; and so time or season, 49¹⁶; occasion; — 3. a con-currence (of circumstances), i.e. a case — see iha. [√i + sam.]

samayocita, a. suitable to the occasion; -am, adv. as the occasion demands. [ucita, √uc.]

samáraṇa, n. battle; Treffen. [prop. 'a coming together,' √ṛ + sam, 1150. 1a: just so, Eng. verb meet sometimes means 'come together with hostile purpose,' and Eng. noun encounter is used mostly of 'a hostile meeting.']

sam-artha, a. (having an agreeing or accordant object [1305], i.e.) suiting its object, *and so* suitable; capable; able, *w. inf.*

sam-alaṁkṛta, *a.* well adorned. [see alam: sam intensive, 1077b end.]

samavatta-dhāna, *a.* containing gathered pieces. [see 1087e.]

samaha, *accentless adv.* somehow, 80⁵. [1 sama: cf. 1100a and 1104⁸.]

samāgama, *m.* — 1. a coming together, meeting; — 2. meeting with, *i.e.* intercourse. [√gam + sam-ā.]

samāná, *f.* -í, *a.* — 1. like; one and the same, 78¹⁶; -am, *adv.* in the same way, 103¹⁸; — 2. common (to different persons *or* countries), 73⁴, 98¹⁷; united, 73¹⁶. [2 samá, 1245d.]

samāna-grāma, *m.* the same village.

samānagrāmíya, *a.* belonging to the same village. [samāna-grāma, 1215.]

samāsa, *m.* — 1. a putting together; *and so* (*cf. Lat.* con-trahere, 'draw together,' then 'abridge') — 2. a condensation; abridgment; -ena *and* samāsatas, succinctly. [√2 as, 'throw,' + sam.]

samídh, *f.* (*like Eng.* kindlings) fuel. [√idh + sam, 'kindle.']

samīpa, — 1. *a.* near; — 2. *as n.* nearness, neighborhood, presence; *used like* antika, *q.v.*; — 2a. samīpam, *w. gen. or in cpd*, (to the presence of, *i.e.*, simply) to, *w. verbs of going*, 6¹⁰, 27¹⁴, 33⁴, 44¹¹; — 2b. samīpe, *w. gen. or in cpd* (in the presence *or* neighborhood of, *i.e.*, simply): before, 2¹⁶; near, 25⁹; hard by, 34¹⁴; by, 40⁸. [cf. pratīpá.]

samīpa-stha, *a. in cpd*, situated in the neighborhood of, near.

samutsarga, *m.* an ejecting, discharge. [√sṛj + sam-ud, 216. 1.]

samudrá, *m.* a gathering of waters, a sea, an ocean. ['a con-fluence,' √ud + sam, 1188b.]

samunnati, *f.* a rising; elevation, *i.e.*, *fig.*, distinction. [√nam + sam-ud, 1157 and d.]

sáṁṛti, *f.* (a coming together, *and so*) col-lision, shock. [√ṛ + sam, 1157d: cf. samaraṇa.]

sampatti, *f.* success; prosperity; abund-ance, 17¹⁴. [√pad + sam, 1157d.]

sampád, *f.* — 1. success; — 2. (a falling together, co-inciding, *and so* a fitting of the parts to each other, *i.e.*) correct pro-portion, beauty. [√pad + sam.]

sampuṭa, *m.* hemispherical bowl *or* dish; round casket (for jewels); sampuṭe likh, write a thing (*acc.*) in the strong-box of a person (*gen.*), *i.e.* credit it to him. [sam + puṭa, 'a together-fold,' 1289a.]

samprati, *adv.* — 1. just opposite; *and so* — 2. (to the same limit) even, exactly; — 3. (*like Eng.* even) at the very time; *and so* just now. [sám (intensive, 1077b end) + práti, 1314a.]

sám-priya, *a.* mutually dear. [priyá, 1289a.]

sambandha, *m.* con-nection; *and so, as in Eng.*, relationship. [√bandh + sam.]

sambhava, *m.* origin; *at end of adj. cpds*, having · · as its origin, originating in · ·. [√bhū + sam.]

sambhāvya, *grdv.* to be supposed, sup-posable. [caus. of √bhū + sam.]

sambhrama, *m.* extreme agitation, haste arising from excitement. [√bhram + sam.]

sám-miçla, *a.* com-mixed, mixed with, united with. [1289a.]

sam-rājñí, *f.* complete, *i.e.* sovereign ruler; mistress. [for sam, see 1289b end, and 1077b end: for m instead of ṁ, see 213a².]

sa-yatna, *a.* (having, *i.e.* taking pains to, *i.e.*) trying to, *w. inf.*; engaged in, *w. inf.*

sará, *a.* running, moving, going, *in cpds.* [√sṛ.]

saraṇa, *a.* running; *as n.* a running. [√sṛ, 1150. 1a.]

√ saraṇya (saraṇyáti). run, hasten. [saraṇa, 1059d.]

saraṇyú, *a.* hastening, swift; -yú [355c], *f.* Saraṇyū, daughter of Twashtar, and spouse of Vivaswant, to whom she bare Yama and Yamī, 85¹⁵ ɴ. [√saraṇya, 1178h: cf. Ἐρῑνύ-s, 'the swift' goddess of vengeance.]

sarámā, *f.* the bitch of Indra *or* of the gods; *cf.* 83¹⁷ ɴ. ['the runner' *or* 'mes-senger,' √sṛ, cf. 1166.]

sáras, *n.* lake, pool. [orig. 'fluid, *i.e.* water,' from √sṛ, 'run,' just as *fluidus* from *fluere*, 'flow, run.']

saras-tíra, *n.* bank of a pool.

sárasvant, −1. *a.* rich in waters; -vatī, *f.*: −2. Saraswatī, name of a mighty stream, probably the Indus; −3. Saraswatī, a small stream in Madhyadeça, to which the name and attributes of the great stream were transferred; −4. Saraswatī, the goddess of voice and speech, learning and eloquence. [sáras.]

sarít, *f.* stream. [√sṛ, 'run, flow,' 383.3: for mg, cf. Ger. *Fluss*, 'stream,' w. *fliessen*, 'flow,' and Eng. *stream* under √sru.]

sárga, *m.* −1. shot; −2. stream or spurt or jet; −3. a letting loose; −4. that which is let loose, *esp.* a herd let loose from the stall, 76⁴; −5. chapter of an epic poem, *a fig. use of the word in mg* 1 *or* 2. [√sṛj, 216.1.]

sarpá, *m.* (*like* serpent *from* serpere, 'creep') the creeper, snake, serpent, 84¹⁴. [√sṛp, q.v.]

sarpís, *n.* clarified butter, *either* warm and still fluid *or* cold and hardened, *and so not differing from* ghṛta, 'ghee.' [orig. 'fluid' butter, or 'the slippery, fat' stuff, from √sṛp, 'creep, move gently, slip,' 1153: see √sṛp and sṛpra: akin are Hesychian *ἔλπ-ος*, 'olive oil, fat,' and *ἔλφ-ος*, 'butter'; Ger. *Salbe*, AS. *sealf*, Eng. *salve*.]

sárva [524], *pron.* −1. entire *or* complete, 50²⁰, 95¹⁸, 96²; salvus, integer, unharmed; −2. *adj.* all, every; −2a. *subst.*: sing. *m.*, everyone; sing. *n.*, everything; *pl.*, all; −2b. *common at beg. of cpds instead of an adj.*: thus **sarva-guṇāir yuktas**, *for* **sarvāir guṇāir yuktas**, 1¹², *cf.* 2⁸; *so cf.* 10¹⁵ *w.* 10²⁰, 32¹⁵ *w.* 32¹⁴, 51²² *w.* 52²³; *similarly* 6⁴, 17¹·⁹, 21²³, etc.; −2c. idaṁ sarvam, 63²¹, *see* idam; *so for* 66¹⁹;

−*observe that both mgs,* 1 *and* 2, *are common to the post-Vedic literature; that in the oldest parts of the Veda,* sarva *occurs only in mg* 1, *while for mg* 2 *the proper Vedic word is* víçva, *q.v.; but see* 77¹¹ ₓ.

[cf. ὅλος, Epic οὖλος, *οὔλλος, *ὄλϜο-ς,

'whole, entire'; Lat. *salvus*, 'whole, unharmed, well'; Oscan *sollu-s*, 'entire'; Lat. stem *sollu-* in cpds, e.g. *solli-ferreum*, 'all-iron (weapon),' *soll-ennis*, 'of every year, annual,' used of religious ceremonies: no connection w. Eng. (*w*)*hole*, see also **kalya.**]

sarvaṁ-saha, *a.* patiently bearing all things. [sarvam, 1250a, 1270b.]

sarva-gata, *a.* (gone to all, *i.e.*) universally prevalent.

sarvátas, *adv.* −1. from all sides; on all sides, 93¹²; in every direction, 3¹¹, 101¹²; −2. omnino, altogether, 56¹⁶. [sárva, 1098b: acct, cf. 1298c.]

sarvátra, *adv.* −1. everywhere *or* in all cases, 21¹⁹; −2. at all times; always, uninterruptedly, 5¹⁴. [sárva, 1099: acct, cf. 1298c.]

sarvathā, *adv.* −1. in every way; −2. by all means. [sárva, 1101.]

sarvadā, *adv.* always; constantly; for ever. [sárva, 1103.]

sarva-deva, *m. pl.* all the gods.

sarvadevamaya, *a.* containing in himself all the gods, *i.e.* representing *or* being in the name of all the gods, 28¹⁹. [sarva-deva: see maya.]

sarva-dravya, *n. pl.* all things.

sarva-bhāva, *m.* the whole heart.

sarvabhūtamaya, *a.* containing in himself all beings, 56²⁰. [sarva-bhūta: see maya.]

sarva-yoṣit, *f. pl.* all women.

sarva-loká, *m.* the entire world.

sárva-víra, *a.* with unharmed heroes *or* with all heroes, *i.e.* having lost none. [1298.]

sarvaçás, *adv.* wholly, altogether; all together, 6⁸; together, 65¹⁵. [sarva, 1106.]

sarvānavadya, *a.* entirely faultless. [anavadya, 1279¹.]

sarvānavadyāṅga, *a.* having an entirely faultless body. [áṅga, 1298.]

sávana, *n.* a pressing, *esp.* of Soma. [√1 su, 'press out.']

sá-vayas, *a.* of like strength *or* age; *m. pl.* (*like* ἥλικες, ἡλικιῶται, 'equals in age, comrades') comrades. [3 vayas.]

sá-varṇa, a. −1. having the same external appearance, exactly similar, 85[14]; − 2. of thé same caste, 62[7]. [for mgs, see varṇa.]

sa-vitāna, a. having a canopy, with a canopy.

savitṛ́, m. −1. (with the two mgs of Eng. quickener) impeller, enlivener; −2. The Enlivener, Savitar, name of a god, selection xxxvi.; −3. the sun, 23[18]. [√2 su, 'impel.']

sa-vinaya, a. with politeness; -am, adv. politely.

sa-viçeṣa, a. possessing distinction, distinguished; -am, adv. in a distinguished way, especially.

savyá, a. left, 101[19], 102[11], 103[2]; as m. the left hand or foot, 60[5]. [prob. for *syavya (as would appear fr. the Church Slavonic form šuj, 'sinister'), and so perhaps akin with σκαιός, *σκαϝιο-ς, Lat. scaevus, 'left.']

savyathā, a. with sorrow or trouble. [sa + vyathā.]

savyāvṛt, a. with a turn to the left, i.e. turning to the left. [āvṛt.]

sa-çiṣya, a. with his pupils.

√ sas (sásti). sleep, slumber.

sasá, m. or n. herbs; grass.

sasaṁdhya, a. with the morning twilight. [saṁdhyā.]

sa-saṁdhyāñça, a. with the evening twilight.

sa-sambhrama, a. with excited haste.

sa-sarpa, a. with a serpent.

sasyá, n. standing crop; produce of the field, grain. [cf. sasa.]

sasya-kṣetra, n. field of grain.

sasya-rakṣaka, m. keeper or watcher of the standing crop.

√ sah (sáhate; sasáha, sasahé; ásahiṣṭa; sahiṣyáte; soḍhá [222[3]]; sáhitum, sóḍhum; -sáhya). −1. overpower, 99[8]; be victorious, 78[4]; −2. hold out against, withstand; and so bear; endure patiently, 32[7].

[orig. 'be powerful, withstand, hold back, hold': cf. the collateral √sagh, 'take on one's self, bear': cf. ἴσχω, *σι-σχ-ω, 'hold back'; ἔχω, ἔ-σχ-ον, 'hold or

have, had': − w. sahas, *sagh-as, cf. the Germanic stem seg-oz, as it appears in Goth. neut. sigis, AS. sigor, prob. neuter, all meaning 'victory'; the stem appears also in Seges-tes, name of a Cheruscan prince (Tacitus, Annals), and in Sigismund: cf. also AS. sige, Ger. Sieg, 'victory.']

+ ud, −1. hold out, endure; −2. be able, w. inf.; katham svārtham utsahe, how can I (sc. do, prosecute) my own object.

1 sahá, −1. adv. together; saha na etad, in common 'ours (is) that, i.e. we'll own that together, 97[11]; −2. prep. with, along with, w. instr., 1[15], 89[8]. [cf. 2 sa, and 1104[8].]

2 sahá, a. −1. powerful; −2. enduring, patiently bearing. [√sah.]

saha-cārin, −1. a. going together, accompanying; −2. as m. comrade. [for 2, cf. sahāya.]

saha-já, a. born together, con-nate, inborn, natural.

saha-bhasman, a. with the ashes.

sahá-vatsa, a. with the calf. [1304c.]

saha-vāhana, a. having their teams along, with their teams. [1304c.]

sáhas, n. superior power; might, 75[11]; victory; sahasā, adv. (with violence, i.e.) suddenly, straightway. [see under √sah.]

sa-hasta, a. having hands.

sahasyà, a. powerful. [sáhas, 1212d 1.]

sahásra, n. a thousand; esp. a thousand kine; a thousand, in the sense of a great many, 87[6]; for constructions, see 486. [prop. 'one-thousand,' 3 sa + hasra: with hasra, cf. -χιλο-, *χειλο, *χεσλο (in δεκά-χίλοι), and χίλιοι, 'thousand.']

sahásra-nītha, a. having a thousand songs, rich in songs. [nītha, 193, 1300a.]

sahásradakṣiṇa, a. having a thousand kine as his gift or as its reward; as m., sc. yajña, a sacrifice at which such reward is given, 87[15]; of persons who offer such gifts, 91[9]. [dakṣiṇá, 1300a.]

sahásra-dvār [388c], a. thousand-doored.

sahásra-çṛṅga, a. thousand-horned.

sahasrāńçu, a. thousand-rayed; as m. the sun. [ańçu.]

sahasrāńçu-sama, a. sun-like.

sahásrā-magha, a. having thousand gifts. [247.]

sáhasvant, a. mighty. [sáhas.]

sahāya, m. companion, attendant. [lit. 'going together or with,' saha + aya: for mg, cf. Lat. comes, stem com-i-t, √i, lit. 'going with, i.e. companion,' and also sahacārin.]

sahāyatana, a. along with the fire-place. [āyatana.]

sahita, a. united; pl. in company, all together. [quasi-ppl. from 1 saha, like Eng. downed from down.

sahela, a. with levity; -am, adv. playfully. [2 sa + helā.]

√ sā or si (syáti [761d3]; sináti; siṣāya; ásāt; siṣyáti; sitá; situm; -sāya; sāyáyati). bind; used almost exclusively with ava and vi. [cf. luás, stem ⁕σι-μαντ, 'strap, thong'; AS. si-ma, 'bond'; Church Slavonic sě-tǐ, Lithuanian sě-tas, AS. sā-da, Ger. Sai-te, 'string'; Church Slavonic si-lo, AS. sā-l, Ger. Sei-l, 'rope': see also √sīv and snáyu.]

+ava, −1. unbind or unharness (a team); and so turn in; go to rest; go home, 101⁶; ávasita, having turned in, at rest; −2. come to a stop at, i.e. decide upon (e.g. a dwelling-place).

+adhy-ava, caus. bring one's self to a stop at, i.e. decide upon, undertake, 28²².

+ud-ava, set out, esp. from the place of sacrifice, cf. sā + ava, 1; betake one's self, w. loc., 101⁴.

+vy-ava, decide, determine, cf. sā + ava, 2.

+pra, in prasiti, 'continuation.'

sākūta, a. having a (definite) intention; -am, adv. significantly, impressively. [ākūta.]

sākṣa, a. having or with the eyes; −used only in abl. sākṣāt, as adv. −1. with the eyes; −2. plainly, actually, 51¹⁴; exactly, 58²³; −3. (in reality, i.e.) in propria persona, embodied, in person, 1¹⁰, 6¹⁸. [akṣa: 1114c.]

sāgara, m. ocean. [cf. sagara: according to the legend, a basin hollowed out by the sons of Sagara, and filled by Bhagīratha with the water of the Ganges.]

sāgnika, a. having Agni with them, with Agni. [sa + agni, 1304c: for -ka, see 1222c2² and 1307.]

sāńguṣṭha, a. with the thumb. [ańguṣṭha.]

sāta, m. Sāta, name of a Yaksha.

sāta-vāhana, a. having Sāta (in the form of a lion) as his beast of burden, riding on Sāta; as m. Sātavāhana, name of a king, 49¹⁷.

sāttvika, f. -ī, a. −1. (really existent, i.e.) real, 22⁵; −2. standing in relation to the quality sattva (q.v.), proceeding from sattva, governed by sattva, good. [sattvá, 1222e2.]

sādana, n. dwelling. [√sad: for mg, cf. sadana.]

sādara, a. with respect; -am, adv. respectfully. [ādara.]

√ sādh (sādhati, -te; sādhitum; sādháyati). −1. come straight to one's aim, attain one's object; −2. bring straight to one's object; −caus. −1. bring to its object or end; accomplish; −2. attain, win. [cf. √2 sidh, 'succeed.']

sādhú, f. sādhvī, a. −1. leading straight to the goal; straight (path), 83¹⁷; −2. good or noble (of people); faithful (wife), 64¹⁰; as m. noble man, 21¹⁹; as f. excellent woman, 46⁷; −3. as adv. right; regularly, 86¹²; well; as excl. bravo! 14²², 48¹⁶. [√sādh, 1178a.]

sādhuyā, adv. straight, directly. [sādhú, 1112e end.]

sādhyá, grdv. to be won; as m. pl. Sādhyas, a class of deities. [√sādh.]

sānu, n. m. top; surface; ridge; back. [cf. snu.]

sānuçaya, a. full of repentance. [anuçaya.]

sāma-dhvani, m. sound of the sāman. [1249a².]

sāman, n. song; as technical term, esp. a Vedic stanza as arranged for chanting, a sāman; the collection of sāman's, the Sāmaveda.

sāmarthya, n. ability; -aṁ kṛ, do one's utmost; strength, 41⁴. [samartha, 1211.]

sāma-vedá, m. the Veda of sāman or chants, 63⁶. [1249a².]

sāmprata, a. of now, present; -am, adv. at present, now. [samprati, 1208d.]

sāmya, n. equality. [2samá, 1211.]

sāmyatā, f. condition of equality or likeness. [sāmya.]

sāyá, n. —1. a turning in, going to rest; —2. evening; sāyám, adv. at evening.

sāyaka, a. suitable for hurling, missile. [√2si, 'hurl,' 1181a.]

sārañga, a. dappled; as m. antelope.

sārameyá, m. descendant of the bitch Saramā, name of certain dogs, 77⁴, 83¹⁷. [sarámā, 1216a.]

sārdha, a. with a half; dve çate sārdhe, two hundred and fifty; sārdhám, adv., generalized, together; as prep. along with, w. instr. [ardha: the generalization of mg is paralleled by that seen in çālin.]

sāvitrá, f. -í, a. belonging to Savitar; with or without ṛc, a verse to Savitar, esp. Rigveda iii. 62. 10 (= 74¹⁴·¹⁵), regarded as the most sacred in the Veda, and called also gāyatrī, 60¹⁸. [savitṛ́, 1208b.]

sāçru, a. tearful; sāçru, adv. [1111c], tearfully, with tears in (their) eyes, 54¹⁹. [açru.]

sāṣṭāṅgapāta, a. having or with an aṣṭāṅgapāta, q.v.; -am, adv. with profoundest obeisance.

sāsūya, a. with impatience; -am, adv. impatiently. [asūyā.]

sāhasrá, a. consisting of a thousand, milliarius. [sahásra.]

sāhāyya, n. office of attendant, and so (like Eng. attendance) service, aid. [sahāya, 1211.]

√ 1 si, bind, see √sā.

√ 2 si, hurl, in prá-sita, 'darting along,' sáyaka, 'missile,' and sénā, 'weapon.'

siṅhá, m. lion; at end of cpds, the best of · ·, noble or brave · ·, cf. vyāghra. ['the powerful' beast, √sah.]

√ sic (siñcáti, -te [758]; siṣéca, siṣicé; ásicat, -ata; sekṣyáti, -te; siktá; séktum; siktvá; -sícya; sicyáte). —1.

pour out; sprinkle, 49²⁰; —2. esp. semen infundere feminae; —3. (like Eng. found) cast, e.g. molten metal; phenaṁ vajram asiñcan, they cast the foam into (the shape of) a thunderbolt, 97¹². [cf. lx-μás, 'moisture'; AS. seón, ᵒsih-an, 'filter, flow,' Ger. seih-en, 'strain'; Church Slavonic sic-ati, Ger. seich-en, 'mingere': cf. also Swedish sila, ᵒsih-la, 'strain,' whence Eng. sile, 'drain, strain,' whence sil-t, 'drainings, sediment.']

+ abhi, —1. pour upon, sprinkle; —2. sprinkle in token of consecration, and so (like Eng. anoint) consecrate.

+ ava, pour upon.

+ ā, pour into.

+ ni, pour down or in; semen infundere feminae.

sic, f. hem of a garment or robe.

siddha, a. perfected; as m. pl. the Siddhas, a class of demi-gods, with supernatural powers, esp. that of flying through the air. [see √2 sidh, 'succeed.']

siddhi, f. —1. success, 36¹⁰; accomplishment (of a wish), 24²¹; successful performance, 57¹⁴; attainment of an object, 52¹¹; —2. (perfection, i.e.) magic power. [prop. 'the reaching an aim,' √2 sidh, 'hit the mark,' 1157. 1a.]

siddhimant, a. possessing magic power. [1235.]

√ 1 sidh (sédhati; siṣédha; setsyáti; siddhá; séddhum; -sídhya). drive off; scare away.

√ 2 sidh (sídhyati, -te; siṣédha; setsyáti, -te; siddhá). —1. reach an aim, hit the mark; —2. succeed, 18¹⁷; be accomplished, 18²²; become realized, 18¹⁹; be of advantage, boot, avail, 71⁴; —siddha, having reached one's (highest) aim, having attained perfection; esp. perfect in the sense of having attained supernatural or magic powers; as m. a Siddha, q.v. [cf. √sādh.]

+ pra, succeed; prasiddha, known, cf. prasiddhi; aham prasiddho mūṣakākhyayā, I go by the name of M., 47²¹.

sindhu, —1. in V., m. stream; —2. in V. and later, f. The Stream, i.e. the Indus (incolis Sindus appellatus — Pliny); —3.

the land on the Indus and its inhabitants (*pl.*). [cf. the Old Persian form *hindu* (in an inscription of Darius Hystaspis at Persepolis), as name of the land on the Indus: hence, w. loss of aspiration, the classical form 'Ἰνδός; hence also Persian *Hind*, 'India,' and *Hind-u-stan* (*stan* = sthāna, 'abode, land').]

sisṛkṣu, *a*. desirous to create. [fr. desid. of √sṛj, 1038, 1178f: euphony, 184c².]

√ **sīv** (sī́vyati; syūtá; -sīvya). sew. [prop. siū (765): cf. √sā, si, 'bind,' sū́tra, 'thread,' sūcí, 'needle': cf. κασ-σύω, ἐκατα-σύω, 'sew down, stitch together, cobble'; Lat. *su-ere*, 'sew,' *sū-tor*, 'shoemaker'; AS. *siw-ian*, *seowian*, Eng. *sew*; AS. *seām*, Eng. *seam*, Ger. *Saum*, 'hem, border.']

√ **1 su** (sunóti, sunuté; suṣā́va; saviṣyáti, soṣyáti; sutá; -sútya). press out, extráct, *esp.* the Soma *or* éxtract; sunvánt, *as m.* the Soma-presser; — sutá, extracted; *as m.* the éxtract, *i.e.* Soma-juice, 70⁸; draught of Soma, 73¹⁰.

√ **2 su** *or* **sū** (suváti; suṣuvé; ásāvīt; sutá, sūtá; -sútya). impel, set in motion; bring about; occasion; give authorization to; *w. loc.*, *perhaps* set, *at* RV. x. 125. 7. [cf. ἕλω, ϝϝεϝ-δω, 'let go, permit'; αἶμα σύ-το, 'the blood shot *or* spurted.']

+ **ud**, impel upwards; set a-going, begin, *in* utsava.

+ **parā**, drive away.

√ **3 su**, generate, bear, *see* √sū.

sú, — 1. *adv.* [1121d], well; *with* sthā, stand well, *i.e.* firmly, 87⁶; *asseverative or emphatic, and to be rendered variously:* we pray, 79⁴; ni ṣu svapa, sleep in peace; *with* u, 'now,' just now, right soon, 80¹, 74¹¹; — 2. *inseparable prefix* [1304b, 1288b], *with force of either adv. or adj.*, well *or* good; *sometimes intensive, as*, **su-dustara**, 'very bad-to-cross.' [no prob. connection *w. eü*, 'well'; see āyú.]

sukumāra, *a*. very delicate. [cf. kumāra.]

sukumārāṅga, *f*. -ī, *a*. having very delicate limbs. [áṅga.]

su-kṛt, *a*. well-doing, righteous; *as m. pl.* the righteous ones κατ' ἐξοχήν, *i.e.* the departed fathers (85¹⁹), who enjoy the reward of their works in the world of the pious — sukṛtā́m u loké, 84¹¹.

su-kṛtá, *n*. a good deed, good works, 63¹⁶; sukṛtásya loká, world of righteousness, 89⁸, *modernized substitute for the old phrase* sukṛtā́m u loká. [1288 and b: acct, 1284a.]

su-keçánta, *a*. fair-locked. [1304b.]

su-kṣatrá, *a*. having a good *or* kind rule; *as m.* kind *or* gracious ruler. [kṣatrá, 1304b.]

su-kṣétra, *n*. fair field. [kṣétra, 1288b.]

√ **sukṣetriya** (•sukṣetriyáti). to desire fair fields — *denom., found only in the following word.* [sukṣetra, 1059c and c².]

sukṣetriyā́, *f*. desire for fair fields. [√sukṣetriya, 1149⁶.]

sukhá, *a*. pleasant; comfortable; *as n.* pleasure; comfort; joy; bliss, 58¹⁷, 66¹; sukham, -ena, *adverbially*, pleasantly, with pleasure, in comfort, happily, well *or* easily, 24⁹, etc. [cf. duḥkha.]

sukha-duḥkha, *n*. weal or woe. [1253b.]

sukhin, *a*. having comfort, being in comfort. [sukha.]

sukhocita, *a*. accustomed to ease. [ucita, √uc.]

sukhodya, *a*. easily pronounceable. [udya.]

sukhopaviṣṭa, *a*. comfortably seated. [upaviṣṭa, √viç.]

su-gá, *a*. having the going *or* approach easy; easy to attain; *as n.* good path.

su-gata, *a*. well-conditioned, *i.e.* having had a good time.

su-gātuyā́, *f*. desire for welfare. [presupposes a noun •su-gātu, 'welfare' (see gātu), whence the denom. verb-stem •sugātuya, 'desire welfare' (1061), whence this noun — 1149⁶.]

su-cira, *a*. very long; -am, *adv.* very long.

su-jániman, *a*. having good productions *or* creations; skillfully fashioning.

1 sutá, *ppl.* extracted; *as m.* éxtract; *see* √ 1 su, 'extráct.'

18

2 **suta**, *m.* son; **sutā**, *f.* daughter. [prop. 'generated, born,' ppl. of √3 su, see √su: for mg, cf. sūnú, and Eng. *bairn* (under √ bhṛ).]

su-tṛp, *a.* easily satisfied. [vbl. fr. √1 tṛp.]

su-darçana, *a.* having a beautiful appearance, handsome, εὐ-φαρής; *as m.* Sudarçana, name of a king, Εὐφάρης.

su-dāman, *a.* having good gifts, bestowing blessings; *as m.* cloud, as source of rain and therewith connected blessings, blessed rain-cloud.

su-dína, *a.* very bright *or* clear; *as n.* (*like Lat.* serenum) clear weather.

sudinatvá, *n.* (*like Lat.* serenitas) clear weather; *fig.* auspicious *or* blessed time, *always in the phrase* -tvé áhnām, in der Glückszeit der Tage, in the happy days. [1239.]

su-díti, *f.* beautiful flaming *or* flame.

su-dustara, *a.* very hard-to-cross, hard to get over; (of a promise) hard to perform.

1 **sudhá**, *f.* (good place *or* position, *i.e.*) well-being. [sú + 1 dhá.]

2 **sudhā**, *f.* (good drink, *i.e.*) drink of the gods, nectar. [sú + 2 dhá.]

su-nāsākṣibhruva, *a.* having beautiful noses-and-eyes-and-brows. [for nāsākṣibhrū (1315c), *i.e.* nāsā + akṣi + bhrū, 1253.]

su-niçcaya, *a.* having a very firm resolve, very resolute.

sundara, *f.* -í, *a.* beautiful.

sunva, *a.* Soma-pressing. [√1 su, 'press': see 1148.3b and 716.]

supátnī, *a. f.* having a good husband. [su + pati, but in the fem. form, since the masc. would not be used: 1304b: cf. sapatnī.]

su-parṇá, *a.* with good wings; *as m.* bird of prey; eagle, vulture; mythical bird. [parṇá, 1304b.]

su-putrá, *a.* having good sons. [putrá, 1304b.]

sú-pratiṣṭhita, *a.* properly set up.

su-prāví [355b], *a.* very zealous. [1288b.]

sú-prīta, *a.* well pleased. [1288b and 1284.]

su-baddhá, *a.* well *or* fast bound. [1288b and 1284a.]

su-buddhi, *a.* having good wits; *as m.* Bright-wits, Good-wits, name of a crow.

su-bhága, *a.* having a goodly portion, fortunate, happy; *esp.* loved (by one's husband), 89¹⁰; charming; amiable, 61¹². [bhága, 1304b.]

súmakha, *a.* jocund. [perhaps sú + makhá.]

su-maṅgála, *f.* -galí [355b], *a.* having *or* bringing good luck. [maṅgalá: acct irregular, cf. 1304b² end.]

su-madhyama, *a.* fair-waisted.

su-mánas, *a.* —1. good-hearted, well-disposed, 90²; kind; —2. (having good, *i.e.* happy feelings, *i.e.*) cheerful; glad, 78¹⁸; —3. *as f. pl.* (the cheerful ones, *i.e.*) the flowers; *in cpd*, 19²). [cf. the second part of εὐ-μενής, stem εὐ-μενες, 'well-disposed.']

√ **sumanasya**, *only in ppl.* sumanasyámāna, being cheerful; joyous. [sumanas, 1063.]

sú-mahant [450b], *a.* very great *or* important. [1288b.]

sumahākakṣa, *a.* having very-great (enclosures, *i.e.*) halls *or* rooms. [sumahá + kakṣā, 1298a, 334².]

su-méka, *a.* (having a good setting-up, *i.e.*) firmly stablished.

su-medhás, *a.* having good insight *or* wisdom, wise.

sumná, *n.* favor, grace; welfare. [perhaps neuter of an adj. su-mna, 'kindly minded'—see mna: but cf. 1224c.]

súra, *m.* a god. [a pendant to asura, formed by popular etymology from asu-ra, as if this were a-sura, 'non-god'—see asura.]

su-rakṣita, *a.* well-guarded.

su-rátna, *a.* having goodly treasures. [rátna, 1304b.]

surabhí, *a.* sweet-smelling, fragrant.

surabhisrag-dhara, *a.* wearing fragrant garlands. [surabhi-sraj.]

sura-sattama, *m. pl.* the best of the gods.

súrā, *f.* spirituous, *and esp.* distilled, liquor; brandy; liquor. [√1 su, 'express': cf. 1 suta and soma.]

su-rádhas, a. having goodly blessings, bounteous.

surottama, a. *subst.* chief of gods. [ut-tama.]

su-lalita, a. very lovely; (of meat) delicious.

su-locana, a. fair-eyed.

su-várcas, a. having good varcas, *i.e.:* full of life, 83¹⁴; blooming, 90²; fiery, 2²; glorious, 1¹⁶.

su-várṇa, a. having a beautiful color; *as n.* gold.

suvarṇa-kaṅkaṇa, n. gold-bracelet. [1280b.]

su-vidátra, a. kindly noticing, *i.e.* taking kind notice, kindly. [1288b.]

suvidatríya, a. kindly. [suvidatra, 1214a.]

su-víra, a. having good heroes; rich in retainers, 87¹; heroic, 78⁴, 88¹⁴. [vīrá: acct, 1304b² end.]

suvṛktí, f. excellent praise, goodly hymn. [su + ṛkti, with euphonic v.]

su-çéva, a. very kindly. [çéva, 1288b.]

su-çlakṣṇa, a. very smooth.

su-saṁcita, a. well-gathered; -am, *adv.* susaṁcitaṁ saṁcitya, having gathered (in a well-gathered way, *i.e.*) carefully.

sú-samāhita, a. very intent, entirely concentrated upon one thing. [√1 dhā, 'put': acct, 1284².]

su-stha, a. (well situated, *i.e.*) safe and well.

su-hṛd, m. friend. [prop. adj., 'having a good heart, kindly disposed.']

suhṛd-bheda, m. a creating of divisions among friends, separation of friends.

suhṛd-vākya, n. (speech, *i.e.*) words of a friend.

√ sū *or* su (sūte [628]; suṣáva, suṣuvé; ásoṣṭa; saviṣyáti, -te; soṣyáti, -te; sūtá, sutá; sūtvá; -sūya). generate; bring forth; bear; *so perhaps at* RV. x. 125.7. [cf. 2 suta, 'bairn'; *ulós, ·συ-ιο-ς,* 'son'; for pronunciation as trisyllable, *ŏ-ι-ŏs,* cf. Boeotian *ŏυιŏs:* see also under sū and sūnú.]

+ pra, bring forth; prasūta, born of (*gen.*).

sū [351], *vbl.* bearing, *in* vīrasū; *as f.* mother. [√sū, q.v.: with sū-s, cf. *σῦ-ς, ŏ-s,* Lat. *sū-s,* AS. *sū,* Eng. *sow* (qua pecude nihil genuit natura fecundius — Cicero, cf. *verres* under √vṛṣ); also AS. *swin, ·su-ina,* Eng. *swine,* prop. a diminutive of *sū.*]

sūkará, m. swine, boar. [origin uncertain.]

sūkṣma, a. fine, small; subtile, intangible, atomic, 56¹⁹.

√ sūcaya (sūcayáti). indicate; sūcita, made recognizable. [sūci, mg 3: 1061².]

sūcí *and* sūcí, f. -1. needle; -2. generalized, a pointed object; *and so* -3. (like *Eng.* pointer) indicator; index. [prob. fr. √sīv, sīū, q.v.]

sūtra, n. -1. thread; cord; -2. brief rule *or* book of such rules (so called, perhaps, because each rule was a short 'line' or because the collection was a 'string' of rules), *cf.* Whitney xvii. [√sīv, q.v.]

√ sūd (sūdáyati). -1. lead straight on, keep a-going; -2. bring about, finish; -3. finish (*in its colloquial sense*), put an end to, destroy.

+ ni, destroy, *see simple verb.*

sūnára, f. -ī, a. gladsome, joyous. [cf. sūnṛtā.]

sūnú, m. son; *once (at* 57⁵*), as f.* daughter. [√sū: cf. Church Slavonic *synŭ,* AS. *sunu,* Eng. *son:* for mg, cf. 2 suta.]

sūnṛta, a. joyous, gladsome, kind; -ā, *as f.* joy. [sūnára: see 1237³.]

sūnṛtāvan, f. -varī, a. joyous. [sūnṛtā, 1234 and ³: for fem., 1169.2².]

sūpa, m. soup. [despite the identity of mg, no etymological connection has as yet been discovered.]

sūpa-kāra, m. soup-maker, cook.

sūpavañcaná, a. (having an easy faltering-approach, *i.e.*) to which one easily *or* gladly totters (of the grave), *i.e.* easy of approach *or* not repulsive. [upa-vañcana, 1304b².]

sūpāyaná, a. (of easy approach, *i.e.*) easy of access. [upáyana, 1304b².]

sūra, m. the sun. [cf. svàr, gen. sūr-as, 'sun': perhaps a transfer to the a-declension, 399.]

18*

sūrí, *m.* (*prop.* impeller, inciter, *i.e.*) he who engages priests to perform a sacrifice for his own benefit and pays them for it, a sacrifice-master; the same as **maghavan** (*q.v.*) and the later **yajamāna**. [√2 su, 'impel,' 1191.]

sū́rya, *m.* the sun, *selection* xl.; the Sun, *personified, selection* xxxiii.; **sūryā́**, *f.* — 1. the Sun, *personified as a female*; — 2. the hymn of Sūryā's wedding, RV. x. 85, *selection* lviii. [*fr.* **svàr** (**súr**), 1212a.]

sūryā́-vid, *a.* knowing the Sūryā-hymn, RV. x. 85.

√ **sṛ** (**sísarti**; **sasā́ra**, **sasré**; **ásarat**; **sariṣyáti**; **sṛtá**; **sártum**; **sṛtvā́**; -**sṛ́tya**; **sāráyati**, -te). run swiftly, glide, flow; *caus. act.* set in motion. [*cf.* ὁρ-μή, 'rush, onset, spring,' whence ὁρμάω, 'rush on'; ἅλ-μα, 'spring'; ἅλλομαι, 'spring'; ἅλ-το, 'leaped'; Lat. *salíre,* 'spring'; *cf.* **saras**, 'pool,' **sarit**, 'stream,' and, for the root with l, **sal-ila**, 'flowing' and 'fluid, *i.e.* water.']

+**anu**, run *or* go after.

+**apa**, go off; *caus.* remove; take out.

+**ava**, go down, *in* **avasara**.

+**ā**, run unto; run.

+**upa**, go unto, approach.

+**nis**, go out; *caus.* drive out *or* away.

+**pra**, go forth; *caus.* stretch forth *or* out.

+**sam**, — 1. flow together; — 2. go about, wander, **sam** *intensive*, 1077b end; *esp.* wander from one existence to another (of the soul).

sṛká, *m. perhaps* missile, lance.

sṛgālá, *m.* jackal.

√ **sṛj** (**sṛját̄i**, -te; **sasárja**, **sasṛjé**; **ásrāk-ṣīt**; **srakṣyáti**, -te; **sṛṣṭá**; **sráṣṭum**; **sṛṣṭvā́**; -**sṛjya**; **sisṛkṣati**). — 1. let loose (from the hand), dart, hurl; throw; — 2. let go, pour out (streams, rain), discharge; — 3. let loose (herds); — 4. spin *or* twist (cord *or* garland); — 5. (discharge from one's self, *cf.* 571, *and so*) procreate, engender; create.

+**ava**, — 1. shoot off (arrows); throw *or* put in, 572; — 2. let loose (streams); loose (from a bond), 7819; deliver over, 8412; — 3. (*like Eng. colloq.* let slide) let pass unnoticed, forgive, 7818.

+**ud**, — 1. cast; hurl (a bolt); — 2. pour out, 10318; — 3. cast off; lay down (a corpse); — 4. let go, 35.

+**sam-ud**, let go, discharge.

+**upa**, (hurl at, *and so*) plague, distress, vex; **āditya upasṛṣṭas**, *sc.* **rāhuṇā**, the sun vexed by Rāhu, *i.e.* eclipsed.

+**vi**, — 1. throw away, 10517; — 2. discharge; (let go from the hand, *i.e.*) lay down, 10320; *mid., w.* **vācam**, let go the voice, *i.e.* break silence by saying · ', 1008; — 3. create, 578, *cf. simple verb.*

+**sam**, (let go together) mix, unite.

sṛj, *vbl.* creating. [√sṛj.]

√ **sṛp** (**sárpati**, -te; **sasárpa**; **ásṛpat**; **sarpsyáti**, **srapsyáti**; **sṛptá**; **sárpitum**; **sṛptvā́**; -**sṛ́pya**; **sisṛpsati**). creep, crawl; glide; *used* of gentle and cautious motion. [*cf.* ἕρπω, 'creep, go'; Lat. *serp-ere,* 'creep'; *rēpere, serep-ere,* 'creep,' *rep-ti-lis,* 'creeping'; AS. *sealf,* Eng. *salve,* so named from its slipperiness, like **sarpis** and **sṛpra**, see these; *cf.* also ἑρπ-ετόν and Lat. *serpens,* 'snake': no connection w. Eng. *slip.*]

+**ud**, creep out *or* up; rise; *desid.* wish to rise.

+**upa**, go gently unto, approach gently.

+**vi**, — 1. move asunder, disperse; — 2. move about.

sṛprá, *a.* slippery, fatty; smooth. [√sṛp, 1188a.]

1 **sénā**, *f.* a missile; weapon. [√2 si, 'hurl,' 1177a.]

2 **sénā**, *f.* line of battle; acies; army. [akin with **sī́tā**, 'furrow,' **sīmán**, 'parting of the hair': from these a root **si**, 'draw a straight line,' may perhaps be inferred.]

sersya, *a.* with jealousy; -**am**, *adv.* with jealousy. [**sa** + **írsyā**.]

√ **sev** (**sévate**; **siṣéva**, **siṣevé**; **seviṣyáti**; **sevitá**; **sévitum**; **sevitvā́**; -**sévya**). — 1. stay by (*loc.*), *the opp. of* **tyaj**; — 2. stay by, *and so* (*like Eng.* wait upon) serve *or* reverence, 3017; — 3. devote one's self to; practice, 218, 662, 689. [no connection w. σέβομαι, 'reverence,' see √tyaj.]

+**upa**, reverence; be devoted to.

+**ni**, be devoted to, *i.e.* cohabit with.

+**sam**, practice.

sevana, *n.* practice. [√sev.]

sevā, *f.* a serving *or* reverencing. [√sev, 1149.]

sāinika, *a.* belonging to an army; *as m.* soldier; champion *or* fighter. [2 senā, 1222e 2.]

sódaka, *a.* with water, containing water. [udaká, 1304c.]

sóma, *m.* —1. éxtract, *esp.* of certain species of the Asclepias family, *see* 70⁵ n.; Soma, *both literally, and also personified as a god; as pl.* Soma-draughts; —2. the moon, *see* 70⁵ n. [√1 su, 'extráct,' 1166.]

soma-pā [352], *a.* Soma-drinking; *as m.* Soma-drinker.

soma-péya, *n.* a drinking of Soma; *dat.* in order to drink the Soma, *see* 1213c, 982. [acct, 1272a.]

somyá, *a.* having to do with Soma, *i.e., as m.:* Soma-offerer; *pl.* the Manes, 84¹⁸. [sóma, 1212c.]

sāudāmanī, *f.* lightning; *prop., f. of an adj.* ★sāudāmana, 'of the rain-cloud, cloud-born,' *and to be taken in its adj. sense, as epithet of* vidyut, *at* 2⁹. [see sudāman and 1208a.]

sāúbhaga, *n.* happiness. [subhága, 1208f.]

sāubhagatvá, *n.* condition of happiness; weal and blessing. [sāúbhaga, 1239.]

sāúbhāgya, *n.* happiness, *esp.* conjugal felicity, 89¹⁶; charmingness, 2⁵. [subhága (1211, 1204c) —see its mgs.]

sāumyá, *a.* —1. of *or* relating to Soma; Soma-, 96⁶; —2. (moon-like, *i.e.*) having a mild and kindly influence on senses and feelings, *and so* mild, gentle; —3. *voc. sing.* sāumya, O gentle sir, 61⁸. [sóma, 1211.]

sāuryá, *a.* pertaining to the sun; *neut. pl., sc.* sūktāni, hymns to Sūrya. [sūrya, 1211.]

sāuvarṇa, *a.* golden. [suvarṇa, 1208f.]

√ skand (skándati; caskánda; áskāntaīt; skantsyáti; skanná; -skándya, -ská-dya). *intrans.* dart, spring, spurt; drop, be spilled; fall. [cf. σκάνδ-αλον, 'trap-stick' (cf. Ger. *Falle*, 'trap, pit-fall,' w. *fallen*, 'fall'), and 'stumbling-block'; Lat.

scand-ere, 'climb,' *de-scend-ere*, 'climb down'; *scāla*, ★scad-la, 'ladder.']

skandhá, *m.* shoulder.

skandha-deça, *m.* region of the shoulder, *i.e.* shoulder.

skándhas, *n.* ramification; branches of a tree, tree-top.

stána, *m.* the breast of a woman.

stabdha, *a.* immovable, rigid, stiff. [√stabh, 954, 160.]

stabdha-locana, *a.* having immovable, *i.e.* unwinking eyes.

stabdhī-kṛ, make rigid *or* stiff (as if dead). [stabdha, 1094.]

√ stabh *or* **stambh** (stabhnáti; tastámbha, tastambhé; ástambhīt; stabdhá; stábdhum; stabdhvá; -stábhya). —1. make firm *or* steady, prop *or* uphold (heaven *or* earth); —2. *mid.* become firm *or* immovable *or* rigid; —stabdha, immovable, rigid. [cf. στέμφ-υλον, 'olives pressed hard, oil-cake'; στέμβ-ειν, 'mal-treat,' collateral form of στείβ-ειν, 'stamp on, tread'; Eng. *stamp:* for connection of mgs, cf. ἐρείδω, 'make steady *or* firm, fix firm, plant.']

+ud, prop up.

+vi, —1. prop asunder, 78¹⁰; —2. (make immovable, *i.e.*) bring to a stand-still, stop, 6²¹.

stambha, *m.* prop, post, column. [√stambh.]

√ stā (stāyánt). be stealthy. [see stená, stāyú.]

stāyú, *m.* thief. [√stā, 1165: cf. tāyú.]

√ stigh (stiñnóti). proceed, stride; *esp.* proceed against, attack. [cf. στείχω, 'proceed, march, go in line,' rarely 'mount up'; Church Slavonic *stignati*, 'hasten': the root is wide-spread in Ger-manic, but often shows a specialization of mg, 'proceed upward, ascend, climb'; cf. AS. *stīg-an*, which often means simply 'proceed, go,' but also 'ascendere,' and even 'descendere'; Ger. *steig-en*, 'mount up'; AS. *stǣg-er*, 'a step to climb by,' Eng. *stair*; AS. *stigel*, 'step *or* steps for climbing over a fence,' Eng. *stile*; AS. *stīg-rāp*, *stī-rāp*, 'mounting-rope,' Eng. *stirrup*; Ger. *Steg-reif*, 'stirrup'; AS.

stigend, 'rising or sty,' Eng. sty, 'swelling
(on eye-lid)': for change of gh to ñ in
present, cf. 161¹ and ⁴.]

+ pra, get ahead in attacking, succeed
in one's attacks, 93 ⁵,¹⁰,¹¹.

√ stu (stáúti [626], stuté; tuṣṭáva, tu-
ṣṭuvé; ástāuṣīt, ástoṣṭa; ástāvīt;
staviṣyáti, -te; stoṣyáti, -te; stutá;
stótum; stutvá; -stútya, -stáya; stū-
yáte). praise; extol (a god); stuvánt,
(praising, as subst.) worshipper.

+ pra, — 1. praise; — 2. bring forward
as object of mention or subject of conversation (cf. Lat. laudare, prop. 'praise,'
but also 'mention'), and so — 3. generalized, introduce, begin.

stúkā, f. lock or tuft (of wool or hair).
[see stokā́.]

√ stṛ (stṛṇā́ti, stṛṇīté, in mg 1 in Veda;
stṛṇóti, stṛṇuté, in mg 2; tastā́ra, ta-
staré; ástarīt [900]; stariṣyáte; stṛtá,
stīrṇá [957b]; stṛtvá, stīrtvá; -stṛ́tya,
-stírya). — 1. strew, esp. the sacrificial
straw, 88¹⁷; spread out; — 2. (like Lat.
sternere) overthrow (an enemy).

[cf. στόρ-νυ-μι, Lat. ster-n-ere, 'strew,
spread out'; στρω-μα, (like Eng. spread)
'bedding,' στρω-μνή, 'bed,' Lat. strā-men,
'straw,' storea, 'straw mat,' torus, stor-u-s,
'bed'; AS. strea-w, streo-w-ian, Eng. straw,
strew; στρω-τός, Lat. strā-tus, 'bespread';
(via) strata, '(way) bespread' with stones,
i.e. 'paved,' whence borrowed AS. strǣt,
Eng. street; Old Lat. stlā-tus, Lat. lātus,
'spread out, spreading, and so broad,
wide'; see also under noun stṛ.]

+ anu, cover over.

+ ā, spread out.

+ upa, spread upon, spread as a cover;
as technical term of the ritual, with or without ājya, pour the sacrificial butter over
(e.g. the hand) so as to make a coating,
99⁹.

+ pra, spread out.

stṛ́ f [371¹², tā́ras, stṛ́bhis], m., plural only.
the stars. [if fr. √stṛ, we may interpret
the name as meaning either (a) 'the
light-strewers,' or (b) 'the scattered' ones,
those that are 'spread out' over the vault
of heaven; but the connection w. √stṛ is

very uncertain: cf. ἀστήρ, stem ἀ-στερ,
Avestan star, Lat. stella, ster-la, Ger.
Stern, AS. steorra, Eng. star: see also
tārā.]

stená, m. thief. [√stā.]

stoká, — 1. m. drop; — 2. as adj. small,
insignificant. [akin with stúkā, 'tuft':
from these, a root stu, 'drop, dribble,
run together, be compacted into a round
mass,' may perhaps be inferred: for mg
2, cf. Eng. dribble w. driblet.]

stotṛ́, m. praiser (of a god), worshipper,
singer. [√stu, 1182a.]

stóma, m. praise, song of praise. [√stu,
1166a.]

stoma-várdhana, a. delighting in
praise. [acct, 1271.]

strī́ [366], f. woman, female individual,
wife, opp. of pumā́ns, e.g. 104⁹. [prob.
for sútri, 'generatrix,' √sū, 1182².]

strī́-kāma, a. having desire for female
(children). [1296.]

sthá, — 1. vbl in cpds. standing; and so,
generalized (like Eng. stand, 'be situated'),
situated, staying, being; — 2. sometimes,
perhaps, substantively, place (like Eng. noun
stand, 'place'), in go-ṣṭha, sadha-stha.
[√sthā, 333: sometimes -ṣṭha, 186.]

sthála, n. dry land (as opp. to water),
terra firma, Fest-land; sthalī, f. place.
[prob. akin w. √sthā, 'that which stands
firm.']

sthávira, a. — 1. firm, thick, massy,
sturdy; — 2. full-grown, old; as m. old
man. [from sthū, collateral form of
√sthā, 1188e: for mg 1, cf. Eng. steady,
cognate w. stand, and cf. sthira; for 2,
cf. Eng. of long standing.]

√ sthā (tíṣṭhati, -te [671, 749a]; tasthā́u,
tasthé; ásthāt, ásthita [884]; sthāsyáti,
-te; sthitá; sthā́tum; sthitvá; -sthā́ya;
sthīyáte; sthāpáyati, -te [1042d]).

— 1. stand, 13¹⁸, 25¹⁶, 47⁶, 80⁷, 87⁶,
98¹³; stand still, 70¹⁹,²¹; remain standing; — 2. stand by (a friend); hold out
faithfully, 25⁵, 63¹³,¹⁴; — 3. remain, 64¹⁶;
wait, 54⁶; abide, 39¹⁰, 46⁶; pass., impers.:
sarvāiḥ sthīyatām, let all remain, 24¹⁰;
atra sthīyatām, stay here, 39²¹; — 4.
remain or be in a condition, continue in

an action [1075c]: *w. adj. or ppl.*, 28[8], 30[2]; vyāpāditas tiṣṭhati, lies dead, 44[16]; *w. gerund*, 26[16]; *w. instr.*, 41[6];

—5. exist; be present, 10[8], 45[18]; —6. be situated, be, 1[5], 26[18], 33[4]; —7. (remain standing, *i.e.* unmoved *or* untouched, *and so, like Ger.* dahingestellt bleiben) remain unconsidered *or* unmentioned; *thus*, dūre tiṣṭhatu tadvṛddhiṣ, (let the interest of it stand afar off, *i.e.*) to say nothing of the interest of it, 46[2]); —8. sthitá, *see s.v.*; —9. *caus.* cause to stand, set; put, 41[19].

[for **stā**: cf. Doric inf. στᾶ-μεν, Epic στῆ-ναι, Church Slavonic sta-ti, Lat. stā-re, Old High Ger. stā-n, Ger. steh-en, 'stand': this old form of the root appears also in Ger. *Statt*, AS. *stede*, Eng. *stead*, 'place': the prevailing form of the root in Germanic is *stand*; cf. AS. *stond-an*, Eng. *stand*; Ger. preterit *stand*, 'stood': —with á-sthā-t, cf. ἔ-στη, 'stood'; *w.* tí-ṣṭhā-mi, cf ἵ-στη-μι, 'set,' Lat. si-sti-t, 'sets': —for mgs of √sthā, cf. in general those of Eng. *stand*.]

+ **adhi**, stand upon.

+ **anu**, —1. (stand along by, *i.e.*) take one's place along by, *and so* support, help; —2. devote one's self to a thing, *e.g.* virtue, 58[16]; devote one's self to (an undertaking), *and so* carry out (a plan), 33[14]; accomplish; *pass. impers.*: evam anuṣṭheyam, it must be done so, 37[8]; *so* 38[15]; tathā_anuṣṭhite, it having been thus accomplished, this being done, 33[14]; *see* 303b[4] *and cf.* 35[16], 37[18], 39[15,22].

+ **abhi**, set the foot upon, vanquish; withstand.

+ **ava**, —1. stand off, 105[20]; —2. stand; —3. remain, abide; —avasthita: standing; posted, 43[12]; situated; abiding, dwelling; —*caus.* (cause to stand apart, *i.e.*) leave behind, 44[2,9].

+ **ā**, take one's place at; resort to, 10[1].

+ **ud**, stand up; rise up (from sleep *or* inactivity), 30[20]; spring up, 26[17]; get out of (*abl.*), 36[18]; *caus.* cause *or* bid to rise, 102[7]; pull out (of a mire, a vat), 22[9], 36[14]. [s lost, 233a.]

+ **praty-ud**, rise up to meet (in token of respect).

+ **sam-ud**, rise up, spring up.

+ **upa**, —1. stand by, 94[9]; set one's self near; stand opposite, 59[28]; —2. approach, *esp.* with reverence *or* supplication; —upasthita: (having) approached *or* appeared; near at hand, 41[8].

+ **anu_upa**, *mid.* approach one after another; *w.* mā (*the pronoun*), come to my side, 94[4].

+ **sam-upa**, approach; fall to one's lot; samupasthita, on hand.

+ **ni**, stand in, rest on.

+ **pari**, stand round about, encompass; restrain.

+ **pra**, *mid.* arise, *and so* set out to go; go off; prasthito 'bhavat, profectus est; *caus.* send away, dismiss, 36[9].

+ **prati**, stand; be established; get a place *or* foot-hold, 84[9]; pratiṣṭhita: established, resting upon; set up; —*caus.* set.

+ **vi**, *mid.* (stand asunder, *i.e.*) spread itself.

+ **anu-vi**, spread one's self over, pervade (*acc.*), RV. x. 125.7.

+ **sam**, *mid.* —1. remain with; —2. *in the ritual*, come to a stand-still (sam, *intensive*), *i.e.* get through, finish; saṃsthite, *loc. absolute*, if he (end, *i.e.*) die, 101[6].

sthātrá, *n.* station, place. [√sthā, 1185: for mg, cf. Eng. *stead* w. root *sta* under √sthā.]

sthāna, *n.* —1. a standing; —2. a remaining, abiding; —3. standing, *i.e., as in Eng.*, rank; —4. an abode (*see* bhavana); place, 35[5], etc.; —5. *pregnantly* (*cf.* pātra), a proper place; —6. a proper occasion; *concrete*, a proper object for giving occasion to anything; tatkāvya-sya_arpaṇa-sthānam ekaḥ s-, of this poem S. is the sole consignment-occasioner, *i.e.* the only one worthy of having this poem entrusted to him, 54[1]. [√sthā, 1150. 1.]

sthāna-bhraṅça, *m.* abode-ruin, loss of abode.

sthāvará, *a.* standing; not endowed with the power of locomotion, *and so, as collective n. sing.*, the plants, 63[22]; *as m. pl.* plants, 67[1]. [√sthā, 1171a.]

sthāvaratā, *f.* condition of being a plant. [1237.]

sthitá, *a.* —1. standing (*as opp. to going, lying*), 14¹⁸; —2. (of animate and inanimate beings) standing in a place; abiding; sthitas (*supply, as is often necessary, some form of √as, 'be*'), was abiding, *i.e.* abode, 29¹⁸; situated; bhūtale sthitam, being on the earth, *i.e., simply,* on the earth, 6¹⁷; *impers.:* sthitam, it was waited by (*instr.*), *i.e.* (he) waited, 34¹⁸; —3. existing; present, 6¹⁸;

—4. being *or* remaining in a situation *or* condition (*cf. √sthā 4*), *which is expressed: by an adj. in the same case,* 13¹⁰; *by an adv.;* tathā, 26¹⁸; kaḥ sthito 'tra, who (is) being here, *i.e.* who is here, 49⁷; *by a gerund:* ātmānam ācchādya sthitas, after concealing himself (was) remaining, *i.e.* kept hidden, 25¹⁰; *so* 36¹⁴, 38¹⁹, 41⁴; upaviçya sthitās, waited sitting, 43⁹; yāir vyāpya bhāvān sarvān sthito mahān, with which the intellect, pervading all beings, stands, *i.e.* with which it constantly pervades all beings, 66⁹.

[ppl. of √sthā, 954c: cf. στα-τό-s, Lat. *sta-tu-s,* 'standing, set': for mgs above, cf. √sthā.]

sthíti, *f.* —1. a standing; —2. a remaining by a thing; *and so* —3. devotion to (*loc.*), 15¹⁷; —4. (*like Lat.* status) condition; *and so* —5. way, method of procedure, 26⁷. [√sthā, 1157.1a, cf. 954c.]

sthin, *vbl.* standing, *in cpds.* [√sthā, 1183⁸.]

sthirá, *a.* steady; steadfast, 81⁹; firm; *also of persons,* 99⁷; enduring (of might), 78⁶. [√sthā, 1188¹, cf. 954c: for mg, cf. sthavira.]

√ sthū, *assumed as collateral form of* sthā, *cf.* sthāvira, *and see under* √anā.

sthūṇā, *f.* post, pillar. [for ●stul-na, fr. √●stul or ●stal, an extended form of √●sta, Skt. sthā: cf. Ger. Stolle(n), Old High Ger. stollo, ●stol-no, 'prop, post'; στῦλ-os, 'post, pillar'; these words, like στήλη, Doric στάλα, 'prop, post,' presuppose the root in causal mgs, 'cause to stand,' i.e. (a) 'keep from falling, prop up,' and (b) 'set up,' as a pillar: the root

appears also in Ger. *Stall,* Eng. *stall,* 'stand, *i.e.* standing-place,' and in Ger. *still,* Eng. *still,* 'standing, not moving.']

√ snā (snáti; sasnāu; snāsyáti, -te; snātá; snátum; snātvā; -snáya). bathe; perform a religious ablution, *esp.* at the end of religious studentship (62⁶) *or* of a vow. [orig. snā or snū (so sthā, sthū): cf. √σνυ in ἔννεον, ●έ-σνεϜ-ον, 'swam'; Lat. nā-re, 'swim': see also under nāú.]

snātaka, *a.* who has performed the ablution customary at the end of religious pupilage. [snātá, 1222.]

snāna, *n.* a bathing, religious ablution. [√snā, 1150.]

snāna-çīla, *a.* (having bathing as a habit, *i.e.*) practicing religious ablutions. [1302.]

snāyin, *a.* performing religious ablutions. [√snā, 1183³, 258.]

snāyu, *f. n.* —1. sinew, 25⁷. [perhaps 'ligament,' from √sā or si, 'bind, ligāre.' *q.v.:* if so, it is formed from the present-stem sinā (see 1148.3b and cf. sunva), abbreviated to snā, with suffix u (1178b) and interposed y (258): cf. Old High Ger. sēnawa, Ger. Sehne, AS. sinu, Eng. sinew, which point to a Goth. ●sinava: that snā-yu and its older equiv. snā-van are abbreviated forms (for sinā-) would appear from the Germanic cognates.]

snāyu-bandha, *m.* sinew-band, *i.e.* bow-string.

√ snih (sníhyati; snigdhá). —1. be supple, greasy, moist; *and so* —2. stick to, *i.e., as in Eng.,* be attached to, be fond of.

snú, *n. collateral form of* sānu. surface.

sneha, *m.* —1. stickiness; —2. viscid and smooth stuff; oil; fat; —3. attachment, love, friendship. [√snih: for connection of 1 and 3, see snih.]

√ apaç, *older form of* √1 paç, *q.v.*

√ spṛdh (spárdhate; paspṛdhé; spardhitā; spárdhitum). contest the precedence among one another; emulate; strive.

spṛdh, *f.* rival; opponent; foe. [√spṛdh.]

√ spṛç (spṛçáti, -te; paspárça, paspṛçé;

ásprākṣīt, ásprkṣat; sprakṣyáti; spṛṣṭá; spráṣṭum; spṛṣṭvá; -spṛ́çya). touch.
+ upa, —1. touch, 103²²; reach to, RV. x. 125. 7; —2. w. apás, touch water, *technical term for symbolical purification,* by dipping the hand in a dish, by rinsing the mouth, or by washing, 104¹⁷, ²²; *word for water to be understood,* 65⁶.

spraṣṭavya, *grdv.* to be touched. [√spṛ́ç, 241.]

√ sphur or sphṛ (sphuráti, -te; ásphārīt; sphuritá). make a quick or jerky motion: —1. dart, *trans.;* with the foot, kick; —2. dart, *intrans.;* twitch (of the eye, arm); —3. (of the lightning) flash.
[for •spṛ, 'quiver, jerk, kick, flutter': cf. ἀ-σπαίρ-ω, 'struggle convulsively' (as a fish just out of water); Lat. *spernere,* 'kick away, reject'; Eng. *spur,* 'goad with the heel'; *spurn,* 'kick away': see also under parṇa.]
+ pra, shake, tremble.

sphyá, *m.* wooden splinter, shaped like a knife and as long as the arm, for use at the sacrifice.

sma, *enclitic and slightly asseverative particle,* 79¹⁷, 6⁸; *accompanying a verb which is in the present tense but has the value of a past,* 2⁸, 8¹⁹, 12²¹; *explained at* 778b *and* b².

√ smi (smáyate; siṣmiyé; ásmayiṣṭa; smitá; smitvá; -smítya). smile; smile bashfully; blush. [cf. φιλο-μμειδής, 'fond of smiles,' stem σμειδες, as in Hesychian μεῖδος, 'smile'; μειδάω, 'smile'; Lat. *mi-ru-s,* 'wonderful,' *mirāri,* 'wonder' (for mg, cf. smaya, 'wonder'); Middle High Ger. *smie-r-en, smie-l-en,* 'smile'; Eng. *smile, smirk.*]
+ vi, be astonished.

smita, *a.* smiling; *as n.* [1176a], a smile. [ppl. of √smi.]

smita-pūrva, *a.* previously smiling, with a smile. [for irreg. order, see 1291.]

√ smṛ (smárati; sasmára; smariṣyáti; smṛtá; smártum; smṛtvá; -smṛ́tya). —1. remember, *both keep in mind and call to mind;* —2. call to mind, *i.e.* hand down by memory, hand down by tradi-

tion, hand down—*see the important word* smṛti;
—smṛta: —1. remembered; —2. handed down by smṛti or taught by tradition; *and so* —3. declared to be · ·, 61²; passing for · ·; regarded by tradition as · ·, 63⁶; *to be variously paraphrased;* mārgo 'yaṁ smṛtas, this is, we are taught, the path, 21⁷; called, 22⁵, 57⁶.
[cf. μέρ-μερ-α ἔργα, 'memorable works'; μέριμνα, 'anxious thought, care'; μάρ-τυρ, 'rememberer, witness'; μέλειν, 'care for'; μέλλειν, 'hesitate, delay, be going to do'; Lat. *me-mor,* 'mindful'; *memoria,* 'memory'; *mor-a,* 'hesitation, delay.']
+ vi, forget.

smṛti, *f.* —1. remembrance; —2. tradition (*see* √smṛ 2); tradition which is handed down and accepted as authoritative (*except* çruti, *q.v.; defined,* 58¹⁸, *see note;* a work based on such tradition; a law-book. [√smṛ.]

smṛti-çīla, *dual n.* tradition and habits (habits *in collective sense, i.e.* usage). [1253a.]

syá [499a], *pron.* that; *cf.* tyá.

√ syand or syad (syándate; sasyandé; ásyān [890²]; syantsyáti; syanná; syánttum; syattvá; -syádya). run (of animate beings and of fluids); flow.
+ abhi, flow unto.
+ pra, flow forth or away.

syoná, *a.* soft; mild; tender.

srákva, *m.* corner of the mouth; mouth, jaws.

sragvín, *a.* wearing a wreath. [sráj, 1232.]

sráj, *f.* wreath, garland. [√sṛj, mg 4, 'twist;' just as AS. *wrǣð,* Eng. *wreath,* fr. AS. *wríðan,* Eng. *writhe,* 'twist' (under √vṛt).]

srávantī, *f.* flowing (water), stream. [ppl. of √sru.]

√ sru (srávati; susrāva; ásrāvīt; sraviṣyáti; srutá). —1. flow, stream; —2. flow or trickle away, waste away, become lost, 60⁹. [cf. ῥέω, •σρεϜ-ω, Lithuanian *srav-j-ù,* 'flow,' Irish *sruth,* 'stream'; cf. also Church Slavonic *stru-ja,* 'stream,'

Ger. *Stro-m*, Eng. *strea-m*, with *t* between
s and *r* (see under **usra** and **svasṛ**):
further *ῥεῦ-μα*, 'stream'; Lat. *Rū-mo*,
'The River,' old name of the Tiber: w.
á-srav-a-t, cf. *ἔρρεε*, *ἐ-σρεϜ-ε-τ*.]

sruc, *f.* one of the large sacrificial ladles
(as long as the arm), of which there are
three, **juhū**, **upabhṛt**, and **dhruvā**, *see*
102¹¹ ɴ.; used for pouring ghee in the
fire. [akin w. √**sru**.]

sruvá, *m.* a small sacrificial ladle (a cubit
long), used for dipping from the pot and
pouring into the **sruc**. [akin w. √**sru**.]

srótas, *n.* stream. [√**sru**, 1152a.]

svá [525⁴]. —1. *pron. adj.* own; my own,
73¹⁸, 78¹²·²⁰; thy own, 69¹⁶, 86⁴; his
own *or* his, 4¹⁷, 45⁸, etc.; her, 8¹⁰; their
own *or* (each) his own, 14⁸; *indef.*, one's
own, 58²³, 66⁶; *very often at the beginning
of cpds:* my, 10²³, 21¹⁰; his, 31⁹, etc.;
their, 27⁹; our, *etc., see following words;*
—2. *m.* kinsman, friend; —3. (*like*
ātman) one's self, *see* 513²; one's natural
self *or* condition; —4. *n.* (*like* Goth. **sves**)
possessions, property. [cf. *ἑός*, *ϝοεϜό-s*,
and *ὅς*, *ἥ*, *ὅν*, and *σφός*, 'own'; Old Lat.
sovo-s, Lat. *suu-s*, 'own'; Goth. *sve-s*, AS.
swǣs, 'own'; also *ἔ*, *σφέ*, Lat. *sē*, Goth.
si-k, Ger. *si-ch*, 'self.']

svaka, *a.* own; his own, *etc.; equiv. to*
sva. [**sva**, 1222a.]

svá-kṣatra, *a.* (having self-rule, *i.e.*)
free.

sva-cchanda, *m.* own will. [**chanda**,
227.]

svacchanda-vanajāta, *a.* (by its own
will, *i.e.*) spontaneously wood-grown, *i.e.*
growing wild in the wood.

√ **svaj** (**svájate**; **sasvajé**; **svajiṣyáte**;
svaktá; **sváktum**; **svajitvá**; -**svájya**).
embrace.

+ **pari**, embrace.

√ **svad** (**svádati**, -**te**; **sasvadé**; **svāttá**;
svadáyati, **svādáyati**). —1. *act.* make
savory, season; *fig.* make agreeable;
—2. *mid.* be savory, relish, *intrans.;* —3.
mid. relish, *trans.;* take pleasure in. [cf.
ἁνδ-άνω, 'please,' aorist *εὔαδε*, *ἐ-σϜαδ-ε*,
'pleased'; *ἥδομαι*, 'rejoice'; see also
under **svādu**.]

sva-dharma, *m.* own duty.

1 **svadhā́**, *f.* —1. wont, habit, custom,
76⁷; rule; *ἔθος*; —2. accustomed place,
home, *ἦθος*; —3. (wonted condition, *i.e.*)
comfort; joy; bliss, 83¹²; pleasure, 73¹⁴;
svadhā́m ánu nas, according to our
pleasure, *i.e.* exactly to our wish, 73¹³;
svadhā́yā *and* **svadhā́bhis**: in wonted
wise; with pleasure, gladly; (gladly, *i.e.*)
willingly, freely, 84¹². [cf. *ἔθος*, 'custom,'
ἦθος, 'wonted place, haunt,' *εἴ-ωθ-α*, 'am accustomed'; AS. *sidu*, Ger. *Sitte*, 'custom.']

2 **svadhā́**, *f.* sweet drink; *esp.* a libation
of ghee to the Manes. [perhaps for
2 **sudhā**: for the etymology, cf. **sva-
dhā́ adhayat**, 'he drank the sweet
drinks,' RV.]

svadhā́vant, *a.* —1. (having his wont,
i.e.) keeping to his custom, faithful, constant; —2. (having bliss, *i.e.*) blessed,
78¹⁷, 79⁴·¹⁵. [1**svadhā**, 1233: see mgs 1
and 3.]

svádhiti, *m. f.* axe.

√ **svan** (**svánati**, -**te**; **sasvána**; **ásvanīt**,
ásvānīt; **svanitá**). sound, resound, roar.
[cf. Lat. *sonus*, 'sound'; Old Lat. *son-it*,
'sounds'; AS. *swinsian*, 'sound'; Eng.
swan, so named from its song; similarly
in Ger. the cock is called *Hahn*, a name
akin w. Lat. *can-ere*, 'sing' — cf. Hamlet
i. 1. 160, "the bird of dawning singeth."]

svaná, *m.* sound; roar (of wind).
[√**svan**.]

svanas, *n.* roar. [do.]

√ **svap** (**svápiti** [631]; **suṣvā́pa** [785⁸];
ásvāpsīt; **svapsyáti**; **suptá** [954b];
sváptum; **suptvā́**; **svāpáyati**). sleep;
fall asleep; **suptá**, sleeping; *caus.* put
to sleep. [cf. Lat. *sop-or*, 'sleep'; w.
caus., cf. Lat. *sōpire*, 'put to sleep'; see
also under **svapna**.]

+ **ni**, go to sleep; *caus.* put to sleep.

+ **pra**, fall asleep; **prasupta**, fallen
asleep, asleep, sunk in sleep.

svápas, *a.* having good works, *i.e.* wonder-
working. [**sú** + **ápas**, 1304b.]

svapú [352], *f. perhaps* besom. [perhaps
for **su-pū́**, 'cleaning well': for **va** in
place of **u**, cf. 2**svadhā**: for mg, cf.
pavana.]

svápna, m. —1. sleep; —2. dream. [√svap, q.v.: cf. *ὕπ-νο-ς, Lat. som-nu-s, 'sleep'; AS. swef-n, 'sleep, dream'; Chaucerian swefn, 'dream'; Lat. somnium, 'dream': for connection of 1 and 2, cf. 51⁹, where either sense fits.]

svapna-māṇavaka, m. the Dream-manikin, name of a certain magic whose performance brings dreams that become realized, 51⁸.

sva-bhāva, m own way of being, inherent nature, ingenium, as distinguished from acquired qualities, see guṇa 2, and 22²¹; svabhāvāt, by nature [291²], naturally.

svabhāva-dveṣa, m. natural hatred. [1280b.]

svayaṁ-vara, m. self-choice; esp. free choice of a husband, which was allowed to girls of the warrior (kṣatriya) caste, a Swayamvara.

svayám [513], pron. own self, self; himself, etc.; referring to subject, 48⁸, etc.; all by itself, of its own accord, 93⁹; referring to predicate, 1¹⁰. [from sva with nom. case ending -am (cf. tv-am, a-y-am), and interposed y, cf. 258.]

svayam-bhū [352], a. self-existent; as m. epithet of Brahma.

svayam-mṛta, a. dead of himself.

svá-yukti, f. pl. own team [acct, 1274: for mg, cf. the Dutch and the American Eng. span (of horses) w. AS. spannan, 'join.']

√ svar (svárati; ásvārṣīt; ásvārīt). sound. [cf σῦρ-ιγξ, 'pipe, flute'; Lat. su-sur-ru-s, 'a humming'; Eng swar-m.]

svàr [388d], pronounced súar in the Veda, n. —1. the sun, 71¹⁹; —2. sunlight, sunshine; light, 79⁹, —3. (the place of the light, cf. rajas) heaven, 91⁶, 92⁸; —4. one of the three "utterances," see vyāhṛti.

[cf. Ξείρ-ιος, Ξείρ, 'sun, dog-star'; σέλ-ας, 'light'; σελ-ήνη, 'moon'; Lat. ser-ēnus, 'bright'; sōl, AS. sōl, 'sun'; AS swel-an, Eng. sweal, 'burn, glow, waste away by heat'; and the kindred swelter, 'be overcome by heat,' whence sweltry or sultry: if the forms with r and l are fr.

extended forms of a root *su, 'to light,' and if svàr is a direct deriv. of the same √su (sú-ar), we may compare Ger. Sonne, AS. sunne, Eng. sun, AS. sunnan dæg, Eng. Sun-day.]

sva-rūpa, n. own form or shape; true nature, 40¹⁹.

svarūpa-bhāva, m. the becoming or being the true form (of names), i.e. the use of the true form (of a person's name). [1280b: svarūpa is used predicatively.]

svar-gá, —1. a. going or leading to the light or to heaven; situate in the heavenly light, heavenly; esp. w. loka, svargo lokas, the heavenly world, heaven, 103⁵, ¹⁴, ¹⁶ — also as one word, see svargaloka; —2. m. without loka, heaven, 64⁹, 66¹.

svarga-gāmin, a. going to or attaining heaven.

svarga-loka, m. the heavenly world, heaven, 103⁷.

svàr-bhānu, m. Suarbhānu, name of a demon causing the eclipse of the sun, cf. the later rāhu. [poss. 'having, i.e withholding the sun's rays.']

svaryà, pronounced svaria, a. sounding; of a thunderbolt, whizzing. [√svar, 1213.]

svalaṁkṛta, a. well adorned. [su + alaṁkṛta: see alam.]

sváçva, a. with goodly horses. [sú + áçva, 1304b.]

svásṛ [373], f. sister. [cf. Lat. sŏror, AS. sweoster, swuster, Eng. sister: cf. 369³ and 1182f: for t between s and r, cf. Easter, under usra, and stream under √sru.]

svastí, pronounced suasti in Veda, —1. f. (like the Eng. well-being, i.e.) welfare; blessing; —2. svastí, instr. [336⁸ end], with luck, happily; hence —3. the indeclinable nom.-acc. neut. svasti, luck, happiness, 84¹; svasty astu te, a blessing on thee. [sú + an unused asti, 'be-ing,' fr. √1 as, 'be,' 1157 1a. acct, 1288b.]

svasti-dá [352], a. bestowing welfare.

svastyáyana, n. sing. and pl. (luck-progress, i.e.) wel-fare, prosperity; blessing; and so benediction, 101², 106⁴; pl. the blessings, i.e. Vedic hymns con-

taining the word **svasti**, 106[8]. [svasti +
áyana: acct, 1271: with **-ayana**, cf. *-fare*
in *wel-fare*.]

sva-stha, *a.* being in one's natural condition, self-contained, healthy, well.

svādas, *n.* agreeableness, *in* **prá-svādas**.
[√svad, 1151. 1b: cf. ἦδος (sic), Doric
ἇδος, 'pleasure.']

svādú, *a.* tasting good, savory; sweet.
[√svad, q.v., 1178a: cf. ἡδύς, Doric ἁδύς,
•σϜάδυ-ς, Lat. *svāvis*, •*svadv-i-s*, AS. *swēte*,
Eng. *sweet*.]

svādhyāyá, *m.* the reading *or* repeating to one's self, study (of the Veda).
[adhyāya.]

svāmi-kārya, *n.* master's business.

svāmi-kumāra, *m.* the Lord Kumāra,
name of Skanda, god of war, *see* **kārttikeya** *and* **kumāra**.

svāmi-guṇa, *m.* ruler-virtue.

svāmin, *m.* owner, proprietor, master,
lord; *opp. of* servant, subject, wife. [sva,
'own,' 1231.]

svāmi-sevā, *f.* the serving one's master.

svāmi-hita, *n.* master's welfare.

svārtha, *m.* own affair *or* cause. [artha.]

svāhā, *excl.* used when making oblations,
hail, *w. dat.*, 103[3]; *at the end of an invocation, like* Amen, 99[13].

√ **svid** (**svédate**; **svidyati, -te**; **siṣvidé**;
svinná). sweat. [svidyāmi=ἰδίω, 'sweat';
cf. ἶδος, ἰδ-ρώς, 'sweat,' ἱδρόω, 'sweat';
Lat. *sūdā-re*, 'sweat,' denom. of •*sūdu-s*,
'sweat'; *sūd-or*, 'sweat'; Lettish *swidrs*,
'sweat'; AS. noun *swāt*, Eng. *sweat*:
observe that though there is a word for
'sweat' common to most Indo-European
tongues, there is no such common word
for 'be chilly.']

svecchā, *f.* own will; **svecchayā**, according to one's inclination, at will. [icchā.]

svéda, *m.* sweat. [√svid.]

---

ha, *enclitic and slightly asseverative particle*,
64[4]; *in the Veda*, 78[15], 79[12], 92[12]; *in the
Brāhmanas*, 94[8], *and very often (so pages
95–6)*, 103[15] *(quotation from a Brāhmana);
in the Sūtras, to be sure, of course, desig-*

*nating that the author agrees with the view
or method mentioned*, 99[19], 101[5], 103[14, 16];
—*very common at end of half-çloka*, 7[15];
esp. after a 3d sing. perf. ($\cup\_\cup$), 9[4], 10[2];
so iti ha, 12[8]; —*combinations:* · · iti
hovāca, "· ·," he said, 61[13]; *so* hovāca,
hocus, 95[13], 96[13]. [this word appears
also as gha in the Veda: cf. γε, Doric γα,
enclitic asseveratives.]

haṅsá, *m.* goose, gander; *perhaps applied
also to the swan and like water-fowl.
*[prob. a consonantal stem, transferred
(399) to the a-declension, and so orig.
•ghaṅs: cf. χήν, Lat. *ans-er*, Lithuanian
žqsì-s, Irish *goss*, Ger. *Gans*, AS. *gōs*,
Eng. *goose*: even the s of •ghaṅs may be
derivational; cf. AS. *gan-d-ra*, •*gan-ra*,
Eng. *gander*; Old High Ger. *gan-azzo*,
'gander'; AS. *gan-et*, Eng. *gannet*, 'sea-
fowl.']

hatá, *see* 954d.

hatya, *n.* slaying. [√han, 1213c and a
(middle), cf. 954d.]

√ **han** (**hánti** [637]; **jaghána** [794d];
hanisyáti; **hatá** [954d]; **hántum**; **hatvá**;
-hátya; **hanyáte**; **jíghaṅsati** [1028f]).
—1. strike; strike down; smite *or* slay,
70[2], etc.; kill, 28[6], 35[14], etc.; overcome;
—2. destroy, 37[19]; bring to nought; (of
darkness) dispel, 18[8]; —*desid.* wish to
smite *or* afflict, 78[16];
—**hatá**, —1. smitten, slain, 98[4]; killed,
23[21]; —2. destroyed, ruined; lost, 27[13],
42[1]; —3. pounded.

[with **hán-mi**, cf. θείνω, •θεν-jω, 'smite';
w. **ja-ghn-ús**, cf. ἐ-πε-φν-ον, 'slew'; w.
hatá, •**ghata**, cf. φατός, 'slain'; w. **ghaná**,
q.v., 'a slaying,' cf. φόνος, 'slaughter'; w.
ha-ti, 'a smiting, slaying,' cf. Old High
Ger. *gun-d*, AS. *gŭð*, •*gun-ð*, 'battle'; AS.
gŭð-fana, Old High Ger. *gund-fano*, 'battle-
flag'; fr. the last form (not fr. the AS.),
through the French, comes Eng. *gonfanon,
gonfalon*; for mg of *gŭð*, cf. Ger. *schlagen*,
'smite, slay,' with *Schlacht*, 'battle': for
senses under 1, observe that AS. *sleán*
(whence Eng. *slay*) means 'smite' and
then also 'slay.']

+**ava**, strike down; bring to nought.

+**ā**, strike upon; hurl (a bolt) upon (*loc.*

w. adhi); *mid.* strike (one's thigh with one's hand).

+ ud, force up; uddhata [163], raised.

+ ni, strike down; slay.

+ pari, strike around; encompass.

+ prati, strike back at (*acc.*); strike against so as to transfix, to broach (on a lance, *loc.*).

+ sam, strike together; (of the eyes) close; unite, combine.

hán [402], *vbl.* slaying, slayer, *in cpds.* [√han.]

hánta, *interjection.* come! go to!

hantavya, *grdv.* to be slain, occidendus. [√han, 964.]

hantṛ, *m.* slayer, destroyer. [√han.]

√ har (háryati, -te). be gratified, take pleasure; take pleasure in (*acc.*), *and so,* desire, long for. [perhaps a transfer (see 761a and b) from the yá-class, with change of accent, and so properly an irregular pass. to √1 hṛ, 'take' (reg. hriyáte); for the mg, cf. Eng. *be taken,* i.e. 'be charmed,' and hara 2: some take √har as representing Indo-European *ghel* (*ghwel*), and connect it w. θέλω, 'will,' Eng. *will;* cf. also √2 vṛ.]

+ prati, long for, entice.

hara, *a.* —1. taking, receiving; —2. (*like the Eng.* carrying away, taking) charming; —3. carrying off, removing, destroying; *as m.* Hara, the Destroyer, a name of Çiva, 55²¹. [√1 hṛ, see its mgs.]

hárana, *a.* holding. [√1 hṛ, 'hold.']

háras, *n.* grip; *esp.* the seizing *or* devouring power of fire. [√1 hṛ, 'hold.']

hári, *a.* fallow, pale yellow, yellowish; greenish; *as m. du.* (*cf. Eng.* pair of bays, *i.e.* bay horses) the fallow steeds, *esp.* of Indra, his coursers. [√•ghṛ, •hṛ, 'be yellow,' is inferrible, but not quotable: cf. χλω-ρόs, 'greenish-yellow'; χλόη, 'verdure'; Lat. *helus* or *holus* or *olus,* 'greens, vegetables'; *helvus,* 'grayish-yellow'; AS. *geolo,* Eng. *yellow;* also *gol-d* (cf. hiranya).]

harit, *a.* fallow, yellowish; *as f.* fallow mare, *esp.* of the Sun-god. [√•ghṛ •hṛ under hari: 383d 3.]

hárivant, *a.* having fallow steeds; *as m.*

lord of the coursers, *i.e.* Indra, *see* hari. [hári, 1233.]

harmyá, *n.* a strong building; dwelling.

harṣa, *m.* joy. [√hṛṣ.]

halāhala, *m. n.* a certain deadly poison.

háva, *m.* call. [√hū.]

havanī, *f.* sacrificial ladle. [prop. fem. of a substantival nomen agentis, havana, √hu, 1150d, 'the sacrificing' instrument.]

havíṣmant, *a.* having an oblation; *as m.* offerer. [havís, 1235.]

havís, *n.* oblation, which, as gift for the gods, is offered wholly or partly in the fire; *generally,* grain (parched, boiled, as porridge, or as baked cake), milk in divers forms, fat, and — best of all — Soma. [√hu, 1153.]

havyá, *n.* oblation. [prop. grdv., 'offerendum,' √hu, 1213.]

hávya, *grdv.* invocandus. [√hū, 1213a.]

havya-váh [403], *a.* carrying the offering (to the gods); *as m.* oblation-bearer (used of Agni), *selections* lvi., lxvi.

√ has (hásati, -te; jahāsa, jahasé; hasiṣyáti; hasitá; hásitum; hasitvā; -hásya). laugh.

+ pra, laugh out, laugh.

+ vi, laugh out.

hása, *m.* laughter. [√has.]

hásta, *m.* hand; (of an elephant) trunk; (of a tiger) paw; *at end of cpds* [1303² end], having · · in the hand.

hasta-gṛhya, *grd.* taking by the hand.

hasta-grābhá, *a.* grasping the hand. [acct, 1270.]

hastín, *a.* having hands; *w.* mṛgá, the beast with the hand, *i.e.* trunk, Vedic designation of the elephant; *as m.* elephant; Hastin, name of an ancient king. [hásta, q.v.]

hastinápura, *n.* Hastināpura, a town on the Ganges, home of the Kurus, said to have been founded by king Hastin. [cf. pura.]

hasti-rāja, *m.* elephant-king, leader of a herd of elephants.

hasti-snāna, *n.* ablution of an elephant.

√ 1 hā (jíhīte [664]; jahé; áhāsta; hāsyáte; hāná; hātum). move, *intrans..* run away, yield.

√ 2 hā (jáhāti [665]; jahāú; áhāsīt [913];
hāsyáti; hīná [957a]; hátum; hitvā;
-hāya; hīyáte, híyate). — 1. leave, i.e.:
quit; leave in the lurch, 82¹; desert,
86¹⁸; leave behind, 85¹⁵; abandon, cast
off; lay aside, 83¹⁴; relinquish; — 2.
híyate, be forsaken or left behind; fall
short or be deficient; become deficient,
decrease; deteriorate, be lowered, 19⁹;
— hīná: — 1. forsaken; — 2. (like Eng.
abandoned) vicious, low, low-lived, 19⁹;
— 3. at end of cpds, abandoned by · ·,
i.e. destitute of · ·, free from · ·. [cf.
χῆ-ρο-s, '(forsaken) destitute,' χή-ρα,
'widow'; Lat. fa-mes, 'lack, hunger.']
  +pari, — 1. forsake; — 2. pass. be
lacking, decrease; come to an end, see
simple verb.
  +vi, leave; vihāya, passing over.
hā, excl. of pain or astonishment. [1135a.]
hārya, grdv. to be taken away or stolen.
  [√1 hṛ, 'seize,' 963³b.]
hāsin, a. laughing. [√has, 1183³.]
hāsya, grdv. to be laughed at; as n.
laughter; ridicule. [√has, 963³c.]
√ hi (hinóti, hinuté; jighāya; áhāiṣīt;
heṣyáti; hitá). set in motion, drive,
impel.
  +pra, send off or away; deliver over.
hí, particle. — 1. asseverative: surely,
verily, indeed, 18²²·²³, 22²⁰, 23²¹, 28¹⁵,
35²¹, 83¹, etc.; — 2. giving a reason:
because; for, 3¹⁹, etc., 53², 70¹¹; — 3. w.
interrogatives, pray, 11¹, 13¹⁴; — finite verb
accented w. hí [595d], 72¹⁸; hí never at beg.
of sentence.
√ hiṅs (hinásti [696]; jihíṅsa; áhiṅsīt;
hiṅsiṣyáti; hiṅsitá; hiṅsitum; hiṅsitvā;
-híṅsya). hurt, harm, slay. [perhaps,
orig., desid. of √han, see 696.]
hiṅsā, f. a harming, injuring. [√hiṅs,
1149.]
hiṅsrá, a. harming; as m. a savage or
cruel man. [√hiṅs, 1188a.]
hitá, ppl., adj. — 1. put, set; placed; and
so — 2. pregnantly (like Eng. in place, i.e.
'in the right place,' and Ger. gelegen,
'lying aright, i.e. convenient'), fit, convenient, agreeable; yadi tatra te hitam,
if it suits thee there; advantageous, salu-

tary; — 3. as n. welfare, safety. [√1 dhā,
'put,' 954c: -dhita in Veda: cf. θετός,
'set.']
hita-kāma, a. wishing one's welfare,
well-wishing. [see kāma.]
hitecchā, f. desire for the welfare (of
another). [icchā.]
hitopadeça, m. salutary instruction;
Hitopadeça, name of a collection of
fables. [upadeça.]
himá, m. the cold; winter. [the stem
*χιμα, 'winter,' appears in χίμα-ρο-s, lit.
'winter-ling, i.e. a one-winter-old or yearling goat,' named χίμαρος precisely as is
the dialectic Ger. Ein-winter, 'a one-winter-
old goat'; cf. χίμαιρα, 'she-goat, chimera';
see similar names under vatsa: cf. further
-χιμο- in δύσ-χιμο-s, 'very wintry'; Lat.
-himu- in bimus, *bi-himu-s, 'of two winters
or years'; also · χιών, 'snow,' χειμών,
'winter'; Lat. hiems, 'winter.']
hiraṇya, n. gold. [akin w. hari, q.v.]
hiraṇya-garbhá, m. fruit or scion or
child of the gold (i.e. of the golden
egg, 57²), Hiraṇyagarbha or Gold-scion,
name of a cosmogonic power, the personal
Brahmán, 91¹⁶.
√ hiḍ (Vedic forms [Whitney 54, 240³]:
héḷant, héḷamāna; jíhīḷa, jihīḷé hīḷitá;
Epic, héḷamāna). be angry; be incon-
siderate or careless.
hīná, see √2 hā.
√ hu (juhóti, juhuté; juhāva, juhvé;
áhāuṣīt; hoṣyáti; hutá; hótum; hutvā).
pour into the fire, cast into the fire; and
so offer; make oblation even of things
not cast into the fire; hutá: offered; as
n. oblation.
  [orig. *ghu: cf. χέω, *χεϜ-ω, 'pour';
χυ-λό-s, 'liquid, juice'; w. hu-tá, cf.
χυ-τό-s, 'poured'; w. ā-hu-ti, cf. χύ-σι-s,
'a pouring,' Lat. fū-ti-s, 'water-pot';
further, fons, stem font, *fov-ont, 'pouring,' i.e. 'fountain':
  with the extended form *ghud, cf. Lat.
√fud in fund-ere, 'pour,' AS. geōt-an, Ger.
giessen, 'pour'; provincial Eng. gut,
'water-course'; and Eng. gut, w. like
sense, in Gut of Canso.]
  +ā, offer in (loc.); āhuta: offered; laid

in the fire (of a corpse), 84¹²; *as n.* oblation.

huta-homa, *a.* having offered oblation.

hutāça, *m.* fire; the fire-god, Agni. [prop. 'having the oblation as his food,' āça: 1302.]

hutāçana, *m.* fire; the fire-god, Agni. [prop. 'having the oblation as his food,' açana: 1302.]

√ **hū** or **hvā** (hávate *and* huváte, *Vedic; classical,* hváyati, -te [761d2]; juháva, juhuvé; áhvāsīt [912]; hvayiṣyáti, -te [935c]; hūtá; hvátum, hváyitum; hūtvā; -húya). call; call upon; invoke, *esp.* a god [orig. *ghū: w. hū-tá, 'called upon, invoked,' some identify the Goth. stem *gu-þa, gu-da,* 'God,' AS. and Eng. *God.*]

+**ā**, —1. call to *or* hither; summon, invite; —2. *mid.* challenge.

+**upa**, *mid.* —1. call *or* summon to one's self; —2. call encouragingly unto.

hūti, *f.* invocation. [√hū.]

√ **1 hṛ** (hárati, -te; jahára, jahré; áhārṣīt, áhṛṣṭa; hariṣyáti, -te; hṛtá; hártum; hṛtvā; -hṛtya; hriyáte; jíhīrṣati). —1. carry, 102⁵, 104³); hold; —2. carry unto, bring; offer, 105⁹; —3. carry away; remove, 85³; —4. *esp.* take away by violence *or* unlawfully, 46⁴, 53⁷; steal, 30², 67²³, 68⁴, 97⁵,⁹; seize; —5. take lawfully, receive (a gift); come into possession of (as heir), 45⁸,¹⁵; —6. get hold of, 96²³; become master of; —7. (*like Eng.* take) charm, captivate; —8. (carry off, *i.e.* remove, *and so*) destroy. [cf. χείρ, dialectic χέρ-s, 'hand'; εὐ-χερ-ής, 'easy to handle'; Lat. *hir,* 'hand'; *hērēs,* 'heir,' see root, mg 5.]

+**ava**, (carry down, *i.e.*) move down.

+**vy-ava**, move hither and thither, go to work, proceed, act.

+**ā**, —1. bring hither, 34³; fetch; fetch *or* get back, 97¹⁰,¹¹; —2. receive, 47¹²; accept; —3. *used* (*like Eng.* take) *esp.* of food, take, eat; —*desid.* be willing to get back, 97¹⁰.

+**ud-ā**, bring out, *and so* utter, say, tell.

+**praty-ā**, get back again; *at* 11⁶, *incorrect reading for* pra-vy-ā-.

+**vy-ā**, bring out, *and so* utter;

with vācam, speak words to a person (*acc.*), 3¹; *similarly,* 8¹⁹.

+**pra-vy-ā**, utter; speak.

+**ud**, take out.

+**pari**, carry around.

+**pra**, —1. (bring forward, *i.e.* reach out, *e.g.* feet, fists, *and so*) strike, attack, deal blows; —2. throw, *esp.* into the fire.

+**anu-pra**, throw into the fire *or* on a fuel-pile.

+**vi**, —1. take apart, divide; —2. pass (part of one's life), 64²³; —3. pass one's time, *esp.* pleasantly; wander about for pleasure, enjoy one's self, 16⁹,¹², 49¹³; —4. wander about.

+**sam**, bring *or* draw together, contract; withdraw.

+**upa-sam**, bring *or* draw together to one's self, *mid.*; withdraw.

√ **2 hṛ** (hṛṇīté). be angry.

hṛchayá, *a.* lying *or* abiding in the heart [1265]; *as m.* love, 2¹⁹. [hṛd + çaya, 159, 203: acct, 1270.]

hṛchaya-pīḍita, *a.* love-pained, love-sick.

hṛchaya-vardhana, *a.* increasing *or* arousing love.

hṛchayāviṣṭa, *a.* entered by *or* filled with love. [āviṣṭa, √viç, 1085a: acct of cpd, 1273.]

hṛchayāviṣṭacetana, *a.* possessing a love-filled mind. [hṛchayāviṣṭa + cétanā, 1298a, 334².]

hṛd [397], *n.* heart; *esp. as* seat of the emotions and of mental activity in general; *also, properly,* region of the heart. [see under çrad.]

hṛdaya, *n.* heart; —1. *prop.* heart, as an organ of the body, 100²³; —2. *fig.* heart, as seat of the feelings. [see hṛd and 397.]

√ **hṛṣ** (hṛṣyati, -te [761a]; jahárṣa, jahṛṣé; hṛṣitá, hṛṣṭá; -hṛṣya; harṣáyati, -te). be excited, *esp.* with pleasure *or* fear; (of the hair) bristle *or* stand on end by reason of fright *or* pleasure; be impatient; —hṛṣṭa, delighted; —hṛṣitá: (of the hair) standing on end; (of flowers) not drooping, unwithered, fresh; —*intens.* be very impatient, 84¹⁷; —*caus.* excite pleasantly, gladden. [for ghṛṣ: cf. Lat. *horr-ēre*, *⁎hors-ere*, 'bristle, shudder'; *hirsūtus*, 'bristly, rough'; *hor-deum*, Ger. *Gers-te*, 'barley,' so called from its bristly ears.] + **pra**, give one's self up to joy, exult; prahṛṣṭa, delighted, glad.

hṛṣitasragrajohīna, *a.* having unwithered garlands and free from dust. [hṛṣita-sraj + rajo-hīna, 1257.]

hetú, *m.* —1. *prop.* an impeller, *and so* occasioner, causer, occasion, cause; hetos, (*like Lat.* causā) on account of; trāsa-hetos, from fear; —2. reason, argument, proof; —3. means, 41¹⁶. [√hi, 1161a.]

hetu-çãstra, *n.* reason-book, rationalistic work; dialectics.

hema *or* heman, *n.* gold.

hemantá, *m.* winter. [cf. hima: 1172⁴.]

helã, *f.* carelessness; levity. [for heḷā, from √hīḍ, q.v.]

hāima, *a.* golden. [hema, 1208f.]

hótṛ, *m.* —1. priest, chief priest, whose assistant in oldest times was the adhvaryu; Agni, as the chiefest hotṛ, 69², 88⁶; —2. *in the highly developed ritual,* the first of the four chief priests, *see* ṛtvij. [*prop.* 'offerer,' from √hu, 'offer': but the sense of 'invoker,' naturally suggested by his function in the ritual, was popularly associated with it and the word thus connected with √hū, 'invoke.']

hotrá, *n.* offering, sacrifice, *both* the action *and* the thing offered. [√hu, 1185a.]

hóma, *m.* a pouring into the fire; oblation;

sacrifice; *observe that the older word is* āhuti. [√hu, 1166.]

hradá, *m.* pool, lake. [cf. √hlãd.]

√ hras (hrásati, -te; hrasitá, hrastá; hrāsáyati). become less; *caus.* diminish. [w. hrás-īyãṅs, 'less,' cf. χείρων, *⁎χέροιων*, 'worse,' and for the mg, cf. Lat. *dētero*, 'lessen,' w. *dēterior*, 'worse.']

√ hrãd (hrádate; hrãditá; hrādáyati). sound (of drums); rattle (of stones *or* dry bones). [for *⁎ghrad*: cf. καχλάζω, *⁎κα-χλάδ-jω*, 'sound' (of liquids, breakers, rain), κε-χλãδ-ώς, 'resounding' (song of victory); AS. *grǣt-an*, obsolete Eng. *greet*, 'cry, lament'; χαρδã-ρα, 'noisy mountain torrent': see hrãduni.] + **sam**, strike (*intrans.*) together so as to rattle; *caus.* cause to rattle.

hrãduni, *f.* hail-stones, hail. [so called from its rattling sound, √hrãd: cf. χάλαζα, *⁎χαλαδ-ja*, Church Slavonic *gradŭ*, Lat. *grando*, stem *grand-in*, 'hail.']

√ hlãd (hlãdate; hlãdáyati, -te). cool off, *intrans.*, refresh one's self; *caus.* cool *or* refresh, *trans.*

hlãdaka, *f.* -ikã, *a.* cooling, refreshing. [√hlãd, 1181 and a⁸.]

hlãdikãvant, *a.* rich in cooling. [from *fem.* of hlãdaka, substantively?]

√ hvṛ (hvárati, -te; āhvārṣīt; hvṛtá; hvāráyati). go crookedly; bend over, fall. + **vi**, fall; *caus.* overturn.

EXPLANATIONS AND ABBREVIATIONS.

CITATIONS.

All numbers below 107 refer to the text of this Reader, which is cited by page and line; thus, 79² means page 79, line 2. When still more precise reference is needed, the first half of a line is designated by ᵃ and the second by ᵇ.

All numbers above 107 refer to the sections of Whitney's Grammar. Observe, however, that reference is occasionally made to grammar-sections preceding § 107, and that the word "Whitney" is then prefixed to the number to show that the Grammar is meant. The grammar-sections sometimes have subdivisions unmarked by letters or numbers. In referring to these, a small superior number is used, and designates the (typographical) paragraph as counted from the last lettered or numbered subsection. Thus 330⁶ refers to the paragraph beginning "Pl.: nom.-voc. masc."; 371¹² begins with "From stf come"; 1222⁸, with "The accent of derivatives"; 1222c2², with "In the Brāhmaṇas."

SIGNS.

The root-sign (√) is prefixed to roots and quasi-roots to catch the eye or as an abbreviation. It is also set before denominative verb-stems, although these are of course in no sense roots.

The plus-sign (+) is set before prepositions with which verbs appear in composition and before certain other elements used as prefixes.

A star (∗) signifies that the word or stem or root to which it is prefixed does not actually occur in that form.

A half-parenthesis on its side (‿) is used to show that two vowels, which, for the sake of clearness, are printed with hiatus in violation of the rules of euphonic combination, should be combined according to those rules.

A hyphen is sometimes used to avoid the repetition of an element of a compound; thus in the article loka, p. 235, para- stands for para-loka.

In Greek words, the old palatal spirant yod is represented by j, pronounced of course as English y. A very few Slavic and Lithuanian words occur, in which the actual or original nasalization of a vowel is denoted by an inverted comma, thus, ę, ą. Anglo-Saxon æ has the sound of a in man.

ABBREVIATIONS.

It is hoped that most of these, if not all, will be found self-explaining. To preclude any misunderstanding, however, a complete list of the abbreviations is given below, p. 293.

But certain abbreviations and words are used in an arbitrary way and require more explanation than is given in the list.

When both the letters, m. and n., follow a stem, they mean that it shows both masculine and neuter case-forms.

19

An "etc." following a reference that stands after a certain definition signifies that the word is of common occurrence in that meaning.

The abbreviation [do.] is used to avoid repetition of identical items in the square brackets at the end of articles; for examples, see the three words following abhivāda, p. 119.

The etymological cognates are usually introduced by the conventional "cf."; this implies that the words which the reader is bidden to "compare" are akin. The fact that two related words are compared implies as a rule only that they are radically akin, and not that their formative suffixes are identical. Thus with anta is compared English *end*, although this corresponds strictly only to the Sanskrit secondary derivative antya. So asthan, ὀστέον, and *os* are radically identical, though not of entirely parallel formation.

On the other hand, where it is desired to call attention, not to radically kindred words, but to words analogous only in metaphor or in transfer of meaning, the brief phrase, "for mg, cf.," is used; and this is to be understood as standing for the phrase, "for a parallelism in the development of meaning, compare," or, "for an analogous instance of transition of meaning, compare."

Specially important references to the Grammar are marked by the word "see": thus under nārāyaṇá (p. 181), special attention is called to § 1219, which shows that this word is a simple patronymic of nára, and is not what the text (at 57⁶) says it is, a compound of nārá + áyana.

GENERAL ARRANGEMENT OF THE VOCABULARY.

The order of the articles is strictly and solely alphabetical (see below). Respecting words whose alphabetic place changes with their inflection, the following remarks may be made for beginners.

All nouns, whether they be substantives or adjectives, are given under the stem. In order to know the stem, a preliminary study of the more important paradigms and rules of euphonic combination is necessary. Thus the nom. sing. rājā must be looked for under rājan, and the acc. sing. nāma under nāman (Whitney, 424); but nalo, as standing for nala-s (175a, 330), must be looked for under nala. The stems in ṛ or ar are entered in the form ṛ. The stems of the perf. act. ppl. and of the primary comparatives are given as ending in vāṅs and yāṅs. The stems in at or ant are given in the fuller form, ant, and similarly those in mant and vant; and the feminines of these and of the in-stems are not given, since they are always made in antī or atī, matī, vatī, inī.

All verb-forms must be sought under the root. Thus āsīt will be defined only under the root 1 as (636), and not in the alphabetic place which the augment gives it, under long ā. Likewise prepositional compounds of verbs will be found under the roots (see 1076), and not in the alphabetic place under the preposition. The beginner is advised to make himself thoroughly familiar with the list of prepositions (1077) at the outset.

Of the verbal adjectives and nouns (Whitney, chapter xiii., p. 307 ff.), only the gerundives (in ya, tavya, and anīya) have been given regularly in alphabetic place. The participles in ta and na are usually given under the roots; but in some cases, where they have assumed a distinctly adjectival or substantival coloring or have an inconveniently large variety of meanings and uses, they are treated at length in alphabetic place; such, for example, are ṛta, kṛta, gata, jāta, nivṛtta, bhūta, sthita, hita, etc. Gerunds with a- or su- (e.g. a-citvā) are of course treated in alphabetic place.

Such adverbs as are merely case-forms of substantive or adjective stems, are generally to be sought for under those stems. Those from pronominal stems (e.g. kim, tad, yad) receive separate treatment.

The pronouns of the first and second person would require a dozen different articles apiece if all their forms were given alphabetically. The same is true to a greater or less extent of the other pronouns. The student should therefore learn, as early as possible, the forms given at 491, 495, 499b, 501 (especially ayam: asāu is less important), 504, and 509. The uses of sa-s, etc., eṣa-s, etc., and ayam, etc., are given under ta, etad, and idam respectively.

As for compounds, they are given with completeness for the Vedic selections, and with great freedom for the remaining texts, especially for the Nala. The meaning of such as are lacking can be easily learned by looking out their component parts.

THE ALPHABETIC ORDER.

The order of the letters is given by Whitney at § 5 (compare § 7); but several matters which are frequent occasions of stumbling, may be noticed here.

The *visarga* has the first place after the vowels. Thus antaḥ-pura (for antar + pura) stands next after anta, p. 116, and not after antardhāna. But the *visarga* which is regarded as equivalent to a sibilant and exchangeable with it (Whitney, 7[2]), stands in the alphabetic place of the sibilant. Thus the *visarga* of adhaḥ-çāyin, as equivalent to ç (172), brings this word just before adhas (p. 115, top), and not between adha and adhanya.

The sign ṅ, as representing "the *anusvāra* of more independent origin" (Whitney, 73[8]), has its place before all the mutes etc. (Whitney, 5). Thus in aṅç-a, the ṅ represents a nasalization of the radical vowel, and the word comes immediately after a. So haṅsa comes just after ha, p. 284; daṅç and daṅṣṭrin, at the beginning of the letter d.

The sign ṁ, as representing an assimilated m, is differently placed, according to its phonetic value. On the one hand, if ṁ, as product of a m assimilated to a semivowel, sibilant, or h (see 213c, d), represent a nasal semivowel or *anusvāra*, then its place is like that of ṅ. Thus saṁyatendriya follows sa, and saṁhita comes just before sakacchapa (p. 263), and puṁs before puṭa (p. 191).

On the other hand, if, for instance, as product of a m assimilated to a guttural, the sign ṁ represent guttural ñ, then its place is that of ñ; and a similar rule applies to all the other cases under 213b. Thus saṁkaṭa and saṁkalpa follow sagara, and saṁgama follows saṅga, p. 264; so saṁcaya (whose ṁ = ñ) follows sajya; and saṁtati (whose ṁ = n) follows sant, p. 266.

Vedic ḷ is placed after ḍ, and ḷh after ḍh.

THE CONTENTS OF THE SEPARATE ARTICLES.

Homonyms, unless differentiated by accent, are distinguished by a prefixed number (cf. aṅga, vayas); similarly homonymous roots (cf. kṛ).

References to the Grammar in square brackets *immediately after* a declinable stem refer to some peculiarity of declension. Occasionally, typical cases of stems are given. Thus under dṛç are given the nom. and acc. sing. and instr. dual; from these, the other cases (dṛk-ṣu, dṛç-ā, etc., dṛg-bhis, etc.) are easily known.

Each root is followed by a synopsis of its conjugational forms, so far as they actually occur in the literature. The finite forms are given in the third person singular of the indicative, and in the order in which they are treated in the Grammar, namely, present, perfect, aorist, and future; then follow the past participle, the infinitive, and the two gerunds (e.g. āptá, āptum; āptvá, -ápya: observe the alternation of the accents); then follow in order the third sing. present indicative of the passive, intensive, desiderative, and causative, so far as they seemed of importance for the users of this Reader.

19*

Meanings which are synonymous or nearly so, are separated by commas; those which differ considerably from each other, are separated by semicolons or by full-faced dashes and figures (−1., etc.). The colon is often used to show that several meanings which follow it and are separated by semicolons are co-ordinate with each other. Thus on p. 268, under samīpa − 2b., the meanings "before," "near," "hard by," and "by" are co-ordinate, and are equivalent to "in the presence or neighborhood of"; cf. suvarcas.

The arrangement for matter in heavy brackets at the end of articles is: in the case of primary derivatives, first, the root from which the word comes, with reference, if necessary, to the section giving the suffix of derivation; second, cognate words from allied languages; and third, words showing a development of meaning analogous to that shown by the Sanskrit word or illustrative of it. If the derivation of a simple word is not given, it is because it is unknown or too uncertain to be worth mentioning. In the case of secondary derivatives, the primary is given, with a reference to the section showing its treatment. The analysis of compounds is often indicated by a hyphen; but if one member ends and the next begins with a vowel or diphthong, the latter member is given in square brackets at the end of the article; cf. nalopākhyāna.

Where words of different languages are given together, separated only by commas, the definition given after the last applies to them all; or, if no definition is given, the English word in italics at the end is both a cognate and a definition of all at the same time; for examples, see ákṣa ('axle'), aṣṭa, ūrṇa.

The references to the Grammar may seem too numerous; but they are really a device for avoiding the frequent repetition of explanations which would otherwise have to be given in full. It would take half a dozen lines to explain the etymology of manmatha, for instance; but the references to 1148.4 and 1002b make this needless; cf. the references under daridra, çiçu, sunva.

It often happens that the statement in the section referred to does not directly cover the point aimed at in citing it; but a moment's thought will show what is meant. Thus under saṁkrānti, the two references to be compared mean that the derivative suffix is ti, and that before it the root-vowel suffers the same peculiar change that is seen in the past participle. Under saṁyatendriya reference is made to 1298, which states that possessive descriptives "are very much more common than [simple] descriptives of the same form." The real point of the reference is plainly, not to bring out this fact, but to show the beginner in what category of compounds this word belongs. So 1290 states that "other compounds with adverbial prior members are quite irregularly accented"; but the section is cited, e.g., under sadha-māda, to indicate that this is a descriptive compound (see the heading of the preceding right-hand page, 441) in which the first member is an adverbial element with the function (cf. 1289) of an adjective. Many roots form verb-stems in aya, but without causative signification; this is briefly indicated by the reference 1041². In the case of secondary derivatives in vant, mant, tā, and tva, a simple reference to one of the sections treating of these endings (1233, 1235, 1237, 1239) is put instead of a repetition of the primitive.

LIST OF ABBREVIATIONS.

—◦◦◦—

a.	adjective.	inf	infinitive.
abl.	ablative.	instr.	instrumental.
acc.	accusative.	intens.	intensive.
acct	accent.	interr.	interrogative.
act.	active, actively.	intrans.	intransitive, intransitively.
adj.	adjective, adjectively.	irreg.	irregularly, irregular.
adv.	adverb, adverbial.	Lat.	Latin.
advly	adverbially.	lit.	literally, literal.
aor.	aorist.	loc.	locative.
AS.	Anglo-Saxon.	m., masc. . . .	masculine.
assev.	asseverative.	MBh.	Mahābhārata.
B.	Brāhmaṇa.	met.	metaphorically, metaphor.
beg.	beginning.	mg, mgs	meaning, meanings.
caus.	causative.	mid.	middle.
cf.	compare.	N.	note.
colloq.	colloquial.	n., neut.	neuter.
comp.	comparative.	nom.	nominative.
conj.	conjunction.	num.	numeral.
correl.	correlative.	opp.	opposed, opposite.
cpd, cpds . . .	compound, compounds.	opt.	optative.
dat.	dative.	orig.	originally, original.
denom.	denominative.	pass.	passive, passively.
deriv., derivs .	derivative, derivatives.	pcl.	particle.
desid.	desiderative.	perf.	perfect.
e.g.	for example.	pers.	person, personal.
encl.	enclitic.	pl.	plural.
Eng.	English.	poss.	possibly.
equiv.	equivalent.	ppl.	participle.
esp.	especially, especial.	prep.	preposition.
etc.	and so forth.	pres.	present.
excl.	exclamation.	prob.	probably, probable.
f., fem.	feminine.	pron.	pronoun, pronominal.
ff.	and the following.	prop.	properly.
fig.	figuratively, figurative.	q.v.	which see.
fr.	from.	reg.	regularly, regular.
fut.	future.	RV.	Rigveda.
gen.	genitive.	S.	Sūtra.
Ger.	German.	s.	singular.
Goth.	Gothic.	sc.	scilicet.
grd	gerund.	sing.	singular.
grdv.	gerundive.	Skt.	Sanskrit.
Hdt.	Herodotus.	subst.	substantive, substantively.
ident.	identical.	superl.	superlative.
i.e.	that is.	s.v.	sub voce.
imf.	imperfect.	trans.	transitive, transitively.
impers.	impersonally, impersonal.	U.f.	uncombined form or forms.
imv.	imperative.	vbl	verbal.
ind.	indicative.	V.	Vedic, Veda.
indecl.	indeclinable.	voc.	vocative.
indef.	indefinite.	w.	with.

For abbreviations of titles, see next page.

ABBREVIATIONS OF TITLES.

See also pages 315-16, 332, 340, 359, 398, 402.

RV.	. . . . Rigveda Saṁhitā.	AB.	. . . . Āitareya Brāhmaṇa.
SV.	. . . . Sāmaveda "	ÇB.	. . . . Çatapatha "
AV.	. . . . Atharvaveda "	PB.	. . . . Pañcaviñça or Tāṇḍya Br.
MS.	. . . . Māitrāyaṇi "	TA.	. . . . Tāittirīya Āraṇyaka.
TS.	. . . . Tāittirīya "	AGS.	. . . Açvalāyana Gṛhya-sūtra.
VS.	. . . . Vājasaneyi "	ÇGS.	. . . Çāṅkhāyana "
K.	. . . . Kāṭhaka.	PGS.	. . . Pāraskara "

JASB. . . . Journal of the Asiatic Society of Bengal.
JA. . . . . . Journal Asiatique.
JRAS. . . . Journal of the Royal Asiatic Society.
JAOS. . . . Journal of the American Oriental Society.
PAOS. . . . Proceedings " " "
ZDMG. . . . Zeitschrift der Deutschen Morgenländischen Gesellschaft.

AJP. . . . . American Journal of Philology — ed. B. L. Gildersleeve.
Ind. Ant. . . Indian Antiquary — ed. James Burgess.
ISt. . . . . . Indische Studien — ed. Albrecht Weber.
KZ. . . . . . Zeitschrift für vergleichende Sprachforschung — ed. A. Kuhn.

ASL. . . . . History of Ancient Sanskrit Literature, by Max Müller.
BI. . . . . . Bibliotheca Indica — publ. by the Asiatic Society of Bengal.
BR. . . . . . Böhtlingk and Roth's Sanskrit-Wörterbuch — see *Brief List*, p. xviii, no. 5.
GKR. . . . . Geldner, Kaegi, and Roth's Siebenzig Lieder — see p. xix, no. 15.
HIL. . . . . History of Indian Literature, Weber — see p. xx, no. 21.
IA. . . . . . Indische Alterthumskunde, by Christian Lassen.
ILuC. . . . . Indiens Literatur und Cultur, Schroeder — see p. 359, § 100.
OLSt. . . . . Oriental and Linguistic Studies, Whitney — see p. 359, § 100.
VP. . . . . . Viṣṇu Purāṇa — Bombay text; or Wilson's translation, ed. 1 or ed. 2 (F. Hall).

SBE. . . . . Sacred Books of the East — transl. by various scholars and ed. F. Max Müller.

Vol.		Vol.	
i.	Upaniṣads. 1.	xv.	Upaniṣads. 2.
ii.	Laws. 1. Apastamba, Gāutama.	xxiii.	Avesta. 2. Yashts, etc.
iv.	Avesta. 1. Vendidād.	xxv.	Manu.
vii.	Laws. Viṣṇu.	xxvi.	Çatapatha Brāhmaṇa. 2.
x.	Dhammapada, etc.	xxix.	Gṛhya-sūtras. 1. ÇGS., AGS., PGS.
xii.	Çatapatha Brāhmaṇa. 1. See p. 356, N.9.	xxx.	Gṛhya-sūtras. 2.
xiv.	Laws. 2. Vasiṣṭha, Bāudhāyana.	xxxi.	Avesta. 3. Yasna, etc.

Bergaigne . La religion védique — see p. 359, § 100.
Kaegi . . . . Der Rigveda — see p. 352, § 70.
Ludwig . . . Der Rigveda — see p. 359, § 100.
Muir . . . . Original Sanskrit Texts — see p. xx, no. 26.
Si-yu-ki . . . Buddhist Records of the Western World. Transl. by S. Beal, London, 1884.
Zimmer. . . Altindisches Leben — see p. xx, no. 22.

The Vocabulary will often serve as an index to the Notes.

PART III.

NOTES.

SELECTION I.

The Story of Nala and Damayantī.

§ 1. The trend of Aryan migration in India has been from the extreme north-west to the south-east, across the region drained by the Indus and its affluents, and called the Panjāb or Land of the Five Rivers; and again south-east, down the valleys of the Jumna and Ganges. One prominent group of Aryan immigrant tribes was that of the Kosalas, Videhas, and Magadhas, who settled in the *lower* valley of the Ganges, *east* of its confluence with the Jumna, in the districts now named Oudh and Behar, the Palestine of Buddhism.

§ 2. Another group of tribes had their home on the upper Indus, in the north-west of the Panjāb. Theirs was the religion and civilization of which the Vedas are the monument. Later we find them advancing south-eastward, and establishing themselves on the *upper* course of the Jumna and Ganges, in Madhya-deça, The Mid-Land. Foremost among them are the tribes of the Bhāratas, the Kurus, and the Panchālas. Here arose the system of Brahmanism; here the simple nature-religion of the Vedas developed into a religion of priests and sacrifices; here the Bhāratas attained a kind of religious primacy and the lustre of a great name, although gradually merging their tribal individuality with that of kindred tribes; here were fought the battles of the Bhāratas; and here, to ever-ready listeners, in school or forest-hermitage, at a sacrifice or a burial, were told the tales of these battles and their heroes. These are the tales that form the nucleus of the Great-Bhārata-Story (mahā-bhārata_ākhyāna, or, more briefly), the Mahā-bhārata.

§ 3. These tales were probably first circulated in prose, until some more clever teller put them into simple and easily-remembered metrical form. The date of these first simple epics we do not know. They may well have existed several centuries before our era; but neither their language nor the notices of the Greeks afford any satisfactorily direct evidence upon the subject. Around this nucleus have been grouped additions, — historical, mythological, and didactic, — until the Great-Bhārata, as we now have it, contains over one hundred thousand distichs, or about eight times as much as the Iliad and Odyssey together.

§ 4. Only about one-fifth of the whole poem is occupied with the principal story. This, in the briefest possible summary, is as follows. The two brothers, Dhritarāshtra and Pāndu (dhṛta-rāṣṭra, pāṇḍu), were brought up in their royal home of Hastinā-pura, about sixty miles north-east of modern Delhi. Dhritarāshtra, the elder, was blind, and so Pāndu became king, and had a glorious reign. He had five sons, chief of whom were Yudhishthira, Bhīma, and Arjuna. They are called Pāndavas, and are the types of honor and heroism. Dhritarāshtra's hundred sons, Duryodhana and the rest, are usually called the Kuru princes, and are represented as in every way bad. After Pāndu's death, his sons are brought up with their cousins. The kingdom devolved on Dhritarāshtra, who in turn made his nephew Yudhishthira the heir apparent.

§ 5. Yudhishthira's exploits aroused the ill-will of his cousins, and, to escape their plots, the Pāndu princes went away to the king of Panchāla, whose daughter, Draupadī, became their common wife. In view of this strong alliance with the Panchālas, Dhritarāshtra thought it best to conciliate the Pāndus. So he divided the kingdom, and gave Hastinā-pura to his sons, and to his nephews a district to the south-west, where they built Indra-prastha, the modern Delhi. Here the Pāndavas and their people lived happily under king Yudhishthira.

§ 6. On one occasion Dhritarāshtra held a great assembly of princes at his capital. The Pāndavas were invited and came. Yudhishthira was challenged to play with Duryodhana, and accepted. The dice were thrown for Duryodhana by his uncle Çakuni. Yudhishthira loses everything — wealth, kingdom, brothers, wife. A compromise, however, is made, by which the Pāndavas give up their part of the kingdom for twelve years, and agree to remain incognito for a thirteenth. With Draupadī, they retire to the Kāmyaka forest, on the Saraswatī.

§ 7. For twelve years the Pāndu princes dwell in the wood. Many legends are told to divert and console them in their exile; and these stories, with the description of the forest-life of the princes, combine to make up the third or 'Forest-book,' the **vana-parvan**, which is one of the longest in the whole poem.

§ 8. The thirteenth year arrived and passed. "Then in the fourteenth the Pāndavas demanded back their possessions, but received them not. From this arose the conflict. They overthrew the ruling house, slew prince Duryodhana, and then, although losing most of their warriors, they got back again their kingdom." MBh. i.61.51=2280. Thus ended the Bhārata, doubtless, in its oldest and simplest form.

§ 9. The poem, as we now have it, spins out the story of the combat through several books and through thousands of distichs. At length Yudhishthira is crowned in Hastinā-pura, and Bhishma, the leader of the Kurus, although mortally wounded, instructs him, for about twenty thousand distichs, on the duties of kings and on other topics, and then dies. In the seventeenth book, the Pāndus renounce the kingdom, and in the next, the last, they ascend to heaven with Draupadī.

§ 10. The Nala-episode illustrates very well how loose is the connection of the episodes in general with the main thread of the Bhārata. The story of Nala is one of those inserted in the third book (above, § 7), and its setting is as follows. Arjuna had gone to the heaven of Indra to get from him divine weapons. The other Pāndavas, remaining in the forest with Draupadī, lament their brother's absence and the loss of their kingdom. Meantime the fierce and stout-armed Bhīma addresses his brother Yudhishthira, and offers to go out and slay their deceitful cousins. Yudhishthira counsels Bhīma to wait till after the thirteenth year, and is trying to calm his impetuous brother, when suddenly there arrives a mighty sage, Brihadaçwa. The holy man is received with honor and with the customary guest's-dish of milk and honey. When he is seated, Yudhishthira sits by him, bewails his sad lot, and asks, " Hast thou ever seen or heard of a man more luckless than I am ? I believe there never was one more unhappy." " On this point," replies the sage, " I will tell thee a story of a king who was even more luckless than thou. King Nala was once cheated out of his kingdom by a false dice-player, and dwelt in the forest, and neither slaves, chariot, brother, nor friend was left him; but thou art surrounded by heroes, brothers, and friends, and oughtest not to grieve." Thereupon Yudhishthira begs him to relate the story at length. Accordingly, to console the king, and to show him that there is hope of regaining his kingdom, just as Nala regained his, Brihadaçwa begins as in the extract given in the Reader (1³).

§ 11. CHAPTER 1. Nala was a prince of Nishadha. Damayanti was the lovely daughter of Bhima, the king of Vidarbha. By the miraculous interposition of swans, the prince and princess become mutually enamored.

§ 12. CHAP. 2. Bhima accordingly holds a swayamvara ('self-choice') for her. The neighboring kings are invited, and she is permitted to choose for herself her husband from them. The chief gods hear of it and determine to go also. On their way, they meet Nala, who is bound on the same errand.

§ 13. CHAP. 3. The gods request Nala to sue for them. Reluctantly consenting, he enters the chamber of the princess and tells how the gods desire her hand.

§ 14. CHAP. 4. Damayanti refuses to listen to the arguments in favor of the gods. She desires that the swayamvara be held in the usual form, and that the gods be present, and informs Nala that she intends to show openly her preference for him. All this Nala reports to the gods.

§ 15. CHAP. 5. The gods and kings assemble. The four chief gods assume the appearance of Nala. Unable to distinguish the real Nala, the princess, distressed, prays to the gods, and they, in answer, resume their proper forms and peculiar attributes (see 14 ¹² N.). Thereupon she chooses Nala. The kings express their sorrow, and the gods their delight. The gods give Nala the magic power of having fire and water whenever he wishes, and a wonderful skill in cookery. The wedding-feast is celebrated. Nala returns to Nishadha with his bride. They live happily, and have a son and daughter. — Here the extract in the Reader ends.

§ 16. CHAPTERS 6–26. These tell of Nala's misfortunes, and their final happy issue. He loses everything, even his kingdom, by gambling, and wanders, hungry and half naked, in the forest. He is transformed into a dwarf, and becomes charioteer of Rituparna, king of Oudh. Damayanti, at her father's in Kundina, is led by certain tidings to suspect that Nala is at Oudh. By way of stratagem, she holds out hopes of her hand to Rituparna, if he will drive from Oudh to Kundina, some five hundred miles, in a single day, knowing well that only Nala's skill in horsemanship (see 1⁴) is equal to this task. Rituparna gets Nala to drive him thither through the air. Nala receives as reward perfect skill in dicing. His wife recognizes him by his magical command of fire and water, and by his cooking. He resumes his true form, plays again, and wins back all he had lost, and lives happy ever after.*

§ 17. When Brihadaçwa had finished the story of Nala, Yudhishthira, pleased, asked him for perfect skill in dicing; and the hermit, granting him his prayer, departed.

§ 18. This story is unquestionably one of the oldest and most beautiful episodes of the Mahā-bhārata. It was extremely popular in India; and to this is due the fact that it escaped the bad influence of Vishnuism, whose adherents have worked over the vast epic, changing and interpolating, and always for the worse.

* The student may read the entire story in any of the numerous translations — by Milman, Bopp, Rückert, and others. The most easily obtained is the very spirited English rendering of Edwin Arnold, in his *Indian Idylls*, Boston, Roberts Brothers, 1883, $1.00.

§ 19. Even the Nala, especially in the first chapter, has suffered much from later hands; but on the whole it is one of the least corrupted episodes. Its antiquity is shown by the simplicity of manners implied in its incidents — the prince, for example, cooks his own food, — by the character of Indra (cf. 14²¹ N.), and in other ways. See Holtzmann's *Indische Sagen*, Stuttgart, 1854, p. xiv. Bruce has attempted to reject definite passages throughout the poem, and has published, at St. Petersburg in 1862, a text of the Nala, reduced from 983 to 522 distichs.

§ 20. The story begins at iii.53.1 (folio 58 b) of the Bombay edition of 1877, and at iii. 2072 of the Calcutta edition of 1834.

§ 21. THE METRE. The stanza (çloka) or distich consists of four octosyllabic verses (pāda). The first and second pādas form together a half-çloka or a line, divided at the middle by the caesura: likewise the third and fourth. The more important rules follow.

a. Odd pādas end usually with a first epitrite, $\cup$ _ _ _, or antispast, $\cup$ _ _ $\cup$.

b. Even pādas end in a diiambus, $\cup$ _ $\cup$ _, or second paeon, $\cup$ _ $\cup$ $\cup$.

So the type of the half-çloka is $\circ \circ \circ \circ | \cup$ _ _ $\vee \| \circ \circ \circ \circ | \cup$ _ $\cup \vee$. **But**

c. In no pāda may the syllables 2, 3, 4 form a tribrach, $\cup \cup \cup$, or anapaest, $\cup \cup$ _ ;

d. Nor, in the even pādas, an amphimacer, _ $\cup$ _.

NOTES TO PAGE 1.

LINE 1. atha, see p. 114, s.v. atha 3. —nalopākhyāna-m, nom.s.n. (see 330) of nalopākhyāna: this last is a compound stem, see s.v., p. 180: its analysis is indicated in the manner mentioned at p. 292, paragraph 2, end: the second member is upākhyāna, as given in the square brackets, p. 180: its initial, u, has evidently combined with the final vowel of the first member to o: according to the important rule 127, that final must have been an *a*-vowel (a or ā), and, since there is no stem nalā, the first member must be nala: since this logically determines the second member, i.e. distinguishes the 'Nala-episode' from all other episodes, the compound is to be classed as a determinative, see 1262.

2. bṛhadaçva, u.f. bṛhadaçva-s (175b), nom.s.m. of bṛhád-açva, see s.v., p. 202: as shown in the square brackets, the first member of the cpd is bṛhánt, which, by 1249a, enters into composition in its weak form bṛhát: by the law of regressive assimilation (159, the most important rule of Sanskrit phonetics), the t becomes d. The combination bṛhad-açvá, with the accent on the ultima, means 'a great hórse'; the same

combination, with the acct of the prior member, is a secondary adjective cpd, and means 'having great horses': here the secondary adjective is used as a substantive, '(man) having great horses, i.e. Gre*át*-horse': see 1293² and cf. the difference between *a great heárt* and Bunyan's *Mr. Greát-heart*. For the ligature çv, see Whitney 13⁶. —uvāca, √vac, p. 236, perf. act. 3d sing., see 800e. —For the connection of this line with the story, see p. 298, § 10.

3ª. āsīd, u.f. āsīt, by the law of regressive assimilation, just mentioned: as was said at p. 290, paragraph 8, the meaning must be sought under √1 as, p. 122: the form is imf. 3d sing., 636. —rājā, see p. 290, paragraph 7, and for declension, 424. —nalo, u.f. nala-s, 175a: declension, 330. Nominatives in as are extremely common, and so of course is the change of as to o. —nāma, acc.s.n. (424) of nāman, see s.v. 3.

3ᵇ. vīrasena-suto, u.f. -suta-s, 175a: the word is a dependent noun-cpd and = vīrasenasya sutas, see 1264: the stem vīrásena (see s.v.) is itself also a cpd, and of the same kind as bṛhád-açva. —balī, see 440.

4ᵃ. upapanno, u.f. upa-panna-s (175a), √pad+upa, p. 186. As a prepositional cpd, this must be sought under the root, not under the preposition — read p. 290, paragraph 8. For the form panna, see 957d : lit., it has only an indefinite past sense, not a passive sense, see 952². —guṇāir, u.f. guṇāis, 174 : declension, 330. —iṣṭāi, u.f. iṣṭāis, which becomes iṣṭāir (174 again) before the following sonant initial; and since this is r, the final r is dropped — see 179: iṣ-ṭá is ppl. of √1 iṣ, 953: the t of ta becomes ṭ by progressive assimilation (197), which is far less common than regressive assimilation. —The half-line means, 'endowed with (desired, i.e. desirable or) excellent virtues.' For the use of the instr., see 278.

4ᵇ. rūpavān, see 452 and 453, and cf. 447. For rū, cf. Whitney 10d. —açvakovidaḥ, u.f. açvakovidas, 170a, an extremely common change. Nala's skill in the manege is a point of prime importance in the story — see p. 299, § 16.

5ᵃ. atiṣṭhan, u.f. atiṣṭhat (161) is 3d s. imf. act. of √sthā, 742. [The a is augment, 585: ti is reduplication (for t, see 590c ; for i, 660) : the i alters s to ṣ (180 and 184c), and this ṣ involves the conversion of th to ṭh (197 — cf. iṣṭa). Orig. sthā belonged to the reduplicating class (671 — cf. ῑ-στη-μι, ῑ-στη-ς, ῑ-στη-σι), but has been transferred (749) to the commonest of all classes, the a-class, and is inflected as if the stem were tiṣṭha, i.e. as if we had in Greek ῑ-στω, ῑ-στεις, ῑ-στει.] —manujendrāṇām, gen.pl. of manujendra : after the lingual r, the n of the ending is changed to lingual ṇ — see 189 and 190a : for the combination of manuja+indra, see 127 ; for dr, Whitney 14.

5ᵇ. mūrdhni, loc.s. of mūrdhan, 424 : for rdh, see Whitney 14. —devapatir, u.f. devapatis, 174 : declension, 339. —yathā, see s.v. 4. —'He (stood, i.e.) was at the head of princes, as Indra (sc. is at the head of gods)' : i.e. 'He was as much superior to other princes as Indra to other gods.' "As handsome as Indra" was a proverbial expression.

6ᵃ. upary, u.f. upari, 129 : the word is repeated for emphasis, 1260 : 'above, above,' i.e. 'far above.' —sarveṣām, gen.pl. of sarva, 522 and 524 : for construction, see s.v. upari and 1130 end.

6ᵇ. āditya, u.f. ādityas, 175b. —tejasā, 414 : as referring to the sun, it means 'splendor,' and as referring to Nala, it has the transferred mg, 'majesty': the instr., prop. the 'with'-case, is here best rendered by 'by,' i.e. 'in virtue of.' —The force of atiṣṭhat extends through the çloka or distich. 'He was far above all in majesty, as the sun (is) in splendor.'

7ᵃ. vedavic çūro, u.f. vedavit çūras : the final t is changed to the palatal c, before the palatal sibilant ç (regressive assimilation, 203), and the sibilant ç is also changed to the mute ch, 203 : the same changes appear in paryupāsac chacīm, 2⁷, abhūc chṛṇvatoḥ, 2¹⁸, hrochayaḥ, 2¹⁹, and tac chrutvā, 4⁵, 4¹⁶ : vedavit is nom.s.m. of vedavid (391), the d being changed to t (159) before the s of the case-ending, which last, however, is dropped — see 150.

7ᵇ. niṣadheṣu, 'among the Nishadhans' or 'in Nishadha'. —mahīpatiḥ, u.f. mahīpatis, 170a : declension, 339.

—It is not known where Nishadha was. Vidarbha, the modern Berar, is at the headwaters of the Tapti, between Nagpore and the Nizam's Kingdom, and about five hundred miles from Oudh. The general run of the story makes it highly probable that Nishadha was between Berar and Oudh. From chapter ix., it would seem to have been north of Oujein (ujjayinī). From an allusion in the Çatapatha-brāhmana, ii.3.2, Weber thinks it is in the south (i.e. from Madhyadeça). These premises give some ground for the inference that Nishadha was in the valley of the Sind, which traverses Gwalior State, Central India. On the Sind is Narwār ; and local tradition connects this place with "King Nala" in a story whose leading features bear a striking resemblance to those of our poem. Finally, Nala is said, chap. xv., to have reached Oudh on the tenth day after quitting Damayanti, and this time suits the distance — some two hundred miles — very well.

8ᵃ. akṣapriyaḥ, u.f. akṣapriyas, 172: for kṣ, cf. Whitney 13 end. —satyavādī, nom.s., 440. —As a dependent cpd (1265), akṣapriya may mean, 1. 'dice-beloved, lucky at gaming,' or, 2. 'dice-loving, friend of dice, fond of gaming': on the whole, mg 2 is perhaps to be preferred.

8ᵇ. mahān, nom.s., 450b.

9. See īpsita, which is ppl. (1037) of the desid. —nara-nārī, declension, 364: for ṇ, cf. 1⁵ᵃ N. end: nārī, see under nāra: for use of case, 296b. —udāraḥ, 172 again, like akṣa-priyaḥ, 1⁸, and çreṣṭhaḥ and manuḥ, next line, etc. etc. —saṁyatendriyaḥ, read p. 291, paragraph 6: saṁyata, √yam, 954d.

10. rakṣitā, 373. —dhanvin-ām, 440. —sākṣād, u.f. sākṣāt, 159. —manu-ḥ, 341. —Render 'as it were, Manu himself, in visible presence.'

11. tathāivāsīd, u.f. tathā eva āsīt, 127, 126, 159: see tathā, mg 3. —bhīmá-parākrama, possessive form of the descriptive cpd bhīma-parākramá: see references in vocab.

12. sarva-guṇāir, u.f. sarva-guṇāis, 174, cf. 1⁴ᵃ N.: for mg, see sarva 2b: a descriptive cpd, 1279. —yuktaḥ, u.f. yukta-s (170d), ppl. (953, 219 and 217) of √yuj: see √yuj 4, 'yoked with' (hence instr., 278), and so 'possessed of'. —prajākāmaḥ, observe accent and references in vocab. —sa cāprajaḥ, u.f. sas ca aprajas, 176a (as exception to 170c): for sa-s, 495: ca, though coalescing with aprajas in euphony (126) and in print, is really an enclitic and so belongs w. sa: 'and yet he (sc. was) childless.'

13. akarot, 3d s. imf. of √1kṛ, 714. —'He (in the matter of, i.e.) for the sake of children made the greatest effort,' i.e. he performed pious rites, etc.; or else, 'He had the matter of children greatly at heart, all intent (upon it).'

14. tam, 495, 274a. —abhy-agacchad, √gam+abhi, see references after pres. form gacchati in vocab.: this is 3d s. imf., 742. Respecting the spelling cch, see Preface, p. v. note 6. —brahmarṣi-r: for r, 174: de-clension, 339: formation, see references in vocab. There were three kinds of Rishis (see ṛṣi): the rājarṣi, or prince who adopted a life of devotion; the devarṣi, or sage who was also a demigod, as Nārada; and the brahmarṣi, or priestly sage.

—Bhārata, like rājendra, kāunteya, viçām pate, prabho, mahārāja, rājan, pāṇḍava, kāuravya, etc., is an interjected vocative, addressed by Brihadaçwa, the narrator, to Yudhishthira, see p. 298, § 10.

15. sa, see p. 291, paragraph 1, and vocab., s.v. ta4. —toṣayām āsa, periphrastic perf. of caus. of √tuṣ, 1070, 1071a: the auxiliary is the 3d s. perf. (800a) of √as, 'be.' —dharma-vit, nom.s.m., declined like veda-vit, 1⁷.

16. mahiṣyā, instr. (364) of mahiṣī. —suvarcas-am: declension, 418: goes with tam. —15–16. 'Along with his queen, Bhīma, desiring children (and) knowing his duty, gratified him (tam, Damana), the glorious, with hospitality.'

17. tasmāi, 495. —pra-sanno, √sad+ pra, cf. upa-panno, 1⁴ N. —sabhāryāya, dat.s.m. with tasmāi, 'to him having an accompanying wife, i.e. to him and his wife': observe that bhāryā shortens its final ā in composition, 334². —dadāu, √dā, 'give,' 800c.

Notes to Page 2.

1. kumārāṅç ca, u.f. kumārān ca (208), or rather, kumārāṅs ca (170c); for the so-called "inserted sibilant" is in the acc.pl. a historic survival, the original ending having been ns. —trīn, 482c. —mahā-yaçās (418) goes with damanas.

2. damayantīm, 364.

3. Cf. 1⁴ and 1¹¹ and notes.

4. tejas-ā, 414: so yaças-ā. —çriy-ā, stem çrī, 351.

5. prāpa, 3d s. perf. √āp+pra, 783c³, 800a. —4–5. 'Fair-waisted D. won fame among men by her beauty, majesty, fame, grace, and comeliness.'—Reprehensible tautology.

6. tām, 495. —vayas-i prāpte, loc. absolute, 303b: prāpta, ppl. of √āp+pra. —dāsīnām, 295 end.

7. paryupāsac cbacīm, u.f. pary-upa-
āsat çacīm, see 1[7a] N.: **āsat**, 3d s. imf. of
a-class (742 — augment 585) fr. √**ās**; this is
reg. of the root-class, 628, and mid. voice.
—6-7. Lit. 'Now, her marriageable age
having come, of slaves an adorned hundred,
and a hundred of friends sat around her
(**tām**), as (they do) around Çacī.'

8. rājate, √**rāj**, 735. —**sarva-ābharaṇa-**
bhūṣitā, 'adorned with all (her) jewels,' a
dependent cpd (1265), whose first member,
sarvābharaṇa, is itself a cpd, like sarva-
guṇa, see 1[12] N.

9. sakhī-madhye, see madhya 1. —**ana-**
vadyāṅgī, initial elided, 135: the cpd is the
possessive form of a descriptive, 1297-8.
—vidyut, 391. The Hindu epos often likens
maiden beauty to the brilliantly flashing
lightning of the rain-cloud.

10. rūpa-sampannā goes with bhāimī.
—U.f. çrī-s (174) iva āyata-locanā, 'like
long-eyed Çrī.'

11. U.f. tādṛk, nom.s.f. — **rūpavatī**,
nom.s.f. of rūpavant, 452.

12. U.f. mānuṣeṣu (129) api ca anyeṣu
dṛṣṭa-pūrvā (sc. āsīt) atha vā çrutā.
—api ca continues the force of the preceding
negatives, 'nor also.' —For dṛṣṭa-pūrva,
see reference in vocab.: dṛṣ-ṭa, ppl. of
√dṛç, 218. —atha vā, see atha 6. —çrutā =
çruta-pūrvā, 1316[3].
—Omission of copula (asi, asti, smas,
santi, āsīt, 'art, is, are, was,' etc., 636) is
extremely common; esp. so w. past pples,
which thus do duty as finite verbs — cf.
3[10] N., 7[6-7] N. So also in German.

13. citta-pramāthinī, fem., 438, 440 end.
—devānām, 1316, first example. —Lines
11–13 belong together: 'Neither among gods
nor Yakshas (sc. was) such a beauty seen
before or heard of, nor also among other
beings, (namely) mortals': bālā is added in
apposition to the subject.

14. nalaç, 170c. —bhuvi, 351.

15. kandarpa, 175b. —mūrtimān, 453.
—abhavat, 742. —'In beauty he was like
K. himself incarnate or having bodily form'
—w. pregnant mg, since K. is said to be
'bodiless,' an-aṅga.

16. U.f. tasyās, 495. —pra-çaçaṅsuḥ, 3d
pl. perf. (800a) of √çaṅs+pra, p. 254: subject indef., 'they' or 'messengers.'

17. punaḥ punaḥ, u.f. punar punar, 178.

18. tayor, 495. —'bhūc chṛṇvatoḥ, u.f.
abhūt çṛṇvatos, see 1[7a] N.: abhūt, 829: çṛ-
ṇv-at-os, loc. du., 447, of pres. ppl., 705, of
√çru, 710.

19. anyonyam, see vocab. —kāunteya,
see 1[14] N. end. —vy-avardhata, √vṛdh+vi,
742.

20. a-çak-nuv-an, negatived pres. ppl.,
705 (cf. 697[3] and 129[2]), of √çak. —dhār-
ayitum, inf., 1051[6], of √dhṛ, whose pres.
is made from a caus. stem, 1041, 1042b.
—hṛd-ā, 391.

21. antaḥpura-, read p. 291, paragraph
4. —vana, u.f. vane, 133. —ās-te, 612.
—gata-s, ppl. of √gam, 954d. —'Stays in a
wood near the harem, having gone secretly.'

22. dadarça, 3d s. perf. √dṛç, strong
stem dadarç, weak dadṛç, 792, 793c, 800.
—haṅsān, 202[2]. —pariṣkṛtān, ppl. of √1 kṛ
+pari, 1087d, 180. —'Gold-adorned' — 'of
golden plumage '.

23. vi-caratām, gen. pl. of pres. ppl. of
√car+vi. —teṣām, 495. —jagrāha, 3d s.
perf. of √grah, 590b, 800.

NOTES TO PAGE **3.**

1. vācam etc., see under vāc. —vy-ā-
jahāra, 590b, 800.

2. Lines 2–4 are the words of the bird.
—asmi, 636. —te, enclitic, and tava, are
gen.s. of 2d pers. pron., 491: use of case,
296b. —rājan, 424. —kariṣyāmi, 933. —See
priya 2a.

3. tvām, 491, object of kathayiṣyāmi,
fut. of denom. stem kathaya, 933. —Supply
tathā as correl. of yathā na, 'ut non',
next line.

4. See yathā 6. —tvad, 491, abl. w.
anya, 292b. —maṅsyati, 933, √man, mg 4.

5. ut-sa-sarj-a, √sṛj+ud, 800.

6. te must be from ta, 495, since the enclitic te (491) could not stand at beg. of
verse. —sam-ut-pat-ya, gerund of √pat+
sam-ud, 990. Note how the gerund, as
instr. of accompaniment of a verbal noun

(read 989), gets its mg: 'with a flying,' i.e.
'flying' or 'having flown.' —vidarbhān,
274a. —agamaṅs, u.f. agaman, 208, aor. of
√gam, 846.

7. ga-tvā, gerund again, 991: the root,
gam, shows the same form as in the ppl.
ga-ta, 954d. —U.f. tadā antike.

8. nipetus, √pat+ni, 800d, 794e. —dadarça, 2²² N.

9. dr̥ṣ-ṭvā, √dr̥ç, 991, 218. —U.f. sakhi-
gaṇa_āvr̥tā, 'surrounded by (her) friend-
crowd,' 1265: sakhi- is demanded by the
metre, instead of sakhī-, p. 300, § 21d: ā-vr̥-
tā, ppl. of √1 vr̥+ā.

10. hr̥ṣ-ṭā, ppl. of √hr̥ṣ, 197. —grahī-
tum, inf., 968, 972²: used here with verb of
motion (√kram — see 981³), Latin, 'subiit
captum'. —khagamāṅs, u.f. -āṅ, 208; but
the s is here a true historic survival, cf. 2¹ N.
—U.f. tvaramāṇā upa-, 127: √tvar, 741:
upa-ca-kram-e, √kram+upa, 590b, 800a, 3d
s. mid.

11. See √sr̥p+vi, and 800.

12. ekāikaças refers to both subject and
object — 'singulae (puellae) singulos (an-
seres).' —sam-upa_adravan, √dru, 742.

13. sam-upa_adhāvat, √dhāv, 742. —
antike, 'in the presence, i.e. near,' is superfluous with 'ran on unto.'

14. kr̥-tvā, √1 kr̥, mg 3, and 991. —a-
bravīt, 3d s. imf. of √brū, w. acc. of person,
274b. —13–14. Observe that the relative
clause comes first, w. incorporated antecedent, 'ad quem anserem D. accurrit, is . . .
dixit': cf. 512, and vocab. ya 4.

15. With mahīpatis supply asti, 'there is
a prince . . .': cf. 2¹² N. end.

16. The first half-line goes w. line 15:
supply santi in the second. —The two genitives are explained at 296b.

—The caesura, be it observed, here marks
the beginning of a new clause. This is often
the case. So 3², ³, ¹³, ²¹, 5⁶, etc.

17. bhāryā, predicate nom. —U.f. bha-
vethās, 177, 738. —var-, voc.s., 304, fem.,
440 end.

18. bhavej, u.f. bhavet, 202, 738. —
janma, 424. —U.f. rūpam ca idam, 'pul-
critudoque haec'. — 'Fruitful (of good)

would be thy birth, and this beauty (of
thine),' i.e. it would then prove a fortunate
thing that thou wast born and art so
beautiful.

19. For the long cpd, see 1247 I²: divide
-mānuṣa-uraga-, 127: the whole is object of
dr̥ṣṭa-vant-as (supply smas, 'sumus'—2¹²
N. end), which is exactly like the Eng. '(are)
having seen' = 'have seen': read 959 and
960. —In the later mythology, the serpents
are divine beings with human face, whose
beauty is often praised: cf. 13¹.

20. U.f. na ca asmābhis (491), 'neque a
nobis.' —dr̥ṣṭapūrvas, supply āsīt and see
N. to 2¹². —tathāvidhas, substantively, of
course: '(a man) of such sort'.

21. U.f. tvam ca api, supply asi, as in
2¹² N. —nārīṇām, 364, in vocab. under nāra.
—nalo, supply asti, as in 2¹² N.

22. U.f. viçiṣṭāyās, 177, gen.s.f., ppl. of
√çiṣ+vi. —For use of instr., 284. —'Ex-
imiae cum eximio congressus.' —For saṁgama, read p. 291 ¶ 7.

23. For viçām pate, 'O prince', s.v. viç
2, see 1¹⁴ N. end.

NOTES TO PAGE 4.

1. abravīt, see 3¹⁴ N. —nale, 304a. —
'Do thou speak so to Nala also' (sc. as
thou hast to me). The api ought to follow
nale.

2. See iti, mg 2, and tathā, mg 2. —
uktvā, √vac, 991: the root shows same
weak form as in ppl., 954b — cf. 217.

3. ā-gam-ya, 990. —nale, as in line 1.
—See √1 vid+ni: imf. 3d s. of caus., 1042a,
cf. 1043. —2–3. 'The bird, saying "Yes"
to the maid (274b) of Vidarbha, ..., communicated all to Nala.'

4. See iti, mg 2e. —In this poem, adhyāya (not sarga) is the proper word for
'chapter.'

6. For tac chrutvā, see N. to 1⁷ᵃ: tat,
495: çru-tvā, 991. —bhārata, see N. to 1¹⁴
end.

7. prati, here used as a true "preposition", or rather postposition, connecting
nalam with svasthā — see 1123. —babhūva,
√bhū, 789a.

8. U.f. **tatas**, 170c. —For an explanation of the nature of these and the following long cpds, look up the references under them in vocab.

9. **niḥçvāsa-**, read p. 291 ¶ 4.

10. **unmatta-darçanā**, 1299: for un-, 161.

11. U.f. **kṣaṇena atha.** —The complete analysis of the long word is indicated by references in vocab.

12. First cpd, see 1253a. —**vindati**, √2 vid.

13. **çete**, √1 çī, 629. —U.f. "**hā hā**" iti. —See √rud and 619. —See punar 2.

15. **asvasthām**: observe the use, common in Skt., of a predicate adj. or subst. instead of subordinate clause: thus, 'announced D. as ill', where we should say, 'announced that she was ill': so 4[19] **kāryam.** —**nareçvare** (like nale, 4[1,3]) is loc. w. nyavedayat and in logical apposition w. the dat. vidarbhapataye, despite the difference of case.

16. See **N.** to 4[6]. —Observe how the idea of 4[14b] is here put in one cpd.

17. **cint-**, see **N.** to 1[15]. —'Considered this important matter (in respect to, i.e.) concerning his daughter.'

18. See √īkṣ and 992. —**prāp-**, see 1308. —'Considering his daughter who had reached nubility,' i.e. taking fully into account the fact of her marriageability (though he knew it well enough before).

19. **apaçyad**, 759, 760.6. —See **ātman** 3, and 514. 'Saw D's swayamvara requiring to be instituted by himself, saw that he must hold D's sw.': cf. **N.** to 4[15].

20. Periphrastic perf. of denom. **mantraya+sam-ni**, 1070, 1071a.

21. **anubh-** is 3d s. pres. imv. pass., √bhū +**anu**, 771.4. —**ayam**, read p. 291 ¶ 1, and see 501. —**iti** marks the four preceding words as the precise words of Bhīma's invitation: 'Let this swayamvara be heard *or* taken notice of, O heroes, i.e. Understand ye that one will take place here.' —**prabho**, 341, see 1[14] **N.** end. —Observe that we have ◡◡▁◡▁ as the first half of the first pāda, a not infrequent irregularity.

NOTES TO PAGE 5.

1. **sarve**, 524, cf. 495.

2. **abhijagmus**, √gam+abhi, 590b, 794d. —For abl., see 291[3].

3. The aggregative cpd **hasty-açva-raths** (1252) makes w. **ghoṣa** a genitively dependent cpd (1264): **hasti** for hastin, 1249a[2]. —**pūrayantas** (√1 pṛ), agrees w. subject of preceding clause.

4. Divide, **vicitramālya+ābharaṇa**, as descriptive, 1280b. —**balāis**, 279. —'(They came) . . . with troops, splendid (and) well adorned with variegated-garland-ornaments.

5. **teṣām** (495) **pārth-**, objective gen. w. **pūjām.**

6. **akarot**, 1[18] **N.** —**te** begins new clause —see 3[16] **N.** —U.f. **avasan**, 135, 208, √3 vas.

7. U.f. **etasmin**, 210, 499b: see vocab. under **etad.** —'The two best of the Rishis (1264) of the gods': the verb is in line 10.

8. See √aṭ and 741. —U.f. **mahātmānāu**, 134. —**gatāu**, 954d.

9. U.f. **ca eva**, 127, see eva, end. —**mahā**-stands in adverbial relation to **-prājña** ('greatly, i.e. very, wise'), since the whole is a descriptive *adjective* cpd — see 1279.

10. Third pers. dual, perf. mid., √viç, 800a. —See **sú** 2, inseparable prefix.

11-12. U.f. **tāu**, 495. —**arc-**, gerund from caus. stem of √ṛc, 1051[7]. —**papraccha**, 590, 794c. —U.f. **anāmayam ca api.** —**gata** (like -bhūta, see 6[7] **N.**, and 1273c) is a mere means of turning **sarva-** [=sarvatra] into attributive form: so also in **sarvatragatam**, line 14, which should be printed as a cpd, and means, like **sarvagatam**, 'under all circumstances, i.e. in all their goings and doings.' Amend vocab. accordingly.

—'Saluting them, Maghavan then asked after the welfare unbroken and also diseaseless of them two under all circumstances — he, the mighty one': i.e. (cf. the principle explained 4[16] **N.**) 'asked if it had gone constantly well with them and if they had been entirely free from sickness.'

14-15. **āvayos**, 491. —Copulas omitted — 2[12] **N.** —'Of us two (there is) welfare, O god, under all circumstances, O lord: and in the whole (kṛtsne) world, O Maghavan, the princes (are) prosperous, O mighty one.'

18-20 are prefatory to the question proper in line 21ᵃ: 'The princes (proleptic nom. independent) . . ., who (509) go to death by the sword (280) . . ., — this (501) imperishable world, i.e. heaven, (is — cf. 2¹² N. end) granting every wish of them, just as (yathā‿eva) of me (it grants every wish).' The idea is, Since the brave warriors can here obtain their every wish, why do they not come up?

21. 'Where now (are) those princes, heroes?' — Observe caesura: cf. 3¹⁶ N.

22. āgacchataḥ, √gam+ā, 741, 447, agrees w. tān.

NOTES TO PAGE 6.

2. çṛṇu, 710, 703. — me, 491, 297b. — dṛçyante, 768, 771.

3. Supply asti, 'there is' (a daughter) . . . —See iti, mg 2 f. — √çru+vi.

4. Ppl. of √kram+sam-ati (955a) 'having excelled = excelling.'

5. tasyās, 495. — bhavitā, 944.

7. See bhūta 2, and reference, 1273c, and cf. 5¹² N. — Pres. ppl. of denom. stem arthaya+pra, 1068.

8. kāṅkṣanti governs tām.

9. 'While this (499b) is being told' (pres. ppl. pass. of kathaya, 1068, cf. 1052a), loc. absolute, 303b. — Study references under sāgnika, an important kind of cpd: lit. 'having an accompanying (sa-) Agni', where sa- is equiv. to an adj. Others in line 13.

10. √gam+ā, cf. 5² N.

11. √çru, 3d pl. perf., 800b.

12. U.f. çrutvā eva ca abruvan (632) hṛṣṭās. — gacchāmas: for tense, 777a.

13. mahārāja, see 1¹⁴ N. end.

14. yatas, supply āsan, 'were.'

15. kāunteya, see 1¹⁴ N. end.

17. path-i, loc.s., 433. — dadṛçus, 2²² N. — sthitam, superfluous, see sthita 2.

18. 'In reality almost, the god of love, present (see sthita 3) with definite shape, (by reason of beauty =) so handsome was he.' Cf. 2¹⁶ N.

20. tasthus, 590c, 794f, 800c. — √smi+vi.

21. viṣṭabhya, √stabh+vi, 185, 992.

22. rājann, 210: see 1¹⁴ N. end. — √tṛ +ava, 992², 242.

23. U.f. bhos, see 176a. — bhavān, see bhavant and 456, and supply asti, 514.

NOTES TO PAGE 7.

1. 'Do thou (714) assistance of us' (491). Observe caesura.

4. √jñā, 989. — U.f. kariṣye, 133, 93:. —'Nala, promising them "I will do (the assistance)", . . .'.

5. etān, 499b. — √sthā+upa, 954c.

6-7. Now review declension of pronouns — very frequent hereabouts: interrogatives, ke, kas, kim, 504; demonstratives, tad, 495, ayam and asau, 501; personal, aham, mayā, asmān, and vas, tvam, tvām, 491.

Note frequent omission (2¹² N.) of copula: u.f. ke bhavantas (santi, 514)? kas ca asāu (asti), yasya aham īpsitas (asmi) dūtas? kim ca (asti) tad vas mayā kāryam ('mihi faciendum')? — yasya dūtas, 'as messenger to whom.' — kath-, 1068, 1043.4.

8ᵃ. See 303bᴬ.

9. √budh+ni, 739. — 'Know us as gods, i.e. know that we are gods' — cf. 4¹⁵ N. — See artha.

10. U.f. aham indras (asmi), ayam agnis ca (asti), tathā eva ayam apām patis (asti). — ayam, 'this one here', with a gesture of introduction. — apām, see ap. 'Lord of waters' is Varuṇa.

11. nṝṇām, gen.pl. of nṛ, 371⁵. — U.f. yamas ayam (asti).

12. 'Announce us as assembled' — cf. 4¹⁵ N.

The last three lines (13-15) of Indra's speech contain in oratio recta the message which he wishes Nala to deliver.

13. Lit. 'The world-protectors, having Great-Indra as first, i.e. Great-Indra and the other world-protectors': for this important kind of cpd, study 1302c 1, and ādi in vocab. — √yā+sam-ā, 611. — See reference under didṛkṣu.

14. 'The gods seek (√1 iṣ, 608) to win (√āp, 968) thee.'

15. 'Choose thou', √2 vṛ, 1043.4.

17. 'Me, come hither (sam-upa-itam, √i: for one and the same purpose.' —Inf. of √2 iṣ+pra, 1051.

18-19. 'Pray how can (√sah+ud) a man who is in love say (√vac, 968) such a thing to a woman (striyam 366, 274b) for another?'

20. ūcus, √vac, perf., see references.

21. sam-çru-tya, 992. —For loc., 304a.

NOTES TO PAGE 8.

1. kar-, 933. —Observe caesura.

4. veç-, object of praveṣṭum, which is inf. of √viç+pra, 218.

5. U.f. pra-vekṣyasi (√viç, fut., 932, 218) iti . . . eva abhy-.

6. √gam. —See iti, mg 2.

7. Third word is vāidarbhīm. — See √1 vṛ+sam-ā.

8. √dīp, intens. 1000, 1002a, 1016. — vapuṣ-ā, 414.

10. √kṣip+ā, 752.5.

11. Join tasya w. kāmas, and tām w. dṛṣṭvā. —√vṛdh, 800.

12. See satya 3. —cik-, √1 kṛ, desid., 1027, 1028b. —√dhṛ, 1070, 1071a.

13. √bhram+sam, 955a.

14. √pat+sam-ud, 794e. —√dhṛṣ.

16. U.f. na ca enam, see ena and 500.

18. U.f. kas ayam (asti)? —For rest of line, see atha 6 and 948² end.

19. √çak, 697¹·³. —See √hṛ+vy-ā: inf. —See 1 ka 2c and 507.

20. Nom.pl.fem. of lajjāvant, 452³.

21-22. 'Then to him smiling, Dama-yantī — with a smile addressing — unto the hero Nala spake, amazed.'

NOTES TO PAGE 9.

1. U.f. prāptas (√āp) asi, 636. —'Thou art having come like a god, i.e. thou camest invisibly?' Observe caesura. —U.f. asi na lakṣitas (ppl. of lakṣaya), 'wast thou not noticed.'

2. U.f. ca iha (āsīt). Caesura. —U.f. asi na lakṣitas (ppl. of lakṣaya), 'wast thou not noticed.'

3. Caesura. —U.f. ca eva ugra-.

5. viddhi - ʟ𝜃ı: see √1 vid 2 and 617.

6-7. Cf. 7¹⁴·¹⁵. —çobh-, voc.s.fem.

8. U.f. praviṣṭas aham (asmi), √viç.

9. √viç, 752.5. —See 1 ka 2d and 507. —U.f. apaçyat, na api avār- (√1 vṛ caus.).

10. preṣitas (asmi), √2 iṣ.

11. √1 kṛ+pra, 2d s. imv. mid. 714.

14. From here on, the use of virāma with a final consonant to prevent its combining in print with a following initial is given up. Thus in nalamabravīt, we allow the a, which — if unannulled by virāma — is inherent in the nāgarī sign for ma, to serve as the first letter of abravīt. Cf. 9⁴ with the identical 10².

See 992 for the two cpd gerunds.

15. √nī+pra, 739: for ṇ, 192a. —See √1 kṛ 2, 714, 578.

16. U.f. yat (202) ca anyat (161) mama asti: see √1 as 2. —'For both I and what other good soever I have —'

17. 'That all (is) thine.' —kuru, 714. —īçvara = Nala.

18. Explained at 512a, q.v.

19. √pat+sam-ni, pass. ppl. of causative, hence long ā, 1051.

20. √khyā+praty-ā, 932: 948² examples.

NOTES TO PAGE 10.

1. āsthāsye, √sthā+ā, 932. —Suicide by hanging etc. is referred to: so also Pañchatantra iv. fable 2.

2. Identical with 9⁴.

3. √sthā 5: loc. (741), absolute, 303b. —'The gods being present, how seekest thou a man (as husband, in preference)?'

4-5. As at 3¹³·¹⁴ (see N.), the relative clause comes first, with incorporated antecedent: lit. 'Of what world-creating noble lords I (am) not equal to the foot-dust (instr., see 281a), let thy mind on those be busied' (√vṛt 4, 739). More natural to us would seem teṣu lokakṛtsu īçvareṣu mahātmasu. "He's not as good as the dust on my feet" was prob. a proverbial expression of reproach: so Mālavikā, act i.

6. U.f. hi ācaran, pres. ppl. —devānām limits vipriyam, 296 b. —rochati, see √ṛ.

7. √trā, 617. —Cf. 2⁹ N. and 7¹⁵ N.

8. See tathā 3. Nala tells her (lines 8-9) what she may enjoy if she chooses a god.

9. devān prāpya, √āp, 992, 'by obtaining
gods (in wedlock).' —bhuṅkṣva, √2 bhuj,
689.

10. U.f. yas: its antecedent is tam.
—imām, 501. —√kṣip, 992. —See punar 3.

12–13. Explained 291². —yasya limits
only daṇḍa-, not the whole cpd, 1316. Yama
is meant here.

16–17. kriyatām (770c) varaṇam, 'let a
choice be made'. —yadi manyase, √man 3.
—suhṛdvākyam. —çṛṇu, 6² N.

19. √plu+sam-ā, past ppl., instr. dual.
—See atha 4. —See vāri and 339.

21. √2 vṛ, 718. —Declension of bhartṛ,
373. —satyam etad bravīmi, see satya 3.

22. √vip, 741. —kṛtāñjalim, here fem.,
346, 344.

23. āgatya, √gam, 992. —U.f. iha utsahe: see √sah+ud 2.

NOTES TO PAGE 11.

1. U.f. hi aham. —For gen., 297a.

2. See √rabh+ā 2. —katham, epanalepsis.

3. U.f. eṣas (176a) dharmas (sc. asti),
forms a clause. —bhavitā, 944. See 949²
near end.

4. See √1 dhā+vi 5 and 770b.

6. See √1 hṛ+praty-ā.

7. 'Here is a safe means (seen — in the
mind, i.e.) thought out by me.'

8. bhavitā = bhaviṣyati, line 12.

9–10. U.f. tvam ca eva … devās ca
… āyāntu (√yā, 611): verb agrees w. nearest subject. Observe caesura in 10. With
yatra supply asti.

11. For saṁnidhi (ṁ=n), read p. 291 ¶ 7.

12. var- governs tvām. —U.f. na evam.

14. U.f. punar, 178. —End, supply āsan.

15. U.f. tam apaçyan (208) tathā
āyāntam (619).

16. U.f. ca enam, 500.

17. For kaccid (kat cid, 202), see kad.

18ª. 'And what did she say to us all?'

20. U.f. bhavadbhis, 456. —See √diç
+ā. —niv-, with praviṣṭas.

21. 'Guarded (vṛ-tam) by warders'
(daṇḍibhis).

22. U.f. na kas cid (1 ka 2d) dṛṣṭavān
(sc. asti) naras, see 959, 960, this example.

NOTES TO PAGE 12.

1. U.f. sakhyas (364) ca asyās (501)…
tābhis ca api… —Copula twice omitted.

2. U.f. sarvās, nom.fem. —vib-, voc.

3. 'While ye are being described by me,'
303b.

4. √2 vṛ, 718. —sur-, voc. —Cf. 10²¹.

5. In the words āyāntu to bhavitā, line
8, Nala repeats substantially D's plan
(11⁹⁻¹²), but in oratio recta. Hiatus (113) is
allowed at the caesura; otherwise bālā
(unless it had lost a final a, 177) would coalesce with the following initial. Cf. 16¹¹ N.

8. mah-, voc. —bhavitā, 11⁸ N. —See
iti 5.

9–10. U.f. etāvad (nom.n., 453) udā-
hṛtam (√hṛ, sc. asti) mayā, full stop. —
'For the rest, ye (are) an authority, O gods':
i.e. it's your affair alone now.

13. The three substantives are locatives
absolute with prāpte, 303b⁸.

14. √hū+ā : w. 782 cf. 643b. —For
loc., 304.

16. √gam+sam-upa_ā, 1080. — For acc.,
dam-, 271a.

18. U.f. viviçus (cf. 5¹⁰ N.) te nṛpās …
acalam.

19. U.f. āsaneṣu .. āsīnās, 619⁸.

20ᵇ. The cpd is a possessive form (1301)
of a descriptive cpd, 1280b.

NOTES TO PAGE 13.

1. Second word is suçlakṣṇāḥ. —'Like
the five-headed serpents'—because the hand
is quinquepartite. Cf. 3¹⁹ N.

5. √muṣ, 724: fem. irreg., 449c⁸ : 'be-
guiling' — cf. κλέπτειν νόον. —prabhayā,
364. —cakṣūṁṣi, 414 end.

6–7. U.f. teṣām dṛṣṭis, … patitā, …
saktā (√sañj) abhūt (829) —caesura : na ca
(dṛṣṭis teṣām) paçyatām cacāla.

8. 'While the names are being announced' —loc. absolute, 303b, pres. ppl. of
pass. of denom. kīrtaya+sam.

9. See atha 4. —See p. 299, § 15.

10. √īkṣ+sam, 992. —See sthita 4.

11. U.f. saṁdehāt (ṁ=n, p. 291 ¶ 7)
.. na abhy-ajānāt, √jñā, 730², 725.

12. See ya 5. —See √man, 794e. — 'For whichever she saw of them, him she thought (to be) king N.'

13. U.f. buddhyā, 339. —tark-, cf. 1¹⁵ ɴ.

14. Optatives (577) of √jñā, 721, and √1 vid, 816.

17-18. 'What marks of the gods [(are) my heard ones (296b) =] I have heard of from old men, these I do not notice as (being of, i.e.) belonging to even one (ekasya api) of those standing here (iha) on the ground (bhūmāu).'

19. √3 ci+vi-nis, 992. —√car+vi, 1051.

20. 'Thought (it) an arrived-time, i.e. thought that the time had arrived (cf. note to 4¹⁵) for refuge (of the) to the gods.'

22. prā- is predicate adj. w. bhū-tvā, 991. See √bhū. —U.f. vepamānā idam.

23. 'As surely as N. (was) chosen by me on hearing . . :' see yathā 4.

NOTES TO PAGE 14.

1. patitve, 'in marriage,' goes with vṛtas. —See satya 2 and 280 end. —U.f. tam = Nala.

2. U.f. na abhicarāmi.

4. 'Ordained (as my, i.e.) to be my husband'—√1 dhā+vi 3, and 954c.

6. 'As this ceremony (vrata) was undertaken by me (in the —) for the winning of Nala..'. —√rabh+ā: rabh-ta = rabdha, 160.

8. √1 kṛ 3, 714: should be mid. See p. 290, § 15.

9. See yathā 6. —√jñā+abhi, 721.

10. √4 cam, 992. —U.f. tad.

11. √1 kṛ, 800f.

12-13. 'She saw (apaçyat) all the gods, free from sweat (asvedān) unwinking, having unwithered garlands and free from dust, standing (see sthita 1) without touching (aspṛçatas) the ground.' The "unwinking eyes" are a survival of the old Vedic conception of the gods that "neither slumber nor sleep." The other marks of anthropomorphic divinity are natural enough. The opposites of all five attributes are ascribed to Nala, besides a shadow.

14. U.f. mlānasrak, nom.s.m., 391. — rajaḥ-sveda- (1252), in instr. relation, forms a cpd (1265) w. sam-anv-itas, √i.

15. 'And (ca eva) the Nishadhan, . . line 14 .., (was) made recognizable, (by) standing on the ground, and (ca) by winking.'

17. √2 vṛ, 1070. —pāṇḍava, see 1¹⁴ ɴ. end.

18. See √grah 1. —Cf. 2¹⁰.

21. 'The cry "Ah, ah" (hā hā_iti — cf. 4¹³) was uttered (√muc).'

22-23. Same construction. 'The cry "Bravo" was uttered (īritas, √īr) by . . . praising (√çaṅs) N.' —Note the generous magnanimity of the gods.

NOTES TO PAGE 15.

1. kāuravya, see 1¹⁴ ɴ. end.

2. √çvas+ā, caus. imf. —U.f. antar-ātmanā.

3. See yad 3: correl. in line 4.

4ª. Cf. 9⁵ and ɴ.

4ᵇ. 'Delighted (√ram 3) with such (see evam, end) words of thine' (as thou hast spoken in choosing me). Loc., 303.

5. See yāvant 2. —See √dhṛ 6.

6ª. √bhū, construed prop. w. loc. of thing (e.g. dāne), means 'be in or on' (e.g. giving), i.e. 'devoted to' (charity): here the construction seems extended in like mg to a person. 'So long will I be devoted to thee' —tvayi. —Line 6ᵇ = 10²¹ᵇ.

7-8. See vāc (391) and nand+abhi. A line, containing the principal verb with Nala as subject, seems lacking.

9-10. √pri 3. —U.f. tu agni-: see -puro-gama. —See √gam 5. —'But the two, mutually pleased, beholding Agni and the others, perceived those very gods as their refuge, i.e. perceived that the gods had been good to them.'

11-12. vṛte, 303b. —U.f. nalāya aṣṭāu (483³) .. dadus (800c). —The four gods give each two gifts, and, besides, one gift in common, a couple of children (mithunam, 19). It is by his exercise of the supernatural powers now given to Nala that Damayantī in the sequel (chap. 23) recognizes her lost and transformed husband. In passing through a low door-way, he does not stoop —the lintel rises; when he wants fire and water for cooking, they come at his wish; and he seasons the food exquisitely.

13-14. U.f. gatim ca an-, 'and a most excellent gait': this includes the ability to pass through the low door-way, as above. —√prī 2, 760.5.

15. The god of fire and the god of the waters (18) give N. magic power over their respective elements — see above and p. 299, §15. —U.f. pra-adāt (√1 dā, 829) yatra.

16. U.f. lokān ātmaprabhān (208) ca eva: 'places-in-heaven, having his (the Fire-god's) splendor, or a splendor of their own' (heaven has "no need of the sun, neither of the moon, to shine in it"): this amounts, perhaps, to 'hopes of future blessedness'; but the Hindus make a deal of loose talk about 'worlds' (lokās).

17. U.f. yamas tu. —anna-rasam, 'subtle taste for food' — as the sequel shows — see above: vocab. wrong.

18. With apām patir supply prādāt and see 7 [19] N.

19. U.f. srajas ca ut-.

20. U.f. evam pra-dāya (992) asya (501), explained 297a.

21-22. Construe, anu-bhūya vivāham asya damayantyāç ca: 'learning of the wedding, i.e. that it would take place duly' — they went back home.

NOTES TO PAGE 16.

1. √1 kṛ, caus., 1070, 1045.

2. uṣya, √3 vas, irreg. (990²) for uṣitvā.

4. U.f. bhrājamānas añçumān: after elision (bhrājamāno 'ñçumān), the anusvāra belongs to the o, and so — in nāgarī — has to be put over the o and to the left of the avagraha.

6. U.f. īje (√yaj) ca api. —Yayāti was an ancient king, whose piety is celebrated even in the Rigveda, where the gods are besought to bless the sacrificer with their presence, as in old time they did for Yayāti. His story is told MBh. i., chap. 75.

7. U.f. anyāis ca bahubhis, dhīmān, kratubhis ca āptadakṣiṇāis: the second ca seems superfluous.

8. U.f. punar (178) ca . . . upavaneṣu (126).

9. √hṛ+vi, cf. 3¹ N. and 16¹².

10. √jan, 1070, 1045: w. loc., 'begat upon (the body of) D.'

11. Observe hiatus at the caesura — cf. 12⁵ N. —By penance the great ascetics could become as gods and thrust even Indra from his throne. The anxious god's most effectual means to defend himself from the power of their austerities was to seduce them by sending a nymph so lovely that they could not resist her charms. 'Indra's weapon' (indrasenā, see vocab.) is therefore a very complimentary name for Nala's daughter. To name her brother, a corresponding masculine was formed, which has, of course, no other than grammatical appropriateness.

12. U.f. viharan ca, 208.

SELECTIONS II.-XXI.

From the Hitopadeça, the 'Book of Good Counsel.'

§ 22. The first book ever printed in Sanskrit was Kālidāsa's 'Seasons' (ṛtusaṁhāra), edited by Sir Wm. Jones, and printed in Bengālī letters in 1792. The first Sanskrit book ever printed in Nāgarī letters was the Hitopadeça. It was edited by Carey, and printed at Serampore in 1803. The publication was undertaken, said Henry T. Colebrooke, "to promote and facilitate the study of the ancient and learned language of India in the College of Fort William." It was chosen as the first for this purpose because of its easy style and intrinsic interest and because two English translations of it existed, one by Wilkins (Bath, 1787), and the other by Jones (London, 1799). To pedagogical reasons, accordingly, may be assigned in great part, the importance of this work: it has become important in the West, because the text is so well suited for tyros in Sanskrit; and in the Orient, because of the intrinsic value of its contents.

§ 23. The book belongs to the ethico-didactic class of literature, and is what the Hindus call a nīti-çāstra or 'cónduct-work.' The term nīti (see this in the vocabulary) came to have special reference to the conduct of kings in their domestic life and in their foreign relations; a nīti-çāstra is, accordingly, a 'Prince's handbook of political and social ethics,' a kind of 'Mirrour for Magistrates.' The Hitopadeça consists of mingled verse and prose. The verses are mostly proverbs and maxims — often of the choicest practical wisdom; and their validity is proved, illustrated, and enforced by the fables, which are in prose.

§ 24. The frame in which the work is set is simple and meagre. The sons of King Sudarçana of Pāṭaliputra[1] (Patnā) are ignorant and vicious. He therefore convokes the wise men and asks if any one is able to reform the princes. Viṣṇuçarman offers to do so, and accordingly takes them in charge, and relates to them the stories which make up the body of the collection.

§ 25. The Hitopadeça is not an original work, but, rather, an excellent compilation of ancient material. The time of its composition has not been even approximately determined. The palm-leaf MS. brought by Mr. Cecil Bendall from Nepāl was written in the year 493 of the Nepāl era or A.D. 1373. And Professor Peterson's[2] old paper MS. from Jeypore is of about the same age. At present we can hardly say more than that the work is at least 500 years old. In the working over of the material, the metrical portions would naturally be changed less, on the whole, than the prose; and in fact, many of the proverbs can be traced back in their identical form to works of antiquity. And travellers report that just such proverbs are current to-day in the talk of the lower classes of India.

The author or editor of this collection of fables, according to the colophon[3] of the Jeypore MS., was named Nārāyaṇa, and his patron and publisher was the prince Dhavalacandra.

§ 26. The sources of this compilation are expressly said (end of the preface, 17⁸) to be "the Pañcatantra and another work." The first part of this statement is borne out by the fact that, out of forty-three fables in the Hitopadeça, twenty-five are found also in the Pañcatantra. The latter work, as its name implies, consists of five books; while the Hitopadeça is divided into four, whose titles are given in the preface, 17⁷. The correspondence is as follows. The first book of the Pañcatantra answers in its frame-work to the second of the Hitopadeça and the second of the Pañcatantra to the first of the Hitopadeça. Five stories from the third book of the Pañcatantra, along with seven from the first, are scattered through the last two books of the Hitopadeça. From the fourth book of the Pañcatantra only one story, "The ass in the tiger-skin," appears in the Hitopadeça; and from the fifth book, only three. It thus appears that, in the main, only the first three books of the Pañcatantra were drawn upon by the author of the Hitopadeça; and Somadeva, in his Kathā-sarit-sāgara (chapters 60–64, much of whose substance is from the Pañcatantra, i.–iii.), has followed a similar course.

§ 27. What the "other work" is we can hardly say with entire certainty. In it ought to be found together — if the statement of the preface is accurate — at least

---

[1] From this point the spelling of proper names will no longer be anglicized.

[2] See Preface to his Hitopadeça, p. i, ii, v.

[3] Peterson's ed., p. 161 : cf. p. iv, v.

the eighteen fables of the Hitopadeça which do not occur in the Pañcatantra. Had the preface said "other works," the problem would be easier. Thus the story of the two giants, iv. 9, may be traced to the Mahā-bhārata, and the prototypes of other single stories are doubtless to be found in one and another ancient collection. Professor Peterson [1] thinks that the "other work" is the Nītisāra of Kāmandaka. The identification deserves further study.

§ 28. The contents of the Pañcatantra have been made the subject of one of the most important contributions to the literary history of the world by the late Professor Benfey. His principal results were published in his *Pantschatantra* (1859, see above, p. xviii, no. 8), and in his introduction to Bickell's edition of the *Kalilag und Damnag* (1876). The latter contains, pages VI–X, a brief résumé of these results. The summary given by Keith-Falconer (1885, see p. 315) is a systematic and lucid account of the history of the fables, and is the one most to be commended to English-speaking students. Some of the most important items follow.

A. The Indian original. In the sixth century of our era, there existed in India a Buddhist Sanskrit work, in thirteen chapters, treating of the conduct of princes. [2] Its doctrines were inculcated in the form of beast-fables, or stories in which animals play the part of human beings.

B. This Indian original was translated by a Persian physician named Barzōī, into the Pehlevī, the literary language of Persia, by command of the Sassanian king, Khosru Anūshīrvān, called The Just (531–579 A.D.).

§ 29. **C1.** Both the Indian original and its Pehlevī version are irrecoverably lost; but from the latter were made two very notable translations. The first was into Syriac, made about 570 A.D., and called *Kalilag and Damnag* after the two jackals, Karaṭaka and Damanaka, who figured prominently in the introduction of the Sanskrit original. A single notice of this version had been preserved in a catalogue of Syriac writings made by Ebed-jesus (died 1318), and published by Assemani at Rome in 1725. A Chaldean bishop, Georgius Ebed-jesus Khayyāth, on his way to the ecumenical council in 1870, stumbled upon a manuscript of this Syriac version in the episcopal library at Mardīn. Through the mediation of Ignazio Guidi in Rome, and by a wonderful combination of lucky accidents and persistent efforts, the existence of "the lost manuscript" was made known to the eager inquirers in Europe, [3] and at last published in text and German translation by Bickell.

§ 30. **C2.** The second translation from the Pehlevī was the *Kalilah and Dimnah* or *Fables of Pilpay* in Arabic, made by Abd-allah ibn al-Moqaffa, a Persian convert to Islam, who lived under the caliph al-Mansor and died about 760. This version was published, though not in the best recension, by Silvestre de Sacy at Paris in 1816, and an English translation of it was given by the Rev. Wyndham Knatchbull, Oxford, 1819.

According to the Arabic introduction, Dabshelim (deva-çarman) was the first king of the Indian Restoration after the fall of the governor appointed by Alexander

---

[1] See his Introduction, p. 29, 43, Notes, p. 3. The Nītisāra was edited by Rājendralāla Mitra, in the Bibliotheca Indica, vol. iv.

[2] Such was Benfey's conclusion. It was questioned by Weber, *Indische Streifen*, iii. 437. Barzōī's Pehlevī version (B.) may have been based on several *different* works—among them a Pañcatantra. Indeed, from the second chapter of the Arabic Kalilah

and Dimnah, 'The mission of Barzōī' (Knatchbull, pages 40–41; cf. Keith-Falconer, p. xxi), and from other evidence (Keith-Falconer, p. liv f), this is the much more probable view.

[3] The story of the discovery is told by Benfey, in Bickell's book, pages XII–XXIII, as also in various periodicals there cited, p. XXII note, e.g. *London Academy* for Aug. 1, 1871.

at the close of his campaign in the Panjāb, B.C. 326. When firmly established, Dabshelim gave himself over to every wickedness. To reclaim the king, a Brahman philosopher takes up his parable, as did Nathan before David, and at last wins him back to virtue. The wise man is called in Arabic *bid-bah*[1] and in Syriac *bid-vag*. These words are satisfactorily traced by Benfey, through the Pehlevi, to the Sanskrit vidyā-pati, 'master of sciences.' Accordingly, *bidbah*, which has become Bidpai or Pilpay in our modern books, is not really a proper name, but an appellative, applied to a 'Chief Pandit' or 'Court-scholar' of an Indian prince.

The Arabic version is of prime importance, since from it have flowed other versions, which have been of the utmost influence in shaping the literature of the Middle Ages.

§ 31. **D.** These versions are: **1.** The Later Syriac, made in the tenth or eleventh century, edited by Wright, and translated by Keith-Falconer; **2.** the Greek one, made about 1080, by Symeon Seth, a Jewish physician; **3.** the Persian, made some fifty years later, by Nasr Allah of Ghaznī; **4.** the Hebrew, ascribed to Rabbi Joel, and probably made before 1250, and published, with French translation, at Paris in 1881, by Joseph Derenbourg; **5.** the old Spanish, made from the Arabic in 1251, and published at Madrid in 1860 by Gayangos.

§ 32. **E.** Of the descendants in the fifth degree from the original, only two need be mentioned: **3.** The Persian *Anwār-i Suhailī* or 'Lights of Canopus,' a simplified recast of Nasr Allah's, made about 1494 by Husain Wāiz al-Kāshifī. English translations of this have been published by Eastwick and by Wollaston, see below. **4.** The *Directorium humanae vitae*, made from the Hebrew about 1270 by John of Capua, and printed about 1480.

§ 33. **F.** From John of Capua's version flowed the famous 'Book of examples of the ancient sages,' *Das bûch der byspel der alten wysen.* It was made at the instance of Duke Eberhard im Bart, whose name and motto, EBERHART GRAF Z[U] WIRTENBERG ATTEMPTO, appear as an acrostic in the initials of the first sections. It was first printed about 1481, and has since been admirably edited by W. L. Holland, Stuttgart, 1860. Holland used, besides three manuscripts, two printed editions *sine loco et anno*, and enumerates 17 dated editions that appeared between 1483 and 1592. Four dated editions appeared at Ulm between 1483 and 1485! The great number of editions of the work and their rapid succession are the best proof of its importance as a means of instruction and amusement in the fifteenth and sixteenth centuries.

Another offshoot from the *Directorium* is the Italian version of A. F. Doni, entitled *La moral filosophia*, and printed at Venice[2] in 1552. This is of special interest, because from it came (**G**) the English translation of Sir Thomas North, London, 1570.

It may here be added that La Fontaine, in the second edition of his Fables (1678), which contains eleven books, says[3] that he owed the largest part of his new material (books vii–xi) to Pilpay, the Indian sage. The edition of Henri Regnier (Paris, Hachette, 1883–85, 3 vols.) gives abundant references to the sources of each fable, and is especially to be commended to those who would compare the well-known French offshoots with the Indian originals.

---

[1] See Benfey, in Bickell, p. XLIII f.
[2] With wood-cuts. Harvard College has a copy.
[3] *Avertissement* prefixed to book vii, Regnier ii

§ 34. From Benfey's investigations it appears that the truest extant representative of the Indian original is the Syriac version, *Kalilag and Damnag*. Next to the Syriac stands the *Buch der Beispiele*, which, besides, is in language remarkable for its dignity, strength, and beauty; upon this latter version, moreover, are based almost all the printed ones previous to 1644. To the German version almost exclusively, therefore, is Europe indebted for the wide-spread knowledge of this cycle of literature from the last part of the fifteenth to the middle of the seventeenth century.

§ 35. After this account of the direct descendants of the Indian original in the Occident, it remains to speak of the history of that original in India, and of its sources. Whether Barzōī translated from one work of thirteen chapters (cf. § 28) or from several independent works, the fact remains that the originals of all of his sections may be certainly identified on Indian ground save three:[1] five, namely, form the Pañcatantra; two other sections figure as a supplement to the first book of a later recension of the Pañcatantra; and yet other sections, three in number, appear in the Mahā-bhārata.

The first three books of the Pañcatantra (above, § 26) were recast by Somadeva about 1070 A.D., in his Kathā-sarit-sāgara, chapters 60–64. Somadeva's abstract of these three books shows that they had the same form then as at the time of the Pehlevī translation (570). As representatives of the Indian original, the offshoots of the Pehlevī version surpass even the Indian offshoots. These latter, as respects their truthfulness in reflecting the Indian original, are arranged by Benfey as follows: first, the recension of the Indian original used by Somadeva; second, the one on which the Southern Pañcatantra (of Dubois) is based; third, the one from which the Hitopadeça is made; and last, the one from which proceed the common Sanskrit recensions of the Pañcatantra.

§ 36. At the time when Barzōī made his Pehlevī version, Buddhism was already on the decline in India, and Brahmanism regaining its lost supremacy. It was not to be expected on the one hand that the Brahmans would allow a work of such great artistic merit as the original *Mirrour for Magistrates* to be lost and forgotten, nor, on the other, that they would preserve it without transforming its whole spirit, which was that of fanatical hatred for Brahmanism. They have, therefore, omitted or transformed such parts as showed most Buddhist animus, leaving, however, many marks uneffaced which betray its Buddhist origin.

In one other way, too, the original was modified. In most of its sections a doctrine was inculcated by means of a single fable or story, and only a sparing use was made of inserted apologues. But gradually the means became an end; into the main story were inserted others, and others still into these, until the main story became a mere frame, and the result was comparable to a set of Chinese boxes.[2]

§ 37. Respecting the sources of the Indian original only a general statement can be made. There were current among the Buddhists, fables and parables which they ascribed to Buddha, and whose sanctity they sought to increase by identifying the best character in any story with Buddha himself in a former birth. Hence the tales were called *Jātakas* or 'Birth-stories.' There is evidence of the existence of a collection with that name as early as the Council of Vesālī, about 380 B.C.; and in

---

[1] Of the remaining three, one is shown by its spirit of deadly hatred towards the Brahmans to be the work of Buddhists, and the other two are in Benfey's judgment genuinely Indian.

[2] Pedagogical reasons forbade the retention of this arrangement, except by way of specimen. Thus selection ix is boxed into viii, and xv and xvi into xiv.

the fifth century after Christ the Jātakas were put into the form in which they now
appear in the Sutta-piṭaka. They are distinguished for quaint humor and gentle
earnestness, and teach the duty of tender sympathy with animals and even of
courtesy to them. With these stories may be identified many if not all of the
fables of the Hitopadeça.

§ 38. The relation of the earliest Greek and Indian fables has been the subject
of much discussion. Wagener tried to show that the Greeks derived their apologues
from the Hindus; Weber, that the Hindus got many from the Greeks. Correspondences there undoubtedly are; but the difficulty is that the earliest forms of the
fables — which would furnish the only safe basis for comparison — are irrecoverably
lost. Aesop and his fables are mentioned by Plato and others as very well known:
but whether he was a Phrygian, a Jew, or an Egyptian is matter of dispute; and
even the Μυθίαμβοι Αἰσώπειοι of Babrius (ca. 100 A.D.), which tradition offers us as the
oldest extant collection, are removed some 700 years from the traditional date of
Aesop. The collection on which the common modern fable-books are based was
made by the Byzantine monk Maximus Planudes, ca. 1325.

At all events, the oldest extant documentary collections of Greeks or of Buddhists are much later than Alexander's invasion; and considering the intercourse of
the Greeks with India after that event, it is quite possible that the influence and
borrowing were in both directions.

§ 39. We have seen how, under the New Persian Dynasty, and afterwards
under the Caliphs, with the spread of Islam, the Indian stories were carried over
western Asia and all southern and western Europe. But this is not all. The pious
pilgrims to India from China took home with them Buddhist apologues, which were
translated into Chinese, and wandered then to Korea and Japan. They have since
been translated from Chinese into French by Stanislas Julien (*Les Avadânas*, Paris,
1859). Among the Mongols, too, Benfey has discovered many of these apologues;
and through the Mongols during their supremacy these stories came to the Slavic
peoples, and even to the Finns and Samoyeds.

§ 40. BIBLIOGRAPHY. First the titles of some books cited often below.

[1. Pāli.] The Jātaka, together with its com-
mentary, being tales of the anterior births of Gotama
Buddha. For the first time edited in the original
Pāli, by V. Fausböll. London, Trübner & Co., 1877-.
Buddhist birth stories; or Jātaka tales. Trans-
lated by T. W. Rhys Davids. London, Trübner &
Co., 1880. Vol. 1 (the only one) goes to Jātaka 40.
It contains very useful lists of books illustrating the
history and migrations of Buddhist tales.

[2. Sanskrit.] Pantschatantra: Fünf Bücher
indischer Fabeln, Märchen und Erzählungen. Aus
dem Sanskrit übersetzt mit Einleitung und Anmerkungen von Theodor Benfey. Leipzig, Brockhaus,
1859. 2 volumes. See p. xviii, no. 8. This work is
cited as "Benfey."—The fables are cited by the
numbers of Benfey and Kosegarten.

[3. Old Syriac version.] Kalilag und Damnag.
Alte syrische Uebersetzung des indischen Fürsten-
spiegels. Text und deutsche Uebersetzung von
Gustav Bickell. Mit einer Einleitung von Theodor
Benfey. Leipzig, Brockhaus, 1876.

[4. Arabic.] Kalila and Dimna, or the fables
of Bidpai. Translated from the Arabic. By the
Rev. Wyndham Knatchbull. Oxford, 1819.

Calila und Dimna, oder die Fabeln Bidpai's. Ver-
deutscht von Ph. Wolff. Stuttgart, 1839. 2 vols.

[5. Later Syriac version.] Kalilah and Dimnah or the fables of Bidpai: being an account of
their literary history, with an English translation of
the later Syriac version of the same, and notes. By
I. G. N. Keith-Falconer. Cambridge University
Press, 1885. Price 7 shillings 6 pence.

[6. Persian.] The Anvár-i Suhailí; or, the
lights of Canopus; being the Persian version of the
fables of Pilpay · · : literally translated into prose
and verse. By Edward B. Eastwick. Hertford,
1854. There is another translation by A. N. Wollaston, London, 1877.

[7. Latin.] Directorium huma|ne vite alias
parabo|le antiquorñ sapientñ.| By John of Capua.
(Sine loco et anno, gothic type, folio, 82 leaves,
quaint wood-cuts.) Copy in Harvard College Library.
Printed about 1480. Joseph Derenbourg is now pub-
lishing a critical edition of this work, with notes,
Paris, Vieweg, 1887-.

[8. German.] Das Buch der Beispiele der
alten Weisen. Herausgegeben von Dr. W. L. Holland. Stuttgart, 1860.

§ 41. The LITERARY HISTORY of the Indian apologues has often been treated. So by Silvestre de Sacy, Loiseleur Deslongchamps, H. H. Wilson (*Works*, London, 1864, iv. 1–159), Lancereau (in his Pantchatantra, Paris, 1871), Max Müller (On the migration of fables, *Chips*, London, 1875, iv. 145–209), Rhys Davids (Introduction to his translation of the Jātakas, London, 1880), J. Schoenberg (in the very readable introduction to his German translation of the Hitopadeça, Vienna, 1884). Keith-Falconer's account is on the whole the best (§ 40).

The French translation of the Hitopadeça by É. Lancereau (Paris, Maisonneuve, 1882) is especially useful on account of the full and convenient references to the books where the analogues of the different fables may be found. · This book is intended by the citation "Lancereau."

§ 42. EDITIONS AND TRANSLATIONS. The most accessible text edition is that of Professor Peter Peterson (Bombay, Government Central Book Depot, 1887. Price 1 rupee 10 annas). It contains an introduction most helpful for reading the text in course. It forms no. xxxiii of the Bombay Sanskrit Series. The text edition used most often as a standard of reference is that of Schlegel and Lassen (Bonn, 1829).

A literal English version has been given by Fr. Pincott (London, W. H. Allen, 1880). A cheap reprint of Wilkins's translation appeared in Henry Morley's Universal Library (London and New York, Routledge, 1885).

§ 43. METRES. Aside from the common çloka — see p. 300, § 21 — there occur in this book several other metres requiring description. The following five are monoschematic — i.e. the stanza consists of one metrical scheme four times repeated. The first two are simple and natural iambic-choriambic rhythms and are common in the Veda. The name vasanta-tilakā means 'Grace of the spring-time'; mālinī, 'Garlanded'; rathoddhatā seems to mean 'Car-proud.'

a. ⩗ ⏓ ∪ ⏓ | ⏓ ∪ ∪ ⏓ | ∪ ⏓ ∪ ⏓   jagatī, 22¹¹.

b. ⩗ ⏓ ∪ ⏓ | ⏓ ∪ ∪ ⏓ | ∪ ⏓ ∪   triṣṭubh, 26¹.

c. _ ⏓ ∪ ⏓ | ⏓ ∪ ∪ | ⏓ ∪ ∪ ⏓ | ∪ ⏓ _   vasanta-tilakā, 18¹⁴, 26⁹.

d. ·⏓ ∪ ∪ | ⏓ ∪ ∪ | ⏓ _ | ⏓ ∪ ⏓ | ⏓ ∪ ⏓ | _   mālinī, 22²².

e. ⏓ ∪ ⏓ | ⏓ ∪ ∪ ⏓ | ∪ ⏓ ∪ ⏓   rathoddhatā, 56¹¹.

The triṣṭubh is simply a catalectic form of the jagatī; but the catalexis gives the new cadence a trochaic effect instead of iambic. The rhythm of the vasanta-tilakā is closely analogous to that of the triṣṭubh. The rathoddhatā is essentially similar to a jagatī without its anacrusis.

§ 44. THE āryā METRE is based on the number of morae — not on the number of syllables. See Whitney, §§ 76–79. A light syllable counts as one mora; a heavy syllable, as two. In general, the āryā-foot consists of four morae. These appear either as two heavy syllables, or with one heavy one at the beginning or at the middle or at the end, or as four light syllables. In each half-stanza, a caesura occurs at the end of the third foot, and the eighth or last foot of each half-stanza is catalectic. The sixth foot of the first half-stanza must be an amphibrach, ∪ _ ∪, and that

Thus:
- _
- ∪∪
∪ _ ∪
∪∪ _
∪∪ ∪∪

of the second must be a single light syllable. No odd foot may be an amphibrach.
The metre occurs at 26⁸ and 56⁵ to 56¹⁰. The scheme is:

$$- - \ | \ - - \ | \ - - \ \| \ - - \ | \ - - \ | \ \cup - \cup | \ - - \ | \ -$$
$$- - \ | \ - - \ | \ - - \ \| \ - - \ | \ - - \ | \ \cup \ | \ - - \ | \ -.$$

Applying this scheme, for example, to 56⁵⁻⁶, we have, with the proper resolutions:

$$\cup\cup \ - \ | \cup - \cup | \ - \ - \| \ - \ - | \cup\cup - | \cup - \cup | \ - \ - | \ -$$
$$\cup\cup \ \cup\cup | \ - \cup\cup | \cup\cup - \| \cup\cup - | \cup\cup - | \ \cup \ | \cup\cup \ \cup\cup | \ -.$$

NOTES TO PAGE 16.

LINE 16. SELECTION II. Preface and introduction to the Hitopadeça. U.f. saṁskṛta-
ukti, 'cultivated expression.'

17. See √1dā. —ca belongs to nītiv-.

19. gṛh-, 956⁴. —iva, 'as if.' —Join
mṛt- w. gṛh-.

NOTES TO PAGE 17.

1. 'Just wisdom (is) the best thing, they
say' (√ah).

2. 'By reason of' the qualities denoted
by the three ablatives, 291².

3. 'The knowledge (of) weapons and the
knowledge (of) books (are) two kinds-of-
knowledge (for acquisition=) that one may
acquire.'

4. 'The first (is) for laughter — is ridicu-
lous.' This dative is explained at 287 mid.:
similar uses 17¹⁵, 20¹⁴. —√dṛ+ā.

5-6. U.f. yad nave · · · na anyathā · · ·
tad iha. —'Since ornamentation put upon
an unburned dish does not change, therefore
to children (297a) nīti is communicated
etc.,' i.e. as one decorates a dish *before* burning it, in order to have the result permanent,
so worldly wisdom should be taught to children while they are still young. Cf. Horace,
Epist. i.2.67–70. —See iha.

8. U.f. tathā anyasmāt granthāt. 7-8.
'Friend-acquisition · · · is delineated (by the
author) drawing (his materials) from · · · .'
See page 311, § 26.

9. The Rāmāyaṇa (i.36–44 = 37–45) and
MBh. (iii. chap's 106–109) tell why and how
Bh. brought the Ganges down from heaven.
See also M. Williams, *Indian Wisdom*, p. 363.
—'Town having P. as name,' 1302. In

Buddhist books it is called Pāṭali-gāma,
'Trumpet-flower Village.' Wilson thinks
Pāṭali-putra is a mere corruption of Pāṭali-
pura, 'Trumpet-flower City.' This certainly
accords well with the K'usumo-pulo (Skt.
Kusuma-pura, 'Flower-City') of the Chinese
Buddhist pilgrims — see Beal, *Si-yu-ki*, ii.83–
85. The Kathā-sarit-sāgara (chap. iii.) gives
a legend telling how the town was founded
by a king Putraka and his wife Pāṭali.
This is perhaps an invention suggested by
the corrupted form.

—The site of P. is discussed at length in
Cunningham's *Archaeological Survey of India
Reports*, viii.1–34 and Note prefixed to the
vol. See also Journ. As. Soc. of Bengal,
xiv.¹137f, with map.

10. Divide thus, sarva-svāmiguṇa; not
sarvasvāmi-guṇa: upeta, vi+upa. —King S.
need not be regarded as a historical person.

11. çuçrāva, √çru, 793a, 800b.

12-13. Construe yasya na asti (see
√1as2) çāstram, andha eva (see this) sas
(asti): -ucchedi and darçakam are attributive adjectives to çās-, and loc- is in
apposition w. çās-.

15. 'One by itself, even (api), is harmful
(17⁴ₙ.); but how much more (kim4) all four
together!'

16-17. See iti 2 and ākarṇaya. —'The
king, distressed (udvignamanās, 418) by the
shaster-neglect (-ananuṣṭhānena) of his (ātmanas) sons, who did not study books (see
1308²) · · · '.

18. See 1ka 1. 'What profit (is there)
with a son born, i.e. in the birth of a son,
who · · '.

—Observe the use of the ppl. where we
use a verbal noun: this is common in San-

skrit, e.g. 17²², 25¹², 38²⁸, and also in Latin, e.g. *post conditam urbem.*

19ᵇ is the answer to 19ᵃ.

20. 'Of (the three,) an unborn (i.e. no son at all), a dead one, and (1253a) a fool, · · ·': see 2vara. —See ca5.

21. U.f. duḥkhakarāu (supply **stas**) ādyāu.

22. See ca3. —jāto, lit. '(is) born'; pregnantly, 'is born in reality or to some noble purpose.'

NOTES TO PAGE 18.

1. Respecting the metempsychosis, see 65⁹ to 68ᵇ and notes. —vā marks the rhetorical question as a rejoinder to an objector's statement. —jāyate, lit. 'is born,' √jan, refers to the mere physical fact of issuing from the womb.

—Render the proverb: 'He (alone) is born in reality, by whose birth (see 17¹⁸ɴ.) his family attains to distinction: or (if you object to that), who, in the circling round of existence, when dead, does nót come out of some womb again?' — True, every one does so issue; but the fact *by itself* has no noble significance.

—The entire point lies in the antithesis between the mg of jāyate and the pregnant sense of jāto. Such pregnant uses of a word are common in gnomic poetry: so 21²³, 22⁶.

2. 'The best thing is one good son; but (ca5) not with even hundreds of fools (is there any profit).' The ellipsis — though harsh and condemnable — is made clear by such phrases as that at 17¹⁸ and the others under 1ka 1.

3ᵇ. Supply tamo hanyate.

4ᵃ. See ta3. For gen., 296b. —'Though born (of whomsoever =) of humble parentage.'

5. See √1kṛ6. —Note the puns in vañca-viçuddhas and nirguṇas, which words thus stand in covert and playful contrast w. yasya tasya prasūtas and guṇavān.

6. U.f. na adhīta (see vi+adhi) · · etāsu.

7. See vidvāńs. —See go. —√sad2.

8 end. Passives, 770c, 769. —U.f. yad ca ucyate, explained under ya2.

9. 'What is not to be, that will not be:

if it is to be, then it will not be otherwise': the do-nothing argument or ignava ratio. —See ced: na, if it belonged to the protasis, would precede ced.

10. 'This · · remedy, embraced-in-the-words (= iti) "What · · · otherwise,"— why is it not drunk?' —√1pā, 770b.

—Lines 9–10 are in apposition w. yad (end of 8), and contain the "sloth-talk" condemned in line 11.

12. 'One should not give up his exertion (udyogam), thinking, "Fate (will do or prevent all)."'

14. Metre, vasanta-tilakā, p. 316, § 43. —U.f. upa˳eti lakṣmīs.

16. √han+ni, 992². —kuru, 714. —ātma-has the force of a possessive of the *second* person here: cf. ātman3.

17. The loc. absolute expresses one condition, and yadi na sidhyati a second.

20–21. The collective result of a man's words and thoughts and deeds is his karman: this alone exists after death and is a powerful determinant of his course in the next birth. —kuryāt, cf. 25²¹ɴ.

23. suptasya, 954b.

NOTES TO PAGE 19.

1. See tāvant2.

2. See tāvant2. —U.f. kim cid na.

3. kār-, made (959) from the past pass ppl ~f the *caus.* of √1kṛ, 1051⁵.

4. See √ṣru3 and 770a. —asti kaç cid 'is there anyone · · · ?' see ya1.

5. putrāṇām limits punarjanma. —Cf. 17¹⁶.

7. dhatte, √1dhā9, 668.

9. hīyate, cf. pīyate, 18¹⁰ and ɴ.

11. See atra1. —Long cpd is analyzed at 1248².

—Viṣṇuçarman, if not the name of a real person, is chosen as a reminder of the synonymous Viṣṇugupta, an epithet of Cāṇakya, the wise and famous minister of Candragupta = Σανδρόκυττος or Σανδράκοττος. — See Benfey, Pantch. i.31, and Böhtlingk, Indische Sprüche, 2d ed., no. 7061. Cf. above, p. 311, § 24.

13. U.f. tad, 161. —Explained √çakA1.

14. U.f. na adravye. —nihitā, 954c.

15. Pass. of *caus.* of √paṭh, 1052a.

16. U.f. asmin (208) tu · · na apatyam.

20. U.f. -saṅgāt, 'by sticking to · ·,' 291².

22. 'You (are) an authority for · · ·.'

23. For gen., 297a. —sam-arpitavān, like kāritavān, 19³ₙ.: √ṛ+sam, 1042d.

NOTES TO PAGE 20.

2. 'By way of introduction.'

3. See √gam2.

5. 'Tale of the crow, tortoise, and so forth' (-ādi 2), not given in this Reader.

7. √stu+pra (770a)—cf. prastāva.

8. SELECTION III. The old tiger and the traveller. Hitopadeça, book i., fable 2.—The *motif* of this tale is feline hypocrisy (whether of tiger or of cat), and appears again in selection v., as also in Pañcatantra, iii.2, Kalilag und Damnag, p. 65f, MBh.v. 160.15–43 = 5421–49, Jātaka, i. p. 460, no. 128. Cf. 21²⁵ₙ.

—aham, namely, the Pigeon-king, who tells this story to dissuade his followers from taking the rice with which a snare was baited. —carann, 210. —See eka3. —The ablution and sacred grass were intended as outward symbols of inward piety. A pretender to virtue is called 'one who acts like a cat,' see Manu iv.195.

11. Observe the impersonal construction (999), which will now be extremely frequent. Logical subject in instr., 282. —See √kṛṣ+ā and √loc+ā.

12. See kim4. —asminn, 210.

13ᵃ. 'In getting even a desirable (object) from an undesirable (source)'—e.g. bracelet from tiger.

14. Observe caesura and exact order of original. —mṛtyave, '(is) deadly,' 174ₙ.

16–17. Nothing venture, nothing have. —Join na w. paçyati (16). Both gerundclauses are conditional.

18. U.f. tad. —See tāvant 3a.

19. pra-sārya, 1051 and ⁵.

20. U.f. prāk eva, 'formerly,' w. emphasis: eva, as much as to say, 'not now, of course'—preliminary hint at a general reformation of character.

NOTES TO PAGE 21.

1. Note how Brahmans are distinguished from men: so 95¹. —U.f. -vadhāt me, 'from my killing · ·, because I killed.'

2. Another me need not be expressed with putrās and dārās: whose they are is clear from nirvañço 'smi.

3. upadiṣṭas: the upadeça consisted of the three words marked by iti.

4. U.f. -upadeçāt, 'in accordance with (his) advice,' 291.

5. kathaṁ na, sc. asmi.

6. Cpd, 1253a: 2d member, adhyayana.

7. See iti 3. —"The noble eight-fold (aṣṭavidha) path" is a favorite Buddhist topic. Buddha defines it in the famous "Sermon at Benares." —See smṛta3.

8. See tatra 1: 'among those (eight things).'

9. U.f. na a-mahātmasu, emphatic litotes.

10. U.f. ca etāvān, 206. —See gata4.

11–12. See ya5. —See tathā4. —'The common saying, "vyāghro · · khādati" is · ·.'

13–14. Third word is kuṭṭanīm. —See pramāṇaya. —Cow-slaying is a heinous offence (64³), coordinated with man-slaying, 21¹. —A dvija's 'second or spiritual (61¹⁵) birth' is when he is invested with the sacred girdle, Manu ii.169.

—'The world keeps on in the old ruts, and does not, in a question of right, take as authority a bawd who gives good advice as (quickly as it does) a Brahman, even if he be a cow-killer.' People heed the social position of the adviser rather than the real character of the adviser or the intrinsic value of the advice.

15. adhītāni, √i+adhi: cf. 20¹¹ₙ.

16ᵇ. 'So (is) food (in =) to a hungry man.'

17. 'To a poor man (304a) is given a fruitful gift,' i.e. fruitful is the gift given to a poor man— cf. 22⁴ and St. Luke vi.33–35. —Observe that the logically important idea is often put in a grammatically subordinate word.

18. See ātman3 and √liṣ+abhi. —Cf. Dhammapada, stanza 129, and SBE. x.36.

20. Note the use or the omission of ca

according to the convenience of the metre:
so 22¹⁸, 26¹·², 32⁴·⁵.

—Lines 18–21 are positive forms of the
Golden Rule: cf. St. Luke vi.31; interesting
negative forms appear at MBh.v.39.72–73 =
1517–18, at the beginning of the Διδαχὴ τῶν
δώδεκα ἀποστόλων, in the Confucian Analects
xv. 23, Legge's edition, and in the Babylonian
Talmud (Story of Hillel).

22. mātṛvat = mātaram iva: similarly
the rest. —The accusatives are objects of
the first paçyati (√1 paç6).

23. Second paçyati, pregnantly, cf. 18¹ₙ.
—This proverb, along with the one quoted
by the cat at 29⁵, is quoted in substance by
the hypocritical cat in the tale of the 'Cat
as Judge,' Kalilag, p. 66. Cf. 20⁸ₙ.

NOTES TO PAGE 22.

2ᵇ. U.f. pra-yaccha (747) īçvare, 304a.

3. See 1ka 1. The idea is identical with
that in St. Luke v.31.

4. dātavyam (999) iti, 'with the thought
"It ought to be given (impers.), i.e. giving
is a duty."'

5ᵃ. Words used pregnantly, cf. 18¹ₙ.

6. √grah+prati, 722 end.

7. U.f. yāvat asāu (= pānthas) · · · tāvat
· · ni-magnas (√majj).

9. See atas 1. —√sthā+ud, 233a, caus.
1042d.

11. Metre, jagatī, p. 316, § 43. —'The
fact that "He reads the law-books" is not
a ground for a judgment' that the reader —
be he man or tiger — has a good and harm-
less nature.

13. 'Just the inherent nature here (atra)
is the surpassingly predominant thing (√ric
+ati) so

14. 'as by nature cows' (361c) milk is
sweet.' —Religious study will not change
the bad inborn nature of a man or a tiger
any more than sugar would turn sour milk
back into sweet milk again. Compare lines
20–21.

15. 'Of those having uncontrolled senses
and mind, the (religious) action is like the
bathing of elephants,' i.e. is mere external
action and without significance as an index
of character. One might infer from their

frequent ablutions that the elephants were
very religiously minded. Cf. 36⁶ₙ.

16. 'Knowledge, without action (to correspond), is a burden, like · · · .'

17. Explained under yad2.

18. Use of ca, 21²⁰ₙ. —Instead of -pāṇī-
nām, we have, for sake of metre, -pāṇīnām,
as if from -pāṇin.

19. See eva. —Note that the gen. and
loc. here express the same relation. So the
dat. and loc. above, lines 4–5.

20. √īkṣ+pari, 'are considered' (namely,
by wise people) = 'should be considered':
so Mālavikā i.17, kāraṇa-kopās, 'are (only)
cause-angry' = 'should not be angry without a cause.' Cf. 41¹³ₙ.

21. √i+ati, 992. —See guṇa2, and note
the difference between that and svabhāva.

22. Metre, mālinī, p. 316, § 43.

NOTES TO PAGE 23.

1. 'Even yonder (asāu) moon (sky-
wandering, etc., p. 22) is eclipsed (grasyate)
· · · .' The demon Rāhu got a part of the
drink of immortality — cf. 32¹²ₙ. The Sun
and Moon betrayed him to Viṣṇu, who cut off
his head. The head, grown immortal, avenges
itself on Sun and Moon by swallowing them
at times. Cf. introd. to selection xl.

2. 'Who is able to wipe out (√uñch)?'
The Hindus thought that every one's destiny
was written on his brow, although invisible
to human eye. Like enough the sutures
of the skull, which look very similar to the
written characters of some Indian alphabets,
gave rise to this belief. Now-a-days, writing
materials are placed beside the new-born
babe in the lying-in room, in order that
Vidhātṛ may write the child's destiny on its
forehead. See Shib Chunder Bose, The
Hindoos as they are, 2d ed., p. 25.

4. SELECTION IV. The deer and the crow,
and the jackal. Hitopadeça, book i., fable
3. — In the Indian fables, the jackal plays
the rôle which the fox plays in the European; see Pañc. book iii., stanza 73 ed. Kosegarten, = 76 ed. Bombay.

5. bhrāmyan, 763.

7. U.f. etad. **=bhavatu**, see this under
√bhū.

8. 'I'll first get his confidence.' **=U.f.**
upa-sṛtya, 992.

11. ā-sādya, grd of *caus.*

12. adhunā etc., explained at 999.

13. astaṁ gate etc., loc. absolute.

17–18. 'This (ayam) is the jackal, (who
is) come seeking (icchann) · · · .'

19. See √yuj5.

20. '(Is) not to be given to any one (gen.
297a) whose · · · .'

21. The story which is announced in this
line, and which the crow tells to serve as the
"example" to the saw of line 20, is inserted
in the original between this line and ity
ākarṇya (24¹), but is here taken out for the
sake of continuity and given separately as
selection v.—cf. p. 29 end.

NOTES TO PAGE 24.

1. iti refers to the story in selection v.
=√ah. **=mṛgasya,** subjective gen. w.
-darçana-. **=U.f.** bhavān api, 'you (= the
crow) too'—no less than I (the jackal) now.

2–3. U.f. adya yāvat (see yāvant 3)
etasya (= mṛgasya) sneha_anuvṛttis.

5. Ppl. of √2as+nis forms possessive cpd
w. pādape, see 1299. **=U.f.** deçe, 133.

6. '"ayam · · vā" is the gaṇanā of · · ,'
i.e. only the small-minded take into account
or stop to ask whether or not a man belongs
to their own party or race.

7. See eva. **=**The proverb expresses a
truth that underlies the doctrine of free-
trade.

9. U.f. kim (see 1ka 1) anena (501) ut-.
=Join anu-bhavadbhis (741) w. sarvāis.

10. sthīyatām, see √sthā3; imv. pass.,
770b, used impers., 999. 'Let all remain in
one place, enjoying pleasure by means of
familiar conversations.'

11. 'No one is any one's friend, no one
any one's foe'—i.e. by nature; we must
have actual dealings (vyavahāra) with each
other to bring out the friendship or enmity.

14. U.f. etasmin eva vana_ekadeçe =
(see 1316) etasya eva vanasya ekadeçe, cf.
33⁵ɴ.

16. tathā · · sati, read 303b⁴ and cf. √las3.

18. U.f. baddhas, 160. **=mām,** object
of trātum. **=** Join itas (= asmāt) with
vyādha-pāçāt.

19. (ko) mitrād anyas, 'who other than
my friend = who but him.'

20. U.f. ā-gatya upa-sthitas. **=** See
denom. √phala.

21–22. U.f. etasya (= mṛgasya) utkṛt-
yamānasya (√kṛt) māṅsa_asṛg-anuliptāni
asthīni (431) mayā · · .

23. √las+ud. cf. 162. **=chinddhi,** √chid,
689. **=**See tāvant 3b.

NOTES TO PAGE 25.

2. U.f. · · jānīyāt (730, 721—'one may
recognize'), yuddhe çūram, ṛṇe çucim.

3. bhāryām, 'a true wife,' one who has
really taken her husband "for richer for
poorer." **=**√2kṣi.

4–5. A friend in *need* (as well as in joy)
is a friend indeed.

6–7. 'Firm-bond-bound indeed (see tāvant 6) is this deer.' The jackal 'thought'
this—he did not say it aloud.

7. -nirmitās, √1mā+nis. **=**Properly, the
Hindus designated the days as first, second,
third, etc. of the lunar half-month—see
tithi. For the (comparatively modern)
names of the days as governed successively
(like those of our week) by the seven planets,
see JAOS. vi.176–7.

8. etān = pāçān: cf. the ecclesiastical
prohibition of meat on Fridays. **=**End, see
√man1.

9. U.f. yad tvayā ucyate, tad · · , 'what
you say, that I'll do.'

10. See sthita 4.

11. U.f. mṛgam anāgatam (cf. 4¹⁶ɴ.)
ava-lokya, itas tatas anv-iṣya, tathāvidh-
am dṛṣṭvā, uvāca. Note how the gerunds
mark each the end of its clause; so 26¹⁶.

12. avadhīrita-, under the denom. √ava-
dhīraya. 'This is the result of rejected
friend-words = (17¹⁸ɴ.) of rejecting them.'

15. 'His trouble is near' (√1dhā+saṁ-ni).

18–19. 'The fact that "I've done no
wrong"—that is not a ground of confidence
(cf. 22¹¹); for there is (√2vid3), from the
malicious, danger even for the good:' although—having done to the bad no wrong

calling for revenge — they might fairly expect to be let alone.

21. √vṛj, 'one should shun' — subject indefinite: this is very common, when the 3d pers. optative is used; e.g. 18²¹, 26⁸, 30¹⁷.

NOTES TO PAGE 26.

1-2. Metre, triṣṭubh, p. 316, § 43. — Note use of ca — cf. 21²⁰ɴ. — √lap+sam, pass. ppl. of caus. — See çrad and 668. — The four genitives refer to arthinām. — See kim3. — Line 2ᵇ, 'Is there a to-be-practised-deceit of the needy, i.e. ought they to be deceived?'

3-4. Metre, āryā, p. 316, § 44. — 'Who perpetrates wrong upon (loc.) · · ·.' — U.f. a-satyasaṁdham. — bhag-, voc. s. fem.

5. See 2sama 2. — kār-, see √lkṛ, caus. end, and 25²¹ɴ.

6. U.f. ca aṅgāras : see caib end.

7. atha vā = 'or rather, to express myself more to the point, — this (iyam) is the way (sthitis) of scoundrels.'

8. Metre, vasanta-tilakā, p. 316, § 43.

9. 'In your ear pleasantly something beautiful he gently hums (√ru).'

10. Gerund of √rupaya+ni.

12. Anacoluthon : 'a scoundrel, though (see ca 6) saying pleasant things, — that is not a ground of confidence (= 25¹⁸ᵇ) :' i.e. 'a scoundrel may say · ·; but that's no reason for trusting him.'

14. U.f. laguḍa-hastas (1303²) tam · · āgacchan · · ava-.

16. See √dṛç+sam and √lpṛ. Note how the three gerunds mark each the end of its clause : cf. 25¹¹ɴ. — See √sthā4.

17. utthāya, 233a ; gerund.

17-18. 'The deer waited just so as the crow said.'

18. U.f. harṣa‿utphulla-locanena, 'having joy-expanded eyes, his eyes wide open with joy.'

19. asāu = the farmer.

19-20. Note the position of the gerunds as a help to the correct phrasing.

20. U.f. bandhanāt, 290 ; not acc.

21. 'The farmer having withdrawn,' √i+antar.

22-23. See diç+ud. 'The jackal was killed by the farmer, throwing the cudgel at him in anger.'

NOTES TO PAGE 27.

1-2. 'One reaps the fruit · · right here on earth, (with =) after three · · ·, (or) three days,' i.e. sooner or later.

3. In the *original*, the fables always begin with the moral, which is then repeated at the end, in abbreviated form, with the introductory words, 'Therefore I say.' This arrangement is retained, e.g., 32¹⁰–33⁷.

4. See 1181a end.

5. 'Trap-caught (from the jackal, 291 =) by his plots.'

6. SELECTION V. The blind vulture, the birdlings, and the cat. Hitopadeça, book i., fable 4. — Cf. 20⁵ɴ., 21²³ɴ.

— The Vulture-peak, Pāli Gijjhakūṭa, is near Rājagṛha, and famous as a sojourn of Buddha.

7. 'From the evil issue of fate = as hard fate would have it.'

8. Instr., 280 end.

9. U.f. sva‿āhārāt. — See 1ka 2d and 1260. — √ldā, 668.

10. Use of inf., 981⁸.

11. U.f. tam ā-yāntam, 619.

12. See lidam near end: 'τίς δ' οὗτος ἔρχεται;'

14. U.f. api : the idea is, 'To say nothing of my disappointment at not getting the young birds to eat, I'm so very near the vulture that *even escape is impossible.*'

15. Same phrase at 23⁸.

17. U.f. dūram apasara (classical pres. imv. √sṛ+apa): no ced, han- (163).

20. 'Is any one ever punished (or) honored on account of mere rank?'

NOTES TO PAGE 28.

2. The lunar penance is described 65⁵⁻⁶.

3. U.f. ācaran tiṣṭhāmi, see √sthā4. — U.f. yuṣmān (= vulture, respectful plural) object of stuvanti. — dharma-jñāna-ratān, see √ram3.

5-6. 'And you (it seems, are) such (etā-dṛçās, q.v.) a jurisconsult that you (have)

undertaken (√yam + ud) to slay me — a
guest!!'

6. U.f. eṣas (see etad) refers forward
here! On the duty of hospitality, see Manu
iii. 99f. —√īr + sam-ud.

7. 'To an enemy (arāu, 304) even, ··
should be shown.' So Plautus says, Trin.
679 and Rud. 438, that one does not withhold
fire and water even from a foe.

8. U.f. chettum api āg-·· na up-, 'even
(in the case of one =) from one come to hew
(it) down ···.'

10ᵇ. 'And joyous or kind (sūnṛtā, as adj.,
omitted in vocab.) words as a fourth thing.'

11. U.f. na uc-, √chid + ud, 202.

13ᵇ. See √gam + abhy-ā, and guru3.

14. Render loc. by 'towards.' —Cf. 21¹⁹.

15. cāṇḍ-, loc. as in 28⁶.

16-17. yasya limits gṛhāt and refers to
tasmāi (and to a tasmāt, understood w.
ā-dāya). —sa = atithis. —dat-tvā, 991 cf.
955c. —See √gam1.

21. First evam, 'so,' namely as at 27¹⁷.

21-22. Touching the feet (Nala xxiv.) or
the head (Manu viii.114) was a kind of ordeal
used in solemn asseverations in order to call
down harm on the one touched in case of
falsehood; at Hitopadeça, p. 122⁵ = book iv.,
fable 11 (cf. Pañc. book i., fable 11), touching the ground and ears seems to be a sign
of detestation for a suggestion just made.
Here the touching seems to partake of both
significations.

23. U.f. -rāgeṇa idam ··· adhy-ava-
sāyitam, √sā.

NOTES TO PAGE 29.

1-2. U.f. iti atra āika-: see atra1. 'The
law-books, though contradicting (√vad + vi)
··, have unanimity on this point, "ahiṅsā
paramo dharmas:"' ahiṅsā is a cardinal
virtue among Buddhists.

3. See nivṛtta. —See ya3.

4. svarga-: for lingual ṇ, see 193.

5. 'There is just one friend, virtue,
who ··:' cf. 63¹⁸ɴ. and ¹⁸; also 21²³ɴ.

6. U.f. sarvam anyad hi (163) 'for all
else' (but virtue).

7-8. See ya6, 2antara3, and √muc + vi.

9-10. See iti2a and çakya3. —Lit. 'What

sorrow (of a =) in a man arises at ···, by
this forming-of-a-conception ···:' we should
expect tad-anumānena as cpd, 'by forming
a conception of this (sorrow).' If we will
think how we should feel if we were in our
enemy's place and about to die, it is possible
that we may spare even *his* life.

11-12. √lp + pra, 770c. —kaḥ kuryāt
(714), rhetorical question, cf. 18¹ɴ.

13. vi-çvāsya, grd of caus., 1051 and ⁸.

15. U.f. yeṣām ···, tāis ·· vi-lapadbhis.

16. √rabh, 160. —U.f. koṭarāt.

18. -asthini, 431. — U.f. "anena (=
gṛdhreṇa) eva ·· khāditās" iti niçcitya,
√ci + nis.

21-22. The story winds up with the distich given p. 23 end, cf. ɴ.

NOTES TO PAGE 30.

1. SELECTION VI. The ass, the dog, and
the thief. Hitopadeça, book ii., fable 3.—
Weber thinks that the attribution of stupid-
ity to the ass in the Sanskrit fables is wholly
un-Indian and due to foreign (western) influences.

4. çvānam, 427. —āha, 801a. —See
tāvant5. —See iti2b.

5. See √3gṛ and 1020, and cf. 30¹⁵.

6. māma, Böhtlingk's suggestion; MSS.
read mama. —jānāsi, 730.

7. See yathā7. —etasya (= rajakasya)
limits gṛha-, 1316. —See yatas2: correl.
tena. —See √lvṛ + nis.

8. Second mama (gen., 297a) depends on
-dāne, 1316.

12. U.f. sam-bhāvayet (caus.) yas tu kār-,
'who honors them (only) in the time for
action, i.e. waits till he is in a strait before
he treats them well.'

13. See √çri + ā. —Caesura here divides a
cpd; this is very unusual.

15. U.f. pāpīyān (208,464) tvam (sc. asi).

16. Explained under yathā6.

17-18. U.f. sevayet, subject indef., cf.
25²¹ɴ. —U.f. a-māyayā. —19. Read so 'tiva.

20. U.f. -kopāt, abl. 291. 'Because of
anger at ···, he got up (992) and beat (√taḍ,
1070) ···.' ·

22 and 31¹. U.f. para_adhikāra- ···
-icchayā. —See √sad + vi.

NOTES TO PAGE 31.

2. SELECTION VII. The lion, the mouse, and the cat. Hitopadeça, book ii., fable 4.

3. See √lçī+adhi, 629, and 619.

4. buddhvā, 991, 160. — 4–5. 'Not catching the hole-hidden mouse · · ·.'

6. U.f. bhavet yas tu, vikramāt na · ·, lit. 'Who is a · ·, he is not subdued by might,' with a play on the name of the lion.

8–9. Note position of gerunds, each marking the end of its clause. 'A cat was kept (dhṛtas) by him (tena), · · reflecting, · · going, · · satisfying, · · bringing.' —mānsa_ādi-āhāra, 'flesh-etc.-food.'

9 end. U.f. tad-bhayāt, 'from fear of it (i.e. the cat).'

10. √sṛ+nis, Epic present, 734. —U.f.asāu.

13. U.f. saṃcaran, 208.

14. See kadā end.

15. See 17¹¹N. — U.f. tadā (correl. of yadā) upayoga_abhāvāt tasya · ·: the gen. depends (297a) on -dāne (1316); cf. 30⁸N.

18. 'A servant, making (= if he made) · ·, would be or fare (syāt, 636) like D.'

19. SELECTION VIII. The crows and the serpent. Hitopadeça, book ii., fable 10. — It is told by Damanaka to Karaṭaka (see p. 312, § 29), and into it is inserted the story of the lion, the old hare, and the well (selection ix., see 32¹²N.), told by the crow to the crow-hen.

—Selection viii. answers to Pañcatantra, book i., fable 6, which is told in like manner by Damanaka. He makes the crow and crow-hen ask a jackal for advice, and the latter tells them the inserted story of the heron, the fishes, and the crab (= selection xviii.). Damanaka then finishes his story about the crows (= selection viii.), and further enforces its moral by the story of the lion (selection ix.). The *motif* of selection viii. is analogous to that of selection xvi., cf. 39⁸N.—A few references for further comparison:

Old Syriac version. Kalilag, p. 12, 13.
Arabic. Knatchbull, p. 113, 115. Wolff, i.40, 44.
Later Syriac version, p. 23–26.
Anvār-i Suhailī, book i., story 11.
Directorium, Cap. II., p. 7 and p. 9 of signature c.

Buch der Beispiele, p. 35³, 36¹⁴.
Benfey, i.167 f; ii.57. Lancereau, p. 322.

—U.f. kasmin cid tarāu · · · apatyāni.

NOTES TO PAGE 32.

1. 'By a tree-hollow-abiding-black-serpent' — see √sthā+ava.

2. tyajyatām, 771.4.

3. U.f. tāvat āvayos (491): see kadā.

4–5. U.f. bhṛtyas ca ut-. — ca, cf. 21²⁰N. —mṛtyus is predicate. —See eva.

6. etasya = sarpasya.

7. soḍhas, √sah, 954, 222⁸, 224b. —āha, 801a. —anena, 501.

9. See alam w. instr.: anayā, 501.

10. Knowledge is power. 'Whose is wit, might is his; but of a witless one, whence is the might?' Repeated at the end, 33⁷, as a *quod erat demonstrandum.*

11. Just as before (23²¹, see N.), this line announces the tale which serves as an "example" to the aphorism of line 10.

12. SELECTION IX. The lion, the old hare, and the well. Hitopadeça, book ii., fable 11. — See 31¹⁹N.

—Selection ix. answers to Pañcatantra, book i., fable 8. The Buddhist version, the Banyan Deer Jātaka, has deep moral significance as showing the beauty of self-sacrifice and the excellence of loving "all things, both great and small." This Jātaka is mentioned by name and illustrated on the bas-reliefs of the tope or *Stūpa of Bharhut,* Cunningham, plate xxv, dating from 200 B.C. or earlier. In the Sanskrit forms, the Jātaka has developed into a simple story that shows how the weak animals get the better of a powerful tyrant, not by force, but by cunning. Somadeva gives the story at lx.91–107. Compare further

. Pāli. Jātaka, no. 12: translation, i. p. 205.
Old Syriac version. Kalilag, p. 14.
Arabic. Kalila. Knatchbull, p. 117. · Wolff, i.46.
Later Syriac version, p. 27.
Anvār-i Suhailī, book i., story 14.
Directorium, Cap. II., p. 10 of signature c.
Buch der Beispiele, p. 37¹.
Benfey, i.179; ii.62. Lancereau, p. 333.

—The first three phrases of this line (12) are specimens of the regular conventional way of introducing the fables. —The mythical mount Mandara was used by the gods as a churning-stick when they churned the ocean to get the drink of immortality — cf. 23¹N. In this book, a real hill may be intended, namely Mandara, a little south of Bhāgalpur, on the Ganges, east of Magadha.

14. See √dhā+viś and √ās3. —Note that the gerund kṛtvā goes with the logical subject of the sentence.

15. See √jñā+vi, caus., and 1042d².

17. 'If that is agreeable to you · · ·.'

18. √kḷp+upa, caus. —See √ās3.

20–21. See hetu, ced, 1kal, and anu-naya. —"I would put on my good behavior, if I thought I had any chance of my life."

NOTES TO PAGE 33.

1. U.f. apa-rāddhas (√rādh) · · dhṛtas · · agre. —See 2antara 4.

2. Note use of acc. w. caus., 'to cause my master to know:' so mām, next line.

4. tam = siṅham. —gṛhītvā, see √grah1, and 254².

5. U.f. "paśyatu svāmī" iti uktvā. —tasmin kūpa-jale = tasya kūpasya jale, cf. 24¹⁴N. —tasya (= siṅhasya) eva, 'his own.'

6. darç-, 959, from caus. —U.f. asāu (= siṅhas) darpa_ā-dhmātas (√dham) tasya (= pratibimbasya) upari ('upon') · · ·.

7–8. 'Therefore I say (the proverb) having yasya buddhir balaṁ tasya as its beginning,' 32¹⁰N. See ity-ādi.

9. The main story of the crows and the serpent is here resumed: cf. 31¹⁹N.

10. See √sad+ā. —ā-gatya, 992.

11. √tṛ+ava, ppl. of caus. —U.f. cañcvā dhṛtvā, ānīya, · · ·.

12. ni-rūpyamāṇe, loc. absolute, pass. ppl. of denom.

13. Gerundives have future force.

14. 'That (plan) was carried out; that being done, that (predicted result of the plan) took place:' see under √sthā+anu2, and cf. 303b⁴.

16. U.f. kuryāt ('one may do'), yad na · · ·.

18. SELECTION X. The birds and the apes. Hitopadeça, book iii., fable 2.

—This story corresponds to Pañcatantra, book i., fable 18, which is itself only a subsidiary form of fable 17. This latter is given by Somadeva lx. 205–210. Compare Jātaka, no. 321 (vol. iii.), and further

Old Syriac version. Kalilag, p. 28.
Arabic. Kalila. Knatchbull, p. 150. Wolff, i. 91.
Later Syriac version, p. 55.
Anvār-i Suhailī, book i., story 24.
Directorium, Cap. II., p. 1, 2 of signature ᴇ.
Buch der Beispiele, p. 55¹⁵.
Benfey, i.269–271 : ii.112 and 111.

19. 'In the interior of constructed (√mā +nis) nests.'

20. 'The sky being covered (ā-vṛte) with cloud-veils, as it were with dark-garments, · · ·.'

NOTES TO PAGE 34.

1–2. U.f. avasthitān (203) çitārtān kampamānān · · ·: 'by the birds, seeing · · ·, it was said.'

3. 'We have constructed nests with straws brought hither (-āhṛtāis) by the beak-merely' (see mātrā 2, and references).

4. 'Endowed with hands, feet, and so forth (see ādi 2), why are you in distress (√sad+ava)?'

6. U.f. tāvat (see tāvant3) vṛṣṭes upa-çamas, 'now there is a stopping of the rain.' —Better perhaps, without the punctuation-bar after bhavatu: 'So let there be for a while a stopping of the rain,' i.e. 'wait till the rain stops a bit and we'll see about it.'

8. bhagnās, √bhañj, 957c. —U.f. aṇḍāni ca adhas.

10. U.f. vidvān eva upa-: caesura; na avidvān tu.

11. U.f. · · upadiçya ajñān · ·, yayus (√yā, 800c).

12. SELECTION XI. The ass in the tiger-skin. Hitopadeça, book iii., fable 3.

—This story corresponds to Pañcatantra, book iv., fable 7, which has been worked over by Somadeva, lxii.19–23. Its oldest Hindu form is the Lion-skin Jātaka. It seems to have been lacking in the Pehlevi version. Plato makes Socrates say, "Since I have put on the lion's skin, I must not be faint of heart "—Kratylos, 411ᴀ. The tale appears in the Chinese Avadānas, vol. ii., p. 59, no. 91. Compare also

Pāli, Jātaka, no. 189 (vol. ii.); transl., i. p. v.
Fab. Aesop., 'Ονος λεοντην φέρων, no. 336, ed. Lucian, Piscator, § 32. [Halm.
La Fontaine, book v., no. 21; Regnier, i. p. 431.
Benfey, i.462–3; ii.308.

13–14. 'By the washerman, covering (him) with a tiger-skin, that one (asāu=gardabhas) was let loose · · ·.' —pracchādya, see √chad ; pra, and 227. —See √muc, and 1051⁸.

15. See buddhi2.

16. See √car3. —16–18. The instr. is logical subject of the impers. pass. sthitam: see sthita2 end, and 999. —'Having a-gray-blanket-made body-cover (1293), i.e. having covered himself with a gray blanket.' —U.f. sajjī-kṛtya (992), avanata-kāyena (√nam), ekānte.

18–19. 'The ass, seeing · ·, thinking "gardabhī iyam," making (714, ppl.) · ·, ran · · ·.'

20. See iti 2a end.

Notes to Page 35.

1–2. See √car3. —See çreyāṅs and 464. —-paricchannas, √chad, 957d.

3. Selection XII. The elephant, the hares, and the moon. Hitopadeça, book iii., fable 4.
—This story corresponds to Pañcatantra, book iii., fable 1, and is given by Somadeva at lxii.29–44. It is unquestionably of Hindu rather than Greek origin, since it turns on the Hindu belief that there is a hare in the moon (36³ʀ.). Compare

Old Syriac version. Kalilag, p. 63–65.
Arabic. Knatchbull, p. 223. Wolff, i.192.
Later Syriac version, p. 135–137.
Anvār-i Suhailī, book iv., story 4.
Directorium, Cap. V., p. 10–11 of signature ʜ.
Buch der Beispiele, p. 104²⁵.
Benfey, i.348; ii.226. Lancereau, p. 337.

—U.f. varṣāsu api, vṛṣṭes abhāvāt, tṛṣā-ārtas · · āha.

5–6. 'And we, who from want of bathing are almost blind, —where shall we go, or · ·?'

7–8. U.f. tattira-avasthitās · · ·āhatibhis bahavas cūrṇitās, 'were crushed in great numbers by the (blows, i.e.) tread of · · ·.'

9–10. ā-hūya, gerund. —See √ākulaya.

—U.f. eva atra āgant-, see √gam+ā end. —vinaṅkṣyati, see √naç.

11. viṣīdata, see √ṣad, and 185.

13. 'How shall I speak · · ?' — See yūthapa.

14. spṛçann, etc., 210. —See √ghrā.

16–17. See √ḷas3 and √sthā+anu, end.

19. ucyatām, 769.

20–21. 'Even when the weapons are raised (udyateṣu, √yam), an envoy speaks not falsely; always, because he is inviolable (sadā eva avadhya-), he is, surely, the speaker of pure-truth.'

Notes to Page 36.

1–2. The moon-god's message goes from yad ete to prasiddhis. —See yad2. —'As for the fact that these hares, · · ·, by thee have been driven away (√sṛ+nis, caus. pass.), therein not rightly (see √yuj5) hast thou done.'

3. See prasiddhi, and cf. çaça, çaçāṅka, and çaçin. The Jātaka tells how the rabbit offered up its own life for Çakra and how Çakra in grateful recognition placed the hare's image in the moon's disk as an enduring memorial of the self-sacrifice — see Jātaka, no. 316, vol. iii., p. 51, and S. Beal, Si-yu-ki, ii. p. 60.

4. U.f. bhayāt idam (=τāδε, see idam) āha: idam (= 'my misdeed, just mentioned') · · ·.

5–6. See atra1. —pra-ṇamya, 192a. — See √gam 1.

6–7. tena (çaçakena), · · nītvā, etc. See √1kṛ, caus. —Here the elephant is made to worship the moon; but Pliny, Nat. Hist. viii.1, gives a curious belief about the voluntary moon-worship and religious ablutions of elephants. Fa-hian, the Chinese Buddhist pilgrim, chap. xxiii., records a like story, Beal, Si-yu-ki, i. p. li.

8–9. The rabbit is the elephant's spokesman : deva, 'O (moon-)god.' —U.f. ajñānāt eva anena (= gajena) · ·; tad kṣamyatām. —pra-sthāpitas, 1042d, 1051⁸.

12. Selection XIII. The blue jackal. Hitopadeça, book iii., fable 7.
—This story corresponds to Pañcatantra,

book i., fable 10. It is not found in the
Arabic version nor in Somadeva, and so was
probably not a part of the Indian original —
Benfey, i. p. 223. But cf. Jātaka, no. 188.
The *motif* is similar to that of the fable of
the whitewashed jackdaw among the doves,
Κολοιὸς καὶ περιστεραί, *Fabulae Aesopicae col-
lectae*, ed. C. Halm, no. 201ᵇ. See La Fontaine, book iv., fable 9, Regnier, i.298f.

—**svecchayā** ·· bhraman: same phrase,
w. the other form (763), at 23⁵.

13. tatas (= bhāṇḍāt, 1098), see tatas 1.

13–14. 'Kept pretending to be dead:' see
√dṛç+sam, caus., and sthita4.

14–15. U.f. -svāminā asāu (= sṛgālas)
utthāpya (1051⁵, 1042d). The two gerunds
go with the logical subject, -svāminā.

15–16. Note how the gerunds, gatvā,
avalokya, mark each the end of its little
clause.

16. uttama-varṇas, w. double mg, 'of the
best color' (royal purple), and 'of the
highest caste' (cf. 28¹³). —See ātman2,
and note how it is used as reflexive of all
three persons — here '*myself*.'

17–19. Construe: aham (asmi) abhiṣik-
tas (√sic) -devatayā araṇya-rājye sarva-
oṣadhi-rasena.

19–20. U.f. adya ārabhya (see √rabh+ā3)
asmad-ājñayā asmin ···. 'By our command
conduct must be made = you must do as I
command.'

20. viçiṣṭa-varṇam, 1299.

21. U.f. pra-ṇamya (192a) ūcus (800e).
—yathā ājñāpayati devas, 'as the king com-
mands' (sc. so will we do), is a common
response in the drama.

NOTES TO PAGE 37.

1. U.f. araṇya-vāsiṣu. — tasya, pred.
poss. gen., see √bhū.

1–3. Construe: svajñātayas dūrīkṛtās
avajñayā tena, ·· (see -ādi) prāpya, ··
avalokya, ···.

3. vi-ṣaṇṇān, √sad, 185, 189.

4–6. U.f. evam ced anena anītijñena ···,
tad yathā ayam ··, 'if thus by this ·· (we're
treated with contempt), then that this one
··:' see √idhā+vi5 end. — naçyati: for
mode, see 581c² and cf. yathā6.

6. amī, 501. —varṇamātra-vipralabdhās,
'fooled by (his) mere color,' see mātrā2,
and √labh+vi-pra.

7. amum, 501. —See √3ci+pari and 770a.

6–8. yatas ·· kuruta: the sentence is
constructed like the sentence evam ·· vidheyam, lines 4–6.

8. See √sthā+anu2.

9–10. tatas ·· tena api çabdas karta-
vyas, 'Then he too will raise a howl.'

11. U.f. syāt, tasya asāu (= svabhāvas).
—'What inherent-nature anyone (yasya)
may have, that (nature — asāu) of him is
hard to overcome :' see yaθ.

12. U.f. tad kim na açnāti. 'If a dog
(427) is made well-fed, i.e. put on good
rations, will he not then gnaw a shoe ?'

13. 'He'll be killed by (some) tiger,
recognizing (him) by his howl.' —tathā
etc., cf. 33¹⁴ and ɴ. and references: for sati,
see √las3.

16. 'And (consumes) destroys, as (does)
a hidden fire (antargatas analas) a dry
tree.'

18–19. ca, used loosely to connect ratas
with the logically, but not grammatically,
coordinate parityajya. — See √ram3.
—mūdhas, see 223⁴. —-vat, see 1107.

20. SELECTION XIV. The two geese
and the tortoise. Hitopadeça, book iv.,
fable 2.

—This story appears in the Pañcatantra,
book i., fable 13, and is given by Somadeva,
lx.169–177. The Pāli form of the fable is
probably the oldest, and corresponds in moral
and incident with the Chinese form, *Avadānas*,
vol. i., no. xiv. The Aesopian form, Χελώνη
καὶ ἀετός, Babrius, no. 115 of Schneidewin's
ed. (cf. no. 419 of Halm's collection), differs
in both these respects. Compare

Pāli. Jātaka, no. 215 (vol. ii.); transl., i. p. viii.
Old Syriac version. Kalilag, p. 24.
Arabic. Knatchbull, p. 146. Wolff, i.85.
Later Syriac version, p. 49.
Anvār-i Suhailī, book i., story 23.
Directorium, Cap. II., p. 10 of signature ᴅ.
Buch der Beispiele, p. 52ʳ.
Benfey, i.239; ii.90. Lancereau, p. 340.
La Fontaine, book x., fable 2. Regnier, iii. p. 12f.

21. mitram, nom. neuter: the name-adj.,
kamb-, agrees in gender with kūrmas.

NOTES TO PAGE 38.

1-2. yad, untranslatable, like ὅτι, introducing a direct quotation: cf. οἱ δὲ εἶπον ὅτι ἱκανοί ἐσμεν; so St. Luke viii.49, etc. —U.f. adya asmābhis atra uṣitvā (see √3vas). —Lit. 'Now once by fishers, going there, it was said, "By us, staying (over night to-day=) over this night here, to-morrow the tortoises, fishes, and so forth shall be killed."'

4. āhatus, 801a. —See tāvant 3b. 'Let the facts be ascertained first; afterwards, what is fitting (yad ucitam, √uc), · · ·.'

5. U.f. mā evam. —'For I (am) having a seen disaster here = (1308) have seen a · · ·.'

7-8. For the three names, see vocab. The third is of a kind with which Bühler compares the early 'Christian name 'Quodvult-dea,' and the Puritan 'Fight-the-battle-of-faith,' etc. —U.f. dvāu · · edhete (√edh). —'Both Forethought and (is) Readywit, these two · · :' the yas merely fills out the metre, see ya3.

9. SELECTION XV. The three fishes. Hitopadeça, book iv., fable 3.

—This story corresponds to Pañcatantra, book i., fable 14; see Benfey, ii. p. 137 and 91. Very similar is book v., fable 6. Somadeva gives a version at lx.179. An excellent version occurs in the MBh. xii.137. 1 = 4889. Cf. also

Pāli. Jātaka, no. 114, vol. i.
Old Syriac version. Kalilag, p. 15.
Arabic. Knatchbull, p. 121. Wolff, i. 54.
Later Syriac version, p. 31.
Anvār-i Suhailī, book i., story 15.
Directorium, Cap. II., p. 12 of signature c.
Buch der Beispiele, p. 39⁹ᵗ.

9-10. U.f. purā etasmin eva · · evaṁvidheṣu · · upasthiteṣu (303b) -trayeṇa.

11. tatra = teṣu matsyeṣu, see tatra 1.

12. See 2antara4.

13-14. See √1dhā+abhi. —'In a matter (still) future, from lack of anything to judge by, where shall I go?'= since the danger is vague and uncertain, I'll keep still for the present. —See √pad+ud.

16-17. Explained in notes to p. 18, lines 9-10.

18. See √dṛç+sam, and cf. 36¹⁸⁻¹⁴.

19. U.f. apa-sāritas (pass. of caus.) · · ut-plutya.

21. U.f. -ityādi refers to lines 7 and 8 above. Cf. note to 33⁷⁻⁸.

22. SELECTION XIV., continued. 'Therefore (tad), this to-day (tad adya) must be brought about, that I reach (yathā prāpnomi) · · :' cf. passages cited under yathā6 end.

23. prāpte, 'reached = in reaching,' see 17¹⁸ɴ. Similarly gacchatas te, 'of you, going = of your going.'

NOTES TO PAGE 39.

1. U.f. bhavadbhyām saha. See vartman.

3. kāṣṭham is subject of avalamb-.

5. 'That is an expedient; but —.'

6. 'A wise man should consider the (expedient or) advantage (of a certain course), and likewise the (inexpedient or) disadvantage of it he should consider.' Note the etymology of upāya and apāya, and the contrast.

7ᵃ. Gen. absolute, 300².

8. SELECTION XVI. The herons, the serpent, and the ichneumons. Hitopadeça, book iv., fable 5.

—This story corresponds to Pañcatantra, book i., fable 20. Cf. also introduction to selection viii., 31¹⁹. Somadeva gives the story very briefly at lx.235. Cf. also

Old Syriac version. Kalilag, p. 30.
Anvār-i Suhailī, book i., story 26.
Buch der Beispiele, p. 57³⁴.

9. Since this Vulture-peak is placed near the Nerbudda, we can hardly identify it with the one famed in Buddhist story (27⁶ɴ.), which was near the Ganges.

13-14. U.f. · · āniya, · · ārabhya (see √rabh+ā 3), · · yāvat (see yāvant 3), paṅkti-krameṇa · · dhatta (668).

15. svabhāva-dveṣāt: the enmity of ichneumons and serpents was proverbial: "They fight like cats and dogs;" cf. Pañcatantra, p. 110²²f, ed. Kosegarten, = book ii., p. 7¹¹f, ed. Bombay; and selection xxi.

15-16. tathā etc. = 37¹⁵: cf. 33¹⁴ɴ.

17. U.f. tāis (= nakulāis) · · ā-ruhya, · · sarve · · ·.

18. āvām, 491. ▬Cf. 33[7-8]N.
19. Selection XIV., concluded. ▬See eva2 near mid.
20. uttaram dā: cf. uttara-dāyaka, 32[4].
21. U.f. sarvathā atra eva. ▬See kim3.
22. U.f. evam anuṣṭhite sati, 303b[4].

Notes to Page 40.

1. sam-uhyate, √vah, 769, 252. ▬āha, 801a.
2. U.f. tadā, atra eva paktvā, khād-, 'Then he shall be eaten, with a cooking (of him) right here' = we'll cook and eat him on the spot. Note that the gerund, as simple instr. of accompaniment of an action-noun, is generally the adjunct of the logical subject of the clause, although the latter (as here) is not always expressed.
4. vismṛta-saṁskāras, 1299.
5. vadann eva, cf. cintayann eva, s.v. eva2.
7–8. Construe: yas na karoti iha vacas suhṛdām · ·, sas etc. ▬bhraṣṭas, √bhraṅç. ▬With line 7, cf. 25[14].

9. Selection XVII. The hermit, and the mouse that was changed to a tiger. Hitopadeça, book iv., fable 6.
▬This story, and the one at MBh. xii.116. 1 = 4254, are ultimately identical with Pañcatantra, book iii., fable 12 (Benfey, ii. p. 262, 281), although very different from their prototype and inferior to it. Benfey traces the connection in a most interesting way, i. p. 373. To his references, add Somadeva, lxii.125, Kalilag, p. 72, Later Syriac, p. 149, Beispiele, p. 116.
9–10. U.f. tena āç- · · · dṛṣṭas, 'he saw.'
11–12. khāditum (981[2]) anu-dhāvan: inf. hantum used similarly, 40[20], 41[2].
12. tapaḥ-prabhāvāt: the austerities of the holy men gave them supernatural powers, cf. 16[11]N.
13. biḍālas, predicate. See √kṛ9. ▬kukkurāt, 292a: so vyāghrāt, next line. ▬See √bhī and 643b.
15. 'Looks upon even the tiger as a mouse.'
17–18. See √nī. ▬yāvat etc., see 999.

19. U.f. svarūpa-ākhyānam, 'report about my true-nature.'
20. See √yam+sam-ud. ▬See √kṛ, desid.
20–21. U.f. "punar mūṣikas bhava" iti uktvā. ▬See eva.

Notes to Page 41.

8. Selection XVIII. The heron, the fishes, and the crab. Hitopadeça, book iv., fable 7. ▬ See note to 31[19].
▬The story occurs in the Pañcatantra, book i., fable 7. Somadeva has it at lx.79. The Buddhist form appears in the Jātaka. A hypocrite is called ' one who acts like a heron,' Manu iv.196 (cf. 20[8]N.).

Pāli. Jātaka, no. 38; translation, i. p. 317.
Old Syriac version. Kalilag, p. 12.
Arabic. Kalila. Knatchbull, p. 113. Wolff, i.41.
Later Syriac version, p. 24.
Anvār-i Suhaili, book i., story 12.
Directorium, Cap. II., p. 8 of signature c.
Buch der Beispiele, p. 35[14].
Benfey, i.174; ii.58. Lancereau, p. 344.
La Fontaine, book x., fable 3. Regnier, iii. p. 18.
Arabian Nights: Night 717 (Weil, iii.914).

4. U.f. tathā ud-vignam iva, 'so, as if terrified.' See √dṛç, caus., and cf. sthita4.
5. pṛṣṭas, 220. ▬See iti 2b.
7–8. U.f. te ca atra avaçyam eva. 'And these here very surely · · will be killed: I heard (√karṇaya) a plan to that effect (iti).'
8–9. See itas3. ▬U.f. -abhāvāt asmad-maraṇam. ▬kṛtas, 'am made = have become.'
10–11. See iha and tāvant4. ▬'This (heron, ayam) appears to be actually (eva) our benefactor; therefore let him be asked (√prach, 768) · · ·.'
13–14. U.f. upakartrā ariṇā saṁdhis. 'Alliance (is proper — cf. 22[20]N.) with a foe who does us a service, not with a friend who injures us (apakāriṇā — cf. 39[6]N.); surely service and injury are to be considered as the essential characteristic of these two.' The fact that one is called foe and the other friend is of no account. ▬lakṣyam agrees with predicate.
18–19. U.f. kasmin cid deçe, 'in a certain place.' ▬sthāpitās, 1051[2], 1042d.
20–21. U.f. bakas api apūrva-kulīra-māṅsa-arthī · · · kulīras api: the api's may

be rendered by 'and' or 'but,' as the sense requires — cf. apí5.

NOTES TO PAGE 42.

1. -ākīrṇām, √3kṛ+ā.

3. 'One should *fear* danger (bhayāt, 292a) so long (only) as the danger is future.'

5-6. U.f. paçyet na kim cid hitam (163). —mriyate, 773. —'Surely, if one sees not any salvation for himself (in a non-fight =) without a fight, then · · ·.'

9ᵇ is one copulative cpd adj., utta-, 1257.

11. SELECTION XIX. The Brahman and his jar. Hitopadeça, book iv., fable 8. Count not your chickens before they be hatched.

—This story corresponds to Pañcatantra, book v., fable 9. The history and literature of the fable are treated at length by Max Müller, *Chips*, iv.145-209.

—The tale recurs in the *Arabian Nights*, Night 716 (Weil, iii.910): and the Barber's story of his fifth brother, Night 166 (Weil, i.540: Lane, chap. V.) is essentially similar. Ultimately dependent on the Indian original are Grimm's Lazy Heinz and Haggard Liese, *Märchen*, no's 164 and 168. Compare also

Old Syriac version. Kalilag, p. 63.
Arabic. Kalila. Knatchbull, p. 269. Wolff, ii.3.
Later Syriac version, p. 170.
Anvār-i Suhailī, book vi., story 2.
Directorium, Cap. VII., p. 7 of signature K.
Buch der Beispiele, p. 130¹⁴.
Benfey, i.499; ii.345. Lancereau, p. 345.
La Fontaine, b'k vii., fable 10. Regnier, ii.145,495.

—For -çarman in names, see 50¹³ and N., and see viṣṇuçarman in vocab.

11-12. The feasts of the winter and summer solstices (corresponding to Christmas and Midsummer), originated in the worship of the sun at his 'entrance' (saṁkrānti) upon his 'north-course' and his 'south-course' respectively, and were celebrated with lavish alms-giving, as appears from the Pañcatantra, book ii., fable 2 (where Kosegarten, 119¹, reads uttarāyaṇa-, and the Bombay ed., 14²¹, reads dakṣiṇāyana-: see this last in vocab.).

—The vernal equinox was also the occasion of great festivities, whence, doubtless, the fulness of the Brahman's jar. This feast survives as the *Holī* or Indian Carnival — described by H. H. Wilson, *Works*, ii.222-43.

12-14. U.f. tatas tam (= çarāvam) ā-dāya, asāu (devaçarmā), çayyā-nikṣipta+dehas (1297) san (redundant, √1as3), rātrāu acintayat. —The long cpd : 'in a dish-filled-pot-maker's-shed-part (ekadeçe).'

14-17. Construe : yadi aham, imam · · vikrīya, · · prāpnomi, tadā (introduces verb of apodosis, karomi) tāis (= kapardakāis) · · çarāvān tatas ghaṭa-ādīn upakrīya vikrīya, anekadhā vṛddhāis · · · -ādikam upakrīya, · · utpādya, · · karomi. As a help to the correct phrasing, note that the interjected adverbial clauses end each with its gerund. —tatas, line 15, 'then,' equiv. to 'and': 'dishes and jars and so forth.'

17-18. U.f. tāsu · · yā adh-, tasyām · · : 'who among those wives (is) most beautiful, on her I bestow · · ·.'

18-20. 'Thereupon, when her co-wives (tat-sapatnyas), jealous, quarrel, then I (will) beat them so' (ittham, said while he throws the cudgel to show how). —U.f. abhidhāya utthāya.

NOTES TO PAGE 43.

1-2. 'By the potter, (who came=) who was brought by the noise of the breaking of the pots, seeing that, the Brahman, scolded (see tiras), was expelled (bahiṣ-) · · ·.'

5. SELECTION XX. The Brahman with the goat, and the three rogues. Hitopadeça, book iv., fable 10.

—This story occurs in the Pañcatantra, book iii., fable 3, and, as usual, in a more elaborate and better form. Somadeva has it at lxii.62. Of the frequent imitations, *Gesta Romanorum*, Cap. 132 = 124 (see ed. of H. Oesterley, p. 486 and 733) may be mentioned. Compare also

Old Syriac version. Kalilag, p. 67.
Arabic. Kalila. Knatchbull, p. 233. Wolff, i.206.
Later Syriac version, p. 141.
Anvār-i Suhailī, book iv., story 7.
Directorium, Cap. V., p. 2 of signature I.
Buch der Beispiele, 109²¹.
Benfey, i.355; ii.238. Lancereau, p. 363.

6. U.f. grāma-antarāt (202) · · gacchan.

7-9. U.f. · · dhūrtās "yadi eṣas (176a) chāgas (227) *supply* asmābhis, kena api upāyena (tam chāgam) prāpya, khādyate, tadā ·· bhavati" iti ālocya, ·· upaviçya, sthitās (see sthita4).

10-11. abhi-hitas, see √1dhā. —See iti 2b. —U.f. skandhena uhyate, 769 and 252.

12. tad eva, 'just that' = 'the same thing.'

14. dolāyamāna-: Grierson, Bihār Peasant Life, p. 45, gives a good picture of the dooly.

16. U.f. "niçcitam eva ayam k-" iti matvā.

17. snātvā, to remove the supposed impurity arising from touching a dog. — yayāu, 800c. —Read cchāgas for -go.

19-20. See √1vid4. —vañcyate, pass. of caus. —chāgatas, see 1098c².

Notes to Page 44.

1. Selection XXI. The Brahman and his faithful ichneumon. Hitopadeça, book iv., fable 13.

—This story corresponds to Pañcatantra, book v., fable 2. It is undoubtedly of Buddhistic origin — Beal, *Academy*, Nov. 1882, p. 331. It is discussed by Benfey, i.479, who gives a Mongol version and a Tamil imitation. Somadeva has the story at lxiv.3. Lancereau mentions numerous versions and imitations, p. 384. Especially famous is a parallel story, which is told of Llewellyn the Great and his faithful hound Gellert, and goes back to 1205. It is familiar to English readers through the well-known ballad of Wm. R. Spencer. A highly interesting English version is found in *Ye Seven Wyse Maysters of Rome*, printed by Wynkyn

de Worde, in 1520, reprinted London 1885, ed. G. L. Gomme, p. 28. Compare also

Old Syriac version. Kalilag, p. 54.
Arabic. Kalila. Knatchbull, p. 268. Wolff, ii.1.
Later Syriac version, p. 169.
Anvār-i Suhailī, book vi., story 1.
Directorium, Cap. VII., p. 8 of signature x.
Buch der Beispiele, p. 131¹⁴.
Benfey, i.479; ii.326. Lancereau, p. 384.

—Through ujjayinī ran the prime meridian of Hindu astronomers.

2-3. 'For (see kṛte) the Br., from the king, a call to offer a çrāddha came.' —çrāddha, see p. 402.

4. sahaja-dāridryāt, 'from connate poverty = a born beggar as he was.'

6-7. 'Of receiving, ···, quickly, (if it is) not done, Time drinks the juice of it :' i.e. if you have anything to receive or give or a deed to do, do it quickly or it'll not be worth doing.

9. U.f. cira-kāla-pālitam ···-rakṣārtham.

11. Natural enemies — cf. 39¹⁵ₙ.

12-13. U.f. asāu ·· āyāntam. —'Having blood-smeared snout-and-paws.'

14. See √dhṛ+ava : his conclusion was "mama ·· bhakṣitas:" anena = nakulena.

15-16. U.f. asāu upasṛtya. —See √sthā4.

16-17. 'Finding out that the ichneumon was his benefáctor, (and) possessing a discovered (√bhū+vi) deed (kṛtyā), i.e. discovering what he had done, with a pained heart (418) ···.'

19-20. 'Who, without ·· (a-vijñāya), goes to or gets under (gatas) the power of passion ···.'

SELECTIONS XXII.-XXVII.

Extracts from the Kathā-sarit-sāgara.

§ 45. The work from which the following extracts are taken holds a rather exceptional place in Hindu literary history, inasmuch as its date and authorship are quite definitely known. According to the author's fancy, it unites in itself all stories as does the ocean all rivers, and he therefore calls it the 'Ocean of the Streams of Story' or Kathā-sarit-sāgara. Following out the metaphor, he divides the work into one hundred and twenty-four chapters, called taraṅgas or 'billows.' By another division, independent of the one just mentioned, the work is broken into eighteen books, called lambakas, which Brockhaus, without authority, conjectured to mean 'surges.' The work contains about 22,000 distichs, that is, about one-

quarter as much as the Mahá-bhárata, and not quite twice as much as the Iliad and
Odyssey together. An analysis of its contents is given by H. H. Wilson, *Works*,
vol. iv. 109–159.

§ 46. BIBLIOGRAPHY. The following discussions connected with the literary
history of this work should be mentioned.

Fitzedward Hall, the Vāsavadattā, Calcutta, 1859,
Introduction, pages 22, 23.

George Bühler, On the Vrihatkathā of Kshemen-
dra, *Indian Antiquary*, i.302f, Bombay, 1872. Cf.
Weber's Remarks, ibidem, ii.57.

George Bühler, Detailed Report of a tour in search
of Sanskrit MSS. made [in 1875] in Kaçmīr etc., published at Bombay in 1877 as an Extra Number of the
Journal of the Bombay Branch of the Royal Asiatic
Society, with vol. xii. Preliminary reports had appeared in the *Ind. Ant.*, v.27f, and vi.264f.

George Bühler, Ueber das Zeitalter des Kaçmi-
rischen Dichters Somadeva, *Sitzungsberichte* der
phil.-hist. Classe der Kais. Akademie der Wiss.,
cx.545f, Vienna, 1885.

Sylvain Lévi, La Brhatkathāmañjarī de Kshe-
mendra, *Journal Asiatique*, 8.vi.397f, vii.178f. Vol.
vi. contains chapters 1–8 in text and translation.

The text has been edited by H. Brockhaus,
Leipsic, 1839, 1862, and 1866. A complete translation has been given by C. H. Tawney, Calcutta,
1880–84.

§ 47. The concluding verses of the work were printed from new and trustworthy
manuscript material by Bühler.[1] From them it appears that the author was named
Soma, i.e. Somadeva, and was the son of the virtuous Brahman Rāma. Somadeva
says that he made this collection of stories to please the queen Sūryavatī, and gives
some of the facts relating to the royal house of Kaçmīr then regnant. These facts
are supplemented and confirmed by the Rājataraṅginī or 'Chronicles of Kaçmīr,'
written by Kalhaṇa, about 1148–1157 A.D.[2] Combining these sources, Bühler
reaches conclusions which may here be summarized briefly.

§ 48. In the year 79, i.e. 4079, of loka-kāla,[3] Saṃgrāmarāja, a descendant of
Sātavāhana (or Çāta-), succeeded to the throne of Kaçmīr. This was A.D. 1003. He
was followed in 1028 by his son Ananta. Anantadeva is described as weak-minded,
rash, and impetuous, but as brave even to fool-hardiness. He married Sūryavatī,
daughter of the king of Jālandhar (jālaṃdhara). She brought him entirely under
her power, and induced him, in 1063, to abdicate in favor of his son Kalaçadeva.
He soon repented his hasty step and got control of the government again. Meantime, Kalaça abandoned himself to every vice, and, in rage, his parents determined
to punish him, and give over the kingdom to his eldest son Harṣa. In fact, Ananta
retired with his court to Vijayakṣetra, the modern Bījbahār, in [41]55 = A.D. 1079,
and after two years of feud with Kalaça, took his own life in 1081, leaving the power
in the hands of Kalaça, who held it till 1089, when he was succeeded by Harṣa.
Sūryavatī burned herself on the funeral pile of her husband Ananta. Now since,
according to Somadeva, Kalaça was king when the work was finished, and since it
was written for Sūryavatī, the date of the composition must fall between Ananta's
first abdication and his wife's death, i.e. between 1063 and 1081 A.D.

§ 49. The real source of the Kathā-sarit-sāgara is stated by Somadeva[4] to be
the Bṛhat-kathā or 'Great Narration' of Guṇāḍhya. This work, according to
Bühler,[5] goes back to the first or second century of the Christian era; but no manuscript of it has yet been published. On the other hand, important evidence of its
general character and contents is afforded by the two works that have flowed from

[1] *Ueber das Zeitalter* etc., pages 547–549.
[2] Bühler's *Report*, p. 52f; *Zeitalter*, p. 554, 557.
[3] The popular calendar (*loka-kāla*) of Kaçmīr
is counted from a date corresponding to 3076 B.C.
The era is connected — in some real or fanciful way
— with Ursa Major (*saptarṣayas* — see ఋఇ2), and so

is called the Saptarshi era. It is still in use. In giving a date, the hundreds and thousands are usually
omitted. See *Report*, pages 59–60.
[4] See Kathā-sarit-sāgara, i.3 and cxxiv.250, and
Reader 56[5].
[5] *Report*, p. 47. Cf. Wilson, l.c., p. 119f.

it, the Bṛhat-kathā-mañjarī and the Kathā-sarit-sāgara. Each is a recast of Guṇā-ḍhya's original. The former was made by Kṣemendra Vyāsa-dāsa, a contemporary of Somadeva. Its date is not far from the year 1037 A.D., and it is therefore some thirty or forty years prior to Somadeva's work.[1] Both Kṣemendra and Somadeva distinctly assert that they translated from an original in the pāiçācī bhāṣā or 'Goblin dialect'; and internal evidence[2] confirms their assertions, and, further, makes it certain that each worked independently of the other. But Somadeva seems to have been well aware of the faults of his predecessor, and his work is a decided improvement upon that of Kṣemendra, whose recast is only about one-third as long as Somadeva's, and sacrifices poetic merit in the effort to be brief.

§ 50. Although Somadeva was a Brahman, there are yet many remaining traces of the Buddhist character of his original, and even direct allusions[3] to the Buddhist Birth Stories occur. Indeed, Weber maintained[4] that Guṇāḍhya was a Buddhist. The name pāiçācī bhāṣā seems to have covered a number of Low Prākrit dialects[5] spoken by the most ignorant and degraded classes in many different parts of India. In one of these dialects the Bṛhat-kathā is actually written.

§ 51. It remains — partly by way of introduction to selection xxvii. — to complete and summarize the half-mythical account there given of the origin of the stories.

In a retired spot on the Himālayan peak Kāilāsa, the god Çiva, to please his wife Pārvatī, was telling her (Kathā-sarit-sāgara, i.48) the adventures of the Seven Fairy Kings. Unfortunately, he was overheard by his Gaṇa or attendant (see gaṇa), Puṣpadanta. Puṣpadanta foolishly told the tale to his wife, and she recited it in turn to Pārvatī. This made it appear that Çiva had palmed off upon her an old story. Even on learning the truth, she was still exceedingly enraged, and cursed Puṣpadanta to be born as a mortal. She also inflicted the same curse on the Gaṇa Mālyavant who interceded for him.

At their entreaty, however, she set a limit (anta) to the curse of each, speaking (i.59) to this effect: "There is a Yakṣa named Supratīka, who, cursed to become a mortal, is living in the Vindhya as a Piçāca, under the name of Kāṇabhūti. When thou, Puṣpadanta, shalt see him, and tell him the tale which thou overheardest Çiva telling me, then thou shalt be released from thy curse. When Kāṇabhūti shall have told it to thee, Mālyavant, he shall be released. And when thou, Mālyavant, shalt have published it to the world, thou shalt be free also."

§ 52. Puṣpadanta, accordingly, is born as Vararuci or Kātyāyana, meets Kāṇabhūti, narrates to him the seven stories of adventure in seven hundred thousand stanzas (ii.26), and is released.

Kāṇabhūti, meantime, remained in the Vindhya, waiting the coming of Mālyavant. The latter is duly born as a Brahman (vi.19, 20), with the name Guṇāḍhya, at Supratiṣṭhita (vi.8) in Pratiṣṭhāna.[6] This is identified with Paiṭhān on the Godāvarī (vi.72), about 150 miles from Bombay, east by north. After travelling in the Deccan, Guṇāḍhya returns to the splendid royal city of Supratiṣṭhita (vi.24) and is appointed a minister (vi.70) of Sātavāhana, the king of whom the story in selec-

---

[1] Lévi, Journ. As., 8.vii.216-220.

[2] Ind. Ant., 1.308-309. Journ. As., 8.vi.413.

[3] E.g., at lxxii.120, to the Boar Jātaka. See Weber, Indische Streifen, ii.367.

[4] Ind. Ant., ii.57.

[5] For the views of the Hindus and others concerning these dialects, see Muir, Orig. Sanskrit Texts,

ii².43f, esp. p. 48 and 50. Cf. also Jacobi, Ausgewählte Erzählungen in Māhārāshṭrī, Einl. § 2, § 15.

[6] Its Prākrit form is Païṭṭhāna; this is the ΠΑΙ-ΘΑΝΑ of the Περίπλους and the Βαίθανα of Ptolemy. See McCrindle, Ancient India as described by Ptolemy, pages 175-6, and J. Burgess, Arch. Survey of Western India, iii. (Bidar, etc.) p. 56.

tion xxvi. is related. In consequence of a wager with his colleague Çarvavarman
(52[1]), Guṇāḍhya forswears the use of Sanskrit, Prākrit, and the local vernacular.
Since he knows no other language, he is forced to keep silence, and so to give up his
position as minister. With two pupils he retires to the Vindhya, and, falling in
with a host of Piçācas (vii.26), learns their dialect. In this he addresses Kāṇabhūti,
who exists himself at the time as a Piçāca. Kāṇabhūti tells the tales in 'his own
dialect' (svabhāṣayā, 53[4]), i.e. Pāiçācī, to Guṇāḍhya. The hearer writes them down
in Pāiçācī, and with his own blood, since he had no ink by him. Kāṇabhūti is then
released.

Guṇāḍhya, in order to "publish the stories to the world," sends the manuscript
to Sātavāhana. The king, puffed up by his newly-acquired knowledge of Sanskrit
grammar (52[28]), rejects the stories on account of their dialect. Guṇāḍhya, overcome
with grief, reads aloud to his two pupils six hundred thousand distichs and casts the
manuscript, leaf by leaf, into the fire, while the beasts stand about in a circle and
listen with tears in their eyes.[1] One hundred thousand couplets Guṇāḍhya keeps,
because they especially pleased his pupils. At last the king hears of the strange
proceeding, comes, and takes what is left,[1] namely the Bṛhat-kathā. The pupils
expounded the poem to the king and he composed the first book or lambaka, called
Kathāpīṭha (56[10]N.), to serve as a general introduction to the rest, after Guṇāḍhya
had ascended to heaven (56[4]), released.[2]

---

[1] Compare the stories of Orpheus and of the
Sibyl.

[2] According, then, to Somadeva (and to Kṣemendra, as well, *Ind. Ant.*, i.307), the παράδοσις of the
stories is, in turn, from

1. Çiva,   to
2. Puṣpadanta (= Vararuci, Kātyāyana),
3. Supratīka (= Kāṇabhūti),
4. Mālyavant (= Guṇāḍhya),
5. Sātavāhana,   and
6. The world.

NOTES TO PAGE 45.

LINE 2. SELECTION XXII. King Putraka
and the seven-league boots. Kathā-sarit-
sāgara, Taraṅga iii.45. — Kṣemendra gives
the tale in his Bṛhat-kathā-mañjarī, at ii.48.
Tawney, i.14, adduces many parallels, among
them, Grimm's Fairy Tales, no. 197, The
Crystal Ball. See also Jātaka, no. 186 (vol.
ii.); transl., i. p. xvi.f.

2–3. See atra 1. — King Putraka's uncles
had bribed assassins to kill him. By a
greater bribe and a promise to go far away,
the king induces the murderers to spare his
life : this in explanation of the "meantime,"
the "promise," the "Vindhya," and the "dis-
gust." — For Putraka, see 17[9]N. — See
√raj + vi.

4–5. The sense-divisions do not correspond
with the metrical divisions here as they do
in the Epos. U.f. bhraman ava_āpa asāu
-ekatatparāu puruṣāu dvāu; tatas tāu etc.
— see iti2.

6. U.f. maya_asura-sutāu āvām sc. svas.

8. 'On account of this (is) our fighting.
Who (is) mighty (= proves to be the stronger), he may take it.' — Brockhaus reads
tannimittam — against the metre.

9. U.f. etad tad-vacanam ·· pra_uvāca.

10. U.f. ·· puṁsas (394)? tatas sam-
avocatām (see √vac, and 854 and 847
end).

11. U.f. pari-dhāya ('by putting on') ··
ava_āpyate.

12. U.f. yad (162) likhyate: see ya5.

13. See ya5. —'Is thought of.'

14. avādīt, √vad, 898, 899c. Aorists are
not very uncommon in this poem, though
very few have been met before in this
Reader. See 826. — U.f. kim yuddhena?
astu ayam paṇas. See 1ka 1.

15. U.f. sas eva etad (= dhanam) haret
(163).

16. See under iti2. —mūḍha, 223[4].

17. U.f. adhy-āsya, ud-apatat vyoma.

19. √tṛ + ava, with abl.

NOTES TO PAGE **46**.

1. SELECTION XXIII. Story of Mousey, the thrifty merchant. Kathā-sarit-sāgara, Taraṅga, vi.28. — It is introduced as a story which Guṇāḍhya hears on his return to Supratiṣṭhita — see p. 333, § 52. It may be called a kind of pendant to selection xix. It is identical with the Cullaka-seṭṭhi Jātaka, no. 4(vol.i.), transl., i.p.168.

2. 'By me, utterly without (vinā eva) capital, wealth was gained' (√sad+ā, caus.).

4. man-mātus, abl., 'from my mother:' man-, 161, 494.

5. tad-bhayāt: tad- (494) = tebhyas, i.e. gotrajebhyas. —See garbha3.

7. 'And there was I born, (as the =) to be the means of support of that excellent-woman.'

8. See √vṛdh, caus. —kurvatī, 714⁵.

9-10. U.f. athā abhy-arthya. — See √çak B 1. —Lit., 'And then by her, the sad one, having entreated a teacher, I was gradually made to learn writing and ciphering somewhat.'

13. For gen. w. √dā, 297a.

15-16. agamam, 846. — so 'pi marks beg. of new clause and is little more than a ổ ở̀è with viçākhilaḥ. —'Thus (i.e. as follows, lines 17-20) spake (854) to a certain · · .'

17-18. See 1 idam, near end. —paṇyena, appositive to etena.

19. punar: the antithesis is between a dead mouse and good hard cash.

—The Roman dēnārius had long been known to the Hindus. The borrowed word appears, e.g., in an inscription of the time of Kumāra Gupta (ca. 430 A.D., Ind. Ant. xv.192), given by Gen. Cunningham, Arch. Survey of India Reports, iii. 54-56.

20. See √sthā7. —te 'pi (sc. dīnārās), 'even the principal.'

22. tvattas, 1098a.

NOTES TO PAGE **47**.

1-2. Construe: asya sampuṭe (see this) tam (='mouse') likhitvā, gato 'bhūvam (829) aham, so 'pi ahasat.

3-4. -yugmena, instr. of price, 281b: mūl-, appositive. —mārj- depends on kṛte; and the other genitives go w. dattas, 297a.

7-8. Construe: aham çrāntāgatāya -saṁghāya adām (829) ambhas, etc.

9-10. dve dve, see dva: 'two apiece,' 1260. —U.f. vikrītavān (960) āpaṇe.

11-12. See tatas5: the second is a mere stop-gap. —See √hṛ+ā.

13-14. mayā, logical subject of krītam: tebhyas, abl.

15-16. Loc. absolute. —The rains made the roads impassable for the wood-men. —paṇ-, 486b. —çatāis, 281b.

19-20. 'A golden mouse was sent (1042d) by me, making (it), to that V.; and he gave (adāt) · · .'

21-22. See √sidh+pra. —U.f. lakṣmīs iyam. —satā, 'being.'

NOTES TO PAGE **48**.

1. SELECTION XXIV. King Çibi, the falcon, and the dove. Kathā-sarit-sāgara, Tar. vii.88. — This story is famous, old, and widespread. It is of distinctly Buddhistic origin and character — see S. Beal, Si-yu-ki, i. p. 125 and note. Benfey, Pañcatantra, i. p. 388 f, gives a great many Buddhist and other parallels. It occurs in the Jātaka as no. 499 (vol. iv.). It is frequently figured on Buddhist sculptures: so on the tope of Amarāvatī — see James Fergusson, Tree and Serpent Worship,² plate lxxxiii. 1, and p. 225, and plate lx. left, and p. 194; also on the great Javan temple of Bōrō Boudour. The Amarāvatī tope dates from about the beginning of our era — see J. Burgess, Arch. Survey of Southern India (Amarāvatī, etc.), p. 12, 101.

—In the Cariyā-piṭaka, Pāli text, ed. Morris, p. 77, Çibi appears as an incarnation of the Future Buddha. Sakka, in the form of a blind old beggar, asks him for one of his eyes, and he gladly gives up both of them. This is represented in a mural painting of a cave at Ajaṇṭā —J. Burgess, Cave Temples of India, p. 315. Beal gives a Chinese version of the story in his Buddhist Literature in China, p. 31-41. And the tale occurs in Mohammedan forms with Moses in place of Çibi, and Michael and Gabriel in place of Indra and Dharma (or Agni).

—In Sanskrit works the Çibi-story is common. We find it in the Southern Pañ-

catantra, French version by J.-A. Dubois,
p. 173. It occurs three times in the MBh.
It is told at iii.130.21 = 10557, of Uçīnara,
the father of Çibi (translated by P. E. Fou-
caux, *Le MBh., Onze épisodes*, p. 231); at
iii.197.1 = 13274, of Çibi himself; and at
xiii.32.3 = 2046, of Vṛṣadarbha, the son of
Çibi.

— Çibi Āuçīnara is the traditional author
of RV. x.179.1, and seems to be the heros
eponymos of a clan that dwelt between the
Indus and Akesines. See Zimmer, *Altindisches Leben*, p. 130, 431.

1. King Suçarman, having been deceived
by a Gaṇa in the form of a Brahman, says,
"This is no Brahman, but a god come to
deceive me; for such things are constantly
happening in this world; and so (tathā ca —
introducing the following story as a similar
instance), in old times, there was (abhūt) a
king, etc."

2. U.f. **sarva-sattva_abhaya-pradas**,
'giving a feeling of safety to all creatures:'
see 29¹N.

3-4. The inf. denotes purpose: cf. 987
w. 982. —'Indra himself, having taken on
· · ·, pursued (anv-apatat) Dharma' — see
dharma3.

5. U.f. **aṅkam açiçriyat**: see √çri3; for
aorist, 859², 864.

7. 'This (is my) proper food. Surrender
(758) to me (297a) · · ·.'

8. For Indra and the reader, who know
the secret of the dove's real nature, there is
a play upon the word dharmas.

9-10. U.f. enam (274b) · · a-tyājyas; tad
('therefore') dadāmi anyad · · tava (297a).

11. See evam. —ātma-, see 18¹⁶N. —See
747.

13. See yathā5. —√kṛt+ud. —aropayat,
1042e end.

15-16. See √ruh+adhi. — U.f. "· · tu
etad" divyā vāk ud-abhūt. '"That indeed is equal"', referring to the promise
contained in line 10, etat-samam.

18-19. U.f. tuṣṭāu akṣ- (pred. adj.) · ·
dattvā (991, 955c) ca · · anyān tāu · ·
īyatus (783b²).

20. SELECTION XXV. Story of Ahalyā.

Kathā-sarit-sāgara, Tar. xvii.137. — Çaci is a
pattern of wifely virtue, but Indra does not
requite her with equal fidelity. His amours
are as notorious as those of Zeus. Indra is
invoked with the words ahalyāyāi jāra, as
early as the ÇB. (iii.3.4¹⁸). He is reproached
for his affair with Ahalyā, at MBh. v.12.6 =
373; and this is narrated at length in the
Rāmāyaṇa, i.48 Schlegel, or i.49 Gorresio.
His attempt upon Ruci is told at MBh. xiii.
40.16 = 2262, excerpted by Muir, *Texts*, i².466.
Later books smooth over these immoralities
by interpreting them allegorically — see
Müller, *Ancient Skt. Lit.*, p. 529. — So Holtzmann, ZDMG. xxxii.302 (cf. 294); Muir,
Texts, iv².48.

NOTES TO PAGE 49.

2. U.f. -lubdhas (√lubh) tām. — See
√arthaya+pra, 959 and 960.

3. Construe: matis pra-, vibhūti-andhā,
dhāvati aviṣaye.

4-5. U.f. sā anu-mene (794e) · ·; tad
('that occurrence') ca prabhāvatas (1098,
291²) buddhvā (160), tatra agāt · ·.

6-7. See √lkṛ3. —See sthita4.

8-9. 'She answered her husband with a
speech, (provincially ambiguous, i.e.) ambiguous on account of its dialect, (but yet)
having some regard for (verbal) truth, "This
is, of course, a cat *or* my lover"' — see
majjāo. Gautama takes it in the latter
sense and replies tvaj-jāra.

11. 'He caused to fall on her a curse,
truth-regard-limited' (-klptāntam), i.e. not
an endless curse, but one with a definite
limit, because she did not lie outright.

12. The curse. —ava_āpnuhi, 703.

13. The limit — cf. p. 333, § 51. —See
ā 4 and 293c. —See 2antara 1. —'Until
forest-interior-wandering-Rāghava-sight, i.e.
till thou seest R. wandering in the wood.'
"Rāma removed the guilt of Ahalyā by
merely looking at her," says the Viṣṇu-
purāṇa, iv.4.42.

14. datta-çāpas, 1299, 1308. —yayāu,
800c.

16. SELECTION XXVI. The king who
didn't know his Sanskrit grammar. Kathā-

sarit-sāgara, Tar. vi.108–164, omitting 111–112, 124–133a, 154–158, 161–162. — Kṣemendra gives this story in brief at vi.35–52, *Journ. As.*, 8.vi.446. The king is called Sātavāhana; but this is merely the family name of a dynasty that reigned in the north-west of the Deccan in the first and second centuries of our era. See Oldenberg, *Ind. Ant.*, x.225 f. Çarvavarman was a protégé of this family — p. 334, § 52. Somadeva, as we saw, makes Harṣa a descendant of Çāta-vāhana; and for the last, he adds (vii.13), Çarvavarman wrote the easy grammar called Kātantra — Bühler, *Report*, p. 74.

16–17. Guṇāḍhya, who had been inter-rupted by Kāṇabhūti, resumes his story here with tatas. — adhy-āsta, 620. — tad, 'that' (garden), whose creation by Durgā (see deva2c), Guṇāḍhya had narrated a little before (vi.84). It was just outside of the capital of Pratiṣṭhāna (p. 333).

19. √tṛ+ava, 957b. — Inf. of purpose.

NOTES TO PAGE 50.

2. 'Çirīṣa-delicate-limbed, i.e. having limbs as delicate as a Ç. blossom.' — U.f. abhy-agāt.

4. 'She said "Don't with water (mā udakāis — cf. line 8) pelt me."' He under-stands it as "With comfits (modakāis) pelt me."

5. ānāyayat, √nī+ā, caus. imf.

7. rājann, 210. — See 2antara 1.

8. The order of the words is inverted to remove the ambiguity. — iti uktam · · tava (297a), 'Thus I said to thee.'

9. 'Knowest thou not the mere (mātrā2) euphonic combination of the mā-word and the udaka-word?'

12. hasati, present ppl., loc. absolute. — -ākrāntas, 955a. — See jhaṭ-iti.

13. 'Having abandoned-water-play,' 1308.

14–15. U.f. pra_aviçat · · muhyan āhārādi-.

17–18. Construe: "caraṇam me ('sti) p- vā, mṛtyus vā" iti · ·. — 'Having bed-thrown-limbs,' √2as+pari-ni.

19–20. Construe: parijanas, · · dṛṣṭvā, abhavat sambhrāntas, "kim etad" iti ('saying "What's that?"').

21–23. aham, i.e. Guṇāḍhya. — tām, i.e. avasthām. — pary-ahīyata, 770b. — prātar āvām ('I. and Ç.').

NOTES TO PAGE 51.

1–2. sarvasya, subjective gen. w. praveçe, which is loc. absol. w. ruddhe. — See ka-tham. — mama begins new clause. — See paçca.

3–4. Construe: nṛpas vijñaptas (1042d2) mayā, upaviçya · ·. — See √vṛt7.

5–6. 'S., tho' he heard it, kept silent (just so, tathā eva, i.e.) nevertheless.' See √1as4. — U.f. tatas ca idam.

7–8. U.f. · · kuru" iti prāk · · tena · · adya · · niçi — see adya.

9–10. See svapna. — U.f. nabhasas cyu-tam (nom.) — see √cyu4. — See √kas+vi.

11–12. tasmāt = ambujāt. — dhavala-ambarā, like the one Socrates sees, *Crito* 44.

13. iyat (451) dṛṣṭvā. — See √man 1.

15–16. 'Ç. having thus announced his vision'— see √1vid+ni and 1308. — U.f. asta-māunas · · avadat.

17–18. The question goes to pāṇḍityam. — See √çak B1, pass. of caus. of desid. — kālena: for instr., 281c. Similarly var-ṣāis, line 21.

19. tena = pāṇḍityena. — eṣā, 'this' that you see about me. — na pratibhāsate = 'sordet.'

20. Observe caesura, and see 1ka 1. 'What pray has a fool to do with power, as it were a block with ornaments?' i.e. he has no more to do · ·, than a block · ·.

21–22. In the introduction to the Pañ-catantra, also, the time needed for learning Sanskrit grammar is put at twelve years. — See mukha4.

23. See √çak B1, caus. — tad = grammar.

NOTES TO PAGE 52.

2. kuryāt, √1kṛ 1.

5–7. Protasis ends w. ced: tatas begins apodosis; 'then by me are renounced (tyak-tam) these three languages which pass cur-rent' (√bhū+sam3). See p. 334, § 52. — See tadvat. — Kṣemendra (vi.52) has apa-bhraṅça for Somadeva's deçabhāṣā. Both of these terms denote indeed a Prākrit dialect; but, in contrast with the word prākṛtam in this connection, they denote a vernacular of a lower order than prākṛtam.

8–9. U.f. na ced evam · ·, -abdān (276) vahāmi eṣas · · : eṣas, emphatic, 'I, this one,' 'I, Ç. here, (will) carry · ·.'

10–11. tasminn = Ç.   — agamam, 846. —See √man 1.

12. ca vīhastaḥ is Boehtlingk's emendation for cavīhastaḥ.

15. 'Without S., no other way of escape appears.' She is led to look to S. or Kumāra for help, because a kumāra (see this) opened the lotus (51¹⁰).— Tawney. Weber conjectured that the war-god Skanda owed his name and existence to Alexander the Great.

18. Caesura. —**19.** prāpa, 783c².

21. 'Showed (√lkṛ 1) favor to him (tasya, 297a), i.e. to Ç.'

22–23. 'Having magic power by K.'s gift.' —See cintitop-: for a like magic, see 45¹⁸.

NOTES TO PAGE 53.

1–2. U.f. prādus āsan ca tās (sciences) tasya (= dat.) · · tatkṣaṇam. · · · hi (163).

3. SELECTION XXVII. The pathetic history of the stories. Kathā-sarit-sāgara, Tar. viii. — It forms Kṣemendra's eighth chapter (of only 16 couplets), *Jour. As.*, 8.vi.449. For a general explanation of the Taraṅga, see p. 333, § 51f.

3–4. 'So, by G's request (vii.113), that tale was told by K. in his own (piçāca) dialect.'

5–6. 'And by G., likewise in (lit. with) that dialect, in (lit. with, 281c) seven years (varṣāis), it (sā) was written down as seven couplet-lacs' (appositively).

7–8. U.f. mā (580) · · hārṣus (882) iti : 'Thinking "Let them not steal it," i.e. Fearing lest they might.'

—Both Somadeva and Kṣemendra state that the stories were written down in blood: S. gives the lack of ink as a reason; K. gives none. But the statement may rest on a popular superstition like the Germanic one which ascribes peculiar virtues to pure spittle (cf. also St. Mark viii.23) and to blood. Life rests in the blood, the "vital fluid"; from it a drink of immortality is made; and with it pacts are made or subscribed (cf. Faust, l. 1383).

—At present (1878), all available information points to a Phoenician-Aramaic origin of the Indian alphabets. Writing was probably introduced not earlier than 400 B.C., and was, certainly, little used in India before 250 B.C. So says Burnell, *Palaeography*,² p. 9. See also Whitney, § 2. The material was the palm-leaf, and in Kaçmīr, birch-bark. Paper was introduced by the Mohammedans, i.e. not till after 1000 A.D. For ink, see maṣī in vocab.

9–10. 'The sky (ambaram) became filled (nirantaram) with S. etc., who came (āyā-tāis) to listen, [became filled *or* covered] as if (iva) with a canopy.'

12. See √gam4. K. was orig. a yakṣa, see p. 333, § 51. —çāpa-muktas would be better.

15–16. 'I must make my B. famous on earth; and this business (of making it so) was enjoined on (lit. announced to, ud-īritas) me by Durgā when she told how my curse would end (lit. in the declaration, -uktāu, of the end, -anta-).' See p. 333, § 51.

19–20. The two nominatives in l. 19 are in partitive apposition to çiṣyāu · · ubhāu, the subject of ūcatus.

NOTES TO PAGE 54.

1. Explained under sthāna6.

4. pra_ahiṇot, 192c. —dattvā : cf. 991 w. 955c.

6. The garden mentioned at 49¹⁷ — see N.

7–8. 'That MS. was shown to S. (genitive, 297a²) with the words "This is G's work."' —The gender of the pred. determines that of the subject, eṣā.

11. See pramāṇa. "The length of the poem (700,000 distichs) is a weighty argument in its favor, but—" This is quite in accord with later Hindu taste. As if the 100,000 distichs of the extant MBh. were not enough, the preface (MBh. i.1.106a = 104c) tells us that there was a version of 3,000,000 couplets for the use of the gods. Fortunately their years were lengthened out so as to give them plenty of time to hear it—see

58⁸ₙ. The Manes had to get along with a version of 1,500,000. Guṇādhya is said (54²², 56¹) to keep only one-seventh of his poem; but even this is an exaggeration (it contains less than 22,000 couplets — p. 331). Similarly Manu is said to have been abridged from 100,000 to 12,000 and then to 4,000. It contains less than 3,000 — strictly, 2685, cf. p. 341, § 56.

18. vivikta-ramya-, 1257 : √vic+vi. — bhūbhāgam, in appos. w. çil-.

19–20. √īkṣ+vi. —√vac and çru, caus.

23. U.f. tasmin·· paṭhati, loc. absol.

Notes to Page 55.

1–3. These three lines and the preceding line make one sentence; the last word is the subject. —pari-tyakta-, 'having abandoned grass-food, quitting their pasturage.' —U.f. āsan abhyetya (√i+abhy-ā, 992): cf. sam-etya, line 10.

—Compare the story of Orpheus. In the MBh., iv.39.6 = 1290, horses shed tears. The horses of Achilles lament the death of Patroklos, Il. 17.426: cf. Pliny, *Nat. Hist.*, viii. 42 = 64.

5. See √vad4. —See ja.

8–9. U.f. ūcus·· girāu·· ko 'pi··.

14–15. 'He saw him completely (abhitas) overspread (√3kṛ) with tangled locks, (that were) like (iva) the smoke of what was left of the fire of his curse, which was [practically] extinguished' [but still smouldering; for G. was almost, but not quite, released from his ban — p. 334].

—Lit., 'as it were, the smoke-of-extinguished-remaining-curse-fire.' The long cpd receives a fem. pl. ending to conform w. jaṭābhis; but it is a genitively dependent subst. (1264 — not adj.) cpd, whose prior member, praçānta-çeṣaçāpāgni, is a descriptive noun cpd (1280); çeṣa-çāpāgni, again, is a descriptive noun cpd (1280); and çāpa-agni, finally, is a descriptive noun cpd (1280b), with a bold metaphor. Cf. Kathā-sarit-sāgara, xix.104.

18ᵃ. '(The adventures) of himself as P.': there is no objection to this grammatically (cf. τῇ ἐμῇ χειρὶ Παύλου); but G. and P. were never identical — see p. 334. The reading puṣpadantasya ca svaṁ ca would be correct in sense and metre.

19. kathā_avatāraṁ tam is in apposition w. -ceṣṭitam; 'the adventures (which were that coming down, i.e.) which were the occasion of that coming down of the divine story from heaven to earth.'

20. See gaṇa2. — 'Recognizing him as··.' —U.f. pāda_ānatas, √nam. —See p. 333, § 51.

Notes to Page 56.

1. See 1idam, end. 'But here are 100,000 (making) one story; take that.' Compare the story of the Sibyl.

3–4. See √mantraya+ā, and pada4.

5–6. Metre, āryā, p. 316, § 44. —U.f. ādāya·· agāt (830) nija-. The long cpd (q.v.) goes w. kathām.

7–8. Metre, as before. —The dual cpd is in the accusative — see √bhaj+saṁ-vi 2. For the long cpd, see 1253a.

9–10. Metre, as before. — 'And with (the help of) those two, King S., having comforted that Kathā, in order to narrate (vaktum) her *or* its descent-to-earth in that (pāiçācī) dialect, composed (cakre) the Kathāpīṭha.' This is the name of the prefatory lambaka; but there is a double mg, 'he made the pedestal of Kathā (personified), the next book being called 'head of K.,' Kathāmukha. He consoles (√çvas+ā, gerund of caus.) Kathā or Story, by studying it, and so atoning for the indignity he had offered it, 54¹².

11–12. Metre, rathoddhata, p. 316, § 43. — 'And that Story, full of varied beauties, made men forget the stories of the gods [lit. (was) possessing forgotten god-stories], by reason of its interest (kutūhalāt, 291²). Then (atra3), after accomplishing that in the city, it attained to uninterrupted fame in the three worlds.'

SELECTION XXVIII.

EXTRACTS FROM THE MÂNAVA-DHARMA-ÇÂSTRA.

§ 53. BIBLIOGRAPHICAL. The Manu literature is now very extensive. Only several of the most important and recent works need be mentioned here.

Arthur C. Burnell and Edward W. Hopkins. The ordinances of Manu. Translated from the Sanskrit. With an introduction. London, Trübner & Co. 1884. 8°. Price 12 shillings.

George Bühler. The laws of Manu. Translated with extracts from seven commentaries. [=SBE. vol. xxv.] Oxford, at the Clarendon Press. 1886. 8°. Price 21 shillings. The volume contains an elaborate and valuable introduction.

Julius Jolly. Mânava-Dharma-çâstra, the code of Manu. Original Sanskrit text, with critical notes. London, Trübner & Co. May, 1887. 8°. Price 10 shillings 6 pence.

Burnell's introduction contains an argument on the date of our Manu text. Professor Hopkins has summed up and criticised this argument (JAOS. xiii. p. xxviii = PAOS. May, 1885), and concludes that it brings us not one step nearer a solution of the problem.

Bühler's introduction (p. civ-cxviii) gives a learned discussion of the date. Of this, Hopkins makes a résumé (JAOS. xiii. p. cxcviii = PAOS. May, 1887). He finds Bühler's conclusions probable, but does not think them absolutely proved by the proofs adduced.

The text-edition of Loiseleur Deslongchamps (Paris, 1830) is hardly obtainable now. It is safe

to say that Jolly's robs all preceding ones of their value, inasmuch as it is the result of far-reaching critical studies. The principal places in which Jolly's text varies from that of the Reader are i.97; ii.11,76, 125; xii.23,37,42,45,90,95,96.

The general theory of the origin of the Laws of Manu was summed up and criticised by Whitney (JAOS. xiii. p. xxx = PAOS. May, 1885). Meantime, however, Bühler's Introduction has put the question in a new light.

The relations of our text to the Mahâ-bhârata are ably discussed by Hopkins, JAOS. xi.239-275 (cf. PAOS. Oct., 1883). Here may be found, conveniently assembled, quotations from Manu in the Sûtras and inscriptions, the legendary material about him in the Epic, and a careful discussion of the passages in the Epic which profess to be the declarations of a personal Manu.

By way of calling attention to the interesting subject of the knowledge of the Greeks concerning India, occasional citations are given. The references to Strabo's Γεωγραφικά (of which book xv., chap. 1, §§ 1–73 describe India) follow Casaubon's paging.

The following introduction is in the main a brief abstract of some of the more important points of Bühler's introduction.

§ 54. The native tradition respecting the origin of the Mânava-dharma-çâstra takes the book to be the work of an individual law-giver. In accordance with this tradition, until quite recently, it has been usual for English writers to call the treatise 'The Laws of Manu.' And this designation may still be used, provided only it be used with an intelligent mental reservation, which takes due account of the results of modern criticism. For in the light of critical study, the figure of Manu, as a historical person, fades away; but, on the other hand, we find that Manu as a name is one of the greatest and most reverend of the Hindu antiquity. Questions thus arise: Whence the greatness of this name? What was the real origin of this law-book, and how came it to be called Mânavan?

§ 55. The word mânu originally means simply 'man' (see vocabulary). As we speak of human beings as the 'children of men,' so the Rig-veda speaks of them as the 'offspring of man' (mânu); and in this way arose the conception of a personal Mânu, the father of mankind. He is, in fact, the heros eponymos of the human race.

In the Veda[1] he appears as 'Father Manu, child of the Sun,' as a holy seer, the originator of prayer, praise, and sacrifice, and as the object of the special favor of the gods. In the Brâhmaṇas, Manu is the progenitor of the new race after the flood. That he was regarded as a type of wisdom, is evidenced by the ancient saw, 'Whatever Manu said, that is medicine' (TS.ii.2.10²). And again, that he was an eminent type of goodness appears from the fact that his actions came to be looked upon as

[1] For the Vedic legend of his birth, see 85¹⁵ᴺ. The ancillary books make Manu the author of RV. viii. 27-31. For ancient legends about Manu, see Bühler's *Manu*, p. lvii f; Muir, i².161f, and esp. 181f.

examples highly worthy of imitation. Thus the Veda says (TS.iii.1.9⁴), 'Manu divided his property among his sons'; and this is quoted by Bāudhāyana in his Dharma-sūtra as such an example. Such simple beginnings are entirely natural; but they are also sufficient to show how, with the growth of legal literature, the authors of law-books came to cite all kinds of (supposititious) sayings and doings of Manu as authoritative precedent. For, after the custom of referring to Manu as authority was once started, the oftener he was thus cited, the greater his factitious authority and the temptation to cite him would become. Accordingly, if we examine the four oldest Dharma-sūtras, we find much more frequent reference to Manu in Vasiṣṭha, the latest of them, than in Gāutama, the oldest. And thus, at last, what had been a mere name, a part of the traditional inheritance of the mythical past, attained to greatness as a personal authority and actual law-giver.

§ 56. Before proceeding to our other questions, let us rehearse briefly the native account of the origin of the work. In Sanskrit, the book is entitled mānava; and this may mean either 'of Manu' or 'of the Mānavans.' The Hindus say, 'of Manu'; and accordingly the opening stanzas represent the great sages as approaching 'Manu, the son of the Self-existent,' and asking him to declare unto them the law. He accedes; but deems it necessary to go back to a time before the Creation, in order to show how he derives his lineage (Manu i.33), and hence also his authority, directly from the Supreme One, Brahmán. 'He,' says Manu (i.58–60), 'composed this law-book, and taught it to me alone in the beginning; I taught it to Bhṛgu; and Bhṛgu will recite it to you.'

Bhṛgu accordingly takes up Manu's cosmogonical discourse, continues with an account of the Four Ages and of other matters, dwells on the excellence of Manu's Laws, and ends book first with a table of contents of the twelve books of which the treatise consists. And in order that we may not forget that it is all (or all but i. 1–60) put into the mouth of Bhṛgu, we are frequently reminded of the situation by an 'I will next declare' or the like, especially at the beginning of books v. and xii., where Bhṛgu is mentioned by name as the promulgator of the laws in question. In accordance with all this, the work is entitled the Bhṛgu-saṁhitā of the Mānava-dharma-çāstra, and it may conveniently be so designated. It contains 2685 çlokas or 5370 lines; compare 54¹¹ₙ.

§ 57. For the incredibility of this native account the reasons are near at hand. First, all the passages involving Bhṛgu as promulgator of the work can be separated from the rest as easily as a picture-frame from the canvas which it surrounds. Indeed, the entire first book is a most palpable later addition. And, more than this, Bhṛgu himself is cited (at iii.16), with three others, as an authority on a disputed point. Clearly, the later editors of the work were nodding here; else they would have expunged this stanza. And who knows how many more of a like sort they may have expunged?

Moreover, against the claim that Manu (to say nothing of the Supreme Spirit), was the author and the first law-giver, the case is equally plain. For the work appeals to the authority of Manu here and there, just as the other works of its class do, thus showing that its earlier editors at least did not pretend that Manu was the author of the whole. Nor was he a law-giver without predecessors or rivals; else we should not find, as we do, divergent opinions of other ancient sages cited along with what purports to be his. Moreover, the work itself (ii.6 = 58¹⁴f) admits that the law is based on the Veda, the usage of virtuous men, etc.; and it plainly mentions (at iii.232) Dharma-çāstras, which must be either contemporaneous, or else earlier than itself.

§ 58. Secondly, then, What was the real origin of the work? The first half of the answer is as follows. The Vedic works, as explained below, fall into the three classes of Saṁhitā, Brāhmaṇa, and Sūtra. Chief among the works of the last class is the Kalpa-sūtra, or 'Ceremony-rules.' No Kalpa work had catholic validity among all Brahman families. On the contrary, many of the most important old families had each its own Kalpa-sūtra. In these clannish differences, doubtless, originated the Caraṇas or 'Schools,' in which Brahman science was cultivated and sacred tradition handed down from generation to generation. Thus among the adherents of the Black Yajur-veda, we find the family of Āpastamba; and, bearing his name, we find not only a Brāhmaṇa, but also a complete Kalpa-sūtra in its three subdivisions of Çrāuta-sūtra or 'Rules for the fire-sacrifices,' Gṛhya-sūtra or 'Domestic usages,' and Dharma-sūtra or 'Sacred law.' The Kalpa-sūtra of Bāudhāyana doubtless had a similar make-up. Good editions of various Gṛhya- and Dharma-sūtras are now accessible in text and translation. They treat [1] of the sacraments, of the duties of a Brahman in the various stages of his life, as student, householder, hermit, beggar, of the duties of a king, of the law of inheritance, and so on.

Now these are the very subjects treated also in the Dharma-çāstras. But there is one great difference, the difference of form. The Sūtras are in mingled prose and verse, the latter including both triṣṭubh and anuṣṭubh stanzas; while the Çāstras are in the ordinary epic çloka. To a mind acquainted with the veriest rudiments of criticism it is quite clear from their form and language alone that the Çāstras are later than the Sūtras — a view which is in entire accord with the stanza ii.6 = 58[14], cited above. The conclusion, then, that the Dharma-çāstras, in general, as shown by their contents and form, are the outgrowth, by a very natural process of evolution, from the Dharma-sūtras, is unimpeached.

§ 59. The other half of our answer is that the Mānava-dharma-çāstra, in particular, is a later metrical recast of a lost Mānava-dharma-sūtra: in other words, that it is the 'Law-book of the Mānavans.' This is a particular thesis, quite different from the general conclusion just stated; and, although very widely accepted, it is not universally so. The theory [2] of this connection proceeds as follows. Among the schools of the Black Yajur-veda, especially among those of the Māitrāyaṇīya branch thereof, we find the school of the Mānavans.[3] According to the investigations of Dr. von Schröder,[4] the Māitrāyaṇīya seems to have been one of the oldest and most important of all the schools of the Yajus-period.[5] Of these Māitrāyaṇīyas there are still some representatives surviving in Western India; and their Sūtras are entitled Mānava-sūtras. Manuscripts of the Mānava-çrāuta-sūtra and the Mānava-gṛhya-sūtra are still extant.[6]

§ 60. Unfortunately, the Mānava-dharma-sūtra, the link most important to connect our Bhṛgu-saṁhitā with the Vedic schools, is still missing. The researches

---

[1] Compare p. 358, § 96f, below.

[2] This theory was broached by Weber (ISt. i.69) and Müller (see SBE. ii. p. xi) in 1849. It was confirmed or elaborated by Johäntgen in 1863, *Das Gesetzbuch des Manu*, p. 100f; by West and Bühler in 1867, see *Digest*[2], p. 27; by Schröder in 1879, *Monatsberichte der Berliner Akad.* for 1879, p. 700, and

in 1881, ed. of Māitrāyaṇī-saṁhitā, i. p. XVIII; and finally by Bühler in 1887, in his *Manu*, p. xviii-xlv.

[3] See Caraṇa-vyūha, ISt. iii.258.

[4] In the places just cited.

[5] Compare p. 356, § 90, below.

[6] See ZDMG. xxxvi.442-48, where von Bradke describes some of them, and states their contents.

of von Bradke,[1] too, failed to show any striking correspondences between the
Mānava-gṛhya-sūtra and our treatise.   But, on the other hand, Bühler has discovered[2] important correspondences between it and the Mānava-çrāddha-kalpa.
Moreover, as has been repeatedly pointed out,[3] the Dharma-sūtra of Vasiṣṭha contains a quotation (iv.5–8) which has every appearance of being a veritable fragment
of the original Mānava-dharma-sūtra.   In this quotation we have, first, the prose
rule (5); next, the stanzas which support it (6, 7), and which agree entirely or
nearly with Manu v. 41 and 48; and, last, a Vedic passage (8) to support both rule
and stanzas.   This is the arrangement usual in the Dharma-sūtras.   And the prose
rule (5) is characterized by the words iti mānavam as a quotation from the Sūtra
of a special school; for works valid for all Aryans are not so cited.[4]

§ 61.   Other quotations[5] are found in Vasiṣṭha at iii.2, xiii.16, xix.37, and xx.18,
in close correspondence respectively with Manu ii.168, iv.117, x.120, and xi.152 of
our text, and introduced by the formula, 'And on this point they quote a Mānavan
stanza.'   From this, one might think that Vasiṣṭha was quoting from our Bhṛgu-
saṃhitā.   But this inference is barred by the evident posteriority of our text, as
shown by its form and by other general considerations, and in particular by the fact
that the stanza at xix.37 is in the triṣṭubh metre.   We conclude, then, that the
Mānava-dharma-sūtra known to Vasiṣṭha closely resembled our text, but was not
identical with it.

§ 62.   Now granting all that precedes, there is a very strong inherent probability
in the conclusion that our Bhṛgu-saṃhitā is a metrical recast of the Dharma-sūtra
of the Mānavan school.   More than this cannot be said; for it is not a necessary
conclusion.   Its probability, however, has been greatly increased by the considerations
respecting the occasion and method of the recast adduced by Bühler.

§ 63.   The occasion was the development (beside the sectarian schools which
studied exclusively a single branch of the Veda and the rudimentary works ancillary
thereto) of the non-sectarian schools of special sciences, whose teachings claimed
validity for all Aryans.   In the old Vedic schools, the pupils had to learn the texts
of the Mantras and Brāhmaṇas of their sect, and the short ancillary treatises, on
ritual, etymology, metre, etc., called Aṅgas or 'Limbs' of the Veda.   With the
development of these subjects to elaborate disciplines, it became impossible for a
student to master them all.   He must either content himself with a thorough verbal
but unintelligent acquaintance with the texts and short treatises of his own sect; or
else he must become a specialist in the ritual, the law, or some other subject, and
renounce an extensive knowledge of the sacred texts.

§ 64.   That this truly describes the course of things is shown by the present
state of learning in India.   A good Vāidik is able to recite all the texts of his branch
of the Veda.   But in order to have an elaborate sacrifice performed, there is need of
a Çrotriya specialist, who, though ignorant of the other Aṅgas, is yet a master of
the ritual.   In the case of two of the Aṅgas, grammar and astronomy, the Vedic
schools possess no sectarian text-books of their own.   These subjects, it would seem,
had been abandoned to the specialists at an early period.   For a good while longer
the sacred law was cultivated in the Vedic schools, as appears from the existence of

---

[1] In the ZDMG. xxxvi. 417–77 (1882).   [4] See Bühler's *Manu*, p. xxxvii.
[2] Bühler's *Manu*, p. xl f.   [5] See Hopkins, JAOS. xi.242–43; and cf. Bühler,
[3] See Bühler, SBE. xiv. p. xviii f and esp. 26;   SBE. xiv. p. xviii–xx.
Manu, p. xxxi.

the numerous sectarian manuals on the subject. But even in these (see Bühler,
Manu, p. lii, p. xxv, N.3) we find mention of persons who know several different law-
books, that is, who were specialists in the law. And this fact alone would lead us
to infer the existence of special law-schools.

§ 65. Granting the existence of these schools, we have precisely the combination
of circumstances which would lead to the production of such a work as our Manu-
text. The schools had before them plenty of Sūtra-material, sectarian, of only local
validity, unsystematic, and incomplete. In the very nature of things, the schools
would tend to be non-sectarian, to widen their influence, and to systematize and complete the work of their predecessors. And this is exactly what they have done in our
Manu-text. It is absolutely non-sectarian. As contrasted with its forerunners, it
emphasizes the practical rather than the moral side of the law, treating strictly legal
topics at much greater length. It shows the signs of being a school-book. And
finally, it aims at general validity among all Aryans. This explains the fact that
our Manu shows so little correspondence with the texts of the Vedic Mānavan
schools. The recast was the work of men whose interest in their subject exceeded
their interest in a sect.

§ 66. Finally, the greatness of the name of the legendary and semi-divine Manu
suggests the reason why a special law-school should have chosen the Mānavan
Dharma-sūtra rather than any other as the basis of their new manual. In con-
structing a treatise that aspired to universal acceptance, they must *ipso facto* withdraw any claim thereto which rested on the high standing of the Sūtra-original as a
sectarian work. The problem then was, in accomplishing this task, to avoid too
violent a break with tradition. Had they taken the Gāutama-sūtra, and recast it,
waiving for it all claim to general validity on the score of Gāutama's authority, it
would indeed have been a bold proceeding to father it upon Vyāsa or Manu or any
of the great sages of yore. By choosing the Mānava-sūtra, after their silent waiver
on the one hand, they had only, on the other, to interpret its title expressly as
meaning 'of Manu,' when, — presto — without the smallest offense to tradition or
grammar, they had a name of unsurpassed authority to commend their work to the
Aryan world.

§ 67. A great deal of the recast — Bühler, p. lxxiii, thinks one half — cannot
have been derived from the Sūtra-original. The entire first book is most clearly such
a later addition; and such is likewise the twelfth book, whose classification of actions
and existences according to the three guṇas (66²f) is based on the teachings of the
Sāmkhya, Yoga, and Vedānta systems of philosophy.

What now is the source of these later additions? The Mahā-bhārata offers very
many correspondences with our Manu-text. A comparative study of the two works
shows that the editors of the latter have not drawn on the former, but rather that
both works have drawn upon a common stock of popular metrical maxims (Hopkins,
JAOS. xi.268), which embodied much of the traditional legal lore, and were ascribed
(as is attested by extant inscriptions) now to one and now to another of the ancient
mythical sages — Vyāsa, Manu, and the rest.

§ 68. As for the method of conversion of the Sūtra into our Manu-text, Professor Bühler is of opinion (p. xcii) that it took place at one time, and that our text
is not the result of many successive recasts.

§ 69. Coming, finally, to the date of the recast, Professor Bühler concludes

(p. cxiv, cxvii) that it existed in the second century A.D., and was made between that time and circa 100 B.C. General considerations make this conclusion seem far from improbable. Our Manu-text is doubtless the oldest of the class of secondary law-books, like those of Yājñavalkya and Nārada, to which it belongs (p. civ). And again, while it is doubtless posterior to the older portions of the Mahā-bhārata, our Manu-text — in some form or other — is probably prior to the later portions of the great Epic, books xii. and xiii. But we do not know the time of Yājñavalkya nor of the Epic; and at present it seems quite vain to seek for an accurate date.

SYNOPSIS.

NOTES TO PAGE 56.

15. This account of Creation (çlokas 5–13), with others, is given and translated by Muir, iv². 30f. —See idam. —'Darkness'—cf. RV. x.129.3.

16. adhyā- 1, i.e. prathamo 'dhyāyaḥ.

17–18. 'He, (himself) not-manifest, making manifest (vy-añjayann) this (universe), the grosser elements and so forth, · · revealed himself' (u.f. prādus āsīt).

19–20. U.f. yas asān atī- etc., sas · · ud-babhān.

NOTES TO PAGE 57.

1–2. Join the ablatives w. siṣṛkṣus. —U.f. apas · · ādān. Primeval waters: cf. Muir, iv². 24f; also Strabo, xv.59, p. 713.

3–4. 'That (seed) became a golden (u.f. hāimam) egg, having sun-like splendor

(prabhā).' —Brahmán is conceived as too distant to be a father; cf. ZDMG.xxxii.295.

—The idea of the mundane egg may be traced to the Veda — cf. 91¹⁶. It plays a part in divers Indian cosmogonies: see ÇB. xi.1.6¹; Chāndogya Upaniṣad, iii.19 (SBE. i.54); Viṣṇu Purāṇa, i.2.52f (see esp. Wilson's Transl.², i.39f and notes); these passages are given by Muir, iv².24f, 41f. Cf. also Preller, Griech. Mythol., i³.35f; and Pott's Anti-Kaulen, 68f.

5–6. 'The waters are called "nārās," (because) the waters are indeed the offspring of the Primal Spirit (nara). Since these were his ancient place of motion (ayana), therefore is he called Nārāyaṇa' ('having the nāra = nārās as his ayana,' 1302). This oft-recurring etymology, as found in MBh. and Purāṇas, is discussed at length by Wilson and Hall in notes to Viṣṇu Purāṇa, i.4.6, Transl.², i.56–8. Cf. Lassen, IA. i².769. For correct derivation, see nārāyaṇa.

7–8. 'What (was) that cause (etc.— see sadasadātmaka), thence-created (was) the Puruṣa, (and) in the world he is called "Brahmán."' Cf. ZDMG. xxxviii.193–4, 206.

9–10. ātmano dhyānāt, 'by his meditation' (291²). —See √1kṛ 10.

11–12. See √1mā + nis. —See diç.

13–14. U.f. -ravibhyas. —See bráhman 3. — U.f. yajña-siddhi-artham ṛc-yajus-sāman-lakṣaṇam. —Cf. AB. v.32.

15–16. The -tas puts the whole aggregative cpd in an ablative relation (1098 b). —The older designation of the second caste was rājanya, which term is used at RV. x.90.12, of which stanza this çloka is a paraphrase. For many other mythical accounts of the origin of the castes, see Muir, i².7-160, esp. p. 10 and p. 159.

18ᵇ. 'Day (is) for performance of works.'

19-20. The dark and light lunar fortnights (= one human month) form respectively the day and night of the Manes; for
with them everything is reversed. See ÇB.
ii.4.2 or AJP. iii.403. They are fed once a
month. —The *older* Greek division of the
month was in two fortnights (cf. Hesiod,
Works and Days, 780): çukla = μὴν ἱστάμενος;
krṣṇa = μὴν φθίνων.

21-22. U.f. ahas tatra (= rātry-ahnos)
udag-ayanam.

23 f. Lit. 'Attend ye to that (tan) which is
the extent both of a night-and-day of Brahman and of the ages.'

NOTES TO PAGE 58.

1. See tu 4. —Respecting the ages, see
Roth, *Ueber den Mythus von den fünf Men-
schengeschlechtern bei Hesiod und die indische
Lehre von den vier Weltaltern*, Tübingen, 1860.
The conception of a past golden age is common. The scheme of ages as here presented
is post-Vedic (see Roth, p. 24f), and based
on the simple descending arithmetical pro-
gression, 4, 3, 2, 1. Description of the four
ages, MBh. iii.149.11 = 11234, f. Criticism
and numerical details: Whitney, JAOS. vi.
152f; Viṣṇu Purāṇa, i.3.10f, Transl.², i.49f;
Monier Williams, *Indian Wisdom*, 333. Gold-
en age described by the Brahman Κάλανος,
Strabo, xv.64, p. 715.

2-3. 'Four thousand of years, they say,
(is) the kṛta yuga (see kṛtá). Its morning
twilight has just as many hundreds; and its
evening twilight is similar.' 400+4000+400
=4800.

4-5. itareṣu, sc. yugeṣu, i.e. the Tretā,
Dwāpara, and Kali, which last respectively
3600, 2400, and 1200. Total of all four,
12,000. —See √vṛt2.

6-7. See ādi 1. — 'What is that quad-
ruple-age, just now reckoned up completely,
that, consisting of 12,000 (years), is called
an age of the gods.' Cf. Whitney, l.c., 154 top.

8-9. sahasram etc., cf. Psalm xc.4; II.
Peter iii.8. —brāhmam ekam ahar: here
then are distinguished periods of Brahmán's
repose (universal death) and of his activity
("new heavens and a new earth"); see
ZDMG. xxxviii.191, § 25.

10-13 = MBh. v.6.1-2 = 109-110, with
variants.

14-15. No real difference between çīla
and ācāra. See also Bühler's *Manu*, p. lxvii.
—tad-vidām = veda-vidām. —ātmanas
tuṣṭis may decide in cases where no rule of
morals and no usage is involved. —L. 14
agrees exactly with Gautama's Dharma-
çāstra, i.1-2, except that it is in metrical
form.

16-17. -uditam, √vad. —See vi+pra.

18-19. Observe that çruti and smṛti (see
these) or 'revelation' and 'tradition' have
come to be important technical terms. Concerning their significance, see M. Müller,
Ancient Sanskrit Literature, 86f. —dharma-
çāstram, collectively: see Bühler's *Manu*,
p. xxv. —U.f. sarva_artheṣu am-.

20-21. mūle: Jolly reads tu_ubhe. —
U.f. hetuçāstra_āçrayāt, 'from support of
or relying on hetuçāstras.' Such treatises
on dialectics are mentioned a number of
times in the *Si-yu-ki* (Beal), e.g. ii.218f.

22-23. 'What is agreeable to one's own
self' — same as ātmanas tuṣṭis. — See
lakṣaṇa 1 end.

NOTES TO PAGE 59.

1-2. 'The body-consecration, having the
niṣeka as its first (rite), is to be performed
etc.' Saṁskāra (see this) is here collective,
including the various single sacraments.

—Observe that there are rites for all
stages of a Brahman's existence from before
his birth till after death. Megasthenes gives
an interesting account of the Brahmans (preserved by Strabo, xv.59, p. 712f), and notes
that even from the time of conception in the
womb (ἤδη εὐθὺς καὶ κυομένους) they are under
the care of wise men.

—The saṁskāras or 'sacraments.'
1. garbha_ādhāna, 'conception.'
2. puṁ-savana, 'male-ceremony.'
3. sīmanta_unnayana, 'hair-parting.'
4. jāta-karman, 'birth-ceremony.'
5. nāma-dheya, 'name-giving.'
6. niṣkramaṇa, 'going out.'
7. anna-prāçana, 'rice-feeding.'
8. cūḍā-karman, 'tonsure of scalp.'
9. upanāyana, 'investiture.'
10. keçānta, 'tonsure of beard.'
11. samāvartana, 'return from study.'
12. vivāha, 'marriage.'

Most of these are described at length,
AGS. i.13f or SBE. xxix.179f or 46f or M.
Williams, *Indian Wisdom*, 246, 201. Number
2 is done to bring it about that the child
prove a male. No. 3 is a consecration of the
pregnant woman by the parting of her hair.

3–4. gárbhāis homāis: 'the oblations
relating to pregnancy' are involved in sacraments 2 and 3. —The ligation of the girdle
accompanies investiture (9). — U.f. enas
apa-mṛjyate.

5–6. See vrata4. —U.f. ijyayā, 'offering' to Gods, Rishis, and Manes, while he is
a student. —sutāis: procreation of sons is
a duty. 'A Brahman is born laden with
three debts. He owes Veda-study to the
Rishis; sacrifice to the Gods; and sons to
the Manes.' TS. vi.3.10⁵. — The 'great
sacrifices' are five, to the Gods, Beings,
Manes, Bráhman, and men: enumerated
ÇB. xi.5.6¹ or AGS. iii.1 (= SBE. xxix.217)
or Manu iii.69f. —yajñāis, such as a certain
Soma-ceremony called jyotiṣṭoma, says a
Scholiast. —U.f. bráhmī, 'holy, fit for
union with Bráhman.'

7–8. See prāñc3. —'Feeding of gold-
rubbings, honey, and ghee.' See AGS. i.15.1.

9. kārayet: note that in Manu the prescriptive use of the optative with indefinite
subject ('a man' or 'one') is very common.

10. Here the vā's are = eva and mean
'just.' — Scholiast.

11–12. Subject, náma. —See √yuj+sam.
—See √gup. —"Nomen, omen." This is
an old belief: cf. ÇB. iii.6.2²⁴. The ÇGS.,
i.24.4–6, mentions two names, one of which
is kept secret by the parents to protect the
child from witchcraft. See Stenzler's note
to AGS. i.15.8. Cf. Weber's 2d Nakṣatra
essay, *Abh. der Berliner Akad.*, 1861, p. 316f.

13–14. The scholiast Kullūka gives as
examples: Çubha-çarman; Bala-varman;
Vasu-bhūti; Dīna-dāsa.

15–16. Sc. náma syāt. —See āçīrv-.

17–18. U.f. yad vā iṣṭam (see √1 iṣ) etc.,
'or what passes for auspicious in the family,'
sc. tat kartavyam. The rules allow some
latitude for diversities of customs in families, villages, etc. See 98¹⁶ and note. Cf.
Manu viii.46.

21–22. See garbha 1. —garbhāṣṭame =
garbhād aṣṭame. —upanāyanam. this
most important ceremony is described AGS.
i.19–22 or SBE. xxix.187f.

1. prad-, see 99¹N. —U.f. pari_itya (992).

2–3. bhavatpūrvam, see vocab. The formulae are: bhavati, bhikṣām dehi; bhikṣām, bhavati, dehi; bhikṣām dehi, bhavati.
Similar distinctions, 61⁷N.

4–5. vyatyasta-pāṇinā (√2as), 'by (sc.
the pupil) having crossed hands.'

6–7. adhy-eṣyamāṇam (√i, 939) etc., 'To
(the pupil) about to recite, the teacher should
say, "Ho, recite (617)!" and should stop
(ā-ramet) him with the words · · ·.'

—India presents a thousand striking and
interesting contrasts with the Occident. So
especially in her way of handing down lore
from age to age. This is described by the
RV. Prātiçākhya, chap. xv.; and reported
by Weber, ISt. x.128f; Zimmer, 210; Kaegi,
Fleckeisen's Jahrbücher, 1880, p. 451. Or see
SBE. xxix.112f,119f.

8–9. brahmaṇas (see bráhman 2) limits
ādāu and ante. —See √1kṛ7. —sravati,
subject bráhma. —√1çṛ+vi.

10–11. a+u+m = om. —Prajāpati belongs
to the period succeeding the RV., and is later
supplanted by Brahman. —nir-aduhat, 635.
—See iti 4. —Compare 57¹³.

12–13. adūduhat (856) —see √duh, caus.
—'Extracted one verse of the stanza beginning with "tad" (74¹⁴) from each of the
three Vedas.' U.f. tad iti ṛcas.

14. etām, sc. ṛcam.

16. hi, 'for,' has pertinence only as connecting this çloka with 119. —U.f. sthavire
ā-yati (619), loc. absol.

19. Hiatus, without combination, at caesura: cf. 12⁶N.

20–21. See param. —'Saying "I am so-
and-so by name," he should announce his
name.' —The older one or the one superior
in station speaks or salutes first. Thus, when
the great Yayāti is falling from heaven and
meets in mid-air Aṣṭaka and others, Aṣṭaka
asks him, "Who art thou?" but not without
excusing himself, as the inferior, for bold

incivility in speaking first.—MBh. i.88.10 =
3573. So Od. 3.24:

αἰδὼς δ' αὖ νέον ἄνδρα γεραίτερον ἐξερέεσθαι.

22–23. See abhivāda. — na jānate,
from ignorance of Sanskrit. Cf. Burnell,
Introduction, p. xxvii. —striyas: thus in
the prologne to act iv. of the Çakuntalā,
Durvāsas, behind the stage, cries out to the
women, ayam aham, bhoḥ, 'Ho there, it
is I.'

NOTES TO PAGE 61.

1–2. 'The word bhos one should repeat
(at the end of =) after one's name in salutation. For the use of bhos instead of a
person's real name is declared by the Rishis
(to be the same as) the use of the true form
of a person's name.' See bhobhāva and
svarūpabhāva. The bhos is of course in
lieu of the name of the *person addressed*.

4. 'And the vowel a must be pronounced
(added) at the end of his name, with the
previous syllable protracted'—reading pūr-
vākṣaraplutaḥ (see Bühler). Thus Devadatta and Harabhūte are to be pronounced
Devadattā3a and Harabhūtā3ya — see
Whitney, 78.

7–8. This rule is observed, e.g. in the
drama, by the Rishis and the king, Çakuntalā, mid. of act v. For other differences
in the modes of address used for or by the
different castes, see 60²ᴺ.; ÇB. i.1.4¹² (or
SBE. xii.28 or Weber's *Ind. Streifen*, i.49).
The rule is disregarded in the Epos, e.g. at
MBh. i.71.5 = 2899.

Analogous distinctions: E. W. Hopkins,
Mutual relations of the four castes, 61; Weber,
ISt. x.11f; Manu, viii.88 and 113.

9–10. 'A d- is not to be addressed by
name even if he is younger (cf. ɴ. to 60²⁰);
but with bhos or (some case-form from the
stem) bhavant a dh- should speak to him
(enam).' Thus, bho dīkṣita! idaṁ kuru!
or, bhavatā yajamānena! idaṁ kriyatām!
For the long adverb, see vocab.

11–12. U.f. "bhavati" iti evam: see iti4.

13–14. U.f. ṛtvijas. 'One should say [to
those in line 13] "asāu aham," rising up to
meet (them, even if they are) the younger.'

15–16. The 'second' or 'spiritual birth'

of the 'twice-born' (see dvija) is the upanāyana. The teacher is the spiritual father.
See SBE. ii.3,174; xiv.9.

17–18. U.f. adhy-āpayām āsa (1042e,
1045) pitṝn (see pitṛ 2) çiçus. —See ha.

19–20. 'They, (having arrived-anger =)
getting angry, asked the gods about the
matter. And the gods, assembling (sametya),
said (ūcus) to them *etc.*'

22. See iti2f and 1102a² near end.

23. See ṣaṭtriṅçat and ābdika. The
Brahmanical school-term lasted 4½ months,
began with the upākarman and ended with
the utsarga — see Bühler's *Manu*, p. xlvi,
and note to iv.95. —See guru4. —'The
course (vrata) in the three Vedas is to be
followed, (lasting 36 =) for 36 years.'
Twelve years for each Veda (see véda2),
AGS. i.22.3. This is sober earnest for a
Hindu. The idea would make a Greek laugh
—cf., e.g., Lucian's Ερμότιμος, chap. i.f, and
esp. vi.

—Not even mighty Indra can absolve
those who fain would know the Veda from
the necessity of studying it. See the charming tale of Yavakrīta, MBh. iii.135.15–42 =
10706f, outlined at ZDMG. xxxii.318.

—Caesar's account of the Druids (B.G.
vi.14) comes near the truth for the Brahmans
in several respects. Magnum ibi numerum
versuum ediscere dicuntur. Itaque annos
nonnulli vicenos in disciplina permanent. Etc.
Cf. also Roth, KZ. xxvi.53.

NOTES TO PAGE 62.

1. See 2antika: adjectives go w. vratam.

2–3. vedān (as contrasted w. dual and
sing.) = '3 Vedas.' AV. not included. —
yathākramam, first the Mantras, then the
Brāhmaṇas, in order. —Two principal elements characterize the 'course' or vrata,
viz., study (adhy-ayana) and holy living
(brahma-carya). —adhi_itya · · ā-vaset:
cf. Megasthenes, in Strabo, xv.59, p. 712,
ἔτη δ' ἑπτὰ (!) καὶ τριάκοντα οὕτως ζήσαντα
ἀναχωρεῖν εἰς τὴν ἑαυτοῦ κτῆσιν ἕκαστον etc.

4–5. 'Him (= the student), approved (on
account of [280] his =) for doing his duty,
· · · he (= the "father," sc. pitā) should presént with a cow.' —pitus, 'from his father,'

meaning his spiritual "father," i.e. (61¹⁵ɴ.) his teacher, who may also be his natural father.

6-7. See √man+anu. —snātvā, technical, see √snā. He thereby becomes a snātaka. —sam-ā-vṛttas, technical — see sacrament no. 11, p. 346. —savarṇām: οὐκ ἔστι γαμεῖν ἐξ ἄλλου γένους, Strabo, xv.49, p. 707. — lakṣaṇa-, cf. 96⁷ˑ⁸.

8-9. 'Let him give up all affairs which hinder his study (296b), but (be) teaching anyhow (see yathā5); for that is the condition of having done his duty *or* of having attained his end.' —'Teaching anyhow,' i.e. 'maintaining himself as best he can while teaching.'

10-11. çuklāmbaras: Ἰνδοὺς ἐσθῆτι λευκῇ χρῆσθαι καὶ σινδόσι λευκαῖς καὶ καρπάσοις etc., Strabo, xv.71, p. 719. The castes wore clothes of different colors. The priests regularly wore white during religious ceremonies. —See yuj2.

12-13. There is so frequent need of water for ceremonial purification that a Brahman should never be without it (see Bāudhāyana, i.6 and 7, esp. i.7.1, or SBE. xiv.160f); hence the jar. —See vedá — not véda. — 'Gold ear-rings:' χρυσοφοροῦντα μετρίως ἐν τοῖς ὠσί, Strabo, xv.59, p. 712.

14-15. U.f. na īkṣeta ud-yantam. —See √sṛj+upa and 23¹ɴ. —See gata4.

16-17. See √vṛṣ. —See rūpa 1.

18-19. 'Let him make · · · (to be) standing on the right' — see 99¹ɴ. Prad- is an adj.; and is neuter, since sexless things are among the substantives. —Places where four ways meet have been the object of awe and of many superstitions: cf. W. Menzel, *Die vorchristliche Unsterblichkeitslehre*, i.145, 163. —vanaspatīn: for an instance of tree-worship, see Kathā-sarit-sāgara, xx.26. Cf. also J. Fergusson, *Tree and Serpent Worship*, passim.

20. U.f. vāyu-agni-vipram. —apas: a similar respect for the waters (which are divinities — 83¹) was shown by the Persians (Hdt. i.138; Strabo, xv.3.16, p. 733) and the Greeks (Hesiod, *Works and Days*, 757). — paçyańs, 'facing.'

22-23. If the earth be regarded as a flat surface, under which the sun passes by night in the same plane of motion as by day, the sun will be to the north of the dwellers of Northern India at night, just as it is to the south of them in the day.

The point of the prohibitions is that the parts of shame be not turned to the Sun-god or (as at 62²⁰) any other sacred or venerable thing. The prohibition recurs in very many Sanskrit books (e.g. MBh. xiii.104.75=5029,f; VP. iii.11.10f; for other parallel passages, see SBE. vii.194), and may be traced, with similar ones, back to the AV. (xiii.1.56).

—Entirely identical is the Pythagorean πρὸς ἥλιον τετραμμένος μὴ οὔρει.—Frag. philos. Graec., ed. Müllach, i. p. 506. This coincidence, with others, is discussed by L. von Schröder, *Pythagoras und die Inder* (Leipzig, 1884), 31-39. But Weber points out that the same thing occurs in Hesiod, *Works and Days*, 727. Cf. Pliny, *Nat. Hist.* xxviii.6 end = 19.

NOTES TO PAGE 63.

1-2. ā-cakṣīta, 616. 'Nor let him tell (the fact that she is drinking — √dhā) to any body' (297a). —U.f. divi in-.

3-4. U.f. -dhvanāu ('at the sound of') ṛg-yajuṣī (1253a) na adhi_iyīta (616) · · adhi_itya vā api antam etc. See vā 1 end. —Respecting this and the next çloka (SV. impure), see Muir, iii².25f, Aufrecht, *Rig-veda²*, i. p. xxxviii, and Hopkins's note to Burnell's *Manu*, iv.124.

7-8. See go3. 'Like the earth, iniquity done in the world does not bear fruit at once; but *etc.*' —See √vṛt+ā. —mūlāni: same figure at Proverbs xii.3. —√kṛt. — Cf. MBh. i.80.2 = 3333,f.

9-10. 'If (punishment falls) not on (the doer) himself, (it falls) on his sons, *etc.*' Cf. the second command of the Mosaic decalogue. —See tu3.

13. Lines 13-20: these and 29⁴ˑ⁶ (= Manu viii.17) are translated by Muir, i².380; and (with classical parallels) in the same author's *Metrical Translations from Skt. Writers*, p. 26.

17-18. See 2sama2. —vimukhās, very naturally! but the rules also forbid looking around (103¹⁷).

21-22. See idam.

23 f. See api 2 beg. —"Thus gazelles eat herbs; tigers eat gazelles; men eat fish; lions eat elephants."—Scholiast.

NOTES TO PAGE 64.

2-3. U.f. kuryāt, 59ᵃɴ. —See saṅga2. —See tu 3.

6-7. U.f. bhakṣayitā (1050, cf. 944) ··· iha admi aham. —'Me eat in t'other world will he, whose *meat* in this world eat do I. That the wise declare to be the meatness of meat = That is why meat is called meat.' An example of Hindu etymologies, which are often little better than mere puns — as here, mām sa and mānsam. Hopkins notes that this is given in varied form, MBh. xiii. 116.35 = 5714. Cf. Whitney, AJP. iii.402; also 94¹⁶.

8-9. See upoṣita. — See √gru, desid. —See yena2. —Cf. Strabo, xv.59, p. 712: ταῖς δὲ γυναιξὶ ταῖς γαμεταῖς μὴ συμφιλοσοφεῖν τοὺς Βραχμᾶνας etc. Notable exceptions to this statement are found in the ancient legends of Māitreyī and Gārgī —SBE. xv. 108,130,136.

10-11. 'Any thing disliked of her husband (296b), displeasing to him.' —It is noteworthy that widow-burning (see p. 382) is quite ignored here. It is not mentioned anywhere in Manu; and the same is true of Yājñavalkya, Nārada, Gāutama, Āpastamba, and most of the others.—Jolly, *Sitzungs-berichte der Bairischen Akad.*, 1876, p. 447. He thinks it originated among the lower classes.

12-13. See kāmam, adv. —√2kṣi, caus. —See √grah5. —parasya limits nāma.

14-15. U.f. āsīta (616) ā maraṇāt. — √kṣam.

16-17. evam, 'so,' as described in book iii.

18-19. Prescriptions quite the reverse of those at 62¹⁰.

20-21. U.f. pañcatapās (see vocab.) ·· varṣāsu abhrā-. Compare, e.g., the penances of Yayāti after he retires to the forest, MBh. i.86.11 = 3544,f; and those exhibited to Alexander, Strabo, xv.61, p. 714; and see xv.63, p. 715.

22. vihṛtya, √hṛ+vi 2.

NOTES TO PAGE 65.

2. pra-vrajan, technical (see vocab.), describing the pravrājaka.

3. THE ORDERS. See āçrama. Perhaps the best English names are: 1. 'Student,' for brahmacārin; 2. 'Householder,' for gṛhastha; 3. 'Forest-hermit,' for vāna-prastha; and 4. 'Ascetic' or 'Pious mendicant,' for yati. The last is often called 'Beggar' (bhikṣu) or 'Wanderer' (pra- or pari-vrājaka).

5-6. Lit. 'One should diminish one mouthful at a time in the dark fortnight etc.,' i.e. 'diminish one's food by one mouthful etc.' —See triṣavaṇa. —This, the diminuendo-crescendo form of the lunar fast, is called pipīlikā-madhya or 'ant-middled.'

7-8. 'One should follow the same rule entire, in (case of) the yava-madhyama (see this), intent, performing (caraṅç) the lunar penance with the bright fortnight first.' —These are fully described, e.g. by Gāutama, xxvii. (transl. SBE. ii.296f), and by Bāudhāyana, iii.8 (SBE. xiv.303f).

9 f. Cf. below, p. 357, § 90. —For a summary of this schematic exposition of the doctrine of metempsychosis, see *Indian Wisdom*, 280.

9-10. 'Resulting in weal or woe (is our) karman, which originates in mind, voice, and body.' Thus qualified, karman comprehends 'virtuous and sinful thoughts, words, and deeds.' —See gati4.

11-12. tasya, sc. karmaṇas. —See api2 beg. — See dehin. — 'One should know that the mind is the prompter in this world (iha) of this (action) which is three-fold [viz. best, worst, and middling, cf. 65¹⁰] and has three manifestations [viz. as thoughts, words, and deeds, 65⁹], is connected with the body, (and) has ten kinds [3+4+3 kinds, enumerated in çlokas 5, 6, 7].'

17. avidhānatas: hereby are excluded from this category injuries to sacrificial victims when required by the ritual, or to a man when inflicted as a lawful penalty.

19. U.f. manasā eva ayam (lit. 'this one' = 'a man') upa-bhuṅkte. See √2bhuj+upa2

NOTES TO PAGE **66**.

1. 'And (ca) he [if he does right for the most part and wrong a little] enjoys bliss in heaven, invested (√1vṛ+ā) with those very elements (see bhūta5), *i.e.* with a corporeal body.' — 'Those very' before-mentioned at Manu xii.16.

3. 'Deserted by the elements' = 'after death.' — Scholiast.

4–5. See jīva. — See the mention of the five elements, Strabo, xv.59 end, p. 713. — The spirit, after purgation, takes on a human form again. The purgatorial idea is prominent in book xviii. of the MBh.

6–7. 'Considering (dṛṣṭvā) these gatis (which result) from right-doing and from wrong-doing' (1098). — See √1dhā3.

8–9. See sattva2, rajas4, tamas3, and esp. guṇa3, and also ātman5, and mahant2, all technical terms here. — 'One should know goodness, passion, and darkness as the ātman's three qualities, with which the mahant constantly pervades all these existent things without exception.' See p. 344, § 67. Line 9 is explained under sthita4.

10–11. ca ·· ca: the sense requires 'or ·· or.' — 'As having the quality of darkness as its attribute:' tāmasam modifies only the prior member, guṇa-; the verbally strict phrase would be tamo-guṇa-lakṣaṇam (cf. line 15).

14–15. 'What (deed) one wishes (to be) known by everybody *etc.*' — jñātam: conjecture of BR. at vi.489. — lajjati, metri gratia, for -te.

18–19. See ya6 and sarva2c. — 'But the transmigrations which (a man) enters upon by reason of any (quality of them =) of these qualities, these (of all, *i.e.*) through all this world in order I will briefly state.'

20–23. A summary of the scheme following.

NOTES TO PAGE **67**.

1–18. çlokas 42–50. Scheme of the nine sets of gatis. On him who is governed by it, each guṇa entails a gati: to wit,

I. tamas, the gati of a beast (42–44);
II. rajas, the gati of a man (45–47);
III. sattva, the gati of a god (48–50).

Each gati is of three kinds:

a. lowest; b. middling; c. highest.

The scheme is not strictly adhered to. In line 1, for instance, 'plants' are put among the beasts; and in 15, the 'Vedas,' among the gods. But we are not surprised to find 'Çūdras' (line 3) among the beasts, and 'Brahmans' (line 13) among the gods (see 94¹⁸).

6. U.f. tāmasiṣu (sc. gatiṣu) uttamā.

7–8. See jhalla. — √saṅj + pra.

11–12. ye merely fills out the verse — see ya3 beg. — 'Likewise all Apsarases.' On the Apsarases, see Holtzmann, ZDMG. xxxiii.631f.

17. Technically used words — see vocab.

19–20. 'A Brahman-slayer enters the womb of dogs (çvan), swine, asses, camels, cows, goats (aja), sheep (avi), *etc.*,' in order to be born therefrom as dog, etc.

22–23. U.f. pretās antyastrī-: pronounce, pretāntyastrī-, in violation of 177. — 'By stealing grain, one becomes a mouse; ·· (by stealing) water, (one becomes) a duck; *etc.*' The same construction runs on to 68⁸. Note that some of the gatis have a special appropriateness.

NOTES TO PAGE **68**.

4–5. 'Women also in like manner (see kalpa) by stealing would incur guilt. They become mates of these very creatures (mentioned above).'

8–9. See pravṛtta and nivṛtta. — eti, 'one attains to.' — aty-eti etc., 'gets rid of the five elements,' i.e. 'obtains final liberation.'

10–11. 'And whatsoever heterodox philosophies (there are).' See 1ka2b: the first ca = 'and.'

12–13. 'Whatsoever doctrines (yāni kāni cid, sc. çāstrāṇi), differing (anyāni) from this (atas = vedāt), spring up and come to nought, — these (tāni) *etc.*'

14–15. See çreṣṭha and 2vara: and for abl., 292b. — vyava-, 'the resolute' who *practice* what they learn.

16. SELECTIONS XXIX. and XXX. Two specimens of vakrokti, 'play on words' or

'Calembourg.' Both come from the Subhâ-çitârṇava, and are taken by me from Böht-lingk's *Indische Sprüche*, 2d ed., no's 1428 and 6846. Other specimens are no's 4042 and 6389.

16-17. 'Nineteen wives went to the wood to play. Twenty came home. The rest were eaten by a tiger.' —Solution : **ekonā viñçatir nāryaḥ** = 'wives twenty lacking one' (477a) ; or, dividing **eko nā** (stem nṛ), 'one man (and) twenty wives.'

18-19. U.f. **mama ājñayā.** —Solution : **na tena,** 'not by him,' when joined, gives **natena** (√nam), 'by him bending over.'

SELECTIONS XXXI.–LXXV.

Extracts from the Vedic Literature.

§ 70. Selections xxxi. to lxxv. comprise Mantra (or "Veda" in its narrower sense), Brāhmaṇa, and Sūtra. They are taken for the most part from the Rigvedic literature (or "Rigveda" in its broader sense). Professor Kaegi's little work, entitled *Der Rigveda* (2d ed.), and described above, *Brief List,* p. xx, no. 23, is recommended as a most useful intro-duction to Vedic study, on account of its general excellence, and, in particular, on account of the ful-ness of its bibliographical details. It is, moreover, now easily accessible in an English version by Dr. Robert Arrowsmith, published by Ginn and Co., Boston, 1886, price $1.65. Kaegi's book will be fre-quently cited in the sequel, as "Kaegi," with the page-number of the translation first, followed by that of the original in parenthesis. The Note-numbers are alike in both.

§ 71. For grammatical forms peculiar to the Veda, reference to Whitney will be made when needful; but the student should read systematically the sec-tions that describe Vedic noun-inflection and verb-conjugation. For the former subject, the small-print lines of 330, 340, and 342 are important; and for the latter, the paragraphs on the subjunctive, 557–563, 736, 700, and those on the mode-forms of the different aorists, chap. xi. The accent, explained by Whitney, 80–86, is important for the exegesis and otherwise. The accent-rules are given at 92–97, 314–320, 591–598, 1082–86. The notation of the accent is explained at 87–90.

§ 72. The Vedic literature is based on the songs of the early Aryan tribes immigrant into India. These tribes were life-loving, brave, and warlike, and show their nature clearly in their songs. But they were remarkable above all for the strength of their religious instinct. This is a cardinal fact — the prime determinant of the character of the early Indian literature; for that literature is one of prevail-ingly religious content. The Veda is thus distinguished from the later literature of the Epic and the Classical periods by its contents, and also — no less — by its language and style. But within itself, the Vedic literature (or "Veda" in the broader sense of the word) shows differences which serve to divide it into three great groups.

§ 73. To assign a definite chronological period for each of these groups is neither feasible nor necessary.[1] But it is interesting and quite possible to establish an inner chronologic sequence among the groups themselves and the sub-groups, and even among individual books and parts of books. To the first group belong the ancient songs themselves, which are in metrical form and are known as the Vedic hymns or Mantras. The term "Veda" is often used in a narrower sense to denote them. To the second belong the Brāhmaṇas, the oldest Indo-European prose extant, which presuppose and are dependent on the Mantra-literature. The third group comprehends the Sūtras, collections of brief rules upon liturgical and other subjects, which, in turn, presuppose both of the foregoing groups.

[1] Indeed, to do so would give a very false impres-sion. The periods overlap; and the styles of litera-ture shade off from one into another — so, for example, in the Yajurveda.

§ 74. A great mass of Mantra-material originated and was handed down by
memorial tradition orally from generation to generation long before the existence
of any such collections of Mantras as have come down to us.[1] The Mantras fall into
several different classes. To one belongs the hymn-stanza (ṛc); to another, the
sacrificial formula (yájus); and to another, the magic charm (bráhman). From the
stock of Mantras of one class — for example, the yájus — a certain collection with
definite arrangement became established by popular usage in a certain community,
and thus arose a Veda, for example, a Yajurveda — not a certain definite book, but
some one of many possible and probable collections of Mantras of a certain definite
class. From the same stock of the same class another collection was formed in
another community, and thus arose another Veda, for example, another Yajurveda.
The period in which the oldest hymns of the Rigveda originated may be set back
into the second pre-Christian millennium;[2] but this only on certain general considerations — not as a matter of precise argumentation. Geographically, the early
Vedic Aryans may be referred to Kābul and the Panjāb.[3]

§ 75. The Mantras have come down to us, for the most part, in several collections, diverse in form and purpose. There was, besides, more or less Mantra-material
which was never embodied in any collection,[4] but of which we find remnants scattered
about in various books. The great collections of Mantras are the Rigveda, the
Sāmaveda, the Yajurveda, and the Atharvaveda. The text of the Mantras forms
what is often called a Saṁhitā. To each Saṁhitā is attached a body of dependent
or ancillary works of the Brāhmaṇa and Sūtra groups: so that the oldest Indian
books are classed, first, according to the Veda to which they belong; and, secondly,
according to their character as Mantra, Brāhmaṇa, or Sūtra. It is to be remembered
that "Veda" has a narrower and a broader sense, and that "Rigveda," for instance,
may mean either the Rigveda-saṁhitā or also the entire body of works belonging to
that Veda.

§ 76. The Saṁhitā of the Rigveda is a historical[5] collection. It consists of
1017 hymns, each containing on an average about ten double lines,[6] so that the text is
in volume somewhat less than that of the two Homeric poems together. There is
a purely external and mechanical division of the text into 'Eighths,' 'Lessons,'[7]
'Groups,' and 'Stanzas' (aṣṭaka, adhyāya, varga, ṛc); but this need not specially
concern us now. Of deep historical significance is the other division into 'Books,'
'Chapters,' 'Hymns,' and 'Stanzas' (maṇḍala, anuvāka, sūkta, ṛc).

§ 77. There are ten 'Books' (literally, 'Circles'). And of these, books ii. to
viii. are the so-called "Family-books" — that is, they contain each the hymns
ascribed to a single family or clan, in which they doubtless originated, and by which
they were handed down as a sacred inheritance. Thus, book ii. contains the hymns
of Gṛtsamada and his clan. Those of Viçvāmitra and his tribe follow in book iii.;
and then in order those of Vāmadeva (book iv.), Atri (book v.), Bharadvāja (book
vi.), Vasiṣṭha (book vii.), and Kaṇva (book viii.). The ninth book is made up of

[1] See Roth's *Atharvaveda in Kaschmir*, p. 9–10.
[2] See Whitney in *The Century Magazine*, 1887,
xxxiii. 921; or Kaegi, note 38. Cf. Ludwig, iii. 178f.
[3] See Whitney, l.c., p. 913; Kaegi, note 39; Ludwig, iii. 198f.
[4] The Hindus say that the Vedas are infinite. See
Ludwig, iii. 15; Muir, iii². 17.

[5] As distinguished from a liturgical collection —
see § 95. Respecting the purpose of the RV. collection, see Roth, KZ. xxvi. 56.
[6] For the number of stanzas, words, and syllables,
and for some convenient tabular statements, see
Müller, ASL. p. 220f.
[7] There are eight 'Lessons' in each 'Eighth.'

hymns addressed to the deified drink Soma. The tenth comprises hymns ascribed to very different authors;[1] while the first consists of fifteen[2] minor groups, each attributed to some ancient poet-sage.

§ 78. The general history of the text of the Rigveda was touched upon by Professor Roth in a very instructive little essay[3] entitled *Vedische Studien*. Some of his conclusions may be briefly stated. The assembling of the Mantras into a collection was accomplished by the aid of writing.[4] The first Rik collections were probably single books and parts of books, each an aggregation of material of such moderate compass as to be easily handled by a single collector. The small collections were later united into one large collection, which, completed by the addition of books ix. and x., and uniformly edited, constitutes our RV. Samhitā.

§ 79. Roth recognizes three stages in the tradition: 1. the oral transmission from the authors to the time of the collectors; 2. the reduction from the oral form to the written form; and 3. the transmission of the written text to us. We may admit that in the last stage the text — carefully preserved as it was, see § 98 — has suffered no very important corruptions. The collectors themselves, however, did not by any means write down the texts precisely as they heard them. The reciters from memory must have recited rhythmically. The collectors (writers — redactors or diaskeuasts) have often destroyed the rhythm by putting the texts into the strait-jacket of the rules of grammar, and especially by writing the words according to the later rules of saṁdhi. To the first stage are to be referred the many mistakes which are ascribable to carelessness in listening,[5] and which may be called blunders of the ear rather than of the eye.

§ 80. That the hymns themselves are of diverse origin, both in respect of place and of time, is probable *a priori* and is shown by internal evidence.[6] Accordingly, if we find, for example, two hymns involving inconsistent conceptions of the same deity or of different deities, this is to be deemed quite natural, inasmuch as they originated among clans dwelling in diverse regions. Moreover, after the aggregation of the small collections into the large one, interpolations and later additions were still made. To discriminate between the different elements that now make up the canonical Vedic text is therefore an important problem.

§ 81. Again, in the course of time, and in part as a result of the wrangling pedantry of narrow teachers, the stock collections became ramified into slightly divergent recensions. These were called çākhās or 'branches,' because so related to each other as are different branches from the same tree-stock. The Çākhās often supply to criticism the various readings for which the classical philologist looks to good and independent manuscripts. The community in which such a Çākhā attained definitive authority was called a caraṇa or 'school.' There once existed, presumably, many branches and schools[7] of the RV. The school of the Çākalas,[8] however, seems

---

[1] The orthodox Hindu conception of the hymns is that they had existed from eternity; it recognizes no human authors. The Hindus do not call Atri, for example, the "author" of a given hymn, but rather the "Rishi," i.e. the "seer," who was so fortunate as to "see" it the last time it was revealed. — Müller, ASL. p. 95.

[2] Bergaigne, JA. viii.8.263 (= 71).

[3] Published, 1883, in KZ. xxvi. 45–68. See especially p. 52–62.

[4] This is entirely consistent with the facts that the tradition in the schools was oral and by memory, and that the open use of a written text was disgraceful. Compare, e.g., *Sarva-sammata Çikshā*, ed. A. O. Franke, rule 36. But this thesis of Roth is denied by some scholars.

[5] Such as *ndmasā* for *mdnasā*, etc., Roth, l.c. p. 62.

[6] Cf. Ludwig, iii. p. IX.

[7] See Müller, ASL. p. 368.

[8] See Müller, RV. Prātiçākhya, *Einleitung*, p. 7.

to have gained exclusive predominance, and the extant recension of the RV. Saṁhitā
bears their name. The Çākhā of the Bāṣkalas is also mentioned.

§ 82. The manuscripts of the RV. Saṁhitā exhibit almost no diversities of
reading; so that, in the absence of çākhā-differences, the criticism of the text has
to rest on intrinsic evidence, and on a comparison of the other Saṁhitās, and on a
study of the RV. citations in the RV. Brāhmaṇas and Sūtras. Other criteria have
been brought to light by the study of the arrangement of the collection. Thus,
within each of the books ii.–vii., the hymns addressed to the same deity are grouped
together and arranged according to the decreasing number of stanzas of each hymn.
The same simple principle goes farther, governing, for example, the order of the
groups within a book.[1] Violations of the principle may arouse suspicion as to the
originality or genuineness of the passages concerned.

§ 83. The first written form of the text would seem to have been the saṁhitā-
pāṭha or 'combined reading,' wherein the words are combined according to the more or
less artificial rules of grammar.[2] These combinations often admit of several different
resolutions. To obviate the resulting uncertainties, there was constructed the pada-
pāṭha or 'word-reading,' which aims to give each word in its true independent form
without reference to any rules of combination. The Pada-text of the published RV.
is attributed to Çākalya,[3] and is the oldest conscious exegetical work upon the Veda
now known. It is far from infallible.[4] For its secondary use, see § 98N.

§ 84. The Sāmaveda is a Veda of sāmans. A sāman is properly a 'tune' —
not a text; but in this connection the word means an ṛc so modified[5] as to be better
adapted for chanting, especially during the ceremonies of the Soma-sacrifice. Of
the 1549 stanzas of the Sāmaveda, 1474 occur also in the Rigveda.[6] The SV.
exhibits many variations from the readings of the RV. Saṁhitā, some of which
are of value for the criticism of the latter text.[7] In general, the relations of the
SV. to the RV. still present many difficult problems.[8]

§ 85. The Saṁhitā of the Atharvaveda, as compared with that of the RV.,
represents a lower plane of life and thought, as it is also later in respect of form
and language. It contains magic incantations for the warding off of the most
diverse malign influences, and prayers and charms for success in the various affairs
of life, as love, gaming, quarrels, journeys, and the like. It has a high degree of
interest for the student of popular superstitions. The Saṁhitā has come down to us
in at least two recensions. The one is called the Paippalāda Çākhā.[9] The other was
published in 1856 by Roth and Whitney.[10] About a sixteenth part of the RV. stanzas
occur also — with more or less interesting variants — in books i. to xix. of this text.
Shankar P. Pandit of Bombay is now editing the AV. with Sāyaṇa's comment.

§ 86. The Yajurveda belongs to the period[11] of the highly developed ritual,
and originated in the sacred and famous Madhyadeça.[12] The Saṁhitās contain the

[1] For details see A. Bergaigne, *Recherches sur
l'histoire de la saṁhitā du RV.*, JA. 8.viii.193f
(esp. p. 199), and 8.ix.191f. Cf. also Oldenberg,
ZDMG. xli.508f; and Bergaigne, JA. 8.x.488f.
  [2] This is the text given in the Reader.
  [3] See Weber, HIL. p. 32f.
  [4] A critical estimate of its exegetical value is given
by Roth in the afore-mentioned essay, KZ. xxvi.45–62.
  [5] By protraction of vowels, insertion of sundry
sounds, repetitions, etc. — Whitney, OLSt. 1.13–15.
  [6] See Whitney, ISt. ii.347–63.

[7] Whitney, JAOS. xi. p. clxxxiv=PAOS. Oct. 1883.
  [8] See Oldenberg's interesting discussion, ZDMG.
xxxviii.439–80, and esp. 464–65.
  [9] Described by Roth, *Der Atharvaveda in Kaschmir*, Tübingen, 1875.
  [10] See *Brief List*, p. xix, no. 18. For bibliography
of translations, see Kaegi, note 13.
  [11] The civilization of this period is treated with
especial fulness in Schröder's *Indiens Literatur und
Cultur* — see below, § 100.
  [12] Cf. p. 297, § 2; also Schröder, ILuC. p. 163.

formulas (see **yajus** in vocab.) which accompanied the sacrificial ceremonials, and
are, as it were, the hand-books of the **adhvaryus** or priests who did the actual
manual labor of the sacrifices.[1] With the growth of ritualism and its spread over
a wide extent of territory[2] there naturally grew up many differing usages in connection with the sacrifice, and many centres of ritualistic study.[3] In this wise it
happened that the sectarian schools of the Yajurveda were especially numerous and
flourishing.

§ 87. The Black Yajurveda. The various schools of this, the older Yajurveda,
bear the names of men reputed to be the pupils — directly or indirectly — of Väiçam-
päyana, a name great in the Epos. At least five schools[4] possessed special Samhitäs,
of which four are still extant: to wit, the Samhitä of the Kaṭhas (Καθαῖοι) or the
Käṭhaka; that of the Kapiṣṭhala-Kaṭhas (Καμβίσθολοι); that of the Mäiträyaṇīyas;
and that of the school of Äpastamba, a subdivision of the Täittirīyas. The one last
mentioned, the Täittirīya Samhitä, was the first to be printed in a scholarly edition.[5]
The Mäiträyaṇī Samhitä has recently been published by Dr. L. von Schröder, Leipzig, 1881–86. The others are still unedited. In all these texts of the old Yajus
Samhitäs, the sacred formulas are commingled with prose passages, explanatory and
prescriptive. A single such passage is a **Bráhmaṇa**,[6] 'the dictum of a brahmán or
priest,' 'a priestly discourse.'

§ 88. The White Yajurveda. To remedy this confusion, a new school of
Adhvaryus, called the Väjasaneyins, arranged a Samhitä of 'clear formulas' (çukläni
yajūṅṣi), i.e. a text in which the formulas or Mantras were separated from the
priestly discourses or Bráhmaṇas.[7] Not without some little animus, doubtless, they
turned to account the double meaning of çukla, 'clear' or 'white,' and fixed the
name of "Dark" (kṛṣṇa, 'dark' or 'black') upon the mingled or uncleared texts of
their older rivals. The Samhitä of the White Yajurveda or Väjasaneyi Samhitä has
come down to us in the recension of the Käṇvas and in that of the Mädhyaṁdinas,[8]
and was published by Weber, Berlin, 1849–52.

§ 89. The separate collections of the formulas naturally suggested a similar
treatment of the priestly discourses. In the school of the Väjasaneyins, the result
of this treatment was a collection of the formerly detached **Bráhmaṇas**, which collection is itself also called a **Bráhmaṇa**,[9] and is practically an encyclopedic digest of the
wisdom of their school.[10]

§ 90. The oldest collection of Mantras, the Rigveda, is in the main the reflex
of the life of a vigorous, active, and healthy people — a people that prayed most for
length of days, for sturdy sons, abundant cattle, doughty retainers, and victory over
their enemies; a people whose religion was a simple worship of the deified powers
of nature. But even during the Vedic period, there comes a profound change. The
Yajurveda represents a turning-point in the development of the Hindu character.
The centre of Vedic life is shifted to Madhyadeça; and here were made the first

[1] Ludwig, iii.27.
[2] Schröder, ILuC. p. 164–65.
[3] Cf. Schröder, ILuC. p. 88–89: also Eggeling, SBE. xii. p. xxv f.
[4] Schröder, *Einleitung* to his ed. of MS., book i. p. IX f. Cf. ILuC. p. 89.
[5] By Weber, as vol's xi. and xii. of ISt., 1871–72.
[6] See this in vocab. and cf. it with *bráhmaṇá*.

[7] See Eggeling, SBE. xii., p. xxvii; also ÇB. xiv. 9.4^{33} or SBE. xv.226.
[8] Or Μαδιανδιναί: see HIL. p. 106.
[9] Specifically, the Çatapatha Brähmaṇa. It was published by Weber, Berlin, 1855. Books i.–iv. have been translated by Eggeling, SBE. xii. and xxvi.
[10] Eggeling, SBE. xii. p. xxii f.

great advances in the arts and institutions of civilization, in trade, and in science.
Here also priestly families and warrior-families attained to such importance as to
assert their independence of the people, and so bring about the strongly marked
class-distinctions that grew into the rigid system of caste. And here, with the
waxing power of the priesthood, the old Vedic religion was converted into an
infinitely complex system of sacrifices and ceremonies. To this period belongs the
belief in metempsychosis — a dreadful and universal reality to the Hindu mind.
With the growing tendency of the Hindu character towards introspection comes the
system of hermit-life and the asceticism which are so prominent in the Hindu
Middle Age, and which in turn led naturally to the habit of theosophic speculation.
The sultry air of Ganges-land has relaxed both the physical and the mental fibre of
the Hindu, and he has become a Quietist.

§ 91. The Hindu character has been transformed almost beyond recognition.
The change is wonderful. It would be also incomprehensible, but for the literature
of the Brāhmaṇas.[1] As a whole and by themselves, they are puerile, arid, inane.
But as the sole and faithful reflex of an immensely important phase in the development of an ethnic type, they have a great interest — an interest heightened by the
fact that the annals of human evolution hardly present another type whose history
can be studied through so many centuries in unbroken continuity.

§ 92. The sacerdotal class, ever magnifying its office, has invested the sacrifice
with a most exaggerated importance and sanctity. The sacrifice has become the
central point of the Brahman's life and thought. About it he has spun a flimsy web
of mystery, and in each of its events he sees a hidden symbolism.[2] Everything is
not only that which it *is* but also that which it *signifies*. So lost is the Brahman in
these esoteric vagaries that to him the line of demarcation between "is" and "signifies" becomes almost wholly obliterated.[3] What we deem the realities of life are as
pale shadows. The sacrifice and its events are the real facts, and to fathom their
mysteries[4] is omnipotence and salvation.

§ 93. It must not be forgotten that the phases of development represented by
the Mantras and Brāhmaṇas are not separated by hard and fast lines. The oldest
Yajus texts are of the transition type. They are called Saṁhitās, and contain
indeed Mantras in abundance; but the Mantras are mingled with prose passages
which are the first Brāhmaṇas. Descriptions of the sacrificial ceremonies, attribu-
tions to them of hidden meanings, accounts of their origin, legends to illustrate their
efficacy — such are the contents of the older Brāhmaṇas. Conscious philosophic
speculation plays a subordinate part: its beginnings we can trace to the RV.
Saṁhitā;[5] but the great mass of it is contained in the later Brāhmaṇa literature.

§ 94. In this, the later Brāhmaṇa period, the descriptions of the ritual are
relegated to systematic treatises (§ 95); and the theosophic and philosophic passages
become more lengthy and important, and receive — as containing material appropriate for the meditations of the ὑλόβιοι or Forest-hermits — the special names of
Araṇyakas[6] or 'Forest-treatises' and Upaniṣads.[7] Some of the best of these have

---

[1] Characterized by Eggeling, SBE. xii. p. ix f, esp.
p. xxii-xxv. Enumerated by Kaegi, note 14 a.
[2] See Oldenberg, *Buddha*, 19(20)f.
[3] A point of prime importance in reading the endless identifications of the Brāhmaṇas.
[4] Hence the constant refrain, *ya evaṁ veda* — cf.
97[1]x.

[5] See selection lxii. and x.
[6] See Deussen, *System des Vedānta*, p. 8; Müller,
ASL. 318f; or Kaegi, note 16.
[7] Upaniṣad: lit. 'a sitting at the feet of another,'
and then 'the hidden doctrine taught at such a
session.'

been handed down by tradition as separate works with separate names; and other tracts of the same general style and contents have been written; but it must be remembered that the original Āraṇyakas and Upaniṣads were integral parts of the digested Brāhmaṇas.[1]

Brahmanical speculation culminates in pessimistic Pantheism, in the doctrine of the misery of all earthly existence, from which we can hope for redemption only through reabsorption into the universal All-in-One. This is the result of Brahmanical thought, on which as a foundation was built up the doctrine and order of Buddha; this the link that unites the Brahmanic and the Buddhistic chains of development.[2]

§ 95. The Brāhmaṇas presuppose a thorough acquaintance with the course and details of the sacrifice, and do not undertake a systematic exposition thereof. But when the ceremonies had grown to tremendous length and complexity, it became necessary to have manuals giving full and orderly directions for the use of the celebrant. Such works are the 'Rules for the sacrifices' or Çrāuta-sūtras, so called because they stand in most intimate relation to the Veda or 'sacred texts' (çruti), and continually cite these texts, and prescribe the manner and the occasions of their employment with the various ceremonies.

§ 96. Usage and observance, crystallized into sacred ceremony, invest the whole life of an Aryan Hindu — nay, even his pre-natal and post-mortem existence. These usages differed considerably in different localities, and in the lesser details among the different families of the same locality. In part, perhaps, to counteract the tendency to diversity, books were made describing the observances recognized as normal in a certain school or community. They are called Gṛhya-sūtras, or 'Rules of domestic usages.' Here, too, as well as in the sacrifice, everything proceeds with the recitation of Mantras; so that these books also attach themselves to certain Vedas or Vedic schools. The legitimate subjects of these Rules are the 'Sacraments' (saṁskāras), and the 'Simple-sacrifices' (pāka-yajñas) of the householder.

§ 97. There is also a third class of Sūtras, called Dharma-sūtras, which prescribe rules for the every-day life of those who would conform to the example of the virtuous. Since they have to do with 'agreement-conduct,' i.e. the 'conduct' (ācāra) which has for its norm the 'agreement' (sam-aya, lit. 'con-vention') of those who know the law, they are also called Sāmayācārika-sūtras. The matters belonging more properly to the Gṛhya-sūtras are sometimes treated also in the Dharma-sūtras. But the legitimate subjects of the latter are far more varied than those of the former. They embrace all sorts of injunctions and restrictions relating to etiquette, to eating and sleeping, to purification and penance, and to the details of the daily life of the student and householder and hermit, and even extend to the duties of the king and to the beginnings of civil and criminal law. In the order of development they are plainly posterior to the Gṛhya-sūtras.·

§ 98. As the sacred texts of the Mantras grew in sanctity, their dialect and style of thought became obsolescent. For the transmission of the sacred lore, a learned apparatus became necessary. To preserve the written text of a given 'branch' (çākhā) of the Veda from any change in "one jot or one tittle," by establishing the relations of the saṁhitā and pada pāṭhas (§ 83) of that branch, there were composed the phonetic treatises, which, because attaching each 'to a

---

[1] See Whitney, AJP. vii.1-2.
[2] The genetic relationship of Buddhism to Brah- manism is admirably sketched by Oldenberg, *Buddha,* Introd., chap's ii.–iii.

(certain) branch' (**prati-çākham**), are called Prātiçākhyas.[1] These give with the utmost minuteness of detail the rules for the retroversion of the pada to the saṁhitā readings, and thus enable us to establish with great accuracy the text as it was in their day.[2]

§ 99. To preserve the knowledge of the sense of obsolescent words, there were made collections of synonyms and of hard words (γλῶσσαι), called the Nighaṇṭavas, the oldest Vedic Glossary. Upon the Glossary there was written, by the ancient sage Yāska, a comment called Nirukta, which is the oldest extant work of formal Vedic exegesis, but which itself acknowledges a number of predecessors. Among its successors, the most famous is the great commentary of Sāyaṇa[3] Ācārya, ca. 1350 A.D. The Anukramaṇis are little works which give the divinity, the "seer," and the metre of each hymn of a Saṁhitā.

---

[1] See Whitney, JAOS. vii.339–40; iv.259–60.
[2] The word-texts were thus converted "from instruments more especially of exegesis, into a complete and efficient apparatus for securing the preservation of textual purity."—L.c. iv.260.
[3] Weber, HIL. p. 41–42.

---

§ 100. It remains to give a brief bibliography of the literature of the Rigveda Saṁhitā with mention of the principal ancillary works appertaining to it. For the bibliography of the other Saṁhitās, reference may be made to Kaegi, notes 8–26, or to Weber's *History of Indian Literature.*

1. Rigveda. Saṁhitā. a. Text-editions. The first complete edition was issued by Aufrecht, 1861-63, as vol's vi. and vii. of the ISt. Müller's great six-volumed quarto, with the full Saṁhitā and Pada texts, Sāyaṇa's commentary, an index, etc., was begun in 1849 and completed in 1874. Then came the editions mentioned at the beginning of this Reader, in the *Brief List*, no's 11 and 12.

b. **Exegesis.** The greatest achievements in Vedic exegesis must be ascribed to Roth. They are contained principally in the St. Petersburg Lexicon, *Brief List*, no. 5. Grassmann's Dictionary and his Translation are described in the *List*, no's 13 and 14. Professor Alfred Ludwig of Prague has published a large work in five volumes (Prag, Tempsky, 1876-83), entitled *Der Rigveda.* Vol's i. and ii. contain a translation of the hymns arranged according to deities and subjects. Vol. iii. contains an introduction to the translation, entitled *Die Mantra-litteratur und das alte Indien.* Vol's iv. and v. contain a commentary on the translation.

c. **General Works.** Abel Bergaigne's work entitled *La religion védique* (Paris, Vieweg, 1878-83, 3 vol's) is a systematic and encyclopedic exposition of the religious and mythological conceptions of the RV. The work of Geldner and Kaegi (*List*, no. 15), and those of Weber, Zimmer, and the rest (no's 21-26), all bear more or less directly on the study of the Veda. Whitney's *Oriental and Linguistic Studies* (New York, Scribner, Armstrong, & Co. 1st series, 1873) contain among other things valuable essays on the history, interpretation, and contents of the RV. Very recently has appeared a book by L. von Schröder, *Indiens Literatur und Cultur in historischer Entwicklung* (Leipzig, 1887), the first third of which is devoted to the Veda, and especially to the period of the Yajurveda.

2. Rigveda. Brāhmaṇas etc. The Aitareya Brāhmaṇa was edited by Aufrecht — see *List*, no. 16.

Haug had already published the text with a translation (Bombay, 1863), criticised and corrected by Weber, ISt. ix.177–380.

The Aitareya Āraṇyaka is associated with the Brāhmaṇa of the same name. It has five books and was edited with Sāyaṇa's comment by R. Mitra in the *Bibliotheca Indica*, 1876. See SBE. i. p. xcif.

Aitareya Upaniṣad is the name borne by certain parts of the Āraṇyaka, viz. book ii., chap's 4, 5, 6 — see SBE. i. p. xcvi. The text was edited and translated by Röer, BI., 1849-53. Müller gives another translation, SBE. i.200f.

The Çāṅkhāyana or Kāuṣītaki Brāhmaṇa was edited by Bruno Lindner (Jena, Costenoble, 1887). A translation is soon to follow.

The Kāuṣītaki Brāhmaṇa Upaniṣad was edited (with Çaṁkara's comment) and translated by Cowell, BI., 1861. Another translation, by Müller, SBE. i.271f; introduction, ibidem, p. xcviii.

3. Rigveda. Sūtras etc. Āçvalāyana's Çrauta-sūtra was edited by R. Vidyāratna, BI., 1874.

Āçvalāyana's Gṛhya-sūtra was edited (with translation) by Stenzler — see *List*, no. 17. English version by Oldenberg, SBE. xxix.

Çāṅkhāyana's Çrauta-sūtra was edited by Alfred Hillebrandt, BI., 1886.

Çāṅkhāyana's Gṛhya-sūtra was edited in 1878 by Oldenberg, ISt. xv.1-166, with translation. English version by Oldenberg, SBE. xxix.

No Dharma-sūtra is certainly known to be attached especially to the RV. Saṁhitā.

The RV. Prātiçākhya was edited by Regnier (JA., 1856-58), and by Müller (Leipzig, 1856-69). Each editor gives a translation.

The Nirukta, with the Nighaṇṭavas, was edited and elucidated by Roth (Göttingen, 1848-52).

The Anukramaṇī of Kātyāyana was edited with valuable accessories by Arthur A. Macdonell in the *Anecdota Oxoniensia*, Oxford, 1886.

NOTES TO PAGE 69.

Selection XXXI. RV. i. 1. Hymn to Agni, the Fire-god. — Translated by Whitney, *Century Magazine*, 1887, xxxiii. 915. Respecting Agni, see Kaegi, p.35(50)f, and n.119f.

—THE METRE is gāyatrī. Each stanza (ṛc) consists of three octosyllabic pādas with iambic cadence — see Kaegi, p.24(34) and n.85. Observe that, if the stanza be a triple one, the strophe usually consists of three stanzas and the hymn of a multiple thereof.

—In respect of frequency, the order of the metres in the RV. is: first the triṣṭubh (about ⅖ of RV.); then the gāyatrī (about ¼); then the jagatī (about ⅛) — see Haskell, JAOS. xi.p.lx = PAOS. May, 1881.

LINES 1–2. īḷe, vīḍ: accentless, 592: for the new letter, see p. 291 ¶ 8, and Whitney, 5 end. —RV.x.2.5 plays on the etymology of ṛtv-íj thus: agnír · · deváṅ ṛtu-çó yajāti. —For superl., 471.

3. pūrvebhis, 330, Vedic instr.: for r final w. initial ṛ, Whitney, 14 end.

4. U.f. deváṅs ā ihá. This interesting combination is really the result of a historic survival, and is fully explained at 209. Observe that āṅ, though transliterated with two letters, is a simple nasalized vowel, 209 a. —ā · · vakṣati: position of prefix, 1081; accent of verb form, 1082; √vah, aor. sub., 893[1].

5–6. açnavat, 700: use of mode, 576: subject indefinite. —divé-dive, 1260. — yaçásam, 1151.2a.

7–8. ágne, acct, 314[8]. —ási, acct, 595 a. —Position of clauses, 512a. —Locative, 304 a.

10. ā gamat, true aor. subjunctive (836[2]), corresponding to the ind. ágan (833): see 558.

11–12. tvám may be read tuám. Observe that in the Veda, when rhythmically read, hiatus is common — 113[3]. —ágne is at the beg. of a new pāda, 314[3]. —U.f. táva íd tád satyám. —Lit. 'Just what pleasant thing thou wilt (= willest to) do for the pious man, of theé indeed that (is) real *or* unfailing' — *i.e.* 'Whatever blessing thoú

dost purpose to grant, that thou never failest to bestow.'

13–14. U.f. úpa tvā (491[3]) agne (accentless) · · · ā imasi (548[1]), √i+upa_ā.

15–16. The accusatives are to be taken w. tvā. —We *may* pronounce adhvarāṇaām (113[3]), or leave the pāda catalectic. —U.f. gopám. —In pāda *c*, we *must* pronounce suē, in order to produce an iambic cadence.

17–18. sā · · bhava, see ta 2. — U.f. sūnáve ágne: for treatment of the acct in combination, see 135, example 4.

—Observe that — as the metre here shows — pādas *a* and *b* are always independent of each other as regards euphonic combination, and that — as here — the written text, with perverse consistency, always combines them when this is possible.

—sácasvā, pada, sácasva, 248 c. —Pronounce su-astáye.

NOTES TO PAGE 70.

SELECTION XXXII. RV. i. 32. Indra slays the dragon. — Respecting Indra and the natural significance of the myths about his battles, see Kaegi, p. 40(57)f, n.141 f; and Perry, JAOS. xi.117f.

—The "hymn" appears to consist of two separate pieces — see N. to 70[2]. The catenary structure is noticeable in some pairs of stanzas (1–2; 3–4) — see Kaegi, p. 24(34).

—THE METRE is triṣṭubh. The old Vedic triṣṭubh is much more free than that of the classical Sanskrit; but its most important feature, the cadence, is the same — see p. 316, § 43.

For statistics, see Haskell, JAOS. xi.p.lxii = PAOS. May, 1881. For a discussion of its development, see Oldenberg, ZDMG. xxxvii.55f.

1. Pronounce vīriāṇi and (line 3) svariam, and see Whitney, 84 b. —prá vocam, augmentless aorist (847 end), as improper subjunctive (563), with future mg (576).

2. U.f. áhan (637) áhim; ánu apás tatarda. Note juxtaposition of perf. w. impf. and see 823[2]. —prá abhinat, √bhid, 692.

3. çiçriyāṇám, 807. — Indra's special
attribute is his "beloved thunderbolt," of
which the Epos fables much, ZDMG. xxxii.
296.

4. 'Like lowing kine, — flowing suddenly
to a sea, down came the waters.' The point
of comparison is the noise. —samudrám,
perhaps 'to *a* gathering of water, so as to
form one' — not necessarily 'to *the* ocean.'

5ª. Pronounce avṛpīta, 135⁴ (important):
in the AV., ii.5.7, the augment is written.
Cf. 70¹⁷ɴ. —sómam: see Kaegi, p. 72(99),
and notes 288–94; also Roth, ZDMG. xxxv.
680f and xxxviii.134f.

5ᵇ. Pronounce tríkadrukeṣu a-, and observe that final -u is almost never to be
pronounced as -v when so written. —Cf. RV.
ii.15.1, which seems to consist of reminiscences of the beg. of this hymn.

6. 'The Rewarder took the missile bolt —
smóte him, the first-born of dragons.' —
áhan (593) has for direct object the enclitic
enam, 'him,' or, more correctly, 'im,' since
the English pronoun *him* loses its *h* when
enclitic. The enam is then explained by an
appositive. So 79⁷.

7–8. U.f. yád indra áhan · ·, át māyínām
áminās prá utá · ·.   'When, O Indra, thou
smotest · ·, and (utá) thereupon broughtest
to nought the wiles of the wily, thereupon
bringing forth the sun, the day, the dawn, —
then soothly foundest thou no enemy.'

—The first át continues the force of yád
through pāda *b*, as the acct (595a) of áminās
(√2mi) shows. —Position of prá, 1081². —
Order in pāda *c* is unnatural: expect 'dawn,
sun, (full) day.' —Pronounce súriam. —
dyám, 361d: vocab., under dív. —uṣásam
and kīlā: see references in vocab.; the prolongations are in the even syllables of the
cadence. —vivitse, 798a.

9. Pronounce viáṅsam: cf. Whitney, 84a.

10. kúliçenā, 248b. —vi-vṛkṇā, nom. pl.
neut., common in Veda, for -āni: √vraçc.
—çay-a-te, transition-form (749) from root-
class, for çe-te (629).

11. á hí juhv-é (alternative form for
juhuv-e), √hū+á: acct, 595d: subject, Vritra.

12ª. 'He (Vritra) did not escape (vtṛ,
899a) the shock of his (Indra's) weapons.'

12ᵇ. 'The (cloud-) rifts he crushed
together, who had Indra as his conqueror.'
That is, the monster, in his retreat or his
fall, crushed into a shapeless mass his
already riven cloud-castles. This is forced.
If we dared emend the áᴡ. λ. rujánās to
rujānás (840²), we might render, 'Broken,
he was (then) completely crushed' (998b).

—indra-çatru: later books, e.g. ÇBr. i.6.
3¹⁰, lay great stress on the correct accentuation of this word; indra-çatrú, 'conqueror
of I.,' would be blasphemy. See *Indische
Studien*, iv.368; or Roth, *Nirukta*, p. xix.

13ᵇ. U.f. á asya · · jaghāna, see √han+á.
Subject here is Indra.

14. See vṛṣan. —See √bhū, desid. —
açayat, 629. —Pronounce vi-astas, Whitney, 84a.

15. 'Over him, lying so, crushed like
(ná) a reed, the waters go, flowing for mankind (lit. the waters of man, flowing, do go).'
So Pischel, ZDMG. xxxv.717–24. P. thinks
that the original text was mánorúhānāáti,
i.e. mános (cf. 73¹⁹) úhānās (√vahá, pres.
mid. ppl., 619⁸) áti, and that the author of
the pada text divided it wrongly, máno
rúhānās, changing, of course, n to ṇ.

—If mánas, like áñjas, could pass for an
instr., we might render '(With a will, i.e.)
Lustily rising, the waters overwhelm him.'
—amuyá, 'so,' w. a sneer: cf. átra, 89⁴ɴ.

16. pari-átiṣṭhat, acct, 595a, 1083. —
tásām limits only the first member of the
foll. cpd.

17. Note relation of acct and mg in
vṛtráputrā. —U.f. índras asyās: observe
the accordance between the written and
spoken form here — see 135⁴, and cf. 70⁶⁴ɴ.
—vádhar, 'weapon' of V's mother, not of
Indra.

18. Translated, 777b. —dānus, fem.,=
V's mother. —çaye, see 613: similarly
duhe, 80¹⁶, íçe, 92⁸.

19–20. 'The waters overwhelm V's hidden body, that was put down in the midst
of · ·.   In long darkness lay (á açayat,
629) he who was vanquished by Indra.'

—Here the narration comes to an end.
Stanzas 1–10 form a brief but complete epic.
The same general theme is treated again by

stanzas 11–14. Rik 15 seems to be a later
addition

21. dasápatnīs: after I's victory, the
waters are called (x.43.8) aryá-patnīs, 'having the Aryans as masters,' or 'having a
gracious (god) as master.' — panīneva
gávas (see gó): the rain-giving clouds are
often called 'cows.' These are pent up by
a malicious demon (Paṇi), and their milk,
the refreshing water of heaven, is withheld
from man.

Curiously, the natural basis of this simple
myth is so far forgotten that the myth itself
is here made to furnish a simile for the very
phenomenon from which it is the poetic
outgrowth.

NOTES TO PAGE 71.

1. 'The orifice of the waters which was
closed up — he who slew (805, 209) Vritra
opened that.' Waters conceived as if pent
up in some mighty cask.

2–3. 'A horse's tail becamest thou then,
O Indra, when on his lance he (V.) impaled
thee. — As god alone, thou conqueredst · · ·.
Thou didst let loose the seven streams (but
see saptá) to flow' (lit. 'for flowing,' vaṛ,
970b, 982).

— In fighting with demons, Indra sometimes gets roughly handled for a while (so
iv.18.9). Such I conceive to be the situation here. Pāda a is the crux. Possibly a
magic transformation is intended. V. im-
pales I. on his lance; but straightway the
god becomes a great sweeping trail of vapor.
Very differently Bergaigne, Rel. Véd. iii.
61–62.

— It seems unavoidable to join devá ékas
with c: cf. i.33.4 and i.165.6 = 73¹⁴. — Second
ájayas begins a new clause: hence acct, 593².

4. Explained under yā́s: asmāi means
Vritra. — ákirad dh-, 163. — Cf. what is
said of Yahve at Psalm xviii.13,14.

5. yuyudhā́te, 800a. — U.f. utá aparí-
bhyas (see ápara). — vi jigye, 787. —
'Indra was victor (both for the time) while
he and Ahi fought and (utá) for the future.'

6–7. 'What avenger of Ahi sawest thou,
Indra, when in the heart of thee having slain
(him) fear did come — when nine and ninety

streams as an affrighted hawk the skies thou
didst cross?' This may refer to a time
when — after all the aerial commotion (i.e.
Indra's battling) — the rain refused to fall
and the uncleared heaven signified Indra's
retreat. Reminiscences of this legend occur
at TS. ii.5.3: cf. MBh. v.9.27 = 255 and
10.43 = 334,f. — jaghnúṣas, 805.

8–9. See √yā 1 and √sā. — U.f. sás íd u
(176b) ·· arán ná ··. — Gen., 297c. —
Tenses, 823².

SELECTION XXXIII. RV. i.50. To Sūrya,
the Sun-god. — Respecting Sūrya, see Kaegi,
p. 54(76). The hymn is rubricated at 106².
It is still used in India, at the Midday Service. It was made the text of a linguistic-
mythological comment of 225 pages by W.
Sonne, KZ. vol's xii.–xv.!

In the textus receptus, the hymn has 13
stanzas. I have given only 1–9. In the
first strophe, stanzas 1–3, the god is mentioned only in the 3d person. In the second
strophe, he is addressed in the 2d person;
and so also in the third strophe, excepting
— as often — the final stanza (9).

— That stanzas 10–13 are later additions is
proved by their contents and language and
their (differing) metre. This proof is confirmed by the fact that the corresponding
passage of the AV., xiii.2.16–24, has only
stanzas 1–9; and also by the fact that only
1–9 are prescribed to be used in the ritual —
see Bezzenberger's Beiträge, viii.198, ZDMG.
xxxviii.475, JAOS. xi.p.cxcii = PAOS. May,
1884, and AGS. ii.3.13 and comment, and cf.
871⁰ₙ. Moreover, the addenda are at the end
of an anuvāka — cf. JA. 8.viii. 207 = 15.

10. See u2. — jātávedasam, see vocab.:
although 'All-possessor' was very likely the
primary mg (Whitney, AJP. iii.409), yet the
mg 'All-knower' also seems to have been
associated with the word early and commonly
(Eggeling, SBE. xxvi.p.xxxi). For analogous
cases, see hótṛ and yamá in vocab.

In the present — very unusual — application of the epithet to Sūrya,

δς πάντ' ἐφορᾷ καὶ πάντ' ἐπακούει,

the latter phase of mg predominates.

11. 'That every man may see the sun,
lit. for every one for beholding the sun.'
See dṛç and read 969, 970a, and 982. —
viçvāya, 524².

12–13. tyé belongs logically with nák-
ṣatrā[ṇi], but is conformed in gender to
tāyāvas. —With this simile, cf. RV. x.
189.2. —See yathā4. —yanti, no acct,
595a². —sūrāya, 'for the sun, i.e. to make
way for the sun.' Render :

> Off — like as robbers — slink away
> Yon constellations with their beams
> Before the all-beholding Sun.

14. ádṛçram (834b end) · · vi (1081²) —
passively, 998b : equiv. to vy-adṛkṣata, 882.
—jánāṅ, 209.

18–19. See pratyáño3. —Pronounce de-
vānaām, 113². —pratyáññ, 210. —Pronounce súar (Whitney, 84b): reg. written
súvar in TS. —súar dṛçé, 'a light to behold' (cf. θαῦμα ἰδέσθαι), here equiv. to 'a
glorious light.'

20 and 72¹. yénā, 509 end. —pávaka:
see ref's in vocab.; this word the redactors
persist in miswriting; it is a typical mistake
belonging to the second stage of the tradition — see p. 354, § 79, and KZ. xxvi.60.

—jánāṅ ánu: if joined w. ppl., render
'stirring *or* busy among (so RV. viii.9.2b)
his fellows;' if w. páçyasi (acct, 595a),
'over the peoples thou dost look on busy
man.' —Pronounce tuám.

—STROPHE 2, stanzas 4, 5, 6. Some join
6 with 7 — possible, but very hard. It is
better to regard 6 as a parenthesis in which
the poet turns suddenly from Sūrya to
·Varuṇa. The latter is the personified vault
of heaven, and the sun is naturally his eye
(RV. vii.63.1), and to mark the deeds of
restless man is his proper function [Kaegi,
p.65(90)]. Yénā then refers to súar, and
cákṣasā is in explanatory apposition w.
yénā. We may render 4, 5, 6 thus:

> Thou goest onward, all-beheld.
> Thou makest light, god Sūria.
> Thou shinest to the end of heaven.
> Turning thy face upon the folk
> Of gods, of men, of all the world,
> Thou risest up, thou glorious light—
> With which, as eye, bright Varuṇa,
> Over the peoples thou dost look,
> To mark the deeds of restless man.

NOTES TO PAGE 72.

2–3. U.f. ví dyám (see dív) eṣi, rájas
(171⁴) pṛthú, áhā (425d) mímānas (√1mā4 :
see 661, 655) aktúbhis ('with beams'),
páçyan (202²). —'Beholding (in pregnant
sense) the generations, i.e. while generations
come and go.'

4–5. J. Burgess, *Arch. Survey of Western
India, Kāṭhiāwāḍ and Kacch*, p. 216, mentions temple-images of Sūrya with a halo
(cf. çociṣkeça) and borne by 'seven steeds,'
see plate lxv.2. Cf. Kaegi, N. 205.

6–7. áyukta (834b), 'hath just yoked.'
—See 356 and 356⁴. —sváyuktíbhis, Sāyaṇa
rightly, svakīya-yojanena.

SELECTION XXXIV. RV. i.97. To Agni.
See Preface, p. v, note 4.— Rubricated at
106². Recurs AV. iv.33. The refrain or
burden, pāda c, of each stanza, is a mere
repetition of pāda *a* of stanza 1; it has no
necessary connection with the rest of each
stanza, although it happens to fadge well
enough in the first and in the last three.

Grassmann and Ludwig make ápa · ·
çóçucat of the refrain a 3d s. subjunctive
(1008²) — 'let him drive · · ·'; but this would
require an accentless çoçucat.

We may therefore disregard the refrains
entirely and group the remaining eight
couplets [each consisting of two octosyllabic
verses], two and two, into four stanzas of
four verses each.

8–11. See √çuc+apa and çuc+ā: ápa · ·
çóçucat is pres. ppl. of intensive conjugation (1012) — no nasal, 444. —U.f. çuçugdhí
á, perf. impv. of primary conjugation, 813.
—Three instrumentals (line 10), 365.1.

STANZA 1 [made by grouping stanzas 1̃,2̃]
may be rendered :

> Driving away with flames our sin,
> Agni, bring welfare with thy light.
> [Driving away with flames our sin.]
> With prayer for fertile fields, for wealth,
> And prayer for good, we sacrifice—
> [Driving away with flames our sin.]

12. With prá, supply jáyeta in *a* and
jáyeran in *b*. —bhánd-iṣṭhas (superl. to
bhad-rá, √bhand, 467), 'brightest, luckiest' ?
—asmākāsas, 330 end.

14. prá yát sc. jáyeran (760.3), 'that they may be propagated = that offspring may go forth from them' — and so in the other clauses of lines 12 and 14.

—In lines 12 and 14, the yad's seem to introduce final clauses expressing the purpose of yajāmahe, line 10. In line 16, Whitney makes yád = 'as, just as.' For all the yád-clauses, Grassmann seeks principal clauses in the refrains.

STANZAS 3,4 and 5,6. '[We sacrifice,] in order that (offspring may go) forth from the luckiest of them (?); and forth from our patrons; that offspring may go forth from thy patrons, Agni, — forth from us (who are) thine,

'As forth from mighty Agni on all sides go the rays. For thou, O (God) who hast a face on all sides, on all sides dost protect.'

20. 'Bring us across the (stream of) foes as with a boat.' See nāú and √2pṛ+ati.

NOTES TO PAGE 73.

2. Pronounce sá naḥ sindhvīva nāváyā, w. elision of -m and combination: instance of a text-error of the second stage of the tradition — see p. 354, § 79 and KZ. xxvi.61, and cf. 78⁷. — See tá2 end. — áti parṣā (248c), √2pṛ, impv. of s-aor., 896.

SELECTION XXXV. RV. i.165. Indra and the Maruts. — Respecting the Maruts and their relations to Indra, see Kaegi, p. 39 (56), and Bergaigne, La religion védique, ii. 369f, 302, and esp. the interesting article of Oldenberg, Ākhyāna-hymnen in RV., ZDMG. xxxix.60–65. The hymn is the first of a collection of eight Marut hymns (165–172), concerning whose arrangement, see Oldenberg, l.c. We have here the beginnings of poetry in epic-dramatic form — cf. Preface, p. iv, note 7. This hymn has been admirably translated by Roth, ZDMG. xxiv.302 (or Siebenzig Lieder, p. 84); English version by Whitney, North American Review, 1871, cxiii.182 = OLSt. i.144. It is also translated with comments by Max Müller, RV. Sanhita, translated, etc., i.162f. I give the "story of the hymn" abridged from Roth-Whitney.

STANZAS 1–2. The poet inquires whither the Maruts are going and how they are to be detained at the sacrifice. The implicit answer is 'With praise.' This then is accomplished in the dialogue, where, although greatest glory is given to Indra, the god in turn lauds them generously.

STANZAS 3–4. The Maruts ask why Indra is going alone, without them, his usual companions. — Indra answers evasively that he is on the way to a sacrificial feast.

STANZAS 5–6. The Maruts are eager to go with him. — He retorts that they were not so eager when he went, alone, and slew the dragon.

STANZAS 7–8. The Maruts remind him that they have helped him do great things and can be most useful allies in the future. — Not inclined to share his glory with them, he boasts again of his exploits.

STANZAS 9–12. The Maruts acknowledge his might this time without reserve and to his satisfaction. — Indra, vaunting himself once more (10), thanks them for their homage (11), and declares that the sight of them delights his heart (12).

STANZAS 13–15. The poet (Agastya) turns to the Maruts directly and asks them to recognize and reward his skill and devotion.

4. √myakṣ+sam, perf. (785, 794b) as preterito-present. —Lit. 'With what common course (?) have they kept together? i.e. upon what common journey are they together?'

5. matí, Classic matyā, 340. — U.f. kútas á_itāsas (vi, 330 end) eté? árcanti (accent-combination, 135²) çúṣmam — acc. as in ἀγωνίζεσθαι τάλην. —vasūyā, as at 72¹⁰.

7. See mánas2. — √vram4: read 869, 864, and 856.

8. Pronounce tuám indra, as 5 syllables. — máhinaḥ sánn, 'being (usually) gay': Roth-Whitney, 'though (else so) blithe'; concessive force doubtful: perhaps they mean a gentle reproach for his slighting their company — 'Why go'st thou alone, and so merry withal?'

9. 'Thou talkest (usually), when going along with (us) moving onward.' —See √ṛ+sam. Both ppls are of the root-aorist, 840³. —vocés, 854. —harivas, 454b. — yát te asmé (loc. 492²), 'which (is) to thee

on our score, lit. on us,' i.e. 'which thou hast against us.'

10ᵃ. çám, '(are) a joy,' pred. to all three subst.

10ᵇ. See çúṣma2. —iyarti, √ṛ, 643c. —prá-bhṛtas, '(is) ready,' begins a clause.

11. 'They [men] are making supplication (to me); they are enticing (me) with invocation (ukthá, as instr. s.). These two (imá, 501 end) coursers here are carrying me (lit. us) unto (áccha) them' (tá = táni, 495 end: the good things mentioned in pāda a).

12. vayám, 'we,' i.e. the few who are conceived as speaking for the whole troop. —See √yuj3: cf. 840ᵃ. —Pronounce tanúaḥ çúmbh-: notation explained by Whitney, 90bᵇ. See tanú under tanú and see √2çubh. —The spokesmen designate their 'companions' as 'free' in order to magnify the value of their readiness to follow Indra.

13. U.f. étán (not etán): the Maruts drive a dappled team of does or mares. —See √yuj+upa: yujmahe is a root-class present (612a), used with future mg (777a). —U.f. nú | índra (314ᵇ). —See 1 svadháṣ3. —babhútha, 798b.

14. kvà syá, Whitney, 90bᵇ: pronounce kúa siá ·· svadháṣid. —syá, 'that' (wish for my company), just mentioned, line 13. They did leave him in the lurch once — see 82¹ɴ. — U.f. yád ·· sam-ádhatta: see √1dhá+sam and 668.

15. Pada-text ahám hí ugráḥ. —See under √nam: for gen., see 297c end, and cf. 77⁸.

16. bhúri, acc. n., may be either pl. (340) or sing. —Pischel shows that asmé may be used as instr. (or gen.) also. 'With (= in company of) us combined, (and) by our united prowess.' — Pronounce yújiebhis, pãúṅsiebhis.

17. kṛṇávāmā (248c), pres. subjunctive (700) of √kṛ, 715. —krátvā, Classic kratuná, 342. —maruto, voc.: the spokesmen call on their companions to bear them witness. But the reading marúto, nom., has been suggested. —See yád4 end. —váçāma, 614.

18. vádhīm, 904a. —babhūván, 802.

19. Compare 70¹⁵ɴ.

20. See á-nutta and ánu-tta in vocab. —See á3. —See √2vid3 and 619³. —Either, 'Entirely invincible for thee is surely nothing. Not (one) like thee is found among the gods'; or, 'Entirely granted thee is (the fact) that surely no one (nákis ·· ná, double neg. = single) like thee etc.' Cf. KZ. xxvi. 611 and JAOS. xiii.p.c = PAOS. May, 1886.

NOTES TO PAGE 74.

1. náçate: acct, 596 and 597, cf. 89ᵃɴ.; the object (tvā) is to be understood from what precedes. —Roth emends to kariṣyáḥ, see 938.

2. Pronounce ékasya cin me vibhú astu ójas. — yá = yáni. See nú3. 'Whatsoever things (I am) having ventured, (those) I will accomplish (subjunctive = fut. ind., 576) wisely (365.1).'

3. This vidánas may be referred to √1vid. —cyávam, 563, 743. —íçe, as 1st pers. here. — 'What things I may undertake, just I, Indra, am master óf thèm.'

4. U.f. ámandat mā marutas st-, 173a: cf. 74¹²ɴ. —yád ·· bráhma cakrá, a subject-clause co-ordinate with stómas.

5. máhyam, appositive to me. —sákhye, 343a. —tanúe tanúbhis, 'for myself, by yourselves (vestra sponte), i.e. for me, spontaneously or heartily.'

6. See evá 1 end. —Roth suggests the emendation ánedyáḥ (ánediáḥ), as nom. pl. m.; or else anedyaçraváḥ. —U.f. á íṣas dádhānās.

7. sam-cákṣiā, 993a. —ácchānta (cch, 227), a-chánt-s-ta, 883, 233b. See √2chad. —chadáyāthā (248c), subjunctive, 1043.2. — 'In very truth these (are) appearing good unto me, blameless, putting on glory (and) strength. Ye of shining hue have delighted me, upon looking at (you), O Maruts, and delight ye me now.'

8. See √mah. — prá yātana, 618. — sákhīñr, 209.

9. See √vat. —bhúta, 835. —návedās, 415e, as nom. pl. m.

—The accent-rules for the oblique cases of the pron. root a (cf. 502) are simple and entirely natural. Thus:

A. If the form is used adjectively, distinguishing 'thís' thing from others, it is accented (74⁹; 92⁸, 79¹⁸). **B.** So also if used as an emphatic substantive pron. (83¹⁵, 103⁴ asmát).

C. But if used as an unemphatic substantive pron., 'his, her, him, their, them,' it is accentless (83¹⁶, 70³, 71¹⁴, 74³, 88¹⁷, and very often). In this case the form cannot stand at beg. of pāda.

10. The á has pregnant mg (cf. √çuç+á and +apa) and goes w. both duvasyát (562²) and cakré. —Both verbs depend (595) on yád. —Pronounce máaniásya. —'When the singer entices (you) hither as to an oblation, (and when) the wisdom of Mána's son has brought us hither —.'
—Roth would expunge one d and read duvasyá, instr. (365.1) of duvasyá (1149⁶), 'with an honoring, i.e. reverently.' The passage is a desperate one.

11. U.f. á u sú vartta (irreg., 839) · · áocha. See sú 1 and √vṛt+á. — imá = imáni. —arcat, 743.

12. va stómo, u.f. vas stómas, 173a: similar combinations at 79¹⁷, vípras st-; 81¹⁷, ájayas sp-; 87¹; 92⁸; 74⁴; per contra, 47¹¹. —iyám here refers back — see 1 idám. —See gír.

13. U.f. á iṣá yāsiṣṭa (914³) · · vidyáma (√2vid, a pres. opt. of the root-class) iṣá-m. —Pronounce vayáām ? —'Hither with refreshment come ye. For ourselves as a strengthening may we get refreshment (and) a well-watered dwelling-place.'
—It would seem that the poet Agastya was the son of Māna, of the race of Mandāra. This entire final stanza recurs at the end of hymns 166–168. The awkward repetition of 'refreshment' leads Roth to suspect that the original pāda d of the stanza is lost and replaced by the one in the text, which is a stock-verse recurring at the very end of twenty subsequent hymns.

SELECTION XXXVI. RV. iii. 62. To Savitar. — Respecting Savitar, see Kaegi, p. 56(79). The last "hymn" (62) of the third maṇḍala is really a collection of six short hymns to various divinities. Each hymn contains three stanzas, and the triad to Savitar is the fourth of the six.

—The first stanza of this triad is the most celebrated stanza of the RV., and is called the sávitrī (sc. ṛk), or the gāyatrī κατ' ἐξοχήν. It has held, and holds even now, the most important place in the worship of the Hindus. In the Proceedings of the *International Congress of Orientalists* (1881) *at Berlin,* ii.2.160–187, and in *Religious Thought and Life in India,* p. 399f, Monier-Williams discusses the place of the RV. in the religious services of the Hindus of the present day.

He says that the worshipper must first bathe, then apply ashes to his limbs and forehead, bind his hair, sip pure water, and inhale pure air and retain it in his lungs for a while. The worshipper then utters RV. iii.62.10, which — like the Lord's Prayer among Christians and like the Fātihah among Muhammadans — takes precedence of all other forms of supplication. [Cf. Manu ii.101f.] Later on, the gāyatrī is muttered 108 times with the help of a rosary of Tulsī wood.

—Much has been fabled about the stanza and its virtues. See, for example, Manu ii.77–83. And it recurs frequently in the other Vedas; thus, four times in the VS., twice in the TS., and once in the SV. "No good and sufficient explanation of the peculiar sanctity attaching to this verse has ever been given." — Whitney, reprinted in Kaegi, n.222. The stanza has naturally been imitated a great deal: so even in the RV. (v.82) we find verses run in the same mould. And it is interesting to find the RV. stanzas iii.62.10 (gāyatrī) and v.82.1 repeated in juxtaposition in the Tāittirīya āraṇyaka at i.11.2 and i.11.3. After the pattern of the gāyatrī have been made a good many wooden and halting stanzas: so TA. x.1.5,6.

14–15. dhīmahi, root-aor. opt. mid. (837) of √dhā — see √dhā3. See also Whitney in Kaegi, n.222. —yó · · pracodáyāt (1043. 2), 'and may he inspire.'

16–17. púraṁdhiā, perhaps 'with exaltation(of spirit).' —ímahe, see √i and reference.

18. náras, nom. pl. of nṛ́.

NOTES TO PAGE 75.

SELECTION XXXVII. RV. iv. 42. Indra
contests the supremacy of Varuṇa. — Respecting Varuṇa, see Hillebrandt, *Varuṇa
und Mitra*, 1877, and Kaegi, p. 61(85), notes
241f. This hymn has ten stanzas; but the
last three have nothing to do with the rest.

— Varuṇa is by far the noblest and loftiest
character of the Vedic pantheon, and seems
to have held the most prominent position in
the earliest period. Later — as appears if
we consider the RV. as a whole — the warlike and national god Indra is plainly most
prominent. The gradual supersession of
Varuṇa by Indra[1] is reflected in a considerable number of passages — among them, this
hymn — and especially in x.124.

— In stanzas 1–4 of this hymn, Varuṇa
claims the godhead, supreme and from the
beginning, in virtue of his creating and sus-
taining the world. — Indra responds (5–6)
by asserting his irresistible might as god
of battle. — And the hymn ends with an
acknowledgment on the part of the poet
(st. 7) of the claims of Indra. This is essentially the interpretation of most of the
authorities.[2]

— But the general drift of the hymn has
been — no less than its details — the subject
of very much discussion and difference of
opinion. Bergaigne[3] considers stanzas 1–6
as a monologue of Indra. Barth[4] rejects
the theory of the decadence of the Varuṇa-
cultus and regards RV. x.124 as one of the
few survivals of a class of myths in which
Varuṇa is not the god of a smiling and
gracious heaven, but a malignant divinity.
Finally, Whitney urges that this is not a
question of supremacy and subordination,
but rather of comparative prominence. —
This selection, I confess, is out of place in
a Reader.

[1] Discussed by Muir, OST. v.116f; and, in connection with RV. x.124, by Hillebrandt, p. 107–111.
See also Grassmann's introduction to x.124 and his
translation of it.
[2] So GKR., p. 26; Grassmann, Translation; and
Hillebrandt, esp. 72(159), 104–105.
[3] La religion védique, iii.142, printed 1877.
[4] The religions of India, p. 18.

1. **máma**: note that every one of the
stanzas 1–6 begins with an emphatic form
of the first personal pron. — **dvitā́**, if rendered 'equally,' means 'as well as thou, O
Indra, who disputest my sovereignty,' or
else 'as well over all creatures as over
gods;' but Kern defines dvitā́ as 'from
everlasting' or 'to everlasting:' the mg is
uncertain and has been so since the time of
the nighaṇṭavas (cf. Nirukta, v.3). — Pronounce **rā́ṣṭrám**. — See viçvā́yu in vocab.
— Grassmann would emend **yáthā naḥ** to
yátānāḥ, root-aor. ppl. of √yat, 'joining
themselves together, united:' 'mine (are)
all immortals together.' Otherwise we must
take naḥ as plural of majesty and equiv. to
máma.

— 'To me, the ruler, forever (belongs) the
sovereignty over all creatures, just as all
immortals (are) ours, i.e. our vassals.'

2[b]. Taking vavrí in mg 1, 'I am king of
the folk's highest cover, i.e. king of heaven,'
or else 'I am king of the folk of the highest
cover, i.e. king of the folk of heaven, *or* king
of the gods.' — GKR. quite otherwise.

3. **rā́jā** as pred. — **prathamā́(ni)**, 'first'
in order of time. — See √dhṛ5.

5. **índro**: excellent authorities emend,
and read **indra**. — **té urví** (342) etc. are
accusatives dual neuter, object of the verbs
in next line. — **mahitvā́** (330) 'by might.'

6. **sám airayam**, √ir, 585. — **dhāráyam**
ca makes a new clause, hence acct, 593[2].

7–8. 'I made the dropping rains to stream.
I uphold heaven in the place of eternal order.
And in accordance with eternal order, the
sacred son of Aditi (i.e. Varuṇa) spread out
the threefold world.' The sending of rain
is a function proper to Varuṇa — cf. Hillebrandt, p. 85–86. In the assignment of *this*
stanza the authorities differ and waver most.

9. Pronounce **máam ·· suáçvās**. — **vṛtás**,
'the chosen ones, πρόμαχοι' (√2vṛ), or else
'hemmed in, sore beset' (√1vṛ2): opinion
about equally divided. — **vhū**.

10. **maghávā_ahám índras** may make a
sentence by itself or be taken appositively
with the subject of **kṛṇómi**. — See √ṛ and
reference.

11. **cakaram**, 817, 818[2]. — **nákis** begins

new clause. —varate, √1vṛ8, root-aor. subj. (836).

12. mamádan, perf. subj., 810a. —yád ukthâ(ni) sc. mâ mamádan. —rájasî, 138a.

13. U.f. vidús (790a) te, 188b: similarly 80¹⁵. — 'All beings have knowledge of thee as such a one (tásya). These things thou proclaimest to Varuṇa, O true one.'

14. Pronounce tuám, both times. — çrạviṣe, 699² end, see √çru2. 'Tu hostium interfector clues.' —jagh-, 805: cf. 71¹. —vṛtán, √1vṛ2. —ariṇâs, 725.

SELECTION XXXVIII. RV. iv. 52. To Uṣas, the Dawn-goddess.— See Kaegi, p. 52(73). The monograph by Brandes, Ushas og Ushas-hymnerne i Rigveda, Copenhagen, 1879, gives translations of all the 21 hymns in juxtaposition. Cf. also Easton, JAOS. x.p.lxix = PAOS. Oct. 1873.

—Stanzas 1, 2, 3 (= SV. ii.1075-7) form a strophe. Stanzas 5, 6, 7 seem to form a second. Stanza 4 seems to be an addendum to the prior strophe.

15-16. U.f. syâ, 188a. —√1vas+vi. = svásus, cf. RV. i. 113.3. — práti adarçi (844), note force of práti.

17-18. citrâ as pred. —mâtâ, cf. Hesiod, Theogony, 378-82. —gávâm, 361c. The 'kine' are the fleecy morning-clouds, the children of Dawn — cf. Kaegi, note 197. —See ṛtávan: the idea in Job xxxviii.12ᵇ or Psalm civ.19ᵇ is similar. "The sun knoweth his going down."

> Bright as a ruddy steed became
> The faithful mother of the kine,
> Uṣas, the friend of Açvins twain.

19. Note how all three pâdas of this stanza begin with utá. — Pronounce sá-khâsi, u.f. sákhâ asi.

NOTES TO PAGE 76.

1. U.f. utá uṣas (voc.). —vásv-as, 342, 297c. —íçiṣe, 630.

3. práti · · abhutsmahi (√budh), 882 and 155: 'we have awaked with praises to meet thee (tvâ)' — vocab. wrong.

4-5. práti adṛkṣata (√dṛç), 879b, 882, 218. —U.f. â uṣás aprâs (889).

> Gladsome before our eyes appear
> Her beams — like herds of kine let loose.
> The wide expanse of air she fills.

6-7. â-paprúṣi, sc. jráyas, or with Sâyaṇa, jagat, 'the world,' 'all': the stems of this perf. ppl. are papriváṅs- and paprúṣ-, cf. 803 and 459. —Pronounce ví âvar (√1vṛ, 831², 585²). —'According to thy wont, be gracious.'

8-9. dyâm, see dív. —U.f. â_antárikṣam, sc. tanoṣi (√1tan+â, 698B). — See priyâ3. —Note the radical connection of the assonant words and render by 'radiant ray,' 'effulgent flame,' or the like.

SELECTION XXXIX. RV. v. 24. To Agni. —The stanzas are dvipadâ, i.e. consist of two pâdas, one of 8 and one of 11 or 12 syllables. Most nearly like this hymn in metre is RV. x.172; but the stanzas of RV. viii.12,13,15, and 18 are essentially similar (8+8+12).

—It is very worthy of note that three of the stanzas occur in immediate juxtaposition in the other samhitâs, and as follows: in the order 1, 2, 4, at SV. ii.457,458,459, at VS. xv. 48ᵃ,48ᵇ,48ᶜ, and at VS. iii.25ᵃ,25ᵇ,26ᵃ (here stanza 3 follows as 26ᵇ); and in the order 1,4,2 at TS. i.5.6 and iv.4.4. Finally, to judge from the legend given below, and from the prescriptions of the ritual — of the sacrifice to the Manes, for example — this hymn would appear to be a tṛca or triad of riks (see Sâyaṇa to RV. v.24 and to PB. xiii.12.5).

—Tradition (Kâtyâyana) ascribes this hymn and also x.57-60 to the Gâupâyana brothers, Bandhu, Subandhu, Çrutabandhu, and Viprabandhu. In his comments to x. 57-60, Sâyaṇa gives the pertinent legendary material taken from ancient sources; and this, with other matter, is given in translation, in JRAS. NS.ii.441f, by Max Müller, who discusses the legend at length.

—The Bṛhaddevatâ says that king Asamâti sent away the four brothers who were his priests, and put in their stead two Brahman wizards. These took shape as doves, bewitched Subandhu, and plucked out his soul. In order to cause the spirit to return, the *three* remaining brothers recited x.58 etc., and 'praised Agni with the dvipadā hymn as it is among the Atris,' i.e. in the book of the family of Atri, the fifth. Then Agni gave back to Subandhu his soul, and the brothers, delighted, sang the rest of x.60 (7-12) and laid their hands (cf. 91²ɴ.) on the one thus resuscitated.

10. ágne, acct, 314⁵. —Pronounce tuám. —bhavā, 248c : so uruṣyā́ and çrudhī́, line 12.

11. ácchā, 248a. — nakṣi, √2naç, 624. —Superl., 471. —dā́s, 835.

12. sá, see tá2 end. — nas, 297b. — bodhi, see 839 end : here from √budh, see √budh3. —çrudhī́ for çrudhí : aorist impv., 839 : acct, 593² mid. — ṇo, u.f. nas, 194. —aghāyatás, pres. ppl. ablative, 290 : acct, 316, 318a. —See īsama.

13. See under tá2. —dídivas, √dī, perf. ppl., voc., 462a. —īmahe, see √i.

SELECTION XL. RV. v. 40. Indra and Atri, and the sun eclipsed by the demon.— For a critical analysis of the hymn, see Grassmann, Translation, i.190 and esp. 540. Stanzas 6, 7, 8, here given, are quite independent of the rest.

—Ludwig identifies the eclipse here referred to with that of April 20, 1001 B.C., O.S.—see *Sitzungsberichte d. böhmischen Gesell. d. Wiss.*, 1885. His argument is reported by Whitney, JAOS. xiii.p.lxi f = PAOS. Oct. 1885, and by Bergaigne, JA. 8.vi.372f. No fair interpretation of the text furnishes data precise enough for an exact identification.

—Stanzas 6 and 8 are spoken by the poet; stanza 7, by the Sun. The Sun's foe, Súarbhānu (accent!), is 'he who has the sun's beams,' and is later identified with Rāhu, the demon who 'swallows,' 'devours,' or 'seizes' (√2gr, √gras — cf. 23¹ɴ., √grah) the sun or moon, and so causes eclipses. The Sun is in terror, and implores Atri for help; and the latter rescues the orb by prayer and praise.

—Atri's mythical exploit is often mentioned in the Brāhmaṇas (see texts in Lud-

wig, v.508; and cf. SBE. xxvi.346). Thus the PB., at vi.6.8,11, narrates how, at the request of the gods, Atri restored to brightness the sun, which the demon had smitten with darkness. On this account, it continues, a present of gold, the symbol of brightness, is made to a descendant of Atri at a sacrifice now-a-days.

—Interesting are the Greek ideas about the τάγκοινον τέρας that bringeth to nought men's strength and wisdom — see Pindar's *Fragments* [74], Bergk⁴ i.411 f and notes.

14. ava ̇áhan (593), cf. 70² and note.

15. gūḷhám, √guh. —ápa-vrata, 'having action off, i.e. baffling,' or, as in vocab. — 'The sun, hidden · ·, Atri found (avindat) by the fourth prayer.'

—Ludwig reasons thus : The other priests had a regular liturgy of three prayers for combating eclipses. On this occasion, these proved ineffectual. Atri knew a fourth, and that brought the sun out. Hence the totality must have been very long. This matter is discussed in full by Whitney, l.c., p. lxv(=xxi). Bergaigne, l.c., p. 383(=14), says it is a mere case of the use of a sacred number plus one — cf. *Rel. védique*, ii.128.

16. mā́m (pronounce mā́am) imám, 'me here, i.e. in this plight;' Sāyaṇa, ī́dṛg-avastham. —U.f. atre : the Sun is addressing Atri. —irasyā́, 365.1. —bhiyás-ā́, '(me, who am thine) with fear, i.e. who am thine, (but) sore in terror:' or, the word *may* be taken actively, as the accent (1151.2c) and Sāyaṇa's gloss ('fear-inspiring') suggest, and joined with the subject—'with a frightening.' —mā́ · · nī gārīt: √2gr; aor., 899a; combination w. mā́, 579.

17. Pronounce tuám mitró asi · · tā́u mehávatam. —mitró, 'friend.' —U.f. tā́u (see tá2 end) mā ihá avatam: 'so do ye two help me here, (thou) and V.' With the peculiar omission of tvám compare that of ahám, 79¹⁰ɴ. So RV. viii.1.6.

18 and 77¹. brahmā́ = átris of next line. —yuyujānás (80¶), see √yuj2. —kírī may rather mean 'praise.' — upaçíkṣan, see √çak+upa. — U.f. cákṣus ā̇ ̇adhāt (830). — ápa aghukṣat, √guh, 920, 916.

NOTES TO PAGE 77.

SELECTION XLI. RV. vii. 55. Magic
spells to produce sleep. — Ascribed to Vasiṣṭha. The hymn consists of three parts
differing in metre and disconnected in contents. For a general discussion of it, see
Colebrooke's *Essays* ²i.27, and Whitney's
note, ibid. p. 112; JAOS. iii.336f; and esp.
Aufrecht, ISt. iv.337f. Sāyaṇa reports the
native traditions about the hymn. Thus:

Vasiṣṭha came by night to the house of
Varuṇa — to sleep, say some; to steal grain,
say others. He was assailed by the watch-
dog, which bayed at him, and fain would
have bitten him; but he laid the hound
asleep with the stanza beginning,

When, silv'ry Sārameya, thou,

and the one following. — Later superstition
uses the hymn to quiet uncanny creatures
at night: see Rigvidhāna, ii.26.

—FIRST PART. The hymn next preceding
this in the RV., vii.54, is to Vāstoṣpati, the
Lar familiaris, and consists of three stanzas.
The first part of our hymn, vii.55.1, is a mere
addition to these three stanzas, and belongs
accordingly to vii.54 rather than to vii.55,
as appears from the fact that the four
stanzas are all recited together in the ceremony of moving into a new house. See
ÇGS. iii.4, AGS. ii.9.9, and esp. PGS. iii.4.7
—all in SBE. xxix.; and cf. MS. i.5.13.

The joining of this stanza to hymn 55 is a
simple misdivision of which the NT. shows
many parallel instances. Thus Mark ix.1
belongs to viii.; chap. ix. should begin with
the Transfiguration. A converse misdivision
is at AV. vi.63–64 as compared with RV.
x.191.

—SECOND PART. Stanzas 2–4 are part of
a scene at the entrance to Yama's kingdom
or the regions of the blessed. Yama's two
watch-dogs (cf. 83¹⁷N. and introd.) guard the
pathway and keep out the wicked. Here
one of them barks at some who would come
in; and these, in turn, protest that they
are godly men, and so have a right to
enter in peace. See Kaegi, N.274; Zimmer,
p. 421.

—THIRD PART. Stanzas 5–8 are the incantations by which the entire household is
put to sleep. According to Aufrecht, l.c.
(or Zimmer, p. 308), it is while a maid is
receiving the visit of her lover; but that
seems a little doubtful because we have
plurals nas and sám hanmas and vayám,
lines 12, 13, 15, and not duals.

With stanzas 5, 6, 7, 8 correspond respectively stanzas 6, 5, 1, 3 of AV. iv.5, and the
variants are interesting. The third part has
nothing to do with the second; but the diaskeuasts have juxtaposed them because in
both a dog is put to sleep.

2–3. vāstoṣpate, see above: for ṣ, see
187. —viçvā for viçvāni, 330. —edhi, 636.
—Yāska, Nirukta x.17, says yad yad rūpaṁ
kāmayate devatā, tat tad devatā bhavati.
Sāyaṇa quotes him from memory thus, yad
yad rūpaṁ kāmayante, tat tad devā
viçanti.

4–5. See dánt. —vìva, accent!, 128 end:
cf. 83¹⁵. U.f. ví iva bhrājante ṛṣṭáyas.
—See úpa2. —See vbhas and 678. —'They
(the teeth) shine like spears, in the jaws of
the devouring one.' —ní ṣú (188a) svapa
is a refrain.

The dog here addressed is partly white
and partly reddish brown, as Sāyaṇa rightly
observes; and this is in accord with the adj.
çabála, 'brinded,' applied to both of them
at 83¹⁷.

6–7. punaḥsara: for the mg, see vocab.
and cf. Hamlet i.4.51–53. —kím, 'why?'

8. For the genitives, see 297c end, and
cf. 73¹⁵. —See √ldṛ and 1010 and 1011.
—Probably the swine as a domestic animal
is meant here. In that case, this stanza is
a later addition to 2 and 3, and is based on
a conception of the situation such as the
native tradition presents.

10. Quoted at 593², which see.

11. In the Veda, 'complete' is sárva and
'all *or* every' is viçva. Later, viçva dies
out and sárva does double duty. In the
Veda, the use of sárva in the proper mg of
viçva (as here, 77¹⁷, 85²⁰, 91¹) marks the
passage as late. See vocab. under sárva.

—ayám etc., 'these here people on all
sides, all the people around here.'

—STANZA 5 may be spoken by maid or by lover or by both. With the AV. reading, svápantu asyãi jñātáyaḥ (see 365.3), it must be spoken by the lover. Stanzas 6–8 may be spoken by both.

12–13. nas, expect nãu — see above. — See under yáthã2 and cf. yá2.

14–15. See vṛṣabhá 1. — téna sahasyèna (248b), 'by (aid of) this mighty one.' —vayám, expect ãvám?. —√svap+ni, caus., 548.

16–17. nárīs, nom. pl., 365.2. —Pãda c may be read as catalectic.

SELECTION XLII. RV. vii. 56. To the Maruts or gods of the storm-winds. — Compare selection xxxv. (73⁴) and introduction. The hymn consists of two parts, of which the first, here given, ends with stanza 10. Number 11 is only the fragment of a stanza. The rest (12–25) is in an entirely different metre.

—The metre of the ten stanzas is without doubt a secondary one, being simply a form of the triṣṭubh syncopated at the sixth place, i.e. with the prevailingly light sixth syllable left out (cf. JAOS. xi.p.lxiii = PAOS. May, 1881). Thus,

$$\smile \measuredangle \cup \measuredangle \smile [\cup] \cup \measuredangle \cup \measuredangle \smile.$$

Each of the parts into which the verse is broken is a 'syllable-pentad' or akṣarapañkti; and each is an independent pãda, since verbs at the beginning of the even pentads are accented, e.g., at vii.34.3ᵇ, 3ᵈ, 4ᵇ, 6ᵇ. A pentad-couplet is sometimes joined with a simply broken but unsyncopated triṣṭubh verse to form a half-stanza or stanza (e.g. i.67.8ᶜᵈ; 70.4ᶜᵈ, 10ᶜᵈ; x.46.1ᵍʰ); and this fact seems to suggest the derivative character of the pentads.

—The gãyatrī-stanza has 3 verses of 8 syllables; and the strophe has 3 stanzas, a multiple of the number of verses. The pentad-stanza has 4 or 8 verses of 5 syllables; and the hymn has 5, 10, or 20 stanzas, a multiple of the number of syllables. The hymns RV. i.65–70 have each 5 stanzas of 8 pentasyllabic verses; while vii.34A and vii.56A and ix.109 probably consisted originally each of 10 or 20 stanzas of 4 pentasyllabic verses. Compare Bollensen, ZDMG. xxii.572f.

18. U.f. ké īm víaktãs·· ádha suáçvãs.

NOTES TO PAGE 78.

1. U.f. nákis hí eṣām: cf. John iii.8, οὐκ οἶδας πόθεν ἔρχεται (τὸ πνεῦμα). —vidre, 790b, 798a.

2. sva-pûbhis, 'with their (sva-) wings,' taking -pū in the sense of pávana. Pávana, lit. 'a cleaner,' from √pū, sometimes means a 'sieve' or a 'fan.' At 104¹² (see note), the pávana used to clean or winnow the ashes from the bones of a cremated corpse may perhaps be a 'wing-like winnowing-fan;' and observe that German Schwinge means 'winnowing-fan' and 'wing.' —abhí·· vapanta, 'bestrew, cover.' —aspṛdhran, see √spṛdh and 834b end.

—Here the storm-gods are pictured as lusty eagles, each sportively striving with the others for precedence, and spreading his wings over them in turn, to put them down and master them.

—Ludwig interprets, 'They vie in overwhelming each other with their blasts' (pávana has also the mg 'wind'). This view accords with the character of the playful, boisterous, and roaring gods, but not with the conception of them as eagles; and it would seem to require the reading abhí ·· vápantaḥ.

—Roth, and after him the vocab., suggests that svapú is a 'besom (that raises the dust)': 'they bestrew each other (in sport) with dust.' At best, the line is doubtful.

3. ciketa, 787, √cit3. —See yád2. The storm-gods are cloud-born, i.e. children of the cloud conceived under the figure of a dapple cow, pṛçni. This stanza (4) ought to come immediately after the second.

4. See víç2. —sáhantī, active: the forms are usually middle. —See √puṣ2. —'The host heroic, with the Maruts (as a part of it or as allies), must be ever victorious, displaying deeds of manhood.' Similarly stanza 7. The víṭ seems to mean the Maruts in alliance with Indra (cf. p. 364) or with some mortal protégé (cf. vii.56.23, i.64.13).

5. Lit. 'As to going, the best-going; most adorning themselves with adornment; united with beauty; terrible with strength.' Their abundant ornaments are much spoken of (e.g. v.54.11). Note the radical connection of ójas and ugrá.

6. 'Terrible is your strength; steadfast your power; therefore (ádhā) is a troop, with the Maruts (as allies), mighty.'

7. krúdhmī, nom. n. pl., 340. — Pronounce mūnīva (cf. 73²ɴ.) or mūnir 'va. — 'Clear is your whistling. Your hearts are wrathful as the wild onward-rush of a doughty troop.' Otherwise Bergaigne, *Mélanges Renier*, p. 85.

8. yuyóta: irreg. impv. (654) of √2yu; accented, as standing at the beg. of a pāda (see above). — prápañ naḥ, u.f. prá-nak (192a, 161) nas: nak, for nak-t, √2naç, 833, 218²; augmentless aor. as subjunct., w. mā.

9. Classic, priyāṇi nāmāni (425d). — huve: we should expect huvé. — U.f. á yád tṛpán (3d pl., 848 end: pada-pāṭha wrongly tṛpát). — See yád3 and √vaç2. — We have here an unsyncopated verse — see above. Grassmann emends. — 'I invoke the dear names of you the mighty, in order that they (among you) who desire (our praise) may be gladdened, O Maruts.'

SELECTION XLIII. RV. vii. 86. To Varuṇa. — Respecting Varuṇa, see vocab. and cf. p. 367. The hymn is rendered by GKR., p. 6. The comments of Ludwig, vol.iv.p.88, deserve careful attention.

— The poet is ill and deems his sickness a punishment sent by Varuṇa for some sin. He acknowledges the wisdom of the majestic god; but ventures to approach him with confession of sin and prayer for forgiveness and renewed self-consecration to the divine service. Compare Kaegi, p. 66(92).

10–11. dhírā = dhíraṇi. — See tú2. — mahiná, poss. like colloquial Eng. 'mightily, *i.e.* very.' — urv-í, acc.du.f. — papráthat, classed doubtfully as an augmentless reduplicated aor., 869⁶. — Note how the accent or the lack of accent of the verb-forms affects the exegesis.

— 'Wise in sooth is his nature (with

might =) and mighty [? *or* Stable in sooth are the creatures by his might], who propped asunder the two wide worlds, even. He set the great lofty firmament in motion, the stars (*collectively*) for ever [*or* the stars as well, *cf.* 75¹ɴ.]; and he stretched out the earth.' — Biblical parallels, Kaegi, p. 62(86).

12–13. Accent-marks, Whitney, 90b²: tanúā sám · · nú antár. — bhuvāni, 836ᴸ². — See kím3. — abhí khyam, 847 middle.

— 'And with my (sváyā) self I say this (take counsel thus), "When pray am I to be in Varuṇa's presence ? " *etc.*'

14. tád énas, τὸ ἀμάρτημα, 'the (admitted) sin.' — U.f. didṛkṣu | úpa u emi — see u2 end. Ludwig takes didṛk-ṣu as loc.pl.m. of didṛç, 'seer.' Thus case-form, stem-form (see 1147b), and construction (cf. German *bei Jemand anfragen*) are entirely regular. Others take didṛkṣúpa for didṛkṣus úpa (nom.s.m. with elision and crasis, cf. 78¹⁷ɴ.); but the acct is wrong — see vocab.

— 'And unto the wise (√cit, 787, 802) I go to find out by inquiry' (√praçh+vi, 970a, 981³).

15. kaváyaç cid — not my conscience only. — U.f. āhus, 801a. — √2hṛ.

16. 'What was, O Varuṇa, the sin most grievous (lit. principal) ? ' — See yád3. — See √han and 1028 e and f.

17. prá vocas, 'tell,' 848⁸, 847 end. — U.f. svadhāvas | áva (135²) tvā anenás nāmasā turás iyām (616³). Pronounce, with elision and combination, turéyām.

18–19. See √vṛj+áva 3 and 2. — Note prolongations of finals in sṛjā, sṛjā, and cakṛmā. — With the second áva, supply sṛja tāni: yá = yáni. — Pronounce dámano (425f end), abl. — Vasiṣṭha, the seer to whose family all the hymns of this seventh book are ascribed.

20. 'It was not my own will, it was infatuation · ·.' Note how the pronouns conform in gender with the predicates. — 'Liquor, dice'—ancient and perennial sources of crime: cf. Tacitus, *Germania*, xxiv.

NOTES TO PAGE 79.

1. 'The older is in the transgression of the younger. Not even (canā 1) sleep itself

(1d) excludes wrong.' I, Vasiṣṭha, have not entirely overcome the sins of my youth. Thoughts of malice or impurity trouble even my sleep. — Interpretation doubtful.

2–3. áram (not arám) karáṇi, 'I will serve,' root-aor. subjunctive (836¹) of √1 kṛ. —ánāgās, now that my sin has been, as I hope, forgiven. —'Made the unknowing to know.' —'The wise (man) unto wealth the still wiser (god) doth speed' (√jū).

4–5. ayám · · stómas, referring back to the hymn just ending — see idám. —See √çri+upa. —See kṣéma2. —See u 1 end. —'Ye gods, O keep us evermore with blessings' — refrain of the Vasiṣṭha-hymns; see Kaegi, note 83c, and Ludwig, iii.129.

SELECTION XLIV. RV. vii. 88. To Varuṇa. — Translated by GKR., p. 10. Like enough stanza 7 is a later addition.

—The poet, forsaken by Varuṇa on account of some sin, calls sadly to mind the by-gone days when he walked so happily with the god, and also the scene when, gliding over the waters with the god of the waters, he received the sacred appointment of Rishi. He asks forgiveness and restoration to divine favor. See Kaegi, p. 68(94). —It is not unnatural that Vasiṣṭha should address himself (cf. Ps. ciii.1) or speak of himself as a third person.

6–7. Pronounce práy-iṣṭham and cf. 470³. —īm, enclitic pron., with which vṛṣaṇam is in epexegetical apposition — cf. 70⁶ɴ. — kárate, root-aor. subjunctive, 836. —See vṛṣan3, and cf. the Hebrew conception of the sun that "rejoiceth as a strong man to run a race," Ps. xix.5.

8. maṅsi, √man2, s-aor. mid. 1st pers. s., 882. — 'So now, having come (805) to the sight of him, as Agni's face I deem Varuṇa's.' When I contemplate Varuṇa, his face seems to me like blazing fire.

9. áçmann, 210, 425c. —abhi · · niníyāt (accentless), put doubtfully as a present opt. of the reduplicating class, 651. — 'The light which in heaven [is], and the dark, let the lord unto me bring, a wonder to see.' The beauty of the heaven by night no less than by day was a wonder.

10. á · · ruháva implies the subject āvám, i.e. (ahám) váruṇaç ca: see 76¹⁷ɴ. At KZ. xxiii.308 is adduced the AS. parallel, vit Scilling song āhōfon, 'we two, Scilling (and I) raised a song.' — See vīr+pra. — See mádhya3.

11. ádhi apám snúbhis, 'ἐπ' (εὑρέα) νῶτα θαλάσσης:' pronounce sánubhis. — U.f. preṅkhé. —prá · · īṅkhayāvahāi (1043.2) is apodosis, as the accent shows. —See 1 çúbh and kám.

12. U.f. nāvi á_adhāt (829). —Pronounce su-ápā(s).

13. sudinatvé áhnām (430a): cf. εἴποτε εὐημερίας ἡμέραν ἐπιτελοίη, 'if ever he makes a jolly day of it,' Alkiphron's Letters, i.21. —U.f. yắt (see this) nú dyávas (361d) tatánan (810a), yắt uṣásas (tatánan). Cf. Psalm lxxii.5,7,17.

14. Pronounce kúa tyáni nāu sakhiá and see kvà. —sácāvahe: tense, see 778a; depends on yắd. —See yắd3. —Muir compares Psalm lxxxix.49.

15. jagamā (248c, 793b), 'I had access to:' we might expect jagámā, accented, and so co-ordinate with sáo. — V's golden house is built (AV. vii.83.1) on the waters:

apsú te rājan varuṇa
gṛhó hiraṇyáyo mitáḥ.

16–17. See explanation under yá7. — Pronounce tuám. — kṛṇávat, 715, 700. — 'Doeth sins against thee.' —sákhā te, '(he is yet) thy friend,' as apodosis to the concessively taken yás kṛṇávat. So Ludwig. —See √2bhuj5. —U.f. yandhí (617, 212) sma (188a, 248a) vípras (see 74¹²ɴ.) stuvaté (619).

18–19. GKR. transpose pādas b and c. —tvāsú: u.f., as given rightly by the pada-pāṭha, tvā (object of vanvānás) āsú (loc. pl. fem. 501). 'In these fixed or secure dwellings dwelling, thee we (are) beseeching (√van, 713, 705) for grace from the lap of Aditi.' —vi · · mumocat, 809, 810a. — Refrain as before, 79⁵ɴ.

NOTES TO PAGE 80.

Selection XLV. RV. vii. 89. To Varuṇa. — The hymn has been often translated:

so by Müller, ASL. p. 540; Muir, v.67; GKR.
p. 12; Hillebrandt, *Varuṇa und Mitra*, p. 64;
Bergaigne, *Religion Védique*, iii.155.

—It is the prayer of a man who is varuṇa-
gṛhīta, 'seized by Varuṇa, i.e. afflicted with
the dropsy.' V. is god of the waters (cf.
7¹⁰ᴺ., 79¹⁵ᴺ.), and the disease is supposed to
come from him and as a punishment for sin :
see AV. iv.16.7; also AB. vii.15, atha
ha_āikṣvākaṁ varuṇo jagrāha; tasya
ha_udaraṁ jajñe; and ÇB. ii.5.2². Cf.
Hillebrandt, p. 63–65, 54. Ludwig's interpretation is quite different: see his notes, vol.
iv. p. 91.

1-2. mó, see u2. —ṣú, 188a. —gṛhám,
Kaegi, note 329: cf. also the AS. poem in
Thorpe's *Analecta*, p. 142, entitled *The Grave*,
and familiar through Longfellow's translation. —gamam, 833, 835: with mā, 579.
—mṛḷá, 248c, √mṛḍ.

3-4. 'When I go, tottering along, like a
bag, puffed up,—have mercy.' — √sphur
implies quick or vigorous motion—see vocab.
Here the iva is not a particle of comparison;
it modifies the mg of the root to that of a
languid shake or wabble such as is characteristic of a dropsical person. So pra-hasan,
'laughing out;' pra-hasann iva, 'smiling.'

—dhmātás, 'puffed up' (with wind) or
'bloated' (with serum), has reference not
only to the bag, but also to the understood
ahám. Grassmann, 'schnaufend,' i.e. 'blown,
winded, puffing.' Otherwise Bergaigne, iii.
155ᴺ. —adrivas (454b), always of Indra,
except here, and at ix.53.1 (of Soma)! —
On this stanza the exegetes differ much.

5-6. krátvas, gen., 342. —dīnátā, 365.1.
—jagamā, 79¹⁵ᴺ.

7-8. Line 7 has trochaic cadences. —
'On (me, thy) singer, (though) standing
(803) in the midst of water, thirst has got
hold' (avidat, √2vid2). See Horace's description, Odes, ii.2, *Crescit indulgens*, etc.

9-10. See yád5. —See 2idám. —See
jána: for loc., 303a. —dhármā, 425d. —
yuyopimā, 793e. —See √riṣ: caus. aorist,
1046, 859; augmentless form as subjunctive
w. mā, 579.

— 'If we mortals do anything (kíṁ ca,
neut.) here (that proves to be) an offense

(masc.) against the gods, if with folly thy
steadfast decrees we have thwarted, do not
(cause us to take harm from this sin =)
chastise us for this sin.'

—METRE, jagatī. This stanza is not a
part of the hymn. The stanza is an oft-
recurring one—Schroeder, MS. iv. p. 290.
Its repetition daily for a year is prescribed
at Manu xi.253: cf. Ṛigvidhāna, ii.29.1.
The interesting stanza at RV. iv.54.3 = TS.
iv.1.11¹ is probably a reminiscence of this.
The AV., at vi.51.3, modernizes ácittī (340)
yád to ácittyā céd.

SELECTION XLVI. RV. viii. 14. To Indra. — Indra and Namuci. — For the introduction to the Namuci-myth, see 81¹⁵ᴺ. For
the later forms of the myth, see selection
lxxii., p. 975ᴺ.

—Division into five strophes of three
stanzas is possible. In respect of contents,
the first three stanzas and the last three
make very good strophes. Stanzas 1, 2,
and 3 form a strophe at SV. ii.1184–6; but
5, 7, and 8 form another at 989–91. The
hymn is unsymmetrically divided into three
at AV. xx.27–29.

11-12. íçīya: form, 616; acct, 628; mode,
581b, note the second example. Similar idea
at 87²⁰f, and often in RV., e.g. viii.19.25,26.
—vásvas, gen. 342.

13-14. See √çak B2 and 1030. —dít-
seyam, 1030; accented at beg. of clause,
though not at beg. of pāda, 593². —Note
the old mg of çácī-páti (vocab.), whence was
evolved the later 'Mrs. Might' (see çácī).

15-16. U.f. dhenús te, 188b: similar combinations at 87¹⁹, 84¹⁵. —sūnftā, cf. 28¹⁰ᵇᴺ.
—sunvaté, √1 su, 705; acct, 318. — 'Kine
and horses,' see under gó 1. —pi-py-úṣ-i, √pī,
802 end, 459. —duhe, 613, and 70¹⁸ᴺ.

17-18. 'Nor god nor mortal is a restrainer
of thy blessing, when ⋰.'

19. U.f. yád ('when') bhūmim ví ávar-
tayat: cf. "He taketh up the isles as a very
little thing," Isaiah xl.15; also 12.

NOTES TO PAGE 81.

1. cakrāṇás, √1 kṛ8, and 807. 'Putting
his plume in the heaven = touching the

heaven with his plume.' Just so, RV. x. 125.7[4].

2–3. See √vṛdh3 and 807[2]. —ji-gy-úṣ-as (787 —strong stem ji-gī-váñs) goes also with te. —U.f. índra ā́ vṛṇīmahe (718).

4–5. U.f. ví antárikṣam (Whitney, 90b[2]) atirat (√tṛ). —ā́bhinat, √bhid, 692. — valám, cf. Indra's epithet, 5[17].

6–7. U.f. úd gā́s (361c) ājat (√aj). — āvíṣ-kṛṇván, 187, 1078.

8–9. dṛḷhā́ni dṛṅhitā́ni ca, ' (were) made stable and (were) established,' both from √dṛh. —parā-ṇúde: form of inf., 192a, 970a: use of inf., 982c. — ' Steady, not for thrusting away = so steadfast they may not be moved.' Cf. Ps. xciii.1 or 2 ; xcvi.10.

10–11. See under √mad 1. —See √rāj+vi and 902.

12–13. Pronounce tuám. —U.f. índra̱ ā́si : acct, 595d. — stotṝṇā́m (acct, 372), objective gen. w. bhadrakṛ́t, which has noun construction rather than verbal.

14–15. U.f. indrám íd keçínā (441). — vakṣatas, 'let them bring,' 893[2]. — See úpa2. —surā́dhasam might be joined with either índram or yajñám.

16–17. NAMUCI-MYTH. ' With foam of the waters, Namuci's head, O Indra, thou didst cause to fly asunder, when thou wast conquering all thy foes.' It appears to me likely that the natural phenomenon to which this refers is a water-spout ('Trombe') on an inland lake. This fear-inspiring thing may well be personified as a demon. The verb úd avartayas means ' didst cause to move out or fly asunder with a gyratory or centrifugal motion.' This accords well with the facts of the not infrequent phenomenon as seen by unscientific eyes. See Major Sherwill on Bengal waterspouts, JASB. 1860, xxix.366f, with good pictures, and Th. Reye, *Die Wirbelstürme*[2], p. 17f. The line MBh. v.10.37 = 328 seems to favor my view. The whole passage is a reminiscence of the Namuci-myth.

The head of the column is twisted and made to burst asunder and scatter itself (phénena, instr. of accompaniment, lit. ' with foam,' i.e.) in abundant foamy masses. Then, with the dispersion of the column, often

comes (Sherwill, 370 ; Reye, 32) a heavy rain. All this is set forth as gracious Indra's prowess. —U.f. ájayas spṛ́dhas, see 74[13]N.

Bergaigne's discussion, ii.346–7, may be compared and also RV. v.30.7,8 and vi.20.6.

—The form of the myth as it appears in the Brāhmaṇas originates in a misconception of the case-relation of phénena (see above), which they take as an instr. of means, i.e. as the weapon by means of which Indra slew Namuci. So Sāyaṇa : phenena vajrī-bhūtena ; see vocab., √sic3. Cf. notes to selection lxxii., p. 97.

18–19. ut-sisṛpsatas (√sṛp) and ā́-ruruk-ṣatas (√ruh), acc.pl.m. of ppl., 1027, 1029. —dyā́m, 361d. — dásyūnr, u.f. dásyūn, prop. dásyūñs, see 209 and b and 338[2]. — See √dhū+ava and 706. — Cf. the legend at Odyssey xi.305–20, and see Eggeling, SBE. xii.286.

20–21. viṣūcim (408), 'so that it was parted asunder *or* scattered,' as factitive predicate of ví-anáçayas (√1 naç). —See úttara 1. ' Becoming victorious (after *or* as result of) quaffing the Soma.'

NOTES TO PAGE 82.

SELECTION XLVII. RV. viii. 85. 7, 8, 9. Indra and the Maruts, and Vṛtra. — For the corresponding Brāhmaṇa legend, see selection lxvii., p. 94[4]. Cf. also Muir, v.93.

—All three stanzas are addressed to Indra ; and might be put in the mouth of the Maruts, were it not for havíṣā, st. 8[d]. If, on the other hand, they are put in the mouth of the worshippers, then úpa ā́ imas cannot serve as verb to marútas nor govern tvā́ of st. 8[a]. I therefore suspect that either pāda *b* or *d* of stanza 8 is a foreign intrusion. If it is the former, the original may have contained ánu yanti or the like.

1. See víṣ. —víçve devā́s, other than the Maruts ; for here, presumably, they are not included among the friends who desert Indra ; and the Brāhmaṇa says expressly that they do not desert. But at RV. viii.7.31 the contrary is affirmed ; cf. p. 364. —ajahus, √2hā (661, 657) : its object is tvā́.

2. Explanation under átha2. Similarly átha is used after an impv. implying a con-

dition (572²), at 06¹⁷, 97¹⁰. —jayási, 736.
—Half-line, cf. 88¹⁵.

3-4. Numerical construction, 486b. —
vāvṛdhānás (807²), 'growing strong, rejoicing in strength.' —úpa tvémaḥ (acct!) u.f.
úpa tvā á_imas (127, end). —kṛdhí, 839.
— 'Thy impetuosity = thee, the impetuous.'
—enā, 502².

— 'Thrice sixty Maruts, in their strength
rejoicing, (do follow?) thee, like hosts of
morning, reverend. Unto thee come we.
Grant thou us a blessing.' Etc.

5-6. áyudham and áníkam are best made
co-ordinate with vájram. —See ásura2.

SELECTION XLVIII. RV. viii.91. To
Agni. —Stanzas 7,8,9 and 13,14,15 form
strophes in the SV. The rest of the hymn
(16-22), after rejection of one stanza, forms
two strophes: 16,17,18 may be safely grouped
together; and of the remaining four, I have
followed Grassmann in rejecting st. 21, on
account of the contents and language. Moreover, the tense of idhe is proper to a final
stanza — cf. Delbrück, Tempuslehre, p. 106-7.
On the other hand, it must be admitted that
stanzas 20 and 21 occur in juxtaposition at
MS. ii.7.7, TS. iv.1.10¹, VS. xi.73-4, and elsewhere.

7-8. Four explanations of dhītí. 1. Grassmann, for díti, q.v.; instances of the confusion of dhi and di are adduced. 2. Ludwig, 'durch die künstlichen mittel des ghṛta,'
see 2dhītí. 3. Sāyaṇa takes it from √dhā,
'put,' and renders by nidhānáis, 'with the
deposits' of ghee. 4. Best taken as
'draughts,' √dhā, 'drink,' see 1dhītí and
reference, and cf. RV. x.115.1.

—tepānás, 794e, 807. —vakṣi, √vah, 624:
so yákṣi (√yaj); accented, 593² middle, cf.
76¹², 77¹⁰, 78¹¹, 80¹³, etc.

9-10. tám tvā: see examples under tá2.
Sāyaṇa renders tám by prasiddham, 'illum;'
similarly tás, at 83¹, he glosses by tādṛçyas.
—ajananta (a-class and mid.!), classic ajan-
ayan. —See mátṛ: cf. RV. iii.29.1-3.

11-12. Pronounce tuā. —ní ṣedire (185),
see √sad +ni2; subject, 'men.' Cf. 88¹⁷.

13-14. Pronounce ásti (595d) ághniā.
—Perhaps, 'There is no ax (with me) de-

siring (it), i.e. I have no ax by me, = own
none.' —See etādṛç.

—I have no cow from whose milk I might
make ghee for an oblation, nor an ax to
cut sticks for the sacrificial fire. So I offer
thee such as I have, i.e. gathered bits of
wood. — 'One should sacrifice, if only a
bit of wood,' says tradition: cf. the widow's
mites; and see ASL. p.204 and Bhagavad-
gītā, ix.26.

15-16. VS., kāni kāni cid; MS. and TS.,
yāni kāni ca; AV., yāni kāni cid; see
1 ka2d. —√dhā + ā2; ending, 548. —Pronounce yaviṣṭhia: the anomalous ending is
solely for the sake of the metre, since
yaviṣṭha makes just as good a catalectic
diiambus as yaviṣṭhya. 'Youngest,' for he
starts into life anew every day.

—In old times Agni would not devour fuel
that was not ax-hewn. The Rishi Prayoga,
who was too poor to own an ax and had to
pick up his wood, made it toothsome for
Agni with this stanza, yád agne yáni káni
ca. So TS. v.1.10¹.

—Note how the other texts make 20 and
21 into two anuṣṭubh stanzas by inserting
21ᶜ in the one and adding 20ᶜ to the other.

17-18. See vídh or indh. —See mánas 1.
—idhe, 'I have enkindled,' tense, see above.
Perfect used to state a thing to some one
who has just seen it transpire.

NOTES TO PAGE 83.

SELECTION XLIX. RV. x.9.1-3. To the
Waters. — Rubricated at 105²¹, funeral service. This hymn in the RV. has nine stanzas; but the first three form a strophe which
recurs very often in other texts: so TS.,
thrice; MS. and VS., twice; K., SV., AV.,
and TA.

—The Gṛhya-sūtras prescribe the use of
this strophe, with the pouring or sprinkling
of water, at the wedding-ceremony, ÇGS.
i.14, in the choosing of a house-site, AGS.
ii.8.12, in the consecration of a new dwelling,
ib. ii.9.8, and in certain funeral rites, ib. iv.6.
14 = 105²¹. Indeed, so frequent is their use
that they have a name and are called the
"three āpohiṣṭhíya stanzas" — cf. 1215a.
The modern Hindus use them daily in their

mārjana, see Monier-Williams, as cited at p. 366.

1-2. ṣṭhā́, u.f. sthā, 188a, 248c. —tā́s, see 82⁹ɴ. —√1 dhā2 and 669. —cā́kṣase, √cakṣ, 970c. —Lit. 'Bring us to vigor, to great gladness, to behold:' attraction, 982a.

3-4. See √bhaj, caus. — uçatī́s, fem. ppl., √vaç.

5-6. U.f. tásmāi, the master of the new dwelling. —gamāma, 848³. — janáyathā (248c), 'produce, i.e. bring:' for aught the accent shows, it may be co-ordinate with jínvatha (595) or also not (see 594a).

— 'For him may we satisfy you, to whose dwelling ye hasten, Waters, and bring us '— whatever that may mean. It seems to have pertinence only as said by officiating priests in performing the above-mentioned conse-cration.

Selection L. RV. x.14.1-2, and 7-12. Funeral-hymn.—Rubricated at 102ᴸ²¹, 103¹² —see p. 402. See Whitney's essay, On the Vedic doctrine of a future life, OLSt. i. 46-63 (= Bibliotheca Sacra, 1859, xvi.404f); also Zimmer, p. 408-22. On immortality as an Indo-European belief, see Kaegi, ɴ. 265 and literature there cited, and ɴ. 283a. On the funeral rites, see introduction to selection lxxv. and literature there cited. Translations of this hymn: Muir, v.292; GKR. p. 146; and Whitney, l.c., p. 58.

—Although maṇḍala x. on the whole is late, it yet contains antique passages; and among these the following seems to belong: so Roth. The hymn contains 16 stanzas, of which 13-16 are palpably later additions. Only 7-12 are actually prescribed by Āçva-lāyana for use in the funeral service; but 1 and 2, although not rubricated, are given for their intrinsic interest.

—The passage as it stands consists of an introductory summons to the assembled mourners (1-2); and of an address to the departed (7-8); then, after bidding the mourners disperse (stanza 9), the spokesman implores the favor of the kindly-disposed hounds of Yama, for the departed (11) and for the company (12).

—In stanza 10, on the other hand, these hounds are conceived as ill-disposed crea-tures standing guard to keep the departed out of bliss—see p. 370; and possibly the stanza which originally belonged with 9 has been displaced by the one in our text. Or is stanza 9 itself the intruder ? See Bezzen-berger's Beiträge, viii.202.

—The stanzas of RV. x.14 recur else-where, with more or less interesting variants. Those in the Reader correspond respectively with AV. xviii.1.49,50,54; 3.58; 1.55; 2.11, 12,13. Compare also MS. iv.14.16; ii.7.11; TA. vi.1.1; 4.2; 6.1; 3.1,2. For st. 9, see note thereto, 83¹⁵.

7-8. parā́_īyivā́ṅsam, √i, 803, 783b². — 'Along after (ánu) i.e. unto the mighty heights,' i.e. to the other world. —anu-paspaçānám, √1 paç, 807. —vāivasvatám, cf. 85¹⁵ɴ. So also in the Avesta, Yima is V's son. — 'Gatherer of the peoples;' pre-cisely so in the Avesta, Vd. ii.21, Yima makes a gathering (hañjamanem) of mortals. Cf. Ἀιδης ἀγησίλαος, Preller, Gr. Myth.³ i.660, Kaegi, ɴ. 276. —Note that Yama is a king, and not, like Varuṇa (line 12), a god.

—Yama is the first mortal (see yamá in vocab.); the first to reach the other world (AV. xviii.3.13); the leader of the endless train of them that follow him; and so the king of the blessed (see yamá-rājan). The comparison of Yama with the Avestan Yima is very interesting: see Roth, die Sage von Dschemschid, ZDMG. iv.417-431; and SBE. iv.p.lxxv., and p.10-21.

—We read at AV. xviii.4.7,

tīrthā́is taranti praváto mahír íti,

By passes pass they to the mighty heights, 'tis said.

This is most interesting as a reminiscence of the same traditional material of which RV. x.14.1 is another outgrowth.

9-10. 'Yamus nobis perfugium primus repperit:' gātúm, q.v., pregnantly, like τόπον at John xiv.2. —eṣā́ gávyūtis, i.e. the gātú, just mentioned. — ápa-bhartavā́ u: the pada-pāṭha reads -tavāí u (133); form of inf., 972³; use of inf., 982c. — For the thought, see an Avestan parallel, Kaegi, ɴ. 270. — yátrā, 248a. —parā́_īyús, 783b².

—jajñānás, √jan2, 807, '(their) children,' sc. párā yanti.

11–12. prá_ihi, 617, see vocab. —The AV. modernizes the forms a little, reading rájānāu, mádantāu. —paçyāsi, subjunctive (760.2), w. future mg, as in Homer. —Note the appropriate connection of this stanza with st. 2 and observe the identical pādas.

13–14. The derivation and mg of iṣṭā-pūrtá are discussed most carefully by Windisch, *Festgruss an Böhtlingk*, 1888, p. 115f. — hitváya, √2hā, 993b. — púnar ástam á_ihi, 'Go back home,' as if the soul had come from heaven. Illustrative material in Kaegi, N. 275. Cf. *zu Gott heimkehren* = 'die.' —Pāda *d* is metrically defective: te tanúā, 'with thy (new) body,' is suggested, Kaegi, N. 278, which see; te tanúā suvárcasā is suggested by Sāyaṇa's comment. Cf. the Christian conceptions at Philippians iii.21, I. Cor. xv.40f.

15–16. U.f. ápa_ita, ví_ita, ví ca sar-pata_átas. asmāi (accent, 74⁹N.) etám · ·. áhobhis adbhis · · ví-aktam (√añj). —vīta, acct, 128 end; so vīva, 77⁶N. —akran, 831. —Second asmāi, accentless, cf. 74⁹N.

—Pāda *c.* '(A place of rest) adorned with days, with waters, with nights:' i.e. where the delights of earth are found again, the change of day and night, cooling waters, etc. Note the especial mention of waters in the enumeration of the joys of heaven at RV. ix.113.7f, and in the description of the 'Assembly-hall' of Yama Vāivasvata, MBh. ii.8.7 = 317. And observe how very frequent are the allusions to the waters in the mentions of Paradise in the Koran, e.g. xlvii. 10–20; lxxvi.5; xiii.35.

—This pāda at best is bad. It is avoided by the noteworthy, but not very helpful, variants of the Yajurveda. VS. xii.45 reads

ápeta vīta ví ca sarpatáto
yé átra sthá purāṇā yé ca nútanāḥ.
ádād yamó avasánam pṛthivyā
ákrann imám pitáro lokám asmāi,

and substantially so read MS., TS., TB. The scholiast to VS. takes this as an address to 'Yama's men.' It *is* a little forced to refer it to the mourners.

17–18. In *this* stanza, these dogs, the off-spring of Saramā, are ill-disposed (dur-vidátra) — see introduction. — Pronounce çuānāu. — 'Four-eyed:' later this is taken to mean 'with two eyes and two round spots above the eyes.' Note the Parsi custom of having such a dog (cf. Vd. viii.16) view the corpse before exposure — Monier-Williams, *Mod. India*, 173–6, ed. 1878.

—Respecting Saramā, see Kaegi, N. 149. Respecting the dogs, see ib., N. 274, 274a, and Muir, v.294. Homer mentions the 'dog of Hades,' Od. xi.623f, Il. viii.368. Not till later is he called 'many-headed' and Κέρβερος. With Κέρβερος is identified çabála — see Benfey, *Göttingische Nachrichten*, 1877, p. 8f = *Vedica*, i.149f. In Avestan belief (Vd. xiii.9), dogs guard the entrance of the other world. These beliefs are compared, SBE. iv.p.lxxxvii.

19. In this stanza and the following, the dogs are kindly creatures.

NOTES TO PAGE 84.

1. Pronounce tábhiām. —Verbs, 668.

2–3. U.f. asutṛpāu: admits several ex-planations — see vocab., and Bergaigne, iii. 72. —These messengers go about to con-duct to the other world those who have received the summons of Yama. —sūryāya, attraction, explained at 982a. —U.f. púnar dātām (839) ásum adyá_ihá: 'may the two give back again —,' for the mourners have been in the shadow of death.

SELECTION LI. RV. x. 16. Funeral-hymn, used at the ceremony of cremation. — Rubri-cated are only stanzas 1–9 and 14 — see p. 402. The rubricated stanzas are translated by Max Müller, ZDMG. ix.p.viiif, and the whole hymn by Zimmer, p. 402. Most of the stanzas are addressed to Agni; but 3, 6, and 7, to the dead man. The hymn has two parts, clearly sundered by the metre.

—In the first, Agni is to burn the corpse, not rudely, but gently, just enough to "make it done." To this end, a sacrificial goat (st. 4) is provided, and (st. 7) the corpse is covered with a caul, in order that Agni may spend his fury on these things and spare the

corpse from too severe a burning. The
original purpose of this custom may have
been different. The Greeks had the custom
— see Il. xxiii.165f, Od. xxiv.65f.

Moreover, Agni is to carry up the departed
to the Fathers or Manes, who have their seat
in the 'fore-heaven' (AV. xviii.2.48, Whitney, OLSt. i.59). Perhaps st. 8–10 did not
belong originally to the first part.

—The second part consists of heterogeneous material, vagrant stanzas, having some
connection, verbal or logical, real or apparent,
with the words or ideas of the first.

—Every stanza of the hymn, save st. 11,
appears in the AV., and some elsewhere also,
and with interesting variants.

4–5. enam: the minds of all present are
so exclusively upon the departed, that the
first reference to him may be made by
an accentless and gestureless word without
unclearness. Similarly asya. —ví dahas,
abhí çocas, 743, 579. The AV. reads çúçucas
(869). —cikşipas, 869, 579. —krņávas,
700. —U.f. átha ím enam. —prá hiņutāt:
ņ, 192c; form, 570, 704, cf. 915; mg, 571.

6–7. Pāda d = atha devān vaçaṁ neşya-
ti, 'he shall bring the gods into his control'
(cf. RV. x.84.3), i.e. 'win their favor.'

8–9. Note the combination of trişţubh
and jagatī pādas (11, 12, 12, 11). Pronounce
diâm. —See dhárman. —apás, óşadhişu,
cf. x.58.7. —See hitá2. —çarirâis, Sāyaņa,
'çarira_avayavāis' ('members').

—For this stanza there is abundant and
interesting illustrative material. See Muir,
v.298,319; Kaegi, N. 275,275a. Man is a
microcosm. Each element in him comes
from some element in nature with which it
has most affinity and thereto it returns (cf.
Eurip. Suppl. 532f). These affinities are
pointed out with much detail in ÇB. xiv.
6.2¹³.

yatra_asya puruşasya mŗtasya_ agniṁ
vág apyeti, vátam prāņaç, cakşur ādityam,
manaç candraṁ, diçaḥ çrotram, prthivíṁ
çariram, ākāçam ātmā_, oşadhir lomāni,
vanaspatin keçā, apsu lohitaṁ ca retaç ca
nidhiyate, — kva_ayaṁ tadā puruşo bhavati ? 'In case the dead man's · · · soul goes
to the ether, the hair of his body to the

plants, the hair of his head to the trees, and
his blood and seminal fluid in the waters are
put, what then becomes of this spirit ? '

Cf. the formula recited at the slaughter of
the sacrificial victim, AB. ii.6.13,

> sūryaṁ cakşur gamayatāt,
> vátam prāņam anvavasŗjatāt,
> antarikşam asum,
> diçaḥ çrotram,
> pṛthivíṁ çariram.

Dissolution into the five elements (see bhūta)
is later the stereotyped phrase for death (see
pañcatva). Cf. the four elements ἐξ ὧν
συμπέτηγγε τὸ σῶμα, γῆς πυρὸς ὕδατός τε καὶ
ἀέρος, Plato, Timaeus, p. 82.

—The affinity of the eye and the sun is
universally palpable: cf., for example, Plato,
Repub. 508, ἡλιοειδέστατόν γε οἶμαι [τὸ ὄμμα]
τῶν περὶ τὰς αἰσθήσεις ὀργάνων. Not less so
is that of breath and wind. Bones and earth,
Timaeus, 73E; blood and plants, ib.80E. Cf.
Darmesteter, SBE. iv.187, who cites Iliad
vii.99 and Empedocles, 378–82 (ed. Müllach).

10–11. 'The goat [laid limb by limb on
the corpse on the fire] (is thy) portion.
Burn it with burning; that let thy heat
burn; that, thy flame.' — But deal gently
with the dead man. —Note the emphatic
position of the last two tám's. —The goat
is the animal most fit for sacrifice—see the
legend, AB. ii.8. Later, ajá is taken as a-já,
the 'unborn' part: so Sāyaņa; cf. Ludwig,
iii.p.435–6; Pañcatantra, book iii., fable 2;
MBh. xii.338.3 (= 12820) fol. 255ᵇ; ISt. i.428.

—Agni has 'dreadful forms' (ghorás
tanúas) as well as 'kindly' ones. —See
loká 2b and sukŗt. The Hindus regard u
as a particle; but it may be part of a word
uloká, which combination appears in old
texts, and even at the head of a pāda, where
u (as enclitic) could not stand.

12–13. See √hu+á. 'Who, offered to
thee, goes freely.' The corpse may have
been conceived — now as yielding easily to
the devourer, and now as struggling against
it. Otherwise Zimmer, p. 403N.

— 'Putting on life (as a garment), let him
seek after offspring.' Where is to be found
expressed the wish for children in the new
life ? It is repulsive. But that carnal inter-

course was by no means excluded from the (doubtless later) ideas of heaven would appear from the material gathered by Muir, v.307–9, esp. from AV. iv.34.2 and xiv.2.32. Add AB. i.22.14, and cf. Zimmer, 413.

—After all, may not çéṣas here mean simply 'those whom we leave behind us,' viz. at the grave (see 63¹⁷.¹⁸), in order to continue the journey of life without them, i.e. 'those who have gone before?' These the dead man is now to rejoin.

—Pāda d: cf. 83¹⁴ and ɴ.

14–15. kṛṣṇáḥ çakunás is one of ill-omen. —utá vā: function of utá like that of átha in átha vā, see athaó. —U.f. agnís tád (80¹⁵ɴ.) viçva_át. — See brāhmaṇá: no necessary allusion to caste here. —If unclean creatures have done any harm to the corpse, Agni is to remove from it the traces of such imperfections, i.e. 'make it whole.' The 'soma' seems to stand for some purifying sacrifice at which it was used in conjunction with the fire.

16–17. Rubricated at 102²⁰. Cutting out the caul of the anustáraṇi, the celebrant covers the head and face of the dead man with it, for the purpose mentioned in the introduction. —góbhis, see gó2: the caul, suet, and fat are meant. —√vyā+pari: see the orig. mg of √vyā. —U.f. sám prá_ūrṇuṣva (712): acct, 1083–84. —See néd and references. —√hṛṣ, intens., 10₁2. —vi-dhakṣyán, √dah, fut. ppl. —Subjunctive form, 1068, cf. 736.

—Lit., then, 'Wind a protection (várma) from the fire (abl.) around thyself by means of the caul etc., i.e. envelop thyself with the caul as a protection from the fire [addressed to the dead man, although the celebrant actually does the enveloping]; cover thyself completely with suet and fat: in order that the bold one (Agni), very impatient, may not with his grip firmly clasp thee around, to devour thee.'

18–19. vi jihvaras, √hvṛ, 858¹, in form and use like cikṣipas, line 4. —Pāda c: metre faulty; read eṣá u or eṣá íd? —See √mad, caus. 2. —This stanza seems to have pertinence only as an accompaniment of the

ritual (103¹). The hymn proper may have ended with st. 7.

20. For ṇ, 192c. —yamárājñas, cf. 83⁸ɴ.

NOTES TO PAGE 85.

1. U.f. ihá_evá_ayám ítaras, jātávedās, 'Right here is this other one, Jātavedas,' i.e. agní havya-váhana, as distinguished from agní kravya-váhana. The cremation has now proceeded far enough; so the corpse-consuming Agni is dismissed to the Manes, and the oblation-bearing Agni summoned.

2–3. This continues the thought of st. 9. In the presence of the Manes (who don't mind the heat), the dismissed Agni may burn as fiercely as he likes and drive his flames in or to the highest place. — 'Him I remove or dismiss (√1 hṛ3) to the pitṛyajñá:' this Ludwig, v.p.423, takes to be a sacrifice to the gods conducted by the Manes; otherwise vocab. —invāt: form, 736; quasi-root inv.

4–5. The diaskeuasts have put this stanza here on account of the mention of kravya-váhana and the Manes. —yákṣat, 893², √yaj. —U.f. prá íd u ‥. — 'Both to the gods and to the Manes' — so Sāyaṇa, Mahī-dhara (to VS. xix.65), and vocabulary under á2. But Ludwig (see transl.) says 'to the gods also, from the Manes.'

6–7. See √vaç. —tvā, the sacred fire. —ní dhīmahi (cf. 74¹⁴) and sám idhīmahi, 837. — 'Gladly would we set thee down, gladly make burn brightly' (sám gives to idh this intensive force). The optative does not imply that they do not suit the action to the word. — 'Glad, bring thou hither the glad Fathers, to the oblation (982a) to eat' (√ad, 970b).

8–9. 'Him cool thou off (see √1 vā+nis), i.e. let him whom thou wast consuming cool off again.' And let the burning-place be so cool and moist that even water-plants (pādas c d) may grow there.

10–11. Rubricated at 104¹¹. —The four words in line 10 may be either voc's s.f. or loc's s.m.n.: accent, indecisive; the i before k (1222d) favors the first view. —sám gamas (active!), 848². —The stanza seems to be meaningless rubbish.

SELECTION LII. RV. x.17.1–2 and 3–6.
Funeral-hymn. — Under x.17 are included
divers elements : **A**. the fragmentary legend
of the Children of the Sun (1–2); **B**. the
funeral-hymn proper (3–6); 'C. a prayer to
Sarasvatī (7–9); **D**. sundry fragments.

— **A**. STANZAS 1–2. This famous fragment
begins a new anuvāka and has nothing to
do with the funeral-hymns. It smacks of
antiquity; and it has become the nucleus of
later legends. Of these, the oldest is that
reported by Yāska, in the Nirukta, xii.10;
and the next is that of Çāunaka, in the
Bṛhaddevatā, vi.33 to vii.2. Ç's version is
quoted in full by Sāyaṇa, in his comment to
RV. vii.72.2, in order to prove that the Rishi
Vasiṣṭha was a relative (first cousin) of the
Açvins. Both legends are given in the
original and in translation by Muir, v.227–9;
also by Kuhn, KZ. i.440–43; L. Myrian-
theus, *Die Açvins oder arischen Dioskuren*,
Munich, 1876, p. 1–4; and in substance by
Max Müller, *Lectures*, 2d series, no. xi., p.
501 Am. ed. of 1865 = 528 Eng. ed. of 1873.
Late form of legend, VP., b'k iii., chap. 2.

— The verbal exegesis of the two stanzas
is beset with uncertainties : see Roth, in the
essay cited above (83⁸ɴ.), ZDMG. iv.425;
Grassmann, Transl., ii.p.466; Bergaigne, ii.
318; and the very suggestive discussions by
Ludwig, iii.332–5 and v.391–2.

— As for their interpretation from the
mythological point of view, see Roth, l.c.
p.425 (reported by Müller, l.c., p.503 = 530);
ISt. xiv.392f; Kuhn, l.c., p.443f; Müller, l.c.,
p.528 = 556, and 502 = 529; Grassmann, l.c.;
Bergaigne, ii.506–7; and esp. Ludwig, iii.
332–5 and v.391–2.

12. U.f. íti_idám. — Note that pari-
uhyámānā is from the same root as vah-
atúm. — Tvaṣṭar, a god, gives the wedding;
yet it takes place on the earth !

13. yamásya mātá : proleptically; prop.,
she who afterwards became Y's mother.

14. kṛtvī, 993b. — adadus, 668.

15. U.f. utá_açvínāu abharat yád tád
ásīt | ájahāt (2hā 1) u. — dvā́ mith-, 'two
pairs' (Yama, Yamī; Açvins): Yāska, 'the
two (Y. and Y.) that formed a pair' ('she
forsook').

"Tvaṣṭar's making a wedding for his daughter "—
At this news all the world here comes together.
Yama's mother, during her wedding,
The wife of mighty Vivasvant, vanished.
They hid away the immortal from mortals.
Making a like one, they gave her to Vivasvant,
And she bare the two Açvins when that happened,
And left two pairs behind her— Saraṇyū.

— "A braw story, but unco short." The
actual text is tantalizingly fragmentary. We
can hardly hope to recover the legend with
any satisfactory completeness. Yāska gives
it thus :

Tvaṣṭar's daughter, Saraṇyū, bare twins
(Yama and Yamī) to Vivasvant. She foisted
upon him another female of the same appearance (sávarṇām), and, taking on the form
of a mare, fled forth. Vivasvant took on
the form of a horse, followed her, and
coupled with her. From that were born the
two Açvins or ' Horse-men.' Of the sávarṇā
was born Manu.

That is — Vivasvant, the Sun, and Saraṇyū,
were the parents of Yama and Yamī (83⁸,
92¹⁴), the first human pair. But there was
a coexisting belief in Manu (see manu in
vocab., and cf. SBE. xxv.p.lvii) as the father
of mankind. Are not RV. x.17.1–2 the fragment of a legend which attempted to recon-
cile the two beliefs by fabling a sávarṇā
who should give birth to Manu, so that,
according to either myth, the human race
are the Children of the Sun ?

— Yāska *tells* more than does the text; yet
we are not sure that he (to say nothing of
Çāunaka) *knew* anything more than is contained in the two stanzas. We are therefore
not obliged to interpret the stanzas so as to
fadge with Yāska's story.

A possible rendering of line 14 is (see
Ludwig) : 'They disclosed (ἀπεκάλυψαν) the
immortal to mortals (*dat.*). Endowing her
with visible form, they gave her to V.'
Lit. 'making her (to be) sá-varṇa,' i.e. (see
2 sa and 1304c) 'making her (to be) having
an accompanying varṇa *or* making her (to
be) endowed with external appearance.'

B. STANZAS 3–6. The funeral-hymn
proper, addressed esp. to Pūṣan ψυχοπομπός,
and rubricated at 103¹³. Respecting Pūṣan,
see Kaegi, p. 55(77), and notes 209–12. As
sun-god and heavenly herdsman, he knoweth

well the ways through the heaven and the
spaces, and so is a safe guide to conduct
the souls of the dead to the regions of the
blessed. Translation by Muir, v.173.

16-17. U.f. tvā (= the dead man) itás
cyāvayatu prá (goes with cyāv-, 1081²)
vidván. —pári dadat, 650⁸.

18-19. pári pāsati, √2pā, 893². —See
prápatha. —U.f. yátra ásate (628). —
See sukṛt.

20. U.f. imás áçās. — See √1 vid+anu.
—sárvās, see 77¹¹ɴ. —neṣat, √nī, 893⁸

NOTES TO PAGE 86.

2-3. ajaniṣṭa, 902, √jan2; as we say, 'he
was "born and bred" there, i.e. is at home.'
— 'On the distant-way of ways ⋅ ⋅ ⋅ : on the
distant-way of heaven; etc.' No matter how
long or where the journey is, P. is at home
on it.

— 'Unto the two most wonted places —
both to and from, he goes, knowing the way.'
The construction is faulty — and yet plain
enough: abhí sadhásthe harmonizes with á
carati; but párā carati requires sadhásthe-
bhyas (abl.).

SELECTION LIII. RV. x.18. Funeral-
hymn. — Rubricated, all except the last stanza, in the later ritual — see p. 402. The
simple ceremonies originally used are inferrible from the hymn. Very different are
those of the later ritual. For illustrations
of these differences, see Roth, ZDMG. viii.
471f. The hymn is given, with the concord-
ants and variants of the AV., TB., TA., and
VS., and the scholia of Sāyaṇa and Mahi-
dhara to the concordant passages, by Windisch, in his Zwölf Hymnen (see p. xviii,
no. 10 of my Brief List).

—The hymn has been translated by Roth,
ZDMG. viii.467f (reprinted by Zimmer, 404f);
Max Müller, ZDMG. ix., appendix; H. H.
Wilson, JRAS. xvi.201f = Works, ii.270f;
Whitney, Bibliotheca Sacra, xvi.409 = OLSt.
i.46f; GKR. p. 150; Ludwig, no. 943; Grass-
mann, no. 844; Rājendralāla Mitra, Indo-
Aryans, ii.122f; and most of it by Kaegi,
76(105)f. Roth, Whitney, GKR., and Kaegi
give "the action" of the hymn.

—The hymn is remarkable for its intrinsic
interest and beauty. And it has acquired
great notoriety in connection with the discussions of Suttee (= satī) or Hindu widow-
burning. Properly, satī (see sant 4) means
a 'virtuous wife.' Improperly, but more
commonly, it has come to be used of the
rite of self-immolation which she practised.
See the admirable article Suttee in Col. H.
Yule's Anglo-Indian Glossary, with some forty
pertinent extracts.

—That Suttee is an ancient custom appears
from many references to it in classical authors. See Cicero, Tusc. disp. v.27.78; Pro-
pertius, iv.12.15; Plutarch, Moralia, p.499;
Nicholas of Damascus, fr. 143 = frag. hist.
graec., ed. Müller, iii.463; Strabo, xv.30, p.
699; 62, p. 714; and esp. the story in Diodorus Siculus, xix.33-34, according to which
the rite is authenticated for 316 B.C. These
passages are given in full by J. Grimm, in
his masterly essay, Ueber das Verbrennen der
Leichen, Abh. der Berliner Akad., 1849, p. 261f
= Kleinere Schriften, ii.298f. And Peter von
Bohlen, in Das alte Indien (1830), i.293-302,
cites a great deal of interesting pertinent
literature.

—The custom was abolished by the British
during the administration of Lord William
Bentinck, in 1829. The story of the aboli-
tion is well told by H. H. Wilson, in his continuation of James Mill's History of British
India, vol.iii.(= ix.),185-192. For descriptions, statistics, etc., see Parliamentary Doc's,
1821.xviii.; 1823.xvii.; 1824.xxiii.; 1825.xxiv.;
and esp. the Calcutta Review, 1867, vol. xlvi.
p.221-261. Other descriptions in Quarterly
Review, lxxxix.257f; Shib Chunder Bose, The
Hindoos as they are, chap. xxi.; Das Ausland,
for 1857, p. 1057f.

—From Müller's Essay on Comparative
Mythology, Chips, ii.34f, or Selected Essays,
vol. i. (ed. of 1881), p. 333f, it would appear
that the seventh stanza of our hymn had
played a great rôle in Hindu history. At
any rate, this idea is current, and seems
traceable to the Essay. Here it is stated
that the stanza was purposely falsified by an
unscrupulous priesthood, and that a garbled
version of it, reading agnéḥ for ágre, was

directly responsible for the sacrifice of thousands of innocent lives. That the author is in error on these points is argued with great detail by Fitzedward Hall, JRAS. ns.iii.183–192. He shows that the misreading can be traced to Raghunandana, ca. 1500 A.D., and no further; and that Suttee was deemed to be amply justified by warrants other than those of the Vedic saṃhitā, which was by no means the ultimate appeal for the mediæval Hindu.

— In the literary discussions of Suttee, on the other hand, the stanza has indeed played a rôle. There is probably no other stanza in the Veda about which so much has been written. It was first cited, in mangled form and as sanction for Suttee, by Colebrooke, in 1794, *On the duties of a faithful Hindu widow*, *Asiatick Researches*, 1795, iv.209–219 = *Essays*, i.133–140. It was discussed by Wilson, in 1854, in his paper *On the supposed Vaidik authority* for Suttee, JRAS. xvi.201–14 = *Works*, ii.270–92. In answer to this, Rājā Rādhākānta Deva, in 1858, endeavored to adduce good Vedic authority for the rite, JRAS. xvii.209–17 (reprinted in Wilson's *Works*, ii.293–305). The most exhaustive treatment of the various readings of the stanza is that by Hall, l.c. Finally must be mentioned the paper read by Rājendralāla Mitra in 1870, *On the funeral ceremonies* etc., JASB. xxxix.1.241–264 (reprinted in his Introduction to the TA., p. 33–58, and with additions in his *Indo-Aryans*, ii.114–155); see esp. p. 257f (= 50f = 147f).

— The Rigveda gives no warrant for the custom. Çāunaka, in the Bṛhad-devatā, furnishes important positive evidence against it (see *Chips*, ii.37); and likewise Manu, v. 156–8(= 64¹⁰f, see N.). Cf. Kaegi, N.51.

— The hymn was originally used at a burial which was not preceded by cremation. The situation and action are as follows. The corpse lies on a raised place; and by it is the widow.

STANZAS 1-2. The spokesman adjures Death to remove, and to harm not the living (1); and pronounces for them absolution from impurity (2).

STANZAS 3-4. The conductor of the cere-mony dwells with joy on the fact that, thanks to the efficacy of their prayers, they have not joined the company of the dead (3). Now, for the better safety of the survivors, and wishing them long life, he sets a stone near the grave as a symbolic boundary of the domain of Death, as a barrier, so that he may not pass to the space beyond or domain of the living.

STANZAS 5-6. The wish and prayer for long life is here continued.

STANZAS 7-8. The women are now summoned to make their appearance together, and, provided with ointments, 'to go up to the place,' i.e. of course, where the dead man and the widow are (7).

Here we must infer that they adorn the widow (as a sign that she is to re-enter the world of life), and that the dead man's brother (devṛ́, 'levir') then takes her hand in token of the levirate marriage.

The priest then bids her leave her lifeless spouse, and makes solemn declaration of the new relation into which she has entered (8).

STANZA 9. The bow is now taken from the dead man's hand, in order that the power and glory of which the weapon was the symbol may remain with the survivors; and a closing benediction is said for them and for the departed.

STANZAS 10-13. "And now, with gentle action and tender words, the body is committed to the earth."

4–5. ví+anu-parā. —te suás, cf. 55¹⁵N. —ítara, w. abl., like anya, 3⁴. —devayānát, 'going *or* leading to the gods,' sc. pathás, abl. — U.f. mā · · rírisas (80¹⁰N.), mā utá. Note how utá follows the repeated portion of the second clause.

6-7. See pad43. —Discussions of √yup, Ludwig, v.514, Whitney, AJP. iii.402, Roth, *Festgruss an Böhtlingk*, 1888, p. 98–99. — áíta, 620. —See √1 dhā7. —√pyā+ā.

6ᵃ. Either 'Clogging Death's foot [by a bundle of brush (kūdí) or a billet of wood, tied to the corpse's foot], as ye came;' or else, 'Effacing Death's foot-print' [by the same means]. I confess, I incline to the former view. But, whichever way we take padáṁ yop-, the simple symbolism amounts to the same thing. The clog is attached to the foot of the corpse, which represents Death, in order that Death may not get back or find his way back so easily to harm the living. See AV. v.19.12 (explained by Roth, l.c.) in connection with xii.2.29. Roth adduces the device of Hermes, in the Homeric Hymn to Hermes, 80-84.

8-9. U.f. **vi mṛtáis** (283²) **á̱̇avavṛtran** (√vṛt+vy-á): Whitney takes the form as a 3d pl. (550⁴) impf. mid. of the redup. class, present-stem **vavṛt** irreg. like **cakṛ** (expect **vivṛt**). —**ábhūt,** 'hath been,' 928. —Pāda c refers — not to "mirth in funeral," but rather — to a fresh start on a new stretch of life, in which, leaving the dead behind, they look for much joy.

10-11. Note radical connection of **pari-dhím** and **dadhāmi.** —U.f. **má̱̇eṣām nú gāt áparas** ('an other'). — 'A hundred autumns, numerous, may they live.' Prayers like this are frequent. The love of long life is very clear in the Vedic texts as contrasted with those of the later period. We must not think of 'hundred' as just '99+1.' —See √1 dhā+antar, and note carefully the development of the mg. 'May they hide Death by a mountain, i.e. put a mountain (symbolized by the rock or **paridhí**) betwixt themselves and Death.' See **párvata** 2 and 4.

—There is much evidence that the age of a hundred years was deemed entirely normal. This appears from RV. i.89.9. Again, to a question about a funeral lustration, Pāraskara (PGS. iii.10.14,15) prescribes the use of a special answer "in case the departed was not yet a hundred years old." Weber, ISt. xvii.500. SBE. xxix. 356. The 'tenth decade of life' has a name, **daçamí** (see BR.). In the Jātaka (Fausböll, vol.ii.p.16), the Bodhisat says to his father, when the latter sneezes,

> O Gagga, live a hundred years,
> And twenty others added on. · ·
> Live thou a hundred autumns yet.

See also Bhartṛhari's fine stanza, **āyur varṣaçatam nṛṇām** etc., Vāirāgya-çataka, 50 Bohlen = 107 Telang. — Among Semitic peoples, the sacred age was 120 years; while the pious Egyptian prayed to Osiris that he might live to be 110. — Krall.

—Very interesting are the classical stories of Hindu longevity. Sometimes, according to Onesikritos, they capped a hundred with thirty more — Strabo, xv.34,p.701. The Uttara Kurus are said, MBh. vi.7.11 = 264, to live 1000 or 10,000 years, and to this fable is probably due the report of Megasthenes περὶ τῶν χιλιετῶν Ὑπερβορέων in Strabo, xv.57,p.711 — see McCrindle's Megasthenes, p.79ɴ., or Lassen, IA. i².613.

—Note that years are counted, now by winters, now by autumns, and now by rainy seasons (see **hima** and **varṣa** in vocab.), and that these differences correspond in general with differences of habitat of the people. ISt. xvii.232, Zimmer, 371-2.

12-13. U.f. **yáthā áhāni, yáthā ṛtávas** (see 127²): pronounce **yáthāháni · ·** | **yáthartáva.** —'As a following one deserts not the former one, i.e. as each season lacks not a successor.' —See **evá** 1 : contrast 18¹⁸,¹⁹. — See √klp : 'so dispose their lives, i.e. make them move on in the same unbroken way.'

14-15. **yáti ṣṭhá** (188a), 'quot estis.' —**karati,** true root-aor. subjunctive, 836¹. —**jīváse,** 970c, 982. —'Attain ye to (long-life, **áyus,** i.e.) fulness of days, old age your portion making, one after another, in turn (**yátamānās**) all of you' (**yáti ṣṭhá**). Otherwise OLSt. i.53.

16-17. STANZA 7. See introduction, and Kaegi, ɴ.328. —**nárīs,** classical **náryas,** 365. 2. —See √viç+sam. —Pāda d : 'Let the wives ascend to the (raised) place (on which the corpse lies), to begin with' (**ágre**). — After which, they are to do their errand, see introduction to stanzas 7-8. It does not mean, 'Let them go (away from the bier) up to a sacrificial altar first, i.e. before others;' for this we should expect **prathamás** rather than **ágre**.

18-19. U.f. **úd íṛṣva** (√īr) **nāri · ·.** — **gatásum etám úpa çeṣe,** lit. 'With this one whose life is gone liest thou.' —U.f. **á̱̇ihi.** —'To take the hand' is the essential preliminary of wedding — see 89⁵ɴ. — U.f. **didhiṣós táva idám.** See 2**idám.** —**pátyus** (343b) **janitvám** means 'condition of being **jáni** of a **páti**;' and the whole line 19 (see **bhū**+**abhi-sam**) means simply 'Thou hast

entered into the state of being wife of a
spouse (who was) a hand-grasper (and is)
thy suitor now.'

—Hillebrandt, at ZDMG. xl.708f, shows
plainly that this stanza, RV. x.18.8, belonged
originally to the ritual of the human sacrifice. Weber describes the ceremony at
ZDMG. xviii.269f = *Indische Streifen*, i.65f.
The king's first queen was obliged to lie
with the dead victim. The situation is evident from the connection in which RV. x.
18.8 occurs at AV. xviii.3.1–4. She is bidden
to rise with our stanza, úd íryva nāri — see
Çāṅkhāyana Çrāuta-sūtra, xvi.13.13.

In this light, the logical connection of
pādas *a b* with pādas *c d* becomes clear. She
is to forsake the corpse and "come hither"
to the king.

Rise up, woman, to the world of the living.
Fled is the soul of him with whom thou liest.   Come hither.

Quitting the embrace of hateful Death, the
queen rises and approaches him who had
already once taken her hand in wedlock and
now stands waiting for her as a suitor once
more. Upon thus resuming her proper relation of wife again, she is greeted with the
words:

To him who grasped thy hand, thy suitor now,
As wife to husband art thou become related.

—As appears from AGS. iv.2.18 = 102⁷,
this stanza was at an early date appropriated
for the funeral-service, where — as an accompaniment of the levirate marriage — it fits
very well (didhiṣú means also 'a second
husband'). Regarding leviration, see Kaegi,
N.51. Its existence in Vedic times is proved
by RV. x.40.2. — Compare also Deuteronomy
xxv.5–10.

20. U.f. dhánus hástāt á-dádānas (668)
mṛtásya | asmé (dat., 492²) kṣatrāya etc.
'(I, the spokesman,) taking from the dead
man's hand the bow, for us for power · · i.e.
that ours may be the power, glory, might'—.
Here the construction breaks off short, but
without a jot of unclearness. —Note that
the bow is left in his hand till the very last.
This was their noblest and chiefest weapon:
cf. RV. vi.75; the stories of Arjuna's bow,
Gāṇḍīva; and Strabo, xv.66,p.717.

NOTES TO PAGE **87**.

1. U.f. átra_evá tvám ('thou,' the departed — sc. jayes); ihá · ·. See átra2. The
adverbs are contrasted as in εὐδαιμονέστεροί
εἰσιν οἱ ἐκεῖ τῶν ἐνθάδε, Plato, *Ap.* 41c. —
U.f. víçvās, cf. 74¹²ᴺ. —abhímātis, as adj.,
'plotting against (us)' — cf. √man+abhi2.

2–3. Addressed to the departed. —The
earth, 'a maid soft as wool to a pious man
(dákṣiṇāvate) — she shall protect thee from
destruction's lap.' —Pāda *c* has 12 syllables.

4–5. Vçvañc+ud: note mg of çvañc and
its concinnity with the metaphor of yuvatí.
—mā́ ní bā́dhathās (743): compare the
formulae

sit tibi terra levis!
ne gravis esse velis!
tu levis ossa tegas!

etc., cited by J. Grimm, l.c., p. 193 = 214.
—asmāi and enam, cf. 84⁴ᴺ. —U.f. bhūme.
—√1 vṛ+abhi, 712.

6–7. mít-as, nom. pl.: cf. 486b. —
gṛhā́sas: cf. 80¹ and N., and Kaegi, N.329.
—Pronounce santu átra. —The like beautiful conception of committal to a place of
security pervades the Eng. word *bury*, the
Old High Ger. *bi-fĕlan*, and Goth. *ga-filhan*.

8–9. Pronounce tuát pári: see pári. —
U.f. ni-dádhat. —See u and 1122a². —
riṣam, 848². —té 'trā, u.f. te | átra: te is
accentless (135²) and so belongs of course to
pāda *c*.

—Pāda *b*: 'And laying down this clod
may I not get harm.' This seems to refer
to the *glebam in os inicere* (a custom which
still accompanies the "earth to earth, ashes
to ashes, dust to dust" of Christian burial),
and to betray the natural "uncanny feeling
at having to do with a corpse." Cf. Kaegi,
N.330.

—Pāda *c*. The 'pillar' or 'prop' may be
a rude beam or tree, laid over the corpse so
as to keep the earth from caving in on it:
cf. AV. xviii.2.25,

"Let not the tree press hard on thee,
Nor yet the earth, the great, divine."

Sometimes the tree was hollowed out as a
coffin (AV. xviii.3.70): cf. the Germanic
Todtenbaum of sacred oak — Weinhold, *Altnordisches Leben*, 497, 491.

10–11. U.f. áhani | ißvãs · · á dadhus. 'On a fitting day me, as the plume of an arrow, have they set.' —The stanza seems to express the poet's satisfaction at having made a good hymn at the right time and place and with as good skill as a skilful horseman has. Whitney renders,

> They've set me in a fitting day,
> As one the plume sets on the shaft.
> I've caught and used the fitting word,
> As one a steed tames with the rein.

—The stanza is fully discussed, JAOS. xi. p.cxci = PAOS. May, 1884. It is interesting as illustrating the varieties of cumulative evidence that may be brought to bear on the criticism of the Veda. Thus: 1. The stanza is at the end of the hymn and out of connection. 2. It is in a different kind of metre. 3. The metre is bad of its kind. 4. The form ißvãs is bad Vedic — for ißos; and 5. pratícim is a late form for pratícim. 6. The stanza is ignored by Āçvalãyana; and 7. by Sãyaṇa.

SELECTION LIV. RV. x.33.4–9. The aged priest to the young prince. — The hymn has nine stanzas. The first three have nothing to do with the rest. The rest (4–9) forms two tṛca's. This passage has more than common freshness, and also directness of connection with the life of Vedic time. The situation would seem to be somewhat as follows.

—The old priest stood well with the gods, so that the efficacy of his intercession with them was of unusually good repute. Accordingly, the foes of king Kuruçravaṇa had once tried to win the Rishi over to their side and away from his master, Kuruçravaṇa; but in vain. He had remained faithful to the royal family in whose service he long had been.

Now at last king Kuruçravaṇa has passed away, leaving Upamaçravas as his son and heir. And in presence of the young prince, the priest tells with pride and pleasure of the old times, and speaks with regret of the loss of his departed patron.

—Ludwig, iii.182, has called attention to the genealogical series of the RV. These cover oftenest, of course, only three genera-

tions, since memory, unaided by records, does not easily go further back. But for preserving that amount of genealogical tradition there was frequent need (Weber, ISt. x.78–88, esp. 82): thus, at the offering to the Manes, the priest has to address by name the father, grandfather, and great-grandfather of the sacrificer; see ÇB. ii.4.2¹⁶ or SBE. xii.365 or OLSt. i.60: similarly at the pravara; cf. ISt. ix.322–3 or x.78–9 or Müller, ASL. 386.

In the present instance, however, we have a series of five at least. Trasadasyu is a prince of the Pūru tribe, and of the *line* of Purukutsa (he is not necessarily the latter's son — RV. vii.19.3), and is often mentioned for his generosity and for the special favors shown him by the gods. The series is

Purukutsa
⋮
Trasadasyu
⋮
Mitrãtithi
|
Kuruçravaṇa
|
Upamaçravas.

Compare Bergaigne, JA. 8.vi.373–4, and Kaegi, 80(110), and N.340. The Pūrus were one of several tribes that were ultimately fused together in the famous Kurus — Oldenberg, *Buddha*, 403 = 411.

12–13. ãvṛṇi: augment, 585²; impf. mid. (725), 1st sing. 'I, the Rishi, preferred king K.' (to his enemies); i.e. I chose to keep him as my master, in order to go out to battle with him, etc. A choice was inevitable. It would appear that priests who sacrificed for many or for a village were despised (Yãjñavalkya, e.g. i.161,163, Manu, iv. 205). The purohitas marched out with their kings to battle (AGS. iii.12), as did the μάντεις, e.g. to the battle of Plataea (Hdt. ix.33,37), and for similar motives — μεμισθωμένοι οὐκ ὀλίγου — κατὰ τὸ κέρδος.

14–15. tisrás, 482c. —stãvãi (626, 617), 'I will praise,' sc. tám, meaning Kuruçravaṇa. —sah-, sc. yajñé. —K's horses (triga) still come to fetch the priest in state to the sacrifice.

16–17. yásya: K. is still meant. — úcúṣe, 803, √vac. — 'Of whom, (namely) of U's father, the words (were) highly pleas-

ing to (me) the intercessor, as a lovely home.'
[! The text is awkward and unclear.] Time
was, when king K., to offset the overtures
of his enemies, had to make very persuasive
offers to the priest. No false delicacy restrains the latter now from alluding to these
with satisfaction in the presence of his future
patron. —The mention of K. as 'father of
U.' is peculiar. Somewhat analogous is the
Semitic fashion: cf. *Abd-allah*, 'Gott-schalk.'

18–19. ádhi goes w. ihi, ví, q.v. —U.f.
nápāt · · pitús te (80¹⁵ɴ.). —pitús limits
vanditá as a possessive (not objective) genitive. The objective gen. would be devânām.
—asmi: the present does not necessarily
imply that K. is still alive.

20. yád íçīya, cf. 80¹¹ɴ. "Had it de-
pended on me, my maghavan K. should have
lived. But—." — But for utá, the vā
would have to follow mártiānaām — cf.
athaô.

NOTES TO PAGE **88.**

1. U.f. íd. —See maghávan 1.

2–3. See vratá 1. —Passage explained
under caná2. — 'Accordingly, with my
yoke-fellow (K.) I have parted' —√vr̥t+vi.

SELECTION LV. RV. x.40.10. "Wedding-
stanza." — Rubricated at 100¹² and ÇGS. i.
15.2. Recurs with variants at AV. xiv.1.46.
The ritual prescribes that it be recited, if,
on the way from the wedding to the groom's
home, the bride chance to weep. For such
an occasion, its relevance lies solely in the
fact that it contains the word 'weep.'

4–5. See √mā or mī+vi: form made
after the model of nayante. —ánu dīdhyus
(AV. dídhyus), 786². —U.f. yé idám sameriré (AV. correctly, sam-íriré), 'who have
come together here:' íriré, perf. of primary
conj. (not caus.— vocab. wrong) of vīr.
—√svaj+pari, 970a.

—The import of the very obscure (if not
hopelessly corrupt) stanza is possibly this.
The first half tells what happens at the
burial of a wife. While the rest lament
aloud, the men show their sorrow for the
bereaved husband by pensive silence. The
second half contains reflections on the joys

of wedlock, whose appositeness is clear, if
we assume that they are uttered in the tone
of mournful regret. [But cf. ISt. v.200.]

— 'They weep for the living one (the
widower). They cry aloud at the service.
The men thought over the long reach (of
his happy wedded life now past).

'A lovely thing for the fathers who have
come together here, — a joy to husbands, —
are wives to embrace.'

SELECTION LVI. RV. x.52. The gods
install Agni as oblation-bearer. — The *motif*
is akin to that of the much superior hymn
x.51, given by Böhtlingk (no. 30), and also
by GKR. (no. 43), who add a translation of
the Brāhmaṇa form of the legend of Agni's
hiding (selection lxvi.). The hymn is in
dramatic form.

STANZAS 1–2. Agni asks the gods for
directions concerning his service at the sacrifice (1); and, with the help of the Açvins
and with everything in readiness, he pro-
poses to resume his work (2).

STANZA 3. Some gods raise doubts as to
his fitness (pādas a b). Others answer that
he is ready whenever needed (pāda c).

The poet accordingly announces Agni's
installation, in narrative form (pāda d).

STANZA 4. Agni accepts the office (pādas
a b); and the gods bid him set about his
duties (c d).

STANZA 5. Agni promises due performance.

STANZA 6. The poet adds a kind of *envoi*
in narrative form.

6–7. víçve devās: see devá 2b; note
accentual unity, 314⁴ (JAOS. xi.61). —çās-
tána: acct, 594a; form, 618. —manávāi:
√man5; form, 713, 700. —yád seems superfluous. —See √sad+ni.

— 'Teach me (the way) in which, chosen
here as hótr̥, I am to be minded (= what I
am to have in view), when (*sic*) having taken
my place. Declare to me (the way) in which
your portion, the path by which your oblation, I am to bear unto you.'

8–9. U.f. áhar-ahar, 1260. — 'Every day,
O Açvins, the office of adhvaryú (ádhv-) is
yours.' —U.f. samít, nom. s. of samídh.
—bhavati, 'is on hand.' —U.f. sā̆ áhutis.

10–11. Explained under yá3. As Yama
is king of the blessed Fathers (83⁶ɴ.), Yama's
hotṛ must be competent to satisfy them at
the monthly çrāddha (p. 402). — 'Has he
(see kám2) grasped (√2ūh+api), i.e. does he
know, (that) which the gods take (see √añj
+sam4, and Böhtlingk's smaller dictionary,
s.v.), i.e. does he know what they like?' —
Is he equal to both sets of duties?

—In pāda c the objections are met. Agni
is born anew every day for the agnihotra
(ISt. x.328), at which the gods take their
food; and anew every month, when the
Manes take theirs.

12–13. Pronounce máām. — See √1 dhā5.
—√mluc+apa: 'hidden' in the waters — see
93¹⁶. — Classic, bahúni kṛcchráṇi: see
√car3. —kalp- (1043.2), 'let him—.' —
Pāda d (= RV. x.124.1b): The victims of
the animal sacrifice were five, 'man, horse,
ōx, sheep, goat' (see AV. xi.2.9 or ISt. xiii.
292); and its later surrogate is called 'five-
fold' as containing the 'essence' of all these
victims (ÇB. i.2.3⁵ — see Eggeling's note).
But it may be ill-judged to try to attach
special significance to these numbers. 'Three'
and 'seven' are of course sacred numbers.

14–15. á yakṣi: see √yaj+á; form, s-aor.
mid. 1st sing., 882. At first the gods were
mortal (96³f). —See yáthā6. —Pronounce
bāhuór. —á dheyām, 837². —U.f. átha_
imás: átha · · jayāti, 'then (if I do), he
shall win,' cf. 82² and ɴ.

16–17. See 486 for construction. '3339
gods.' — √ukṣ, 585. —ástṛṇan, 725. —
U.f. asmái | át íd hótāram.

Notes to Page 89.

Selection LVII. RV. x.53.6 and 8.
Burial and wedding-stanzas.— Rubricated as
burial stanzas at 105⁹ and 105¹⁸. The eighth
is also used (100¹¹) as a wedding-stanza, in
case the bride has to embark and disembark
on her wedding-journey. See also AB. iii.
38. Interesting variants of the stanza and
reminiscences of its traditional material at
AV. xii.2.26,27,28ª.

1. tanván (705), see √tan4. The metaphor is frequent. —rájasas appears to be
abl. and to refer backwards as well as for-

wards, i.e. to tanván as well as to ánv-ihi.
—Note that rakṣa and Eng. keep coincide in
having the mgs 'guard' and (as here) 'not
quit.'

2. vayata, see √2vā. —See jógū and
352. —mánu, here as the typical originator
of prayer, praise, and sacrifice — see vocab.,
and cf. ÇB. i.5.1⁷, manur ha vā agre
yajñena_īje; tad anukṛtya_imāḥ prajā
yajante. —Note again that janáyā and
Eng. produce coincide in having the mgs
'generate' and (as here — cf. i.31.17, á vahā
dáiviaṃ jánam, and 82⁸) 'fetch along or
bring to view.'

—Stanza 6 is really a prayer to Agni and
his flames to help in the work of devotion.
As the immortal messenger (see Muir, v.201)
between men and gods, he is to go from
earth, traverse the atmosphere (see rájas in
vocab.), and pursue his way to the gods
through the súar. Here he is to keep to
the paths (cf. TS. v.7.7) which are made by
the prayers and oblations that go up to the
gods,— the devayānās or 'god-paths,' as
the AB. at iii.38 calls them, on which the
gods descend to man. Pāda c, continuing
the metaphor of a, is addressed to Agni's
flames; and d, to Agni.

Stretching devotion's weft from gloom to light go on.
Keep to the radiant pathways which our prayers have made.
Without a blemish weave ye now the singers' work.
Be Manu thou. Bring to our sight the heavenly race.

3–4. 'It (sc. nadī) flows stony,' the logical predicate being áçmanvatī — cf. ῥέουσι
μεγάλοι, Hdt. ii.25; cum flueret lutulentus,
Horace, Sat. i.4.11. Others, not so well,
make áçm- a proper name (die Stein-ach),
or refer it to the stream from the press-
stones, i.e. the Soma. —Note that √tṛ has
special reference to water: thus, ava-tṛ, 'go
down into the water' (49¹⁹); ut-tṛ, 'come
up out of it;' pra-tṛ, 'advance in crossing
it.' —átra, 'thére,' with a sneer: cf. amuyá,
70¹⁵ɴ. —yó ásann (636⁸) áçevās, 'qui in-
felices sint:' not so well the vocab. —út-
tarema_abhí, see √tṛ+abhy-ud.

—Stanza 8. The situation is perhaps
this. A band of men, hotly pursued by their
enemies, are in the middle of a stream, which
they hope soon to have put betwixt themselves and the foe. They call out to each

other encouragingly the words of the stanza.
The famous hymn RV. iii.33 involves a situation which is similar (Muir, i².338), and, indeed, familiar elsewhere (Hebrews xi.29; Hdt. viii.138).

> The stream is stony. Hold ye well together.
> Your footing keep. On! make your crossing, comrades!
> There let us leave them in a mood unhappy,
> While we go out and on to happy conquests.

SELECTION LVIII. RV. x.85.36, 24-26, 32-33, 27, 43-47. The wedding-hymn.—The stanzas are here given in the order in which they are rubricated at 98¹⁹†—see p. 398. Their uses in the ritual are discussed by Haas in his treatise on the ancient wedding customs of India, ISt. v.267-412.

—The hymn is called the sūryā-sūkta or "The marriage of Soma and Sūryā," and has received at the hands of Dr. J. Ehni, ZDMG. xxxiii.166-176, a mythological interpretation, briefly summarized in AJP. i.211. The hymn has 47 stanzas, with an appendix given by Aufrecht, *Rigveda²* ii.682, and comprises somewhat heterogeneous matter (ISt. v.269). Most of the hymn occurs in AV. xiv.1 and 2, with many variants. Partial concordance :

RV. x.85.	AV. xiv.	RV. x.85.	AV. xiv.
36 =	1.50	27 =	1.21
24 =	1.19,58	43 =	2.40
25 =	1.18	44 =	2.17
26 =	1.20	45	
32 =	2.11	46 =	1.44
33 =	2.28	47	

—Besides the translations of Ludwig and of Grassmann, there is one of hymn and appendix by Weber, ISt. v.177-195. This is followed by one of AV. xiv. (pages 195-217) and of the other wedding-stanzas of the AV. (pages 218-266) — see also Ludwig, iii. p. 469-76. Most of the Reader-stanzas are translated, with explanations, by Zimmer, 311-313. See also Kaegi, 74(102), and notes 317-325.

STANZA 36. Said to the bride by the groom in the very act of taking her hand in token of wedlock.

STANZAS 24-26 and 32-33. Said just before the bride's departure for her new home. Stanzas 24 and 32 are said by a third person; 25, 26, and 33 *may* be put in the mouth of the groom. St. 33 may, as the Sūtra says,

be spoken on the way, when people come out of their dwellings to gaze.

STANZA 27. Pādas *a, b*, and *c* are said to the bride, and *d* to the couple, on their arrival.

STANZAS 43-47. The groom first prays to Prajāpati on behalf of himself and his bride (43 *a b*), and addresses the latter with good wishes and solemn benedictions (43 *c d*, 44); prays to Indra that the bride may be fruitful (45) ; bids her hold her own with her new relatives (46) ; and, finally, beseeches the gods, on behalf of himself and his wife, that they two may dwell in unity (47).

5–6. gṛbhṇāmi ·· hástam : this, the dextrarum iunctio, is the essential feature of the simplest wedding-ritual, see Haas, 277, 316 ; cf. hasta-grābhá (86¹⁹) and pāṇi-grāha (64¹⁰); the AV. modernizes, reading, gṛhṇāmi. With the concordant stanza of the AV. are grouped several others (48, 49, 51) of like import. — 'With me as husband' (343b). —yáthā_ásas, 'ut sis.' — U.f. máhyam tvā_adus (829). —gárh-, 'for (our) being heads of a household, i.e. that we may establish a family.'

7–8. ábadhnāt, 730. —See ṛtá2. —See loká 2b and cf. sukṛtá with sukṛt. This phrase is equiv. in *form* to the older one (84¹¹), but refers here rather to the 'world of the pious' on earth.

> I loose thee from Varuṇa's bond,
> With which kindly Savitar bound thee.—
> At the altar, in the company of the good,
> I put thee unharmed with thy husband.

—The first half-stanza is an allegorical, and the second a literal address to the bride. In the allegory, the bond of Varuṇa is night (Hillebrandt). Savitar is the 'Impeller,' not only of the rising, but also of the setting sun (RV. i.35.3ª). He brings rest (ii.38.3,4) by sending night, whose gentle bond he lays (Muir, v.235-7) upon his daughter, Sūryā, 'The Sun,' till she is released for her bridal with Soma, 'The Moon' (masc.), a union which is the prototype (cf. Haas, 328) of human marriages.

From the more literal point of view, the bond of Varuṇa, as the upholder of the established order of things, is (not night—

still less sickness — but) the tie by which a
maid is bound to her father till a man come
to loose and take her. — See the discussions
of Haas, 319–20, 277–8, and of Hillebrandt,
Varuṇa, p. 59.

9–10. prá · · muñcámi : acctl 596, 507 ;
similar cases at 74¹ and 92¹⁶ ; supply either
imā́m, or (since a change of address to Indra
is quite natural) tvám. — U.f. amútas (171⁴)
karam (831²) | yáthā_iyám · · ásati, 'ut
haec sit.' — mídhvas, 462a.

— Sāyaṇa comments thus : itaḥ pitṛ-kulāt
pra muñcāmi tvām ; na_amuto bhartṛ-
gṛhāt pramuñcāmi. amuto bhartṛ-gṛhe
subaddhāṁ karam.

11–12. Said to the bride as she gets into
the wagon. Pūṣan is the best of guides for
earthly travellers also — cf. p. 381–2. — See
gṛhá, *pl.* — U.f. yáthā_ásas. — See √vad + ā.

13–14. Said just as the wedding-train
starts. — √2vid, 848. — AV. modernizes,
reading sugéna. — áti_itām, 617. — Pronounce ápa drāntu (617).

15–16. imā́m sam-á_ita, pácyata ' come
near to this one together, i.e. crowd around
her, (and) take a look.' Cf. note to 100¹⁵.
— dat-tváya, 993, from the quasi-root dad
(955c). — U.f. átha_ástam ví párā_itana
(618).

17–18. priyám (priya 2b), subject of
sám-ṛdhyatām. — enā (502², here = anénā)
etc. : ' with this (man) as husband unite
thyself.' — ádhā jívrī etc., said to both.
'Old,' i.e. until ye become so.

19. This stanza'(43) has interesting variants in AV., and at MS. ii.13 end. — Pronounce sám-anaktu (689).

NOTES TO PAGE 90.

1. patilokám, 'husband's home :' not till
later, 'husband's heaven.'

2–3. edhi, 636. — Pronounce vīrasúur
· · sionā. — AV. reads devṛ́-kāmā.

— Note that 44a, b, and c are of 11 syllables,
while 44d (= 43d) is of 12. Although this
discrepancy is not very rare, it yet helps to
bring out the character of d as a *formula
sollennis* :

— ' Be a blessing to our bipeds, a blessing
to our quadrupeds.' It is most interesting

to note that a similarly comprehensive formula occurs elsewhere : in the Avesta, Yasna
xix.8(18–19), Vd. xv.19(59), see KZ. xxv.
195 ; and on the Iguvine Tables, VI b 10–11,
see Bréal's ed., pages XL, 125.

4–5. U.f. dáça_asyām putrā́n á dhehi
(668). There is no end of evidence (e.g.
Zimmer, p. 319) to show that the desire for
male children was very strong, and that the
birth of daughters was unwelcome. A wife
who bears only daughters may be put away
— Manu ix.81. — kṛdhi, 839. — ' Put ten
sons in her. Make her husband an eleventh.'
The logical incongruity is paralleled by *Paradise Lost*, iv. 323–4, and by the Greek classics.

6–7. Pronounce çvaçruám : specimen of
a very rare form of transition to the devī-
declension, see 358. — Pronounce nánāndri :
AV. reads nánāndus. — See ídhi.

— This throws an interesting light on
ancient family-life. — Note that of the Ger.
correspondents to çváçura and çvaçrū́, viz.
Schwäher and *Schwieger*, the former has died
out and given place to the term *Schwieger-
vater*. The mothers-in-law have thus made
their mark in the language — see Kluge.

8–9. U.f. sám (sc. añjantu) ápas hṛda-
yāni (note neglect of dual) nāu (gen.). A
real anointing of both took place. — In line
9, a dadhātu goes with each sám, and nāu is
acc. — Dhātṛ́ is esp. the deity who ' puts'
fruit in the womb — RV. x.184.1. — See
u l end.

SELECTION LIX. RV. x.137. Exorcism
for a sick person. — Tradition assigns each
stanza to one of the Seven Rishis as author.
Stanza 4 is spoken by the Wind, personified ;
the rest, by the exorcist. Respecting the
general character of the hymn, see Kaegi,
85–86(115). See also the beautiful essay of
Kuhn, KZ. xiii.49–74 and 113–157, who compares similar Vedic and Germanic spells.
Nearchus says (Strabo, xv.45, p. 706) that the
Hindus trust to wandering enchanters (ἐπῳδοί)
for cures, and that this is about all their
ιατρική amounts to. The hymn is translated
by Aufrecht, ZDMG. xxiv.203. It corresponds in general to AV. iv.13 ; but see note
to stanza 6.

10–11. Note the accentless and accented vocatives. —See vní+ud and 248c. —U.f. utá́ ā́gas cakrúṣam (= cakṛváṅsam, 462c). The disease is a punishment for sin, cf. p. 374.

12–13. See 1 idám end. —Zimmer queries, p. 45, whether the two Monsoons are here meant. —á́ síndhoṣ, see á́ 4. — 'Away let the other blow what infirmity (there is,' 512b).

15. Pronounce tuám. —See vi.

16–17. á́ · · agamam and á́ abhárṣam (882): note use of aorists (928) — 'I have just come and brought,' says the Wind. — átho, 1122a², 138c. —√2su+pará.

18–19. Pāda c, bad metre. —ayám, the sick man.

20. U.f. íd vāí, see vāí.

NOTES TO PAGE 91.

1. 'The waters are healers (lit. healing) of everything.' On use of sárva, see 771¹¹N. The AV.-concordants of this stanza are at AV. vi.91.3 and iii.7.5 and read víçvasya.

—STANZA 6. In place of this stanza the AV. has interpolated RV. x.60.12, evidently because it has to do with the laying on of hands — see the following.

2–3. That the laying on of hands has especial virtue is a wide-spread belief — cf. Acts viii.17f, and above, p. 369ᵃ top. The Greeks attributed to each of the Δάκτυλοι 'Ιδαῖοι a name and a particular healing power. The finger next to the little finger (see note to 104¹¹) is called, *digitus medicus* by Pliny, and *medicinalis*, in the laws of Henry I. of England; and it has a special and beneficent magic power. —W. Grimm, *Kleinere Schriften*, iii.440f, 442.

— 'With hands, ten-fingered (the tongue is leader of the charm), healing, — thee with these thee we touch.' The parenthesis may mean that the tongue brings out a charm to precede the laying on of hands. Text probably corrupt; AV. variants interesting.

SELECTION LX. RV. x.154. To Yama.— Funeral-hymn. — Rubricated at 103¹⁸, see p. 402. Recurs at AV. xviii.2.14–18, with interesting variants. Translated, Muir, v.310. To judge from the ritual, the subject of ápi gacchatāt in each stanza is the spirit of the departed. He is to go and join the Fathers — saints, warriors, poet-sages, — a description of whom makes up most of the hymn. In stanzas 4 and 5, gacchatāt (see 570) is a 3d sing., 'O Yama, let him go;' in the rest, it may be a 2d or a 3d. — Ludwig, ii.394, v.311, interprets otherwise, taking mádhu as subject of ápi gacchatāt (√gam+api).

4–5. 'Some · · others' (éke), i.e. of the Fathers, "who revel in bliss with Yama" (83¹⁸). —See vās+upa. — 'For whom mádhu flows :' Yama and the Fathers are the eager recipients of sweet drink-offerings — cf. AV. xviii.2.1–3, and RV. x.15 passim. —táñç cid = 'thóse :' táñç cid evá = 'júst those.'

6–7. Pronounce súar. — 'Who made tápas their glory.' —Heaven can be won only by the pious and (stanza 3) the brave: cf. MBh. iii.43.4 = 1759, and 42.35 = 1748f.

10–11. See cid2. —U.f. pū́rve ṛtasā́paṣ. —Cf. 85⁴.

12–13. 'Who keep (= confine themselves to) the sun, i.e. who hover about the sun' The righteous after death are transformed into rays of the sun or into stars (Muir, v. 319f; see 100⁸N.). Thus ÇB. i.9.3¹⁰, ya eṣa tapati, tasya ye raçmayas, te sukṛtas. So MBh. iii.42.38 = 1751f :

> ete sukṛtinaḥ, Pārtha,
> yān dṛṣṭavān asi, Vibho,
> tārārū́pāṇi bhūtale.

SELECTION LXI. RV. x.155.5. Burial-stanza. — Rubricated, 105²¹. The preceding four stanzas are a *deprecatio* addressed to Arāyī, a vile and murderous witch. This stanza, the last, dwells upon the safety of the godly.

14–15. pári · · aneṣata and pári · · a-hṛṣata, 882; akrata, 834a. Note the use of the aorists, 928 — where all is translated. —á́ dadharṣati, perf. subj., 810b.

SELECTION LXII. MS. ii.13.23. Hiraṇya-garbha. — The god Ka or Who (see notes to selection lxviii.). — The RV. version (x.121) of this famous hymn has been translated by Max Müller, ASL. 569, and *Chips*, i.29; by Ludwig, no. 948; and by Muir, with comments, iv².15–18.

—STRUCTURE of the hymn. The seven stanzas here given (or perhaps only 2–6) constitute the original stock of the hymn. To this is added, in the MS.-version, an eighth stanza, quite impertinent to the rest; and in the RV.-version, three stanzas (8, 9, 10), whose character is determinable by various and interesting criteria.

Pāda *d* of each stanza is a refrain, ' Whom as god shall we worship with oblation ? i.e. Who is the god that we are to worship with oblation ? ' The later Vedic texts understand it, ' We will worship the god Who or Ka,' making of the interrogative pronoun a deity whom they identify with Prajāpati (selection lxviii.). The other pādas of stanzas 2–6 are relative clauses with yás, yásya, yéna, yásmin. These may refer

A. To devāya: ' Who (interrog.) is the god, — who (relative) became king, etc. etc., — that we are to worship ? ' Ludwig: ' Ka, the god, — who is become king, etc. etc., — we would wait upon with havis.'— Better, perhaps,

B. To hiraṇyagarbhás, although stanza 1 (and 7 as well) looks as if it might have been an afterthought. This leaves the connection of the refrain with the rest of each stanza very loose; but this is perhaps just what it ought to be.

—The hymn corresponds to RV. x.121. The comparative study of the differing versions of the same traditional material, as it appears in different Vedic texts, is interesting and instructive; and there is no better opportunity for it than this (see Preface, p. v, n.2).

The hymn occurs also at TS. iv.1.8; in the VS., with the stanzas scattered, at xiii.4, xxiii.3, xxv.13, xxv.12, xxxii.6,7, xxvii.25; and at AV. iv.2. The TS. version follows that of the RV. most nearly. Disregarding the order, the same is true of the VS. The AV. version looks like an unsuccessful attempt at writing down a half-remembered piece.

—ACCENT-MARKS, etc. The vertical stroke designates the acute accent; the horizontal hook, the circumflex. Details in L. von Schroeder's ed., book i., preface, p. XXIX.

Phonetic peculiarities, ibidem, XXVIII. Final m before sibilants, y, r, and v, is marked by the 'dot in the crescent,' e.g. praçíṣam, line 4. See also Preface to this Reader, p. v, note 7.

16. Cf. 57ᵃɴ.

NOTES TO PAGE 92.

1. dyám · · imám, see dív3.

2–3. pra_aṇatás (192b), gen. s., pres. ppl. —íçe: form, 613, cf. 70¹⁸ɴ.; acct, 628. — asyá, acct l, 74⁹ɴ. —dvipádas etc., see 90⁸ɴ. —RV.-reading better in this stanza.

4–5. ' On whose command all wait, on whose (command) the gods (wait)—.' — chāyá etc.: cf. Bhagavad Gītā, ix.19.

6–7. mahitvá, as instr. sing., 280. Müller's rendering — ' Whose greatness (as acc. n. pl.) the mountains and sea (neuter, as at vi.72.3) with the Rasā proclaim'— would require pra_āhús. —devís, as adj. (see devá 1), 'heavenly = of heaven,' not 'divine.'

—Pāda *c*: díç, q.v., is 'a point of the sky : ' of these there are usually four; sometimes are mentioned 5, 6, 7, 8, and 10 (explained by BR. s.v. díç). When five are mentioned, we may understand them as N., E., S., W., and the zenith : cf. AB. vī.32, pañca vā imā díçaç : catasras tiraçcya, ekā_ūrdhvā. Occurring *with* díças, the word pradíças may mean 'intermediate points,' and, with the zenith, count as five. But considering the (faulty) concordant of RV., TS., and VS.,

yásya imáḥ pradíço yásya bāhú,

further, RV. ix.86.29ᵇ, AV. i.30.4ᶜ, and esp. iii.4.2ᵇ,

tuám imáḥ pradíçaḥ páñca devíḥ,

I am inclined to deem the pāda before us a jingle of incoherent reminiscences.

Whose (are) all these mountains, by reason of (his) greatness;
Whose (possession) they call the ocean, with the Rasā;
The points, whose are the five fore-points of heaven; · · ·.

8–9. dṛḍhá, spondee, 224a. —U.f. súar, see 178 and 173a, and 74¹²ɴ. —The adjectives ugrá and dṛḍhá may be attributives, and stabhitá or stabhitás supplied as predicate for the substantives of line 8. — Pāda *c* = RV. ii.12.2ᶜ. — vi-mamé, √1 mā. Respecting the tripartite world, see under rájas, and Kaegi, 34(49) and notes 117–8. — antárikṣam: ÇB. i.2.1¹⁶, antarikṣeṇa hi_ime dyāvā-pṛthivī viṣṭabdhe; cf., at Od. i.54, the κίονας

μακρὰς, αἳ γαῖάν τε καὶ οὐρανὸν ἀμφὶς ἔχουσι.

10–11. Pronounce -pṛthvi. — See ádhi and √tan+vi. — U.f. súras éti: in the MS., final -as and -e if accentless, become -ā before an accented initial vowel. So 93¹².

12–13. U.f. yád mahatis víçvam áyan (620). See víçva 1c. — The RV., TS. [with nír for sám], and VS. read

táto devánām sám avartata_ásur ékaḥ.

The athetesis of the hypermetric ékaḥ, made by Bollensen, *Orient und Occident*, ii.485 (1864), and again by Grassmann, is here beautifully confirmed by the MS.

SELECTION LXIII. MS. i.5.12. Legend of Yama and Yami.— The creation of night. — Respecting Yama and Yami, see notes to 85¹²f.

— 'The prose of the Brāhmaṇas is not difficult. In reading it, the chief thing is some familiarity with the style, i.e. ability to divide up the discourse aright into the little clauses and choppy sentences with which it proceeds. As a help to this it is important to observe that the particle *átha* marks the beginning of a new clause, and that the postpositive *vái* marks the foregoing word as the first of its clause. Analogous is the use of *náma* to distinguish a proper name from an identical appellative. Cf. Pliny, *Epp.* vi.31, evocatus in consilium ad centum cellas (hoc loco nomen) ' '.

As my colleague, Professor A. P. Peabody, has observed in his translations of Cicero's *Offices* and *Tusculans*, there are certain connectives and illatives which are employed as mere catchwords for the eye. In manuscripts (Greek, Latin, Sanskrit) written with letters of one size, with no separation of words, and with very few stops, these particles serve the purpose effected now-a-days by capitals, by division or spacing, and by punctuation. In spoken language it is often wrong to render them otherwise than by inflection or by stress of voice.

14. U.f. vái. — See √brū+apa.

14–15. U.f. tám yád ápṛchan (207), sá abravīt: "adyá amṛta" íti. té abruvan: "ná vái iyám etc." — Difference between imperf. amriyata and aor. amṛta (834a) illustrated at 928⁵. — Accent of té, Whitney 84d, 135.

15–16. Lit. 'Not (if things keep on) in this way (itthám) does she forget him.'

16. Note the fine distinction. The gods use the solemn old Vedic form rátrim; the narrator, the later and more colloquial

rátrim. Similar distinction at ÇB. xi.5.4⁴: cf. 98²⁰ɴ., 103¹⁴ɴ. Not uncommon is the assumption that the gods have words or a dialect peculiar to themselves. Thus ná with the gods means the same as iva, AB. ii.2.14,15. Cf. Iliad i.403, ii.814, xiv.291, xx.74, Od. x.305; and A. F. Pott's *Antikaulen*, p. 71.

— sṛjāvahāi, faulty reading for -mahāi? — U.f. áhar vává tárhi ásīt, ná rátris· verb-acct, cf. 89⁹ɴ.

— 'Yama died. The gods sought to console Yami for the loss of Yama.— When they asked her, she said, To-day hath he died. They said, In this way she will never forget him. Night let us create. Only day in those times existed — not night. The gods created night. Then came into being the morrow. Then she forgat him. Therefore they say, 'Tis days and nights make men forget sorrow.'

SELECTION LXIV. MS. i.10.13. Legend of the winged mountains.— The myth is often alluded to by the later poets: see Stenzler's note to Kumāra-sambhava, i.20, and Bollensen's to Vikramorvaçī, str. 44. BR. observe that it is often difficult to distinguish between the mgs 'mountain' and 'cloud' which belong to párvata. In letting loose the heavenly waters, Indra splits open the 'mountains' as well as the 'clouds.' The Maruts house on the 'heights' or in the 'clouds,' etc.

19. Explained under yá3.

NOTES TO PAGE 93.

1. U.f. parā-pátam (995) ásata, yátra-yatra (1260 — see yátra) ák-. — iyám, see 1 idám, middle: so imám, line 2.

2. téṣām = párvatānām. — achinat, 692. — tāis = párvatāis, used evidently in the manner of paper-weights. — adṛ́nhat, √dṛh. The like achievement at RV. ii.12.2.

3. Explained under yá3.

4. U.f. yónis hi eṣām (accentless, 74⁹ɴ.) eṣás, 'For this is the'r place-of-origin.'

SELECTION LXV. MS. ii.1.12. The potency of the sacrifice.— A passage much resembling this occurs at TS. ii.4.13 = Muir, 1².21. Respecting the myths of Indra's birth and Aditi's motherhood, see Hillebrandt, *Aditi*, p. 43; Perry, JAOS. xi.127f, 148f; and *Literatur-Blatt für Orient. Philol.*, ii.4.

5. 'The Āindrābārhaspatyan oblation he should offer (nír-vapet), who, as a sovereign, shouldn't exactly succeed in his attacks.' This is a typical Brāhmaṇa passage. It invents a legend showing the efficacy of some ritual observance in former times, to prove the usefulness of repeating the same rites in analogous circumstances. —Peculiar interest attaches to this occurrence of the √stigh — see Schroeder's ed. of MS., Introduction, p. XIV; also ZDMG. xxxiii.194f, where the substance of the passage is given.

6. U.f. odanám apacat. —úñçiṣṭam, see this: final t (= d) before ç becomes ñ in MS. —āçnāt, √2aç.

6-7. U.f. tám vái índram antár evá·· sántam·· ápa‿āumbhat (√ubh; augment, 585): 'Indra, being (yet) an embryo, withín (her), she bound with an iron bond.' — ápa‿ubdhas, 160.

8. ayājayat, see √yaj, caus.

9-10. tásya = índrasya. —vyápadyata = of course, ví-apadyata: cf. Whitney, 84a. — U.f. abhi-pary-ā‿avartata, 1080, 1083.

10. U.f. yás··, tám eténa yájayet··, 'One should teach him to sacrifice with this Āindrābārhaspatyan (oblation), who etc.'

11. eṣás, same as yó and tám, line 10.

12-13. U.f. nir-upyáte, impers. 'it is offered:' combination, 921N.; form, √vap, 769; accent!, 596. kriyate, √1 kṛ 12, 'it is sacrificed.' — 'Offering is made to B., sacrifice is made to I.: (then) on áll sides (the god) releases him' (enam). 'Him,' i.e. the sin-bound king of lines 10-11, who is also the subject of abhi-pary-ā-vartate.

SELECTION LXVI. TS. ii.6.6. Legend of Agni the oblation-bearer, and of the fish.— This is the Brāhmaṇa form of the myth which is the subject of RV. x.51, and is adverted to in x.52 = selection lvi. To their version of x.51, GKR. add on p. 106 a translation of the selection before us (lxvi.). It is also rendered by Muir, v.203, and by Eggeling, SBE. xii.452. Ludwig, v.504-5, gives other Brāhmaṇa forms of this myth: cf. esp. ÇB. i.2.3¹ = SBE. xii.47. For Epic forms of the same, see Ad. Holtzmann, Agni nach den

Vorstellungen des MBh., p. 11, and esp. MBh. iii.222.7 = 14214f.

14-15. tráyas, 482c. —√2mi+pra, 770a.

15-16. 'Agni feared, (thinking,) " In this way, surely, he (syás) will get into trouble, i.e. if things keep on in this way, I shall get into trouble."' He speaks of himself here (as also at x.51.6ª) in the 3d person (syás). Note the common root of ā‿artim and ā‿ariṣyati.

16. nílāyata: in strictness, to be divided thus, níl-āyata, 'he went out, took himself off, hid.' This is for nír a-ayata, an imperf. mid. of √i (after the model of a-jayata from √ji) with the prefix nis or nir; for according to Pāṇini (viii.2.19), the r of a preposition with forms of the verb-stem aya is regularly changed to l— cf. 1087c.

In the Hindu mind, these forms of the verb-stem nil-aya were evidently confused with those of ni-laya, which yield a like mg — see BR. under √lī+ni. On this account, doubtless, the pada-pāṭha, which usually gives the division of compound verbs, refrains here. The confusion is further attested by the analogous passage of the ÇB., which has, in the Mādhyaṃdina text (i.2.3¹), ni-lilye, and in the Kāṇva text, ni-layáṁ cakre — see SBE. xii.p.xlvi. The proper form from √lī in the passage before us would of course be ny-ālayata.

16-17. U.f. pra‿éṣam (see √2iṣ+pra2 and ref.) āicchan (√1 iṣ, 585). In the metaphor, Agni is implicitly likened to a hunted beast.

17-18. tám açapat etc., 'Him (the fish) he (Agni) cursed (as follows): "dhiyā·· pra‿ávocas."' See dhī 1. — vadhyāsus (form! 924) and ghnanti (637) have as subject 'people.' —The loose use of sás, tám, etc., is one of the chief stylistic faults of the Brāhmaṇas.

19. ánv-avindan: √2vid; subject, 'the gods.' —See √vṛt+upa‿ā.

NOTES TO PAGE 94.

1-2. U.f. gṛhītásya (sc. ghṛtásya) ā-hutas-ya (see √hu)·· skándāt (736), tád me·· asat. —bhrātṛṇām: the TS. reg. has short ṛ in the gen. pl. of these words. — 'He said: "Let me make a condition (√2vṛ): Just what of the (sc. ghee) (when) taken (into the

sacrificial ladle, but) not (yet) poured into
the fire (á-hutasya), may fall outside the
enclosure, let that be the portion of my
brothers."'

SELECTION LXVII. AB. iii.20. Legend
of Indra and the Maruts, and Vṛtra.—Translated, Muir, v.93. In selection xlvii. = RV.
viii.85.7f, the Maruts are praised because
they stood by Indra when all the other gods
forsook him. The passage before us is an
expansion of that myth, a "reproduction
plus ou moins amplifiée d'un cliché emprunté
au livre des hymnes."

From other passages, it would appear that
the Maruts also were faithless, cf. Muir, v.
92 and 82¹ₙ. Both views are involved in the
explanation of the Mid-day Soma Feast, ÇB.
iv.3.3⁶f, where the Maruts first withdraw
from Indra and afterwards help him (SBE.
xxvi.334f).

4–5. haniṣyan, 948². —U.f. "anu mā
upa tiṣṭhadhvam; upa mā hvayadhvam"
(√hū). Note the free position of the prefixes (1081). — tathā̲iti, '"Yes," said
they.'

5–6. U.f. sas (Vṛtra) avet (see √1 vid3,
and 620): "mām etc.; hanta! imān bhi-
ṣayāi" (√bhī, caus., 1042f, 1043.2).

7. √çvas+abhi-pra: imperf., 631. —
adravan: simple root dru, without prefix;
note that the prefix ā with √dru exactly
reverses its meaning; so with √√dā, hṛ, and
muc.

8–9. U.f. m- ha enam na ajahus (√2hā,
661,656): "prahara bhagavas! (454b) jahi!
(637²) vīrayasva!" iti eva enam · · upa_
atiṣṭhanta. See vác.

9–10. tad etad (see etad) = 'this.' —See
√vac+abhy-anu. — 'The Rishi, seeing this
(occurrence), described (it) in the Vedic
words, "At Vṛtra's snorting, thee."' These
words are a quotation of the beginning of
RV. viii.85.7f, and illustrate the way in
which the Vedic stanzas are cited in the
secondary literature.

10–11. U.f. sas (Indra, this time) avet:
"ime · ·; ime · ·; hanta! imān asmin ukthe
ā bhajāi." See √bhaj+ā: the subjunctive
has the force of a future.

SELECTION LXVIII. AB. iii.21. Legend
of Indra and the god Ka or Who. — Compare selection lxii. and see Müller, ASL. 432f.
The identification of Prajāpati with Ka is very
common: see, e.g. ÇB. i.1.1¹⁸, vii.4.1¹⁹, xi.5.4¹.

13–14. U.f. · · vi-jitya, abravīt prajā-
patim: "aham etad asāni (636), yad tvam
(sc. asi); aham mahān asāni."

15. U.f. "yad eva etad avocas." The
etad, q.v., goes appositively with yad, marking the thing designated by yad as something
preceding, and so may be rendered by 'just'
or 'a moment ago.' P. asks, '"Who am I,
then?" "Exactly what thou just saidst,"'
replied Indra.

15–16. 'Then P. became Ka by name =
got the name of Ka. (For) P. is Ka by
name = has the name Ka.' Note that the
predicate comes first.

16–17. See yad2. 'As for the fact that
Indra became great, therein (lies) Great-
Indra's Great-Indra-ness' (cf. ÇB. ii.5.4⁹).
This is a specimen of the verbal and ety-
mological explanations of the Brāhmaṇas:
cf. 64⁷ₙ.

SELECTION LXIX. ÇB. ii.2.2⁶. The two
kinds of deities, the gods and the Brahmans.
— A little oratio pro domo of an oft-recurring kind (see ISt. x.35). Translated by
Muir, i².262 (he quotes TS. i.7.3¹ by way of
illustration), and Eggeling, SBE. xii.309.

18. U.f. devās (predicate) aha eva devās
(subject): 'The gods of course are gods.'
So mártyā ha vā́ ágre devá̄ āsuḥ, 'In the
beginning, the gods were mortals' (not 'The
mortals were gods'). — Delbrück, Altindische
Wortfolge, p. 26.

18f. 'Then (they) who are the Brahmans,
the learned (√çru 1), the scholars (see √vac
+anu, and 807), — they are the human gods.'

NOTES TO PAGE 95.

2–3. 'For (lit. of) the gods, (the sacrifice
is) just the oblations; for the human-gods,
the B., the learned, the scholars, (it is) the
dakṣiṇā.' — pṛiṇāti, subject indefinite.

4. U.f. brāhmaṇān çuçruvuṣas, 203. —
Note the fond repetition. —enam, same
as subject of pṛiṇāti.

SELECTION LXX. ÇB. ii.2.2¹⁹f. Truth,
untruth, and silence. — Translated by Delbrück, *Wortfolge*, 29,79; Eggeling, SBE. xii.
312,452.

6-8. abhi-siñcet, 758. — 'Of this fire-
consecration a (concomitant) duty is TRUTH.
He who speaks the truth, — as (if) the enkindled fire, it with ghee he should besprinkle,
so he makes it blaze up; of him greater and
greater the dignity becomes; from day to
day better he becomes.' — Note the childish
verbal anticipations and repetitions, esp. of
pronouns.

11-12. U.f. tad u ha api: Eggeling renders all four particles by a simple 'Now.' —
'"Thou'rt old (enough). Establish thy two
fires."' See √1 dhā + ā3. This ceremony was
an essential preliminary to matrimony and
to setting up in life as a householder.
Described at ISt. v.285f, x.327f.

12-14. U.f. sas ha uvāca: "te mā etad
brūtha: ' vācaṁyamas eva edhi.' na vāi
· · vaditavyam; na vadan jātu, na anṛtam
vadet. etc." 'He said: "What ye say to
me, then, amounts to this: 'Just hold thy
peace.' By no means by an āhitāgni may
untruth be spoken. By not speaking at all,
one would not speak untruth. (I.e. Only by
silence can one wholly avoid untruth.) To
such an extent (of silence, namely), is truth
a duty."' — See ha end. — See ta2. Lit.
'Ye, those, to me this are saying.' — See
tāvant2.

SELECTION LXXI. ÇB. x.4.3¹f. How the
gods got immortality and how Death got his
share. — Translated, Muir, iv².57f; in part,
v.316f. Cf. iv.54f and v.12f. Metrical paraphrase by Monier-Williams, *Indian Wisdom*,
34, = Hinduism, 35, = *Religious Thought and
Life in India*, 24. On the symbolism of the
Brāhmaṇas, see p. 357, § 92; Oldenberg's
Buddha, 19(20)f; Schroeder, ILuC. p. 127f.

15-18. 'Death (subject) is this thing
(eṣas, predicate, masc. to conform in gender with mṛtyus — cf. 78²⁰ and N.), what the
Year is. For this one, by means of days
and nights, exhausteth the life of mortals.
So they DIE. Therefore 'tis this one that is
called DEATH. The man who knoweth this

Death to be the Year, not of him doth this
one before old age by days and nights exhaust the life. To perfectly complete duration of life attaineth he.' — U.f. sarvam
ha eva āyus: cf. 86¹¹N.

19. U.f. āyuṣas antam gacchati, see
√gam3.

3-5. U.f. antakāt · · bibhayām cakrus
(1071d) yad (see 38¹N.) etc. 'The gods were
afraid of this Ender, Death, the Year, Prajāpati, [hoping] "May this one by days and
nights not get at the end of our (no) life."'
Similar construction (yad · · na and optative)
after verb of fearing, ÇB. iv.3.3¹¹.

5. U.f. te · · yajñakratān tenire (794e).

5f. THE SACRIFICES are described by
Weber, ISt. x.321f. The Hindus did not
class them according to their purpose, as
thank-offerings, expiatory offerings, etc.
They grouped them

A. according to the MATERIAL used, as:
1. oblations of milk, ghee, corn; 2. animal
sacrifices; 3. libations of Soma. And again
B. according to the TIME, as: 1. at the
beginning (x.328) of each day and of each
night (agnihotra); 2. at the beg. (x.329) of
the lunar half-month; 3. at the beg. (x.337)
of the three seasons, — spring, rains, autumn;
4. at the beg. (x.343) of the two harvests.
The offering of first-fruits or nava-sasya-
iṣṭi; in the spring, of barley; in the autumn,
of rice; 5. at the beg. (x.344) of the solar
half-year, the paçu-bandha; 6. at the beg.
(x.352) of the new year, the Soma-sacrifice.

With this last, often occurs the elaborate
ceremony of building the fire-altar of bricks,
ISt. xiii.217-292. This ceremony is called
the 'Fire-piling,' agni-cayana (see √1 ci), or
briefly agni.

Schröder gives in brief compass a sketch
of a specimen-sacrifice, ILuC. p. 97-109.

7. U.f. na amṛtatvam ānaçire (788⁴). te
ha api agnim (= agni-cayanam) cikyire
(787). — That the gods were once mortal
(94¹⁸N.) is doubtless a late notion. The path
of Death is itaro devayānāt, 86⁶: cf. also
ZDMG. xxxii.300.

8-9. See √1dhā + upa. — U.f. yathā idam

(see 2idam) api etarhi eke upa-dadhati:
"A polemical hit aimed by the author of
the Brāhmaṇa at some contemporaries who
followed a different ritual from himself."—
Muir. Cf. Chāndogya Upaniṣad, i.12.4 =
SBE. i.21. —See iti 1.

10–11. Ppls w. cerus, see √car2 and 1075b.
—See √1 rudh+ava, desid., 1027.

11–13. U.f. "na vāi · · · upa dhattha:
ati vā eva · ·; na vā · ·; tasmāt na · ·."

13–14. See ha end. —See explan. under
ta2. —See yathā6.

15–18. The protasis-clauses begin with
ṣaṣṭim and ṣaṣṭim and atha lokampṛṇās:
the apodosis-clauses, with atha me and atha
amṛtās. The second protasis-clause has an
appendix, adhi ṣaṭtriṅçatam, see adhi. —
For impv. with conditional mg, cf. example
under atha2, and 82²ⁿ. —For daça etc.,
see 480.

— 'Put ye on 360 P's; 360 Y's, and 36 besides; then 10,800 L's. Then (if ye do) shall
ye etc.' The days of the year number 360;
and 360 × 30 = 10,800. But see also Weber,
ISt. xiii.254–5. Note that 108 = 2² × 3³.

18–19. The acquisition of immortality is
otherwise related, ÇB. ii.2.2⁹f, Muir, ii⁵.372.

21–23. U.f. "na atas · · asat (636²):
yadā eva · · harāsāi (736), etc." See atas3.
'"From this time on, not any other with his
body shall be immortal: just when thou this
(thy) allotted-portion shalt seize, then parting
with his body he shall be immortal, who is
to be immortal either by knowledge or by
works."'

23f. See yad2 end. 'As for their saying
thát, "Either by knowledge or by works,"—
this is that knowledge, (lit. which is agni =)
namely agni; and these are those works,
namely agni.' Here agni = agni-cayana.
—Cf. 66²⁹.

NOTES TO PAGE 97.

1–2. U.f. te, ye evam etad vidus, ye vā
etad karma kurvate, etc. Promises to them
"who have this knowledge" recur times un-
numbered in the Brāhmaṇas. As between
'knowledge' and 'works,' knowledge is the
better: ÇB. xiv.4.3²⁴ = SBE. xv.96. On this
passage, see Oldenberg, Buddha, 46 = 47.

4. U.f. te etasya (= mṛtyos) eva annam.

SELECTION LXXII. ÇB. xii.7.3¹f. Legend
of Indra and Namuci.— For the origin of
this story, see 81¹⁵f and notes. Translated,
Muir, v.94. Other forms of the story : Muir,
iv².261; Ludwig, v.145. The MBh. has it at
ix.43.33 = 2433f; see ZDMG. xxxii.311.

6–7. 'N. stole I's strength etc., along with
his surā.'

7–10. U.f. sas (Indra) · · upa_adhāvat:
"çepānas asmi (see √√çap, as) namucaye,
'na tvā · · · na ārdreṇa;' atha me idam
ahārṣit. idam me ā jihīṛṣatha ?" iti. —
Note the difference (929, 928) between aharat
and ahārṣit. —Note reversal of mg (94⁷ⁿ.)
effected by ā with jihīrṣatha (1028b): '"Are
ye willing to fetch it back for me ?"'

10. "astu nas atra api; atha ā harāma:"
'"Let there be of us in this also (a share);
in that case, we'll fetch (it) back."'

10–11. '"Together ours (is) that; so
fetch it back." Thus said he.'

11. iti (the one before tāu açvināu) =
'on the strength of that agreement.'

12. asiñcan: see √sic3.

13. vy-uṣṭāyām (√1 vas) rātrāu, 303b.
So an-udite āditye.

14. √3vas+ud — a queer verb to use for
this mg. — U.f. ṛṣiṇā abhy-anu_uktam
"apām phenena" (81¹⁶) iti.

SELECTION LXXIII. Nirukta ii.16. Explanation of RV. i.32.10, selection xxxii.,
page 70¹⁹·²⁰.— See Roth, Erläuterungen, 21f,
and Muir, ii⁵.174f.

15–16. The iti marks aniviçamānānām
as a gloss to the quoted "átiṣṭhantinām."
So asthāvarāṇām is a gloss to the "ani-
veçanānām" of the sacred text; and in like
manner, meghas to "çáriram."

16. Starting from the 3d pers. s. pres.
ind. act. of a verb-root (e.g. çamnāti from
√3çam), and treating it as a declinable noun-
stem, like mati, the Hindu forms an ablative
sing., e.g. çamnātes, to express "derivation
from a root." Render: 'çarira is from the
root çṛ break, or from the root çam harm.'
So with drāghati and the following two.

19f. After the verbal explanations, comes
the mythological discussion. 'Who then is
Vṛtra? "A cloud" say the etymologists.

"An Asura descended from Tvaṣṭar" say the tellers of old legends.' There were, then, already schools of conflicting opinions. Cf. Muir, ii².170f.

Notes to Page 98.

1. The genitives limit miçribhāva-, 1316.

2–3. -karmaṇas is abl. — 'In this process (tatra), ·· battles, so to speak, take place.'

3. ahivat etc.: 'The m- and b- (sc. speak of V.) as a dragon.'

4. √1 vṛ+ni (1045): subject, Vṛtra.

5. U.f. tadabhivādini eṣā ṛk bhavati.

Selection LXXIV. Wedding-customs and the wedding-service. Āçvalāyana Gṛhya-sūtra, book i., chap's 5, 7, 8. — Stenzler published the text in the *Abhandlungen für die Kunde des Morgenlandes*, vol. iii., 1864; and the translation, vol. iv., 1865. Cf. Weber, *Indische Streifen*, ii.296f. The text appeared with a Hindu comment in the *Bibliotheca Indica*, 1866–69. English translation by Oldenberg, SBE. xxix.159f.

—On the subject-matter of this selection, the following essays and books may be consulted. The most important is the essay of Haas, with additions by Weber, ISt. v.267–410; cf. esp. the synoptic index, 410–12. Haas gives the text and an annotated translation of our selection at pages 289f, 362f.

See also notes to selection lviii., p. 389. Further, Kaegi, 74(102), and notes; Zimmer, 309f; Kaegi in *Fleckeisen's Jahrbücher*, 1880, 456f; and Colebrooke's *Essays*, i.217–38.

—Birth, reproduction, and death are the three great facts of all organic life. It is therefore natural that the customs connected with marriage and burial should take so important a place in the traditions of primitive peoples. It can hardly be doubted that a considerable body of these customs have their root in Indo-European antiquity. For we find, as between the various members of this family, many and most striking coincidences of usage. The systematic exposition and criticism of these coincidences form one of the most interesting chapters of comparative philology. It is not feasible to point them out in detail here. In lieu of this may be cited —

For purposes of comparative study: Joachim Marquardt, *Privatleben der Römer*, i². 28f; A. Rossbach, *Die Römische Ehe*, Stuttgart, 1853; G. F. Schömann, *Griechische Alterthümer*³, ii.529–36; K. Weinhold, *Die Deutschen Frauen* (Wien, 1851), p.190–274, or *Altnordisches Leben* (Berlin, 1856), 238–59; Spiegel, *Erānische Alterthumskunde*, iii.676–81.

—Synopsis of the subject-matter (with references to passages in vol. v. of the ISt., where Haas and Weber treat of the Hindu customs or cite analogous ones): —

Chapter v. Test of the bride by means of exorcised lumps of earth. See ISt. v.288f.

Chap. vii. The marriage ceremony. Dextrarum iunctio (v.277,311). Bride led around the fire and water (v.318n.2, 396n.). Amo 'ham asmi (v.216). Mounting the stone (v.318n.1). Oblation (v.318n.3). Loosing braids (v.320). Seven steps (v.320f, 321n.).

Chap. viii. Wedding journey (v.327f). Arrival at new home (v.329). Pellis lanata (Rossbach, 113f, 324; Marquardt, 50). Continence (v.325f, 331).

Vedic Citations. If the entire first pāda of a stanza is quoted, the entire stanza is meant. If only part of the first pāda of a hymn is quoted, the entire hymn is meant. If more than a complete pāda is quoted, then three stanzas are meant. — Stenzler, note to AGS. i.20.9.

Synopsis of RV.-mantras cited at

98¹⁹	gṛbhṇāmi te	= 89⁵
99²²	pra tvā muñcāmi	= 89⁷
99²³	'The following'	= 89⁹
100¹⁰	pūṣā tveto	= 89¹¹
100¹¹	açmanvati (½ stanza)	= 89⁸
100¹²	'The following' (½ stanza)	= 89⁴
100¹²	jivaṁ rudanti	= 88⁴
100¹⁴	mā vidan	= 89¹³
100¹⁵	sumaṅgalir	= 89¹⁵
100¹⁵	iha priyam	= 89¹⁷
100¹⁸	ā naḥ prajām (4 stanzas)	= 89¹⁹
100¹⁹	sam añjantu	= 90⁸

6. 'The family (of the intended bride or groom) in the first place one should consider, according to the rule, "Who on the mother's and on the father's side, —" as aforesaid.'

The rule referred to is in Āçvalāyana's Çrauta-sūtra, ix.3.20 (p. 714, *Bibl. Ind.*), and continues thus,

" — for ten generations back, are endowed with knowledge, austerity, and works of merit." See Weber's interesting discussion of ancestor-tests, ISt. x.84–8.

8-11. U.f. aṣṭān piṇḍān kṛtvā (127²), · · · piṇḍān abhimantrya, kumārim brūyāt, "eṣām ekam gṛhāṇa." (722). 'Making eight lumps (of earth), conjuring the lumps with the mantras "ṛtam · · · · dṛçyatām," he should say to the girl, "Take one of these."' —Germanic bride-tests cited, ISt. v.288ɴ.

11-12. U.f. kṣetrāt ced ubhayataḥ-sasyāt gṛhṇīyāt, "annavatī asyās prajā bhaviṣyati," iti vidyāt. 'If she take (the lump made) from the field that bears two crops a year, "Rich in food will her children be," thát he may know.' —'Two crops:' cf. Megasthenes, as preserved by Diodorus (ii. 35,36) and Strabo (xv.20, p. 693).

12-15. Most of the remaining seven conditional periods are abbreviated to two words : thus goṣṭhāt answers to kṣetrāt and paçumatī to annavatī; and the rest is to be supplied from the first period. No's 4, 5, and 7 begin respectively with avidāsinas, ādevanāt, and iriṇāt. But patighnī is predicate to a supplied kumārī rather than to prajā.

14. dvi-pravrājinī: to be preferred, perhaps, is the reading vipravrājinī (√vraj+vi-pra), 'wandering hither and thither;' but the mg amounts to the same thing.

16. In order of extent stand deça, 'country,' janapada, 'district,' nagara, 'town,' grāma, 'village,' kula, 'family.' But at weddings and funerals, village-customs stand first in importance—PGS. i.8.11,13 or SBE. xxix.285. On conflicts, cf. Stenzler's note to AGS. i.7.2, and 59¹²ɴ. —tān begins new clause. —prati_iyāt, 616.

17-21. dṛṣadam açmānam, 'a millstone (which is) stone' (not, e.g. burnt clay). Apposition, cf. 101¹². —See √rabh+sam-anv-ā: sc. kumāryām, loc. absol. —Note how the quoted sacred text has gṛbhṇāmi, while the later one has gṛhṇīyāt: cf. 92¹⁶ɴ. —kāma-yita (1043.3), as if of the 1st gen'l conj., instead of kāmayeta. So vācayita, 101², 106⁴; kalpayiran, 105¹. —pumānsas etc.; δύνασθαι · · τοιεῖν καὶ ἀρρενογόνους καὶ θηλυ-γόνους etc., Megasthenes, in Strabo, xv.60, p. 713; also ÇB. xiv.9.4¹⁴f or SBE. xv.219f.

— 'To the west of the fire, a millstone setting, to the north-east, a water-jar, while she touches him, he, offering, standing facing west, of her, facing east, seated, with RV. x. 85.36, the thumb only should grasp, in case he should desire "pumānsas · · jāyeran."'

1. pari-ṇayam : we should read pari-ṇay-añ or (BI.) -an, pres. ppl. — 'Leading (her) thrice to the right around the fire and the water-jar.' The analogies are remarkable : cf. ἐπιδέξια, the Roman dextratio, the Gaelic "walking the deasil," etc. Consult SBE. xii.37, 45, 272, 442; Rossbach, 231, 314f: Marquardt, i².51 and ɴ.1. Circumambulations followed the course of the sun on occasions of joy; and were reversed (104²¹) on occasions of sorrow.

2-3. Pronounce : sā tvam asi ; amo aham. —These interesting formulae occur at AV. xiv.2.71; ÇB. xiv.9.4¹⁹; PGS. i.6.3; AB. viii.27; ÇGS. i.13.4. For pāda d, the first three have sāmāham asmi; ṛk tuam.

—The sāman is conceived as male (ÇB. iv.6.7¹¹), and as sprung from the ṛc (as it is), or as husband of it (ÇB. viii.1.3⁶). But to the Hindu mind this lugging in of sāma has a charming mystic significance, inasmuch as sā plus ama makes sāma (see AB. iii.23; and SBE. i.13). —The conception of heaven as male and of earth as female is common — see Preller, *Gr. Mythologie*³, i.37f.

—The Vedic formula has a general significance not unlike that of the ancient *quando* (or *ubi*) *tu Gaius ego Gaia* and the German *Wo ich Mann bin, da bist du Frau, und wo du Frau bist, da bin ich Mann*. For the Latin formula, see Rossbach, p. 351; ISt. v.216; Fleckeisen, 1880, p. 457; and esp. the discussion by Marquardt, i².49ɴ.2. For the German, see ISt. v.216. Another use of the Vedic formula, ISt. x.160.

4-5. ehi, used just like ἄγε or φέρε; but cf. the variants noted ISt. v.332ɴ. —If we could read priyāu, the metre would be in order (8+8+11+8); but cf. TS. iv.2.5¹.

6. Force of repetition — 'With each leading-around' (1260). —She mounts the stone or puts her foot on it as a symbol of the way in which she is to put her foot on her enemies.

9. U.f. vadhv-añjalāu (184 end) upa-
stīrya (see √str+upa). The loc. is adjunct
of ā-vapati as well as of the gerund.

9-11. The first pouring (upastaraṇa) of
ājya and the two strewings of parched grain
on the bride's hands, and the second sprinkling (pratyabhighāraṇa) of ājya, constitute
the four portions "cut off" or separated
from the havis or sacrificial food. The first
is done by the groom; the rest by the brother.
The descendants of Jamadagni used to "cut
off" five such portions (ISt. v.366; x.95)
and so had to strew grain three times.—
Oldenberg's note. —eṣas, refers back.

— '(The groom) having poured the sacrificial butter on the bride's hollowed-and-
joined-hands, her brother or brother's representative strews parched grain (on her hands)
twice [Thrice (is the custom) of the Jamad-
agnians.], sprinkling again (sc. ājya) over
the havis (= what he has left of the grain in
the basket) and over the avatta (= what grain
he has strewn on her hands). This (as just
stated) is the cutting-off-usage.'

12-17. ayakṣata, 882. —pra·· muñcātu
(cf.89⁹), impv., w. lengthening (ISt. v.340ɴ.):
so nudātu, svadātu. —These stanzas are
mere adaptations of blank forms, so to say.
For examples of the changes (called ūhās)
which circumstances demand, see AB. ii.6.6;
cf. AGS. iii.8.7. The forms are filled out
(see nigama in BR.) with a deity-name,
which, as here, does not always fit the metre.

18. 'With the above mantras (uttered
by the groom), she, not-parting (fem.) her
joined-hands, should offer (the grain in
them), as with a sruc.' The nose of the
sruc is at the side. She is therefore to pour
out the grain so,—not over her finger-tips.

—For the case of families who do not
strew grain but twice, we must assume that
the bride, when making her second oblation,
does not offer all the grain in her joined-
hands, but leaves some for her third oblation.
Her fourth is from the basket.

18-19 (§ 14). 'Without (any) leading
around (on the part of the groom), (the
bride should offer grain) with the nose of
the basket towards herself in silence the
fourth time.' The "silence" refers of course

to the groom. The bride does not say anything at any time (cf. SBE. xxix.37).

—As prescribed above, the rites are performed in the order following:

I. II. First and second rounds:
  a. leading around, § 6;
  b. mounting stone, § 7;
  c. strewing grain, § 8;
  d. oblation w. mantra 1 or 2, § 12.
III. Third round:
  a. leading around;
  b. mounting stone;
  c. sprinkling ājya, § 10;
  d. oblation w. mantra 3, § 13.
IV. Fourth time:
  a, b, and c fall out;
  d. oblation in silence.

19-20. U.f. ā_upya ā_upya (127 end)
ha (see ha) eke etc. 'Some lead her around
after each strewing (of) the grain. In this
way (tathā) the last two oblations do not
fall together.' That is, some do the rites in
the order:

  c. strewing or sprinkling;
  d. oblation w. mantra;
  a. leading around;
  b. mounting stone.

In this way, the fourth oblation comes directly
after the third mounting of the stone.

20-21. asyāi, 365.3. 'Then he loosens
her two braids, if they are made; (i.e. if)
two braids of wool at her two temples are
tied.'

22. He loosens the right one with RV.
x.85.24. —uttarām (sc. çikhām) uttarayā
(sc. rcā): see uttara 3, 4.

23. The AB. at i.14.5f tells why the NE.
is called a-parājitā. See also A. Kuhn,
Entwicklungs-stufen der mythenbildung, Abh. der
Berliner Akad., 1873, p. 126f.

NOTES TO PAGE 100.

1-3. U.f. iṣe ekapadi (sc. bhava), etc.,
'be taking one step for strength = take one
step for strength; two for vigor;' and so on.
—The body consists of five elements. At
one period, the seasons are reckoned as
six: çiçira, vasantá, grīṣmá, varṣá, çarád,
hemantá.

4. See saptapada in vocab. Seven, as a
sacred number, became the symbol for
'many' or 'all.' Doubtless the word always
suggested both the literal and the transferred mgs. Orig., sakhā saptapado bhava,

'Be a constant friend,' was a mere general formula, used on sealing a friendship, e.g. between two men, who would take seven steps together hand in hand by way of ratifying their bond. Sāptapadam māitram, 'Friendship (if genuine) is constant,' became a common proverb.

—The application of the formula to the wedding-ceremony is prob. only a secondary and special use; although it came to be exceedingly important. Here saptapadī being taken with strict literalness, it became necessary to lead up to it by six other formulae — as in the text. The matter is explained at length and illustrated, by Haas and Weber, ISt. v.320-22 : cf. BR. s.v. saptapada; and AV. v.11.10.

6. The two gerunds seem to go with the subject of abhy-ut-krāmayati, i.e. the groom.

8. vaset : subject, the bride. —sapta ṛṣin, 127². —See iti 3.

8-9. dhruvam, as symbol of fixity and constancy (see PGS. i.8.19 and ÇGS. i.17.3). For the legend of Dhruva's translation to the skies, see Viṣṇu Purāṇa, book i, chap. 12. —arundhatīm : cited, with many other examples of faithful and happy wifehood, at MBh. i.199.6 = 7352 and v.117.11 = 3970; cf. also ISt. v.195. There was a superstition that one whose life was near its close could not see these stars (ISt. v.325 : Indische Sprüche, 2d ed., no. 2815). —ṛṣin : here, as so often, the heavenly lights are the souls of pious sages and saints departed — see note to 91¹². —The bride has nothing to say during the ceremony, and keeps silence after it until (cf. 103²⁰) starlight.

10. U.f. prayāṇe (loc. 303b), the wedding-journey, from the bride's village to the groom's. See ISt. v.327f.

11-12. Rules 2 and 3 are for the case that they have to cross a stream.

12. rudatyām, 'if she weeps,' loc. abs.

13. So in Rome a boy went ahead with a nuptial torch. Cf. Rossbach, 362-3.

14-15. 'At every dwelling' — as the wedding-train passes it. The procession called out eager gazers then, as now. Indeed, to judge from AV. xiv.2.73, even the Manes were supposed to crowd about for a look at the bride (ISt. v.277). —U.f. ·· iti ikṣakān ikṣeta.

17. U.f. ānaḍuham carma ā-stīrya : compare the pellis lanata (Rossbach, 112, 324). —tasminn = carmaṇi. The two foll. words are loc's s. fem., supply kumāryām (303b).

18-19. cataṣṛbhis, sc. ṛgbhis.

19-20. dadhnas (431) etc.: 'Partaking of curds, he should offer (them) in turn (to her); or, with the rest of the ājya, he anoints (anakti, √añj) his and her heart.' hṛdaye : better as dual, on account of the nāu (dual, 90⁸) in the stanza which accompanies the action.

20-21. See ūrdhvam. —brahma-cāriṇāu : see ISt. v.325n.3, 331. —U.f. alam-kurvāṇāu, 714.

22. Counting of time by nights : see Kaegi, n.68* and citations, and Zimmer, p. 360. — 'Or, "(They should be continent) a year," (say) some : a Rishi is born in this way (iti).' 'In this way' = 'on condition and as reward of such self-restraint.'

NOTES TO PAGE 101.

1. Marital intercourse is declared by Āpastamba to be a duty resting on the authority of Holy Writ (brāhmaṇa-vacanāc ca saṁveçanam, ii.1.19 = SBE. ii.101). The Scripture-passage, acc. to Bühler, is TS. ii.5.1⁵, kāmam ā vijanitoḥ sám bhavāma, 'Let us have intercourse after our heart's desire till a child be begotten.' Explicit is Bāudhāyana, iv.1.17 = SBE. xiv.315; MBh. xii.21.12 = 626. Cf. Ludwig, v.549 (N. to RV. i.179.2), and iv. 315: also Exodus xxi.10f, and I Cor. vii.3.

2. See √vac, caus.: form, cf. 982³N.

SELECTION LXXV. The customs and ritual of cremation and burial. Āçvalāyana Gṛhya-sūtra, b'k iv., chap's 1-6. —Text and translations as at the beginning of introduction to selection lxxiv. Roth compares the ceremonies here described with those implied by the text of RV. x.18 in his essay, die Todtenbestattung im indischen Alterthum, ZDMG. viii.467-75, reprinted in part by Zimmer, p. 404f. The same subject is treated at length by Max Müller, ZDMG. ix.p.I-LXXXII. We may mention also Colebrooke's

Essays, i.172–95; the papers of Wilson and of Rājendralāla Mitra, cited above, p. 382f; and especially Monier-Williams, in *Religious Thought and Life in India*, chap. xi., *Death, Funeral Rites, and Ancestor-worship*, and in *Ind. Ant.* v.27. Cf. also in general the intro-duction to selection liii., p. 382f.

The ceremonies in question have three main parts: the cremation; the gathering and burial of the bones; and the expiation. —These are followed by the çrāddha, de-scribed at AGS. iv.7, SBE. xxix.250f, 106f.

Synopsis of RV.-mantras cited at

102¹	apeta vīta	= 83¹⁶
102⁷	ud irṣva nāri	= 86¹⁸
102⁸	dhanur hastād	= 86²⁰
102²⁰	agner varma	= 84¹⁶
102²¹	ati drava	= 83¹⁷
103¹	imam agne	= 84¹⁶
103¹²	prehi prehi	= 83¹¹
	and 23 others, see note	
103¹⁷	ime jīvā	= 86⁸
104¹¹	çitike	= 85¹⁰
104¹⁴	upa sarpa	= 87²
104¹⁵	'The following'	= 87⁴
104¹⁵	'The following'	= 87⁶
104¹⁶	ut te stabhnāmi	= 87⁸
104²⁾	kravyādam (½ *stanza*)	= 84²⁰
105⁵	ihāivāyam (½ *stanza*)	= 85¹
105⁹	tantuṁ tanvan	= 89¹
105¹¹	ā rohatāyur	= 86¹⁴
105¹²	imaṁ jivebhyah	= 86¹⁰
105¹⁴	param mṛtyo (4 *stanzas*)	= 86⁴
105¹⁵	yathāhāni	= 86¹²
105¹⁷	imā nārir	= 86¹⁶
105¹⁸	açmanvati	= 89²
105²¹	āpo hi ṣṭhā (3 *stanzas*)	= 83¹
105²¹	parime gām	= 91¹⁴
106³	'Sun-hymns,' *see note*	
106³	'Blessings,' *see note*	
106³	apa nah (8 *stanzas*)	= 72⁶

—For purposes of comparative study (cf. p. 398) we cite: Joachim Marquardt, *Privatleben der Römer*, I².340f; Schömann, *Griechische Alterthümer²*, ii.539f; K. Wein-hold, *Altnordisches Leben* (1856), 474–504; the same author's *Heidnische Todtenbestattung in Deutschland* (with illustrations), *Sitzungs-berichte der Wiener Akad.*, 1858, 1859; Spiegel, *Erānische Alterthumskunde*, iii.701–6; Geiger, *Civilization of the Eastern Irānians*, i.84f; and finally the masterly essay of J. Grimm, *Ue-ber das Verbrennen der Leichen, Abh. der Berlin-er Akad.*, 1849, p. 191f = *Kleinere Schriften*, ii.

211f, who treats of the custom among almost all peoples of Indo-European stock. See p. 230 = 261f for the custom among our Anglo-Saxon forefathers, a remembrance of which lives in the modern English *Bale-fire*. Cre-mation is common throughout the MBh. — Holtzmann, *Agni*, p. 10.

3–4. Protasis, ·· ced upa-tapet; apodosis, ··· ud-ava-syet (√sā).

5. enam, the sick householder.

6. U.f. ·· paçunā iṣṭyā iṣṭvā (√yaj), ava-syet. See Stenzler's note to § 4. —See √sthā+sam.

7–8. The quarter and the slope are in general to the south, the region of the dead (cf. ÇB. i.2.5¹⁷).

9. ity eke, see iti 2c. —tāvad-āyāmam (sc. khātam ayāt), 'the trench should be having so much length.'

10. vitasty-avāk, 'span-deep': or, for vitasti-mātram avāk. — 'On all sides, the çm- should be an open space.'

11. '"But thorn-plants and milk-plants" as aforesaid' [viz. at AGS. ii.7.5, "he should dig out with their roots and remove them"]. Cf. 98⁶ɴ.

12. çm- is both a burning-ground and a burial ground: here, the former, as is shown by ādahanasya. For a similar definitive apposition, cf. 98¹⁷.

13. 'This has been stated above' — at Çrāuta-sūtra, vi.10.2, given in Stenzler's note.

14. Rule 17, sc. 'should be.'

16. etām diçam, 'to that quarter,' men-tioned 101⁷.

16–18. Rules 2–7: nayanti may be re-peated w. the accusatives. Rule 2, cf. 104⁹.

20. The cord is usually worn over the shoulder; cf. Stenzler's note to AGS. iv.2.9. —On returning (103²¹), the order of march is reversed.

21. evam, in the order named. —kartā, subject of pra‿ukṣati, next line. —pra-savyam, cf. 99¹ɴ.

Notes to Page 102.

2–8. The oblation-fire, the householder's fire, and the southern fire are the three sacred fires which are to be started and maintained in every family. Here they are set respectively in the SE., NW., and SW. parts of the sacred place.

3-4. enam, 'for him,' i.e. the dead man (Oldenberg), or the conductor of the ceremony (see Stenzler). This second accusative with (idhmacitim) cinoti is strange.

4-6. The first tasmin, masc., refers to -citim, fem. 1; the second, neuter, to -ajinam. 'On it they set the dead man, carrying (hṛtvā) him to the north of the g-, with his head towards the ā-.'

6. 'To the north (of the corpse) they set the wife; and a bow for a Kṣatriya.'

7-8. U.f. tām (= patnīm) ut-thāpayet · · · vā, "ud īrṣva nāri etc." See 86¹³N.

8. 'The conductor of the ceremony should repeat (the stanza) in case of a Çūdra (= in case a Ç. raises her up from the pile).'

9. dhanus, sc. apa-nayet. — Rule 21 = exactly 'Ditto in case of a Çūdra.'

9-10. 'Having strung it, without (= before) piling the pile (of things mentioned below), breaking (√1 çṛ) it, he should throw it on the fuel-pile.'

11 f. Müller gives pictures of these various implements, ZDMG. ix.p.VII f, LXXVIII f.

14. bhittvā ca ekam, 'and breaking (it in two pieces, in case there is only) one (sruva).'

18. āsec-, sc. pātrāṇi. — See √1 pṛ. — putras, the dead man's.

19. 'And the metallic ware (and) pottery.'

21-22. U.f. vṛkkān (134 end) ud-dhṛtya (√1 hṛ). —dakṣiṇe (sc. pāṇāu) dakṣiṇam (sc. vṛkkam ā-dadhyāt), etc.

22-23. '"And two meal-cakes," (say) some [, he should put on the hands of the corpse]. "(Only) in the absence of the kidneys," (say) others.' — sarvām, sc. anustaraṇīm.

NOTES TO PAGE 103.

1-2. See √mantraya+anu: 'accompanies the fetching · · w. the stanza "imam etc."'

2-4. U.f. · · jānu ā_acya, · · juhuyāt, "agnaye svāhā etc." — pañcamīm (sc. ājya_āhutim juhuyāt) urasi pretasya —

4-5. U.f. "asmāt (accent, asmāt, 74⁹N.) vāi (see vāi) · · · tvat adhi (see adhi) jāyatām," a metrical mantra, substantially identical with VS. xxxv.22. — asāu, voc., 'O so-and-so.'

6. See √2iṣ+pra3.

6-8. 'If the āh- should reach ̗the corpse) first, "In the heaven-world it has reached him"—this may one know. Happy will that one be in that world: so (will) this one, that is, the son, in this (world).' U.f. rātsyati (√rādh) asāu amutra: evam ayam asmin, iti putras. The last iti marks putras as an explanation of ayam.

8-11. Rules 3-4 are counterparts of 2.

11-12. Rule 5: loc. = 'in case of.' — ṛddhim vadanti, see √vad3. — "The higher the smoke of the pyre rises, the more distinguished will the departed be in the other world."—Weinhold, Altnord. Leben, 480-1.

12. tam, like sas (line 13) and eṣas (16), refers to the departed.

12-13. · · · iti samānam, 'with the mantras "prehi prehi etc." in the same way'— as indicated, namely, in the Çrāuta-sūtra, at vi.10.19-20 (p. 505-6), i.e. with the 24 stanzas there enumerated. They are RV. x.14. 7,8,10,11 ; x.16.1-6; x.17.3-6; x.18.10-13; x.154.1-5; and x.14.12. The text of all these stanzas is given in the RV. order in the Reader, pages 83-91.

14. svargam lokam: note the fine distinction between this and the later svarga-lokam (as cpd). The old two-word form is used in lines 14 and 16, as virtual quotations from an older text; and above, at line 5, a quoted mantra; but the cpd is used in the Sūtra proper, line 7. Cf. 92¹⁶N.

15. U.f. avakām, çīpālam iti (marks çī- as a gloss to avakām) ava-dhāpayet. tatas (= gartāt) ha (see ha) vāi etc.

17. With regard to the pertinence of the mantra, see Roth, ZDMG. viii.472, 468. — savyāvṛtaṣ, cf. 99¹N.

18-20. The end of each clause is marked by a gerund. —U.f. udakam a-vahat · · un-majjya, · · gṛhitvā, ut-tīrya, · · enāni (= vāsānsi, i.e. the ones they had on before changing) ā-piḍya, · · āsate. —See 44. — Similarly, the bride keeps silence till starlight, 100²N.

—See nāman2. —Each of the relatives, facing southward, performs the lustration,

saying to the departed, "O thou of the family
of the Kāçyapans, O Devadatta, this water is
for thee" (kāçyapagotra, devadatta, etat
te udakam). — Scholiast.

21. 'Or, while (a bit) of the sun is (still)
seen, they may go home.' — Rule 12: cf.
101²⁰ɴ.

22. U.f. prāpya agāram, · · · a-kṣatān,
tilān, apas etc.

NOTES TO PAGE 104.

1. More fully, kritena vā, utpannena vā
(sc. annena) : see √pad+ud.

3f. Render the locatives by 'in case of,'
i.e. here 'in case of the death of.' —dāna-
adhyayane, acc. dual n., 1253a.

8. See ūrdhvam. —'Tenth' (see daçamī)
—counting from the day of death. —
kṛṣṇapakṣasya ayujāsu, sc. tithiṣu. —See
eka-nakṣatra. Of the 28 lunar mansions,
six form three pairs, named 'former' and
'latter' Phalgunī (9–10), Aṣāḍhā (18–19),
and Bhadrapadā (24–25). Accordingly,
under these asterisms, or in the lunar months
named after them, the gathering is forbidden.
See Whitney, OLSt. ii.351f, 360. But cf.
Weber, Abh. der Berliner Akad., 1861, p. 322.

9. 'In a plain male urn (they put) a man
(i.e. his bones); in a plain female (urn—sc.
kumbhyām), a woman.' If the urn has pro-
tuberances on it, like a woman's breasts, it
is regarded as a female urn. Many such
have been found by Schliemann — see his
Ilios, numbers 986, 988–93. A male urn is
one without these breasts.

9–10. § 3, cf. 101¹⁷. —prasavyam, 99¹ɴ.

11–12. U.f. aṅguṣṭha_upakaniṣṭhikā-
bhyām (cf. 105¹⁶) ekāikam asthi a- etc.
Even the Brāhmaṇas give evidence of a well-
developed body of popular beliefs about
the fingers: cf. ÇB. iii.1.3²⁵; iii.3.2²·¹⁶f, and
Eggeling's Index, SBE. xxvi.461, s.v. fingers.
See the beautiful essay of W. Grimm, Ueber
die bedeutung der deutschen fingernamen, Kleinere Schriften, iii.425–50.

But with the finger next the little one is
associated — now something mysterious, now
something uncanny (as here): this appears
from the fact that it is the 'nameless' one

not only in Sanskrit (a-nāmikā), but also
with Tibetans, Chinese, Mongols, Lithua-
nians, Finns, and North American Indians.
See Grimm, l.c. 441–47; and 91²ɴ.

13. The scholiast takes pavana as a
'winnowing-basket' used to sift out the
small bones yet remaining among the ashes,
and not picked up by hand. Is it not rather
a 'fan to blow the ashes from the carefully
gathered bones in the urn'?

13–14. U.f. yatra · · na abhi-syanderan,
anyās varṣābhyas, tatra (sc. kumbham)
· · ava-dadhyus. 'Whereunto from all sides
no water other than rain would flow.'

15–16. Rule 8: uttarayā (sc. ṛcā) = RV.
x.18.11 = 87⁴. —ava-kiret, √3kṛ. —Rule 9:
uttarām (= RV. x.18.12 = 87⁵), sc. japet.

16–17. U.f. kapālena (sc. kumbham)
api-dhāya, atha an-avekṣam praty-ā-
vrajya, apas etc. —asmāi, the deceased.

18. See √1 mṛ+abhi. For the force of
the prefix, cf. what was said by a little
newsboy, as reported by my colleague,
Professor Lane, "My mother *died on me* and
my father *runned away*." —See √2kṣi+apa.

19. U.f. purā udayāt.

20–22. tam = agnim. —ny-upya, √2vap.
—See under yatra. —prasavyam: the left
is associated with evil or sorrow (see 99¹ɴ.);
cf. Latin *laevum omen* or *numen*. —U.f.
savyān ūrūn ā-ghnānāś (637).

NOTES TO PAGE 105.

1. upa-kalpayiran (for -yeran, see 98²⁰ɴ.),
'they should provide': the verb has 11
objects (lines 1 to 4).

2–3. U.f. çamīmayyāu araṇi. A legend
explaining why the sacred fire is made with
sticks of çamī (see this) is given at MBh.
ix. 47.14 = 2741 f.

4–5. agni-velāyām, 'at the time of the
(evening) agnihotra': cf. 96⁵ɴ.

6. U.f. āsate etc., similarly 103²⁰.

7. U.f. itihāsa-purāṇāni iti (see iti3)
ā-khyāpayamānāś (1042d). Story-telling
followed the cremation in Germanic antiquity also — cf. Weinhold, Altnord. Leben,
482, and the very end of the Beöwulf.

7–10. 'When sounds are hushed (√ram),

or when (the others) have gone home or to bed, starting (pra-kramya) from the south side of the door, a continuous water-stream (the conductor of the ceremony) should offer, with the words "· · ·," (going round) to the north (side of the door — u.f. iti á uttarasmāt).'

10–12. Rule 8: cf. 100¹⁶f.

13–15. uttaratas, with agnes. —U.f. amātyān īkṣeta.

17. U.f. akṣiṇi (343f) ā_ajya (√añj) parācyas (407³) vi-arjeyus (sc. taruṇakāni).

18. añjānās (sc. yuvatis) īkṣeta (subject, 'the conductor,' kartā).

19–22. 'Then, standing off (ava-sthāya) in the NE., while (the others) circumambulate (pari-krāmatsu) with fire, and bull's dung, and a continuous water-stream, with the tṛca "āpo hi ṣṭhā etc.," he should repeat "parīme gām etc."' —ud-ā-haranti, compare 101⁴.

NOTES TO PAGE **106**.

1. U.f. yatra abhi-raṁsyamānās (√ram 939) bhavanti, 'where they are about (= intending) to tarry': not so well the vocab. —See ahata. Respecting the Hindu washerman, his work, and tools, see G. A. Grierson, *Bihār Peasant Life* (Trübner, 1885), p. 81 f.

2. U.f. ā udayāt. udite etc.

3. The scholiast to AGS. ii.3 end, enumerates the "Sun-hymns" and the "Blessings." The "Sun-hymns" are RV. x.158; i.50.1–9; i.115; and x.37. The "Blessings" are RV. i.89; v.51.11–15; and x.63. Cf. SBE. xxix.114. Of all these, only the second is given in the Reader — see Preface, page v, note 4.

3–4. U.f. annam saṁskṛtya (1087d), "apa naṣ çoçucat agham" (= RV. i.97 = 72⁶f) iti pr. hutvā. Cf. Preface, p. v, N.4.

4–5. vācayita (see √vac, caus.): we should expect -yeta — cf. 98²⁰N.

POSTSCRIPT.

Not without grave misgivings can a Vedic commentary be put forth. The hard places are very hard. Nevertheless, an unsatisfactory bit of exegesis may be a valuable approximation to the truth or may even suggest the correct solution of a difficulty.

Inasmuch as Professor Whitney has been so kind as to look over the manuscript of the Notes, it ought to be said that there are various things in the Vedic part of the work of which he does not approve.

The earliest English version of the Fables of Bidpai, *The Morall Philosophie of Doni*, by Sir Thomas North (see above, p. 313), has just been reprinted, with a valuable introduction by Joseph Jacobs, and published by David Nutt, London, 1888.

The second edition of Whitney's Grammar may soon be looked for. The section-numbers are substantially unchanged; but the subsections are marked with a, b, c, etc. The references in the Notes (see p. 289, above) are to the first edition of the Grammar. Users of the second edition will often have to seek, e.g., 844² under 844a, 371¹² under 371k, and the like.

In addition to the lexicons mentioned above, page xviii, there has recently appeared a *Sanskrit-Wörterbuch nach den Petersburger Wörterbüchern bearbeitet von* Carl Cappeller (Strassburg, Karl J. Trübner. 1887. Royal 8°, pages 541. Price 15 Mark). This is so excellent, cheap, and convenient as to deserve the warmest commendation. An English version is in progress.

C. R. L.

HOLLIS HALL, HARVARD COLLEGE,
  CAMBRIDGE, MASSACHUSETTS,
    August, 1888.

HARVARD ORIENTAL SERIES

Founded in 1891 by CHARLES ROCKWELL LANMAN and HENRY CLARKE WARREN.

Edited, with the coöperation of various scholars, by CHARLES ROCKWELL LANMAN, A.B. and LL.D. (Yale), LL.D. (Aberdeen), Professor of Sanskrit (since 1880: Wales Professor since 1903) at Harvard University (founded, 1636).

Member of the American Philosophical Society (founded, 1727); Fellow of the American Academy of Arts and Sciences (1780); President (for 1889–1890) of the American Philological Association (1869); President (for 1907–1908 and 1919–1920) of the American Oriental Society (1842).

Honorary Fellow of the Asiatic Society of Bengal (Calcutta, 1784); Honorary Member of the Société Asiatique (Paris, 1822); the Royal Asiatic Society (London, 1823), and the Deutsche Morgenländische Gesellschaft (Leipzig, 1845).

Honorary Member of the North-China Branch of the Royal Asiatic Society (Shanghai), the Finnish-Ugrian Society (Helsingfors), the India Society (London); Honorary Correspondent of the Archæological Department of the Government of India; Foreign Member of the Bohemian Society of Sciences (Prague, 1759); Member of the Colonial Society of Massachusetts; Corresponding Member of the Academy of Sciences of the Institute of Bologna (1712), of the Society of Sciences at Göttingen (1751), of the Russian Academy of Sciences (Petrograd, 1725), and of the Académie des Inscriptions et Belles-Lettres (1663) of the Institute of France.

Published by the Harvard University Press, Cambridge, Massachusetts, U.S. of America. The home office of the Press is at Randall Hall, Cambridge. The Agent of the Press in Great Britain is Humphrey Milford, Oxford University Press, Amen Corner, London, E.C., England.

Direct application for books of this Series may be made, with remittance, to the Harvard University Press at Cambridge, Massachusetts. The volumes will then be sent by mail or parcel-post direct to the buyer.

The list-prices are subject to a trade-discount. No extra charge is made for postage. This list is here revised up to date of December, 1920. Prices of previous revisions are cancelled.

Descriptive List. A bound volume, containing a list of the volumes, and a brief memorial of Henry Clarke Warren, joint-founder, will be sent free upon application to the Harvard University Press, Cambridge, Massachusetts. — The List tells the general nature and contents of each work of the Series, and the uses which that work is designed to serve. The List gives also extracts from critical notices of those works, taken from various periodicals of high standing. Appended is a partial list of libraries where the Series may be found.

Externals of the volumes. The books of this Series as a whole are printed on paper of a quality and tensile strength far above the average. They are all bound durably in full buckram. The edges are cut, but the margins are ample; and the tops are gilded, not for ornament, but to make cleaning easy. The backs are properly lettered. No work is issued until it is complete. Volume 10 is royal quarto (32 cm.); volumes 7 and 8 are super-royal octavo (28 cm.); the rest are royal octavo (26 cm.).

For sale or public inspection. A complete stock of the publications of the Harvard University Press is carried by the University Press Association, 19 East 47th Street, New York City, and by the Oxford University Press in London. Copies of this Series may be seen also in the Reading Room of the Harvard Library, Widener Hall, Cambridge, and at Randall Hall, Cambridge.

Some of the public libraries in which this Series may be found are given below, in a list, on pages 13–15.

LIST OF THE HARVARD ORIENTAL SERIES
REVISED TO DECEMBER, 1920

Volume 1. Jâtaka-Mâlâ. Stories of Buddha's former incarnations, by Ārya Çûra. Edited in Sanskrit [Nāgarî letters] by Professor HENDRIK KERN, University of Leiden, Netherlands. 1891. Second issue, 1914. Pages, 270. Royal 8°. Price, $3.

A masterpiece, as to language and style and metrical form, of Buddhist literature of the Northern Canon. By the Honorable (ārya) Çûra. Stories used as homilies in old Buddhist monasteries. Editio princeps. Kern (1833-1917), long the honored Dean of the Dutch Orientalists, thought that Çûra flourished not far from 600 A.D., or earlier. English translation by Speyer, London, 1895, Frowde.

Volume 2. Sānkhya-Pravachana-Bhāshya, or Commentary on the Exposition of the Sānkhya philosophy. By Vijñāna-Bhikshu. Edited in Sanskrit [Roman letters] by Professor RICHARD GARBE, University of Tübingen, Germany. 1895. Pages, 210. Royal 8°. Price, $3.

Sānkhya is dualistic. It recognizes souls and primeval matter, but not God. Vijñāna, however, is a pronounced theist. But in spite of his distortions of the original system, his Commentary (about 1550 A.D.) is the fullest source that we have for a knowledge of the Sānkhya system, and one of the most important (Garbe's Preface). Garbe studied the whole work with Bhāgavata Āchārya in Benares. German translation by Garbe, Leipzig, 1889, Brockhaus. Partial English version in J. R. Ballantyne's The Sānkhya Aphorisms of Kapila, London, 1885, Trübner.

Volume 3. Buddhism in Translations. Passages selected from the Buddhist sacred books, and translated from the original Pāli into English, by HENRY CLARKE WARREN, late of Cambridge, Massachusetts. 1896. Sixth issue, 1915. Pages, 540. Royal 8°. Price, $1.20.

In accordance with the author's wish, the original price of this beautiful volume was set very low, at $1.20. In spite of greatly changed conditions, that price has been maintained unaltered.

Buddhism portrayed in the words of the Buddhists themselves. The life of Buddha (a beautiful narrative), his teachings, and his monastic order form the substance of this work. The Pāli passages, done into vigorous English and accurately rendered, are chosen with such broad and learned circumspection that they make a systematically complete presentation of their difficult subject. Warren's material is drawn straight from the fountain-head. It is this fact that has given to his work an abiding importance and value. It has been highly praised by competent judges. Moreover, it has enjoyed a very wide circulation in America and Europe and the Orient. And nearly half of the work was included by President Eliot in *The Harvard Classics* (New York, P. F. Collier and Son), of which a quarter of a million sets and more have been sold. The usefulness of Warren's work has thus been incalculably enhanced.

The life of Henry Warren as a scholar is memorable in the annals of American learning. A brief memorial of his life and public services is appended to volume 30 of this Series, of which he was joint-founder. It is also issued with the Descriptive List of this Series (see above, page 1). The List may be had, free, upon application to the Harvard University Press.

Volume 4. Karpûra-Mañjarî. A drama by the Indian poet Rāja-çekhara (900 A.D.). Critically edited in the original Prākrit [Nāgarî letters], with a glossarial index, and an essay on the life and writings of the poet, by STEN KONOW, Professor of Indic Philology at the University of Christiania, Norway, and Epigraphist to the Government of India.

— And translated into English with introduction and notes, by C. R. LANMAN. 1901. Pages, 318. Royal 8°. Price, $3.

A play of court-intrigue, and the only extant drama written entirely in Prākrit. It presents interesting parallels with the Braggart Soldier of Plautus.

Volumes 5 and 6. Brhad-Devatā (attributed to Çāunaka), a summary of the deities and myths of the Rig-Veda. Critically edited in the original Sanskrit [Nāgarī letters], with an introduction and seven appendices [volume 5], and translated into English with critical and illustrative notes [volume 6], by Professor ARTHUR ANTHONY MACDONELL, University of Oxford. 1904. Pages, 234 + 350 = 584. Royal 8°. Not sold separately. Price, $6.

The Great-Deity (-book), "hardly later than 400 B.C.," is one of the oldest books ancillary to the Rig-Veda. It includes very ancient epic material: so the story of Urvaçī, the nymph that loved a mortal (whence Kālidāsa's great drama, Urvaçī). The text is edited in a way that meets the most rigorous demands of exact philological criticism. The typographic presentation of text, version, and notes (critical and expository) is a model of convenience.

Volumes 7 and 8. Atharva-Veda. Translated, with a critical and exegetical commentary, by WILLIAM DWIGHT WHITNEY, late Professor of Sanskrit in Yale University, Editor-in-Chief of *The Century Dictionary*, an Encyclopedic Lexicon of the English Language. — Revised and brought nearer to completion and edited by C. R. LANMAN. 1905. Pages, 1212. Super-royal 8°. Not sold separately. Price, $10.

The Atharva-Veda is, next after the Rig-Veda, the most important of the oldest texts of India. Whitney (1827–1894) was the most eminent American philologist of his century, and these monumental volumes form the crowning achievement of his life-long labors as an Indianist. For his translation, he expressly disclaims finality; but his austere self-restraint, resisting all allurements of fanciful interpretation, makes of his version, when taken with his critical and exegetical commentary, the sure point of departure for future study of this Veda and for its final comprehension.

The text-critical notes form the most important single item of the work. These give the various readings of the "authorities." The term "authorities" includes not only manuscripts (of Europe, India, Kashmir), but also living reciters (the Hindu equivalents, and in some respects the superiors, of manuscripts); and, in addition, the corresponding (and often variant) passages of the other Vedas. Whitney gives also the data of the scholiast as to authorship and divinity and meter of each stanza; extracts from the ancillary literature concerning ritual and exegesis; and a literal translation. Version and Comment proceed *pari passu*. Prefixed is an elaborate historical and critical introduction, and a sketch of Whitney's life, with a noble medallion portrait. A leaf of the birch-bark ms. from Kashmir is beautifully reproduced in color. The typography is strikingly clear.

Few texts of antiquity have been issued with appurtenant critical material of so large scope. And never before or since has the material for the critical study of an extensive Vedic text been so comprehensively and systematically gathered from so multifarious sources, and presented with masterly accuracy in so well-digested form.

Volume 9. The Little Clay Cart (Mṛc-chakaṭika). A Hindu drama attributed to King Shūdraka. Translated from the original Sanskrit and Prākrits into English prose and verse by ARTHUR WILLIAM RYDER, Instructor in Sanskrit in Harvard University. 1905. Pages, 207. Royal 8°. Price, $2.

A play of such variety, humor, and swift-moving action, that it has often been produced on the modern stage. Version, true and spirited. "The champagne has been decanted, and has not lost its fizz." Noble typography (Merrymount Press). Most books of this Series are technical. This one, like Warren's *Buddhism*, may be happily chosen as a gift-book.

Volume 10. Vedic Concordance: being an alphabetic index to every line of every stanza of the published Vedic literature and to the liturgical formulas thereof, that is, an index [in Roman letters] to the Vedic mantras, together with an account of their variations in the different Vedic books. By Professor MAURICE BLOOMFIELD, of the Johns Hopkins University, Baltimore. 1906. Pages, 1102. Royal 4°. Price, $15.

The Vedas are, in general, the oldest extant records of the antiquity of India, and indeed of Indo-European antiquity. They are the sacred books of the oldest religion of the Hindus. They represent parts of a mass of traditional material, current in the various schools of Vedic learning, and handed down from teacher to pupil by word of mouth. What was originally one and the same stanza, appears in the texts of the various schools in more or less varying forms. The variations are often such as appear in the varying forms of popular ballads or of church hymns. Thus it happens that the texts of these different Vedic schools are often virtually related to each other and to their presumable original, as are the several kindred manuscripts of (let us say) a Greek play to each other and to the archetype from which they are descended. The comparison of these variant forms of a given text is often indispensable for ascertaining its original form and true meaning. This comparison is just what the Concordance enables us easily to effect. It is a tool of the very first importance for future editors and revisers and translators of Vedic texts.

The Concordance covers nearly all the important published texts, and is in one single alphabetic arrangement and one single volume. It is a royal quarto of over 1100 pages, of double columns, containing 125,000 lines or more. For the lines of the Rig-Veda alone, about 40,000 entries are required. The lines of the Atharva-Veda by themselves would require over 18,000 entries, but are often merged with those of their Rig-Veda correspondents. No less than 119 texts have been drawn upon for contributions to the work.

The book was printed (in the early years of the century) in a limited edition of 1000 copies, now half exhausted; and was printed, not from electrotype plates, but from type. The expense in money alone, to say nothing of scholarly labor, was about seven thousand dollars. It is not likely that any publisher or scholar will soon undertake a new edition. For many decades, doubtless, the work will maintain its value unimpaired, an enduring monument to the industry and learning and resolute will of Professor Bloomfield.

Volume 11. The Pañcha-tantra: a collection of ancient Hindu tales, in the recension (called Pañchākhyānaka, and dated 1199 A.D.) of the Jaina monk, Pūrṇa-bhadra, critically edited in the original Sanskrit [in Nāgarī letters; and, for the sake of beginners, with word-division] by Dr. JOHANNES HERTEL, Professor am königlichen Realgymnasium, Doebeln, Saxony. 1908. Pages, 344. Royal 8°.

Volume 12. The Pañchatantra-text of Pūrṇabhadra: critical introduction and list of variants. By Professor HERTEL. 1912. Pages, 246. Royal 8°.

Volume 13. The Pañchatantra-text of Pūrṇabhadra, and its relation to texts of allied recensions, as shown in **Parallel Specimens.** By Professor HERTEL. 1912. Pages, 10: and 19 sheets, mounted on guards and issued in atlas-form. Royal 8°. Volumes 11–13 not sold separately. Price of all three together, $4.

Volume 14. The Pañchatantra: a collection of ancient Hindu tales, in its oldest recension, the Kashmirian, entitled **Tantrākhyāyika.** The original Sanskrit text [in Nāgarī letters], editio minor, reprinted from the critical editio major which was made for the Königliche Gesellschaft der Wissenschaften zu Göttingen, by Professor HERTEL. 1915. Pages, 160. Royal 8°. Price, $2.

For two thousand years and more, the tales of the Panchatantra have instructed and delighted the Hindus. The Panchatantra has exercised a greater influence than any other work of India upon the literature of the world. It was the Panchatantra that formed the basis of the studies of the immortal pioneer in the field of comparative literature, Theodor Benfey. His Pantschatantra laid the foundation of the scientific treatment of the history of the fable. From the Panchatantra there came the lost Pahlavi translation, among whose effluxes are some of the most famous books of south-western Asia and of Europe, the Arabic Kalilah and Dimnah, the Directorium of John of Capua (1270), the Buch der Beispiele (1483) in German of great vigor and beauty, — and so on, down to that gem of racy Tudor English, Sir Thomas North's translation of Doni (1570), reprinted by Joseph Jacobs, London, 1888.

Hertel gives us here one recension of known authorship and date (1199), and another, the Kashmirian, many centuries older. To volume 11, Lanman adds an essay on The Externals of Indian Books. Of the Kashmirian recension, Hertel made a German version (Berlin, 1909, Teubner). The typography of both editions is clear and beautiful. The confusing emboxments of the stories (a second in the first, a third in the second, and so on) are disentangled in a most ingenious and simple way.

Volume 15. Bhāravi's poem Kirātārjunīya, or Arjuna's combat with the Kirāta. Translated from the original Sanskrit into German, and explained, by CARL CAPPELLER, Professor at the University of Jena. 1912. Pages, 232. Royal 8°. Price, $2.

The subject-matter is taken from the great epic of India, the Mahā-Bhārata. Like the Ajax of Sophocles as compared with the Ajax of Homer, this poem is an instructive example for the student of literary evolution or literary genetics. For centuries it has been acknowledged in India as one of the six Mahā-kāvyas or most distinguished specimens of artificial poetry, a masterpiece of its kind.

Volume 16. Çakuntalā, a Hindu drama by Kālidāsa: the Bengālī recension, critically edited in the original Sanskrit and Prākrits by RICHARD PISCHEL, late Professor of Sanskrit at the University of Berlin. Pages, about 250. Royal 8°.

As descendants of Bhārata, the Hindus are called Bhāratans. Their " continent " is called Bhārata-varsha, and their great epic is called the Great Bhāratan (Story or Fight), Mahā-Bhārata. Çakuntalā is the mother of Bhārata, and the beautiful story of her birth and life is told in the Great Epic. This play is a dramatization of that story, and is the masterpiece of the literature of India.

In 1898, Pischel wrote: " Es ist der sehnlichste Wunsch meines Lebens eine korrekte Ausgabe zu machen." His Prākrit Grammar was off his hands in 1900. In 1902 he was called to the Berlin professorship. The six years of his tenancy were crowded with toil (finds from Chinese Turkestan, etc.). Then came the call to Calcutta, and, in 1908, his death at the threshold of India. Under many difficulties, the book (all but a couple of sheets) was printed at Stuttgart (Kohlhammer). Then came the world-conflagration. We hope to complete and issue the work.

Volume 17. The Yoga-system of Patañjali, or the ancient Hindu doctrine of concentration of mind. Embracing the Mnemonic Rules, called Yoga-sūtras, of Patañjali; and the Comment, called Yoga-bhāshya, attributed to Veda-Vyāsa; and the Explanation, called Tattva-vāiçāradī, of Vāchaspati-Miçra. Translated from the original Sanskrit by JAMES HAUGHTON WOODS, Professor of Philosophy in Harvard University. 1914. Pages, 422. Royal 8°. Price $4.

Three works in one pair of covers. The Rules are a set of mental pegs on which to hang the principles and precepts of a system which you must learn from the living teacher of your "school." The Comment is a reinvestiture of the skeleton of the Rules with the flesh and blood of comprehensible details. And the Explanation is of course a commentary on the Comment. The Comment is the oldest written systematic exposition of Yoga-doctrine in Sanskrit that we possess.

Of the Hindu philosophies, by far the most important are the ancient dualism called Sānkhya, the monism of the Vedānta, and the Yoga-system. Kāuṭilya, prime-minister of Chandragupta (300 B.C.), mentions Sānkhya and Yoga as current in his day. But the elements of Yoga, rigorous austerities and control of the senses, are indefinitely antique, and are one of the oldest and most striking products of the Hindu mind and character.

When one considers the floods of pseudo-scientific writing with which the propagandists of Indian "isms" in America have deluged us, one is the better prepared to appreciate the self-restraint of Dr. Woods in keeping all that pertains to miracle-mongering and sensationalism in the background, and in devoting himself to the exposition of the spiritual and intellectual aspects of Yoga. His work " continues the tradition of austere scholarship " which has, from the beginning, characterized the Harvard Oriental Series.

Volumes 18 and 19. The Veda of the Black Yajus School, entitled Tāittirīya Samhitā. Translated from the original Sanskrit prose and verse, with a running commentary. By ARTHUR BERRIEDALE KEITH, D.C.L. (Oxford), of the Inner Temple, Barrister-at-law, and of His Majesty's Colonial Office, sometime Acting Professor of Sanskrit at the University of Oxford, Author of ' Responsible Government in the Dominions.' Volume 18, kāṇḍas I–III; volume 19, kāṇḍas IV–VII. 1914. Pages 464 + 374 = 838. Royal 8°. Price $7. Not sold separately.

The Rig-Veda holds unquestioned primacy in the sacred literature of the Hindus; but their greatest mediæval scholiast on the Vedas, Sāyaṇa, did not write his commentary on the Rig-Veda until after his commentary on the Yajur-Veda, because (as he expressly tells us) of the transcendent importance of the Yajur-Veda for the sacrifice. The Yajur-Veda is the Veda of sacrificial formulas. An accurate edition of the Tāittirīya-Samhitā was published in 1871–2 by Weber. It waited nigh fifty years for a translator.

For the difficult task of translation, no English or American Sanskritist was so well qualified by previous studies as Keith. To it he has brought his wide and varied learning, and with such effectiveness as to produce a work, which, in spite of its large extent, is notable for its well-rounded completeness. The entire text is translated. The commentary runs *pari passu* with the version, embodies the gist of Sāyaṇa's scholia, and is presented with the utmost typographical perspicuity. An elaborate introduction is given, treating of the relation of this text to kindred texts, its contents, language, style, and date ('about 600 B.C.'), and the religious ritual of ancient India.

Volumes 20 and 24. Rig-Veda Repetitions. The repeated verses and distichs and stanzas of the Rig-Veda in systematic presentation and with critical discussion. By MAURICE BLOOMFIELD, Professor of Sanskrit and Comparative Philology in the Johns Hopkins University, Baltimore. 1916. Pages, 508 + 206 = 714. Royal 8°. Not sold separately. Price, $5.

Volume 20 contains Part 1: The repeated passages of the Rig-Veda, systematically presented in the order of the Rig-Veda, with critical comments and notes. Volume 24 contains Part 2: Comments and classifications from metrical and lexical and grammatical points of view, and from the point of view of the themes and divinities of the repeated passages. Also Part 3: Lists and indexes.

The aim of this work is to help us to understand the oldest religious document of Indo-European antiquity. The arrangement of Part 1 enables the student to bring under his eye at one time all the passages that he needs to compare, and to do so with utmost ease and speed. The material of this work was, from a typographical point of view, exceedingly intractable. The result as a whole is a marvel of clarity and convenience.

This work is the first of three natural sequels to Bloomfield's great Vedic Concordance: 1. The Rig-Veda Repetitions; 2. The Reverse Concordance; 3. The Vedic Variants. A draft of the second has been actually prepared by Bloomfield. And he and Edgerton have in hand the first draft of the third, a systematic presentation and critical discussion of the variant readings of the Vedic texts.

Volumes 21 and 22 and 23. Rāma's Later History, or Uttara-Rāma-Charita, an ancient Hindu drama by Bhavabhūti. Critically edited in the original Sanskrit and Prākrit, with an introduction and English translation and notes and variants, etc. By SHRIPAD KRISHNA BELVALKAR, Graduate Student of Harvard University. (Now, 1920, Professor of Sanskrit at Deccan College, Poona, India.)

Dr. Belvalkar, when returning to India in 1914 from his studies at Harvard, shipped his manuscript-collations and other papers and his books by the German freighter, Fangturm. In August, 1914, the Fangturm was interned at the port of Palma, Balearic Islands. In 1919, she was released. In May, 1920, Dr. Belvalkar recovered his papers.

Volume 21 was issued in 1915, complete.

Of volume 22, the first 92 pages, containing the text of the whole play, have been in print since January, 1915, awaiting for nigh five and one-half years the recovery of the material for the rest of the book.

Of volume 23, the material included collation-sheets giving the readings of manuscripts from widely-separated parts of India, from Nepal to Madras, from Calcutta to Bombay. In spite of the generous assistance of His Majesty's Secretary of State for India in Council, the work of getting the loan of these mss. was so great that it seemed best not to try to do it again, but to await the release of the Fangturm. — There is hope now that volumes 22 and 23 may be issued.

Volume 21. Rāma's Later History. Part 1. Introduction and translation. (Prefixed is a convenient synoptic analysis of the play. The introduction treats of Bhavabhūti's life and date and works, and includes a summary of the Rāma-story as given by the Rāmāyaṇa. Lanman adds an essay entitled ' A method for citing Sanskrit dramas.' The method is very simple and practical.) 1915. Royal 8°. Pages 190. Price, $2.

Volume 22. Rāma's Later History. Part 2. The text, with index, glossaries, etc. (This was printed at Bombay, with the exquisitely beautiful type, newly cast for this work, of Jāvajī's Nirṇaya Sāgara Press, and upon paper made expressly for this edition at the Wolvercote Mill of Oxford. Each Prākrit speech is followed by the Sanskrit version in immediate sequence.) See above.

Volume 23. Rāma's Later History. Part 3. Explanatory and critical epilogue. (Critical account of the manuscripts. Running expository comment. The variant readings of the mss. The typographical 'make-up' of Comment and Variants into pages is such that they go *pari passu*. These epilegomena close with an essay on the two text-traditions of the play, a time-analysis, a note on the Hindu stage, etc.) See above.

Volume 24. Rig-Veda Repetitions. Parts 2 and 3. By Professor BLOOMFIELD. Described above, with volume 20.

Volume 25. Rig-Veda Brāhmaṇas: The Aitareya and Kauṣītaki Brāhmaṇas of the Rig-Veda. Translated from the original Sanskrit. By ARTHUR BERRIEDALE KEITH, D.C.L., D.Litt., of the Inner Temple, Barrister-at-law, Regius Professor of Sanskrit and Comparative Philology at the University of Edinburgh. 1920. Pages, 567. Royal 8°. Price $5.

In August, 1915, this work was ready for printing. In August, 1916, it was delivered to the Controller of the Oxford University Press. In 1918, the Press had nigh 350 men at the war. Of the older men who were left, many were busy with urgent war-work, such as a Report on Trench-fever for the American Expeditionary Force. And when, after the armistice, the printing was resumed, the author was engrossed in the work of Lord Crewe's Committee on the Home Administration of Indian Affairs.

The Vedic literature falls into three clearly sundered groups: the Vedic hymns or Mantras; the Brāhmaṇas, ' the priestlies ' or ' priestly (discourses) '; and the Sūtras. Keith thinks that the Aitareya is not later than 600 B.C. The plan of the work is like that of volumes 18–19: elaborate introduction; translation; running comment on the same page. The skill of the priestly story-tellers is at its best in the splendid legend of Çunaḥçepa (threatened sacrifice of son by father: cf. Isaac, Iphigeneia, Phrixos). Despite the pseudo-profundity and puerility of the Brāhmaṇas, they are of genuine significance to the student of Hindu antiquity, social and religious. And they are in fact the oldest Indo-European prose extant.   •

Volumes 26 and 27. Vikrama's Adventures, or The Thirty-two Tales of the Throne. A collection of stories about King Vikrama, as told by the Thirty-two Statuettes that supported his throne. Edited in four different recensions of the Sanskrit original (Vikrama-charita or Sinhāsana-dvātriṇçakā) and translated into English with an introduction, by FRANKLIN EDGERTON, Assistant Professor of Sanskrit at the University of Pennsylvania. Nearly ready.

Vikrama's Adventures is one of the most famous story-books of mediæval India. Vikrama is one of the most noted quasi-historical heroes of his times. His magic throne, hidden upon his death, is discovered by a later king, Bhoja. Each of the thirty-two (dvā-triṇçat) statuettes that support his throne (sinhāsana) tells one story to Bhoja. Hence the alternative title. The theme of the tales is Vikrama, who is meant to serve as a kind of Hindu King Arthur, an example for real kings.

Edgerton hopes that his work may prove suggestive as a model for students of comparative literature. The text of each of the four recensions (Southern, Metrical, " Brief," Jainistic) is printed in horizontally parallel sections, so that each page contains those parts which correspond to each other in substance. And the translation is treated in like manner. Comparisons are thus facilitated to a degree never before attained in a work of this kind.

From all this, Edgerton reconstructs, with some detail, and with reasonable certainty, the original work from which the current versions are derived. This he presents in the form of a Composite Outline, the concrete solution of a problem in literary genetics.

Volumes 28 and 29 and 30. Buddhist Legends. Translated from the original Pāli text of the Dhammapada Commentary, by EUGENE WATSON BURLINGAME, Fellow of the American Academy of Arts and Sciences, sometime Harrison Fellow for Research at the University of Pennsylvania and Johnston Scholar in Sanskrit at the Johns Hopkins University and Lecturer on Pāli in Yale University. 1921. Pages, 366 + 370 + 378 = 1114. Royal 8°. Not sold separately. Price $15.

Dhámma-pada, or Way of Righteousness, is the name of one of the canonical books of the Buddhist Sacred Scriptures. It consists of 423 stanzas. These are reputed to be the very words of the Buddha himself. The Dhammapada Commentary, composed by an unknown author in Ceylon about 450 A.D., purports to tell the circumstances under which Buddha uttered each one of these stanzas. In telling them, it narrates 299 stories or legends. These stories are the preponderating element of the Commentary, and it is these which are here translated.

In style and substance the tales resemble those of the famous Jātaka Book, the Buddhist Acta Sanctorum, a counterpart of the Legends of the Christian Saints. And they present many parallels to well-known stories of mediæval literature, Oriental and European. For the comparative study of such parallels, Dr. Burlingame's Synopses, clear and brief, will prove a very great convenience. His vigorous diction suggests familiarity with such " wells of English undefyled " as the Bible and the Book of Common Prayer. The work gives a vivid picture of the every-day life of the ancient Buddhists — monks, nuns, lay disciples. It is thus, incidentally, an admirable preparative for the study of the more difficult Buddhist books in the original. As especially attractive stories may be cited: Lean Gotamī seeks mustard-seed to cure her dead child; Murder of Great Moggallāna; Buddha falsely accused by Chinchā; Visākhā; the Hell-pot. A critical and historical introduction is prefixed. At the end is an *intelligent* index, modeled after that of George Foot Moore's *History of Religions.*

In September, 1909, Mr. Burlingame came to Harvard University to pursue his studies with Mr. Lanman. It was at the suggestion of the latter that Mr. Burlingame undertook the task of translating into English the Dhammapada Commentary. He first made a table of contents of the work, giving the title of each story and the place of its occurrence in the Burmese text and also in the Cingalese text. He added an index to the titles, and an extremely good analysis of Books 1 to 4. This most useful preliminary work was formally presented to the American Academy of Arts and Sciences on December 8, 1909, by Mr. Lanman. The manuscript of the article was delivered February 5, 1910, and published soon after as pages 467–550 of volume 45 of the Proceedings of the Academy. The admirably elaborated manuscript of the entire translation of the Dhammapada Commentary was delivered by its author on January 10, 1917, just before the War.

THE HARVARD UNIVERSITY PRESS

publishes other works relating to India, as follows:

Sanskrit Reader: Text and Vocabulary and Notes. By CHARLES ROCKWELL LANMAN, Wales Professor of Sanskrit at Harvard University. Seventh issue, 1920. Royal 8°. Pages, 430. Price, $3.

The Reader furnishes the text for 60 or 80 lessons, and with it, the needed lexicon and notes. The notes make constant reference to Whitney's Sanskrit Grammar: see below. These two volumes supply all that is strictly indispensable for the beginner. The text is in the Oriental (Nāgarī) letters; but a transliteration of the first four pages in Roman letters is added. The Reader is designed especially to meet the needs of those who have not the aid of a teacher.

The text is chosen: 1. from Classical Sanskrit works (Nala-story, fables of Hitopadeça, "Manu's Laws"); and 2. from the Vedic literature (Rig-Veda hymns, Brāhmaṇas, Sūtras for wedding and burial). A literary-historical introduction is given for each kind of text. The vocabulary is in Roman letters, and is elaborated with the utmost care. Special heed is given to the development of the meanings (semantics: pāda, foot, leg, leg of lamb, quarter, quarter of a four-lined stanza, line, line of a three-lined stanza), and also to the etymological cognates in English, Greek, and so on (ta-d, τό, ðæ-t, tha-t, is-tu-d).

○ **Parts of Nala and Hitopadesha in English letters.** Prepared by C. R. LANMAN. 1889. Royal 8°. Pages, 50. Price, 50 cents.

A reprint of the first 44 pages of the Reader (see above), transliterated from the Oriental characters into English letters. It corresponds page for page and line for line with its original, so that the references of the Vocabulary and Notes of the Reader apply exactly to this reprint. With the Grammar and Reader and this reprint, the student is enabled to acquire a knowledge of the structure of the Sanskrit and to do some reading, without first learning the Oriental letters.

Sanskrit Grammar: including both the Classical language, and the older dialects of Veda and Brāhmaṇa. By WILLIAM DWIGHT WHITNEY, late Professor of Sanskrit at Yale University. Fourth issue of second edition, 1921. 8°. Pages, 578. Price, $4.50.

The greatest extant repository of the grammatical facts concerning the Sanskrit language. A masterpiece of orderly arrangement. Prefixed is a brief account of the literature of India.

Vedanta Philosophy. Outline of the Vedanta system of philosophy according to Shankara. By PAUL DEUSSEN. Translated by JAMES H. WOODS, Professor of Philosophy at Harvard University, and CATHARINE B. RUNKLE of Cambridge, Massachusetts. Second edition. 1915. 8°. Pages, 56. Price, 50 cents.

This book, a translation of the summary given by Deussen at the end of his monumental work, Das System des Vedanta, was first published in 1906. Since then, thanks to the learning and enthusiasm of Charles Johnston, the whole great work has been made accessible in an English version (Chicago, 1912, The Open Court Publishing Company). Nevertheless, the small book was so inexpensive and practical, that a new edition was made in 1915. The summary, although brief and compact, is yet so lucid and adequate, — in short, so altogether admirable, that it is not likely soon to be superseded by a better exposition of what has been to untold millions at once a philosophy and a religion.

IN PREPARATION

Sanskrit Grammar. The essentials, in briefest form and for beginners, as to sounds and sound-changes and inflection. With an appendix of linguistic Comment, entirely separate from the Grammar, and drawn from English and Greek and Latin. By C. R. Lanman. 1921. Royal 8°. Pages, about 50 + 50. Price, $1.

Of all the Indo-European languages, Sanskrit is incomparably well adapted as an elementary study for the purposes of mental discipline in general and of rigorous linguistic training in particular. The transparency of its structure is absolutely unique. The various elements — prefix, root, derivative suffix, inflectional ending — which in synthesis constitute the word, are easily made the subject of quick and certain analysis by the veriest beginner. Thus Sanskrit serves best to reveal the fundamental principles which underlie the structure of English, Greek, Latin, etc. For these have suffered linguistic erosion to such a degree that their original structural features are often no longer recognizable. The habit and power of alert observation and of linguistic reflection (such, for example, as shows you without reference to any book, the connection of *batch* with *bake*, of *fil-th* with *foul*, of *gris-t* with *grind*) are best won by the study of some foreign language. One single year of Sanskrit may, with proper books, be made so fruitful, that any intending Anglicist or Hellenist or Latinist may well hesitate to forego the unmatched opportunity which it offers for winning a habit and a power that shall enable him to tackle his English or his Greek or his Latin more vigorously and effectively.

For this purpose, the mastery of Oriental alphabets is of no use whatever. The inflections and sound-changes of Sanskrit are far less difficult than is commonly supposed, and are positively easy if you separate the difficulties of the language from those of the writing. Therefore this grammar prints all Sanskrit words in Roman letters. The use of Roman letters makes clear to the eye, instantly and without a word of comment, countless facts as to the structure and analysis of the forms. And by combining ingenious typographic arrangement with the use of Roman letters, it is possible to accomplish wonders for the visualizing memory.

The explanatory or illustrative matter, drawn from English, Greek, and Latin, will be found helpful and often entertaining. Thus palatalization (important in Sanskrit: *k* becomes *ch*, *g* becomes *j*) is illustrated by *drink drench, hang hinge*, and so on. The section-numbers of the Comment correspond throughout with those of the Grammar, so that reference from the one to the other is 'automatic.'

◊ **Bhāratan Readings.** Easy and interesting stories from the Mahā-Bhārata in the original Sanskrit. Printed in Roman letters, with a literal English version. By C. R. Lanman.

These show to the beginner how exceedingly easy the easy epic texts are. They are chosen with common sense and good taste, and are purged of long-winded descriptive passages. They are in simple unstilted language, entertaining, full of swift-moving action and incident. Among them are the story of Çakuntalā (heroine of the masterpiece of the Hindu drama, and mother of Bhārata: see above, page 5), the Flood, the great Gambling-scene, the Night-scene on the Ganges (in which the fallen heroes come forth from the river and talk with the living), Vipula (who restrains Ruchi from a lapse of virtue by hypnotizing her), the Man in the Pit (prototype of the famous mediæval allegory), Nala and Damayantī (cut down from a thousand stanzas to a few hundred), and so on. To make easier and quicker the understanding of the text, each stanza is printed as four lines (not two), and the literal version is given in a parallel column.

The Indic Alphabet called Nāgarī, in which Sanskrit is commonly printed. A brief manual for beginners. By C. R. LANMAN.

This is not to be taken up until the student has acquired a considerable vocabulary of common Sanskrit words, and such familiarity with the inflectional endings and prepositional prefixes and with the rules of sound-combination, as shall enable him quickly to separate the words, which, in the writing of India, are confusingly run together. By printing the little book at Bombay, with the rich and admirable type-fonts of the Nirṇaya Sāgara Press, it will be easy to make many things clear which are now stones of stumbling.

LIBRARIES OF CITIES, UNIVERSITIES, ACADEMIES, ETC.

(A PARTIAL LIST)

IN WHICH THE HARVARD ORIENTAL SERIES MAY BE FOUND

L. (B.) = Library (Bibliothèque, etc.)   U. = University, Universität, etc.
Ac. (Ak.) = Academy (Akademie), etc.   R.A.S. = Royal Asiatic Society

AMERICA, UNITED STATES OF

California
Berkeley, University of California
San Francisco, Public Library
Stanford University, U. Library
Connecticut
Hartford, Trinity College Library
Middletown, Wesleyan University L.
New Haven, Yale University Library
— American Oriental Society's L.
Norwich, Otis Library
District of Columbia
Washington, Library of Congress
— Catholic University of America
Illinois
Chicago, The Chicago Public Library
— The Newberry Library
— University of Chicago Library
Louisiana
New Orleans, Tulane University L.
Maine
Brunswick, Bowdoin College Library
Maryland
Baltimore, Johns Hopkins U. L.
— The Peabody Institute
Massachusetts
Amherst, Amherst College Library
Boston, Public Library
— Harvard Club of Boston
— American Ac. of Arts and Sciences
Cambridge, Harvard College Library
— Radcliffe College Library
Northampton, Forbes Library
Wellesley, Wellesley College Library
Williamstown, Williams College L.
Michigan
Ann Arbor, University of Michigan L.
Minnesota
Minneapolis, Public L. of Minneapolis
— Minneapolis Athenæum
Northfield, Carleton College Library

Missouri
Columbia, University of Missouri L.
St. Louis, Washington University L.
— Public Library of St. Louis
Nebraska
Lincoln, University of Nebraska L.
New Hampshire
Hanover, Dartmouth College Library
New Jersey
Princeton, Princeton University Library
New York
Brooklyn, Brooklyn Public Library
Ithaca, Cornell University Library
New York, Columbia University Library
— Harvard Club L., 27 West 44th St.
— New York Public Library
— University Club L., 5th Ave. at · 54th St.
North Carolina
Chapel Hill, U. of North Carolina
Ohio
Cincinnati, Public L. of Cincinnati
Cleveland, Adelbert College Library
— Cleveland Public Library
Oberlin, Oberlin College Library
Pennsylvania
Bryn Mawr, Bryn Mawr College L.
Philadelphia, Free L. of Philadelphia
— American Philosophical Society
— University of Pennsylvania L.
— Library Company of Philadelphia
Rhode Island
Providence, Brown University Library
— Providence Public Library
Tennessee
Nashville, Vanderbilt University L.
Virginia
Charlottesville, U. of Virginia L.
Wisconsin
Madison, University of Wisconsin L.

CANADA, Dominion of

Montreal, McGill University L. Toronto, University of Toronto L.

EUROPE

Austria
 Vienna, Academy of Sciences
 —— Hof-Bibliothek, Hofburg
 —— University Library
 —— Oriental Institute of the U.
Belgium
 Brussels, B. Royale de Belgique
 Louvain, B. de l'Université
Czecho-Slovakia
 Prague, Universitäts-Bibliothek
 —— Bohemian Society of Sciences
Denmark
 Copenhagen, Royal Danish Academy
 —— University Library
Finnland
 Helsingfors, Finnish-Ugrian Society
France
 Lyons, B. de l'Université
 Paris, B. de l'Institut de France
 —— Bibliothèque Nationale
 —— B. du Musée Guimet
 —— B. de la Société Asiatique
 —— U. de Paris à la Sorbonne
 Strasbourg, B. de l'Université
 Toulouse, B. de l'Université
Germany
 Berlin, Universitäts-Bibliothek
 —— Indogermanisches Seminar der U.
 —— Königliche Bibliothek
 —— Prußian Ac. of Sciences
 Bonn, Universitäts-Bibliothek
 —— Orientalisches Seminar der U.
 Breslau, Universitäts-Bibliothek
 Erlangen, Universitäts-Bibliothek
 Freiburg in Baden, Universitäts-B.
 Göttingen, Universitäts-Bibliothek
 —— Society of Sciences
 Halle, Universitäts-Bibliothek
 —— Deutsche Morgenländische Gesellschaft
 Heidelberg, Universitäts-Bibliothek
 Jena, Universitäts-Bibliothek
 Kiel, Universitäts-Bibliothek
 Königsberg, Universitäts-Bibliothek
 Leipzig, Universitäts-Bibliothek
 —— Indogermanisches Institut, U.
 —— Saxon Society of Sciences

Germany (continued)
 Munich, Bavarian Ac. of Sciences
 —— Hof- und Staats-Bibliothek
 —— Universitäts-Bibliothek
 —— Seminar für Arische Philologie
 Tübingen, Universitäts-Bibliothek
 Würzburg, Universitäts-Bibliothek
Great Britain
 Aberdeen, University Library
 Cambridge, University Library
 Edinburgh, Advocates' Library
 —— University Library
 Glasgow, University Library
 London, British Museum
 —— India Office Library
 —— Royal Asiatic Society L.
 Manchester, Victoria U. L.
 Oxford, Bodleian Library
 —— Indian Institute
 —— Balliol College Library
 St. Andrews, University L.
Greece
 Athens, Ἐθνικὴ Βιβλιοθήκη τῆς Ἑλλάδος
Italy
 Bologna, Reale B. Universitaria
 Florence, B. Nazionale Centrale
 —— Società Asiatica Italiana
 Milan, Biblioteca Ambrosiana
 Naples, Regia B. Universitaria
 Padua, Regia B. Universitaria
 Rome, B. Apostolica Vaticana
 —— Accademia dei Lincei
 Turin, B. Nazionale di Torino
Netherlands
 Amsterdam, Royal Ac. of Sciences
 The Hague, Koloniale Bibliotheek
 Leiden, Rijks-Universiteit
 Utrecht, University Library
Norway
 Christiania, University Library
Russia
 Petrograd, Public Library
 —— Academy of Sciences
Spain
 Madrid, Biblioteca Nacional